EXPLORER

www.Explorer-Publishing.com

Passionately Publishing...

Dubai Explorer 2004/8th Edition

First Published 1996
Second Edition 1997
Third Edition 1998
Fourth Edition 1999
Fifth Edition 2000
Sixth Edition 2001
Seventh Edition 2003
Eighth Edition 2004 ISBN 976-8182-47-4

Front Cover Photograph – Jumeirah International

Printed and bound by Emirates Printing Press, Dubai, United Arab Emirates.

Explorer Publishing & Distribution
Dubai Media City, PO Box 34275, Dubai,
United Arab Emirates
Phone (+971 4) 391 8060
Fax (+971 4) 391 8062
Email Info@Explorer-Publishing.com
Web www.Explorer-Publishing.com

Dear Loyal Readership & New Converts,

Following countless exhausting weeks of late nights and social sacrifices, team dedication that would bring a tear to the eye, and enough collective energy to recreate the world in less than seven days, Explorer Publishing's dream team (although barely alive to tell the tale) is proud to bring you the 8th edition of the shockingly good **Dubai Explorer**.

This edition too, is nothing short of downright genius, and if you buy nothing all year but the **Dubai Explorer**, your budget is wisely spent. So crammed is it with juicy info that, when you open it for the first time, its contents will burst out in a flood of delicious insider knowledge. This prodigy among guidebooks truly does cover everything you need to know to survive (and enjoy) this funky metropolis.

All the well loved sassy sections and informative insights that we cover so well, have been brought bang up to date. Topics such as Exploring, Shopping & Activities are blissfully inspired and, as true slaves to the Going Out section, our food critics have now joined Overeaters Anonymous following months of gorging their way through Dubai's tastiest restaurants.

As ever, our resident team of community 'Know Alls' are at your disposal for any burning questions you need answered, or a comment you wish to get off your chest. Just email us at Info@Explorer-Publishing.com, log on to our Website (www.Explorer-Publishing.com) or simply pick up the phone and holler!

We're listening...

The Explorer Team

Alistair Mackenzie

Media Mogul

Alistair's dream would be to run Explorer Publishing from a remote wadi somewhere in the Hajar mountains; to have a completely functional office setup in the port-a-loo, powered by solar energy reflected from his shaving mirror. As a dedicated and paid up member of the 'You Can't Just Stay In & Watch TV This Weekend Again!' brigade, Alistair is a true inspiration to the non outdoorsy types.

Louise Mellowdew

Meat Packer

Louise is pro at routinely avoiding deadlines. How? She never sits at the same desk twice and hides her stuff in everyone else's In trays. Her theory is that 'hot desking' with wild abandon will leave her mysterious and undetected. However, DNA samples collected from post its all over the office have confirmed her existence, and plans are afoot to trap her by the photocopier before the rest of the crew follows her example.

Amanda Harkin

Publicity Junky

When Amanda marched into our office wearing pin stripes and heels, we thought she'd come to audit our books – so we held her hostage! But since no one will pay her ransom, she now spends her time chewing through her shackles and sending out subliminal help messages embedded in Explorer press releases.

Hema Kumar

Primo Peddler

Hema's international career as a cheerleader for the Australian Rugby Team came to an abrupt end at the Rugby Sevens, when her pompom slipped and whisked off the Cheerleading Association Chairman's toupee. This incident (amidst a crowd of 30,000) closed all pompom doors on her, and she requested asylum in the Media City Free Zone, selling ads in the hope that her triple flips and double axels in the parking lot will have her discovered again.

Yolanda Rodrigues

Chief Bean Counter

Yolanda's two passions, cooking and accounting, have both been put to excellent use with Explorer, where she is required on a regular basis to cook the books in order to make them balance. Still, she's more popular in the office because she's great (and not because she has keys to the petty cash box...)

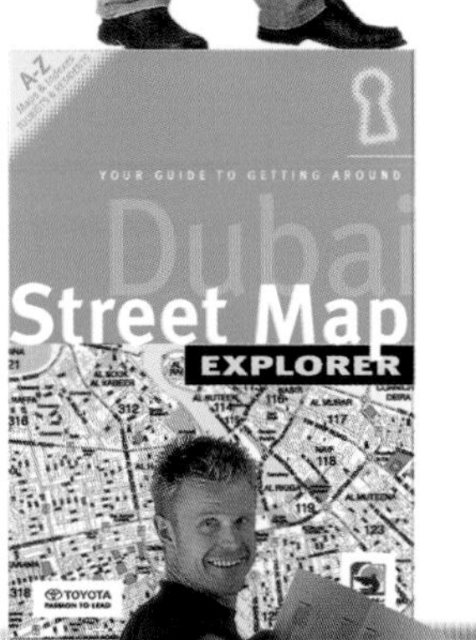

Pete Maloney

Pencil Pusher

As mentioned in last year's edition, Poor Pete moved from Manchester for there wasn't a single girl left in the region that he hadn't dated. Well, history has a way of repeating itself and alas, Dubai is also proving too small a town. He's currently working huge amounts of overtime to fund his purchase of a camel and thus, do away with colossal taxi fares to the outer reaches of Al Ain.

Derrick Pereira

Techno Guru

Following his split from his supermodel girlfriend, and 4 years modelling Y Fronts for a leading underwear manufacturer, Derrick was frustrated at being judged on his looks rather than his IT abilities. We have given him a part time role tinkering with office computers, which he fits in between working with under privileged children and animals.

Lena Moosa

Big Ed

Our own little tinkerbell, Lena buzzes around the office waving her magic wand over our badly written text. She can spot a typo from Sharjah and can make a silk purse out of the dodgiest of sow's ears. In fact, she makes everything look so good that, had she created the world, all the men would resemble George Clooney and chocolate would have the calorific value of a carrot!

Jayde Fernandes

Master Craftsman

Jayde is working with us only until his record deal with a boy band is finalised. He is often spotted practising his MTV Award speech in front of the men's room mirror, whilst considering if he would be better blonde. He's a born performer – the performance he puts up to get out of work each day is amazing!

Helga Becker

Fantasy Foodist

After years of playing with letters in her alphabet soup, Helga decided to continue her career in food by wow-ing Explorer with her unparalleled expertise of fruity teabags. She now spends her time perfecting the art of catching the waiter's eye and researching her first recipe book – 1001 Ways to Boil Water.

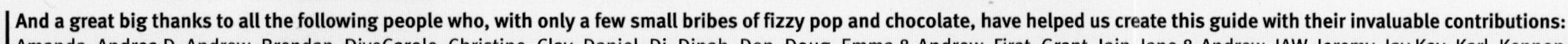

And a great big thanks to all the following people who, with only a few small bribes of fizzy pop and chocolate, have helped us create this guide with their invaluable contributions:

Amanda, Andrea D, Andrew, Brendan, DiveCarole, Christine, Clay, Daniel, Di, Dinah, Don, Doug, Emma & Andrew, Firat, Grant, Iain, Jane & Andrew, JAW, Jeremy, Jay Kay, Karl, Kennon, Kerry, Lena & David, Liz & Simon, Mish & Mike, Nick, Peter B, Peter L, Peter St, Richard, Rober

Online Explorer

Visit us online! Our Website is better than ever, keeping you abreast of the flux with the latest updated information and a full range of our titles. Also, look out for the **Weekly Explorer** on MyTravelChannel.com, and keep a watch for exciting new ideas for the future. Check it all out on **www.Explorer-Publishing.com**.

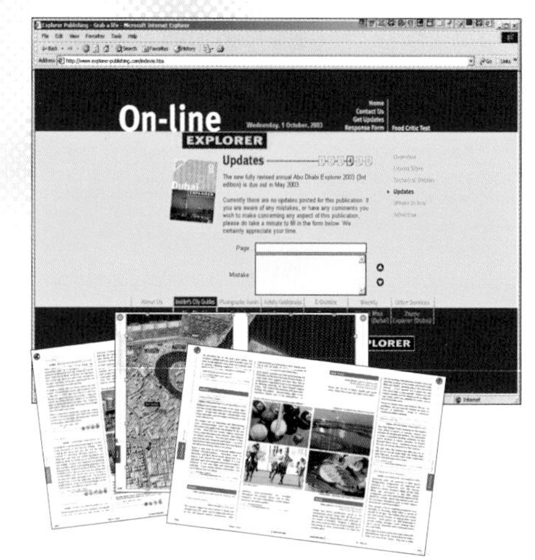

Web Updates

A tremendous amount of research, effort and passion goes into making our guidebooks. However, in this dynamic and fast paced environment, decisions are swiftly taken and quickly implemented. We will try to provide you with the most current updates on those things which have changed DRAMATICALLY.

To view any changes, visit our Website: **www.Explorer-Publishing.com**

1. Click on **Insiders' City Guides** -> **Dubai Explorer** -> **Updates** to check on any updates that may interest you.
2. All updates are in Adobe PDF format*. You may print in colour or black & white and update your guide immediately.
3. If you are aware of any mistakes, or have any comments concerning any aspect of this publication, please fill in our online reader response form. We certainly appreciate your time and feedback.

If you do not have Adobe Reader, download it from (www.adobe.com) or use the link from our Website.

Centerfold!

XXXPLORER

The Explorer 'B' Team

In media & publishing, our team is like no other. Companies will sell you images of dedication and hard work – humourless professionalism drowning in a sea of serious business acumen and policies. We just work hard... then play hard! Hand picked for our abilities and our personalities, we enjoy our clients as they enjoy us, building a unique business relationship full of creativity and respect with our customers. The end result is quality! quality! quality! and a smile...

Alena Hykešová
Sales Supergirl

Alena should be working as a linguist for the United Nations since she speaks most languages known to man. We, however, offered her better career prospects and way better pay. A former Greek spy, she has escaped the Greek & Czech mafia and is residing with us under an assumed name until the United Nations improves their offer!

Nadia DSouza
Nosey Parker

Nadia's ability to calm even the most frenzied of situations came from her vast experience with the LAPD in talking crazies down from high ledges. It's a skill that has come in handy when nearing print deadlines, as she somehow manages to retrieve our editor off the 5th floor window ledge.

Mannie Lugtu
Distribution Demon

Mannie was a 70's disco champion who made quite a name for himself on the New York club scene. Alas, his LA shirt and disco trousers eventually got a bit tight on him, and he retired to Dubai to manage a sequin emporium. He can be found sparkling the length and breadth of Al Wasl Road in our Caddy, tapping his steering wheel to Boney M remixes.

Ivan Rodrigues
Head Honcho

Ivan's ability to answer questions like 'What time is it?' by immediately conjuring up multidimensional spreadsheets in Excel won him the position of Distribution Manager in Explorer. We don't think he actually distributes anything, but his lunch announcements are a timely mid day marker... and the graphs and pie charts look stunning

Abdul Gafoor
Ace Circulator

Gafoor is on the run from the police for tippex-ing digits out of number plates and selling them to rich wannabes. There are currently 3,498,236 cars cruising Sheikh Zayed Road (including 3 Explorer Caddy vans) all bearing the number plate 'DUBAI 1'. He is bound to Explorer for the next 5 years till he pays off the office supply overspend.

Pamela Grist
Happy Snapper

Ever since she was asked to write a feature on whether blondes have more fun, most of Pam's spare time is consumed under a shower cap waiting for the latest hair colour to develop. When she's not indulging her passion for photography, she's auditioning for shampoo ads, which makes sense as she's 'Head & Shoulders' above the competition.

Zainudheen Madathil
Doodle Maestro

We believe that Zainudheen's real name is John, and that he kept changing it to more and more obscure alternatives in a bid to escape Alistair's phone calls. When he ran out of letters and landed at 'Z', he surrendered. What he's left with is a name no one can pronounce and a life of doodling and designing his way back into the real world.

Geraldine Fernandes
The Enigma

Geraldine is so young she was being born when most of us were getting married and starting pension plans. Her youth is reflected in her super energy and she whizzes around the office at the speed of sound, doing things it takes us crumblies hours just to think about. However, working for Explorer, she will also age at the speed of light, so we expect her to be slowing down any time soon

Rani Anthony
Admin Queen

Rani was in charge of a very successful hotel business centre when we forced her at gunpoint to come and work for us. We hid her from the hoard of businessmen wielding briefcases and faxes, chasing us down the street and begging her return. We also assured her that she was doing the right thing. She now jumps every time there's a loud bang, but she's very good at PR, Advertising and pretty much everything else too!

hen B, Tracy, Vanessa

Tracy, Vanessa

Online Explorer

Who Are You?

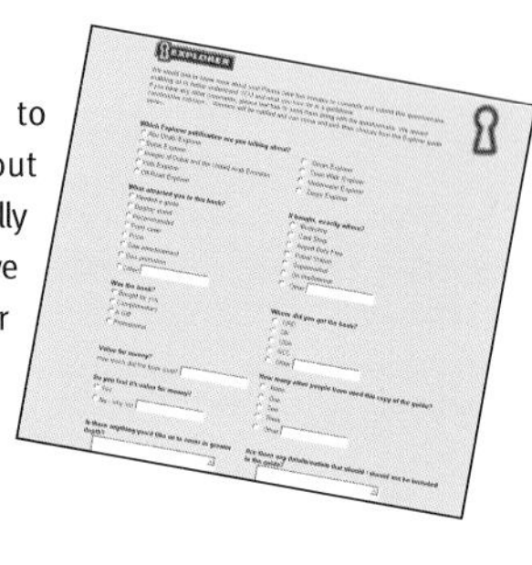

We would love to know more about you. We would equally love to know what we have done right or wrong, or if we have accidentally misled you at some point.

Please take a minute to fill out the Reader Response Form on our Website. To do so:

1. Visit **www.Explorer-Publishing.com**
2. At the top right, click on Response Form
3. Fill it out and enlighten us

Free Fabulous Food – aka 'the FFF'

Gluttons and connoisseurs interested in bona fide, calorified membership to the FFF Fest, know that you can now realise your fantasy of becoming a food reporter. We do have certain prerequisites*. You should:

1. Frequently dine out
2. Know which hands hold the knife and fork
3. Love the challenge of doing restaurant reviews incognito

(*Good looks, charm, wit and humour are a bonus)

Whether it's your grandma, maid, boyfriend, colleague, slave (or even favourite Martian!), reporting knows no boundaries and they can all qualify. Log on to www.EatOutSpeakOut.com for details.

Plate smashing is a form of expression, culturally acceptable only in Greek restaurants. You can now get your point across for all other eateries and still avoid costly lawsuits. Just log on to Eat Out Speak Out, UAE's first online restaurant review forum, and freely spill all thoughts about your dining experience.

Explorer Community

Whether it's an idea, a correction, an opinion or simply a recommendation, we want to hear from you. Log on and be part of the Explorer Community – let your opinions be heard, viewed, compiled and printed.

Explorer Insiders' City Guides

These are no ordinary guidebooks. They are your lifestyle support system, medicine for the bored, ointment for the aimless, available over the counter and prescribed by those in the know. An essential resource for residents, tourists and business people, they cover everything worth knowing about the city and where to do it.

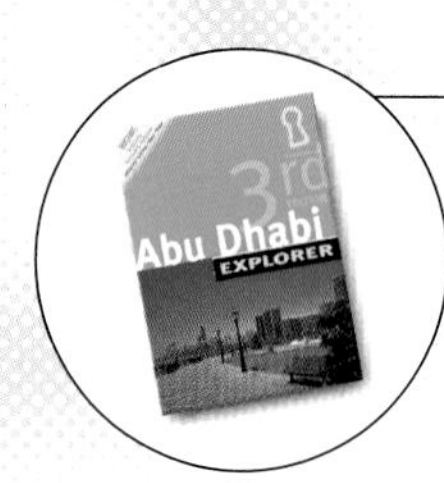

Abu Dhabi Explorer

Just when you thought it couldn't get any better! The 3rd edition of the **Abu Dhabi Explorer** has been radically revised and revamped, making it the ultimate insiders' guidebook. A lifetime of information is sorted into easy reference sections with recommendations, advice and guidance on every aspect of residing in Abu Dhabi & Al Ain. Written by residents with a zest for life, this book is an essential resource for anyone exploring this beautiful emirate.

ISBN 976-8182-38-5 **Retail Price** Dhs.55, €18

Dubai Explorer

The 8th stunning edition of Dubai Explorer has broken the mold in insiders' city guides. A prodigy amongst its peers, and still the best selling in its class, the **Dubai Explorer** has done it again with its newest annual addition.

Full of all of the favourite sections, we bring you even more places to eat, sleep shop and socialise, as well as an enormous amount of must have information on everything you need to know to survive and enjoy the city of Dubai.

ISBN 976-8182-47-4 **Retail Price** Dhs.65 €18

Geneva Explorer

Following the hugely popular style of the **Explorer** city guides, the **Geneva Explorer** too, has raised the bar for quality guidebooks in the region. A resident team of writers, photographers and lovers of life have sold their souls to exhaustive research, bringing you a guidebook packed with insider recommendations, practical information and the most accurate coverage around. Written by residents thoroughly familiar with the inside track, this is THE essential must-have for anyone wanting to explore this multicultural haven. **(Due out 1st quarter 2004)**

ISBN 976-8182-44-x **Retail Price** Dhs.65 €18

Oman Explorer

As the list of fascinating insights grew beyond the city limits of Muscat, the **Oman Explorer** was born. Now covering the whole of this largely unspoilt country, this guidebook has become an in-depth catalogue of the region's life, leisure and entertainment. Based on the legendary formula of the **Dubai Explorer**, every aspect of existence in Oman is covered, with no stone left unturned. This is essential reading for anyone exploring this gorgeous country - be it residents, visitors or business trippers. **(Due out 2nd quarter 2004)**

ISBN 976-8182-07-5 **Retail Price** Dhs.65 €18

Explorer Activity Guides

Why not visit stunning marine life and mysterious wrecks, or stand poised on the edge of a natural wadi or pool in the mountains? Get a tan and a life with our activity guidebooks.

Family Explorer (Dubai & Abu Dhabi)

The one and only handbook for families in Dubai and Abu Dhabi has finally arrived. Jam packed with hundreds of innovative ideas, you can now enjoy a multitude of both indoor and outdoor activity options with your little ones, or follow the guidance and tips provided on practical topics such as education and medical care. Written by experienced parents residing in the Emirates, the **Family Explorer** is, without a doubt, the essential resource for families and kids aged up to 14 years. **(Due out 1st quarter 2004)**

ISBN 976-8182-34-2 **Retail Price** Dhs.65 €18

Off-Road Explorer (UAE)

You haven't truly been to the Emirates until you've experienced its delights off the beaten track. Dear to the hearts of the indigenous and the insane, this pastime involves hours of zooming 4x4's up sand dunes and hours of digging them out again! The **Off-Road Explorer (UAE)** is a brilliant array of outback route maps designed for the adventurous and the anxious alike. Satellite images superimposed with step-by-step route directions, safety information and stunning photography, make this a perfect addition to your four wheeler.

ISBN 976-8182-37-7 **Retail Price** Dhs.95 €29

Underwater Explorer (UAE)

Opening the doors to liquid heaven in the UAE, this handy book details the top 58 dive sites that avid divers would not want to miss. Informative illustrations, shipwreck data & stunning marine life photographs combined with suggested dive plans cater to divers of all abilities. Whether you're a passionate diver or just pottering, you will not want to be without this crucial resource.

ISBN 976-8182-36-9 **Retail Price** Dhs.65 €18

Dubai Tourist Map

This much awaited second edition of the **Dubai Tourist Map**, compiled and published by Dubai Muncipality, offers visitors and residents the best chance of getting from A to B. Key places of interest are highlighted and brief descriptions of the main tourist attractions are enhanced by colour photographs. An index of the community street and building numbering system ensures that the city can be easily navigated. This map is a must for anyone in Dubai.

ISBN 976-8182-16-4 **Retail Price** Dhs.35 €14.95

Explorer Photography Books

Where words fail, a picture speaks volumes. Look at the world though new eyes as the lens captures places you never knew existed. These award winning books are valuable additions to bookshelves everywhere.

Dubai: Tomorrow's City Today

Stunning photographs shed light on the beauty and functionality of contemporary Dubai, a city that is a model of diversity, development and progress. Explore its historical highlights, municipal successes, innovative plans and civic triumphs, as you wonder at the grandeur in store for the future. **(Due out 1st quarter 2004)**

ISBN 976-8182-35-0 **Retail Price** Dhs.165 €45

Images of Abu Dhabi & the UAE

This visual showcase shares the aesthetic and lush wonders of the emirate of Abu Dhabi as spectacular images disclose the marvels of the capital and the diversity of astounding locations throughout the seven emirates. **(Due out 1st quarter 2004)**

ISBN 976-8182-28-8 **Retail Price** Dhs.165 €45

Images of Dubai & the UAE

Images of Dubai shares the secrets of this remarkable land and introduces newcomers to the wonders of Dubai and the United Arab Emirates. Journey along golden beaches under a pastel sunset, or deep into the mesmerising sands of the desert. View the architectural details of one of the most visually thrilling urban environments in the world, and dive undersea to encounter the reef creatures that live there. This book is for all those who love this country as well as those who think they might like to.

ISBN 976-8182-22-9 **Retail Price** Dhs.165 €45

Sharjah's Architectural Splendour

Take a guided tour of some of the highlights of Sharjah's architecture. Through the lens, this book captures small, aesthetic details and grand public compounds, the mosques and souks of this remarkable city. Striking photographs are linked together with text that is both analytical and informative. Whether you are a long term resident or a brief visitor, this volume of images will undoubtedly surprise and delight.

ISBN 976-8182-29-6 **Retail Price** Dhs.165 €45

Other Products

Apart from our wondrous array of city guides, activity guides and photography books, we offer other titles so innovative, they cannot be categorised. From the Hand-Held Explorer (our revolutionary digital guidebook) to the Street Map Explorer (your guide to getting around), these popular products have been bought, used, loved and lived.

Hand-Held Explorer (Dubai)

The **Dubai Explorer** goes digital. Interactive, informative and innovative, this easy to install software for your PDA offers you all the info from your favourite guidebook at your fingertips. Browse through restaurant reviews at the push of a button, scroll through and peruse a multitude of activities, and dive into a mountain of must know data at a glance. Your PDA will be undernourished without it!

ISBN 976-8182-40-7 **Retail Price** Dhs.65 €18

Street Map Explorer (Dubai)

The most accurate and up to date map on Dubai has arrived! The **Street Map Explorer (Dubai)** is a concise and comprehensive compendium of street names, cross referenced with an A to Z index of businesses and tourist attractions. In this fast developing city, this expansive and handy guidebook will soon become your favourite travel mate and a standard tool for navigating this ever-growing metropolis.

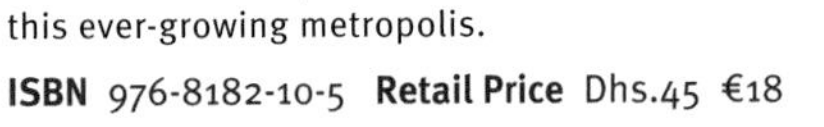

ISBN 976-8182-10-5 **Retail Price** Dhs.45 €18

Weekly Explorer (Dubai)

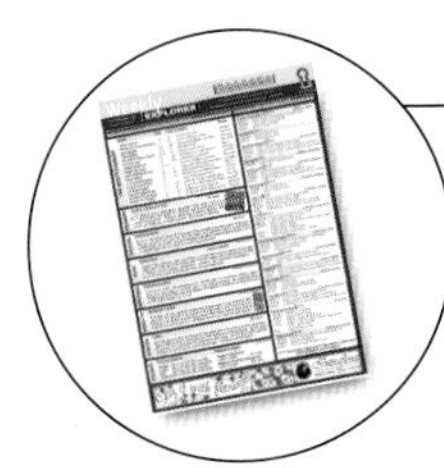

Don't be baffled by the choice of social events clogging your calendar. Just subscribe online to our FREE newsletter, emailed or faxed each week to over 12,000 readers. The **Weekly Explorer** sifts through and picks out the best happenings in town for the week without you having to wade through a sea of happy hours. Better than your social PA, this single page clues you in on what's moving and shaking in the city, providing you with a full listing of events, promotions, exhibitions, movies and more.

ISBN – **Retail Price** Free

Zappy Explorer (Dubai)

Aptly dubbed the 'ultimate culture shock antidote', this guide is **Explorer's** solution to the complexities and perplexities of Dubai's administrative maze. A clear, straightforward set of procedures assists residents through the basics of life in this city, from opening a bank account and connecting your phone to buying a car and marrying your true love. Including detailed information on ministry and government department requirements, what to bring lists, reference maps and much more, the **Zappy Explorer** is your best chance of getting things done next to bribery or force!

ISBN 976-8182-25-3 **Retail Price** Dhs.65 €18

General Information

New Residents

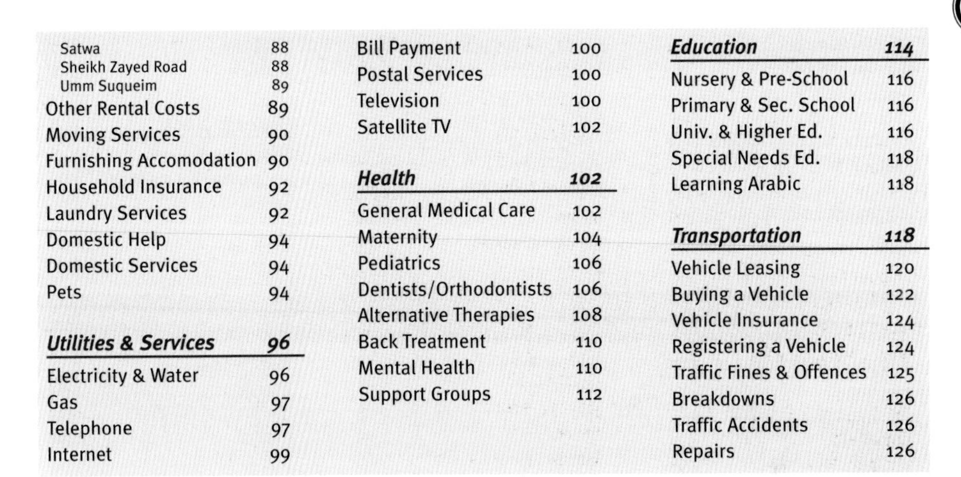

Exploring

Shopping

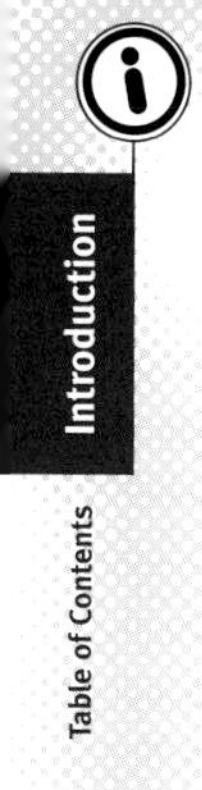
Introduction
Table of Contents

Activities

Going Out

Maps

Index

Jeep is a brand of DaimlerChrysler Corporation.
THE SPIRIT OF ADVENTURE
rom the head-for-the-hills driving fun of Wrangler to the
dvanced capability of Cherokee and the luxurious power of
rand Cherokee, only a Jeep vehicle ensures you don't
iss a thing!
ONLY IN A
Jeep

You'll find it all in the City
DEIRA
CITY CENTRE
Dubai's most popular shopping destination, with over 300 outlets.
www.deiracitycentre.com
okaïdi
NINE WEST
adidas
MANGO
BREITLING

General Information

EXPLORER

General Information

What's new?

Tourism developments

Page 8

Dubai is determined to be a serious contender worldwide in the world tourism industry. Already earning the name as a top favourite tourist destination, the region continues to come up with astounding 'never been done before' projects in a bid to keep those tourists coming. If you want to read up more on these astounding projects, flip forward to the Business section [p.130], and refer to Places to Stay [p.27] for the five star hotels that cater to your tastes and budget.

No passport required!

Page 22

With Dubai International Airport increasing in growth, so do the crowds. Hence, the revolutionary idea of the e-Gate service. Serving as an electronic form of crowd control, the swiping of this smart card enables people to pass through both the Arrivals and Departures halls without showing their passport. This makes travelling an awful lot simpler and is a great decongestion formula for the Immigration hall. Read on about this plastic genius on [p.22].

UAE Overview

Geography

Situated on the northeastern part of the Arabian Peninsula, the United Arab Emirates (UAE) is bordered by the Kingdom of Saudi Arabia to the south and west, and the Sultanate of Oman to the east and north. The UAE shares 457 kilometres of border with Saudi Arabia and 410 kilometres with Oman. It has a coastline on both the Gulf of Oman and the Arabian Gulf, and is south of the strategically important Strait of Hormuz. The geographic co-ordinates for the UAE are 24 00 N, 54 00 E.

The country is made up of seven different emirates (Abu Dhabi, Ajman, Dubai, Fujairah, Ras Al Khaimah, Sharjah and Umm Al Quwain) which were formerly all independent sheikhdoms. The total area of the country is about 83,600 square kilometres, and a major chunk of this land lies in the Abu Dhabi emirate. Dubai, with an area of 3,885 square kilometres, is the second largest emirate.

Emirs or Sheikhs?

While the term emirate comes from the ruling title of 'emir', the rulers of the UAE are called sheikhs.

Golden beaches dot the country's 1,318 kilometres of coastline, of which 100 kilometres are on the Gulf of Oman. The Arabian Gulf coast is littered with coral reefs and over 200 islands, most of which are uninhabited. Sabkha (salt flats), stretches of gravel plain, and desert characterise much of the inland region.

Dubai and its surrounding area consist of flat desert and sabkha. However, to the east, rise the Hajar Mountains (hajar is Arabic for rock). Lying close to the Gulf of Oman, they form a backbone through the country, from the Mussandam Peninsula in the north, through the eastern UAE and into Oman. The highest point is Jebel Yibir at 1,527 metres.

Maps

For in-depth information, your best bet is the Street Map Explorer (Dubai), a street guide with detailed maps charting every nook and cranny of this city. For a one page fold out option, the Dubai Tourist Map (Dubai Municipality) gives visitors a good overview. Both are easily available from all good bookstores around Dubai.

Most of the western part of the country lies in the Abu Dhabi emirate and is made up of the infamous Rub Al Khali or Empty Quarter desert, which is common to the Kingdom of Saudi Arabia and the Sultanate of Oman. The area consists of arid, stark desert with spectacular sand dunes, broken by an occasional oasis. It is the largest sand desert in the world, covering nearly a quarter of the Arabian Peninsula with dunes rising at times to well over 300 metres.

Visitors to Dubai will find a land of startling contrasts, from endless stretches of desert to rugged mountains and modern towns. The city of Dubai is situated on the banks of a creek, a natural inlet from the Gulf that divides the city neatly into two. You can read more about Dubai's geography in the Exploring section [p.156].

History

Dubai's growth over the last fifty years has been astonishing – it is difficult to imagine its transformation from an undeveloped, although flourishing, town to today's modern metropolis. Until 1830, Dubai was an unremarkable backwater whose people existed from fishing, pearling and small scale agriculture. At that time, it was taken over by a branch of the Bani Yas tribe from the Liwa oasis to the south, (now, the Abu Dhabi emirate). The Maktoum family, whose descendants still rule the emirate today, led the takeover.

However, nothing much changed for Dubai until the late 1800s, when the then ruler, Sheikh Maktoum bin Hasher Al Maktoum, granted tax concessions to foreign traders, encouraging many of them to switch their base of operations (from Iran and Sharjah) to Dubai. By 1903, a British

Dubai Creek

shipping line had been persuaded to use Dubai as its main port of call in the area, giving traders direct links with British India and other important trading ports in the region. Encouraged by the farsighted and liberal attitudes of the rulers, Indian and Persian traders settled in the growing town, which soon developed a reputation as the leading commercial market in the region.

Dubai's importance was further helped by Sheikh Rashid bin Saeed Al Maktoum, father of the current ruler of Dubai, who recognised the importance of Dubai's Creek and improved facilities to attract more traders. The city came to specialise in the import and re-export of goods, mainly gold to India, and so it was that trade became the foundation of the wealth of this modern day emirate.

In the broader perspective, Dubai and the other emirates had accepted the protection of the British in 1892 in the culmination of a series of maritime truces. The British regarded the Gulf region as an important communication link with its empire in India, and wanted to ensure that other world powers, in particular France and Russia, didn't extend their influence in the region. In Europe, the area became known as the Trucial Coast (or Trucial States), a name it retained until the departure of the British in 1971.

In 1968, Britain announced its withdrawal from the region and tried to create a single state consisting of Bahrain, Qatar and the Trucial Coast. The ruling sheikhs, particularly of Abu Dhabi and Dubai, realised that by uniting forces they would have a stronger voice in the wider Middle East region. Negotiations collapsed when Bahrain and Qatar chose to become independent states. However, the Trucial Coast remained committed to forming an alliance and in 1971, the federation of the United Arab Emirates was created.

The new state was composed of the emirates of Dubai, Abu Dhabi, Ajman, Fujairah, Sharjah, Umm Al Quwain and, in 1972, Ras Al Khaimah (each emirate is named after its main town). Under the agreement, the individual emirates each retained a certain degree of autonomy, with Abu Dhabi and Dubai providing the most input into the federation. The leaders of the new federation elected the ruler of Abu Dhabi, His Highness Sheikh Zayed bin Sultan Al Nahyan, to be their president, a position he has held ever since.

However, the creation of what is basically an artificial state, hasn't been without its problems. Boundaries between the different emirates have been the main cause of disputes. At the end of Sheikh Zayed's first term as president in 1976, he threatened to resign if the other rulers didn't settle the demarcation of their borders. The threat proved an effective way of ensuring co-operation; however, the degree of independence of the various emirates has never been fully determined. The position still isn't settled but there does seem to be more focus on the importance of the federation as a whole, led by Abu Dhabi whose wealth and sheer size makes it the most powerful of the emirates.

The formation of the UAE came after the discovery of huge oil reserves in Abu Dhabi in 1958 (Abu Dhabi has an incredible 10% of the world's known oil reserves). This discovery dramatically transformed the emirate from one of the poorest states into the richest. In 1966, Dubai, which was already a relatively wealthy trading centre, also discovered oil. The oil revenue allowed the development of an economic and social

Sunset Over Sheikh Zayed Road

infrastructure, which is the basis of today's modern society. Education, healthcare, roads, housing, and women's welfare were all priorities. Much of the credit for this development can be traced to the vision and dedication of the late Ruler, HH Sheikh Rashid bin Saeed Al Maktoum, who ensured that Dubai's oil revenues were deployed to maximum effect. His work has been continued by the present Ruler, HH Sheikh Maktoum bin Rashid Al Maktoum.

Although it seems that the modern story of the UAE is rather short, history is, nevertheless, being made on a daily basis.

Economy

UAE

The UAE has an open economy today, with one of the world's highest per capita incomes (estimated at US $19,000 in 2002), although this is far from being evenly spread amongst the population. The UAE's wealth, once chiefly based on the oil sector, now sees an oil contribution of only around 34% of the country's gross domestic product (GDP). The GDP for 2002 was approximately Dhs.255 billion. Abu Dhabi and Dubai contribute most to the country's GDP – the figures for 2002 put these at 55% and 26% respectively.

Over 90% of the UAE's oil reserves lie in Abu Dhabi, and there is enough at the current rate of production (just over 2.5 million barrels per day) to last a further 100 years. However, although there is a heavy dependence on the oil and gas industry, trade, manufacturing, tourism and construction also play an important part in the national economy. Investment in infrastructure and development projects exceeded an estimated Dhs.250 billion in 2001. The UAE's main export partners are Saudi Arabia, Iran, Japan, India, Singapore, South Korea, and Oman. The main import partners are Japan, USA, UK, Italy, Germany and South Korea.

The situation in the Emirates is radically different from that of 30 - 40 years ago, when the area consisted of small, impoverished desert states. Visitors will find a unified and forward looking state with a high standard of living and a relatively well balanced and stable economy. Current reports note that the country's economy is roughly 36 times larger than it was in 1971, a mere 32 years ago! With an annual growth rate of 4.9%, the UAE has one of the fastest real GDP growth rates in the world and the UAE's credit rating was ranked A2 (tied with Kuwait for first place in the GCC) by Moody's for the year 2003.

Dubai Overview

Other options → Business [p.130]

While oil has been crucial to Dubai's development since the late 1960s, the non oil sector currently contributes some 90% of the total gross domestic product and is continuing to expand in importance. Because of this, Dubai has been less affected by the recent ups and downs in crude oil prices than other countries in the region. Manufacturing and tourism are both growing at a steady rate, helping to create a well balanced and diverse economy.

Trade remains the lifeblood of Dubai's business life, as it has for generations. This long trading tradition, which earned Dubai the reputation of 'the city of merchants' in the Middle East, continues to be an important consideration for foreign companies looking at opportunities in the region today. It is reflected not just in a regulatory environment that is open and liberal, but also in the local business community's familiarity with international commercial practices and the city's cosmopolitan lifestyle.

The relative buoyancy of Dubai's economy is reflected most obviously in the many building programmes around the city. New shops, offices and apartment blocks seemingly appear overnight. Likewise, the growth in new hotels is considerable and the main chains are all well represented.

However, don't be blinded by the healthy economy into believing that the average expat coming to work in Dubai will necessarily be on a huge salary.

Dhows on the Creek

The wealth isn't spread evenly and, except for highly skilled professionals, the salaries for most types of work are dropping. This downward trend is attributed in part to the willingness of workers to accept a job at a very low wage. While the UAE GDP per capita income was estimated at approximately Dhs.80,000 in 2002, this figure includes all sections of the community and the average labourer can expect to earn as little as Dhs.600 (US $165) per month.

Unemployment levels in the national population are high. This is partly due to their desire to work in the public sector (where salaries and benefits are better), and partly because of qualifications not matching the skills required in the private sector. However, the government is trying to reverse this scenario and reduce unemployment in the local sector with a 'nationalisation' or 'emiratisation' programme (this is common to countries throughout the region). By putting the local population to work, the eventual goal is to rely less on an expat workforce. This is being achieved by improving vocational training and by making it compulsory for certain categories of company, such as banks, to hire a determined percentage of Emiratis. In another attempt to get more Nationals attracted to the private sector, the government has a pension scheme where private companies are required to provide a pension for their national employees.

Tourism Developments

Other options ➜ Annual Events [p.50]
Key Dubai Projects [p.134]

With tourism contributing over 40% to Dubai's economy, the emirate is well ahead of other countries in the Middle East, which all seem to be playing a losing game of 'catch up'. Over 4.7 million tourists visited Dubai in 2002; this figure is expected to grow to 15 million by 2010. Good infrastructure, the practically crime free environment, government regulated public transport etc, all add to the draw of the sun, the sands and the shopping.

Really Tax Free?

Taxes. Do they exist in Dubai? Well, yes and no. You don't pay income or sales tax except when you purchase alcohol from a licensed liquor store – and then you'll be hit with a steep 30% tax. The main taxes that you will come across are a municipality tax in the form of a 5% rent tax and 10% on food, beverages and rooms in hotels. The rest are hidden taxes in the form of 'fees', such as your car registration renewal and visa/permit fees.

Dubai International Exhibition & Convention Centre

Revenue generated from the tourism sector stood at approximately Dhs.3 billion in 2001.

Almost all leading hotel chains are represented in Dubai. There are currently 280 hotels with over 23,000 hotel rooms, and more coming on the market on what seems to be a daily basis.

Investment in tourism is truly phenomenal. For Dubai 2003 – World Bank and IMF Summit of Governors – the focus was on the construction of a Dhs.850 million convention centre and hall spread over 11,500 square metres. It is hoped that the new facilities will boost meetings, incentive, conference and exhibition (MICE) tourism. Dubai already hosts over 50 international exhibitions each year. See [p.54] for a listing of this year's main events.

One of the most impressive ongoing projects is Dubai Palm Islands – the world's two largest manmade islands, to be created in the shape of palm trees stretching out 5 km from the Jumeira coastline. When completed, the islands will be visible from the moon by the naked eye and will add 120 km to Dubai's coastline, effectively doubling it! Each 'island' will be six km in diameter, consisting of 17 'fronds' and will be protected by a barrier reef. On the Jebel Ali Palm, the Middle East's first marine park will complement 2,200 villas, 1,500 apartments and 40 luxury hotels. The Palm, Jumeirah's villas and town homes sold out within days of release to the market, and the list of proud home owners includes David Beckham and half the England football team!

Following in its awe inspiring lead, The World project was announced. The first island project of this size and magnitude, The World will comprise 250 artificial islands shaped like countries, spreading five kilometres off Dubai's shores. It is due for completion by late 2005.

The Dubai development bug then dived underwater and the Hydropolis Hotel was announced. This is the world's first underwater hotel, built to a depth of 20 metres. Targeted for completion by 2006, the entire project will comprise a land station as a reception, a connecting tunnel that provides access to the hotel and the submarine complex, which will be the hotel itself.

The hugely successful Dubai Shopping Festival attracts over 2.5 million visitors each year (2.92 million last year), with shopping bargains to be found all over the city and attractions such as the Global Village, where people can visit pavilions from various countries, learn more about each culture and purchase traditional items, plus some real junk! The Dubai Shopping Festival's annual ad campaigns stretch worldwide and cost millions of dollars. Dubai Summer Surprises, held annually during July and August, brings in large numbers of mostly GCC visitors and features numerous events that focus on children and the family.

Inaugurated in 2001, the cruise ship terminal at Port Rashid brings thousands of cruise passengers to the city during the mild winter season. The government is making active efforts to put Dubai on the global cruise map. Dhs.15 million have been invested in Al Minsaf – a luxury vessel which offers lunch, sunset and dinner cruises on the Creek to Dubai bound tourists and executives. The 60 metre boat is light and covered with transparent glass, and has a 350 guest capacity at any given time.

Dubai International Airport, the second fastest growing airport in the world, handled almost 18 million passengers in 2003. The upcoming Terminal 3 and Concourses 2 & 3 aim to accommodate a projected 30 million passengers by 2010.

The construction boom is ongoing, with Dubai Festival City completion planned for fall 2006. Festival City, to be comprised of six concentric bands of buildings following the curve of the Creek, will house apartments, offices, restaurants and hotels, and will be the new focal point for the Dubai Shopping Festival.

The Mall of the Emirates, coming up on Sheikh Zayed Road, held the banner for the highest retail space outside North America until the Dubai Mall project was announced (see below). This mall also includes a snow dome (a 300,000 square feet ski resort!) and a five star hotel with 400 rooms.

Opening in 2004, The Gardens Shopping Centre will feature the world's largest maze, encompassing over 1,200 metres.

As if the largest and the biggest wasn't enough, the tallest has also been covered. Already under construction, the Burj Dubai has been earmarked as the world's tallest tower, and will exceed the height of the Petronas Twin Towers in Kuala Lumpur (currently the tallest). And nestled in its grounds is, not surprisingly, the world's biggest mall – Dubai Mall. The shopping space will be larger than the Mall of America in Bloomington, Minnesota, and it will also contain the world's biggest gold souk.

The tourist attraction that is sure to pull the Disney going crowd to this city in the sands is Dubailand. This project consists of six 'worlds' (Attractions & Experience World, Sport & Outdoor World, Eco-Tourism World etc) and the phenomenal scale is sure to create a unique tourism, leisure and entertainment destination. It will also house Dubai Heritage Vision – a permanent showcase of local and Middle Eastern culture, spreading over 380 hectares of desert. It aims to create a recreational/learning experience about the region.

In addition to the construction boom, steps are continually being taken to ensure that Dubai's image remains spotless. It is now rare to find street vendors hawking Russian army binoculars or woodcarvings, and you'll no longer see newspaper vendors at the traffic lights. Car washing without permission and begging are also illegal. What you may find these days though, are vendors with a very temporary 'stall' set up on the sidewalk, selling pirated DVDs and VCDs from the Far East. The Dubai Police are making a concerted effort to stop this trade, but the vendors seem to multiply faster than the numbers thrown in jail or deported!

The Palm, Jebel Ali

Dubai isn't yet targeting or catering to the backpacker crowd. Instead, it has kept its sights on the more upscale travel market and for the moment, there isn't much to entice backpackers to this region except the six youth hostels spread over the emirates.

International Relations

In its foreign relations, the UAE's stance is one of non alignment, but it is committed to the support of Arab unity. The country became a member of the United Nations and the Arab League in 1971. It is a member of the International Monetary Fund (IMF), the Organisation of Petroleum Exporting Countries (OPEC), the World Trade Organisation (WTO) and other international and Arab organisations. It is also a member of the Arab Gulf Co-operation Council (AGCC, also known as the GCC), whose other members are Bahrain, Kuwait, Oman, Qatar and Saudi Arabia. The UAE, led by Sheikh Zayed bin Sultan Al Nahyan, had a leading role in the formation of the AGCC in 1981 and the country is the third largest member in terms of geographical size, after Saudi Arabia and Oman. All major embassies and consulates are represented either in Dubai or in Abu Dhabi, or both.

Government & Ruling Family

The Supreme Council of Rulers is the highest authority in the UAE, comprising the hereditary rulers of the seven emirates. Since the country is governed by hereditary rule, there is little distinction between the royal families and the government. The Supreme Council is responsible for general policy matters involving education, defence, foreign affairs, communications and development, and for ratifying federal laws. The Council meets four times a year and the Abu Dhabi and Dubai rulers have effective power of veto over decisions.

The seven members of the Supreme Council elect the chief of state (the President) from among its members. The President of the UAE is HH Sheikh Zayed bin Sultan Al Nahyan who is also Ruler of Abu Dhabi. He has been President since independence on December 6, 1971 and ruler of Abu Dhabi since August 6, 1966. The Supreme Council also elects the Vice President, who is HH Sheikh Maktoum bin Rashid Al Maktoum, Ruler of Dubai. The President and Vice President are elected and appointed for five year terms. The President appoints the Prime Minister (currently HH Sheikh Maktoum bin Rashid Al Maktoum) and the Deputy Prime Minister.

The Federal Council of Ministers is responsible to the Supreme Council. It has executive authority to initiate and implement laws and is a consultative assembly of 40 representatives who are appointed for two years by the individual emirates. The council monitors and debates government policies, but has no power of veto.

The individual emirates still have a degree of autonomy, and laws that affect everyday life vary between the emirates. For instance, if you buy a car in one emirate and need to register it in a different emirate, you will first have to export and then re-import it! All emirates have a separate police force, with different uniforms and cars, and while it is possible to buy alcohol in Dubai, it is not in Sharjah. However, while there are differences

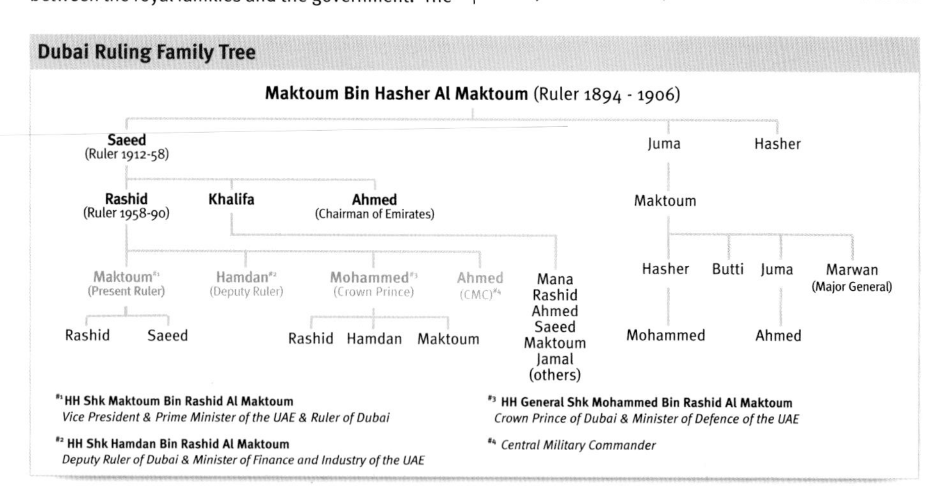

between the emirates, the current move is towards greater interdependence and the increasing power of the Federation.

Facts & Figures

Population

A national census is taken every ten years and the following figures are based on the last one (taken in 1995), as well as Ministry of Planning figures for 2001. According to the Ministry, the population of the UAE stood at 2,377,453 in 1995. The end of year count for 2002 put the total number of UAE Nationals and expat residents at 3,754,000.

Dubai's population stood at 276,301 in 1980 and 674,101 in 1995, while the end of year figures for 2002 put the population at over 1,100,000. The annual growth rate is estimated at around 6%, and there are 2.4 men to every woman in Dubai. A recent Dubai Municipality statistical survey revealed that the average size of a UAE National household is 7.6 members, while that of the expat is 3.7.

According to the United Nations Development Program (UNDP), the UAE has the highest life expectancy in the Arab world at 72.2 years for males and 75.6 years for females.

National Flag

In a nation continually striving for world records, when 30 year anniversary celebrations were marked on National Day 2001, the world's tallest flagpole was erected in Abu Dhabi and the world's largest UAE flag was raised at the Union House in Jumeira, Dubai. The UAE flag comprises three equal horizontal bands: green at the top, white in the middle and black at the bottom. A thicker vertical band of red runs down the hoist side.

Local Time

The UAE is four hours ahead of UCT (Universal Co-ordinated Time – formerly known as GMT). There is no summer time saving when clocks are altered. Hence, when it is 12:00 midday in Dubai, it is 03:00 in New York, 08:00 in London, 13:30 in Delhi, and 17:00 in Tokyo (not allowing for any summer time saving in those countries).

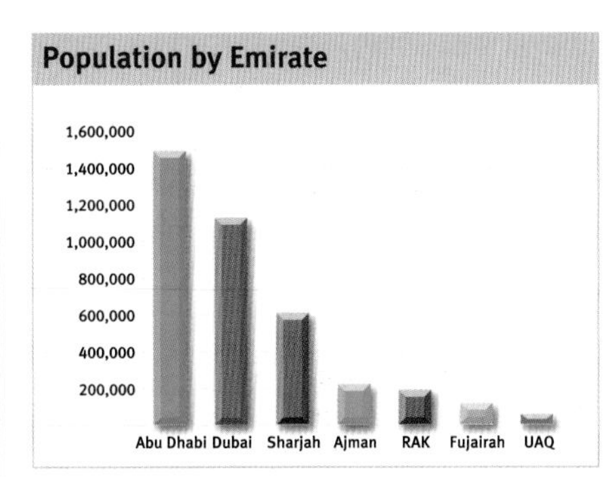

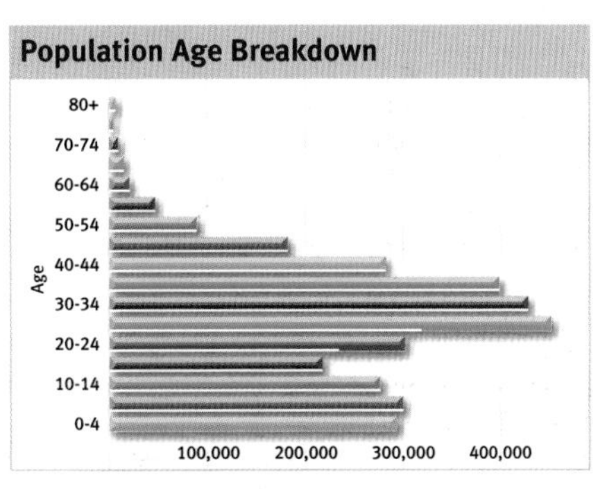

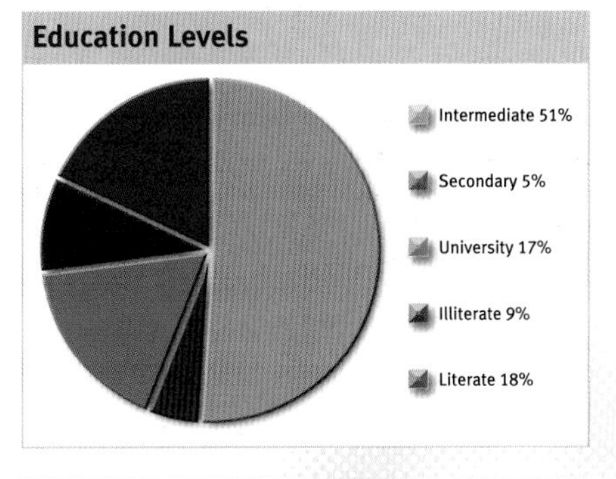

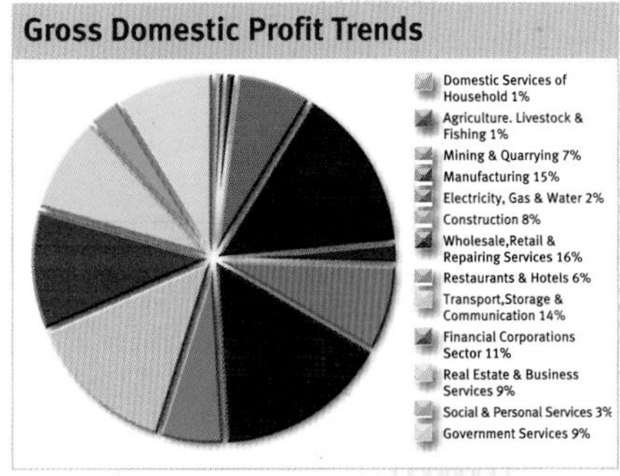

Source: Ministry of Planning

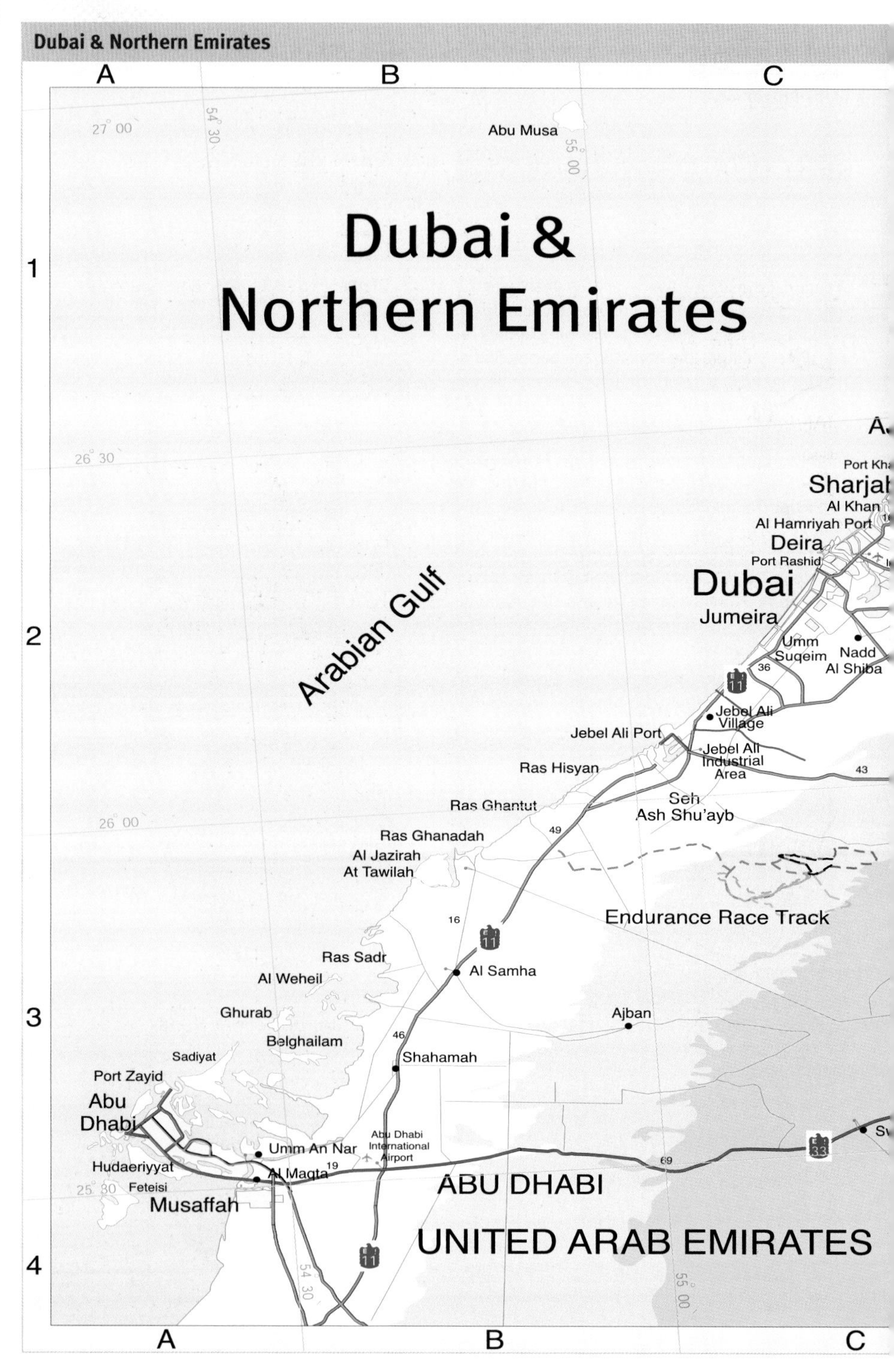
A
B
C
1
2
3
4
27° 00
54° 30
55° 00
26° 30
26° 00
25° 30
Abu Musa
Dubai &
Northern Emirates
Arabian Gulf
Port Kha
Sharjah
Al Khan
Al Hamriyah Port
Deira
Port Rashid
Dubai
Jumeira
Umm
Suqeim
Nadd
Al Shiba
36
Jebel Ali
Village
Jebel Ali Port
Jebel Ali
Industrial
Area
43
Ras Hisyan
Seh
Ash Shu'ayb
Ras Ghantut
49
Ras Ghanadah
Al Jazirah
At Tawilah
16
Endurance Race Track
Ras Sadr
Al Weheil
Al Samha
Ghurab
Ajban
Belghailam
46
Sadiyat
Shahamah
Port Zayid
Abu
Dhabi
Umm An Nar
Abu Dhabi
International
Airport
Hudaeriyyat
Al Maqta
19
69
Feteisi
Musaffah
ABU DHABI
UNITED ARAB EMIRATES
A
B
C

Dhs.100 ~ € 26

SULTANATE OF OMAN
Gulf of Oman
Ras Al Khaimah
RAS AL KHAIMAH
Umm Al Qaiwain
AJMAN
Sharjah
Fujairah
SULTANATE OF OMAN
Al Buraymi
Al Ain
This map is Not an authority on international boundaries
Copyright © 2000 by Dubai Municipality

Social & Business Hours

Other options ➜ Business [p.130]

Social hours are very Mediterranean in style. In general, people get up early, often have an afternoon siesta and eat late in the evening. The attitude to time, especially in business, is often very different from the 'time is money' approach in other parts of the world. So, don't be frustrated if your business meeting takes place a day late – the 'Inshallah' (God willing) attitude prevails!

Traditionally, there is no concept of the weekend, although Friday has always been the holy day. In the modern UAE, the weekend has established itself on different days, generally according to the company. Until recently, government offices had Thursday afternoon and Friday off, but a 1998 ruling established a five day week for government offices and schools, which are now closed all day Thursday and Friday. Some private companies still take half of Thursday and all day Friday off, while others take all day Friday and Saturday as their weekend. Understandably, these differences cause difficulties, since companies may now be out of touch with international business for up to four days, plus families do not necessarily share weekends.

Government offices are open from 07:30 - 13:30, Saturday to Wednesday. In the private sector, office hours vary between split shift days, which are generally 08:00 - 13:00, re-opening at either 15:00 or 16:00 and closing at 18:00 or 19:00; or straight shifts, usually 09:00 - 18:00, with an hour for lunch.

Shop opening times are usually based on split shift hours, although outlets in many of the big shopping malls now remain open all day. Closing times are usually 22:00 or 24:00, while some food shops and petrol stations are open 24 hours a day. On Fridays, many places are open all day, apart from prayer time (11:30 - 13:30), while larger shops in the shopping malls only open in the afternoon from either 12:00 or 14:00.

Embassies and consulates open from 08:45 - 13:30. They are closed on Fridays and in most cases on Saturdays, but generally leave an emergency contact number on their answering machines.

During Ramadan, work hours in most public and some private organisations are reduced by two to three hours per day, and business definitely slows down during this period. Many offices start work an hour or so later and shops are open till late into the night. The more popular shopping malls are crowded at midnight and parking at that time is tough to find!

Public Holidays

Other options ➜ Annual Events [p.50]

The Islamic calendar starts from the year 622 AD, the year of Prophet Mohammed's (Peace Be Upon Him) migration (Hijra) from Mecca to Al Madinah. Hence the Islamic year is called the Hijri year and dates are followed by AH (After Hijra).

The Hijri calendar is based on lunar months; there are 354 or 355 days in the Hijri year, which is divided into 12 lunar months, and is thus 11 days shorter than the Gregorian year.

As some holidays are based on the sighting of the moon and do not have fixed dates on the Hijri calendar, the dates of Islamic holidays are notoriously imprecise, with holidays frequently being confirmed less than 24 hours in advance. Some non religious holidays are fixed according to the Gregorian calendar.

Public Holidays - 2004

New Year's Day (1)	Jan 1 Fixed
Eid Al Adha (4)	Feb 2 Moon
Islamic New Year's Day (1)	Feb 22 Moon
Prophet Mohammed's Birthday (1)	May 2 Moon
Accession of H.H Sheikh Zayed (1)	Aug 6 Fixed
Lailat Al Mi'Raj (1)	Sept 12 Moon
Ramadan begins	Oct 15 Moon
Eid Al Fitr (3)	Nov 14 Moon
UAE National Day (2)	Dec 2 Fixed

The different emirates also have their own different fixed holidays, such as the accession of HH Sheikh Zayed, which is only celebrated in Abu Dhabi. The number of days a holiday lasts is in brackets in the table shown above. However, this applies to the public sector only, since not all the listed holidays are observed by the private sector, and often, the public sector gets a day or two more.

Electricity & Water

Other options ➜ Utilities & Services [p.96]

Electricity and water services in Dubai are excellent and power cuts or water shortages are almost unheard of. Both of these utilities are provided by Dubai Electricity & Water Authority (known as DEWA).

The electricity supply is 220/240 volts and 50 cycles; the socket type is the same as the three point British system; most hotels and homes have adapters for electrical appliances.

The tap water is heavily purified and safe to drink, but most people prefer to drink the locally bottled mineral waters, of which there are several different brands available. Bottled water is usually served in hotels and restaurants.

Photography

Normal tourist photography is acceptable, but, like anywhere in the world, it is courteous to ask permission before photographing people, particularly women. In general, photographs of government buildings, military installations, ports and airports should not be taken.

There is a wide choice of films available and processing is usually cheap and fast, but the quality of reproduction may vary. Ultra violet filters for your camera are advisable. APS, 35mm negative and slide film can all be processed; however, the cost of processing and developing APS is high and very few places around town deal with slide film. Prolab (347 7616) is your best bet for processing slide film, as well as medium or large format film.

Environment

Climate

Dubai has a sub tropical and arid climate; sunny blue skies and high temperatures can be expected most of the year, and rainfall is infrequent and irregular, falling mainly in winter (November to March (13 cm per year)). Temperatures range from a low of around 10° C (50° F) in winter, to a high of 48°C (118°F) in summer. The mean daily maximum is 24° C (75° F) in January, rising to 41° C (106° F) in August.

During winter, there are occasional sandstorms when the sand is whipped up off the desert (the wind is known as the shamal). More surprisingly, winter mornings can be foggy, but by mid morning, the sun invariably burns the cloud away. The summer humidity can be a killer approaching 100%, so be prepared to sweat! The most pleasant time to visit Dubai is in the cooler winter months.

For up to date weather reports, log on to www.bbc.co.uk/weather and choose your destination.

Dubai Temperature & Humidity

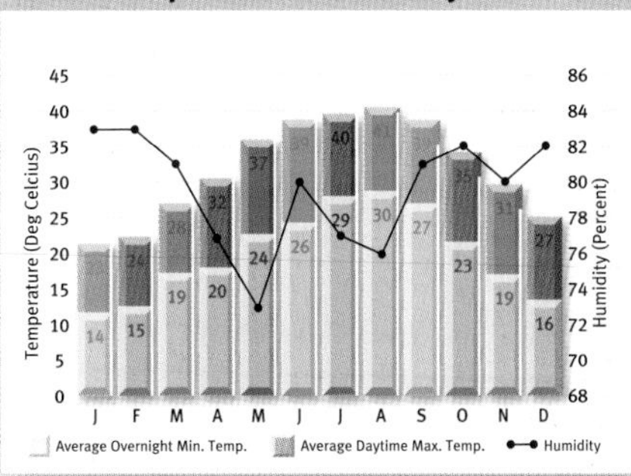

Average Number of Days With Rain

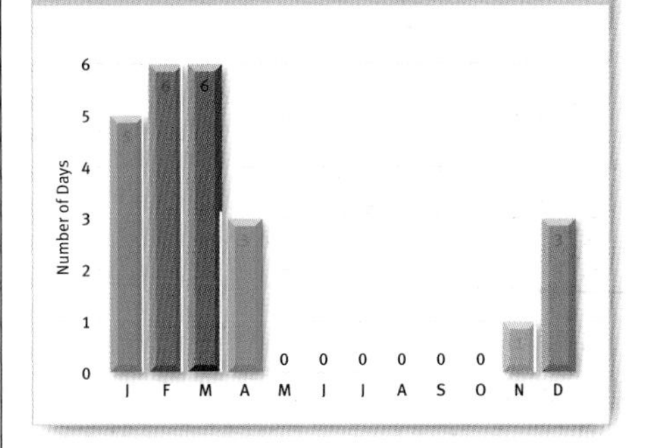

Flora & Fauna

Other options → Arabian Wildlife [p.16]

As you would expect in a country with such an arid climate, the variety of flora and fauna in the Emirates is not as extensive as in other parts of the world. Still, a variety of creatures and plant forms has managed to adapt to a life of high temperatures and little rainfall.

In the city of Dubai, as in all cities in the Emirates to a greater or lesser extent, the Municipality has an extensive 'greening' programme underway. Areas along the roads are incredibly colourful for a desert environment, with grass, palm trees and flowers being constantly maintained by an army of workers and round the clock watering. The city also boasts a large number of attractive and well kept parks (see Parks [p.154]).

The region has about 3,500 endemic plants – amazing considering the high salinity of the soil and the harsh environment. The date palm is the most obvious of the indigenous flora, and this

provides wonderful seas of green, especially in the oases. Heading towards the mountains, flat topped Acacia trees and wild grasses give a feel of an African 'savannah'. The deserts, in places, are often surprisingly green, even during the dry summer months, but it takes an experienced botanist to get the most out of the area.

Indigenous fauna includes the Arabian Leopard and the Ibex, but sightings of them are extremely rare. Realistically, the only large animals you will see are camels and goats (often roaming dangerously close to roads). Other desert life includes the Sand Cat, Sand Fox and Desert Hare, plus gerbils, hedgehogs, snakes and geckos.

Birdlife in the city is limited – this isn't a place for hearing a dawn chorus, unless you're lucky with where you live. However, recent studies have shown that the number of species of birds is rising each year, due in part to the increasing lushness of the area. This is most apparent in the parks, especially in spring and autumn, for the country lies on the route for birds migrating between Central Asia and East Africa. You can even see flamingos at the Khor Dubai Wildlife Sanctuary at the southern end of Dubai Creek.

Off the coast, the seas contain a rich abundance of marine life, including tropical fish, jellyfish, coral, the dugong ('sea cow') and sharks. Eight species of whale and seven species of dolphin have been recorded in UAE waters. Various breeds of turtle are also indigenous to the region. These include the loggerhead, green and hawksbill turtles, all of which are under threat from man. These may be seen by divers off both coasts, and if you are lucky, near the East Coast at Kalba (see Khor Kalba [p.166]). The most popular local fish is hammour, which is a type of grouper and can be found on most restaurant menus.

Protection

The UAE's, and specifically Sheikh Zayed's, commitment to the environment is internationally recognised. At the Environment 2001 Conference and Exhibition in Abu Dhabi, a statement was made that the UAE would invest US $46 billion on projects related to the environment over the next ten years. Sheikh Zayed set up the Zayed International Prize for the Environment and has himself been awarded the WWF's (World Wide Fund for Nature) Gold Panda Award.

Various organisations have been formed to protect the environment, as well as to educate the population on the importance of environmental issues. The Environmental Research and Wildlife Development Agency or ERWDA (02 681 7171) was established in 1996 to assist the Abu Dhabi government in the conservation and management of the emirate's natural environment, resources, wildlife and biological diversity. Sir Bani Yas Island in Abu Dhabi has an internationally acclaimed breeding programme for endangered wildlife. There is also an active branch of the World Wide Fund for Nature in Dubai (353 7761). The Arabian Wildlife Centre in Sharjah also has a successful breeding programme for endangered wildlife, particularly the Arabian Leopard.

The UAE is party to international agreements on biodiversity, climate change, desertification, endangered species, hazardous wastes, marine dumping and ozone layer protection. In addition to emirate wide environmental controls, Dubai has strictly enforced laws governing the use of chemical insecticides. In 2001, the Dubai government banned any further development along the coast without prior government permission.

Al Mamzar Park

Despite all the efforts being made, there are still some serious environmental issues facing the UAE. With no rainfall to speak of for the past few years, the water table is at record low levels and desalination plants work overtime to satisfy a thirsty population and keep the numerous parks and verges green. Desertification and beach pollution from oil spills are other areas of worry; one large spill off the coast in 2001 had hundreds of municipality employees and volunteers cleaning up Gulf beaches for weeks afterwards.

See also: *Environmental Groups [p.328]*

Culture & Lifestyle

Culture

Other options → Business [p.130]

Dubai's culture is firmly rooted in the Islamic traditions of Arabia. Islam is more than just a religion; it is a way of life that governs even the minutiae of everyday events, from what to wear to what to eat and drink. Thus, the culture and heritage of the UAE is tied to its religion. In parts of the world, Islamic fundamentalism has given the 'outside' world a very extreme, blanket view of the religion. However, in contrast to this image, the UAE is very tolerant and welcoming; foreigners are free to practice their own religion, alcohol is served in hotels and the dress code is liberal. Women face little discrimination and, contrary to the policies of Saudi Arabia and Iran, are able to drive and walk around unescorted. Among the most highly prized virtues are courtesy and hospitality, and visitors are sure to be charmed by the genuine warmth and friendliness of the people.

Connected!

'Wasta' means connections. If you've got them, all power to you – they'll take you far! However, most people in Dubai don't have wasta – it's reserved for the select few who have somehow managed to establish the 'right' contacts, either through family or friends. It's pretty much the same as in any other country (very much like an old boys' network); however, here it's more pronounced, as rules and regulations aren't always set in stone.

The rapid economic development over the last 30 years has changed life in the Emirates beyond recognition in many ways. However, the country's rulers are very aware of the danger that their traditional heritage will be eroded by the speed of development and increased access to outside cultures and material goods. They are therefore keen to promote cultural and sporting events that are representative of their past, such as falconry, camel racing and traditional dhow sailing. (Ironically, a large part of local entertainment focuses less on traditional pastimes and more on shopping and shopping festivals!) Nevertheless, traditional aspects of life are still apparent, most obviously in the clothes (see National Dress [p.19]). Arabic culture in poetry, dancing, songs and traditional art is encouraged, and weddings and celebrations are still colourful occasions of feasting and music.

In an attempt to give visitors a clearer appreciation of the Emirati way of life, the Sheikh Mohammed Centre for Cultural Understanding has been established to help bridge the gap between cultures.

See also: *Sheikh Mohammed Centre for Cultural Understanding [p.183].*

Language

The official language of the country is Arabic, although English, Urdu and Hindi are spoken and, with some perseverance, understood! Arabic is the official business language, but English is widely used and most road and shop signs, restaurant menus etc, are in both languages. The further out of town you get, the more Arabic you will find, both spoken and on street and shop signs. Refer to [p.18] for a quick list of useful Arabic phrases to get you around town.

Arabic isn't the easiest language to pick up... or to pronounce! But if you can throw in a couple of words of Arabic here and there, you're more likely to receive a warmer welcome or at least a smile. Most people are happy you're putting in the effort and will help you out with your pronunciation. Just give it a shot – it certainly won't hurt to try and it definitely helps when dealing with officials of any sort!

Religion

Other options → Annual Events [p.50]

Islam is the official religion of the UAE, but other religions are respected. Dubai has a variety of Christian churches: the Evangelical Community Church, Holy Trinity, International Christian Church, St Mary's (Roman Catholic) and St. Thomas Orthodox Church. There is also a Hindu temple in Bur Dubai.

Basic Arabic

General

Yes	na'am
No	la
Please	min fadlak (m) / min fadliki (f)
Thank you	shukran
Please (in offering)	tafaddal (m) / tafaddali (f)
Praise be to God	al-hamdu l-illah
God willing	in shaa'a l-laah

Greetings

Greeting (peace be upon you)	as-salaamu alaykom
Greeting (in reply)	wa alaykom is salaam
Good morning	sabah il-khayr
Good morning (in reply)	sabah in-nuwr
Good evening	masa il-khayr
Good evening (in reply)	masa in-nuwr
Hello	marhaba
Hello (in reply)	marhabtayn
How are you?	kayf haalak (m) / kayf haalik (f)
Fine, thank you	zayn, shukran (m) / zayna, shukran (f)
Welcome	ahlan wa sahlan
Welcome (in reply)	ahlan fiyk (m) / ahlan fiyki (f)
Goodbye	ma is-salaama

Introduction

My name is	ismiy ...
What is your name?	shuw ismak (m) / shuw ismik (f)
Where are you from?	min wayn inta (m) / min wayn inti (f)
I am from ...	anaa min
America	ameriki
Britain	braitani
Europe	oropi
India	al hindi

Questions

How many / much?	kam?
Where?	wayn?
When?	mata?
Which?	ayy?
How?	kayf?
What?	shuw?
Why?	laysh?
Who?	miyn?
To/ for	ila
In/ at	fee
From	min
And	wa
Also	kamaan
There isn't	maa fee

Taxi / Car Related

Is this the road to ...	hadaa al tariyq ila
Stop	kuf
Right	yamiyn
Left	yassar
Straight ahead	siydaa
North	shamaal
South	januwb
East	sharq
West	garb
Turning	mafraq
First	awwal
Second	thaaniy
Road	tariyq
Street	shaaria
Roundabout	duwwaar
Signals	ishaara
Close to	qarib min
Petrol station	mahattat betrol
Sea/ beach	il bahar
Mountain/s	jabal / jibaal
Desert	al sahraa
Airport	mataar
Hotel	funduq
Restaurant	mata'am
Slow Down	schway schway

Accidents

Police	al shurtaa
Permit/ licence	rukhsaa
Accident	Haadith
Papers	waraq
Insurance	ta'miyn
Sorry	aasif (m) / aasifa (f)

Numbers

Zero	sifr
One	waahad
Two	ithnayn
Three	thalatha
Four	araba'a
Five	khamsa
Six	sitta
Seven	saba'a
Eight	thamaanya
Nine	tiss'a
Ten	ashara
Hundred	miya
Thousand	alf

Ramadan

In Islam, Ramadan is the holy month in which Muslims commemorate the revelation of the Holy Koran (the holy book of Islam, also spelt Quran). It is a time of fasting and Muslims abstain from all food, drinks, cigarettes and unclean thoughts between dawn and dusk. In the evening, the fast is broken with the iftar feast. Iftar timings are found in all the daily newspapers.

All over the city, festive Ramadan tents are filled to the brim each evening with people of all nationalities and religions enjoying shisha and traditional Arabic mezze and sweets. In addition to the standard favourite shisha cafés and restaurants around town, the five star hotels erect special Ramadan tents for the month.

Islam

The basis of Islam is the belief that there is only one God and that Prophet Mohammed (Peace Be Upon Him) is his messenger. There are five pillars of the faith, which all Muslims must follow: the Profession of Faith, Prayer, Charity, Fasting and Pilgrimage. Every Muslim is expected, at least once in his/her lifetime, to make the pilgrimage or 'Hajj' to the holy city of Mecca (also spelt Makkah) in Saudi Arabia.

Additionally, a Muslim is required to pray (facing Mecca) five times a day. The times vary according to the position of the sun. Most people pray at a mosque, although it's not unusual to see them kneeling by the side of the road if one is not close by. It is not considered polite to stare at people praying or to walk over prayer mats.

The modern day call to prayer, through loudspeakers on the minarets of each mosque, ensures that everyone knows it's time to pray. In Dubai, the plan is to build enough mosques so that residents do not have to walk more than 500 metres to pray. Friday is the holy day.

The timing of Ramadan is not fixed in terms of the western calendar, but each year it occurs approximately 11 days earlier than the previous year, with the start date depending on the sighting of the moon (see Public Holidays [p.14]). In 2004, Ramadan should commence around October 15th. Non Muslims are also required to refrain from eating, drinking or smoking in public places during daylight hours as a sign of respect. The sale of alcohol is restricted to after dusk, and office hours are cut, while shops and parks usually open and close later. In addition, entertainment such as live music is stopped and cinemas limit daytime screenings of films.

Ramadan ends with a three day celebration and holiday called Eid Al Fitr, or 'Feast of the Breaking of the Fast'. Seventy days later is another Eid holiday and celebration called Eid Al Adha, or 'Feast of the Sacrifice' and this marks the end of the pilgrimage season to Mecca. For Muslims, Eid has similar connotations as Diwali for Hindus and Christmas for Christians.

National Dress

On the whole, the national population still chooses to wear their traditional dress. For men this is the dishdash(a) or khandura – a white full length shirt dress, which is worn with a white or red checked headdress, known as a gutra. This is secured with a black cord (agal). Sheikhs and important businessmen may also wear a thin black or gold robe or mishlah, over their dishdasha at important events, which is equivalent to the dinner jacket in Western culture.

In public, women wear the black abaya – a long, loose black robe that covers their normal clothes – plus a headscarf called the sheyla. The abaya is often of very sheer, flowing fabric and may be open at the front. Some women also wear a thin black veil hiding their face and/or gloves, and older women sometimes still wear a leather mask, known as a burkha, which covers the nose, brow and cheekbones. Underneath the abaya, women traditionally wear a long tunic over loose, flowing trousers (sirwall), which are often heavily embroidered and fitted at the wrists and ankles. However, these are used more by the older generation and modern women will often wear trousers or a long skirt beneath the abaya.

Performers in National Dress

Sharjah has a Decency Law that penalises those who do not abide by a certain dress code and moral behaviour. 'Indecent dress' includes anything that exposes the stomach, back or legs above the knees. Tight fitting, transparent clothing is also not permitted, nor are acts of vulgarity, indecent noises or harassment. If you have offended the law, you will initially be given advice by the police on what decency is, and then warned to abide by the law in future. If the police find you breaking the law again, a more severe penalty will be imposed.

National Weddings

Weddings in the UAE are a serious and very large affair. Homes are lit from top to bottom with strings of white lights and the festivities last up to two weeks. Men and women celebrate separately, normally in a hotel ballroom or convention centre, depending on the number of guests. High dowries and extravagant weddings may be a thing of the past though, as the government has placed a ceiling of Dhs.50,000 on dowries, and lavish weddings can result in a prison sentence or Dhs.500,000 fine!

The government sponsored Marriage Fund, based in Abu Dhabi, assists Nationals in everything to do with marriage – from counselling and financial assistance (long term loans up to Dhs.70,000 for UAE National men marrying UAE National women) to organising group weddings to keep costs down. While marriage between a National man and a non National woman is legally permissible (but frowned upon), National women are not allowed to marry non National men. One of the marriage fund's main aims is to promote a reduction in the rate of foreign marriages by UAE Nationals.

Food & Drink

Other options → Eating Out

Dubai offers pretty much every type of international cuisine imaginable. While most restaurants are located in hotels and are thus able to offer alcohol, some of the best places to eat are the small street side stands around town. Refer to the Going Out section for details on anything and everything that is available to quench both hunger and thirst.

Arabic Cuisine

Modern Arabic cuisine is a blend of many types of cooking, from Moroccan, Tunisian or Iranian to Egyptian and Afghani, but in Dubai, modern Arabic cuisine invariably means Lebanese food. Sidewalk stands selling shawarma (lamb or chicken sliced from a spit and served in pita bread) and falafel (small savoury balls of deep fried beans), are worth a visit at least once. Fresh juices, especially the mixed fruit cocktails, are another highlight not to be missed.

Pork

Pork is not included on the Arabic menu. Do not underestimate how taboo this meat is to a Muslim. It is not just in eating the meat, but also in the preparation and service of it. Thus to serve pork, restaurants need a separate fridge, equipment, preparation, cooking areas etc. Supermarkets too, need a separate pork area in the shop and separate storage facilities. Images of pigs can also cause offence.

Additionally, in Islam it is forbidden to consume the blood or meat of any animal that has not been slaughtered in the correct manner. The meat of animals killed in accordance with the Islamic code is known as halaal.

Alcohol

Alcohol is only served in licensed outlets that are associated with hotels (ie, restaurants and bars), plus a few clubs (ie, golf) and associations. Restaurants outside of hotels that are not part of a club or association are not permitted to serve alcohol.

Nevertheless, permanent residents who are non Muslims can obtain alcohol for consumption at home without any difficulty. All they have to do is get a permit.

See also: *Liquor Licence [p.69]; Purchasing Alcohol [p.214]*

Shisha

Smoking the traditional shisha (water pipe) is a popular and relaxing pastime throughout the Middle East. It is usually savoured in a local café while chatting with friends. They are also known as hookah pipes or hubbly bubbly, but the proper name is nargile. Shisha pipes can be smoked with a variety of aromatic flavours, such as strawberry, grape or apple, and the experience is unlike normal cigarette or cigar smoking. The smoke is 'smoothed' by the water, creating a much more soothing effect. This is one of those things in life that should at least be tried once, and more so during Ramadan, when festive tents are erected throughout the city and filled with people of all nationalities and the fragrant smell of shisha tobacco.

See also: *Shisha Cafes*

Entering Dubai

Visas

Other options → Residence Visa [p.64]
Entry Visa [p.60]

Visa requirements for entering Dubai vary greatly between different nationalities, and regulations should always be checked before travelling, since details can change with little or no warning.

All visitors, except Arab Gulf Co-operation Council nationals (Bahrain, Kuwait, Qatar, Oman and Saudi Arabia), require a visa. However, citizens of the countries listed on this page will be granted a free visit visa on arrival.

Arabic Family Names

Arabic names have a formal structure that traditionally indicates the family and tribe of the person. Names usually start with that of an important person from the Koran or someone from the tribe. This is followed by the word bin (son of) for a boy or bint (daughter of) for a girl, and then the name of the child's father. The last name indicates the person's tribe or family. For prominent families, this has Al, the Arabic word for 'the', immediately before it. For instance, the President of the UAE is HH Sheikh Zayed bin Sultan Al Nahyan. When women get married, they do not change their name. Family names are very important here and extremely helpful when it comes to differentiating between the thousands of Mohammeds, Ibrahims and Fatimas!

Expat residents of the AGCC who meet certain criteria may obtain a non renewable 30 day visa on arrival. Oman visitors of certain nationalities may enter Dubai on a free of charge entry permit. The same criteria and facilities apply to Dubai visitors entering Oman.

Tourist nationalities (such as Eastern European, Chinese, South African and members of the former Soviet Union) may obtain a 30 day, non renewable tourist visa sponsored by a local entity, such as a hotel or tour operator, before entry into the UAE. Other visitors may apply for an entry service permit (for 14 days exclusive of arrival/departure days), valid for use within 14 days of the date of issue, or for a 60 day visit visa (renewable once for a total stay of 90 days) sponsored by a local company. This visit visa costs Dhs.120, plus DNATA (Dubai National Airline Travel Agency) visa delivery fee. Urgent visit visas, delivered in less than four days, can be obtained for Dhs.220, plus DNATA visa delivery fee.

For those travelling onwards to a destination other than that of original departure, a special transit visa (up to 96 hours) may be obtained free of charge through any airline carrier operating in the UAE.

'No Visa Required'

Citizens of Andorra, Australia, Austria, Belgium, Brunei, Canada, Denmark, Finland, France, Germany, Greece, Hong Kong (with the right of abode in the United Kingdom), Iceland, Ireland, Italy, Japan, Liechtenstein, Luxembourg, Malaysia, Monaco, The Netherlands, New Zealand, Norway, Portugal, San Marino, Singapore, South Korea, Spain, Sweden, Switzerland, United Kingdom (with the right of abode in the UK), United States of America and Vatican City now receive an automatic, free visit visa on arrival in Dubai.

A multiple entry visa is available for business visitors who have a relationship with a local business. It is valid for visits of a maximum 30 days each time, for six months from date of issue. It costs Dhs.1,000 and should be applied for after entering the UAE on a visit visa.

Airlines may require confirmation (a photocopy is acceptable) that you have a UAE visa before check in at the airport. If you have sponsorship from a UAE entity, ensure that they fax you a copy of the visa before the flight. The original is held at Dubai International Airport for collection before passport control. Your passport should have a minimum of three months validity left. Israeli nationals will not be issued visas.

Costs: Companies may levy a maximum of Dhs.50 extra in processing charges for arranging visas. The DNATA visa delivery service costs an extra Dhs.10.

Note: Visit visas are valid for 30 or 60 days, not one or two calendar months. If you overstay, there is a Dhs.100 fine for each day overstayed.

Visa Renewals

Visit visas may be renewed for a total stay of up to 90 days. Renewals are usually made by paying for a month's extension (Dhs.500) at the Department of Immigration and Naturalisation (398 1010), Karama, near the Dubai World Trade Centre roundabout (Map Ref 10-B1).

After the third month, you must either leave the country and arrange for a new visit visa from overseas or, for certain nationalities, fly out of the country on a 'visa run' (see next page).

The Airport

If you're lucky enough to have friends or family collect you from the airport, you'll avoid the hassles of fighting for a taxi with all the other passengers who have just arrived in Dubai. If not, find the curb and, along with everyone else, shove your way into the first available cab. You'll face a stiff Dhs.25 pick up charge, but there's nothing you can do about it (unless you don't mind hiking out of the airport with all your bags to hail a non airport licensed taxi).

If you're concerned about finding your friends or relatives when you arrive, have no fear. They have a bird's eye view of you as you stand in line waiting to go through Immigration (look up!), and there's only one narrow exit from the airport once you clear customs.

You'll have a bit of a trek before then, however, as the new terminal is huge. Apparently, it takes six escalators, two moving sidewalks and 3,446 steps to get from the aircraft door to a taxi at the main entrance ...and no baggage trolleys are provided till the end!

Need cash? There are ATM machines dotted around the airport in both the arrivals and departures areas. Currency exchanges are all over the departures area and outside the customs area in arrivals.

'Visa Run'

The 'visa run' (or 'visa change' flight) basically involves exiting and re-entering the country to gain an exit stamp and new entry stamp in your passport. Unfortunately driving over the border into Oman is not an option, since your passport will not be stamped with a UAE exit stamp. Hence, the visa run is a flight to a neighbouring country and back to Dubai.

The flight is invariably to Doha, Muscat or Kish Island and it returns an hour or so later. Passengers remain in transit and hence do not need a visa for the country they fly to. There are several flights daily and the cost is about Dhs.400 for a return flight, depending on the season. The low price is only offered for the visa flight and does not apply if you wish to spend any time in the country to which you are flying. Flights are offered by Emirates (214 4444), Gulf Air (271 3222) and Qatar Airways (229 2229). See also Travel Agents [p.157].

These flights are the cheapest option for those whose residency application has been approved by the Immigration department and now need to change their visa status for their application to proceed.

The visa run is also an opportunity to stock up on good value duty free, and there are sales outlets in both the departure and arrival halls of Dubai Airport.

Holders of passports that are allowed a visit visa on arrival at the airport currently have the option of making a visa run indefinitely.

Until 2000, the visa run was an option for all nationalities that had a Dubai sponsor willing to arrange for a new visit visa. Now, unless the situation reverts, a visa run is only possible for nationalities who can gain a visa stamp on arrival at Dubai International Airport. This was implemented in a crackdown on people working in the country illegally without sponsorship or residency.

E-Gate Service

In 2002, a new rapid passenger clearing service was unveiled by the Dubai Naturalisation and Residency Department and the Department of Civil Aviation. The 'e-Gate Service' allows UAE & GCC nationals, residents and nationals of the 33 countries permitted entry to the UAE without a visa (see [p.22]) to pass through both the departures and arrivals halls of Dubai International Airport without a passport. Swipe your smart card through an electronic gate and through you go, saving a great deal of time otherwise spent in long queues! Applications for a smart card are processed within minutes on the mezzanine floor of the Emirates Holidays building, Sheikh Zayed road; you'll need your passport, be fingerprinted and photographed.

Dubai International Airport

Starter Kit Explorer

Reside in peace. By pairing up the Dubai Explorer with the Zappy Explorer, you now have the ultimate culture shock antidote that shows you where to eat, sleep, shop and socialise, and simplifies your life with step by step procedures on opening a bank account, buying a car or even renting a home.

The smart card costs Dhs.150 and is valid for two years. Payment can be made in the form of cash/credit card. For further information, please contact the e-Gate smart card centre on 316 6966.

Smart Card

Plans are underway to take the Smart Card to a whole new level. This new card will, once developed, be the single most important document for a UAE National and resident expat. To be used as a multipurpose identification document, the card will contain details of the driving license, passport, health card, ATM card and more. It will be issued through registration centres spread throughout the country and will cost Dhs.300 (Dhs.100 for UAE Nationals) – a small price to pay for a considerably lighter purse.

Meet & Greet

Two reception services are offered at the airport to assist people with airport formalities. The Marhaba Service (224 5780) – ideal for children, the disabled and the elderly – is run by DNATA and operates mainly at Terminal 1 (plus a few airlines at Terminal 2), while Ahlan Dubai (602 5515) is run by the Civil Aviation Authority and is at Terminal 2. (Both the words marhaba and ahlan are Arabic for 'welcome'.)

Marhaba provides staff to greet new arrivals and guide them through Immigration and baggage collection. Through this service, you can also get general information and help with visas. To use Marhaba, a booking has to be made at least 24 hours in advance and passengers are met in the arrivals hall before passport control.

Cost: Marhaba cost varies according to the service required, but is usually Dhs.75 for one passenger and Dhs.50 each for 2 – 9 passengers. The cost for children between the ages of 2 – 12 years is Dhs.35. Ahlan Dubai is more limited, only offering help with visas for Dhs.10.

Customs

No customs duty is levied on personal effects entering Dubai. It is forbidden to import drugs and pornographic items.

At Dubai International Airport, after collecting your bags in the arrivals hall, they are x-rayed before you enter the city. Videos, DVD's, CD's books and magazines are sometimes checked and suspect items, usually movies, may be temporarily confiscated for the material to be approved. Unless it is offensive, it can be collected at a later date. The airport duty free has a small sales outlet in the arrivals hall.

There has been talk of restrictions on the import or export of large amounts of any currency since the events of 11 September 2001. We recommend that you check this out before you try it! Additionally, a new anti money laundering law will also, eventually, come into effect, which not only penalises individuals who violate the law, but also financial institutions. The penalty for money laundering will be a prison sentence of up to seven years or a maximum fine of Dhs.300,000. The limit for undeclared cash that can be brought into the country is Dhs.40,000.

Duty Free allowances:

- Cigarettes - 2,000
- Cigars - 400
- Tobacco - 2 kg
- Alcohol (non Muslim adults only) - 2 litres of spirits and 2 litres of wine
- Perfume - a 'reasonable amount'

Travellers' Info

Health Requirements

No health certificates are required for entry to the Emirates, except for visitors who have been in a cholera or yellow fever infected area in the previous 14 days. However, it is always wise to check health requirements before departure as restrictions may vary depending upon the situation at the time.

Malarial mosquitoes are not really a problem in the cities, although they do exist, mainly around the wadis and the mountain pool areas where it's damp. Long term residents rarely take malaria

tablets, but short term visitors who plan to visit the countryside during mosquito season may be advised to take them. Check out the requirements a month or so before leaving your home country.

Health Care

Other Options → Health [p.102]

The quality of medical care in the Emirates is generally regarded as quite high and visitors should have little trouble in obtaining appropriate treatment if they need it, whether privately or from the government run hospitals in case of an emergency. Tourists and non residents are strongly recommended to arrange private medical insurance before travelling since private medical care can become very expensive.

There are no specific health risks facing visitors, although the climate can be harsh, especially during the summer months. It is advisable to drink plenty of water (and to replace lost salts with energy drinks or salty snacks), and to cover up when out in the sun and use the appropriate factor sunscreen – sunburn, heat stroke and heat exhaustion can be very unpleasant.

Travel Insurance

All visitors to the Emirates should have travel insurance – just in case. Choose a reputable insurer with a plan that suits your needs as well as the activities you plan to do while in Dubai. Make sure this insurance also covers 'blood money' (see [p.39]) in case you are involved in an accident involving a death and are found at fault.

Female Visitors

Women should face few, if any, problems while travelling in the UAE. Thanks to a directive by Sheikh Mohammed, men who are caught harassing women have their photo published in the local newspaper. Single female travellers who don't want extra attention should avoid wearing tight fitting clothing and should steer clear of lower end hotels in Deira and Bur Dubai. No matter what, most females receive some unwanted stares at some time or another, particularly on the public beaches. If you can ignore it, you'll save yourself some aggravation! The Dubai Police are very helpful and respectful – call them if you face any unwanted attention or hassles.

Travelling with Children

Dubai is a great place for kids of all ages! Parks and amusement centres abound, and if those aren't interesting enough for the little ones, annual festivals such as the Dubai Shopping Festival and Dubai Summer Surprises offer all sorts of fun filled activities for the whole family. The Activities section will give a better idea of what there is to do with kids, as will the *Family Explorer (Dubai & Abu Dhabi)*. Hotels and shopping malls are well geared up for children, offering everything from babysitting services to kids' activities. Restaurants, on the other hand, have children's menus but tend not to have many high chairs; it's best to ask when making reservations. Discounted rates for children are common – just ask.

Disabled Visitors

Most of Dubai's five star hotels have wheelchair facilities, but in general, facilities for the disabled are very limited, particularly at tourist attractions. Wheelchair ramps are often really nothing more than delivery ramps, hence the steep angles. When asking if a location has wheelchair access, make sure it really does – an escalator is considered 'wheelchair access' to some! The Dubai International Airport is equipped for disabled travellers (see also: Meet & Greet [p.23]) and Dubai Transport has a few specially modified taxis. As for parking, good luck! Handicapped parking spaces do exist, but are often taken up by ignorant drivers who don't need the facility.

Hotels with specially adapted rooms for the disabled include: the Burj al Arab, City Centre Hotel, Crowne Plaza, Emirates Towers Hotel, Grand Hyatt Dubai, Hilton Dubai Creek, Hilton Dubai Jumeirah, Hyatt Regency, Jebel Ali Hotel, Jumeirah Beach Hotel, JW Marriott, Oasis Beach Hotel, The Ritz-Carlton, Dubai, Renaissance Hotel, One&Only Royal Mirage, Shangri-La and the Sheraton Jumeirah.

Dress Code

With its liberal attitude there isn't much that visitors to Dubai can't wear. However, as in all countries, a healthy amount of respect for the local customs and sensibilities doesn't go amiss. Short or tight clothing can be worn, but it will attract attention – most of it unwelcome. Like anywhere in the world, attitudes in the rural areas are more conservative than in the cities.

Lightweight summer clothing is suitable for most of the year, but something slightly warmer may be needed in the evening for the winter months. In winter and summer, be sure to take some sort of jacket or sweater when visiting hotels or the cinema, as the air conditioning can be pretty fierce! In the evenings, restaurants and clubs usually have a mixture of styles; Arabic, Asian or Western – and anything goes. During the day, loads of sunscreen, good quality sunglasses, hats and buckets of sunscreen are needed to avoid the lobster look!

Do's and Don'ts

Do make the most of your stay in Dubai – have fun! But don't break the law. It's a simple and easy rule, and common sense will keep you out of trouble. In the UAE, drugs are illegal and carry a normally lengthy jail sentence. If you are caught bringing drugs into the country, you will be charged with trafficking, which can result in a life sentence. Pornography of any sort is also illegal and will be confiscated immediately.

The best rule of thumb is to respect the local laws, culture and Muslim sensibilities of the UAE. Remember, you are a visitor here. Treat the local population with the same respect you'd expect back home.

Safety

While the crime rate in Dubai is very low, a healthy degree of caution should still be exercised. Keep your valuables and travel documents locked in your hotel room or in the hotel safe. When in crowds, be discreet with your money and wallet; don't carry large amounts of cash on you and don't trust strangers offering to double your money with magic potions. Money and gem related scams run by confidence tricksters are on the increase – be warned!

With the multitude of driving styles converging on Dubai's roads, navigating the streets either on foot or in a vehicle can be a challenge. Quick tips to make your experience on Dubai's streets safer: if your taxi driver is driving too aggressively, tell him to slow down. Cross roads only at designated pedestrian crossings, and make sure all cars have actually stopped for you before crossing. Learn the rules of the road before getting behind the wheel, and drive defensively. Make sure you have insurance!

Tourist Police

In an effort to better serve Dubai's visitors, the Dubai Police have launched the Department for Tourist Security. The role of this department is twofold: to assist visitors through educating them on safety in Dubai, as well as offering quick assistance if visitors face problems of any sort. They act as a liaison between you and the Dubai Police, and offer personal assistance. Dubai police officers are extremely helpful in general. They are calm and understanding, and speak a multitude of languages to better serve Dubai's international population. Their Website (www.dubaipolice.gov.ae) is easy to navigate, helpful, and even lists Dubai's top ten most wanted criminals – always an interesting read!

Contact: Call their toll free number (800 4438) for assistance.

Lost / Stolen Property

To avoid a great deal of hassle if your personal documents go missing, make sure you keep one photocopy with friends or family back home, and one copy in a safe place such as your hotel room safe.

If your valuables do go missing, first check with your hotel, or if you've lost something in a taxi, call the taxi company lost and found department. There are a lot of honest people in Dubai who will return found items. If you've had no luck, then try the Dubai Police or the Department for Tourist Security (see above) to report the loss or theft; you'll be advised on the next course of action. If you have lost your passport, your next stop will be your

Dubai Marina

embassy or consulate. Refer to [p.143] for a list of all embassies and consulates in Dubai.

Dubai Tourist Info Abroad

The Dubai Department of Tourism and Commerce Marketing (223 0000) operates 15 offices overseas, which promote Dubai to both travellers and businesses.

DTCM Overseas Offices

Australia & NZ	Sydney	+61 2 995 6620
East Africa	Nairobi	+25 4 224 6909
Far East	Hong Kong	+85 2 2827 5221
France	Paris	+33 1 4495 8500
Germany	Frankfurt	+49 69 7100 020
India	Mumbai	+91 22 2283 3497
Italy	Milan	+39 02 8691 3952
Japan	Tokyo	+81 3 3379 9311
Nordic Countries	Stockholm	+46 8 411 1135
North America	Philadelphia	+1 215 751 9750
Russia, CIS & Baltic States	Moscow	+7 95 933 6717
South Africa	Johannesburg	+27 11 785 4600
Switzerland & Austria	Zurich	+41 43 255 4444
UK & Ireland	London	+44 207 839 0580

Places to Stay

Visitors to Dubai will find an extensive choice of places to stay, from hotels to hotel apartments, youth hostels, and even an eco tourist hotel (the Al Maha resort located amongst the dunes on the road to Al Ain).

The growth in the number of hotels and hotel apartments over the last few years has been phenomenal. In the past nine years, the number of hotels has risen from 70 to nearly 300, with many more planned. With so many rooms (over 23,000 at the last count!) needing to be filled, it's not surprising that visitors can expect excellent service and facilities – at least at the higher end of the market.

One service that the larger hotels and hotel apartments offer is to act as a sponsor for those needing a visit visa. This service should cost about Dhs.180 (including mark up) for a regular, and Dhs.280 for an urgent visa. The visa is deposited at the airport for collection on arrival; however, the visitor is expected to stay at the accommodation.

Hotels

Hotels range from those costing under Dhs.100 a night to those with a published price, or rack rate of over Dhs.6,000 a night! While the hotels at the higher end of the market offer superb surroundings and facilities, those at the cheaper end vary – you pay for what you get. Refer to the Index for a list of outlets (including restaurants and bars) that can be found at each hotel.

Hotels in Dubai can be split into 'beach hotels' (grouped along the coast to the south of the Creek entrance) and 'city hotels'. Most are located within a maximum 30 minute journey from Dubai International Airport. The larger hotels all offer an airport shuttle service as well as a minibus service to the main tourist spots around the city. A taxi ride from the airport to most hotels will cost around Dhs.40 - 50. Road transport in Dubai is usually quite fast and the majority of journeys will only be of 15 - 20 minutes duration, costing about Dhs.20 - 25.

The Dubai Department of Tourism and Commerce Marketing (DTCM) oversees a hotel classification system which gives an internationally recognised star rating system to hotels and hotel apartments so that visitors can judge more easily the standard of accommodation they will receive.

The DTCM also operates an Internet reservation system for Dubai's hotels on their Website (http://dubaitourism.co.ae). This enables guests to reserve rooms online and allows them a virtual tour of the hotel before they book. Alternatively, the DTCM Welcome Bureau at the airport offers instant hotel reservations, often at a greatly discounted rate.

Refer to the Club Facilities table [p.318] for the list of facilities offered at each hotel. Remember that, as in anywhere else in the world, you can usually manage a discount on the rack rate or published price.

Hotel Apartments

A cheaper alternative to staying in a hotel is to rent furnished accommodation. This can be done on a daily/weekly/monthly or yearly basis and there are a number of agencies offering this service. One advantage is that the place can feel far more like home than a hotel room. Usually the apartments come fully furnished, from bed linen to cutlery, plus maid service. Additionally, there may be sports facilities, such as a gym and a swimming pool, in the building.

Dubai City 5 Star Hotels

Al Bustan Rotana Hotel
Map Ref → 14-D3

Located near Dubai International Airport, this hotel is best known for its excellent steakhouse, and Italian and Thai restaurants. Opened in 1997, it has a visually impressive but cold lobby, a few small upscale retail outlets, and 275 modern rooms overlooking either the pool area or a busy road.

Burj Al Arab
Map Ref → 4-A2

This hotel is very James Bond – all glitz, gold and glamour. This very exclusive seven star hotel (the only one in the world) is built on its own manmade island. It is 321 metres high, and houses five restaurants and 202 duplex suites with a host of butlers to look after your every need.

Crowne Plaza
Map Ref → 9-D2

Another of Dubai's entertainment focused hotels, the older 560 room Crowne Plaza places a good deal of emphasis on its food and beverage outlets – all seven of them. Convenience is key here – not only is it located on Sheikh Zayed Road, but there is a shopping mall beneath this hotel/serviced apartment complex.

Dubai Marine Beach Resort & Spa
Map Ref → 6-D2

Better known as 'Dubai Marine', this independent hotel is best known for its wide variety of restaurants and bars packed into its compact area. The property also includes a small private beach, three swimming pools, a spa and a well outfitted health club. The 195 villa style rooms are nestled in gardens located off the central area.

Dusit Dubai
Map Ref → 9-A2

This architecturally inspired, modern building on Sheikh Zayed Road comprises four restaurants, including a Thai restaurant and bar – both quite popular – 174 guestrooms and serviced apartments. With a Far East flavour, much of the emphasis is on luxury amenities combined with Thai hospitality to meet the needs of business travellers.

Emirates Towers Hotel
Map Ref → 9-C2

At 305 metres high and housing 400 rooms, this is the third tallest hotel in the world. Sophisticated and elegant, with a shopping arcade and consistently popular restaurants on the ground level, this hotel on the Sheikh Zayed Road is twinned with an office block. The entrance lobby is impressive and a ride in the glass fronted lifts recommended.

The Fairmont, Dubai
Map Ref → 9-E1

With four glowing pyramids on top at night, this hotel, across from the Dubai World Trade Centre, is hard to miss. The interior (particularly the funky lobby) is much more inspired than the exterior, and besides 394 rooms and serviced apartments, the Fairmont houses some of the trendiest restaurants in town.

Grand Hyatt, Dubai
Map Ref → 13-E2

With 674 of the largest, most tech smart rooms and suites, Grand Hyatt Dubai introduces a new concept in business/leisure travel, offering top level conference facilities in a resort environment. It also houses ten restaurants and the ever popular club, MIX.

Hilton Dubai Creek
Map Ref → 11-C2

With very flash yet understated elegance, this new ultra minimalist, centrally located business hotel was designed by Carlos Ott and features interiors of wood, glass and chrome. There are 154 guestrooms plus exclusive Gordon Ramsay restaurants for the super cool. As the name suggests, this hotel is on the Creek, and overlooks the Arabian dhow trading posts.

Hilton Dubai Jumeirah
Map Ref → 2-D2

This two year old beachfront hotel has 330 guestrooms and 57 luxury suites, most with sea views. Some of Dubai's best restaurants (and in house entertainers) dwell here, and each outlet features stunning views as well. Located on the 'Golden Mile' Jumeira beach strip, this hotel is family friendly and buzzing with tourists, especially on the beach.

Dubai City 5 Star Hotels

Hotel InterContinental Dubai
Map Ref → 8-C4

This dated hotel is best known for its top notch restaurants ranging from seafood to Italian to Japanese to one of Dubai's trendiest restaurant/bars, all oozing with atmosphere. Facing the Creek in Deira, traffic and parking can be a hindrance in reaching the hotel, but the food's worth the hassle of getting there.

Hyatt Regency Dubai
Map Ref → 8-D2

One of Dubai's older hotels, the recently refurbished Hyatt Regency features 400 guestrooms and serviced suites, each with a sea view and some of Dubai's finer, longstanding popular restaurants. While there's no beach nearby, it's within walking distance of the gold, fish and vegetable souks.

Jebel Ali Hotel & Golf Resort
Map Ref → 1-A1

This resort, open since 1981, has enough activities and facilities to keep guests busy for their entire stay. The 406 roomed hotel is situated amongst acres of secluded beach, landscaped gardens, and one of the region's original golf courses. Guests can also enjoy horse riding and a variety of watersports.

Jumeirah Beach Club, The
Map Ref → 5-D1

In a city that prides itself on knowing how to deliver first class and exclusive, this place stands out. 48 secluded suites (each with their own balcony or garden) and 2 luxury villas are nestled among the club's manicured gardens and private beach, along with a full range of facilities.

Jumeirah Beach Hotel, The
Map Ref → 4-B2

Part of the Jumeirah Beach Resort, along with the Burj Al Arab and the Wild Wadi Water Park, this exclusive hotel is one of Dubai's landmarks. The main building, built in the shape of an ocean wave with a colourfully dynamic interior, features 618 sea view rooms and 25 restaurants along with a host of cafes, bars and shopping outlets.

JW Marriott Hotel
Map Ref → 12-A3

Located on the edge of bustling Deira and conveniently close to the airport, the Marriott boasts 305 rooms, 39 suites, and 13 bars and restaurants. A grand staircase, detailed marble floors and natural lighting provided by 'the Middle East's largest skylight' create a charming lobby, while a landscaped indoor town square provides a relaxing atmosphere.

Le Meridien Dubai
Map Ref → 14-E3

Le Meridien's ultra convenient location, just across from the Dubai airport and a stone's throw from the Aviation Club Tennis stadium, and its very fine array of restaurants, including those of the Meridien Village, are its main assets. One of Dubai's first five star hotels, none of the 383 rooms has an exquisite view, but all feature superlative luxury and service.

Le Meridien Mina Seyahi
Map Ref → 3-A2

Not to be confused with the nearby Le Royal Meridien, this hotel focuses on water bound fun, from hobie cats to fishing charters. There are 211 rooms with seaside ones offering excellent vistas of the well landscaped grounds, beach and Gulf. The clincher for families is the 'Penguin Club', which allows parents to chill while the kids are entertained with supervised activities.

Le Royal Meridien
Map Ref → 2-C2

A bit further out in the Mina Seyahi area is Le Royal Meridien. 500 rooms and 13 bars/restaurants, some of which could be considered amongst the finest in Dubai, leave guests begging for fresh superlatives. One of the highlights is the Caracalla Spa, which offers all of the amenities one would expect from a Roman themed spa.

Metropolitan Palace Hotel
Map Ref → 11-D2

An elegant lobby, 212 tasteful rooms and a nice rooftop swimming pool are this hotel's assets. Additionally, the convenient location, a block from the Creek in bustling Deira, merits a thumbs up. The gem in this hotel's crown, though, is the Tahiti restaurant, one of Dubai's premiere restaurants for groups looking for a good time.

Dubai City 5 Star Hotels

Mina A'Salam

Map Ref → 4-A2

This is fast becoming one of Dubai's prime attractions and a city in itself. Due for completion this year, the project stretches 1 km along Jumeira beach. 2 five star hotels make up 940 luxurious rooms and suites, a convention centre, an amphitheatre, the largest spa and health centre in the region, a cultural village and a trading souk. Landscaped gardens in between 3 km of waterways can be accessed with abras (water taxis).

Mövenpick Hotel Bur Dubai

Map Ref → 10-D4

Located near Lamcy Plaza and Wafi City, this business hotel isn't quite as 'five star' as the other five star hotels in town. With 230 rooms, a coffee shop and a few restaurants serving mostly hotel guests, the main reason Dubai residents will visit this quiet venue is to dine at Fakhreldine, one of Dubai's best Lebanese restaurants.

One&Only Royal Mirage

Map Ref → 3-A2

Aside from the opulent extravagance of the Burj al Arab, this hotel is, if not Dubai's finest, surely its most unique. Traditional Arabian architecture and unparalleled dining and service give one the impression of spending the night in a palace. At the very least, a night tour of the grounds and a trip to Tagine or the fabulous Kasbar are highly recommended.

Renaissance Hotel

Map Ref → 12-A3

A little bit off the beaten path in Dubai's northern Deira (Hor Al Anz) section, this hotel features some of the more popular dining spots in Dubai, Spice Island and Harry's Place. Though not as central as some of the other five star accommodations, the Renaissance is one of the better values around.

The Ritz-Carlton, Dubai

Map Ref → 2-C2

With stunning Mediterranean architecture and 138 guest rooms all enjoying a view of the Gulf and their own private balcony or patio, you'll be spending a lot of time just enjoying the setting. Match that with the hotel's exacting international standards, and you are virtually guaranteed plenty of quality for the money you are sure to spend here.

Safir Deira Hotel

Map Ref → 11-E2

With 32 hotels across the Middle East and North Africa, this Kuwait based chain has strategically appeared in Deira, the heart of Dubai's business district. The contemporary interior designed by Italian designer, Saporiti, holds 126 rooms and 14 suites, a swimming pool, kids' club, business centre and meeting rooms, and a trio of restaurants, attracting both business and leisure clientele.

Shangri-La Hotel, Dubai

Map Ref → 9-A2

This 200 metre high structure is located on Sheikh Zayed road and is minutes away from the World Trade Centre Complex. With fantastic views of the coast and the city, 301 guest rooms and suites, 126 serviced apartments, 2 health clubs, restaurants/bar outlets and a ballroom are a few of the many facilities available.

Sheraton Deira

Map Ref → 12-A3

This hotel is more attractive to the business traveller or heavy duty shopper because of its location (close to the airport and the souks). While it might not be one of the city's highlights, with 230 rooms, a host of respectable dining outlets and relatively reasonable rates, it is probably one of Dubai's better five star deals.

Sheraton Dubai Creek Hotel

Map Ref → 11-C1

Located right on Dubai's creek, this 255 room hotel has undergone massive renovations. And one of Dubai's best Japanese restaurants (Creekside) is housed here. The views from this restaurant are beautiful, the location prime, and the interior, now stunning.

Sheraton Jumeirah Beach Resort

Map Ref → 2-C2

The 255 delightfully decorated rooms are airy and bright here. The hotel offers a full range of sporting facilities and is very close to the Emirates Golf Club. Along with 12 quality restaurants, a stunning beachfront location and a children's club, this is another good choice for families.

Dubai City 5 Star Hotels

Sofitel City Centre Hotel
Map Ref → 14-D1

Adjoining the Middle East's largest shopping centre – Deira City Centre, this hotel is great if you're in town for a shopping holiday. Some of the 327 rooms have a stunning view over the Dubai Creek Golf & Yacht Club. The hotel also features good conference facilities, serviced apartments, four restaurants and an English pub.

Taj Palace Hotel
Map Ref → 11-D2

Centrally located in the heart of Deira, this exquisite hotel pulls out all the stops. Boasting the largest rooms in the city, extraordinary service and magnificent interiors, the Taj Palace has created a niche for itself as the only five star hotel in Dubai to adopt a 'no alcohol' policy in respect of Islamic traditions.

World Trade Centre Hotel, The
Map Ref → 10-A2

Part of the World Trade Centre Complex, this hotel is ideal for convention goers. As one of Dubai's older five star establishments, the lobby feels a bit dated and some of the 333 rooms are a little on the dark side – but all offer comfortable accommodation. Additionally, hotel guests have unlimited access to the Jumeirah Beach Club facilities.

Burj al Arab

Grand Hyatt, Dubai

Hotels

Five Star	Beach Access		Phone	Map	Double	Email
Al Bustan Rotana Hotel		282 0000	14-E3	550	albustan.hotel@rotana.com
Al Maha Resort		832 9900	5-C4	2,800	almaha@emirates.net.ae
Burj Al Arab	✔	301 7777	4-A1	3,500	reservations@burj-al-arab.com
Crowne Plaza		331 1111	9-D2	575	cpdxb@cpdxb.co.ae
Dubai Marine Beach Resort & Spa	✔	346 1111	6-D2	1,320	dxbmarin@emirates.net.ae
Dusit Dubai		343 3333	9-A2	1,200	info@dusitdubai.com
Emirates Towers Hotel		330 0000	9-C2	1,300	eth@emirates-towers-hotel.com
Fairmont Hotel		332 5555	9-E1	800	fbconcierge.dubai@fairmont.com
Grand Hyatt Dubai		317 1234	13-E3	1,275	dubai.grand@hyattintl.com
Hilton Dubai Creek		227 1111	11-C2	350	hiltonck@emirates.net.ae
Hilton Dubai Jumeirah	✔	399 1111	2-D2	775	info_jumeirah@hilton.com
Hotel Inter-Continental Dubai		222 7171	8-C4	1,280	intercon_bc@ihcdubai.co.ae
Hyatt Regency Hotel		209 1234	8-D2	675	dubai.regency@hyattintl.com
Jebel Ali Golf Resort & Spa	✔	883 6000	1-A1	2,300	hoteluae@emirates.net.ae
Jumeirah Beach Club, The	✔	344 5333	5-D1	2,850	info@jumeirahbeachclub.com
Jumeirah Beach Hotel, The	✔	348 0000	4-B2	1,800	info@thejumeirahbeachhotel.com
JW Marriott Hotel		262 4444	12-A3	765	marriott@emirates.net.ae
Le Meridien Dubai		282 4040	14-E3	1,200	lmdxbbsc@emirates.net.ae
Le Meridien Mina Seyahi	✔	399 3333	3-A2	1,200	reservations@lemeridien-minaseyahi.com
Le Royal Meridien Beach Resort & Spa	✔	399 5555	2-E2	1,800	business@leroyalmeridien-dubai.com
Metropolitan Palace Hotel		227 0000	11-D2	360	metpalac@emirates.net.ae
Mina A'Salam	✔	366 8888	4-A2	1,850	reservation@madinatjumeirah.com
Mövenpick Hotel Bur Dubai		336 6000	10-D4	600	hotel.burdubai@moevenpick-hotels.com
Palace at One&Only Royal Mirage, The	✔	399 9999	3-A2	1,560	royalmirage@royalmiragedubai.com
Renaissance Hotel		262 5555	12-A3	468	rendubai@emirates.net.ae
Ritz-Carlton, Dubai, The	✔	399 4000	2-E2	2,150	rcdubai@emirates.net.ae
Safir Deira Hotel		224 8587	11-E2	1,250	safir-deira@safirhotels.com
Shangri-La Hotel		343 8888	9-A2	1,250	sldb@shangri-la.com
Sheraton Deira		268 8888	12-A3	429	sheratondeira@sheraton.com
Sheraton Dubai Creek Hotel & Towers		228 1111	11-C1	1,150	sheradxb@emirates.net.ae
Sheraton Jumeirah Beach Resort	✔	399 5533	2-D2	780	sherjum@emirates.net.ae
Sofitel City Centre Hotel		295 5522	14-D1	600	reservation@citycentre-sofitel.com
Taj Palace Hotel		223 2222	11-D2	660	tajdubai@emirates.net.ae
World Trade Centre Hotel, The		331 4000	10-A2	375	reservation@twtch-dubai.com

Four Star	Beach Access	Phone	Map	Double	Email
Al Khaleej Palace Hotel		223 1000	11-D1	350	kpalace@emirates.net.ae
Ascot Hotel		352 0900	7-E3	350	info@ascothoteldubai.com
Avari Dubai International		295 6666	11-D3	390	sales@avari-dubai.co.ae
Best Western Dubai Grand		263 2555	15-C3	325	dxbgrand@emirates.net.ae
Capitol Hotel		346 0111	7-A2	475	caphotel@emirates.net.ae
Carlton Tower, The		222 7111	8-C4	350	carlton@emirates.net.ae
Four Points Sheraton		397 7444	8-A4	612	fpshrdxb@emirates.net.ae
Golden Tulip Aeroplane Hotel		272 2999	8-E3	300	aeroplan@emirates.net.ae
Holiday Inn Downtown		228 8889	11-E2	350	hidowtwn@emirates.net.ae
Ibis World Trade Centre		332 4444	9-E3	350	novotel.ibis@accorwtc.ae
Jumeira Rotana Hotel	✔	345 5888	6-E3	378	jumeira.hotel@rotana.com
Marco Polo Hotel		272 0000	8-E4	350	marcohot@emirates.net.ae
Metropolitan Deira		295 9171	11-D3	500	metdeira@emirates.net.ae
Metropolitan Hotel	✔	343 0000	5-C4	1,100	methotel@emirates.net.ae
Metropolitan Resort & Beach Club Hotel	✔	399 5000	2-E2	1,250	metbeach@emirates.net.ae
Millennium Airport Hotel		282 3464	14-D3	396	apothotl@emirates.net.ae
Novotel World Trade Centre		332 0000	9-E3	750	reservation@accorwtc.ae
Oasis Beach Hotel	✔	399 4444	2-D2	360	obh@jaihotels.com
Ramada Continental Hotel		266 2666	12-B4	425	ramadadb@emirates.net.ae

Hotels

Four Star	Beach Access	Phone	Map	Double	Email
Ramada Hotel		351 9999	7-E3	390	rhddxb@emirates.net.ae
Regent Palace Hotel		396 3888	11-A1	400	rameedxb@emirates.net.ae
Riviera Hotel		222 2131	8-C3	450	riviera@emirates.net.ae
Rydges Plaza Hotel		398 2222	7-A4	450	rydges@emirates.net.ae
Sea View Hotel		355 8080	7-2E	450	seaviewh@emirates.net.ae
Towers Rotana Hotel		343 8000	9-B2	850	towers.hotel@rotana.com
Three Star					
Admiral Plaza, The		393 5333	7-E2	300	admplaza@emirates.net.ae
Al Khaleej Holiday Hotel		227 6565	11-D2	550	kholiday@emirates.net.ae
Ambassador Hotel		393 9444	8-A2	264	ambhotel@emirates.net.ae
Astoria Hotel		353 4300	8-A2	400	ast@astamb.net.ae
Claridge Hotel		271 6666	8-E4	200	claridge@emirates.net.ae
Comfort Inn		222 7393	11-D2	300	comftinn@emirates.net.ae
Dubai Palm Hotel		271 0021	3-A3	300	palmhtl@emirates.net.ae
Gulf Inn Hotel		224 3433	11-D2	250	gulfinn@emirates.net.ae
Imperial Suites Hotel		351 5100	7-E3	600	imphotel@emirates.net.ae
Kings Park Hotel		228 9999	11-E2	220	kingsprk@emirates.net.ae
Lords Hotel		228 9977	11-D2	250	lords@emirates.net.ae
Lotus Hotel		227 8888	11-D1	400	lotusdbx@emirates.net.ae
Nihal Hotel		295 7666	11-D2	250	nihalhtl@emirates.net.ae
Palm Beach Rotana Inn		393 1999	7-E2	250	palmbhtl@emirates.net.ae
Palm Hotel Dubai, The		399 2222	3-A3	690	dxbprkht@emirates.net.ae
Princess Hotel		263 5500	15-C3	450	princhtl@emirates.net.ae
Quality Inn Horizon		227 1919	11-D2	275	qualitin@emirates.net.ae
Sea Shell Inn		393 4777	7-E2	325	seashellinnhotel@yahoo.com
Vendome Plaza Hotel		222 2333	11-D2	240	vphotel@emirates.net.ae
Two Star					
Deira Park Hotel		223 9922	8-C3	180	deirapak@emirates.net.ae
New Peninsula Hotel		393 9111	8-A2	250	pennin@emirates.net.ae
Phoenicia Hotel		222 7191	8-C3	250	pennin@emirates.net.ae
President Hotel		334 6565	10-D1	300	president@emirates.net.ae
Ramee International Hotel		224 0222	8-D4	200	rameeint@ramee-group.com
San Marco		272 2333	8-D3	180	smhtldxb@emirates.net.ae
One Star					
Dallas Hotel		351 1223	6-E2	200	siavash2@emirates.net.ae
Middle East Hotel		222 6688	8-D3	180	mehgroup@emirates.net.ae
Vasantam Hotel		393 8006	8-A2	160	vhdubai@emirates.net.ae
West Hotel		271 7001	8-D3	150	westwest@emirates.net.ae

Note

The above prices are the hotels' peak season published rack rates. Many hotels offer a discount off the rack rate if asked. Peak or high season is from October - April (except during Ramadan, refer to Ramadan & Public Holidays [p.10], for further details).

For more one star hotels, contact the One Stop Information Centre (223 0000), Department of Tourism & Commerce Marketing, www.dubaitourism.com. For more hotels outside Dubai, refer to the Weekend Break table [p.204].

Classification is based on the DTCM hotel rating in accordance with bylaw No. (1) of 1998 concerning Licensing and Classification of Hotels, Guesthouses and Hotel Apartments in Dubai.

Hotel Apartments

Deluxe	Phone	Area	One B/room Apts (Weekly)	Two B/room Apts (Weekly)	Email
City Centre Residence	294 1333	Al Garhoud	5,700	10,000	cityhotl@emirates.net.ae
Rihab Rotana Suites	294 0300	Al Garhoud	-	-	rihab@emirates.net.ae
Golden Sands X	359 9000	Al Karama	-	4,410	gldnsnds@emirates.net.ae
Al Bustan Residence	263 0000	Al Qusais	4,620	6,300	reservations@albustan.com
Imperial Residence Hotel	355 3555	Bur Dubai	5,250	6,650	impres@emirates.net.ae
Oasis Court Hotel Apts	397 6666	Bur Dubai	2,380	3,080	oasis@gtfs-gulf.com
Pearl Residence	355 8111	Bur Dubai	3,500	-	pearlres@emirates.net.ae
Rolla Residence	359 2000	Bur Dubai	5,400	6,600	rollabus@emirates.net.ae
Marriott Executive Apts	213 1000	Deira	-	-	dubaimea@emirates.net.ae
Rayan Residence	224 0888	Deira	3,850	4,200	-
Al Faris Hotel Apts	336 6566	Oud Metha	3,300	-	afarisre@emirates.net.ae
Wafi Residence	324 7222	Oud Metha	-	-	mkm@waficity.com
Standard					
Al Awael Hotel Apts	271 1211	Dubai	1,050	1,260	alawael@emirates.net.ae
Al Deyafa Hotel Apts	228 2555	Deira	-	2,250	defuap55@emirates.net.ae
Al Faris Hotel Apartment 2	393 5847	Bur Dubai	1,750	2,350	afarisre@emirates.net.ae
Al Faris Hotel Apartments 1	393 3843	Bur Dubai	-	-	afarisre@emirates.net.ae
Al Harmoody Hotel Apts	273 5222	Al Baraha	1,450	-	mohraah@emirates.net.ae
Al Hina Hotel Apartments	355 5510	Bur Dubai	1,750	-	hinarest@emirates.net.ae
Al Mas Hotel Apartments	355 7899	Bur Dubai	1,925	3,500	almasfur@emirates.net.ae
Al Muraqabat Plaza	269 0550	Deira	1,400	2,800	muraqabt@emirates.net.ae
Al Nakheel Hotel Apts	224 1555	Deira	2,100	3,500	alnakhel@emirates.net.ae
Atrium Suites	266 8666	Abu Hail	-	-	-
Baisan Residence	221 9966	Deira	1,750	3,150	-
Blanco	227 3400	Deira	1,260	1,750	sacham@emirates.net.ae
Embassy Suites	269 8070	Deira	1,225	1,750	suite@emirates.net.ae
Galleria Apartments	209 6788	Deira	4,650	5,500	dubai.regency@hyattintl.com
Golden Sands III	355 5551	Bur Dubai	3,045	-	goldensands@emirates.net.ae
Premiere Hotel Apts	359 9545	Bur Dubai	5,000	6,545	preapts@emirates.net.ae
Richmond Hotel Apts	398 8456	Bur Dubai	2,450	2,800	rchmdhtl@emirates.net.ae
Rimal Rotana Suites	268 8000	Deira	-	5,800	rimal.suites@rotana.com
Savoy Hotel Apartments	355 3000	Bur Dubai	2,800	-	savoy@emirates.net.ae
Tower No. One	343 4666	Trade Centre 1&2	1,995	3,000	sales@numberonetower.com
Winchester Grand	355 0222	Bur Dubai	4,900	6,300	wingrand@emirates.net.ae
Winchester Hotel Apts	355 0111	Bur Dubai	3,850	-	winchest@emirates.net.ae
Listed					
Al Shams Plaza	355 1200	Bur Dubai	1,547	2,310	anbmr@emirates.net.ae
London Crown II	351 8888	Bur Dubai	1,750	-	info@londoncrown.com
Sky Hotel Apartments	273 3344	Deira	1,260	-	skydubai@hotmail.com

Note: The above prices are the hotel apartment's peak season published rack rates and are inclusive of tax and service charge. Many hotels offer a discount off the rack rate if asked. Peak or high season is from October - April (except during Ramadan, refer to Ramadan & Public Holidays, General Information, for further details).

For more listed hotel apartments, contact the One Stop Information Centre (223 0000), Department of Tourism & Commerce Marketing, www.dubaitourism.com.

Key: * marked rates for studio apartments

Youth Hostels

The Dubai Youth Hostel (298 8161), located on Qusais Road, near the Al Mulla Plaza, provides the cheapest accommodation in town. A four star wing was added to the hostel in 2002, almost tripling the number of rooms. In the old wing, there are 53 beds, available for Dhs.45 per night (YHA members) or Dhs.60 (non members) in one of 20 clean two bed dormitory rooms, including breakfast. Beds in the new wing are Dhs.65 for members and Dhs.80 for non members, including breakfast. Check in is always open.

Accommodation is available for men, women and families. Annual membership costs Dhs.100; family membership is Dhs.300 and for groups of more than 25, the yearly charge is Dhs.1,000. Single women, especially, should check availability, since the management reserves the right to refuse bookings from single women when the hostel is busy with men. The hostel is well served by a cheap, regular bus service into the centre of Dubai and reasonably priced taxis are plentiful. By car, the hostel is about 15 minutes from airport Terminal 1.

There are hostels in Sharjah, Fujairah and Ras Al Khaimah too, and one in Abu Dhabi.

Camping

Other options → Sports [p.259]

There are no official campsites in the UAE, but there are plenty of places to camp outside the cities. For sites near Dubai, the desert dunes on the way to Hatta are a good option. So is the Jebel Ali beach, where, if you get there early enough in the cooler months, you can have your own shelter and shower right on the beach!

While many people camp around here, they are mostly UAE residents. You will rarely see a tourist with camping gear, ready to set off on a camping holiday in the Emirates.

For the best camping options in the UAE, pick up a copy of the *Off-Road Explorer (UAE)*. This guidebook tells you where to go and how to get there, what to bring and how to prepare, and also where to buy what you'll need for your camping trip.

Getting Around

Other options → Maps
Exploring [p.156]

The car is the most popular method of getting around Dubai and the Emirates as a whole, either by private vehicle or by taxi. There is a reasonable public bus service, but walking and cycling are limited and motorcycles are limited to a few brave (foolhardy?) souls. There are no trains and trams, but the rapid rail transit system, due for completion in the next 4 - 6 years, will see Dubai's first metro running both under and above ground. The 50 km, 37 station system will link Sharjah with Jebel Ali and Dubai International Airport with Port Rashid. Other proposals for transport also include a high speed ferry linking Dubai and Abu Dhabi.

The city's road network is excellent though, and the majority of roads are two, three or four lanes. They are all well signposted and, in this respect, Dubai is probably the best emirate. Blue or green signs indicate the main areas or locations out of the city and brown signs show heritage sites, places of interest, hospitals etc.

Once here, the visitor should find Dubai a relatively easy city to negotiate. However, a bit of insider

Camping in the Dunes

Lane Discipline?

Lane discipline is yet another challenge to the overall UAE driving experience. As so many different nationalities converge on Dubai's roads, there are bound to be some major differences in driving styles, and lane discipline is a particular annoyance of ours! On the Sheikh Zayed Road for example, the majority of drivers seem to believe that the two far right lanes are reserved for trucks and the two left lanes are for cars. This means that on a highway with a posted speed limit of 120 km per hour, and drivers flying down the fast lane at sometimes over 200 km per hour, you will find a small car plodding along in the next lane at far below the speed limit! Now, if you have someone coming up on you very, very fast, flashing their headlights and swerving dangerously, where do you go?

knowledge will help get you from A to B quicker. The Creek divides Bur Dubai (to the south) from Deira (to the north). These are further divided into several different areas, such as Satwa in Bur Dubai and Al Hamriya in Deira. There are three main crossing points on the Creek – Al Shindagha Tunnel, Maktoum Bridge and Garhoud Bridge. The Creek can also be crossed by a pedestrian foot tunnel near Shindagha, or by boat (these water taxis are known locally as abras).

To ease the pressure on inner city roads, a ring road or bypass, called the Emirates Road 311, was built at a cost of Dhs.150 million. This connects Abu Dhabi directly to Sharjah and the Northern Emirates, with the aim to ease the flow of traffic in Dubai. But, although traffic on the Ring Road is increasing steadily, the highway and city roads show no noticeable improvement. Further steps to reduce traffic congestion were taken in 2002, with a ban on all trucks on main routes such as Sheikh Zayed Road and the Garhoud Bridge between 06:00 and 22:00. Although never ending roadworks eventually provide extra lanes and interchanges, they end up creating further road blocks in the process.

e-Service

For traffic updates on Bur Dubai and Deira, log on to www.dm.gov.ae. This e-Service provides a direct traffic broadcast through cameras installed on all important roads and junctions, snapshots of which are uploaded on the Website every 30 seconds. Maps of the areas help you click on to your choice of road (and camera).

Roads are named with white road signs. However, these are not really referred to regularly. People generally rely on landmarks to give directions or to get their bearings, and these landmarks are usually shops, hotels, petrol stations or notable buildings. Similarly, while there is a numbered address system, few people actually use it. Thus an accommodation 'address' may read something like 'Al Hamriya area, behind Abu Hail Centre, near Happyland supermarket in the pink building', rather than Building XX, Road XX, Al Hamriya.

To confuse matters further, places may not be referred to by their 'official' name. For instance, Al Jumeira Road is often known as the Beach Road and Bu Kidra roundabout is invariably called Country Club roundabout.

Recently, Sheikh Hamdan bin Rashid Al Maktoum ordered certain streets around Dubai to be given the names of prominent Arab cities. Thus, various streets are now named 'Amman Road', 'Cairo Road', 'Marrakech Road' etc, to demonstrate the strong ties that exist between the UAE and other Arab nations.

You can avoid all this confusion, however, by simply getting a copy of the *Street Map Explorer (Dubai)*. This detailed street guide is a concise and comprehensive compendium of street names cross referenced with an A to Z index of businesses and tourist attractions. In this fast developing city, this handy guidebook will soon become your favourite travel mate and a standard tool for navigating this ever growing metropolis.

Car

Other options → Transportation [p.118]

Over the past two decades, Dubai has built, and is still building, an impressive network of roads. The Municipality estimates that, in the last ten years, the number of roads in Dubai has literally doubled. There are two bridges and a road tunnel linking the two main districts on either side of the Creek, with another bridge under way. The roads to all major towns and villages are excellent and an eight lane highway heads south from the city to Abu Dhabi, which takes about 1 - 1 1/2 hours to reach. With all this, it is quite obvious that the car is the best option of getting around in this city.

Driving Habits & Regulations

Whilst the infrastructure is superb, the general standard of driving is not. Apparently the UAE has one of the world's highest death rates per capita due to traffic accidents. According to the Dubai Police, one person is killed in a traffic related accident every 48 hours, and there is one injury every four hours – not the most positive statistics! Drivers often seem

completely unaware of other cars on the road, and the usual follies of driving too fast, too close, swerving, pulling out suddenly, lane hopping or drifting, happen far too regularly.

One move to help the situation on the roads was a ban in Dubai on using handheld mobile phones whilst driving. Predictably the sales of hands free systems rocketed before people went back to their old bad habits.

In Dubai, you drive on the right hand side of the road, and it is mandatory to wear seatbelts in the front seats. Children under ten years of age are no longer allowed to sit in the front of a car. This ban is now countrywide, even though you'll still see people driving with their child on their lap.

Fines for any of the above violations are Dhs.100, plus one 'black' point on your licence. Speeding fines are Dhs.400 and parking fines start at Dhs.100. Most fines are paid when you renew your annual car registration. However, parking tickets appear on your windscreen and you have a week or two to pay – the amount increases if you don't pay within the time allotted on the back of the ticket.

ZERO Tolerance!

The Dubai Police exercise a strict zero tolerance policy on drinking and driving. This means that if you have had ANYTHING to drink, you are much better off taking a taxi home or having a friend who has consumed nothing drive you home. If you are pulled over and found to have consumed alcohol, you are likely to find yourself enjoying the hospitality of the police station overnight – at the very least!

Also note, that if you are involved in an accident, whether it's your fault or not, and you are found to have been drinking and driving, your insurance is automatically void. Penalties are severe, so the simple message is to be safe: if you're going to drink, don't even think of driving.

Try to keep a reasonable stopping distance between yourself and the car in front. Ultimately it also helps to have eyes in the back of your head and to practice skilful defensive driving at all times.

If you wish to report a traffic violation, call the Traffic Police's toll free hotline (800 4353). The Dubai Police Website: www.dubaipolice.gov.ae offers all information relevant to driving, such as traffic violations, road maps, contact numbers etc. For complete information on Highway Codes, safety and Dubai's road rules, check out the *Safe Driving Handbook* available from the Emirates Motor Sports Federation (282 7111).

Speed Limits

Speed limits are usually 60 - 80 km around town, while roads to other parts of the Emirates are 100 - 120 km. The speed is clearly indicated on road signs and there is no leeway for breaking the limit. Both fixed and movable radar traps, and the Dubai Traffic Police, are there to catch the unwary violator! In 2001, 361,500 fines were given for speeding – that number amounted to 64% of all traffic violations. On the spot traffic fines for certain offences have been introduced, but in most cases, you won't know you've received a fine until you check on the Website or renew your vehicle registration.

Tune in to the Flow

Be smart. Avoid a traffic jam by tuning in to any of the four Arabian Radio Network (ARN) channels – Arabiya 98.9 FM, Al Khallejiya 100.9 FM, Free FM 96.7 and City FM 101.6. Regular updates about the traffic situation on main roads are provided throughout the day, forewarning you if a certain road is blocked, so you can take alternative routes or side roads.

Driving Licence

Visitors to Dubai have two options for driving. You can drive a rental vehicle with, either an international driving licence or a licence from your country of origin. The latter is applicable only if you are from one of the countries listed on the transfer list (see [p.66]).

If you wish to drive a private vehicle, you must first go to the Traffic Police to obtain a temporary licence. Please note that, unless you have a Dubai driving licence, either permanent or temporary, you are not insured to drive a private vehicle.

Accidents

If you are involved in a traffic accident, however minor, you must remain with your car at the accident scene and report the incident to the Traffic Police, then wait for them to arrive. In Dubai, as long as no one is injured, you must move your vehicle so that it is not blocking traffic. Unfortunately, in Dubai, when you have an accident, you become the star attraction as the passing traffic slows to a crawl with rubberneckers.

Apparently, to lessen the number of traffic jams caused by accidents, a move allowed those involved in a non injury accident to move their cars to the side of the road and deal with the other driver without having to wait for the police. Insurance companies were to supply accident forms to all drivers to comply with this change in regulation; however, we have yet to see one three years on. Better to be safe and call 999 if you have an accident.

Stray animals (mostly camels) are something else to avoid on the roads in the UAE. If the animal hits your vehicle and causes damage or injury, the animal's owner should pay compensation, but if you are found to have been speeding or driving recklessly, you must compensate the owner of the animal – this can be expensive.

See also: *Traffic Accidents [p.126].*

Non Drivers

In addition to dealing with the nutters in cars, you will find that pedestrians and cyclists also seem to have a death wish! The few cyclists who do brave the roads will often be cycling towards you on the wrong side of the road, invariably without lights if it is night. Pedestrians often step out dangerously close to oncoming traffic and a lack of convenient, safe crossings makes life for those on foot especially difficult. However, the numbers of pedestrian footbridges and pedestrian operated traffic lights are gradually (slowly) increasing.

Parking

In most areas of Dubai, parking is readily available and people rarely have to walk too far in the heat. Increasing numbers of pay and display parking meters are appearing around the busier parts of the city. The areas are clearly marked and range from Dhs.1 - 2 for an hour. Try to have loose change with you since there are no automatic change machines available. Meters operate between 08:00 - 13:00 and 16:00 - 21:00 Saturday - Thursday. If you haven't purchased a ticket, you may be unlucky enough to receive one from the police for the bargain price of Dhs.100.

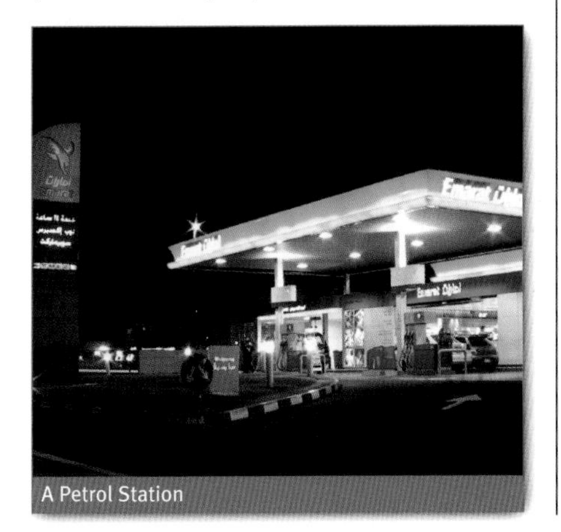

A Petrol Station

Petrol/Gas Stations

Petrol stations in the Emirates are numerous and run by Emarat, Emirates, EPPCO and ENOC. Most offer extra services, such as a car wash or a shop selling all those necessities of life that you forgot to buy at the supermarket.

The majority of visitors will find petrol far cheaper than in their home countries – prices range from Dhs.4 per gallon for Special (95 octane) and Dhs.5 for Super (98 octane). The UAE must be one of the few countries in the world where diesel fuel actually costs more than other fuels!

Blood Money

If you are driving and cause someone's death, even in an accident that is not your fault, you are liable to pay a sum of money, known as 'blood money', to the deceased's family. The limit for this has been set at Dhs.200,000 per victim and your car insurance will cover this cost (hence the higher premiums). However, insurance companies will only pay if they cannot find a way of claiming that the insurance is invalid (ie, if the driver was driving without a licence or, for example, under the influence of alcohol). The deceased's family can, however, waive the right to blood money if they feel merciful.

Car Hire

All the main car rental companies, plus a few extra, are in Dubai and it is best to shop around as the rates vary considerably. It's worth remembering that the larger, more reputable firms generally have more reliable vehicles and a greater capacity to help in an emergency (an important factor when handling the trying times following an accident). Depending on the agent, cars can be hired with or without a driver, and the minimum hire period is usually 24 hours. Prices range from Dhs.70 a day for smaller cars to Dhs.1,000 for limousines. Comprehensive insurance is essential (and make sure that it includes personal accident coverage).

The rental company will also arrange temporary local driving licences for visitors. To rent a car, you are usually required to produce a copy of your passport and valid international or national driving licence and two photographs. Your licence should be from any of the following countries: Austria, Belgium, Canada, Denmark, Finland, France, Germany, Greece, Holland, Ireland, Italy, Japan, Norway, Singapore, Spain, Sweden, Switzerland, Turkey, UK and the USA.

See also: *Vehicle Leasing [p.120].*

Car Rental Agencies

Autolease	282 6565
Avis Rent a Car	224 5219
Budget	282 3030
Diamondlease Rent a Car	881 4645
Hertz Rent a Car	282 4422
Thrifty Car Rental	224 5404
United Car Rentals	266 6286

Taxi

If you don't have a car, taxis are the most common way of getting around. Currently, visitors have the choice of metered taxis operated under franchise from Dubai Transport Corporation (DTC).

In 2000, the DTC cleverly decided to take over the entire taxi business in Dubai and private taxis were phased out by the end of the year. The days of being ripped off by non metered taxi drivers were suddenly a thing of the past, but then again, so was choice! In addition to DTC cabs, three taxi firms operate in Dubai with a fixed fare structure – competition at its best!

Metered taxis are run by Dubai Transport Corporation (sand/camel coloured cars), Cars Taxis (white with blue and red stripes), Metro Taxis (sand coloured) and National Taxis (silver).

Global Positioning System (GPS) equipment is fitted in all 2,000 DTC taxis, giving the car's location with pinpoint accuracy – useful for letting the control point know which is the closest vehicle available to pick you up. Some Dubai Transport vehicles have been fitted with terminals that allow customers to pay with a credit card.

No Passport Required

Although rental companies may ask for one, your original passport must never be handed over. When renting a car, your passport details are added into the system, which has an electronic link with the Dubai Traffic Police Department. Hence, passports need not be surrendered for security anymore. If you are asked to hand over your passport, don't... and report the matter to the police.

The fare is Dhs.3 for pickup (Dhs.3.50 between 22:00 - 06:00), followed by Dhs.1.25 per kilometre. The starting fare inside the airport area is an extortionate Dhs.25 and only Dubai Transport vehicles are allowed to pick up here. The journey to the town centre from the airport costs around Dhs.30 - 35. You can also hire a taxi for Dhs.500 for 12 hours, or Dhs.1,000 for 24 hours. Van service is Dhs.50 per hour.

Towards the end of 2002, three non metered taxi companies were once again permitted to work on Dubai's roads. Under Dubai Transport franchise as well, these non metered cabs allow customers the option of bargaining the fare down. Dubai Taxi, Khaibar Taxi and Palestine Taxi all have their prices fixed by Dubai Transport, and from there... it's bargaining time! A word of warning: determine the fare before the ride and try to find out what the normal cab fare should be first.

Cabs can be flagged down by the side of the road or you can make a Dubai Transport taxi booking by calling 208 0808. Alternatively, if you drop Dhs.1 into one of the 15 electronic booking machines dotted around town, a taxi is immediately despatched to the machine's location. If you make a booking, you will pay a Dhs.4.50 starting fare.

To make life a little more confusing, taxi drivers in Dubai occasionally lack any knowledge of the city and passengers may have to direct them! Start with the area of destination and then choose a major landmark, such as a hotel, roundabout or shopping centre. Then narrow it down as you get closer. If you are going to a new place, try to phone for instructions first – you will often be given a distinctive landmark as a starting point. It's also helpful to take the phone number of your destination with you, in case you're completely going around in circles. If your taxi driver is well and truly lost, ask him to radio his control point for instructions.

Taxi Companies

Cars Taxis	269 3344
Dubai Transport Company	208 0808
Gulf Radio Taxi	223 6666
Metro Taxis	267 3222
National Taxis	336 6611
Sharjah: Delta Taxis	06 559 8598

Airport Bus

The Dubai Municipality, in conjunction with the Dubai Department of Civil Aviation, operates airport buses departing from and arriving at Dubai International Airport every 30 minutes, 24 hours a day. Currently, there are two loop routes: Route 401 services Deira, while Route 402 services Bur Dubai. The fare is Dhs.3 and is paid when boarding the bus. Airport bus route maps are available at Dubai International Airport.

Dubai Municipality Bus Information (800 4848)

Bus

Dubai Municipality's Transport Section operates over 36 bus routes for the emirate serving the main residential and commercial areas, from Al Qusais in the northeast to Jebel Ali in the southwest and some destinations out of the city. Around 150,000 passengers are transported daily. However, the service is gradually being extended, with more buses covering more routes. Efforts are also being made to display better timetables and route plans at bus stations to encourage people to use this inexpensive method of transport. The majority of passengers in buses tend to be lower income workers.

In Deira, the main bus station is near the Gold Souk and in Bur Dubai, on Ghubaiba Road near the Plaza Cinema. Buses run at regular intervals from 06:00 to around 23:00, and fares are cheap at Dhs.1 - 3 per journey. Fares are paid to the driver when you board, so try to have the exact change ready. Also available are monthly discount tickets and e-Go cards (see below). Buses also go from Dubai to Al Khawaneej, Al Awir and Hatta for very reasonable prices; a one way ticket to Hatta, which is 100 km away, is Dhs.10.

e-Go Card

This electronic smart card helps bus passengers save time and avoids the hassle of small change. Available for Dhs.5, the e-Go card can be filled with credits (Dhs.20 for the first time and multiples of Dhs.10 after). When placed on the ticket machine in the bus, the ticket amount is automatically deducted, and the balance is adjusted and stored. The monthly pass (for Dhs.90) gives multiple ride options to bus users as well as offering various shopping discounts.

Dubai Transport Corporation offers a minibus service in addition to their taxis. These buses run to Sharjah, Ajman, Umm Al Quwain, Ras Al Khaimah, Fujairah, Al Ain and Abu Dhabi. The minibuses are modern, air conditioned and offer a good value service to the cities of the UAE. Unfortunately, at present, these services only carry passengers on the outward journeys. Anyone wishing to return to Dubai by public transport must make alternative arrangements.

- *Dubai Transport* – Northern Emirates (286 1616 or 227 3840)
- *Dubai Municipality* – Bus information (800 4848) and lost & found (285 0700)

Train

Currently, there are no trains and trams, but the rapid rail transit system, due for completion in the next 4 - 6 years, will be Dubai's first metro.

Alternative proposals for transport also include a high speed ferry linking Dubai and Abu Dhabi, and a monorail alongside Sheikh Zayed Road.

Air

Other options → Airlines [p.138]
Meet & Greet [p.23]

Dubai's location at the crossroads of Europe, Asia and Africa makes it an easily accessible city. London is seven hours away, Frankfurt six, Hong Kong eight, and Nairobi four. Most major cities have direct flights to Dubai, many with a choice of operator.

Dubai International Airport is currently ranked fourth amongst the world's top international airports, handling almost 14 million passengers in 2003. An ambitious US $540 million expansion programme has transformed the already excellent airport into a state of the art facility, ready to meet the needs of passengers for the next 30 years. Work has already started on an even larger third terminal due to service all Emirates flights.

Currently, more than 90 airlines take advantage of Dubai's open skies policy, operating to and from over 120 destinations. Dubai's award winning airline, Emirates, is based here and operates scheduled services to 70 destinations. Etihad Airways, the national airline of the UAE, has

Dhow on Dubai Creek

recently come on the scene with plans of fast growth (eight carriers and 16 destinations by end 2004). Another newcomer is the budget airline, Air Arabia. The attractions of this airline are reduced costs and ticketless travel.

There are two terminals, which are located on different sides of the airport (a 15 - 30 minute taxi ride, depending on the traffic). Both terminals offer car rental, hotel reservations and bureau de change services. Terminal 2 opened in April 1998 and has the capacity to handle 2.5 million passengers annually. Most of the better known airlines use Terminal 1, but a fine selection of over 20 airlines operates from Terminal 2. Primarily focused on the former Soviet countries, the airlines include Chelyabinsk Airlines, Nizhegorodsky and Zitotrans (yes, they do exist!).

Duty Free shops are located in both the arrival and departure halls, although the arrivals hall outlet is limited. All travellers have the opportunity to enter the prestigious raffle to win a luxury car, which will be shipped anywhere in the world (tickets Dhs.500 each).

Dubai National Airline Travel Agency (DNATA) (316 6666), is home to most of the main airline offices in Dubai. Here, you can make enquiries, collect tickets etc. DNATA is located in the Airline Centre building on Sheikh Zayed Road (Map Ref 5-C4).

Flight Info: 216 6666

Boat

Opportunities for getting around by boat in the Emirates are limited... unless you wish to travel by dhow, and then your opportunities are limitless. Crossing the Creek in low wooden boats (known locally as abras) is a very common method of transport for many people in Dubai. Future possibilities for travel by boat include a high speed ferry linking Dubai and Abu Dhabi, but this is presently only a proposal. There is a cruise ship terminal at Port Rashid, currently the only dedicated complex in the region. It is comprised of a 335 metre quay with simultaneous berthing capacity for two ships, and a 3,300 square metre terminal.

It is also possible to travel from Dubai and Sharjah to several ports in Iran by boat. There are different companies providing this service and prices vary. A hydrofoil operates from Dubai and costs Dhs.215 for the four hour trip. From Sharjah, the boat takes 10 - 12 hours and costs Dhs.130. All prices are for one way tickets. There is also a Dhs.20 port tax. For more information, contact the Oasis Freight Co. (06 559 6325).

Walking & Biking

Other options → Cycling [p.272]
Hiking [p.285]
Mountain Biking [p.294]

Cities in the Emirates are generally very car orientated and not designed to encourage either walking or cycling. In addition, the heat in summer months, with daytime temperatures around 45° C, makes either activity a rather sweaty experience!

In the winter months, however, especially in the evenings, temperatures are perfect for outdoor activities. At this time of year, walking is a popular evening pastime, especially in the parks, along the seafront in Deira and Jumeira, or on the pedestrian paths along both sides of the Creek.

Cycling too, can be an enjoyable way to explore the city – you can cover more ground than on foot and see more than from a car. However, a lot of care is needed when cycling in traffic, since drivers in speeding cars are quite unaware of this method of transport.

In the quieter areas, many of the roads are wide enough to accommodate cyclists as well as cars, and where there are footpaths, they are often broad and in good repair. There are no dedicated bike lanes, apart from a 1.2 km cycling track along Al Mamzar Corniche (which should take all of 6 minutes to cover!). But this at least recognises the need for cyclists to ride without the threat of being mowed down by a speeding car.

Money

Cash is still the preferred method of payment in the Emirates, although credit cards are now widely accepted. Foreign currencies and travellers cheques can be exchanged in licensed exchange offices, banks and hotels – as usual, a passport is required for exchanging traveller's cheques.

There is more confidence in cheques these days; strict enforcement of laws concerning passing bad cheques has helped. It is a criminal offence to write a cheque with insufficient funds in the bank account and a jail term will result.

Local Currency

The monetary unit is the 'dirham' (Dhs.), which is divided into 100 'fils'. The currency is also referred to as AED (Arab Emirate Dirham). Notes come in denominations of Dhs.5, Dhs.10, Dhs.20, Dhs.50,

Dhs.100, Dhs.200, Dhs.500 and Dhs.1,000. Coin denominations are Dhs.1, 50 fils and 25 fils, but be warned, there are two versions of each coin and they can look very similar. Because 5 and 10 fil coins are rarely available, you will often not receive the exact change.

The dirham has been pegged to the US dollar since the end of 1980, at a mid rate of US$1 ~ Dhs.3.6725. Exchange rates of all major currencies are published daily in the local newspapers.

Exchange Rates

Foreign Currency (FC)	1 Unit FC = x Dhs	Dhs.1 = x FC
Australia	2.7	0.37
Bahrain	9.76	0.10
Bangladesh	0.06	16.67
Canada	2.85	0.35
Cyprus	7.61	0.13
Denmark	0.59	1.69
Euro	4.44	0.23
Hong Kong	0.47	2.13
India	0.08	12.50
Japan	0.03	33.33
Jordan	5.25	0.19
Kuwait	12.54	0.08
Malaysia	0.98	1.02
New Zealand	2.93	0.34
Oman	9.57	0.10
Pakistan	0.06	16.67
Philippines	0.06	16.67
Qatar	1.01	0.99
Saudi Arabia	0.98	1.02
Singapore	2.15	0.47
South Africa	0.66	1.52
Sri Lanka	0.03	33.33
Sweden	0.49	2.04
Switzerland	2.87	0.35
Thailand	0.09	11.11
UK	6.32	0.16
USA	3.67	0.27

Rates updated – December 2003

Banks

The well structured and ever growing network of local and international banks, strictly controlled by the UAE Central Bank, offers the full range of commercial and personal banking services. Transfers can be made without difficulty as there is no exchange control and the dirham is freely convertible.

For further information on opening a bank account in the UAE, refer to the *Zappy Explorer (Dubai)*.

Banking hours: Saturday to Wednesday 08:00 - 13:00 (some are also open 16:30 - 18:30). Thursday 08:00 - 12:00.

Main Banks

ABN AMRO Bank	351 2200
Abu Dhabi Commercial Bank	295 8888
Abu Dhabi National Bank	666 6800
Bank of Sharjah	282 7278
Barclays Bank Plc	335 1555
Citibank	324 5000
Dubai Islamic Bank	295 9999
Emirates Bank International	225 6256
HSBC Bank Middle East	353 5000
Lloyds TSB Bank Plc	342 2000
Mashreq Bank	222 3333
Middle East Bank	800 4644
National Bank of Dubai	222 2111
RAK Bank	224 8000
Standard Chartered	800 4949
Union National Bank	800 2600

ATMs

Most banks operate ATMs (Automatic Teller Machines, also known as cash points or service tills) which accept a wide range of cards. For non UAE based cards, the exchange rates used in the transaction are normally extremely competitive and the process is faster and much less hassle than traditional travellers cheques.

Common systems accepted around Dubai: American Express, Cirrus, Global Access, MasterCard, Plus System and Visa. ATMs can be found in all shopping malls, at the airport, at petrol stations and at various streetside locations.

Money Exchanges

Money exchanges are available all over Dubai, offering good service and reasonable exchange rates, which are often better than the banks. Additionally, hotels will usually exchange money and travellers cheques at the standard hotel rate (ie, poor!).

Exchange house hours: 08:30 - 13:00 and 16:30 - 20:30

Exchange Centres

Al Ansari Exchange	335 3599
Al Fardan Exchange	228 0004
Al Ghurair Exchange	222 2955
First Gulf Exchange	351 5777
Orient Exchange Company	226 7154
Thomas Cook Al Rostamani	295 6777
Wall Street Exchange Centre	800 4871
World Link Exchange Co. (LLC)	225 2666

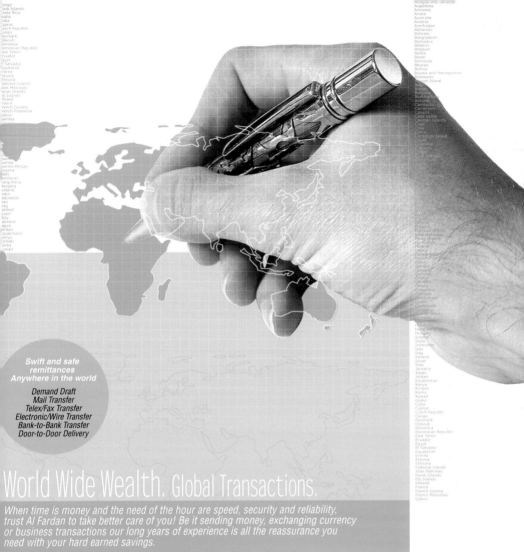

Credit Cards

Most shops, hotels and restaurants accept the major credit cards (American Express, Diners Club, MasterCard and Visa). Smaller retailers are sometimes less keen to accept credit cards and you may have to pay an extra five percent for processing (and it's no use telling them that it's a contravention of the card company rules – you have to take it or leave it!). You can, however, call your local credit card company to lodge a complaint if you are charged this five percent 'fee'. Conversely, if you are paying in cash, you may sometimes be allowed a discount – it's certainly worth enquiring.

Tipping

Tipping practices are similar to most parts of the world. An increasing number of restaurants include service charge, although it is unlikely to end up with your waiter. Otherwise, ten per cent is the usual.

Media & Communications

Newspapers/Magazines

The Gulf News, Khaleej Times and The Gulf Today (all Dhs.2 and Dhs.3 on Fridays) are the daily English language newspapers of Dubai and the Northern Emirates. Arabic newspapers include Al Bayan, Al-Ittihad and Al-Khaleej.

Foreign newspapers, most prominently French, German, British and Asian, are readily available in hotel bookshops and supermarkets, although they are more expensive than at home (about Dhs.8 - 12) and slightly out of date. Also available are good hobby magazines, such as computing, photography, sports, and women's magazines (expect to find censored portions or occasionally, even whole pages or sections missing). These are expensive, usually costing two or three times more than at home (between Dhs.30 - 50).

Newspapers and magazines are available from bookshops, supermarkets and hotel shops. Newspapers used to be sold at major road junctions, but this practice was stopped in late 2001, as it was deemed too dangerous for the vendors.

Further Reading

Visitors will find a variety of books and magazines available on the Emirates, from numerous coffee table books (such as *Images of Dubai & the UAE* or *Dubai: Tomorrow's City Today)* to magazines with details of aerobics classes. Monthly publications range from the free Connector or Aquarius (both focusing on health and beauty) to the event focused Time Out and What's On. Many magazines here seem to almost merge into one; they have no clear cut identity and the audience always seems the same, no matter which one you pick up.

Guides to the region include the Lonely Planet series, as well as Explorer Publishing's *Abu Dhabi Explorer* and *Oman Explorer* (formerly *Muscat Explorer*). *Sharjah The Guide* and the *Spectrum Guide to the United Arab Emirates* also offer more information on the region.

For the finer points on life in Dubai, books to refer to include: the *Family Explorer (Dubai & Abu Dhabi)*, a family guide to life in the UAE; the *Zappy Explorer (Dubai)*, a step by step helping hand guiding you through the administrative procedures and red tape in Dubai; the *Off-Road Explorer (UAE)*, the ultimate outdoor guide to the region; and the *Underwater Explorer (UAE)*, a detailed guide to scuba diving in the area. These can be found in all good bookstores around town.

Post & Courier Services

Other options → Postal Services [p.100]

Empost, formerly known as the General Postal Authority (GPA), is the sole provider of postal services in the UAE. In addition, plenty of courier companies operate both locally and internationally, such as Aramex, DHL, Federal Express, etc. Empost also operates an express mail service, Mumtaz Express.

Post within the UAE takes 2 - 3 days to be delivered. Mail takes 7 - 10 days to reach the USA and Europe, 8 - 10 days to reach Australia and 5 - 10 days to reach India. Airmail letters cost Dhs.3 - 6 to send,

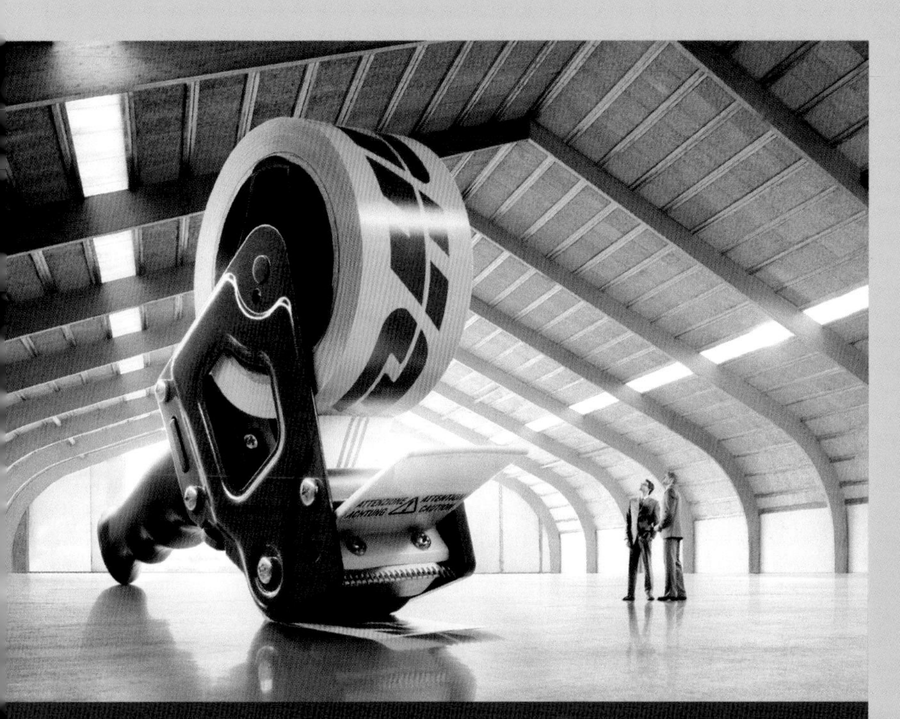

depending on weight, and postcards cost Dhs.1 - 2. Letters are a dirham cheaper if they are posted unsealed. Aerogrammes can be bought for Dhs.2 each from post offices and save the bother of buying a stamp before posting.

Stamps can be bought from post offices and certain shops – card shops often sell a limited range of stamps. Deira City Centre and Lamcy Plaza shopping malls both have full postal facilities, and some Emarat petrol stations now have postal facilities. Red post boxes for outbound mail are located at post offices and near shopping centres. Hotels will also handle your mail if you are staying there.

There's no house address based postal service; all incoming mail is delivered to a PO Box at a central location and has to be collected from there.

Courier Companies	
Aramex	286 5000
DHL	800 4004
Emirates Post	800 5858
Federal Express	800 4050
Immex - Immediate Courier Express LLC	282 4444
Memo Express	211 8111
TNT	285 3939
UPS	800 4774

Radio

The UAE has a number of commercial radio stations broadcasting in a range of languages, from Arabic and English to French, Hindi, Malayalam and Urdu. Daily schedules can be found in the local newspapers.

Operating 24 hours a day, everyday, the English language stations, Dubai FM (92 FM), Free FM (96.7 FM), and Ajman's Channel 4 FM (104.8 FM), play modern music. Operating throughout the UAE, Emirates 1 FM (104.1, 100.5 FM) plays modern music for a 'younger' audience, while Emirates 2 FM (99.3, 106 FM) broadcasts a mixture of news, talk shows and modern music. Sadly, while there are some current affairs programs in English, most are sorely lacking in depth.

Ras Al Khaimah's Radio Asia (1152 KHZ) has programmes in Hindi, Urdu and Malayalam, while Umm Al Quwain's Hum FM (106.2 FM) broadcasts mainly in Hindi with a bit of English.

If you want to hear Arabic music, tune in to 93.9 FM. With the right equipment, the BBC World Service can also be picked up.

Television/Satellite TV

Other options → Television [p.100]
Satellite TV [p.102]

Local television offers four channels: Dubai 2, 10 and 41 show Arabic programmes, while Dubai 33 broadcasts mainly in English. Emirates Dubai Television broadcasts by satellite throughout the world in Arabic and English.

There is also a great variety of services available via satellite. Most hotels and hotel apartments have satellite television available for residents and many apartment blocks have dishes installed, ready for residents to acquire a decoder. Satellite programmes that can be received range from news programmes, international entertainment or films to sports, cartoons and current events.

Telephones

Other options → Telephone [p.97]

Telecommunications are very good, both within the UAE and internationally. All communication is provided by the monopoly organisation, Emirates Telecommunications Corporation, commonly known as Etisalat. Calls from a landline to another landline within Dubai are free of charge and direct dialling is possible to over 170 countries. GPRS, WAP and Hot Spot services are also available in the UAE.

Public payphones are all over the city. A few accept coins, but most require phone cards, which are available at most shops and supermarkets. They come in a variety of values, but for international calls, beware – the units vanish at a truly amazing rate! Etisalat has a new generation of prepaid phone cards called 'Smart Cards', which are available for Dhs.30.

Telephone Codes			
UAE Country Code	+971	Directory Enquiries	181
Abu Dhabi	02	Operator	100
Ajman	06	Etisalat Information	144
Al Ain	03	Fault Reports	171
Dubai	04	Billing Information	142
Fujairah	09	Etisalat Contact Centre	121
Hatta	04	Speaking Clock	140
Jebel Ali	04	Recharge Al Wasel	122
Ras al Khaimah	07	Al Wasel Credit Balance	121
Sharjah	06	To dial a typical Dubai number from overseas, it is 00 **971 4** 391 8060	
Umm Al Quwain	06		
Mobile Telephones	050		

Internet

Other options → Internet Cafés
The Internet [p.99]

With around one third of the population using the Internet, the UAE is among the top twenty countries in the world in terms of Internet use. Internet or cyber cafés around town provide easy and relatively cheap access.

Etisalat is the sole provider of Internet services within the UAE and in order to maintain the country's moral and cultural values, all sites are provided via Etisalat's proxy server. This occasionally results in frustrated users being unable to access perfectly reasonable sites. If you come across such a site, you can report it to Etisalat. Please see [p.57] for helpful Websites and numbers.

Most organisations that are connected have up to an eight character email address. Typical email syntax is: user@emirates.net.ae.

You can also surf the Internet without being a subscriber. All that's needed is a computer with a modem and a regular phone line. To dial 'n' surf, simply call 500 5555. For information on charges, see Dial 'n' Surf on [p.99].

Websites

There are numerous Websites on Dubai and the Emirates in general, and new ones are being uploaded all the time. Some are more interesting, successful and relevant than others. The table on [p.51] lists those that the Explorer team has found to be the most useful – if you have any suggestions for other relevant and helpful Websites, do let us know, and we will include them in the next edition.

UAE Annual Events

Throughout the year, Dubai hosts a number of well established annual events, some of which have been running for years. The events described below are the most popular and regular fixtures on Dubai's social calendar.

Camel Racing — www.nadalshebaclub.com

A traditional sport, the sight of these ungainly animals, ridden by young boys, is an extraordinary spectacle. Racing camels can change hands for as much as ten million dirhams! Morning races start very early during the winter months – be there by 07:00 – and the races are over by 08:30. It is also possible to watch the camels being trained every morning at around 10:00. Admission is free.

Desert Rallies — www.emsf.ae

The UAE provides the ideal location for desert rallying and many events are organised throughout the year by the Emirates Motor Sports Federation (EMSF) in Dubai. The highest profile event is the Desert Challenge, which is the climax of the World Cup in Cross Country Rallying. It attracts top rally drivers from all over the world and is held in the first week of November.

Other events throughout the year include the Spring Desert Rally (4 WD), Peace Rally (saloons), Jeep Jamboree (safari), Drakkar Noir 1000 Dunes Rally (4 WD), Shell Festival Parade, Audi Driving Skills (driving challenge) and the Federation Rally (4 WD).

Contact: For 2004 event details, call EMSF (282 7111). For information on the UAE Desert Challenge, call 282 3441.

See also: *Emirates Motor Sports Federation – Rally Driving [p.296] and UAE Desert Challenge [p.53]*

Dhow Racing — www.dimc-uae.com

Traditional wooden dhows look very atmospheric when racing. The vessels are usually 40 - 60 ft in length and are either powered by men (up to 100 oarsmen per dhow) or by the wind. Fixed races are held throughout the year as well as on special occasions, such as National Day. Most events are held at Dubai International Marine Club.

See also: *Dhow Charters [p.273]*

Dog Show, The — www.nadalshebaclub.com

An event not just for competitors and proud owners, the Dog Show is a popular family outing and the only show of its kind in the Middle East. You are guaranteed to see both pedigree and crossbreed dogs of every shape, size and colour imaginable. One of the most popular events is the Dog Most Like its Owner competition – the likenesses are uncanny!

Dubai Desert Classic — www.dubaidesertclassic.com

Incorporated into the European PGA Tour in 1989, this popular golfing tournament attracts growing numbers of world class players.

Websites

Dubai Information

www.arabiaonline.com	News of the Arab world
www.crazyspin.com	Lists current and upcoming events
www.diningindubai.com	Make reservations online after consulting the Dubai Explorer
www.doctorelite.com	24 hour doctor/pharmacy/medical service
www.dubai.com	Online newspaper type site – Dubai and international news
www.dubaicityguide.com	Updated daily, lists upcoming and current events
www.dubailocator.com	A superb interactive map site for Dubai
www.dubailook.com	Lists current and upcoming events
www.dubaishoppingmalls.com	List of major shopping centres around Dubai
www.expatsite.com	Find out what's going on back home
www.explorer-publishing.com	Our site!
www.godubai.com	Covers all the events and news of Dubai
www.gulf-news.com	Local newspaper
www.khaleejtimes.com	Local newspaper
www.roomservice-uae.com	Deliveries from your favourite restaurants
www.sheikhmohammed.co.ae	His Highness Sheikh Mohammed Bin Rashid Al Maktoum's site
www.sheikhzayed.com	His Highness Sheikh Zayed Bin Sultan Al Nahyan's site
www.uaemall.com	Shop online in the UAE
www.weather.com	Weather in the UAE

Business/Industry

www.dcci.org	Dubai Chamber of Commerce & Industry
www.dm.gov.ae	Dubai Municipality
www.dubai2003.ae	Dubai 2003 IMF site
www.dubaiairport.com	Dubai International Airport
www.dubaipolice.gov.ae	Dubai Police
www.dubaitourism.co.ae	Department of Tourism & Commerce Marketing (DTCM)
www.dwtc.com	Dubai World Trade Centre
www.dxbtraffic.gov.ae	Dubai Traffic Police – great for viewing traffic fines
www.emirates.net.ae	Emirates Internet – Dubai's Internet service provider
www.etisalat.co.ae	Etisalat – Dubai's telephone service provider

Embassies

www.dwtc.com/directory/governme.htm	Embassies in Dubai
www.embassyworld.com	Embassies abroad

Hotels/Sports

Hotel details listed in **General Information** [p.28], and sporting organisations in **Activities**

Wheels

www.4x4motors.com	A little more sand than tar
www.diamondlease.com	Car leasing/rental
www.motorhighway.com	Buy a vehicle online
www.valuewheels.com	Buy a vehicle online

Dubai Marathon
www.dubaimarathon.org

The Dubai Marathon now offers a full marathon as well as a 10 km and 3 km fun run. Attracting all types of runners, the emphasis here is more on fun and participation.

Dubai Raft Race
www.dimc-uae.com

On the weekend of the Raft Race, the marina comes alive with a carnival atmosphere as teams battle against each other on their coloured rafts. Landlubbers can enjoy the spectacle at sea, as well as land activities such as beach games and music by live bands.

Dubai Rugby Sevens
www.dubairugby7s.com

This two day event is a very popular sporting and spectator fixture. With alcohol freely available at the stadium, the party atmosphere carries on until the small hours! Top international teams compete, providing a rare opportunity for local teams from all over the Gulf to try their luck.

Dubai Shopping Festival
www.mydsf.com

A combination of a festival and a shopping extravaganza, DSF, as it is popularly known, is hard to miss as buildings and roads are decorated with coloured lights and there are bargains galore in the participating outlets. Highlights include spectacular fireworks each evening at the Creek, the international wonders of Global Village and the numerous raffles. Other attractions include music, dance and theatrical entertainment from around the world, plus animal shows and a huge funfair. Its success can be gauged from the hotels, which are at 100% occupancy during this month (January 15 - February 15). It is therefore, also dubbed the 'Dubai Traffic Festival' by weary residents facing the resulting traffic congestion in the evenings.

Dubai Summer Surprises
www.mydsf.com

Similar to DSF but smaller, Dubai Summer Surprises is held to attract visitors during the hot and humid summer months. Aimed at the family, DSS offers fun packed activities, which are generally held in climate controlled facilities, such as shopping malls, specially constructed areas and hotels. Events are often based on food, heritage, technology, family values, schools etc.

Alongside DSS, the dramatically reduced summer room rates at hotels have proved a strong attraction for tourists, especially from GCC countries.

Dubai Tennis Open
www.dubaitennischampionships.com

Held in the middle of February, the US$1,000,000 Dubai Duty Free Tennis Open is a popular and well supported event. It is firmly established on the international tennis circuit and offers the chance for fans to see top seeds, both male and female, in an intimate setting, battling it out for game, set and match.

Dubai World Cup
www.nadalshebaclub.com

The Dubai World Cup is billed as the richest horseracing programme in the world – last year's total prize money was over US $15,000,000. The prize for the Group 1 Dubai World Cup race alone was a staggering US $6,000,000. It is held on a Saturday to ensure maximum media coverage in the West, and with a buzzing, vibrant atmosphere, is a great opportunity to dress up and bring out your best hat.

Eid Al Adha

Meaning 'Feast of the Sacrifice', this four day Islamic holiday marks the end of the annual period of pilgrimage to Mecca. The ritual involves the slaughtering of many animals. The holiday is celebrated 70 days after the first Eid.

Eid Al Fitr

This Islamic holiday lasts for three days and celebrates the 'Feast of the Breaking of the Fast'. It is held at the end of Ramadan.

Exhibitions
www.dubaitourism.com

With the increasing importance of MICE (Meetings, Incentives, Conferences, Exhibitions) tourism to Dubai, there are currently two large state of the art exhibition spaces showcasing a variety of exhibitions each year. These are the Airport Expo (Map Ref 15-A4) and the exhibition halls at the Dubai World Trade Centre (Map Ref 10-A2). For details of exhibitions in Dubai, contact Dubai Tourism and Commerce Marketing (223 0000). See [p.54] for a monthly listing of annual events and exhibitions.

Fun Drive
www.gulf-news.co.ae

If your idea of fun is venturing through the wilderness of the UAE with 750 other 4 wheel drives, then this is for you. Spread over two days, the Fun Drive is a popular and very sociable, guided off-road jamboree. The first night is spent at a campsite in the desert where catering and entertainment are provided, as well as large Arabic tents for sleeping (although most people take their own tents). The second day ends in a hotel with more activities. Early booking is advised. Contact the Gulf News Promotions Department for more information.

Great British Day
www.britbiz-uae.com

With a village fête atmosphere, cream teas and fish and chips, Great British Day guarantees a good family day out. It is organised by the British Business Group and usually held on a Friday. Thousands of people of all nationalities attend the event and enjoy competitions, bouncy castles, live music, handicraft stalls etc, and a terrific fireworks display as the grand finale.

Horse Racing
www.nadalshebaclub.com

Nad Al Sheba racecourse is one of the world's leading racing facilities, with top jockeys from Australia, Europe and USA regularly competing throughout the season (November – April). Racing takes place at night under floodlights and there are usually 6 - 7 races each evening, held at 30 minute intervals. The start time is 19:00 (except during Ramadan when it is 21:00).

The clubhouse charges day membership of Dhs.60 on race nights, which allows access to the Members Box. Everyone can take part in free competitions to select the winning horses, with the ultimate aim of taking home prizes or cash. Hospitality suites (catering on request) can be hired by companies or individuals. The dress code to the public enclosures is casual and smart/casual in the clubhouse and private viewing boxes.

General admission and parking are free, and the public has access to most areas with a reserved area for badge holders and members.

Islamic New Year's Day

Islamic New Year's Day marks the start of the Islamic Hijri calendar. It is based on the lunar calendar and should fall on February 22 this year.

See also: *Public Holidays [p.14].*

Lailat Al Mi'raj

This day celebrates the Prophet's ascension into heaven and is expected to occur on September 12 this year.

Powerboat Racing
www.dimc-uae.com

The Emirates is well established on the world championship powerboat racing circuit – in Abu Dhabi with Formula I (Inshore) and in Dubai and Fujairah with Class I (Offshore). These events make a great spectacle, ideal for an armchair sports fan. Just take a picnic and settle in for the day with family and friends. The Dubai Creek also provides a stunning setting for national events in Formulas 2 and 4, which become more competitive every year. The local Victory Team continues to compete in Class I and is ranked the best in the world. Events in Dubai are held at the Dubai International Marine Club (DIMC), (399 4111).

Sharjah World Book Fair
www.swbf.gov.ae

This annual event takes place at the Sharjah Expo Centre and boasts the participation of 35 countries. One of the oldest and largest book fairs in the Arab World, thousands of titles in Arabic, English and many other languages are displayed by private book publishers, governments and universities. Good discounts can be availed and the choice is huge.

Terry Fox Run
www.terryfoxrun.org

Last year, thousands of individuals ran, jogged, walked, cycled, wheeled and even roller bladed their way around an 8.5 km course for charity; over Dhs.270,000 was raised in donations. The proceeds go to cancer research programmes at approved institutions around the world. Check the local media for contact details nearer the time.

UAE Desert Challenge
www.uaedesertchallenge.com

This is the highest profile motor sport event in the country, and is often the culmination of the cross country rallying world cup. Following prestigious events, such as the Paris – Dakar race, this event attracts some of the world's top rally drivers and bike riders who compete in the car, truck and moto-cross categories. The race is held on consecutive days over four stages, usually starting in Abu Dhabi and travelling across the harsh and challenging terrain of the deserts and sabkha to finish in Dubai. For more details, check out www.uaedesertchallenge.com.

Modesh – the official DSS Mascot

Main Annual Events – 2004

January

1	New Year's Day (Fixed)
9	Dubai Marathon
10-12	Sign & Graphic Imaging ME 2003
10-14	18th International Autumn Trade Fair
15	Dubai Shopping Festival begins
16	Dubai Traditional Rowing Race (Heat 1)
18-21	Arab Health Exhibition
21-23	Dubai International Jazz Festival
24-30	Dubai International Sailing Week Regatta 2003

February

2	Eid Al Adha (Moon)
6	Terry Fox Run
6	Dubai Traditional Dhow Sailing Race 22ft
8-10	GEMEX – Global Entertainment & Media
8-10	CABSAT 2004
9-12	Arablab Exhibition
13	Dubai Jet Ski Race (Heat 4 – UAE)
13	Great British Day
14-16	Malayasian Trade Expo
15	Dubai Shopping Festival ends
19-20	Dubai International Kitesurfing Challenge (Heat 2)
22	Islamic New Year's Day (Moon)
23	Dubai Tennis Open commences
26	Dubai Wooden Powerboat Race (Heat 4 – UAE)
26-27	UAE Kite Surfing Challenge (3rd 7 Final Heat)
tbc	Dog Show (mid Feb)

March

4-7	Dubai Desert Classic 2004
5	Dubai Traditional Rowing Race 30ft (3rd & final heat)
6-9	Child Expo
7	Dubai Tennis Open concludes
12-19	Dubai International Kitesurfing Tournament
22-24	International Fashion Exhibition
26	Dubai Wooden Powerboat Race (5th & Final Heat)
27	Dubai World Cup
28-30	Automative Aftermarket Middle East Expo (AAMEE)
tbc	Godolphin 7 Stars

April

1-2, 8	Dubai National Sailing Championship
6-8	Career Fair 2004
6-8	Dubai International Aid
9	"Maktoum Cup" Traditional Rowing Race – 30ft
12-15	Bride 2004
tbc	Nad Al Sheba Gold Cup, UAE Arabian Derby
17-20	Dubai International Boat Show 2004
19-22	Motexha Spring
19-22	Ambient Arabia (Gifts & Homeware)
19-22	The Baby Show
19-22	World of Education
20-23	Gulf Education & Training 2004
26-28	Gulf Beauty
26-29	Agri-Business Expo ME 2004
27-29	Theme Parks & Fun Centres Show 2003
29	Jumeirah Traditional Dhow Sailing Race 43ft (3rd & final heat)

May

2	Prophet Mohammed's Birthday (Moon)
2-6	International Spring Trade Fair
4-7	Arabian Travel Market
7	Dubai Jet-Ski Race (7th and final Heat – UAE)
13	Dubai Traditional Dhow Sailing Race 22ft (Heat 8)
16-19	Gulf Light Exhibition
16-19	Gardening Landscaping & Outdoor Living
16-19	Hardware & DIY Exhibition
16-19	Housewares & Homtech
16-19	Kitchens & Bedrooms
16-19	ME Toy Fair
17-19	The Hotel Show
17-19	The ME Office Interiors & Facilities Man. Exhibition
18-22	International Jewellery Dubai 2004
27	Sir Bu Naa'ir Trad Dhow Sailing – 60ft

June

tbc	Dubai Summer Surprises commences
10-11	UAE National Sailing Championship (4th & Final)

August

6	Accession Day of His Highness Sheikh Zayed

September

11-14	Motexha Autumn
12	Lailat Al Mirage (Moon)
19-22	Gulf Print
22-26	Index 2004 (Furniture & Interior)
27-30	Arab Hunting Exhibition commences
27-30	Arabian Adventure Show
27-30	Arabian Equestrian Show

October

2-8	Gitex 2004
6-8	The Student Show
15	Ramadan begins (Moon)
tbc	UAE Desert Challenge (date to be confirmed)

November

14	Eid Al Fitr (Moon)
20-24	Big 5 Show

December

2	UAE National Day (Fixed)
tbc	Dubai Rugby Sevens (date to be confirmed)
tbc	Dubai Airshow (every two years – next 2005)
tbc	The ME International Motorshow

tbc – to be confirmed

THREE
TIME AWARD
WINNER
images of
Dubai
and the UNITED ARAB EMIRATES

New Residents

EXPLORER

New Residents

What's new?

Make an investment

Page 80

All nationalities are now invited to have 100% home ownership in the area. Freehold properties in the form of scenic community complexes are springing up in prime locations, from Marina penthouse apartments to villas in the Emirates Hills. Check out Residential Areas [p.86]. Freehold property ownership is becoming quite popular, but beware of imposing restrictions - like anywhere else in the world, there are government laws that have to be adhered to.

Don't go West!

Page 102

This healthcare 'oasis' of the Middle East will be a world class hub for modern healthcare, with a premier western healthcare research/teaching institution based within to build local expertise. It also aims to keep potential patients closer to the region (generally, in the past, people have travelled to the West to solve advanced healthcare issues).

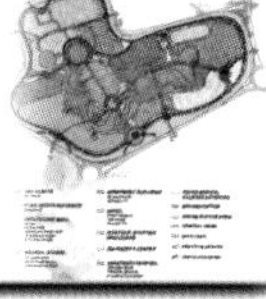

Overview

Dubai has come a long way from the diamond in the rough that it was a mere 30 years ago. Whether it's for fun in the sun or for employment under some serious air conditioning, Dubai is one of the Gulf's top destinations today. With so much expansion, vision and inspiration packed into an average day, there is never a shortage of things to do, places to eat or people to meet! However, do not be fooled into thinking that settling down in this city will be a job of grace and ease. You should be prepared for the paperwork, the heat and the monotonous weather, the conferences and the burgeoning businesses, and the constantly changing policies that come hand in hand with a growing city in the sands.

However, as government departments are encouraged to be more efficient and creative, processes are now displaying a higher degree of professionalism. The Internet is used far more liberally for the issue of documents like trade licences, health cards and visit visas. But, don't expect to find everything online and don't expect the paperwork to be reduced! This government directive is taking its time to filter through, and until the simplification process makes its way through all the individual departments, you can expect to be sent from counter to counter with your documents. This can be confusing, but remember, wherever you go, people are invariably friendly and ready to point you in the right direction.

The following information is meant only as a guide to what you will have to go through to become a car owning, phone owning, Internet connected, working resident. For step by step instructions and details on all the procedures and formalities related to living in Dubai, pick up the *Zappy Explorer (Dubai)*. Remember, requirements and laws change regularly, often in quite major ways. Changes are generally announced in the newspapers and can be implemented literally overnight – so be prepared for the unexpected while living in Dubai!

Remember also, that the following applies only to Dubai, and that while Sharjah and Dubai are close geographically and share many rules and regulations, there are many differences between the two emirates and you should check into Sharjah's specific regulations before engaging in any endeavours.

In The Beginning...

...there was a sponsor. To become a resident in Dubai, you need someone to legally vouch for you. This is usually your employer, who thus turns into your legal sponsor. Once you have residency, you may then be in a position to sponsor your spouse, parents or children, should you wish to do so.

The first step to acquiring residency is to enter the country on a valid entry visa (see Documents [p.60]). The *Zappy Explorer (Dubai)* will also guide you step by step through the visa application process.

A New Way of Looking at Things...

Your employer in Dubai will usually provide your visa. If you do not already have a job secured, you may obtain a visit visa to enter the UAE for a short time (see Visas – Entering Dubai [p.21]). If you are already in Dubai and are applying for a family member or friend, the application form may be collected from the Immigration Department near Trade Centre roundabout (Map Ref 10-B1).

The original entry visa documentation must be presented to airport Immigration on arrival and your passport will be duly stamped. Once you have entered the country on the correct visa, the next step is to apply for a health card, which includes a medical test. After this, you can apply for residency. This should be done within 60 days of entering the country or a fine will be incurred. To legally work, you also require a labour card. Your employer will usually take care of processing all required documentation for you, and sometimes for your family as well.

Labour cards and residence visas are valid for three years and can be renewed (this does not apply to elderly parents or maids – see Residence Visa [p.64] and Domestic Help [p.94]). Health cards are valid for one year. If you are a qualified professional with a university degree or have an established employment history, there should be few difficulties in obtaining the necessary paperwork to become a resident.

Useful Advice

When applying for a residence visa, labour card, driving permit etc, you will always need a handful of essential documents (see below), and you will need to complete countless application forms – invariably typed in Arabic. Don't panic, help is always nearby in Dubai, where a million expats and services exist to make life easier! Most government offices, such as the Immigration Department, Labour Office, Traffic Police, Ministry of Health, government hospitals etc, have small cabins full of typists offering their services in English and Arabic for Dhs.10 - 15. Most also offer photocopying services and some even take instant passport sized photos. If you want to expedite the visa application process, you may pay an additional Dhs.100 ('urgent visa' fee) when you apply for the visa at the Immigration Department.

Essential Documents

For your ease, and to avoid repetition throughout this section, a list of essential documents has been compiled here. These are standard items that you will invariably need to produce when processing documentation. Additional documents will be referred to in the appropriate paragraph.

- Original passport (for inspection only)
- Passport photocopies (personal details)
- Passport photocopies (visa/visit visa details)
- Passport sized photographs

You will need countless photographs over the next few months. Usually two passport photocopies and two photographs will be required each time you file for something, apply for a job, or join a gym. To save time and money, ask for the original negative when you order your first set of photos. Duplicate photos can then be made easily. There are many small photo shops that offer this service; look in your local area.

Although this seems to be fading out, you may have to produce what is commonly known as an NOC, a 'no objection certificate' (or letter) from your employer or sponsor. This confirms who you are and says that they have no objection to you renting a house, getting a driving licence or opening a bank account. It should be on company letterhead paper, signed and stamped with the company stamp to make it undeniably 'official.' Remember to take a photocopy of this document for future use.

e-Dirhams

This rapid passenger clearing service allows UAE & GCC nationals, residents and nationals of the 33 countries permitted entry to the UAE without a visa (see [p.62]), to pass through both the departures and arrivals halls of Dubai International Airport without a passport. Swipe your smart card through an electronic gate and through you go, saving a great deal of time otherwise spent in long queues! Applications for a smart card are processed within minutes on the mezzanine floor of the Emirates Holidays building, Sheikh Zayed Road; you will need your passport, be fingerprinted and photographed. The smart card costs Dhs.150 and is valid for two years. Call the E-Gate smart card centre (04 316 6966) for more information.

Documents

Entry Visa

Other options → **Entering Dubai [p.21]**

Shopping festivals and conferences draw large numbers of tourists and business crowds into Dubai. Hence, it's always smart to keep the happenings of the city in consideration when planning your journey. Also bear in mind the summer heat; it can be an unpleasant welcome, so consider the months between October and May when planning your arrival into the city of golden sands.

Immigration Department Under Construction

In order to initiate your residence visa application process, make sure you enter Dubai on the correct entry visa. This is either a residence or an employment visa. The other two kinds of visa (visit and transit) only allow you to remain here temporarily, as the names imply, and their rules vary depending on your nationality.

In accordance with the Ministry Council Decree No.23/207, it was agreed to issue entry permits (visit visas) at UAE entry ports for citizens of the following countries:

Western European Countries:

Andorra, Austria, Belgium , Denmark, Finland, France, Germany, Greece, Holland, Iceland, Ireland, Italy, Liechtenstein, Luxembourg, Monaco, Norway, Portugal, San Marino, Spain, Sweden, Switzerland, United Kingdom, Vatican

Other Countries:

Australia , Brunei, Canada, Hong Kong, Japan, Malaysia, New Zealand, Singapore, S. Korea, USA

Entry Permit Regulations:

This permit is a visit visa and entitles its holder to stay for 60 days from the date of entry, and it can be renewed.

It is issued without any charges when entering the UAE, but there will be a charge of Dhs.500 for renewal from the Immigration Department

The renewal must be made at the office of Naturalisation & Residency Administration of the port of arrival (eg, airport, port).

Nationalities that can obtain a visit visa on arrival at Dubai International Airport can initially stay for 60 days and renew once, or take an indefinite 'visa run' back home (see also: Entering Dubai [p.21]). Or perhaps you are up for an hour flight to Kish, Qeshm, Bahrain, Doha, or Qatar, and you can re-enter on another visit visa; either way figure for about Dhs.500.

If you manage to secure work while on a visit visa, you will have to transfer to an employment visa in order to apply for your residence visa and labour card. You can transfer your visa status through the Immigration Department. You will need the relevant application form (obtainable from the Immigration Department) typed in Arabic, Essential Documents (see [p.60]), a copy of your original labour contract from your new employer and a copy of your sponsor's original passport, plus Dhs.100. Alternatively, you can fly out of the country and re-enter on the correct visa.

Health Card

Once you have the correct visa status (see above), the next step to becoming a resident is to apply for a health card, which is valid for one year. Your employer may do this for you, and if you work at Dubai Media or Internet Cities, they will process this for you. This entitles residents to relatively low cost medical treatment at public hospitals and clinics. However, the consultation charges of Dhs.50 do not include x-rays and other such necessary care. Some employers provide additional private medical insurance and, as in most countries, this is regarded as preferable to state care, although the usual hospital horror stories apply to both sectors.

Public (Government) Hospital

The current process to apply for a health card starts off with the application form available at any public hospital, like Iranian, Al Baraha, Maktoum or Rashid Hospitals, the Ministry of Health, or any First Health Care Centre, whichever is in your local area. Submit the application form (typed in Arabic) along with the essential documents (see [p.60]), employment verification letter and Dhs.300 (e-Dirham). If you are not employed and are a dependant, you will be required to produce your tenancy contract, electricity and phone bills (original and photocopy of all documents) instead of your employment letter. In return, they will issue you with a temporary health card and a receipt for Dhs.300.

You can then go for your medical test – it is best to go to Al Baraha (Kuwait) Hospital for this as they are best prepared for this. Children under 18 do not need to have a medical test; all you need do is apply for a health card and you can then directly submit their residence visa application.

You will need your temporary health card, a copy of the receipt for Dhs.300, and two passport photos. The test fee is Dhs.205; this includes Dhs.5 for typing the application form in Arabic (done by the hospital). The medical test includes a medical examination, a chest X-ray and a blood test for AIDS, Hepatitis, etc. If you are processing a health card for a maid, you will need to pay an additional Dhs.100 to have him or her vaccinated against Hepatitis, and an additional Dhs.10 for typing out the form (refer to Domestic Help [p.94]).

Your temporary health card will be returned to you, and after one to two working days, you can collect your medical certificate. The temporary health card will have a date on it stating when to collect your permanent health card. This can take anywhere from a week to a few months; in the meantime, the temporary health card can be used at hospitals should you require treatment.

Office locations:

- *Al Baraha (Kuwait) Hospital*, near Hyatt Regency Dubai hotel, Deira (Map Ref 12-A2)
- *Iranian Hospital*, Al Wasl Road, Jumeira (Map Ref 6-D3)
- *Maktoum Hospital*, near Al Ghurair City, Deira (Map Ref 8-D4)
- *Rashid Hospital*, near Maktoum Bridge, Bur Dubai (Map Ref 11-A4)

Residence Visa

Other options → **Visas - Entering Dubai [p.21]**

There are two types of residence visas: one for when you are sponsored for employment, and the other for residence only (sponsored by a family member). As stated, the first step to gaining a residence visa is to apply for a health card.

Once a resident, you must not leave the UAE for more than six months without revisiting, otherwise your residency will lapse. This is not relevant to children studying abroad who are on their parent's sponsorship here, as long as proof of enrolment with the educational institution overseas is furnished.

Office location:

- *Immigration Department*, near Trade Centre roundabout (Map Ref 10-B1)

Sponsorship by Employer

Your employer should handle all the paperwork, and often times will have a staff member (who is thoroughly familiar with the ins and outs of the bureaucracy) dedicated for this task alone. After arranging for your residency, they should then apply directly for your labour card (see below). The Ministry of Labour Website (www.mol.gov.ae) has been expanded to include a feedback section as well as a facility for companies to process their applications and transactions over the Internet.

You will need to supply the essential documents and education or degree certificates. You must have your certificates attested by a solicitor or public notary in your home country and then by your foreign office to verify the solicitor as bona fide. The UAE embassy in your home country must also sign the documents. Of course, it makes life much simpler if you can do all of this before you come to Dubai. However, there are several courier services, such as DHL and UPS, that can ensure fast and secure service of your important papers, making the process a lot smoother.

Family Sponsorship

If you are sponsored and are arranging sponsorship for family members since your employer will not do so, you will have a lengthy and tedious process ahead (see below). Good luck! To sponsor your wife or children, you will need a minimum monthly salary of Dhs.3,000 plus accommodation, or a minimum all inclusive salary of Dhs.4,000. Only what is printed on your labour contract will be accepted as proof of your earnings.

For parents to sponsor children, difficulties arise when sons (not daughters) become 18 years old. Unless they are enrolled in full time education in the UAE, they must transfer their visa to an independent sponsor or the parents may pay a Dhs.5,000 security deposit (once only) and apply for an annual, renewable visa. If they are still in education, they may remain under parental sponsorship, but again, only on an annual basis.

Babies born abroad to expatriate moms holding a UAE residency are required to have a residence visa or a visit visa before entering the UAE. The application should be filed by the father or family provider, along with the essential documents, a salary certificate and a birth certificate. The residence visa for newborns does not require a security check, so the process promises to be faster than most.

It is very difficult for a woman to sponsor her family but there are some exceptions to this rule. Those women employed as doctors, lawyers, teachers etc, earning a minimum stipulated salary, may be permitted to sponsor family members. In most cases though, the husband/father will be the

sponsor. When sponsoring parents, there are certain constraints depending on your visa status, ie, you should be in a certain category of employment, such as a manager, and earning over Dhs.6,000 per month. In addition, a special committee meets to review each case individually – usually to consider the age of parents to be sponsored, health requirements etc. Even when a visa is granted, it is only valid for one year and is reviewed for renewal on an annual basis.

If you are resident under family sponsorship and then decide to work, you will need to apply for a labour card. You will also need a second medical test – this should be paid for by your employer.

The Process

To become a resident, collect a residency application form from the Immigration Department and have it typed in Arabic. Then submit the application along with the essential documents, medical certificate and Dhs.100 (e-Dirham).

It is essential that you fill out the names of your parents (including your mother's maiden name) in the specified section. Once the application is approved (this may take up to a month), you will be issued with a permit of entry for Dubai and you must exit and re-enter the country, submitting the entry permit on re-entry to Immigration (ie, passport control), who will then stamp your passport. You should then submit your original passport to the Immigration Department, the original passport of your nominated sponsor, along with your medical certificate, four passport photos and Dhs.300 (e-Dirham) in order to get your permanent residency stamp. This can take anywhere from ten days to one to two months or longer. Then you can relax!

Once you have your residency stamped, your sponsor or employer may insist that they need to keep your passport. This seems to be the accepted practice amongst many local sponsors. However, unless you work in Jebel Ali, there are currently no legal requirements under UAE law for you to hand over your passport. If you aren't comfortable with them keeping it, don't let them! Additionally, you may need it when visiting your consulate, setting up a bank account etc. Other sponsors will keep your labour card in return for you keeping your passport.

As a full fledged resident, you are now welcome to take out a bank loan, buy a car, rent an apartment in your own name, get a liquor licence etc.

See also: *Visa Run - Entering Dubai [p.21]; refer to the Zappy Explorer (Dubai)*

Labour Card

To work in the UAE, you are legally required to have a valid labour card. This can only be applied for once you have residency. Additionally, expatriate workers who do not renew their labour card will face a penalty of between Dhs.500 and 2,000. A fine of Dhs.500 will be imposed for a card expired six months, Dhs.1,000 for a card expired one year, and Dhs.2,000 for cards expired longer than one year.

Office Towers on Sheikh Zayed Road

If your employer is arranging your residency, the labour card should be processed directly after residency has been approved. You should not need to supply any further documentation. Before your labour card is issued, you will need to sign your labour contract, which is printed in both Arabic and English. It's a standard form issued by the labour authorities and completed with your details. Unless you read Arabic, it may be advisable to have a translation made of your details, since the Arabic is taken as the legal default if there is any dispute (see Employment Contracts [p.76]).

If you are on family residency and decide to work, your employer, not your visa sponsor, will need to apply for a labour card. Your sponsor will need to supply a letter of no objection (also known as an NOC or no objection certificate). Sponsored women are not allowed to work unless they have a work permit, also known as a labour card.

Documents to supply include: the essential documents (see [p.60], NOC, education certificate/s (if appropriate) and usually a photocopy of your sponsor's passport – they may also require the sponsor's original passport.

Expat students on their parent's visa, who wish to work in Dubai during the summer vacation, should apply to the Department of Naturalisation & Residency for a permit allowing them to work legally.

Location: *Labour Department near Galadari roundabout, (269 1666, Map Ref 12-B4)*

Free Zones

Other options → **Free Zones [p.149]**

Employees of companies in free zones have different sponsorship options, depending on the free zone. For example, in Jebel Ali, you can either be sponsored by an individual company or by the free zone authority itself. Whether the Jebel Ali Free Zone, Dubai Internet or Media City, or the Dubai Airport Free Zone, the free zone authorities will handle the processing of your visa through the Immigration Department and generally, they are able to process your visa very quickly. Once Immigration has stamped your residence visa in your passport, the free zone will issue your labour card – this also acts as your security pass for entry to the free zone (your passport will be retained in Jebel Ali, but not in the other free zones). Your visa is valid for three years, and the labour card either one or three years, depending on the free zone.

Certificates & Licences

Driving Licence

Other options → **Transportation [p.118]**

Taking to the roads in Dubai is taking your life in your hands! The standard of driving certainly leaves much to be desired.

Until you acquire full residency, you can drive a hire car, provided you have a valid driving licence from your country of origin or an international licence (this only applies to those countries on the transfer list below). Make sure your driving licence details are registered with the car hire company.

To drive private vehicles, you must first apply for a temporary Dubai licence with the Traffic Police. You will need to fill out the application form, take the essential documents and Dhs.10 to obtain a temporary licence that is valid for one month (licences for longer periods are also available).

Once you have your residence visa, you must apply for a permanent UAE licence. Nationals of certain countries can automatically transfer their driving licence, providing the original licence is valid.

Some of the above licences will need an Arabic translation by your consulate – check with the Traffic Police. You may also be required to sit a short written test on road rules before the transfer will take place.

Automatic Licence Transfer

Australia, Austria, Belgium, Canada, Cyprus, Czech Republic, Denmark, Finland, France, GCC member countries, Germany, Greece, Iceland, Ireland, Italy, Japan, Luxembourg, Netherlands, New Zealand, Norway, Poland, Portugal, Singapore, Slovakia, South Africa, South Korea, Spain, Sweden, Switzerland, Turkey, United Kingdom, United States.

If you aren't from one of the above countries, you will need to sit a UAE driving test. To apply for a permanent driving licence, submit the following documents (see the next page) to the Traffic Police, plus your valid Dubai residence visa and Dhs.100.

Driving in Dubai

Dubai Country Club is an idyllic retreat, offering you an atmosphere of warm hospitality whilst you enjoy the impressive range of facilities. Whatever your pleasure may be - golf, tennis, squash & keeping fit for the energetic, to chilling out by the pool or just experiencing a superb range of restaurants, bars and events for those who enjoy a more leisurely pace - Dubai Country Club has it all. There is more happening, more often than anywhere else - and it is much less expensive than you would think.

The Dubai Country Club is for everyone to enjoy and if you are looking for a warm, friendly atmosphere with plenty of social activity, then this is the club for YOU!

THE DUBAI COUNTRY CLUB

P.O.BOX: 5103, DUBAI, UAE TEL: +971 4 3331155 FAX: +971 4 3331409
E-mail: dcc@emirates.net.ae - Website: www.dubaicountryclub.com

Always carry your Dubai driving licence when driving. If you fail to produce it during a police spot check, you will be fined. Driving licences can be renewed at the Traffic Police as well as other sites around Dubai, including Al Safa Union Co-operative (394 5007, Map Ref 5-B2), Al Tawar Union Co-operative (263 4857, Map Ref 15-C2) and Jumeira Plaza (342 0737 Map Ref 6-C2). The licence is valid for ten years, and if you manage to drive on the UAE roads for this long without going crazy, you deserve a medal!

Driving Licence Documents

- The relevant application form from the Traffic Police typed in Arabic

Plus these essential documents:

- A copy of your sponsor's passport or a copy of the company's trade licence
- An NOC from your sponsor/company in Arabic
- Your original driving licence along with a photocopy (and translation, if requested by the Traffic Police)
- Sometimes your sponsor's original passport is requested as well as a copy. However, this seems to depend on whim more than anything concrete.

Office locations:

- Traffic Police HQ – near Galadari roundabout, Dubai-Sharjah Road (269 2222, Map Ref 15-B1)
- Bur Dubai Police Station – Sheikh Zayed Road, Junction 4 (398 1111 Map Ref 10-A1)

Driving Test

If your nationality is not on the automatic transfer list, you will need to sit a UAE driving test to be eligible to drive in Dubai, regardless of whether you hold a valid driving licence from your country or not. If you haven't driven in your country of origin and need to obtain a driving licence, the following information will apply to you as well.

The first step is to obtain a learning permit – start by picking up an application form from the Traffic Police. You will need the essential documents (see above), the driving licence documents and Dhs.40. You will be given an eye test at the Traffic Police. Then find a reputable driving school – check the Yellow Pages or try one of these:

Driving Schools	
Al Hamriya Driving School	269 9259
Belhasa	668 440
Dubai Driving School	271 7654
Emirates Driving Institute	263 1100

Some driving institutions insist that you pay for a set of pre-booked lessons. In some cases, the package extends to 52 lessons and can cost up to Dhs.3,000! The lessons must be taken on consecutive days and usually last 30 - 45 minutes. Other companies offer lessons on an hourly basis, as and when you like, for Dhs.35 per hour. Women are required to take lessons with a female instructor, at a cost of Dhs.65 per hour, as opposed to male instructors who charge Dhs.35 per hour. If a woman wants to take lessons with a male instructor, she must first obtain NOC's from her husband/sponsor and the Traffic Police. That said, if she has previous driving experience, she will have to sit a test with an instructor (who could be male) before signing up for lessons (no NOC's required for this one!).

When your instructor feels that you are ready to take your test, you will be issued with a letter to that effect and can now apply for a test date. You will need to fill out the necessary application form at the Traffic Police, and also hand in your essential documents, driving licence documents, Dhs.35, and again, you must take an eye test elsewhere and bring the certificate the optician supplies you. The time between submitting your application and the test date can be as long as two to three months.

No UAE Licence?

You cannot drive a privately registered vehicle on an international or foreign driving licence, as the vehicle is only insured for drivers holding a UAE driving licence.

The Infamous Traffic on Sheikh Zayed Road

You will be given three different tests on different dates. One is a Highway Code test, another an 'internal' test which includes garage parking etc, and the third is a road test. Once you pass all three tests, you will be issued with a certificate (after about five days), which you should take to the Traffic Police to apply for your permanent driving licence. Before you are issued with your permanent driving licence, you will have to attend two compulsory hour long road safety lectures, the cost of which is incorporated into the price of your lessons. For detailed, step by step information on licence procedures, refer to the *Zappy Explorer (Dubai)*

Liquor Licence

Other options → **Alcohol [p.20]**

Dubai has the most liberal attitude towards alcohol of all the emirates. If you wish to buy alcohol for consumption at home, you will need a special liquor licence to buy from a liquor shop (alcohol is not available at the local supermarket). In public, only four and five star hotels are licensed to serve alcoholic drinks in their bars and restaurants, as well as some private sports clubs. You won't need a liquor licence to drink at a hotel or a club, but you will require a valid ID to prove you are 21 or older.

The licence allows you to spend a limited amount on alcohol per month – this amount is based on your monthly salary. While no minimum salary level is stated, Dhs.3,500 is generally felt to be the minimum for an application to be accepted. Only non Muslims with a residence visa may obtain a licence, and for married couples, only the husband may apply.

To apply, collect an application form from the Dubai Police HQ. Your employer must sign and stamp the form, then submit it (in both Arabic and English) to the CID at the Dubai Police HQ along with the essential documents, your labour contract (stating your salary), your spouse's passport copy and Dhs.105. Your liquor licence should be processed in less than two weeks. Alternatively, check with either MMI or A&E, the two licensed liquor store chains in Dubai, to see if you can apply for your liquor licence in store, saving you the hassle of visiting the Police HQ.

Buying alcohol from liquor shops can be expensive as you have to pay an additional tax of 30% on all items. However, the range of alcohol for sale is excellent. There are cheaper alternatives for buying alcohol where a licence is not required, such as Ajman's 'Hole in the Wall', near the Ajman Kempinski. Umm al Quwain also has outlets by the Barracuda Resort, next to the Dreamland Aqua Park, and next to the Umm al Quwain Beach Hotel. However, if you decide to make a run for it, beware that it is illegal to transport alcohol around the Emirates without a liquor licence. This law is particularly enforced in Sharjah.

Office location: Liquor Licensing Section, CID, Dubai Police HQ, Dubai-Sharjah road, near Al Mulla Plaza (Map Ref 15-C1)

Office hours: Saturday - Wednesday 07:30 - 12:00

Birth Certificates & Registration

Every expat child born in the UAE must be registered with a residence visa within 40 days of birth. Without the correct documentation, you may not be able to take your baby out of the country.

The hospital that the baby is delivered at will prepare the official 'notification of birth' certificate in English or Arabic upon receipt of hospital records, photocopies of both parents' passports and marriage certificate, and a fee of Dhs.50. Take the birth certificate for translation into English to Dubai Hospital's Preventative Medicine Department (behind Al Baraha (Kuwait) Hospital) where you will be issued with an application form, which must then be typed in English (Dhs.50 fee). You should also take the certificate to be attested at the Ministry of Health (Dhs.10 fee) and the Ministry of Foreign Affairs (Dhs.50 fee).

Once this is done, ensure you register your child's birth at your embassy or consulate. To do this, you will require the local notification of birth

Explorer Baby

certificate, both parents' birth certificates, passports and marriage certificate. In addition, you may want to arrange a passport for your baby. Then, you must apply for a residence visa through the normal UAE channels.

Before the birth, it is worth checking the regulations of your country of origin for citizens born overseas (see [p.143] for a list of embassies and consulates in Dubai).

Marriage Certificates & Registration

Love is in the air! With so many singles in Dubai and all the ladies' nights about town, it won't be long before you, too, are bitten by the marriage bug. While most people prefer to return to their country of origin, Dubai does offer a number of options for you to get married here.

Muslims

As a Muslim marrying another Muslim, apply at the marriage section of the Sharia Court (Dubai Court), next to Maktoum Bridge. You will need two male witnesses and the bride should ensure that either her father or brother attends as a witness. You will require your passports with copies, proof that the groom is Muslim and Dhs.50. You can marry there and then.

For a Muslim woman marrying a non Muslim man, the situation is little more complicated, but possible if the man first converts to Islam. For further information, the Dubai Court (334 7777) or the Dubai Court Marriage Section (303 0406) can advise.

Opening hours: 07:30 - 14:00 & 17:30 - 20:30

Christians

Christians can choose to have either a formal church ceremony with a congregation, or a small church ceremony and a blessing afterwards at a different location, such as a hotel.

At the official church ceremony, you will need two witnesses to sign the marriage register - the church then issues a marriage certificate (you will also need to take copies of your passport and residence visa). You can take the certificate and your essential documents to your embassy in order to attest the document.

Catholics must also undertake a Marriage Encounter course, which usually takes place at St Mary's Church (337 0087) on a Friday. You will need to fill out a standard form and at the end of the course, you are presented with a certificate. You should then arrange with the priest to undertake a pre-nuptial ceremony and again, you are asked to fill out a form. You will need to take your birth certificate, baptism certificate, passport and passport copies, an NOC from your parish priest in your home country and a Dhs.250 donation. If you are a non Catholic marrying a Catholic, you will need an NOC from your embassy/consulate stating that you are legally free to marry. A declaration of your intent to marry is posted on the public noticeboard at the church for three weeks, after which time, if there are no objections, you can set a date for the ceremony.

Anglicans should contact the Chaplain at Holy Trinity Church (337 4947) for an appointment. You will need to fill out a number of forms, basically stating your intention to marry, that you aren't a Muslim and confirming that you are legally free to do so. Documents required are the original passport and photocopies, and passport sized photos. If you have previously been married, you will need to produce either your divorce certificate or the death certificate of your previous partner. You will also need Dhs.520, plus Dhs.50 for the marriage certificate. If you wish to hold the ceremony outside the church, an additional Dhs.500 will be charged.

These marriages are recognised by the Government of the UAE. The chaplain's or priest's signature may be authenticated by taking an Arabic translation of the marriage certificate to the Dubai Court after the ceremony. Filipino citizens are required to contact their embassy in Abu Dhabi before the Dubai Court will authenticate their marriage certificate.

Hindus

Hindus can be married through the Hindu Temple and the Indian Embassy (397 1222). The department publishes a booklet with guidelines on how to get married and you will have to fill out an application form on the premises. Formalities take a minimum of 45 days.

Atheists

Atheists should contact their local embassy or consulate, as they may have regulations and referrals to arrange for a local civil marriage, which can then be registered at their embassy.

Death Certificates & Registration

In the unhappy event of a death of a friend or relative, the first thing to do is to notify the police of your district. On arrival, the police will make a report and the body will be taken to hospital where a doctor will determine the cause of death. A post mortem examination/inquest is not normally performed, unless foul play is suspected or the death is a violent one. Contact the deceased's embassy or consulate for guidance.

The authorities will need to see the deceased's passport and visa details. The hospital will issue a death certificate declaration on receipt of the doctor's report for a fee of Dhs.50. Make sure that the actual cause of death is stated. Then take the declaration of death and original passport to the police who will issue a letter addressed to Al Baraha (Kuwait) Hospital. The letter plus death declaration, original passport and copies should be taken to Al Baraha Hospital, Department of Preventative Medicine, where an actual death certificate will be issued for a small fee. If you are sending the deceased home, you should also request a death certificate in English (an additional Dhs.100) or for other languages, apply to the legal profession.

Then take the certificate to the Ministry of Health and the Ministry of Foreign Affairs for registration. Notify the relevant embassy/consulate for the death to be registered in the deceased's country of origin. They will also issue their own death certificate. Take the original passport and death certificate for the passport to be cancelled.

The deceased's visa must also be cancelled by the Immigration Department. Take the local death certificate, original cancelled passport and embassy/consulate death certificate.

To return the deceased to his/her country of origin, you will need to book a flight through DNATA and get police clearance from airport security to ship the body out of the country, as well as an NOC from the relevant embassy. The body needs to be embalmed and you must obtain a letter to this intent from the police. Embalming can be arranged through Maktoum Hospital for Dhs.1,000, which includes the embalming certificate. The body must be identified before and after embalming, after which it should be transferred to Cargo Village for shipping.

The following documents should accompany the deceased: local death certificate, translation of death certificate, embalming certificate, NOC from the police, embassy/consulate death certificate and NOC, and cancelled passport.

A local burial can be arranged at the Muslim or Christian cemeteries in Dubai. The cost of a burial is Dhs.1,100 for an adult and Dhs.350 for a child. You will need to arrange for a coffin to be made, as well as transport to the burial site. Cremation is also possible, but only in the Hindu manner and with the prior permission of the next of kin and the CID.

See also: *Support Groups [p.112], Zappy Explorer (Dubai)*

Work

Working in Dubai

Working in Dubai is very different from working in Asia, Europe or North America. The greatest advantage is the general proximity of everything – there are no stuffy trains to catch, no real distances to commute... and it's always sunny! Having said that, watch out for the six o'clock traffic on your way home.

Expat workers share a common mission – to seek a better quality to life. They all come from various countries and lifestyles, and many are skilled, educated and have a lot to contribute. There are those who have been seconded by companies based in their home country, and those who have come to Dubai in search of the expat lifestyle. However, don't be fooled – it's not all coffee and sunshine. Setting up life here and establishing a network is still hard work. Additionally, you only have developing labour laws to protect you.

Labourers Loading a Dhow

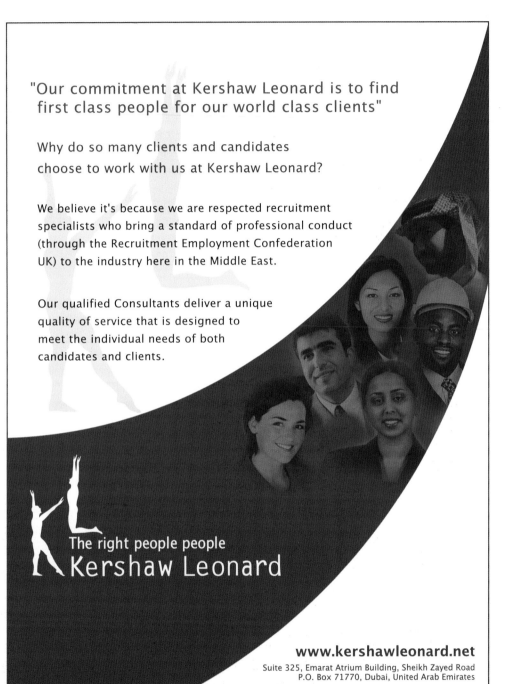

Working Hours

Working hours vary quite dramatically within the emirate, and are based on straight shift and split shift timings. Split shift timings allow for an afternoon siesta and are generally 08:00 - 13:00 and 16:00 - 19:00. Straight shift timings vary from government organisations (07:00 - 14:00) to private companies (09:00 - 18:00). Some companies work five and a half days, with the weekend on Thursday afternoon and Friday. However, more companies are adopting a five day working week with government departments and some private sector companies observing a Thursday/Friday weekend, and other private sector companies observing a Friday/Saturday weekend.

Public holidays are set by the government and religious holidays are governed by the moon. During Ramadan, organisations are meant to reduce their working hours for their Muslim employees, with the public sector working a six hour day. (For further details on holidays, refer to Public Holidays [p.14].)

Finding Work

If you do not have employment on arrival to Dubai, the best way to find a job is to register with the recruitment agencies and to check the small ads and employment pages in the main newspapers. An employment supplement is published in the Gulf News every Sunday, Tuesday and Thursday, and in the Khaleej Times on Sunday, Monday and Wednesday.

A note of caution concerning the use of the words 'UK/US educated' in the papers: this is the 'accepted' form of discrimination here but ironically, UAE Nationals are also told they have priority to get any job in their own country. While efforts are being made to make a move towards 'emiratisation', there are no precise laws to force the private sector to employ Nationals.

Social Life

International Intrigue
You're surrounded by people from all over the globe, so try be open minded and get to know them - you will find yourself knee deep in culture, intrigue, glamour and style.

Glam it Up!
Get out your best duds and take your bejewelled self to the hottest spots. Dubai is a star studded city where you can do more for less, so there's no excuse to stay home. Go dancing, check out the latest restaurants and clubs, have tea at the Ritz, and live the high life.

The Rumour Mill
Now that you're a twinkle on this star studded scape, beware the photographers, the reporters, the local Internet sites and the fact that this is a tiny city with a very healthy grapevine. In the end, everyone knows what's going on!

Recruitment Agencies

There are a number of recruitment/employment agencies in Dubai. To register, check with the agency to find out if they take walk ins. Most only accept CVs via email these days and will then contact you for an interview. For the interview, you will need both your CV and passport photographs. Invariably, you will also have to fill out an agency form summarising your CV. The agency takes its fee from the registered company once the position has

Deira Highrises

been filled. It is illegal for a recruitment company to levy fees on candidates for this service.

Don't rely too heavily on the agency finding a job for you; more often than not, they depend on you spotting a vacancy that they have advertised in the paper and telephoning them to submit your interest. Should you be suitable for the job, the agency will mediate between you and the employer and arrange all interviews.

Below is a list of recruitment agencies operating out of the UAE. You can thank us when you're rich and famous! Some of these agencies are specialised for certain industries, so do your research and register accordingly. Good luck!

Recruitment Agencies	
BAC	336 0350
Bayt (Recommended)	391 1900
Clarendon Parker (Recommended)	391 0460
Dubai Media City	391 4615
IQ Selection	324 2878
Job Scan	355 9113
Job Track	397 7751
Kershaw Leonard (Recommended)	343 4606
Nadia	331 3401
Resources	644 2868
Search	268 6100
Seekers	351 2666
SOS	396 5600
Talent	335 0999

Employment Contracts

Never sign a contract on the spot. You will be thanking us all the way to the bank! Take it home overnight for reflection (and perhaps interjection by a well intentioned friend). This is a binding and legal contract, and severely affects your life in Dubai, so before you leap in, make sure it's the job that you really want. You can even opt to put an initial 3 month introductory period into your contract before processing your visa under the company. Once you have accepted a job offer, you may be asked to sign a copy of your contract in Arabic as well as in English. Be sure to check the Arabic translation before you sign, as this is taken as the legal default if there is a dispute. There have been instances of the Arabic reading differently from the English. You should also refer to a copy of the UAE Labour Law (see below) for details of other benefits and entitlements.

If you are sponsored by your spouse and wish to work, you will need to obtain an NOC (No Objection Certificate) from him before signing a contract with your new employer. Your employer will then apply for your labour card. This card is very important; if an officer asks you to show yours, and you are unable to produce one, you can be fined Dhs.1,200 and sent to jail.

Labour Law

The UAE Labour Law is a work in progress; the most recent version available is from 1980, though updates and amendments occur from time to time. The Labour Law outlines everything from employee entitlements (end of service gratuity, workers' compensation, holidays etc) to employment contracts and disciplinary rules. The law tends to favour employer rights but it also clearly outlines those employee rights that do exist in the UAE.

Labour unions are illegal, as are strikes. Recent moves have been made by the Ministry of Labour to assist workers (particularly labourers) in labour disputes against their employers. The Ministry now punishes companies who do not comply with the Labour Law – licences are withdrawn if warnings are not heeded. Non payment of salaries is a common problem, hopefully to be sorted out one day. However, if you are facing this ugly dilemma, you do have rights. You can file a case with the UAE Labour Department who will then follow up with your employer on your behalf and pressure them to pay you your due wages. You may opt to get a lawyer, which can be less confusing than dealing with a governmental agency, although more expensive as fees can accrue. For recommendations, referrals and consultation, call your embassy.

A copy of the UAE Labour Law may be available from your employer or it can be obtained through the Ministry of Labour & Social Affairs (269 1666). The UAE Labour Guide, published by the Ministry in 2002, also outlines workers' rights.

'Banning'

While it is natural to seek out better work opportunities, many expats live in fear of being banned if they change employer. This is one area of the law which seems to change on a monthly basis, hence it's best to check with the Labour

Department or someone who's in the know for the latest version. No matter what, in most cases, red tape and visa transferring hassles apply, so check out all options before making any moves.

The government's aim is to stop people from job hopping, and the visa laws favour the educated, degree holding specialist. Unless you work in a free zone, hold a Master's degree, or are in a special category of employment, if you resign from your job, you could potentially receive a six month ban from working elsewhere in the UAE. This stands, even if you have an NOC letter from your previous employer. It helps your case if you've worked in your company at least one year, but until the law is set in stone once and for all, this area really is up in the air.

People resigning from a job fall into three groups.

- Those who resign to return to their own country: the residence visa will be cancelled (if they wish to live/work here in the future, they must find a new sponsor and apply for residency etc, from the beginning)
- Those who resign to look for other work: if they are lucky, their old company will supply an NOC and their residency can be transferred. This is provided they have been employed by the company for over one year and that they fall into certain categories of employment
- Those who resign to work for another company: People in this category run the risk of a labour ban and residence visa cancellation. This applies where the person was employed on a specified term contract. For those on an unlimited contract, they may only risk an immigration ban.

For details of the employee categories that cannot be banned, refer to the most recent version of the UAE Labour Law.

Company Closure

Some people and companies move around and see Dubai as a place to make money and run. Employees who face the unlucky situation of bankruptcy or company closure are entitled under UAE Labour law to receive their due gratuity payments, holidays etc, but you had better speak to the labour department for the proper process. Additionally, no employee of a firm which has been closed, is allowed to transfer sponsorship to their new employer unless an attested certificate of closure by their previous employer is issued by the court and submitted to the Ministry of Labour and Social Services. If you are unfortunate enough to have to deal with this, consult with the appropriate government offices to get your paperwork right.

Financial & Legal Affairs

Other options → **Money [p.42]**

Banks

Dubai is not short of internationally recognised banks that offer standard facilities, such as current, deposit and savings accounts, ATMs (otherwise known as automatic teller machines, service tills or cash points), credit cards, loans etc. There are plenty of ATM machines around Dubai (location details can be obtained from the bank) and most cards are compatible with other Dubai based banks (a few also offer global access links).

To open a bank account in most banks in Dubai, you need to have a residence visa or to have your residency application underway. You will need to present the banking advisor with your original passport, copies of your passport (personal details and visa) and an NOC from your sponsor. Some banks set a minimum account limit – this can be around Dhs.2,000 for a deposit account and as much as Dhs.5,000 for a current account. Without a residence visa, Middle East bank, known as ME bank, will open an account for you and provide an

National Bank of Dubai

ATM card, but not a chequebook. ME bank also allows you to apply online for a bank account at www.me.ae/mebank/default.htm.

Opening Hours: Saturday - Wednesday 08:00 - 13:00; Thursday 08:00 - 12:00. Some banks, such as Mashreq and Standard Chartered, also open in the evenings from 16:30 - 18:30.

Financial Planning

Planning for the financial future (unless you take the head in the sand approach) is an important aspect of modern day life and especially necessary for expats.

Before you do anything, you should contact the tax authorities in your home country to ensure that you are complying with the financial laws there. Most countries will consider you not liable for income tax once you prove your UAE residence or your non residence in your home country (a contract of employment is normally a good starting point for proving non residence). As a non resident, however, you may still have to fulfil certain criteria (such as only visiting your home country for a limited number of days each year).

Generally, the main reason for accepting an expat posting is to improve your financial situation. It is recommended not to undertake any non cash investments until you know your monthly savings capacity, even though this may take up to six months to ascertain. In fact, one of the first steps you should take with your new earnings is to begin paying back as much debt as possible (starting with your credit card/s!).

If you have a short term contract, stay away from long term investment contracts. Once you have decided that expat life is for you and that you are ready to plan for the future, you might want to establish the following: emergency cash buffer (3 - 6 months salary), retirement home, retirement income, personal and family protection (life insurance, health coverage) etc.

When selecting a financial planner, use either a reputable name or at least an institution regulated by the UAE Central Bank. If another authority is 'regulating' your advisor, you cannot expect the principal UAE authority to be of assistance to you, and your chances of recourse in the event of a problem may be severely hampered. For financial planners, try any of the major international companies or word of mouth.

Cost of Living

Drinks	
Beer (pint/bottle)	Dhs.25
Fresh fruit cocktail	Dhs.10
House wine (glass)	Dhs.20
House wine (bottle)	Dhs.90 - 120
Milk (1 litre)	Dhs.3
Water	
1.5 litres (supermarket)	Dhs.2
1.5 litres (hotel)	Dhs.10 - 18

Food	
Big Mac	Dhs.9
Bread (large)	Dhs.4 - 8
Cappuccino	Dhs.7 - 15
Chocolate bar	Dhs.1.50 - 2
Eggs (dozen)	Dhs.5
Falafel	Dhs.2
Fresh fruit	Dhs.1-19/kg.
Fresh meat	Dhs.6-40/kg.
Sugar	Dhs.3.5/kg.
Shawarma	Dhs.3
Tin of tuna	Dhs.3

Miscellaneous	
Cigarettes (per packet)	Dhs.6
Film	Dhs.20
Film processing (colour, 36 exposures)	Dhs.35 - 45
Hair cut (female)	Dhs.100+
Hair cut (male)	Dhs.40
Postcard	Dhs.2

Getting Around	
Abra Creek crossing	50 fils
Car rental (compact)	Dhs.90/day
Private Creek tour	Dhs.50
Taxi (airport to city)	Dhs.40 - 50
Taxi (airport to beach)	Dhs.70 - 80
Taxi (+ Dhs.1.25 every km)	Dhs.3 drop charge
City tour (half day)	Dhs.110
Bus from airport to downtown	Dhs.3
Desert safari (half day)	Dhs.270

Entrance Fees	
Beach club (may include lunch)	Dhs.60 - 200
Cinema	Dhs.25 - 30
Museum	Dhs.2 - 10
Nightclub	Dhs.50 - 100
Park	Dhs.3 - 5

Sports	
Fishing (two hours)	Dhs.100
Go Karting (15 mins)	Dhs.75
Golf (18 holes)	Dhs.80 - 375
Jet ski hire (30 mins)	Dhs.100
Parasailing (1 ride)	Dhs.200

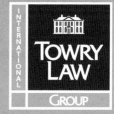

Taxation

The UAE levies no personal income taxes or withholding taxes of any sort. The only noticeable taxes you are obliged to pay as an expat are a 5% municipality tax on rental accommodation and a 30% tax on alcohol bought at liquor stores. In addition, there is a 10% municipality tax and a 15 - 16% service tax at hotel food and beverage outlets (these are no longer shown separately on customers' bills).

Business Groups & Contacts

For information on doing business or setting up a business in Dubai, refer to your local business group or the commercial attaché at your embassy/consulate. The contact numbers may be found in the table on [p.143] in the Business section of this book.

Also worth contacting are the Dubai Chamber of Commerce (228 0000 Map Ref 11-C2) and the Economic Department (222 9922 Map Ref 11-C1), both located along the Corniche in Deira.

For information and details, refer to the Dubai Commercial Directory, Hawk Business Pages and the *Zappy Explorer (Dubai)*. Also see Business Councils [p.144].

Legal Issues

Other Options → **Legal Consultants [p.146]**

The UAE is governed by sharia law – this is Islamic canonical law that is based on the traditions of Prophet Mohammed (PBUH) and the teachings of the Koran – and only a graduate of a sharia college can practice in court here. All court proceedings are conducted in Arabic, so you will find it important to hire legal representation that you trust.

For most people, any sort of brush with the 'wrong' side of the law can be a worrying experience, but in a foreign country and with an alien language, this can be particularly unnerving. If you are in serious difficulties, you should contact your embassy or consulate as soon as possible and follow their advice, plus find yourself a good lawyer.

Warning: Do not fall for any fantasies of opiate nights in the Middle East – such things are highly illegal here and often times, even your embassy cannot get you out of trouble with the local authorities.

For a list of legal consultants in Dubai, refer to [p.146].

Housing

Housing in Dubai

Since freehold property ownership for non Nationals was announced in the summer of 2002, Dubai seems to be taking over the world. There are literally plans to build a small rendition of the world (see [p.135] – The World) with appropriately shaped Jumeira coast islands for individual and residential complex sale. Developers such as Emaar, Nakheel and Damac, and real estate agents such as Better Homes are a good place to start your hunt for a good home. However, most developments offering land ownership won't be complete for several years. So for now, rental is still the main option.

New residents arriving in Dubai on a full expat package may have accommodation included in their employment contract. But don't be fooled by the charm of the expat lifestyle – life in Dubai is expensive and the need to exceed your pocket book is certainly an evil lure.

Search Tips

A Des. Res.?
Check proximity of potential homes to church bells, mosques, rubbish bins, schools, and the airport flight path.

New Buildings
Look out for buildings under construction - it's often a good way to find a place you like and be one of the first on the waiting list. The guys on site should be able to give you the name of the real estate agent or landlord.

Noise Control
In the less built up areas, beware that the area around your new home could be ripe for development - few people really appreciate a noisy building site just a few metres from their bedroom window! Construction work starts at about 06:00 and finishes by 21:00 or 22:00, with the odd 01:00 concrete pour, often seven days a week.

Real Estate Glossary

It is generally best to rent from a real estate agent, as they will handle all the paperwork for you. Single women occasionally have difficulty renting apartments and may need to put their employer's

name on the lease. Several good agents exist and all are helpful and interested in getting you settled in your new home (see [p.89]).

Housing Abbreviations	
BR	*Bedroom*
Ensuite	*Bedroom has private bathroom*
Fully fitted	*Includes appliances (oven,kitchen refrigerator, washing machine)*
L/D	*Living/dining room area*
W/robes	*Built in wardrobes (closets)*
Hall flat	*Apartment has an entrance hall (ie, entrance doesn't open directly onto living room)*
D/S	*Double storey villa*
S/S	*Single storey villa*
C.A/C	*Central air conditioning (usually included in the rent)*
W.A/C	*Window air conditioning (often indicates an older building)*
S/Q	*Servant quarters*
Ext S/Q	*Servant quarters located outside the villa*
Pvt garden	*Private garden*
Shared pool	*Pool is shared with other villas in compound*

Purchasing a Home

While in the past, only GCC Nationals could own residential property, options for expatriate land ownership are on the increase in Dubai. The option of property purchase is yet another method employed by the government to encourage foreign investment in the emirate. Currently, non GCC Nationals are permitted to own land only in certain developments. GCC Nationals, however, may purchase land and, often choose to build large, upscale villas.

For further information on property ownership, contact the developers from the list provided below. Being in its infancy, this area is likely to change radically. Log on to the Explorer Website *(www.Explorer-Publishing.com)* for more information and updates on Dubai.

Main Developers	
Al Nakheel Properties	800 5554
Damac Properties Co. LLC	399 9500
Emaar Properties	399 2299
Estithmaar Realty FZ - LLC	399 1114

Mortgages

Soon after the government announced the granting of freehold status of residential property to foreign nationals, mortgage plans were introduced for investors purchasing property. This is another first in the region and can be seen as an indication of Dubai's seriousness in encouraging foreign investment in real estate. The maximum mortgage granted is Dhs.5 million and financing companies offer up to 90% of the purchase price or valuation to UAE Nationals, and up to 80% to GCC and foreign nationals. Mortgages must be paid back in monthly instalments within a maximum of 25 years. The mortgage amount depends on the chosen mortgage plan and is limited to an amount no greater than 60 times the monthly household (both husband and wife's) income. For more information on mortgages, contact Amlak (800 4337).

Renting a Home

The majority of Dubai residents rent their home for the duration of their stay in Dubai. Rents over the past few years have consistently risen and, in general, are very high. However, it is expected that accommodation at the higher end of the market (over Dhs.65,000 for apartments and Dhs.100,000 for villas per annum) will drop eventually due to supply exceeding demand and freehold property ownership now being an option for all. Prices at the lower/middle end are expected to remain firm due to heavy demand. Rents are always quoted for the year, unless otherwise stated.

Rent Disputes

The Rent Committee of the Dubai Municipality (206 3833) assists both tenants and landlords in rent disputes. Amongst recent cases, the majority of disputes were raised by landlords rather than by tenants. To help improve the system, it's important that you use these services if trouble ever arises.

Government Apartments and Villas

The Dubai Government owns and manages more than 18,000 residential and commercial properties around Dubai with rents suitable for all levels of income. Because these properties tend to be very good value for money, many have long wait lists. To find out more or to put your name on a wait list, contact the Dubai Real Estate Department (398 6666) or log on to www.realestate-dubai.gov.ae.

Dubai Property Group

> ***Renter's Nightmare!***
>
> *The majority of leases in Dubai are fixed for one year and unless you find a really nice landlord who offers you an opt out clause, you are locked in till the end of the year. Penalty? You might not get your deposit back and you certainly won't get the remainder of your rent back!*
>
> *Be careful when you sign your lease as you will have to pay your entire year's rent in one to three cheques, so make sure the apartment or villa you've just found is really the one you'd like to make your home for the next year!*

In 2002, a group of professional real estate companies banded together to work towards ensuring proper conduct in real estate dealings in Dubai. Examining current real estate industry practices, they make proposals for change that will benefit all concerned. Their goal is to try to make a difference for the residents of Dubai, working closely with the Rent Committee and the Government of Dubai (through the Dubai Development Board).

Website: www.dubaipropertygroup.com

The Lease

To take out a lease personally, you need to be a resident. The real estate agent will need a copy of your passport and visa, a no objection letter (NOC) from your company, a copy of your salary certificate and an initial signed rent cheque (plus up to three post dated cheques covering the remaining period of the lease). Unlike elsewhere in the world, rent cheques have to be paid to the landlord up front and not on a monthly basis. This can cause problems as many new residents do not have the cash available to pay this sort of lump sum in advance. Needless to say, banks are quick to offer loans! To rent through your company, you require a copy of the company trade licence, a passport copy of whoever is signing the rent cheque and, of course, the rent cheque/s.

Main Accommodation Options

Apartment/Villa Sharing

For those on a budget, the solution may be to share an apartment or a villa with colleagues or friends. Check the notice boards in supermarkets such as Choithrams, Park 'n Shop or Spinneys, or even sports clubs, for people advertising shared accommodation. The Spinneys Website (www.Spinneys.com) posts details of places to live and people to live with. The classified section of local newspapers also advertises accommodation.

Standard Apartment

There are generally two types of apartments available for rent – those with central air conditioning (A/C) and those with the noisier window A/Cs where the unit is in the apartment wall. Some even have central heating. Central A/C accommodation is always more expensive, although in some buildings, the charge for A/C is absorbed into the rent. Top of the range, central A/C apartments often come semi-furnished (with a cooker, fridge and washing machine), boast 24 hour security, satellite TV, covered parking, gym, pool etc. Normally, the more facilities that come with the apartment, the more expensive the rent.

Villa

The same procedure for leasing apartments applies to leasing villas. Value for money villas are very hard to find and, where you used to be able to find older, cheaper villas in some parts of Jumeira, many are being demolished for redevelopment. As with apartments, villas differ greatly in quality and facilities, such as pool, security, compound etc.

Hotel Apartment

An alternative option is to rent a hotel apartment – ideal if you require temporary, furnished accommodation, although they are expensive. Most hotel apartments are in Bur Dubai near the BurJuman shopping mall. Apartments can be rented on a daily/weekly/monthly or yearly basis. They come fully furnished (from sofas to knives and forks) and serviced (maid service) with satellite TV, and are often complemented by

Villas

sports facilities (pool and gym etc). Water and electricity are also included in the rent. If you can, call around first for rates, as they have high and low seasons based on the heat and the tourism in Dubai.

Residential Areas

Other options → **Exploring [p.156]**

As in all cities, there are obvious areas of desirable residence. The more upmarket areas for villas are Jumeira and Umm Suqeim, with cheaper options in Satwa, Al Garhoud, Mirdif and Rashidiya. The most popular area for apartments tends to be Bur Dubai behind the BurJuman shopping mall, and along Sheikh Zayed Road, which is lined with modern glass skyscrapers. Cheaper options are in Deira, the old Pakistani Consulate area, Satwa and Karama. However, the odd top of the range building can be found in these cheaper areas and likewise, the odd bargain can still be found in the more upmarket areas of Jumeira or Umm Suqeim. There's a good mix of nationalities in most places.

A cheaper option is to live in The Gardens near Jebel Ali, or in the nearby emirates of Sharjah or Ajman. Here, prices for apartments are generally lower by at least Dhs.10 - 20,000 per year, and villas are cheaper still. However, while there are great savings to be made by living in either of these emirates, beware the Sharjah-Dubai highway – renowned for mammoth delays around rush hour. Also beware the Sharjah Decency Law. If your work or social life is based in Dubai, you could find that living outside the city and facing daily delays may not be worth the savings.

A glance through the property pages in the newspapers will give you an idea of what is available where and for how much. You can also check online in the classifieds of Gulf News and Khaleej Times. Check out the following areas and refer to the maps at the end of the book to get a feel for the layout of Dubai. Also, have a look at the Exploring section [p.156] for further helpful descriptions of the various areas within Dubai.

Al Barsha — Map Ref → 3-D3

- Hot tip... rumoured to be the new Jumeira
- Apartments and villas are fast appearing. Prices at one time were extremely affordable for Dubai standards, but are now on the up. The development of The Mall of Emirates will increase the pace (and noise levels) of this presently tranquil district
- Tailing on the outskirts of downtown Dubai, a quieter area but barren in appearance. Watch out for constant road works and other frustrating construction related problems
- A great place in the future, if you can put up with the surrounding distractions for some time.

Al Garhoud — Map Ref → 14-D4

- Centrally located
- A fairly quiet, residential part of town. Close to the airport, however, so depending on the direction of the wind, aircraft noise can be heard
- Villas with less expensive rents than other central areas; very few apartments
- Mix of nationalities - mainly Nationals, Arab and Western expats.

Garhoud Apartments

Al Qusais — Map Ref → 15-D2

- Characterless area located on the border of Dubai and Sharjah
- Some of the lowest rents in town, but noise can be overwhelming and the commute into Dubai similar to that from Sharjah
- Mainly Asian residents in four storey blocks.

Bur Dubai (two main residential areas)

1. Creek — Map Ref → 8-A2

- Lots of hustle and bustle
- Area has character but limited parking
- Apartments with low rents; low income district

Annual Rent

	Apartments	Apartments	Apartments	Villas
B/R	Bur Dubai	Deira & Satwa	Sheikh Zayed Rd	-
1	33,000 - 45,000	28,000 - 40,000	40,000 - 46,000	-
2	46,000 - 55,000	36,000 - 60,000	52,000 - 60,000	40,000 - 65,000
3	55,000 - 80,000	44,000 - 80,000	65,000 - 80,000	55,000 - 135,000
4	70,000 - 110,000	60,000 - 100,000	75,000 - 120,000	70,000 - 150,000
5	-	-	-	100,000 - 200,000

- Mainly Asian residents; 95% of people on the streets are male.

2. Golden Sands (Mankhoul) Map Ref → 7-E4

- Great name, but really just a concrete jungle with no green spaces, apartment buildings up to eight storeys high and plots of sand in between
- Apartments with high rents, yet it's still a popular area
- Limited access to the area results in traffic congestion at certain times of day
- Good mix of nationalities; great if you're female (any age) and like being chatted up on the street by guys in cars.

Deira Map Ref → 8-E2

- One of Dubai's older districts, now mostly a concrete jungle with little neighbourhood feel
- Terrible traffic problems all day
- Lower rent apartment blocks. However, alongside the Creek some upmarket apartment buildings cater to higher income expats (Twin Towers, etc)
- Mostly Arab expats and Asian residents.

Emirates Hills Map Ref → 2-E4

- Part of the new 'downtown' of Dubai
- The hippest place to be (once it's built!) with The Lakes, The Meadows, The Greens and The Springs offering villas, apartments and townhouses to rent or buy
- Prices incline more to the upper middle class and up to the playboy status. Natural and peaceful surroundings with parks, water features and tree lined streets
- A golf fanatic's dream with a residential golf course and 621 villas complete with a clubhouse, spa and golf pro shop, and yes... the freehold prices are a tad high
- Beautiful beaches and five star hotels in walking distance. Internet & Media Cities only minutes away.

Jebel Ali Village/The Gardens Map Ref → 2-A3

- Pleasant atmosphere amongst the older villas as there are trees; however, new villas are concrete and brick compounds with virtually no green spaces
- Bit of a commute unless you work in Jebel Ali or Dubai Media or Internet Cities
- Mix of bungalows and villas; rents are reasonable to expensive for new villas, and very reasonable for older villas
- Popular with oil company expats, many Westerners
- 'The Gardens' is a new community of 3,800 apartments plus villas with the main attraction being the low rents. We're hoping this will spark a much needed rent reduction all-around in Dubai!

Jumeira Map Ref → 5-D2

- Wide, quiet and leafy streets; close to the beach
- Mainly large, walled villas with established gardens
- A suburban feel; many Nationals, Arab and Western expats
- High rents.

The Gardens

Karama Map Ref → 10-D2

- Convenient central location but little green space; another concrete jungle
- 'Calvin Karama' - the nearby souk sells just about everything
- Mostly four storey apartments with inexpensive rents
- Predominantly Asian community feel.

Marsa Dubai Map Ref → 2-D2

- Mainly upmarket villas; very high rents, but your neighbours are five star hotels and royalty
- The beach, Emirates Hills and Internet & Media Cities are all in the vicinity
- Emirates Golf Club and The Montgomerie golf club are minutes away
- Dubai Marina – a freehold property consisting of high rise towers and villas overlooking the marina. The apartments are penthouse posh and for catering to those who have the financial opportunity to splurge on real luxury
- Jumeirah Beach Residence – a multitude of residential towers currently under construction.

Mirdif Map Ref → 16-B4

- Up and coming area of Dubai, but no local supermarkets or shops, and located a ways out of town
- Under the airport flight path – beware!
- Costa del Sol feel with single villas and villa compounds
- Much cheaper rents than other areas
- Residents are mainly Nationals, Arab and Western expats; lots of families, many with children.

Renting the Smart Way

Like anywhere else in the world, Dubai too, has its fair share of cons. To avoid falling into a landlord trap, the Rent Tribunal advises that both parties produce a written agreement. This contract reduces the risk of either party falling out on the rental terms discussed.

Do remember to ask for a copy of the estate agent's identification card and make sure you save copies of all receipts, contracts and other documents.

Oud Metha Map Ref → 13-E1

- Another up and coming, centrally located area
- A fair amount of construction ongoing, but rents are better value for money than other areas
- Convenient access, with one of Dubai's largest malls and lots of restaurants nearby
- Four storey apartment buildings with mostly Arab and Western expats.

Satwa Map Ref → 6-D3

- Older, established and atmospheric part of town; located between trendy Sheikh Zayed Road and prestigious Jumeira
- Mix of housing and rents, plus some decent, but older, inexpensive villas
- Mix of nationalities; possibly not the best place for a single female to live.

Sheikh Zayed Road Map Ref → 9-C2

- No community feel – mostly office workers in the vicinity

Villas Under Construction in Umm Suqeim

- Extremely noisy, although apartments facing away from the road are slightly quieter
- Residential apartments in skyscrapers; very high rents
- Trendy location with a good mix of nationalities and sexes.

Umm Suqeim — Map Ref → 4-C2

- Quiet suburban feel
- Great established compounds; mix of old and new with lots of individual villas. Lower rents than Jumeira, but higher than Mirdif
- Mix of nationalities, but mostly Nationals and Western expats.

Other Rental Costs

Extra costs to be considered are:

- Water and electricity deposit (Dhs.2,000 for villas, Dhs.1,000 for apartments) paid directly to Dubai Electricity & Water Authority (DEWA) and fully refundable on cancellation of lease
- Real estate commission – 5% of annual rent (one off payment)
- Maintenance charge – 5% of annual rent
- Municipality tax – 5% of annual rent
- Fully refundable security deposit – Dhs.2,000 - 5,000)
- Some landlords also require a deposit against damage (usually a fully refundable, one off payment).

If you are renting a villa, don't forget that you may have to maintain a garden and pay for extra water etc. To avoid massive water bills at the end of every month, many people prefer to have a well dug in their backyard for all that necessary plant and grass watering. Expect to pay around Dhs.1,500 - 3,000 to have a well dug and a pump installed.

Apartment Towers on Sheikh Zayed Road

Some of the older villas may also need additional maintenance, which the landlord may not cover. Often, the more popular accommodation has waiting lists that are years long. To secure an immediate tenancy many people offer the landlord 'key money', a down payment of several thousand dirhams to secure the accommodation.

Real Estate Agents

Al Futtaim Real Estate	211 9111	realestate@alfuttaim.ae	www.al-futtaim.com
Alpha Properties	228 8588	lucy@alphaproperties.com	www.alphaproperties.com
Arenco Group	337 0550	narinder@arencore.ae	www.arencore.com
Asteco Property Management	269 3155	asteco@astecoproperty.com	www.astecoproperty.com
Better Homes	344 7714	bhomes@emirates.net.ae	www.bhomes.com
Cluttons	334 8585	simon@cluttons-uae.com	www.cluttons-ikaar.com
Dubai Government Real Estate	398 6666	n/a	www.realestate-dubai.gov.ae
Dubai Property Group	262 9888	dubaipg@hotmail.com	www.dubaipropertygroup.com
Landmark Properties	331 6161	info@landmark-dubai.com	www.landmark-dubai.com
Property Shop, The	345 5711	info@propertyshopdubai.com	www.propertyshopdubai.com
Real Estate Specialists, The	331 2662	Restate@emirates.net.ae	www.dubaiuae.com
Rocky Real Estate	353 2000	info@rocki.com	www.rocki.com
Sherwoods	343 8002	shwoods@emirates.net.ae	www.sherwoodsproperty.com
Union Properties	294 9490	up@unionproperties.com	www.unionproperties.com

Moving Services

Two main options exist when moving your furniture and personal effects either to or from Dubai: air freight and sea freight. Air freight is a better option when moving smaller amounts, but if you have a larger consignment, sea freight is the way to go. Either way, ensure your goods are packed by professionals.

Unless you send your personal belongings with the airline you are flying with, you will need to use the services of a removal company. A company with a wide international network is usually the best and safest option, but more importantly, you must trust the people you are dealing with. Ensure they are competent in the country of origin and have reliable agents in the country to which you are shipping your personal belongings. Most removal companies offer free consultations, plus advice and samples of packing materials – call around.

Moving Tips

- *Book moving dates well in advance*
- *Don't forget insurance and purchase additional insurance for irreplaceable items*
- *Make an inventory of the items you want moved (keep your own copy!)*
- *Ensure everything is packed extremely well and in a way that can be checked by customs and repacked with the least possible damage; check and sign the packing list*
- *Keep a camera and film handy to take pictures at each stage of the move (valuable in case of a dispute)*
- *Do not pack restricted goods of any kind*
- *If moving to Dubai, ensure videos, DVD's and books are not offensive to Muslim sensibilities*

When your belongings arrive in Dubai, you will be called to Customs to be present while the authorities open your boxes to ensure nothing illegal or inappropriate is brought into the country. Assisting in this process can be exhausting; the search may take place outdoors over a few hours, with your belongings thrown on the ground. After this, depending on the agreement you have with the removal company, either their representative in Dubai will help you transport the boxes to your new home, or you can make the arrangements locally.

Relocation Companies	
Global Relocations	352 3300
In Touch Relocations	332 8807
Interem (Freight Systems Co. Ltd)	314 1201
Mover's Packaging	267 0699
Orientation, The	332 4111

Removal Companies	
ADSA International Movers	282 6999
Allied Pickfords	338 3600
Blue Line	06 562 5111
Crown Worldwide Movers	289 5152
Gulf Agency Company (GAC)	345 7555
Interem (Freight Systems Co. Ltd)	314 1201
Mover's Packaging	267 0699

Relocation Experts

Relocation experts offer a range of services to help you settle into your new life in Dubai as quickly as possible. Practical help ranges from finding accommodation or schools for your children to connecting a telephone or information on medical care. In addition, they will often offer advice on the way of life in the city, putting people in touch with the social networks to help them establish a new life.

Furnishing Accommodation

Other options → **Furniture & Household Items [p.228]**
Second-hand Items [p.236]

One of Dubai's best points is that anything can be made for you, be it tailoring or furniture making. You can easily pick out the latest Italian furniture from photos, and after a few hours of research and bargaining along Naif road, that burgundy sofa or leopard spotted chair will be made just for you!

Ready made, good quality furniture and household items can be found at reasonable prices. The most popular furniture outlets in Dubai are IKEA, ID Design, Marina, Feshwari, THE One, Home Centre and Pan Emirates Furniture (both located in Dubai and Sharjah). Other favourites for Indian teak and wrought iron are Khans (06 562 1621), Pinkies and Luckys (06 534 1937) in Sharjah, and Indian Village in Dubai.

You can often buy furniture from the previous tenant through 'garage' sales or from supermarket noticeboards. Many people sell their furniture when they leave Dubai, often leaving behind nice items bought from reputable shops for much cheaper prices. Check the classifieds sections of newspapers. Second hand furniture is widely available in Karama as well, with plenty of shops selling inexpensive, basic furniture, pots, pans and almost every household item.

Garage Sales

One man's trash is another man's treasure. With so many people moving in and out of Dubai, you can find

almost anything at garage sales. Check out the noticeboards at Spinney's, Park'nShop or Safestway for the latest happenings in garage sales. Also read the classifieds section of newspapers for advertised garage sales.

If you're leaving the Emirates and have some items that you don't want to ship back home, hold your own garage sale. It's a great way to earn some cash while getting rid of all the junk that you couldn't fob off on friends! Ask your neighbours if they have some unwanted treasures to dispose of, and then advertise the sale on local supermarket noticeboards and place ads in the classifieds of daily newspapers. If permitted, post some easy to follow direction signs with arrows in prominent locations. Clearly mark the goods with prices. On the day, have plenty of plastic bags, old newspapers for wrapping glass items and loads of change... then be prepared to haggle hard!

Moving within Dubai

When moving from once place to another in Dubai, you can opt for a moving company or rent a truck and do it yourself. If you like taking the lead, the latter is a cheaper option. Just choose a vehicle from the many standing at 'truck roundabout' (near the furniture section of Naif road or on the corner of Mankhool and Kuwait Roads in Bur Dubai) and request the driver's help in moving your stuff. These men are also very helpful when you need to have furniture you bought delivered to your flat at bargain rates. They're a very handy bunch!

Household Appliances

Carrefour, Jashanmal, Jumbo Electronics and Plug Ins have a decent selection of heavy household appliances. Make sure that your purchases come with a warranty! All the main brands are found in the UAE, but the fittings are made for the European market and thus, North American makes can be harder to find.

Household Items

Prices are quite reasonable for new appliances, but if you would prefer to buy second hand, have a look at the noticeboards at the various supermarkets around town. Of course, there is no guarantee with second hand goods, so beware of the souped up junk sellers in this market!

Household Insurance

No matter where you live in the world and how 'safe' a place appears to be, it's always wise to insure the contents of your home. There are many internationally recognised insurance companies operating in Dubai – check the Yellow Pages, or Hawk Business Pages for details.

When forming your policy, the general information insurance companies need is your home address in Dubai, a household contents list and valuation, and invoices for items over Dhs.2,500. Cover usually extends to theft, storm damage, fire etc. For an additional fee, you can insure personal items outside the home, such as jewellery, cameras etc.

Most companies allow you to pick and choose the home owner's or renter's insurance best suited to you. A good coverage gives you flexibility, so you can rest easy when you go on that long vacation or business trip. Coverage generally includes buildings, home contents, decorations, personal belongings and more, for you and family members residing with you. Call around for the best rates and options.

Household Insurance	
BUPA International	324 3514
Millennium Insurance	335 6552
National General Insurance	222 2772
Norwich Union Insurance	324 3434

Laundry Services

Whilst there are no self service launderettes in Dubai, there are hundreds of small outlets plus larger supermarkets and some hotels, offering laundry and dry cleaning services at reasonable rates and next day delivery. You can also take clothes for ironing only, at approximately Dhs.1 per item. It's always a good idea to speak to the laundry man himself, if you have a preference on how you want an item ironed (or if you would like to avoid the 'shiny' look!).

Domestic Help

Other options → **Entry Visa [p.60]**

If you are tired, lazy or just want someone to help out with the kids and the cats, consider hiring a maid or a domestic helper. Maybe you never considered it before, but people in Dubai eventually see the light, as it's comparatively cheap and very easy to arrange for. If you do decide to go for a maid, take your time and make your decision wisely as the government is trying to reduce the amount of 'maid hopping'. No objection certificates will no longer be accepted by the Ministry of Interior for housemaids transferring sponsorship, and there will be an automatic six month ban. The worker will then have to re-enter the country on a new visa. Those who change housemaids frequently or have complaints filed against them for mistreatment will be unable to sponsor housemaids in the future.

Domestic Help Agencies	
Helpers	395 6166
Home Help	355 5100
Maids To Order	336 2555
Molly Maid	398 8877
Ready Maids	339 5722

To employ the services of a full time live in domestic helper, you must have a minimum monthly salary of Dhs.6,000. The helper cannot be related to you or be of the same nationality as you. As the employer, you must sponsor the person and deal with all residency papers, including the medical test etc. Singles and families in which the wife isn't working may face difficulties sponsoring a helper. It's normally best to find someone through an agency dedicated to hiring domestic helpers. You will be asked to sign a contract stating that you will pay your employee a minimum salary of about Dhs.750 each month with an airfare home once a year.

The residence visa for a maid will cost around Dhs.5,000 (Dhs.4,800 for the government fee, Dhs.100 for the residence visa and Dhs.100 for the labour card). Nationals will also soon be charged approximately Dhs.1,500 for sponsoring a housemaid. Residency is only valid for one year. It is illegal to share a maid with another household. You can obtain a residence visa card through the normal channels, after which some embassies (eg, the Philippines) require to see the labour contract of your newly appointed maid. This is to ensure that all paperwork is in order and that the maid is receiving fair treatment. If, for any reason, the domestic worker leaves their employer before their contractual agreement ends, they are banned from working in the UAE for six months and they will have to re-enter the country with a new visa. This applies even if they receive a no objection letter from their employer. Nationals and expatriates caught borrowing or lending a housemaid will be fined Dhs.50,000 and will not be permitted to sponsor a housemaid again. The housemaid will also be deported and banned from entering the UAE for a period of one year.

An alternative and cheaper option is to have part time home help and there is a number of agencies that offer domestic help on an hourly basis. The standard rate is about Dhs.20 - 25 per hour, with a minimum of two hours per visit. It's not a bad idea to ask around; you can also get recommendations from friends who employ maids on a part time basis. The service includes general cleaning, washing, ironing and sometimes babysitting, but your mess level will determine the hours they spend cleaning.

Domestic Services

Need a plumber? Or would you rather continue pretending you can fix that leak on your own? If you've done your best but the overflowing sink still threatens to flood the entire apartment, call a professional. The following are some of the companies that offer handy help (plumbers, electricians, carpenters and more).

Domestic Services	
Al Salam Sanitary & Electrical	261 5977
Al Wahda Carpentry	533 4418
Belhasa	285 1857
Brightest Trading	331 0822
Hassan Foulad Plumbing Works	285 9187

Pets

Bringing Your Pet to Dubai

While many people have brought their pets to Dubai, it does involve paperwork and time. But it is worth the effort if your good times are even better with your furry friend by your side. The following steps need to be taken to import pets into Dubai:

Stop! Take time to enjoy the Finer Details...

- Have the pet vaccinated and its booklet updated (in English) by the veterinarian in your country of origin
- Get an export certificate from the Ministry of agriculture and fisheries of the country from where the animal is being exported, certified by the vet there
- Book a space for your pet with your airline and beware, not all airlines allow them!

Dubai Kennels & Cattery (285 1646), The Doghouse (347 1807) or the Ajman Pet Resort (06 743 1629) can help you obtain an import permit, customs clearance and collection from the airport, delivery and/or boarding of your pet, if required. If you choose not to use their services, either your local vet or the originating country's local embassy will be able to advise you of the necessary requirements. There is no quarantine for pets brought into the UAE.

Taking Your Pet Home

You should also take your pets with you, should you relocate. You will be able to get an import permit from the Ministry of Agriculture and Fisheries (295 8161). The process may take a few weeks. Remember to check with your airline to see if you can take your pet as cargo or carry on, which is generally preferred for small pet owners. The regulations for 'exporting' your pet depend on the laws of the country to which you are moving.

Basic requirements are:

- A valid vaccination card not older than one year but not less than 30 days

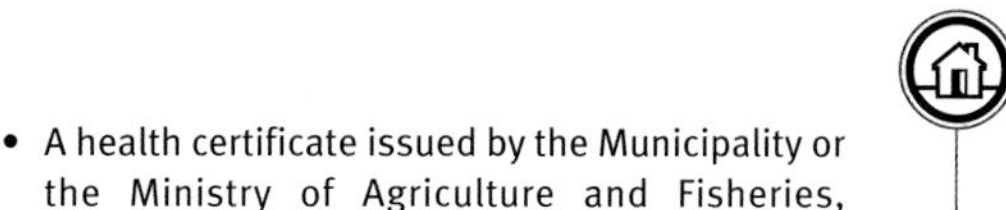

- A health certificate issued by the Municipality or the Ministry of Agriculture and Fisheries, normally issued one week before departure

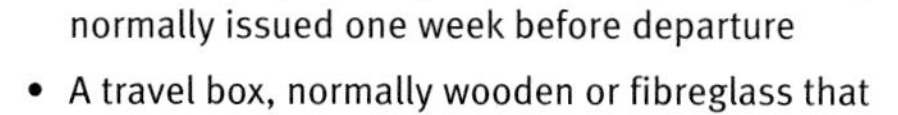

- A travel box, normally wooden or fibreglass that meets airline regulations.

Your local vet, kennels or the airline that you are using can inform you of the specific regulations pertaining to your destination, such as the country's quarantine rules etc.

Getting a UAE Pet Health Certificate

To obtain a UAE pet health certificate, you need to go to the Ministry of Agriculture and Fisheries (Clocktower R/A - look out for building which has the 'Omega' sign on the roof) and do the following:

1. Get an import application form from the Ministry of agriculture
2. Submit a copy of the pet owner's passport, including the residence visa page
3. Submit a copy of the pet's vaccination booklet, along with Dhs.200 (processing fee).

Pet Services	
Ajman Pet Resort	06 743 1629
Doghouse	347 1807
Dogsbody	349 9879
Dubai Kennels & Cattery	285 1646
Pets At Home	331 2186

Cats & Dogs

In the Middle East, animals are generally treated with a lot less sympathy than you may be used to. It is best to keep your animals indoors, as the heat, traffic and attitude of the people here towards animals may be what you would consider cruel. You are also prohibited from taking your dog running with you along the beach or at public parks. Although many people do it, they can be fined. The government is devising an alternative – a 'dog park' – but for now, just be careful when you take Fifi for that morning Jumeira stroll. As usual, your pet must be vaccinated regularly and wear the Municipality ID disc (supplied on vaccination) on its collar at all times. The Municipality controls Dubai's huge stray population by trapping and practicing euthanasia. If your pet is trapped without an ID disc, it will be treated as a stray.

All pets should also be sterilised and kept safely on your premises. Once sterilised, they will wander less and will therefore be less exposed to the dangers of traffic and disease. If you feed the stray population around your home, you will simply

create a problem for yourselves and your neighbours with a burgeoning stray population. To do something proactive to help, or if you see an injured cat and need assistance, contact Feline Friends (050 451 0058). For help with stray or injured dogs, call K9 Friends (347 4611).

Veterinary Clinics

Dr Matt's Veterinary Clinic	349 9549
European Veterinary Clinic	343 2764
Jumeirah Veterinary Clinic	394 2276
Modern Veterinary Clinic	395 3131
Veterinary Hospital	344 2498

Pet Shops

Though regulations governing the sale of animals in pet shops exist, they are rarely actively enforced. Animals are often underage (although their papers state differently), sometimes sick or even pregnant, and the conditions in which they are kept leave a lot to be desired. Rather than encouraging this trade, you would do better to give a home to one of the many stray animals in Dubai. Contact Feline Friends or K9 Friends to see who needs a home. Also check in the classifieds section of the newspapers for lost and found animals and animals that need homes.

Animal Souks

Do not be tempted by visions of becoming the next Seigfreid and Roy, and get a wild animal as a pet. This is highly illegal under international law (and we all know that the tigers finally got their revenge on Roy). Animal souks are a negative mark on Dubai, a city that sells itself as a clean, safe and regulated tourist destination, and much more needs to be done to eradicate this sick trade. The CITES protected list is disregarded in these souks and wild animals are still captured and sold here. Most of the animals are smuggled into the country from Asia and other places, and the conditions in which they are housed are not to be witnessed by the faint of heart. The animals are kept in cramped, overcrowded cages, are often diseased and most definitely disturbed. The sellers may promise 'if you want it, we'll get it for you,' but don't be fooled by the thought of a nearly extinct cat or monkey sitting in a cage in your kitchen, even if they do supply – the misery of an animal in captivity is hardly worth that moment of novelty.

Help!

If you see a cat or dog which is stray, injured or in distress, then please try to get it to the nearest vet (see table above). Most have 24 hour mobiles or pagers. If you need further assistance, call either Feline or K9 Friends, but remember that they are both run by volunteers and would very much appreciate if others would also be 'animal responsible' and help out. Call Feline (050 451 0058) or K9 (347 4611) if you'd like to offer time, assistance or support.

Also beware the diseases and disorders that often arise from these animals. It is very expensive and troublesome, if not impossible, to get the necessary vaccinations, or have enough space that a wild animal needs to be healthy and normal. You will also find it tough to cope with the hormonal changes that inevitably result from their being restricted into captivity. No vet will be able to give proper care to the animal and many of these sad creatures are destined for death. If you love animals, donate to WWF and just opt for a dog from K9 Friends.

Utilities & Services

Electricity & Water

These utilities, along with sewerage, are provided by Dubai Electricity & Water Authority (commonly known as DEWA). The authority provides an excellent service with extremely rare electricity or water shortages/stoppages.

When you sign up, you will have to pay a water and electricity deposit (Dhs.2,000 for villas; Dhs.1,000 for apartments) directly to DEWA. This is fully refundable on cancellation of your lease.

Monthly bills can be paid at any DEWA office through various banks or even on the Internet. Those offering this service are listed on the reverse of the bill. Bills are assessed one month and the meter read the next month.

Main office: next to Wafi Shopping Mall, Bur Dubai (324 4444, Map Ref 13-D2)

Opening hours: Saturday – Wednesday 07:30 - 21:00 bill payments and 07:30 - 14:30 enquiries. Thursday 07:30 - 21:00 bill payments only, and telephone enquiries 08:30 - 14:00

Electricity

There's plenty of it! The electricity supply in Dubai is 220/240 volts and 50 cycles. Socket type is identical to the three point British system. Adaptors can be purchased at any grocery or hardware store.

Jumeira Beach Road at Night

Water

More expensive than oil! Tap water is safe to drink but not always pleasant, and visitors generally prefer the locally bottled mineral water, which is widely available. Bottled water is usually served in hotels and restaurants.

Buying 20 litre water bottles rather than small 1 1/2 litre bottles is more environmentally friendly and can make a considerable cost saving for drinking water. The bottle deposit is usually Dhs.25 - 35 and refills Dhs.5 - 7. These large bottles can be used with a variety of methods for decanting the water. Choices include a hand pump available from supermarkets and costing about Dhs.3, a fixed pump costing about Dhs.60, or a variety of refrigeration units are also available. Prices for these vary, depending on the model, but on average are about Dhs.400. Water suppliers will deliver to your door, saving you some backache.

One of the slightly crazy aspects of life in the Emirates is that during the summer months, if your water tank is on the roof, you won't need to heat water – it's already hot when it comes out of the cold tap! Indeed the only way to have a cold(ish) shower is to keep the immersion heater off and to use the hot tap for cold water.

Water Suppliers	
Culligan	800 4945
Desert Springs	800 6650
Oasis Drinking Water	884 5656

Gas

Gas mains don't exist in Dubai, but there is the option of buying individual gas canisters for cooking if required. These can be connected to a gas oven and generally cost about Dhs.230 per new canister and Dhs.28 - 50 for a refill. There are numerous companies around town supplying gas canisters.

Gas Suppliers	
New City Gas Distributors	351 8282
Oasis Gas Suppliers	396 1812
Salam Gas	344 8823
Union Gas Company	266 1479

Telephone

Emirates Telecommunications Corporation (known as Etisalat, meaning communications) is the sole telecommunications provider in the Emirates – the Dubai headquarters are in the groovy glass building near the Creek with a large ball on the top. They are responsible for telephones, both landlines and mobiles, and the Internet (through its sister company, Emirates Internet & Multimedia).

Etisalat is generally an efficient and innovative company, continuously introducing new services and even cutting bills from time to time. You should have few problems in processing paperwork, receiving services or rectifying problems. You need a residence visa to get a landline, but you can get a SIM card for a mobile phone and corresponding telephone number without residency.

Opening hours: Saturday – Wednesday 07:00 - 13:00, and 15:00 - 17:00 (bill payments only); Thursday 08:00 - 13:00 (bill payments only). The main office in Deira, opposite the Sheraton Hotel & Towers, is open 24 hours for bill payments and pre-paid SIM cards. Jebel Ali Free Zone office: Saturday - Thursday 09:00 - 17:00

Landline Phones

To install a regular landline phone connection in your home, you need to apply directly to Etisalat with the following: Etisalat application form in English (handwritten is acceptable), copy of passport and residence visa, Dhs.250 and a copy of your tenancy agreement.

Once you have submitted the application, it takes between 2 - 3 days until a phone connection is

installed. Even if you have your own phone handset, Etisalat will provide one. If you require additional phone sockets, order them at the same time and pay a further Dhs.50 for the first socket and then Dhs.15 per socket thereafter. The procedure is usually extremely efficient and streamlined.

The Etisalat Building

What's nice about having a landline is you can get a free calling card that enables you to call your home number, and charge the call to your home number – very useful if you are travelling and want to stay in touch. Etisalat offers many additional services, such as call waiting, call forwarding, a 'follow me' service – for more information contact you nearest Etisalat branch, check the Etisalat home page (www.etisalat.co.ae) or have a look at the *Zappy Explorer (Dubai)*.

Quarterly rental: standard landline (for all sockets) - Dhs.45. All calls made locally within Dubai on and to a landline are free. For international and mobile rates, check the phone book. Discount long distance rates are all day Friday and government declared national public holidays. Weekdays (outside GCC): 21:00 - 07:00; weekdays (GCC only): 19:00 - 07:00

Mobile Phones

It's really easy to have a GSM connection in Dubai. You can even register for your new number online and get it delivered straight to your door the same day! Check out the Etisalat 4 Me service at www.e4me.co.ae or call 800 888 3463. Mobiles can be purchased from Etisalat, telecommunications shops, most electronics shops and large supermarkets, such as Carrefour. To get a telephone number, you need to go to Etisalat with your passport in hand and Dhs.100. Remember to renew this with Etisalat annually or your number and service will be cut off!

Etisalat GSM assistance telephone service: dial 101 for enquiries.

Non Resident

If your visa is not fully processed, or if you're visiting the country and want to use your mobile, your only option currently, is Wasel GSM service. This is a popular variation of the GSM service here, available to both non residents and residents, allowing you to decide on the amount of outgoing calls that can be made on your phone, but allowing unlimited incoming calls. For residents, this includes while you are abroad (you will be charged the international roaming rate). However, Wasel subscribers can take advantage of Etisalat's free of charge roaming facility. Log on to www.etisalat.ae to view a list of the 110 countries offering roaming. Outgoing calls can also be made by dialling 111 and then the number (with the country code).

The subscription is for one year and payment for outgoing calls needs to be made in advance. One year's subscription is Dhs.185 and you can apply at any branch office. The annual renewal charge is Dhs.100 and they will SMS you with a reminder. To apply, fill out the application form and submit it along with your essential documents. The service includes connection, one year's rental, SIM card charges and Dhs.10 free credit. You may 'recharge' your card for outgoing calls in Dhs.30 units, and cards can be purchased at any gas station or grocery store.

Resident

If you are a resident applying for a mobile phone connection, pick up an application form from any Etisalat office. Submit the application to any Etisalat branch office, along with your passport and residence visa copy and Dhs.215 (this amount includes rental for the first quarter). You should receive your SIM card there and then, and once you have it installed, you're ready to dial. An alternative to the standard mobile phone agreement is to apply for the Wasel GSM service (see above).

Rental charges: Quarterly rental charge for the standard mobile phone service – Dhs.90.

Local rates: Peak rate - 30 fils per minute (06:00 - 14:00 & 16:00 - 24:00); off-peak rate – 21 fils per minute.

International discount rates: All day Friday and government declared national public holidays. Weekdays (outside GCC): 21:00 - 07:00; weekdays (GCC only): 19:00 - 07:00.

Missing Mobile

Lost your mobile? Call 101 to temporarily disconnect your number (you will need to know your passport number for security). Your SIM card can be replaced, but sadly, all the numbers you had saved in your phone's memory will be gone. To replace the SIM, you will need to go to a branch of Etisalat with your essential documents in hand and Dhs.50. If you need to cancel your mobile number permanently, go to Etisalat and fill in the cancellation forms.

Missing Mobile

If you lose your mobile or have it stolen, call 101 to disconnect your number temporarily. You might need to know your passport number for security.

Internet

Other options → **Internet Cafes**
Websites [p.50]

For connection to cyberspace, Etisalat's sister company, Emirates Internet & Multimedia (EIM) is the sole provider of Internet services through its UAE proxy server. With the proxy server in place, some sites are restricted (if you find a blocked site that you believe is perfectly reasonable, you can report it to Etisalat on help@emirates.net.ae). You can access Emirates Internet from any standard telephone line using an appropriate modem at speeds in excess of 56 Kbps. If you require higher speed access, you can apply for an ISDN line (64 Kbps) or an ADSL line (128 Kbps); for more information, contact Etisalat (800 6100). Check out the Website listing on [p.50] for sites on the UAE.

The Ubiquitous Mobile

To get yourself connected, you will require a landline in your name or your company's name, a copy of your passport and residence visa, and the Internet application form from Etisalat.

Registration charge: Dhs.100 for dialup or ISDN; Dhs.200 for ADSL (plus Dhs.100 for optional software installation by the Etisalat technician).

Rental: Standard Internet connection – Dhs.20 per month; ISDN line – Dhs.60 quarterly; ADSL line Dhs.250 per month.

User charge: For the standard and ISDN connection, there is an additional user charge: peak rate – Dhs.1.8 per hour (06:00 - 01:00); off-peak rate – Dhs.1 per hour. With an ADSL line, you are logged on 24 hours a day and pay no further charges.

Dial 'n' Surf

This facility allows you to surf without subscribing to the Internet service. All that's needed is a computer with a modem and a regular phone (or ISDN) line - no account number or password is required. In theory, you then simply dial 500 5555 to gain access. However, in practice it may not be quite so straightforward, since there are different set ups depending on your software. If you have difficulties, contact the helpdesk (800 5244).

Charges: A charge of 15 fils per minute is made for the connection and billed to the telephone line from which the call is made.

Internet Help

abuse@emirates.net.ae
report hacking, illegal use of the Internet, spamming etc

watch@emirates.net.ae
report inappropriate sites

custserv@emirates.net.ae
comments, billing disputes and general Internet inquiries

help@emirates.net.ae
technical support

www.emirates.net.ae
Etisalat homepage & Emirates Internet & Multimedia products and services, billing inquiries, online change of passwords and change of ISDN access speed

800 6100
Internet Help Desk

Internet Cafés

A cheaper option would be to step out and use the Internet café in the mall or the restaurant below your apartment. Lots and lots of Internet Cafés

exist, from the chic and sleek to the down and dirty. Rates vary dramatically, from Dhs.5 - 15 per hour. Check if the café provides food. If you order a meal, they may let you cruise the Internet for free.

Bill Payment

Bills are mailed monthly and are itemised for international and mobile calls, SMS (short message service) and service charges. For all bill payments, it's possible to pay at Etisalat branch offices, on the Internet, as well as at certain banks such as Emirates Bank International and HSBC (details can be obtained through Etisalat). Etisalat also has cash payment machines at several sites around Dubai, saving you the hassle of queuing at Etisalat or the bank; again, details can be obtained from Etisalat. You can also recharge your Wasel service using these machines.

If you don't pay your landline telephone bill within the first ten days of the month, or your GSM bill within 45 days, your outgoing calls will be cut off and you will only receive incoming calls for up to 15 days before complete disconnection. But Etisalat very kindly automatically calls landlines and sends SMS reminders to people to pay up.

Bill Enquiry Service

Etisalat provides a useful bill enquiry service, enabling customers to obtain the current amount payable on their phone/s up to the end of the last month. The aim is to help customers budget their calls and to facilitate prompt settlement of bills, leading to fewer disconnections.

Central Post Office, Karama

The information is only available for the phone that the call is made from (in theory) and the cost of the call inquiry is charged at the normal rate. To use the service, dial 142 (English) or 143 (Arabic). You may also use Etisalat cash payment machines for this service, and Etisalat's 'online billing service' to pay Internet bills.

Postal Services

Other options → **Post & Courier Services [p.46]**

The postal service is fast and reliable, but there is no house address based mailing system in the UAE. All mail is delivered to the Central Post Office and then distributed to centrally located post office boxes. While many residents direct mail to a company mailbox or a mailbox at their apartment, it's also possible to rent a personal PO Box. To apply, you require an application form from the Central Post Office and Dhs.160. You can then select a PO Box at a convenient location near to your home (if one is available).

Emirates Postal Service (Empost) will send you notification by email when you receive registered mail or parcels in your PO Box. While there is no charge for this service, you do have to register your email address and details with Empost. They will tell you the origin, arrival date, type of mail and its location, and for Dhs.9, you can have your parcel or registered mail delivered to your door. However, you may be required to pay Customs charges on international packages, which are about Dhs.15.

Location: Central Post Office (337 1500), Zabeel Road, Karama (Map Ref 10-E2).

Opening hours: Saturday – Wednesday 08:00 - 24:00; Thursday 08:00 - 22:00.

Television

UAE television is divided amongst the emirates with Dubai, Abu Dhabi, Sharjah and Ajman all broadcasting terrestrially and via satellite. Dubai has four channels - Dubai 2, 10 and 41 show Arabic programmes, whilst Dubai 33 broadcasts mainly in English. It offers a mixture of serials, documentaries and films (chiefly American, British and Australian), as well as films from 'Bollywood' (Indian cinema). Programme details are published daily in the local press.

Emirates Dubai Television broadcasts by satellite throughout the world in Arabic and English. Abu Dhabi has an English language channel, while

Sharjah and Ajman TV transmit mainly Arabic programmes with some in English.

There are numerous video/DVD rental stores around the cities and the latest releases from Hollywood and Bollywood are widely available, usually with Arabic subtitles. Anything that offends the country's moral code is censored – be prepared for some interesting continuity!

The UAE's cable TV network, Emirates Cable TV & Multimedia (E-Vision), is a subsidiary of Etisalat. Subscription currently includes approximately 70 or more Arabic, Asian and Western channels, though this will rise to 100 channels in the future. The basic subscription fee is Dhs.50 and for an extra charge, you can add pay satellite channels. For further information, contact 800 5500 or log on to www.emiratescatv.co.ae.

Satellite Main Dealers	
Arabtec SIS	286 8002
Bond Communications	343 4499
E-Vision	800 5500
Eurostar	225 5777
Global Direct Television	339 5585
Orbit Direct	800 4442
Showtime	808 8888

Satellite TV

The digital home entertainment revolution is sweeping through the Middle East – and Dubai is its epicentre, judging by the number of satellite dishes in the city! Satellite TV offers viewers an enormous number of programmes and channels to watch, and the choice and options available can be rather confusing. Most leading hotels offer satellite in their rooms, showing news, sports, movies, documentaries, cartoons etc.

Considering the diversity of people watching, it's not surprising that programmes of all hues, flavours and tastes are available. Couch potatoes first have to decide what types of programmes they want to watch and then whether they are willing to pay for them.

The various channels available can be split into two types:

1. Pay TV Satellite Channels

These are channels that require payment for installation and equipment, such as the decoder, dish etc, followed by a viewing subscription for the channels you choose to watch. Generally, subscriptions can be paid monthly, quarterly or annually. Take your time making the right choice because the Middle East has a competitive pay TV market with four pay TV networks all offering a range of channels.

2. Free to Air Satellite Channels

These are channels that require payment for the installation and reception equipment, but there is no viewing subscription. There are more than 200 of these types of channels.

Equipment

Equipment can be bought from various locations: directly from the main dealers, electrical shops, second hand shops or classified ads. The majority of dealers offer installation. For apartment blocks or buildings with a large number of viewing points, a central system is recommended, making it economical as well as offering more choice. Persuade your landlord to install the system if the block does not already come with satellite receiving equipment.

Health

General Medical Care

The quality of medical care in the Emirates is generally regarded as quite high and visitors should have little trouble in obtaining appropriate treatment if they need it, as both private and government run hospitals have emergency services. Dubai is planning to expand Rashid Hospital, one of the best and largest, into the largest emergency centre in the Middle East. However, tourists and non residents are strongly recommended to arrange private medical insurance before travelling since private medical care can become very expensive and public hospitals accept only residents at nominal rates.

Ouch!

While there are no specific health risks facing visitors, it is always advisable to take tetanus and hepatitis shots before travelling or upon arrival. Also, Dubai's climate can be harsh, especially during the summer months, so drink lots of water and take energy drinks and salty snacks to replace lost salts. In the few minutes' walk from the refreshing air conditioning of your hotel or home to the car, the dramatic temperature differences will have you in a sweat, so till you get used to it, you will be quite prone to colds. Cover up with hats and the appropriate factor sunscreen when out in the daytime hours – sunburn, heatstroke and heat exhaustion can be very unpleasant.

Hospitals	
Al Amal Hospital	344 4010
Al Baraha Hospital	271 0000
Al Maktoum Hospital	222 1211
Al Wasl Hospital	324 1111
American Hospital	336 7777
Belhoul European Hospital	345 4000
Dubai Hospital	271 4444
International Private Hospital	221 2484
Iranian Hospital	344 0250
Rashid Hospital	337 4000
Welcare Hospital	282 7788

Private Centres/Clinics	
Al Borj Medical Centre	321 2220
Al Zahra Private Medical Centre	331 5000
Allied Diagnostic Centre	332 8111
Belhoul European Hospital	297 6203
Dr Akel's General Medical Clinic	344 2773
Dubai London Clinic	344 6663
Dubai Physiotherapy Clinic	349 6333
General Medical Centre	349 5959
Health Care Medical Center	344 5550
Jebel Ali Medical Centre	881 4000
Manchester Clinic	344 0300
New Medical Centre	268 3131

UAE Nationals and expatriate residents are allowed healthcare for a minimal cost at the government hospitals and clinics. In Dubai, the Department of Health and Medical Services runs New Dubai, Rashid, Al Baraha, Maktoum and Al Wasl hospitals. Dubai Hospital is one of the best medical centres in the Middle East, with specialised clinics, while Al Wasl is a specialized maternity and gynaecology hospital. The department also operates a number of outpatient clinics. Additionally, there are government initiatives to build Dubai Healthcare City to serve as a hub for treatment, prevention, education and research on healthcare in the region.

Diagnostics	
Al Zahra Private Medical Centre	331 5000
Allied Diagnostic Centre	332 8111
American Hospital	336 7777
Dr. Leila Soudah Clinic	395 5591
Medic Polyclinic	355 4111
Medical Imaging Department	309 6642
Welcare Hospital	282 7788

Currently expatriates can go to any hospital as long as they have a valid health card. However, in the future, this may change and some government sectors are pushing to make it mandatory that all expatriates have private insurance coverage. There are various private hospitals and clinics that offer thorough services, such as the American Hospital. Additionally, each emirate must have at least one pharmacy open 24 hours a day. The location and telephone numbers are listed in the daily newspapers and on the Dubai Police Website (www.dubaipolice.gov.ae). The Municipality has emergency numbers (223 2323 or 266 3188), which also give you the name and location of open chemists. Pharmacies are open Saturday – Thursday from 08:30 - 13:30 and 16:30 - 22:30, and on Fridays 16:30 - 22:30, although some pharmacies may open on Friday mornings, 09:00 - 13:00.

Dermatologists	
Al Zahra Private Medical Centre	331 5000
American Hospital	336 7777
Belhoul European Hospital	345 4000
Dr. Simin Medical Clinic	344 4117
International Private Hospital	221 2484
Jebel Ali Medical Centre	881 4000

Maternity

Every expatriate child born in the UAE must be registered at the Ministry of Health within two weeks and hold a residence visa within four months of birth. Without the correct documentation, you won't be able to take your baby out of the country. The hospital you deliver at will prepare the birth certificate in Arabic upon receipt of hospital records, photocopies of both parents' passports, the marriage certificate and a fee of Dhs.50. Take the birth certificate for translation into English to the Ministry of Health Department of Preventive Medicine (there's one in every emirate). They will endorse and attest it for a fee of Dhs.10. Once this is done, make sure you register your child at your embassy or consulate

(you may also want to arrange for a passport for your baby at this time), then apply for a residence visa through the normal UAE channels. Before the birth, it's worth checking the regulations of your country of origin for citizens born overseas.

Ante Natal Care	
Al Zahra Private Medical Centre	331 5000
American Hospital	336 7777
Ballet Centre, The	344 9776
Belhoul European Hospital	345 4000
Dr. Leila Soudah Clinic	395 5591
Dubai London Clinic	344 6663
Fakih Gynecology & Obstetrics Center	349 2100
General Medical Centre	349 5959
Medilink Clinic	344 7711
Royal Medical Centre	345 6780
Welcare Hospital	282 7788

Post Natal Care	
American Hospital	336 7777
Ballet Centre, The	344 9776
Belhoul European Hospital	345 4000
Dr. Leila Soudah Clinic	395 5591
essensuals Aromatherapy centre	344 8776
Fakih Gynecology & Obstetrics Center	349 2100
General Medical Centre	349 5959
Medilink Clinic	344 7711
Royal Medical Centre	345 6780
Welcare Hospital	282 7788

You may opt to give birth in a public hospital, which charges expatriates for their services. Otherwise check around for rates and go with the place you feel most comfortable – after all, you should feel your best in the place you choose to bring your baby into the world.

Public Hospital Maternity Care Fees	
Normal delivery in a shared room	Dhs.2,000
Normal delivery in a private room	Dhs.3,000
Caesarean birth in a shared room	Dhs.4,000
Caesarean birth in a private room	Dhs.5,000

Paediatrics

Your kids deserve the best, so choose wisely and be nosey. Call around and ask for the experience and qualifications you are after, or think your child may need. There are also specialties such as paediatric surgeons and neurodevelopment therapists and doctors that care for children with special needs and learning difficulties.

Gynaecology & Obstetrics	
Al Zahra Private Medical Centre	331 5000
American Hospital	336 7777
Belhoul European Hospital	345 4000
Dr. Leila Soudah Clinic	395 5591
Dubai London Clinic	344 6663
Elixir Medical Centre	343 4090
Fakih Gynecology & Obstetrics Center	349 2100
General Medical Centre	349 5959
International Private Hospital	221 2484
Manchester Clinic	344 0300
Medilink Clinic	344 7711
Royal Medical Centre	345 6780
Welcare Hospital	282 7788

Al Zahra Clinic

Dentists/Orthodontists

The standard of dentistry in Dubai is generally very high. Practitioners and specialists of all nationalities offer services on a par with, or better than those found 'back home'. Prices, however, match the level of service, and most health insurance packages do not cover dentistry, unless it's an emergency treatment brought about by an accident. Word of mouth works particularly well for finding a suitable dentist. Alternatively, phone around to find out what methods and equipment etc, are used.

If you have a health card, you are entitled to dentistry by your assigned hospital, and if they

do not have a dental section, they will give you a reference to another public hospital that does, such as Rashid Hospital. You will be charged Dhs.50 for the visit plus any other services that are performed, such as cleaning, filling etc. Services are generally professional and accurate, but the rates may not be any lower than going to a private dental clinic.

Private Dentists/Orthodontists	
Al Zahra Private Medical Centre	331 5000
American Dental Clinic	344 0668
British Dental Clinic	342 1318
Clinic for Orthodontics & Aesthetic Dentistry	330 0220
Dr M.S. Ahmadi	344 5550
Dr Michael's Dental Clinic	349 5900
Dr. Nicolas & Asp Dental Centre	345 4443
24 hour emergency hotline	*050 551 7177*
Dr Tim Walters	228 3948
Dubai London Clinic	344 6663
Jumeira Beach Dental Clinic	349 9433
Swedish Dental Clinic	223 1297
Talass Orthodontic & Dental Center	349 2220

Alternative Therapies

Years ago, Dubai served as a connection between Europe and Asia, where traders stopped over to refuel and explore the commercial benefits of the little Gulf centre of trade. Arguably, this trade based diversity has become today's most beautiful aspect of Dubai. Given the vast number of Dubai's residents that come from countries practicing traditional, herbal and alternative therapies, Dubai holds a well balanced choice of Western and holistic therapies.

Additionally, the Dubai Herbal & Treatment Centre (335 1200) offers a full range of Chinese, Indian and Arabic herbal Medicines. The facility, which is unique in the GCC region, offers out-patient services and there are plans to expand the facility to offer in-patient services.

Natural medicine can be very specialised, so ask questions, explain your needs and expectations, and talk about your medical history if necessary, to ensure they can help with your situation. Prices vary and can run comparable to Western medicine, and most insurance will not cover the costs.

Dubai residents now have a range of healing methods to choose from in addition to the more conventional approach to medicine. As always, word of mouth is the best way of establishing who might offer the most appropriate treatment.

The UAE office of Complementary & Alternative Medicine is governed by the Ministry of Health, and grants licenses to qualified practitioners of alternative medicine. This legal process helps weed out the quacks.

The following are some of the services offered and the main practitioners in Dubai.

Acupressure/Acupuncture

Among the oldest healing methods in the world, acupressure involves the systematic placement of pressure with fingertips on established meridian points on the body. This therapy can be used to relieve pain, sooth the nerves and stimulate the body, as determined necessary by the therapist. Acupuncture is an ancient Chinese technique that uses needles to access the body's meridian points. The technique is surprisingly painless and is quickly becoming an alternative or complement to Western medicine, as it aids ailments such as asthma, rheumatism, and even more serious diseases. It has also been known to work wonders on the maladies of animals!

Acupressure/Acupuncture	
Dubai Herbal & Treatment Centre	390 1630
Dubai Physiotherapy Clinic	349 6333
Gulf American Clinic	349 8556
Herbalpan Ayurvedic Centre	321 2553
House of Chi & House of Healing	397 4446
Jebel Ali Medical Centre	881 4000

Homeopathy

Homeopathy strengthens the body's defence system. Natural ingredients are used to address physical and emotional problems. The discipline extracts elements from traditional medicines of various origins, but was recently organised into a healthcare system in Europe. Practitioners undergo disciplined training and some are also Western medical doctors.

- Holistic Healing Medical Centre (formerly Dr. Sergei Clinic) 228 3234

Reflexology & Massage Therapy

Reflexology is a detailed scientific system with Asian origins, which outlines points in the hands and feet that impact other parts and systems of the body. In addition to stress reduction and improved health, the pressure applied to these points directly addresses issues in those specific corresponding parts of the body. While many spas and salons offer massage and reflexology, the

following centres have a more focused approach to the holistic healing qualities of reflexology and massage. For a listing of spas that offer massage for relaxation and beauty, see Activities [p.259].

Massage Therapy/Reflexology	
Essensuals Aromatherapy centre	344 8776
House of Chi & House of Healing	397 4446
Royal Reflexology Center	321 2128

Aromatherapy

Essential oils derived from plants and flowers can be used in a myriad of ways to add balance to your health. Specialists use such oils when delivering massages as well as a number of other methods to address your needs. While no certification is required to practice aromatherapy, it's a healthy decision to make sure your practitioner has studied plants and can make the best choices for you. Additionally, for cosmetic and relaxing purposes alone, it is nice to have an aromatherapy facial or massage, which many spas and salons offer. While these are intended to be for pleasure rather than health related, they can work wonders on your soul!

- *Essensuals Aromatherapy Centre* 344 8776

Healing Meditation

Meditation can offer inner peace as well as a disease free mind and body. With quiet settings and various breathing techniques, movements and mantras, group and individual meditation sessions can be a powerful tool in healing and stress relief. More and more of Dubai's residents are trying out meditation as a means to unwind.

Healing Meditation	
Art of Living Foundation	050 646 2507
Serenity Specialised Rehab Centre	321 0110
World Pranic Healing Foundation	336 0885

Back Treatment

Without a strong and healthy back, you're nothing! Luckily, treatment is widely available in Dubai with top notch specialists from all around the world practising here.

Chiropractic and osteopathy treatments concentrate on manipulating the skeleton in a non intrusive manner to improve the functioning of the nervous system or blood supply to the body. Chiropractic is based on the manipulative treatment of misalignments in the joints, especially those of the spinal column, while osteopathy involves the manipulation and massage of the skeleton and musculature.

Craniosacral therapy aims to relieve pain and tension by gentle manipulations of the skull to balance the craniosacral rhythm. Pilates is said to be the safest form of neuromuscular reconditioning and back strengthening available. It is also a form of exercise that's gaining popularity. Check with your gym to see if they offer any classes.

Back Treatment	
Canadian Chiropractic & Natural Health Centre	342 0900
Chiropractic Speciality Clinics	634 5162
Clark Chiropractic Clinic	344 4316
General Medical Centre	349 5959
Gulf American Clinic	349 8556
House of Chi & House of Healing	397 4446
Nautilus Academy, The	397 4117
Neuro Spinal Hospital	342 0000
OrthoSports Medical Center	345 0601
Osteopathic Health Centre	344 9792
Pilates Studio, The	343 8252
Specialist Orthopaedic & Rehab Centre	349 5528

Mental Health

Everyone needs to talk. Instead of dwelling on your imperfections, why not call someone that can give you an objective opinion? Even the most resilient of personalities can be affected by culture shock, or maybe it's just the mountain of heat that sticks to your every move that's weighing you down. Whatever the origin of the stress, a new environment and the natural

American Hospital

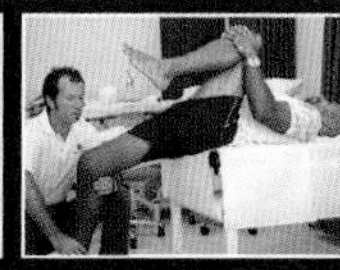
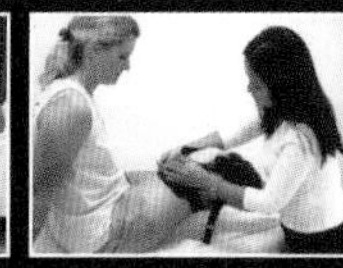

ORTHOSPORTS
MEDICAL CENTER
THE SPORTS MEDICINE SPECIALISTS

adjustment period can be demanding on your nerves. Couple this with a few personal problems and it may be best to talk it over with someone who can give you some sound advice.

The Dubai Community Health Centre offers workshops and other psychiatric services free of charge to all nationalities. The Centre is the GCC region's first dedicated mental health centre, and holds affiliations to the Dubai Police. Additionally, a 24 hour online counselling service is available and suffering surfers can email, chat and ask a dedicated psychologist questions about mental health.

Counselling & Psychology

Counsellers/Psychologists

Comprehensive Medical Centre	331 4777
Dr. Roghy McCarthy Psychology Clinic	394 6122
Dubai Community Health Centre	395 3939
Welcare Hospital	282 7788

Psychiatry

Psychiatrists

Dr Akel's General Medical Clinic	344 2773
Dubai Community Health Centre	395 3939
Welcare Hospital	282 7788

Support Groups

Dubai can be a challenging place to live and with many residents originating from overseas, there is often a lack of the family support that many people are used to. Making the first step of reaching out for help can be tough; however, there are groups out there offering a hand through the difficult patches.

Support Groups

Adoption Support Group	394 6643
Al Anon Family Groups	343 0446
Alcoholics Anonymous	394 9198
Breastfeeding Telephone Support Group	050 453 4670
Diabetic Support Group	309 6876
Fertility Support Group	050 632 4365
Mother to Mother	050 595 2974
Pastoral Care	395 4601
Special Families Support	393 1985
Still Birth & Neo Natal Death Society	884 6309
Twins, Triplets or More!	050 654 0079

Check out the list above, or any of the monthly health focused magazines that are usually available in surgeries, nutrition stores etc, for updates of support groups. If possible, get personal recommendations first, as standards can vary enormously, especially if a group or workshop is linked to a business. Be wise and use your discretion.

Help on the Web

www.doctorelite.com is a Website run by doctors and health professionals in the UAE, containing information on where to find a doctor who speaks your language, health tips, where to find a pharmacy open late at night etc. Basically, the main function of the Website is to provide a search engine that allows you to look for practitioners in the UAE and internationally. It details their qualifications, specialities, medical degrees, etc - very helpful!

The Dubai Community Health Centre (344 6700) offers a pleasant, healing space for support group meetings for no charge, so if your group isn't already in existence in Dubai – be a pioneer and start it!

The following groups do not charge to attend their meetings:

- *Adoption Support Group* (394 6643/394 2387). Meetings held once a month at different locations.
- *Al Anon Family Groups* (AA) (343 0446). Meets Mondays 19:30 at American Hospital Dubai.
- *Alcoholics Anonymous* (AA) (394 9198 – 24 hour hotline).
- *Attention Deficit Hyperactive Disorder* (ADHD) (394 6643). Meets second Saturday of the month at the Community Health Centre.
- *Breastfeeding Telephone Support* (050 453 4670). Meets 08:00 - 20:00, 7 days a week.
- *Diabetic Support Group* (309 6876). Meets every three months on a Wednesday evening at 17:30. Based at the American Hospital Dubai. Contact Nibal.
- *Fertility Support Group* (050 646 5148/050 632 4365/ 050 456 4109). Meets the first Tuesday of every month at 19:00. Based at the Dubai Gynaecological and Fertility Unit, Rashid Hospital. Contact Ram Kumar/Lalitah/Tricia.
- *Mother 2 Mother* (050 595 2974). Support, friendship, fun and advice for all mothers, from those who are expecting to those who have already delivered.

- *Pastoral Care* (395 4601). A listening ear from someone who cares.
- *Professional Single Parents Group* (050 535 6220). Meetings held once a month for single fathers and mothers and their kids.
- *Special Families Support* (393 1985). Monthly meetings on a Friday. For the families of special needs children. Contact Ayesha Saeed.
- *Still Birth & Neo Natal Death Society* (SANDS) (884 6309/395 4564). Meetings held approximately once a month. Contact June Young or Angela Scally.
- *Twins, Triplets or More!* (050 654 0079). Baby Circle (for pregnant mothers and mothers with multiples up to one year) meets every Monday. Double Trouble (for those with multiples aged one year and up) meets every other Tuesday. (www.twinsormore.2om.com). Contact Paula.

Education

In Dubai, due to the diverse expat culture, the education system is extremely varied and there are many private international schools from which to choose, all of which charge fees. It's always best to seek advice from friends or colleagues about a school's reputation. Many schools operate a waiting list and families are not necessarily able to enrol their child at their preferred school. The Ministry of Education has warned secondary students from enrolling in school that are not accredited. For a listing of Ministry approved institutions, log on to www.uae.gov.ae/mohe. For more information on the education system, schools, fees etc, refer to the *Family Explorer (Dubai & Abu Dhabi)*.

School terms: Autumn (mid September - mid December); spring (early January - early April); summer (mid April – early July).

Generally, to enrol your child at a school, the following information is needed:

- School application form
- Copies of student's and parents' passports – both information page/s and residence visa stamp
- Passport size photos (usually eight)
- Copies of student's birth certificate
- School records for the past two years
- Current immunisation records and medical history
- An official transfer certificate from the student's previous school detailing his/her education
- Some schools also require a student questionnaire to be completed

Original transfer certificates must contain the following details:

- Date of enrolment
- Year of placement
- Date the child left the school
- School stamp
- Official signature

The Ministry of Education also requires the following documentation for any student enrolling at any school in the emirate:

Sunset over Mina Seyahi

- Original transfer certificate (to be completed by the student's current school)
- Most recently issued original report card

If the student was attending a school in any country other than the UAE, Australia, Canada, European nation or USA, the transfer certificate and the most recently issued original report card must by attested by the Ministry of Education, Ministry of Foreign Affairs and the UAE embassy in that country.

Nursery & Pre-School

(Age: Babies - 4 1/2 years)

Nursery schools usually like to interview a child before accepting him or her. Most nurseries adopt English as their common teaching language and annual fees can vary dramatically. Call around to find the one that's right for you.

Hours: Most nurseries run for 4 - 5 hours in the morning

Fees: Approximately Dhs.3,000 - 12,000 per annum

Nurseries & Pre Schools	
De La Salle Montessori International	398 6218
Dubai Gem Private Nursery & School	345 3550
Dubai Infants School	337 0913
French Children's Nursery House	349 6868
Gulf Montessori Nursery	282 2402
Jumeirah International Nursery	394 5567
Jumeirah International Nursery School	349 9065
Kids Cottage Nursery School	394 2145
Kid's Island Nursery	394 2578
Ladybird Nursery	344 1011
Little Land Nursery	394 4471
Little Star Nursery	398 2004
Palms	394 7017
Safa Kindergarten Nursery School	344 3878
Small World Nursery	345 7774
Smart Children's Nursery	398 0074
Tiny Home Montessori Nursery	349 3201
Yellow Brick Road Nursery	282 8290

Primary & Secondary School

(Age: 4 1/2 - 11 years) (Age: 11 - 18 years)

Most schools require proof of your child's previous school academic records. You will also need an official letter from a school in your home country detailing your child's education to date and some schools even ask for a character reference! The child may also be required to take a short entrance exam and there may even be a physical examination as well as a family interview. Translated school certificates must have the student's name spelled exactly as it is found on the student's school record and passport. The student's passport must be brought too.

Depending on your nationality and educational requirements, most national curriculum syllabuses can be found in Dubai schools, covering GCSEs, A levels, French and International Baccalaureate and CNEC as well as the American and Indian equivalent.

Standards of teaching are usually high and schools have excellent facilities, with extracurricular activities offered. The Ministry of Education regularly inspects schools to ensure rules and regulations are being upheld, and most schools insist on a school uniform. Some school fees include books and transport to school by bus, but mostly, fees only cover the basic education.

Hours: Most are from 08:00 - 13:00 or 15:00, Saturday – Wednesday.

Fees: Primary: approximately Dhs.10,000 - 20,000 per annum. Secondary: approximately Dhs.15,000 - 45,000 per annum. Other costs may include a deposit or registration.

Primary & Secondary Schools	
Al Mawakeb School	347 8288
American School of Dubai	344 0824
Cambridge High School, The	282 4646
Dubai College	399 9111
Dubai English Speaking School	337 1457
Dubai Infants School	337 0913
Emirates International School	348 9804
English College, Dubai	394 3465
German School	06 567 6014
Horizon English School	394 7878
International School of Choueifat	399 9444
Jebel Ali Primary School	884 6485
Jumeirah English Speaking School, The	394 5515
Jumeirah Primary School	394 3500
Lycee Georges Pompidou	337 4161
Regent School	344 2409
School of Research Science	298 8776
St. Mary's Catholic High School	337 0252

University & Higher Education

A number of universities and colleges around the UAE with American, Australian and European affiliates, offer degree and diploma courses in Arts, Sciences, Business & Management, and Engineering & Technology. Many commercial organisations also offer higher education

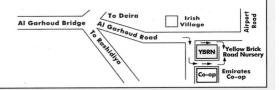

courses for school leavers, mature students and adults alike. Details of these establishments can be found in the Hawk Business Pages or Yellow Pages. Both the American University of Dubai and the University of Wollongong are accredited, and offer undergraduate and graduate degrees.

Universities	
American University of Dubai	399 9000
American University of Sharjah	558 5555
University of Wollongong	395 4422

Special Needs Education

If you have a child or children with special needs, before embarking on your adventure in the Emirates, we recommend that you first contact one or more of the following schools/centres, as student spaces are limited. All centres are charities, rather than government run, and thus rely on donations, sponsorship, grants and a certain amount of voluntary work from outside helpers. Entry into most is generally between the ages of 3 1/2 - 5, unless the child was in a special needs school previously. Generally, teaching is in English, but Arabic language instruction is also available, and in most cases, each child receives an individual programme. All charge tuition fees.

- The Al Noor Centre for Children with Special Needs (394 6088) provides therapeutic support and comprehensive training to special needs children of all ages. The centre also equips its 220 students with work related skills, assisting them to functionally integrate into society as young adults.
- The Dubai Centre for Special Needs (344 0966) currently has 119 students, all of whom have an individual programme, including physiotherapy, speech therapy and/or occupational therapy. A pre-vocational programme is offered for older students, which includes arranging work placements.
- Rashid Paediatric (340 0005) includes physical, occupational and speech therapy. In the afternoons, 13:30 - 17:00, therapists see children on an outpatient basis, also working on early intervention and assisting school children with motor, learning, speech and communication difficulties.
- Additionally, there is a therapeutic horse riding programme for children with special needs – Riding for the Disabled (336 6321)

Note that, in general, the UAE is not set up for those with special needs and you won't find many wheelchair ramps around. Those ramps that we have seen appear to be there to assist with construction rather than wheelchairs, as they all seem to be at a 60 degree angle. When considering employment in the Emirates, check with your future employer whether any medical insurance programme they offer will cover special needs children, as many do not. (See also: Disabled Visitors [p.24])

Learning Arabic

Can you speak the local lingo and know that corner store jive? While it's relatively easy to pick up a few words of greeting, expand your horizons and learn more. There is a number of private institutions that offer very good Arabic language courses. Refer to Language Schools [p.331].

Kids' Cottage Nursery

If you want just a few words to help you get by, have a look at the Arabic expressions table on [p.18].

Transportation

Other options → **Car [p.37]**
Car Hire [p.39]
Zappy Explorer (Dubai)

Cars are the most popular mode of transport in Dubai and those who are licensed, and can afford

it, generally have one. The main options, if you wish to drive, are to buy a vehicle (for which you will need residency), or to lease. Those on visit visas (short or long term) have the option of renting a vehicle from one of numerous rental companies by providing their international driver's license.

The following section covers leasing, buying (new or used vehicles), registration, fines, insurance and traffic accidents.

The Dubai Traffic Police recorded information line (268 5555) or Website (www.dxbtraffic.gov.ae) (Arabic and English) tells you all you ever wanted to know about fines, speeding tickets, registering vehicles, applying for driving licences, emergency numbers, suggestions etc.

Office locations:

Traffic Police HQ – near Galadari roundabout, Dubai-Sharjah Road (269 2222, Map Ref 15-C1)

Bur Dubai Police Station – Sheikh Zayed Road, Junction 4 (398 1111, Map Ref 10-A1)

Vehicle Leasing

Leasing a vehicle has many advantages over buying. Not only is it a good option financially for shorter periods, but there are also fewer hassles when it comes to breakdowns, re-registration etc, since the leasing company should deal with everything. All services are provided inclusive of registration, maintenance, replacement, 24 hour assistance and insurance (comprehensive with personal accident is advisable). You may find that your employer has connections with a car hire company and can negotiate better rates for long term hire than you can on an individual basis.

Leasing is generally weekly, monthly or yearly. Cars typically range from Mitsubishi Lancers or Toyota Corollas to Mitsubishi Pajero 4 wheel drive vehicles. Monthly lease prices range from Dhs.1,500 for a small vehicle to Dhs.1,900 for larger cars and Dhs.3,500 for a 4 wheel drive. As the lease period increases, the price decreases.

Vehicle Leasing Agents	
Autolease Rent-a-Car	282 6565
Diamond Lease	331 3172
FAST Rent-a-car	332 8988
United Car Rentals	266 6286

For short term rental there are many companies offering daily services – check the Hawk Business Pages for the most competitive rates. To hire any vehicle, you will need to provide a passport copy, credit card and a valid driving licence from your home country, or a valid international driving licence.

Driver's Licence

You can only drive in the UAE if you hold an international driver's license, for so long as you are on a visit visa. Once you have processed your residency in Dubai, you are required to get a UAE license. The process varies for different nationalities, and some are required to be on waiting lists, and or take driving lessons from a driving school. Students applying with the larger institutes no longer need to have a no objection letter from their employer.

If you possess a driver's license from anywhere in the EU, North America, Australia or New Zealand, which all double as an international license in the UAE, you can immediately get a UAE driver's license, which is good for ten years. You will need

Tight Parking

to bring your existing foreign license with you, along with your passport to the registration office, near the Dubai Police College. They will take your picture and give you your driver's license within minutes, after the Dhs.100 processing fee.

Note that some Americans and Kiwis have had to sit a test before transferring their licence. As this has not happened to all, the policy seems possibly based on whim.

See also: *Driving Licence [p.66]*

Buying a Vehicle

In Dubai, the car rules as the most popular method of getting around, and buying one gives you far greater flexibility than relying on other means of transport. Choosing a car here can be a tough decision as the market is huge – should it be second hand, a 4 wheel drive, what has a good A/C, what colour's best... ?

Only those with a residence visa can own a vehicle in the UAE. Most people will find that cars are far cheaper here than in their home countries and that, with the low cost of petrol and maintenance, they can afford something a little more extravagant than they would otherwise think of buying.

New Vehicles

If you are going to invest in a brand new vehicle, you will find most models available on the market through the main dealers.

Used Vehicles

Where can you go to buy a second hand vehicle? Due to the relatively low price of cars and the high(ish) turnover of expats in the Emirates, there is a thriving second hand market. Dealers are scattered around town, but areas to start with include Sheikh Zayed Road and Garhoud. Expect to pay a premium of about Dhs.5,000 for buying through a dealer, since they also offer a limited warranty, insurance, finance and registration, unlike a less 'official' sale. Sometimes the main dealers will offer good deals on demonstration cars, which are basically new but have been used by the showroom for test drives.

Alternatively, visit Dubai Municipality's Used Car Complex at Al Awir/Ras Al Khor, where all the cars have been checked by EPPCO's Tasjeel service. If you're online, have a look at www.valuewheels.com.

For other second hand deals, check the classifieds section in the newspapers and supermarket noticeboards (mainly Spinneys or Park N Shop).

Before buying a second hand car, it's advisable to have it checked by a reputable garage - just to 'make sure'. 4 wheel drives especially, need to be thoroughly checked for they may have been driven off-road rather adventurously! Expect to pay around Dhs.300 for this service and it's best to book in advance.

New Car Dealers

Alpha Romeo	Gargash Motors	266 4669
Audi	Al Nabooda Automobiles	347 5111
BMW	AGMC	339 1212
Cadillac	Liberty Automobiles	282 4440
Chevrolet	Al Yousuf Motors	339 5555
Chrysler	Trading Enterprises	295 4246
Daewoo	Al Yousuf Motors	339 5555
Dodge	Trading Enterprises	295 4246
Ferrari	Al Tayer Motors	282 5000
Fiat	Al Ghandi Auto	266 6511
Ford	Al Tayer Motors	282 5000
Galloper	Al Habtoor Motors	269 1110
GMC	National Auto	266 4848
Honda	Trading Enterprises	295 4246
Hyundai	Juma Al Majid	269 0893
Isuzu	GENAVCO Llc	396 1000
Jaguar	Al Tayer Group	282 5000
Jeep	Trading Enterprises	295 4246
Kia	Al Majed Motors	268 6460
Land Rover	Al Tayer Group	282 5000
Lexus	Al Futtaim Motors	228 2261
Mazda	Galadari Automobiles	299 4848
Mercedes	Gargash Enterprises	269 9777
Mitsubishi	Al Habtoor Motors	269 1110
Nissan	Arabian Automobiles	295 1234
Opel	Liberty Automobiles	282 4440
Pontiac	Mirage General Trading	266 0062
Porsche	Al Nabooda Automobiles	347 5111
Rolls Royce	Al Habtoor Motors	269 1110
Saab	Gargash Motors	266 4669
Skoda	Autostar Trading	269 7100
Toyota	Al Futtaim Motors	228 2261
Volkswagen	Al Nabooda Automobiles	347 5111
Volvo	Trading Enterprises	295 4246
Wrangler	Trading Enterprises	295 4246

Used Car Dealers

4 x 4 Motors	Opp Al Bustan Rotana	282 3050
Autoplus	Sheikh Zayed Road	339 5400
Boston Cars	Al Awir	333 1010
Car Store, The	Sheikh Zayed Road	343 5245
House of Cars	Sheikh Zayed Road	343 5060
Motor World	Nr Ports & Customs	333 2206
Off Road Motors	Jct 3, Sheikh Zayed Rd	338 4866
Quality Cars	Trading Enterprises	295 4246

All transactions for vehicles must be directed through the Traffic Police. A Dhs.3,000 fine is imposed on both buyer and seller for cars sold unofficially.

Ownership Transfer

To register a second hand ('pre-owned') car in your name, you must transfer vehicle ownership. You will need to submit an application form, the valid registration card, the insurance certificate, the original licence plates and Dhs.20 to the Traffic Police, plus an NOC from the finance company, if applicable. The previous owner must also be present to sign the form.

Vehicle Import

In the first half of 2002, over 100,000 vehicles were imported into Dubai. A requirement for cars imported by individuals or private car showrooms that were manufactured after 1997/98, is an NOC from the official agent in the UAE or from the Ministry of Finance and Industry (if no official agent exists). This is to ensure that the car complies with GCC specifications (or rather that the local dealers are not outdone by the neighbouring competition!).

Additionally, believe it or not, if you are buying a vehicle from another part of the Emirates, you have to export and import it into Dubai first! This means lots of paperwork and lots of hassle. You will need to take your essential documents, the sale agreement, current registration and Dhs.60. You will then be issued with a set of temporary licence plates, which are valid three days – enough time to submit a new registration application in Dubai.

Cars toting export plates may not drive on Dubai roads. This ban came about because cars have been illegally sold under the guise of a foreign registration – export plates were used to avoid registration in Dubai.

Vehicle Insurance

Before you can register your car, you must have adequate insurance and many companies offer this service. The insurers will need to know the year of manufacture and may need to inspect the vehicle. Take along copies of your Dubai driving licence, passport and the existing vehicle registration card.

Annual insurance policies are for a 13 month period (this is to cover the one month grace period that you are allowed when your registration expires). Rates depend on the age and model of your car and your previous insurance history. The rates are generally 4 - 7% of the vehicle value or 5% for cars over five years old. Fully comprehensive with personal accident insurance is highly advisable. For more adventurous drivers, insurance for off-roading accidents is also recommended. Norwich Winterthur is one of the few insurers who will cover off-road accidents. For details on all insurance companies, look in the Yellow Pages or Hawk Business Pages.

It is wise to check whether your insurance covers you for the Sultanate of Oman as, within the Emirates, you may find yourself driving through small Omani enclaves (especially if you are off-road eg, near Hatta, through Wadi Bih and on the East Coast in Dibba). Insurance for a visit to Oman can be arranged on a short term basis, usually for no extra cost.

Registering a Vehicle

All cars must be registered annually with the Traffic Police. There is a one month grace period after your registration has expired in which to have your car re-registered (hence the 13 month insurance period). Please beware that some second hand dealers may sell you a car that under normal circumstances would not pass the annual vehicle testing. However, with 'friends' at the test centre, they are able to get the car 'passed', leaving you stuck when you come to do it yourself the following year.

There are several ways to test your car. Ras Al Khor boasts a five lane testing centre (Al Ghandi) that is run in conjunction with the Traffic Police. The centre is paperless and this saves you time in necessary procedures. Following this centre's success, EPPCO and Emarat are making life easier for motorists. They even offer a full registration service for a fee, which includes collecting your car, testing and registering it, and delivering it back to you all in the same day. EPPCO Tasjeel offers a service called Al Sayara, which costs Dhs.200, plus the testing and registration fees. Contact EPPCO Tasjeel (267 3940). Emarat also has five full registration and vehicle testing service centres called Shamil. They will test and register your car with the police. You can also pay any traffic fines and visit insurance kiosks. Call Emarat at 343 4444.

The following charge a fee for undertaking registration, in addition to normal registration costs.

Registration Service	
AAA Service Center	285 8989
Al Sayara Tasjeel	800 4258
Midland Cars	396 7521
Protectol	285 7182

The Process

In order to obtain licence plates for the vehicle, the car must first be tested, then registered with the Dubai Traffic Police. If you have purchased a new vehicle from a dealer, the dealer will register the car for you. You do not need to test a new vehicle for the first two years, though you must re-register it after one year. In some cases, dealers will register the car for you. The test involves a technical inspection, checking lights, bodywork, fire extinguisher, emissions etc. Once the car has been 'passed' you will receive a certification document.

Remember to take all your essential documents, insurance documents valid 13 months, the proof of purchase agreement, the vehicle transfer or customs certificate (if applicable) and Dhs.330. Before the registration procedure can be completed, all traffic offences and fines against your car registration number must be settled – a potentially expensive business!

Traffic Fines & Offences

If you are caught driving or parking illegally, you will be fined (unless the offence is more serious). You can also be fined Dhs.50 on the spot for being caught driving without your licence. If you are involved in an accident and don't have your licence with you, you will be given a 24 hour grace period in which to present your licence to the police station. If you don't, you risk having your car impounded and may have to go to court.

There are a number of police controlled speed traps, fixed cameras and mobile radar around Dubai. There is no leeway for breaking the speed limit – not that it seems to bother many people! The fines have been restructured because of the high number of traffic accidents, many of which could be avoided with better care and judgement. The fine for speeding is Dhs.400, parking tickets are Dhs.100 and up. Cars without exhaust control are fined Dhs.150 - 300, and overloaded cars Dhs.150. In addition, a black point penalty system operates for certain offences and you can be fined Dhs.100 for using your horn in excess.

The Dubai Traffic Police Information Line (268 5555, Arabic & English) or their Website: www.dxbtraffic.gov.ae enable you to check the fines you have against your vehicle or driving licence – a handy thing to know rather than being faced with an unexpectedly large bill when you renew your car registration!

Office location: For payment of traffic fines, Traffic Fines Section, Traffic Police HQ – near Galadari roundabout, Dubai-Sharjah Road (269 2222, Map Ref 15-B1). It is also possible to pay road fines at other locations around Dubai. These include Al Safa Union Co-operative, Al Tuwar Union Co-operative and Jumeira Town Centre. Payment of fines online using a credit card at www.dxbtraffic.gov.ae is also possible for a small fee.

Tinted Windows

Currently, the government allows you to avoid the sun somewhat by tinting your vehicle's windows up to 30 percent. Some areas have facilities where you can get your car windows tinted as dark as you like – but don't get carried away and remember to stick to the limit. Random checks take place and fines are handed out to those caught in the dark! Tinting in Sharjah is allowed for a fee of Dhs.100 and Ajman residents may tint for Dhs.200 per annum, but only if they are women.

Car Dealership

Breakdowns

In the event of a breakdown, you will usually find that passing police cars stop to help, or at least to check your documents! We recommend that you keep water in your car at all times – the last thing you want is to be stuck in the middle of summer with no air conditioning, nothing to drink and lots of time to waste waiting for help. Dubai Traffic officers recommend pulling your car over to a safe spot, but if you are on the hard shoulder of a highway, it is suggested that you pull your car as far away from the yellow line as possible and step away from the road until help arrives.

Recovery Services/Towing (24 hour)	
AAA Service Center	285 8989
Ahmed Mohammed Garage	333 1800

The Arabian Automobile Association (AAA) (285 8989) offers a 24 hour roadside breakdown service for an annual charge. This includes help in minor mechanical repairs, battery boosting, or help if you run out of petrol, have a flat tire or lock yourself out. The more advanced service includes off-road recovery, vehicle registration and a rent a car service. It's a similar concept to the RAC or AA in Britain, or AAA in the States.

Traffic Accidents

Other options ➜ **Accidents [p.38]**

Be very careful on the roads in Dubai and don't hesitate to tell your taxi driver to slow down if he's a bit wild behind the wheel. If, however, you are in the unlucky predicament of an accident, in serious cases dial 999 or in less critical cases, call Deira (266 0555), Bur Dubai (398 1111), or Sharjah (06 538 1111). The Dubai Traffic Police Information Line (268 5555, Arabic & English) gives the numbers of police stations around the emirate.

Then you have to wait for the police to arrive. They will assess the accident and apportion blame on the driver. In this part of the world, if you have an accident, you are then the star attraction of a million rubberneckers, but see if you can get them to help out instead of causing more accidents. If there is minor damage, move the vehicles to the side of the road. However, if there is any doubt as to who is at fault or if there is an injury (however slight), do not move the cars, even if you are blocking traffic. Apparently, if you help or move anyone involved in an accident and should something happen to that person, the police may hold you liable.

After having assessed the accident, the police will document the necessary details and give you a copy of the accident report. Submit the paper to your insurance company to get the vehicle repaired. A pink accident report means you are at fault and a green one means you are not to blame. The police may retain your driving licence until you obtain the necessary documentation from the insurance company to say the claim is being processed. Your insurers will then give you a paper that entitles you to retrieve your licence from the police.

And Finally...

Oh the follies of Dubai...

The final amount paid for the number 2 on a vehicle licence plate bought in 2001 was Dhs.1,240,000. Auctioned off over two days initially, personalised licence plates brought in a staggering Dhs.44,000,000 of revenue! Check out the Traffic Police's website for current auction details www.dxbtraffic.gov.ae/en.

Black Points

In addition to a system of fines for certain offences, a black points penalty system operates. If you have a permanent licence and receive 12 black points four times in one year, your licence is taken away and your car impounded. The first time you hit 12 points, you receive a fine and your licence is revoked for anything between two weeks and a month. For the next set of 12 points, the penalty is more severe, and so on.

If you are on a probationary licence and aged between 18 - 21, and receive 12 points within 12 months, your licence is revoked and you have to start the whole process of obtaining a licence from the beginning.

However, it seems that there are no hard and fast rules or amounts when it comes to black points. If you do something serious, your licence can be taken away immediately. If you run a red light, you receive nine black points instantly.

Repairs

By law, no vehicle can be accepted for repair without an accident report from the Traffic Police. Usually, your insurance company has an agreement with a particular garage to which they will refer you. The garage will carry out the repair work and the insurance company will settle the claim. Generally, there is a Dhs.500 deductible for all claims, but check with your insurance company for details of your policy.

Business

EXPLORER

Business

Business

Business

What's new?

Dubai means business

Page 132

For business ventures, Dubai is an exciting place to be. All the latest drawing board developments are unique projects that prove Dubai means business, and that it's marking itself firmly on the map as a world class business and tourist destination. Find out more...

Above the rest

Page 131

In a bid to improve the business economy, the Middle East is slowly changing its views on business ownership. Recognising the economic advantage in opening its gates to international companies, Dubai is beating its fellow comrades to the post, wisely using its physical location and thus, emerging as a leader in international trade and commerce.

All zoned out

Page 149

1985 saw the birth of the first free zone in Dubai, JAFZA (Jebel Ali). The free zone allowed 100% foreign ownership, encouraging international businesses to set up base in Dubai. Exemption from corporate and income tax and customs duties alone proved to be a great incentive. Today, over 13 free zones are in existence, with more on the horizon. Over 5,000 companies are currently thriving from the development, and the economy continues to flourish. Dubai is set to eventually become one big free zone!

Business Overview

General Information

Other options → **Economy [p.6]**

Strategically located between Europe and the Far East, Dubai is clearly the city of choice for both multinational and private companies wishing to tap the lucrative Middle Eastern, Indian and African markets (which have a combined population of 1.4 billion people). Annual domestic imports exceed $17 billion and Dubai is the gateway to over $150 billion (annual) in trade.

There are several reasons for Dubai becoming an attractive location for businesses, but the most important factors driving Dubai's economy are the government's planned yet innovative approach to business and continual investment in developing the city's soft and hard infrastructure. The key objective has been to make Dubai very 'business and investment friendly'.

Looking to the future, Dubai is targeting for the economy to become totally non oil driven by the year 2010 when, it is reported, the emirate's reserves may run out. One of the key planks in this strategy has been the development of a high end tourist industry and a regional hub for large multinationals, hence becoming the 'New York/London' for the region. The success of the latter is obvious from the number of industries that use Dubai as a conference hub for the region. (A multitude of trade shows held here attract customers, vendors and suppliers from many industries). The effort to develop tourism, too, has been very successful. Five to ten years ago, any detailed discussion on Dubai's economy would have made only a cursory mention of tourism. Today, it is one of the most important factors driving the economy of the city.

Business Climate

Other options → **History [p.3]**
Dubai Overview [p.3]
International Relations [p.10]

The pace of economic growth in Dubai over the past 20 years has been incredible – trade alone has grown at over 9% per annum over the past 10 years – and the emirate stands poised for future strong growth with the development of many multi billion dollar coastal extension projects (ie, The Palm Islands, The World, Dubai Marina and more) plus new business and financial ventures. With the vision of the rulers of Dubai and the UAE, both the legislation and government institutions have been designed to minimise bureaucracy and create a business friendly environment.

Government officials take an active role in promoting investment in the emirate, and decisions are taken (and implemented) swiftly. Government departments have also, in recent years, placed increasing importance on improving customer service levels, including free zones, such as the Internet, Media and Healthcare Cities which foster a community environment for the specific industries and are very easy to set up and operate in.

> **Heads Up!**
>
> *Although there are no direct taxes in Dubai, the government has a large number of pricey fees for residence visas, trade licenses and office & apartment rental taxes. Always be wary and ask questions before committing to a contract or agreement.*

The Dubai Rulers' commitment to economic development is pioneering in the Middle East and is seen by many as a best practice model for other governments in the region. While Dubai is probably the most expensive business location in the Middle East, companies are ready to pay this premium to reap the rewards offered, namely: no tax collection and low business fees, a high degree of political stability, steady, strong economic growth rates, excellent infrastructure, and a high quality of life for expatriate residents.

Trade & Trading Partners

While Abu Dhabi is the political capital of the UAE, Dubai is firmly entrenched as the commercial capital. The Dubai emirate accounts for about 75% of the UAE's entire imports, and about 85% of non oil exports; Dubai also enjoys about 80% of the lucrative re-export market to other Gulf, African and Indian subcontinent countries. Overall, trade represents approximately 16% of Dubai's GDP.

Strategically located between Asia and Europe, Dubai counts countries such as Japan, South Korea, China, India, the UK and the US amongst its most important trade partners for both imports and exports. In terms of re-exports, Iran, India, the other Gulf countries and the CIS states are amongst the most important markets for Dubai.

Key Dubai Projects

Dubai's strategic location gives this city an edge over others in reaching its aim – to be marked as the hottest tourist and trade destination on the global map. The government is investing large amounts of capital in major ventures and hence, new developments are constantly popping up on the proverbial drawing board. Below are the top development projects – some completed, others currently underway...

Burj Dubai

Talk about rising high! The competition continues as Emaar Properties attempts the tallest building in history (again). This undertaking will potentially yield the tallest office/residential tower and largest shopping mall in the world. Uniquely, the base will be the shape of the local six petal desert flower.

Contact *800 4990* Web **www.burjdubai.com**

Dubai Autodrome & Business Park

The first automotive and motor sports facility in the Middle East will introduce a world class 5.35 km racing track. Surrounding the FIA standard track is a business park dedicated to all automotive related industries, mixing business with pleasure for the avid motor fan.

Contact *204 6333* Web **www.unionproperties.com**

Dubai Festival City

...And you thought the traffic was bad at DSF! 1600 acres next to the Creek are being turned into a resort style city that will be a complete housing, shopping and recreation paradise. Highlights include a marina and canals, along with a signature 18 hole golf course designed by Robert Trent Jones II. Completion of first phase – 2006.

Estimated Investment *$6 billion*

Contact *213 6213* Web **www.dubaifestivalcity.com**

Dubai Flower Centre

Recognising the increasing demand for imported fresh flowers, this air cargo import, export and redistribution centre will act as the fresh vegetation gateway for the region, reducing transit time and improving quality and variety.

Contact *282 2323* Web **www.dubaiflowercentre.com**

Dubai HealthCare City

This healthcare 'oasis' of the Middle East will be a world class hub for modern healthcare with a premier western healthcare research/teaching institution based within to build local expertise. It also aims to keep potential patients closer to the region (generally, people travel to the West to solve advanced healthcare issues).

Estimated Investment *Dhs.300 million*

Contact *324 5555* Web **www.dhcc.ae**

Dubai Humanitarian City

This philanthropic gesture focuses on creating a central location for international aid providers to manage operations for the region. Completion date – 2005.

Contact *330 2222, 881 2222* Web **www.ddia.ae**

Dubai International Financial Centre

Bankers of the Middle East unite! This financial haven aims to effectively manage the Middle Eastern financial markets. Acting as the bridge between Asia and Europe, it will also allow global players to leverage the trillion dollar market (comprising the GCC, Levant, Maghreb, CIS and the subcontinent).

Estimated Investment *$3 billion*

Contact *330 0100* Web **www.difc.ae**

Dubai Internet City

This area is embracing technology at breakneck speeds and is cashing in on its proximity to one of the largest talent pools of technology workers (the subcontinent). A huge core of companies, from multinational to one man shows, is using this hub to expand their presence into the region.

Contact *391 1111* Web **www.dubaiinternetcity.com**

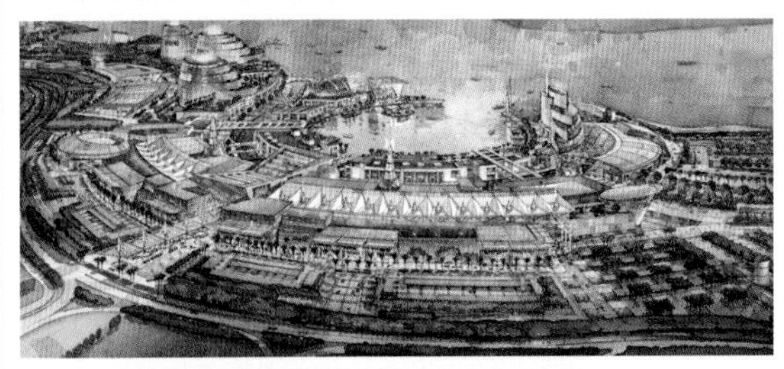

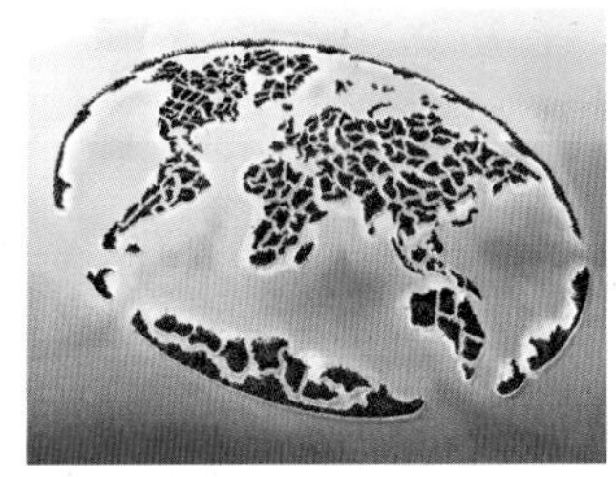

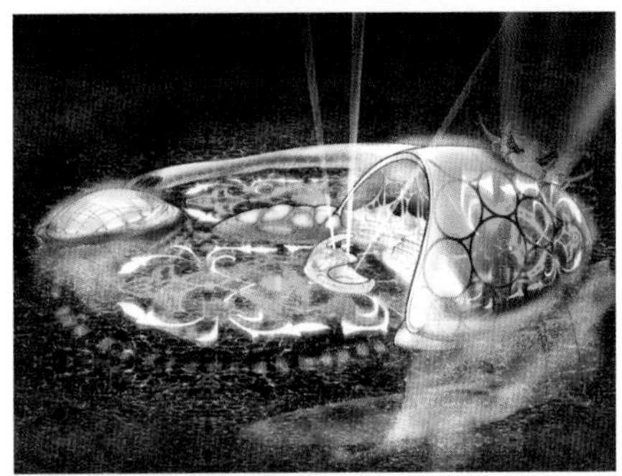

Some of Dubai's Key Developments

Dubai Investments Park

Want to build something and live next to it? This self contained city will provide the infrastructure required for advanced manufacturing along with excellent residential facilities promoting a good lifestyle.

Contact *885 1188* Web **www.dipark.com**

Dubai Mall, The

This mall is boasted to be the largest in the world (the covered area equals 50 soccer pitches put together). It will also house the world's largest gold souk and will be linked to the Burj Dubai by an 800 foot enclosed travellator.

Estimated Investment *Dhs.22 billion*
Contact *399 2299* Web **www.emaar.com**

Dubai Marina

A freehold property consisting of high rises and villas overlooking the marina. The apartments are penthouse posh and luxurious. Panoramic views and 11 km of waterfront walkway complement the first phase (completion date – 2004). Emaar will develop a large segment of the project; the remainder will involve other developers and be completed over 10 years.

Estimated Investment *$4 billion*
Contact *800 4990, 399 2299* Web **www.dubai-marina.com**

Dubai Maritime City

Ahoy mateys! This centre will service the region on all aspects of sea based shipping and place Dubai on the global shipping map.

Estimated Investment *Dhs.650 million*
Contact *390 3819* Web **www.dubaimaritimecity.ae**

Dubai Media City

This hub for broadcasting and entertainment is fast becoming the media capital for the region, creating a local knowledge and talent pool, coupled with a growing freelance directory. In the true spirit of Dubai based free zones, there is very little red tape involved in setting up here.

Contact *391 0000* Web **www.mediacity.com**

Dubai Metro/Railway Project

Finally, the choice of transport is expanding with the long awaited demand for trains to hit the desert! The railway will consist of two lines that cover the city from end to end. Completion date – 2008.

Estimated Investment *$1.6 billion*
Contact *221 5555* Web **www.dm.gov.ae**

Dubai Silicon Oasis

Where there's sand, there's silicon! This ambitious project is going to provide silicon chip manufacturers a solid infrastructure in Dubai, facilitating manufacturing requirements all in one place. A technology institute will further enhance the opportunity to educate local talent in the region.

Contact *202 7741* Web **www.dso.ae**

Dubai Techno Park

Technology seems to make the world go round these days, and Dubai wants to become the regional 'think tank' for using technology to improve our lives. This scheme will allow those with good ideas to develop them regionally.

Estimated Investment *$40 billion*
Contact *332 8835* Web **www.dpa.co.ae**

Dubailand

Disneyland too far for you? Try Dubailand. This world class theme park is intended to be the largest tourism attraction on the planet consisting of six themed worlds, sports and other outdoor activities, parklands, theme and water parks, health retreats, resort villages/hotels and a huge shopping mall... did we leave anything out?

Estimated Investment *Dhs.18+ billion*
Contact *330 2222* Web **www.dubailand.ae**

Gardens Mall, The

This shopping extravaganza (near the 6th interchange) will encompass 5.4 million square feet. Imitating Arabic folklore, five shopping zones will honour the famous Arab explorer, Ibn Batuta, reflecting his travels through Egypt, Morocco, Persia, India and China.

Estimated Investment *Dhs.800 million*
Contact *882 1414* Web **N/A**

Hydropolis Hotel

Like the ocean but not the sun? Here's your chance to sleep with the fishes. This first underwater hotel will be opening its gills in 2006, and will let you experience the uniqueness of living 20 metres under the sea with five star luxuries.

Estimated Investment *$500 million*
Contact *330 2222* Web **www.ddia.ae**

International Media Production Zone

To be completed in 2005, this will be the first media dedicated trade zone for the growing number of media companies in Dubai. The 35 million square feet of land will focus on the printing industry, providing the latest technology and communications services.

Contact *391 4555* Web **www.dubaimediacity.com**

Jumeirah Islands

A country within a country, the Jumeirah Islands will bring global tropical living styles to one location. This exclusive address will consist of 50 islands taking up 300 hectares of land. The project will focus on providing a self contained family community surrounded by canals and landscaped gardens. Completion date – April 2004.

Contact *390 3333* Web **www.jumeirahislands.ae**

Jumeirah Lake Towers

A modern development with 45 towers consisting of retail and office outlets as well as residential units. The whole design will be surrounded by lakes, waterways and landscaped gardens to form yet another stylish community retreat. Ready for occupancy in 2005.

Estimated Investment *Dhs.310 million*
Contact *390 8804* Web **N/A**

Knowledge Village

Next door to the Media and Internet Cities, this is the latest addition to the Dubai Technology and Media Free Zone (TECOM). The goal here is to bring further knowledge to the region through the wonders of technology.

Estimated Investment *Dhs.200 million*
Contact *390 1111* Web **www.kv.ae**

Madinat Jumeirah

This 42 hectare complex on the Jumeira beach consists of courtyard villas and two five star hotels. The theme focuses on the cultural heritage of the region. 3 km of winding waterways run through the entire complex and abras (water taxis) provide easy access to all areas. The in-house souk adds tradition. Completion date - 2004.

Estimated Investment *Dhs.536 million*
Contact *348 4757* Web **www.jumeirahinternational.com**

Mall of Emirates (previously Souk Al Nakheel)

Set to take over the quiet area of Al Barsha, this mall will house the world's largest indoor ski resort (using real snow), a hotel, a 14 screen multiplex cinema and a myriad of shops and food outlets. Completion date – late 2005.

Estimated Investment *Dhs.3 billion*
Contact **294 9999** Web **www.majidalfuttaim.com**

Palm Islands, The

Visible from outer space, these palm frond shaped islands (one off Jumeira and one near Jebel Ali) are the largest man made islands to date and will be a stunning haven for tourists and residents. The Palm, Jumeirah will be completed late 2005/early 2006, and The Palm, Jebel Ali, towards the end of 2007.

Estimated investment *$3 Billion*
Contact *390 3333* Web **www.palm.ae**

Third Bridge over the Creek

Part of the much needed Dhs.400 million project to combat Dubai's traffic congestion problem. This bridge will ease the pressure off Al Garhoud Bridge, Maktoum Bridge and the Shindagha tunnel, and will stretch out 20 km by 2006.

Estimated Investment *Dhs.197 million*
Contact *221 5555* Web **www.dm.gov.ae**

World, The

Nakheel is heading this $1.8 billion project to create 250 islands, which will resemble the shape of the world. Built 4 km offshore, each island will then be sold to private developers to turn into a private water retreat. Billionaires and royalty now have a new winter holiday home. Completion date - 2008

Estimated Investment *$1.8 billion*
Contact *390 3333* Web **N/A**

Both the government and the business community in Dubai have displayed a repeated ability to exploit business opportunities in the region. Such responses are possible due to the excellent infrastructure, flexible rules and regulations (Dubai has one of the most open foreign trade policies in the region), and the huge expatriate community that has a collective ear tuned to the needs of their home countries.

Dubai has used its (limited) oil revenues – 90% of Dubai's GDP is non oil – to maximum benefit by investing heavily in the basic and advanced infrastructure required to make the city attractive to both foreign investors and visitors. Equally important, the government maintains low tariffs (no departure taxes, road tolls, etc), which further stimulates demand.

Both the airport and ports in Dubai have achieved international recognition as regional hubs and offer passenger and freight connections to almost every destination in the world. Connecting these key facilities and other points in the city is an extensive road network, which is constantly being expanded and upgraded to meet future requirements.

International banks such as HSBC, Citibank, Standard Chartered Bank and Lloyds TSB offer advanced financial products for trade and commerce, while the government controlled Etisalat offers a full range of advanced voice and data telecommunication services. Each Dubai government department has a Website and a large number of government services are available online. There is also a government wide initiative to electronify fee collection and management – 'e-Government' – to streamline the process of getting approvals and fees paid for government services.

Telecommunications Services (Telephones)

	2000	2001	% Change
Telephone lines	390,665	407,563	4.33
Mobile phones	523,838	709,224	35.39
Internet	88,531	101,996	15.21

Source: Etisalat

Electricity Consumption

	2000	2001	% Change
Installed capacity (MW)	2,579	2,579	0.0
Energy generated (million kWH)	11,910	12,973	8.93
Number of consumers	223,505	240,855	7.76

Source: Dubai Electricity and Water Authority

Water Consumption

	2000	2001	% Change
Total production	44,495	47,808	7.45
Total consumption	38,442	41,343	7.55
Number of consumers	175,182	190,335	8.65

Source: Dubai Electricity and Water Authority

Total in million imperial gallons

Gross Domestic Product (in billion dirhams)

UAE	2000*	2001*	% Change
Total	210.4	248.3	18.0
Crude-Oil	63.4	69.6	9.8
Non Oil	147.0	178.7	21.6

Dubai	2000*	2001*	% Change
Total	55.5	64.2	15.7
Crude-Oil	6.5	5.4	-16.9
Non Oil	49.0	58.8	20.0

*Preliminary figures

Source: Ministry of Planning

Dubai Creek Skyline

Exports by Top Ten Destinations (in million dirhams)			
Destination	**1999**	**2000**	**% Change**
USA	390	614	57.44
Japan	508	565	11.22
Taiwan	383	381	-0.52
United Kingdom	389	335	-13.88
South Korea	277	297	7.22
Italy	193	271	40.41
Gemany	154	180	16.88
India	165	173	4.85
Indonesia	101	157	55.45
Thailand	175	148	-15.43

Source: Department of Ports and Customs

Imports by Top Ten Countries of Origin			
Country	**1999**	**2000**	**% Change**
China	5,471	7,138	30.47
Japan	5,835	5,953	2.02
United Kingdom	4,903	5,570	13.60
India	4,747	5,306	11.78
France	4,372	5,226	19.53
USA	5,238	4,861	-7.20
South Korea	4,044	4,397	8.73
Germany	4,003	3,768	-5.87
Italy	3,066	3,413	11.32
Taiwan	1,807	1,886	4.37

(Difference in totals is due to the rounding off of figures)

* Export figures exclude crude oil and petroleum gas exports

* Import figures exclude imports into the Free Zones and Duty Free Storage areas

Source Department of Ports and Customs

Dubai International Financial Centre

The finance sector is perhaps the sole area of the economy in which Dubai lags behind another Gulf state, namely Bahrain, which has traditionally been considered as the financial hub for the region.

DIFC

That, however, is expected to change with the inauguration of the Dubai International Financial Centre (DIFC), which was unveiled in 2002 and is expected to start operations soon. Situated on a huge property running from Emirates Towers to Interchange 1 behind Sheikh Zayed Road, the project will include an estimated 9 million square feet of commercial and residential real estate.

DIFC is expected to become the regional hub for corporate financing activities and share trading in the Middle East, and is hoping to become a mid way time zone bridge between the markets of Asia and Europe. Deutsche Bank and Moody's are expected to be some of the initial participants, while NASDAQ has been tipped as a possible operator of the planned stock exchange. The project has received a key publicity boost with the World Bank and International Monetary Fund Annual Meeting, which was held in Dubai in September 2003.

Dubai International Airport

Dubai International Airport has quickly established itself as the key regional air hub in the Middle East – over 100 airlines operate out of the airport and offer direct links to more than 140 cities. Aside from American carriers who have yet to tap the market, all other major airlines (and a lot that you have probably never heard of), operate regular flights. Major cities, such as London, are served non stop by Emirates (thrice daily), British Airways (twice daily), and other carriers such as Cathay Pacific and Royal Brunei. Because Dubai operates under an 'open skies' policy, there are very few restrictions on foreign airlines' ability to pick up passengers in Dubai and carry them to a third country.

Dubai Airport	
DNATA	295 1111
Dubai Airport	224 5555
Flight Enquiry	216 6666

The ultra modern Rashid Terminal, constructed in the year 2000, is being joined by an adjacent twin sister terminal and dedicated to all Emirates Airlines flights. With a fleet of over 42 planes (most under 10 years old) serving over 64 destinations, Emirates Airlines has already become the carrier of choice in the Middle East. While Emirates is seldom the cheapest option, they offer a high level of service on exceptionally modern, well maintained planes. Emirates has more planes on order and expects to increase the fleet size to at least a hundred planes by 2010.

Dubai International Airport

For the business traveller, this means that Dubai enjoys direct connections on reputable airlines to almost any destination in the world. The recently introduced e-Gate card, available for Dhs.150 (for two years) allows UAE residents to avoid Immigration line-ups with a quick swipe of the card and fingerprint scan. For those travelling without checked in luggage, it is now possible to be out of the airport within 15 minutes from arrival at the gate, including a quick stop at the duty free shop in the arrivals hall.

Airlines

Airline	Phone
Air Arabia	06 508 8888
Air France	294 5899
Air India	227 6787
Alitalia	224 2256
Austrian Airlines	294 5675
British Airways	307 5777
Cathay Pacific Airways	295 0400
CSA Czech Airlines	295 9502
Cyprus Airways	221 5325
Emirates	214 4444
Etihad	02 505 8000
Gulf Air	271 3111
KLM Royal Dutch Airlines	335 5777
Kuwait Airways	228 1106
Lufthansa	343 2121
Malaysia Airlines	397 0250
Olympic Airways	221 4761
Oman Air	351 8080
PIA	222 2154
Qatar Airways	229 2229
Royal Brunei Airlines	351 4111
Royal Jet	02 575 7000
Royal Jordanian	266 8667
Royal Nepal Airlines	295 5444
Saudi Arabian Airlines	295 7747
Singapore Airlines	223 2300
South African Airways	397 0766
SriLankan Airlines	294 9119
Swiss	294 5051
United Airlines	316 6942

Dozens of airlines, including Emirates, Air France, Cathay Pacific and Singapore Airlines, operate regular freight services out of Dubai, taking advantage of the Airport Free Zone and well established air – sea cargo trade moving through Jebel Ali Port. Courier companies such as Aramex, DHL, UPS and Fedex offer fast connections through their airport hubs.

Dubai Ports Authority

While Port Rashid, located next to the mouth of the Creek, was historically considered the main trading entry port for the emirate, the future is clearly focused on Jebel Ali Port, which is the largest man made harbour in the world. The two terminals handle a combined annual throughput of over 4 million TEU (twenty equivalent units) of containers in 2002, which ranks the port within the top 20 container terminals in the world. All of the major shipping lines have regular weekly services connecting Dubai with Europe, the Far East and North America.

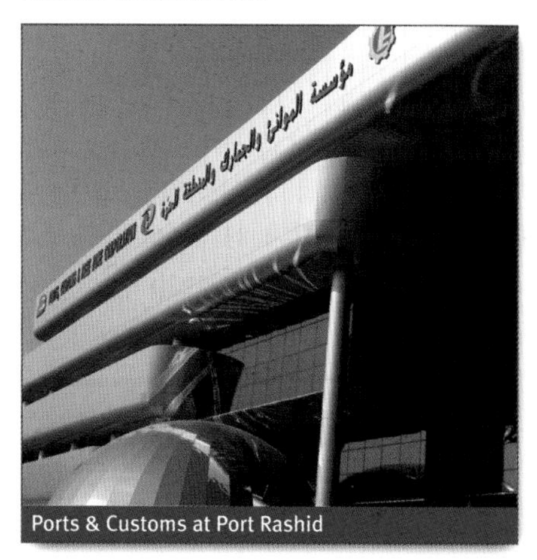
Ports & Customs at Port Rashid

Jebel Ali is also the key transshipment centre for containers and other general cargoes destined for the Arabian Gulf – this trade has been driving up Dubai's traffic to more than 15% per annum over recent years. The wooden dhows at the Creek and Hamriya Port also play a pivotal role in the Dubai economy; demand for these smaller ships, that can discharge almost anywhere along the coast, is largely driven by restrictions and unavailability of the latest consumer goods in other regional countries.

In early 2002, Dubai Ports Authority (DPA) and the Jebel Ali Free Zone Authority (JAFZA) were merged with Dubai Customs to form the Ports, Customs and

Free Zone Corporation. This single corporation controls virtually the entire importation process – from discharging goods (DPA), through warehousing and final processing (JAFZA), and finally, entry into the local market (Customs). The result has been a more business orientated approach to Customs and the introduction of modern, integrated electronic data processes for the arrival and importation of goods into the Dubai market.

Government Departments

Various departments and ministries – both federal and local – are key to setting up and doing business in Dubai. From the Chamber of Commerce, which offers business related services, and the Ministry of Labour, which issues all labour related permits, to the Ministry of Economy, the federal ministry that oversees and regulates all business activity, each now follows recent government mandates to offer advanced e-Government services (often Web based) and improved customer service.

Dubai e-Government recently launched a host of innovative channels, services and initiatives which include mDubai (mobile messages), e4all (a community IT literacy solution), eLibrary (an online library service), e-Job (an online recruiting service), and AskDubai (a contact centre).

Dubai Chamber of Commerce & Industry

The Dubai Chamber of Commerce & Industry (DCCI), located in a modern glass building on the Deira side of the Creek, was set up by the Dubai government to provide a variety of services to the Dubai business community. It promotes commerce through various means, both locally as well as internationally.

Among other activities, the Chamber compiles all business related data for the emirate, issues certificates of origin of commodities and other goods, nominates experts for goods surveying, receives commercial complaints, states and sets standards, defines commercial usage and terminology, and holds economic and commercial conferences.

Every commercial, professional and industrial company must register with the Chamber (very small businesses may be excepted).

Public Relations Officer

Navigating Dubai's various government departments can be an arduous task. Employing the services of a 'Public Relations Officer' (the general term for a professional middleman when dealing with government departments) would prove a sound investment. Generally, these middlemen are savvy persons that have a cultural link to the way government departments function here. The ideal person would be an Arabic speaker and hired by referral ONLY! (There have been cases where PROs have created more problems than solved.)

Dubai Department of Economic Development

Also known as the Economic Department, this is the first department to visit if you plan to open an office. When setting up a business, this institution is key as it is the authority that issues the ever important and necessary trade license. Anyone starting a company outside a free zone will have to deal with this organisation, and will continue to do so as long as they are operating.

The office is located in a modern building in Deira and is always extremely busy – a reflection of the bustling economy.

Government Departments in Dubai

Department of Civil Aviation	224 5333	www.gcaa-uae.com
Department of Economic Development	222 9922	www.dubaided.gov.ae
Department of Health & Medical Services	337 0031	www.dohms.gov.ae
Department of Ports & Drydocks Customs	345 9575	www.dxbcustoms.gov.ae
Department of Tourism and Commerce Marketing	351 1600	www.dubaitourism.co.ae
Dubai Chamber of Commerce & Industry	228 0000	www.dcci.org
Dubai Courts (Department of Justice-Dubai)	334 7777	www.djd.gov.ae
Dubai Development and Investment Authority	330 2222	www.ddia.ae
Dubai Development Board	228 8866	www.dubaidb.gov.ae
Dubai Drydocks	345 0626	www.drydocks.gov.ae
Dubai Duty Free	206 6444	www.dubaidutyfree.com
Dubai Electricity & Water Authority	334 8888	www.dewa.gov.ae
Dubai Municipality	221 5555	www.dm.gov.ae
Dubai Police Headquarters	229 2222	www.dubaipolice.gov.ae
Dubai Ports Authority	881 5000	www.dpa.co.ae

To learn more about the DED's responsibilities or for any trade license related issues, visit their comprehensive Website: www.dubaided.com or www.dubaided.gov.ae, or visit the information counter to collect material. For specific advice, speak to the Corporate Relations Department.

Dubai Municipality

The Municipality is another key government department to deal with when setting up a business outside of a free zone. All companies must gain approval from the Municipality for their premises before setting up; zoning regulations are both devised and enforced here.

Dubai Municipality

Responsible for Dubai's overall structure, the Municipality approves and monitors all construction in this emirate. Besides creating and maintaining urban landscaping, from public parks to 'greened' roundabouts and medians, the department also provides Dubai residents and companies with all municipal services (transportation infrastructure etc) as well as environmental protection and regulation, and public health services. The Dubai Municipality is comprised of numerous departments, each located in a different area within the city; the head office is located in Deira, near Etisalat. The food control section of this department is what controls and approves any import of food items.

Ministry of Economy & Commerce

The Ministry of Economy is the federal institution overseeing all economic activity in Dubai. It plays a supervisory and regulatory role in setting up all commercial companies.

Foreign companies wanting to set up a branch in Dubai, as well as insurance companies, agents and brokers, must obtain approval from this Ministry.

The Ministry of Economy also handles the registration of commercial agents/agencies. Other responsibilities include issuing certificates of origin for national exports and the protection of trademarks.

Dept. of Immigration & Naturalization Services

Once the trade license is issued, the office is set, one would need to have residence visa, and in order to have residence visa for the investor or his/her employees, it is required to have a immigration card (also known as computer card). Normally a PRO (see [p.140]) is hired to deal with all government related matters, especially Department of Labour and Department of Immigration matters. As mentioned previously, it is strongly advised to hire a PRO either full or part time.

Department of Health & Medical Services

It is required by UAE law for all foreign nationals to have a health/medical card (even if they have medical insurance from the private sector, within the UAE or from elsewhere). The health card is issued by hospitals run by the Department of Health and Medical Services (see Health Card [p.62]).

Ministry of Labour & Social Affairs

This Ministry is a federal institution and is responsible for labour issues and approval of all labour related permits (with the exception of some free zones). Only official representatives of companies deal directly with this Ministry, which is particularly strict on who is allowed to enter the building and submit documents. Only an officially authorised person, such as the company owner, sponsor or PRO (public relations officer), may perform the labour related procedures for each company. (PROs have special ID cards, which have to be presented to the officials at the counter.) This Ministry also issues the UAE Labour Law (see [p.76]).

The Dubai Development & Investment Authority

The role of this government authority is to increase the growth rate of Dubai's economy by attracting corporate and private investors and facilitating leading local businesses. Their methods include developing strategies to attract inward private sector investment into Dubai, mobilising domestic capital resources for growth and innovation, marketing the business benefits of Dubai to leading global companies and

helping these companies develop additional value added services. Visit their Website (www.ddia.ae).

Doing Business

Aside from Agency Law (see [p.146]), which is in many cases avoidable by establishing in one of the various free zones, Dubai is an enjoyable and rewarding place to live and do business. There are many exciting business opportunities for companies and entrepreneurs to serve an increasingly sophisticated and growing market.

The sheer scope of public sponsored projects currently being implemented throughout Dubai, such as The Palm Islands (over US$2 billion), The World, Dubai Pearl, Dubai Internet & Media Cities, Knowledge Village, Boutique City, Children's City, Dubai Festival City (over US$2 billion), Dubai Healthcare City (US$1.8 billion), Burj Dubai (which will be the world's tallest building) and the Dubai Airport expansion (approximately US$2.5 billion) will virtually ensure sustained economic growth over the next 5 - 10 years. When combined with huge private sector investments in commercial, manufacturing, distribution, and residential facilities, there are countless opportunities in the trade, retail and service sectors of the economy.

Multinational corporations have also recognised the rewards of setting up a base in Dubai, particularly in the various free zones. The top 10 Fortune 500 firms have a regional office or base in Dubai, along with numerous others, usually conducting international trade in the Middle East and Africa region.

Business Groups & Contacts

In addition to the various government departments specifically responsible for providing commercial assistance to enterprises in Dubai, there are various chambers of commerce and other business groups that help facilitate investments, and provide opportunities for networking with others in the community. Some groups provide information on trade with their respective country, as well as on business opportunities, both in Dubai and internationally. Most also arrange social and networking events on a regular basis.

Embassies or consulates can also be a good business resource and may be able to offer contact lists for the UAE and the country of representation.

Embassies/Consulates	
Australian Consulate	321 2444
Bahrain Consulate	665 7500
Canadian Consulate	314 5555
Chinese Consulate	398 4357
Danish Consulate, Royal	222 7699
Egyptian Consulate	397 1122
French Consulate	332 9040
German Consulate	397 2333
Indian Consulate	397 1222
Iranian Consulate	344 4717
Italian Consulate	331 4167
Japanese Consulate	331 9191
Jordanian Consulate	397 0500
Kuwaiti Consulate	397 8000
Lebanese Consulate	397 7450
Malaysian Consulate	335 5528
Netherlands Consulate	352 8700
Norway, Consulate of	353 3833
Omani Consulate	397 1000
Pakistani Consulate	397 0412
Qatar Consulate	398 2888
Saudi Arabian Consulate	397 9777
South African Consulate	397 5222
Sri Lankan Consulate	398 6535
Switzerland, Consulate of	329 0999
Thai Consulate	349 2863
UK Consulate	397 1070
USA Consulate General	311 6000

The Popular GITEX Exhibition

Trade Centres and Commissions

Canadian Trade Commission	314 5555
Cyprus Trade Centre	228 2411
Danish Trade Centre	222 7699
Egyptian Trade Centre	222 1098
Export Promotion Council of Norway	353 3833
French Trade Commision	331 3887
German Office of Foreign Trade	352 0413
Hong Kong Trade Development Council	223 3499
Indian State Trading Corporation	397 1222
Italian Trade Commission	331 4951
Japan External Trade Organization	332 8264
Korean Trade Centre	332 7776
Malaysian Trade Centre	335 5528
Philippine Embassy	223 6526
Polish Trade Centre	223 5837
Singapore Trade Centre	222 9789
South African Consulate	397 5222
Spanish Commercial Office	331 3565
Sultanate of Oman Office	397 1000
Taiwan Trade Centre	396 7814
Thailand Trade Centre	396 7814
Trade Representative of the Netherlands	352 8700
USA Consulate General	311 6000

Business Councils

American Business Council	331 4735
Australian Business in the Gulf	395 4423
British Business Group	397 0303
Canadian Business Council	335 8975
Denmark Business Council	222 7699
French Business Council	335 2362
German Business Council	359 9930
Iranian Business Council	344 4717
Pakistan Business Council	337 2875
South African Business Group	397 5222
Swedish Business Council	337 1410
Swiss Business Council	321 1438

Business Culture

Other options → **Culture [p.17]**

Customs

Despite its cosmopolitan outward appearance, Dubai is an Arab city in a Muslim country and people doing business in Dubai must remember this fact. Even if your counterpart in another company is an expatriate, the head decision maker may be a UAE National who might take a different approach to business matters. Your best bet when doing business in Dubai for the first time is to observe closely, have lots of patience and make a concerted effort to understand the culture and respect the customs. Once you understand the customs and culture, follow them (and keep a hold of that patience!).

Although women have not made significant inroads into mainstream business, there are both National and expatriate women in Dubai who have risen to positions of prominence.

Remember, as in any community, networking is critical even across industries. Dubai is a very small community with the setting of a large urban city. Business acumen here can, at times, be more important than specific industry knowledge. Keep your finger on the pulse of activity by attending business events and trade shows. Make friends in government departments where your business has direct interfaces, and this will often land you in the front line of opportunities. Likewise, bad news is rarely made public here, so staying in tune with the grapevine can help prevent wrong decisions.

Etiquette

Tea and coffee are a very important part of Arabic life and it may be considered rude to refuse this offer of hospitality during a meeting. Tilting the small Arabic coffee cup back and forth several times with your fingers will signal that you do not want another refill.

Although proper dress is important for all business dealings, the local climate has dictated that a shirt and tie (for men) is sufficient for all but the most important of business encounters; women usually choose a suit or a skirt and a blouse that are not excessively revealing.

In Arabic society, a verbal commitment (once clearly made) is ethically if not legally binding; reasonable bargaining is an important part of reaching any such agreement. And finally, it is important to remember that Dubai is still a relatively small business community, so confidentiality and discretion are of the utmost importance in all business dealings.

Meetings

A strong handshake should not only start each meeting, but also end the encounter – a longer handshake at the end is an indication that the meeting has gone well. It is always preferable to start a meeting with a non business discussion, but avoid enquiring about somebody's wife, even if you know the wife – general enquiries about the family are more appropriate.

Don't be surprised if other people walk in and out during the meeting to discuss unrelated matters, and be prepared for the meeting to run longer than expected.

While meeting agendas, it might be important to ensure that all relevant matters are discussed – they are better used as a checklist (at the end) instead of a schedule for discussions during the meeting.

It is also a good idea not to jump to conclusions at the end of a good meeting. Try to do background work on the people you have met to understand how much influence they wield in a decision making tree. You will rarely have someone admit (due to cultural norms) how little or how great their influence is on a business decision!

Time

While punctuality for meetings is very important, the visitor must always remember to be patient if the host is delayed, due to an unforeseen (and possibly more important!) other visitor. Also remember, traffic accidents on Sheikh Zayed road are a very predictable event (they happen every day), so plan ahead, and don't be forced to use them as an excuse for being late.

Business Hours

Other options → **Social & Business Hours [p.14]**
Ramadan [p.19]
Working Hours [p.74]

Dubai has no set in stone business hours, or even fixed working days for that matter. Government departments generally work between 07:00 - 14:00 (Saturday – Wednesday), although departments providing services to the public sometimes offer extended hours. Many multinational companies prefer the Sunday to Thursday work week, which provides greater overlap with other international offices, while other companies work a straight six day week (Saturday – Thursday). Private sector offices normally work a 08:00 - 17:00 or a 09:00 - 18:00 day, though some take advantage of the Labour Law guidelines and make the most of their employees' time with a 08:00 - 18:00 work day.

Banks remain open until about 13:00 on weekdays but close early on Thursdays, while large supermarkets generally maintain hours between 09:00 and 22:00 throughout the week. Shopping malls are open for about 12 hours, starting from

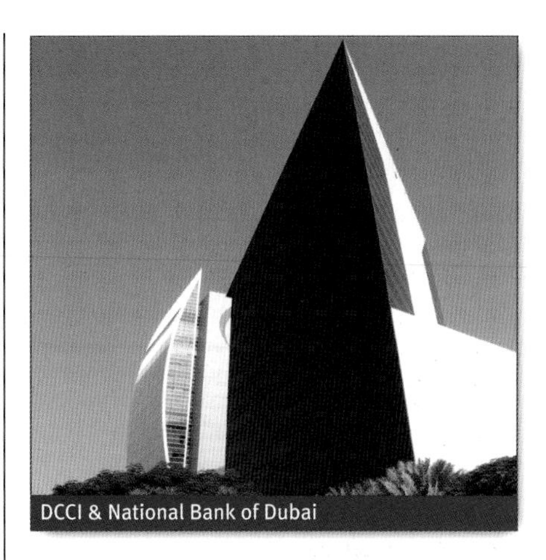
DCCI & National Bank of Dubai

10:00 (later on Friday), while other shops in the city generally close between 13:00 and 16:30.

During the holy month of Ramadan, working hours for government and some private sector companies are reduced by two or more hours, while shops and malls open later in the day and stay open much later in the evening. Call ahead to avoid frustration.

Laws

Laws & Regulations

As with many countries in the Middle East, UAE law requires that companies have a local (UAE National) participant holding at least 51% of the shares. While there has been discussion of easing or even removing these ownership restrictions, no change in the regulations is imminent. 100% foreign ownership is permitted for the following:

- a company located in a UAE free zone (see [p.149])
- a company with activities open to 100% GCC ownership (Gulf Co-operation Council: Saudi Arabia, Oman, Kuwait, Qatar & the UAE)
- a company in which wholly owned GCC companies enter into partnership with UAE Nationals
- a branch or representative office of a foreign company registered in Dubai
- a professional or artisan company practising business activities that allow 100% foreign ownership

Agency Law

By law, foreign nationals intending to set up a company such as a sole proprietorship, a branch of a foreign company or a professional company, must find a National agent and sign a local (national) service agency agreement with him. The local agent is usually referred to as a 'sponsor'.

The sponsor does not have any responsibility for the business, but he is obliged to assist with all government related procedures such as obtaining government permits, trade licenses, visas, and labour cards. His signature will be required for most application forms.

Dubai Courts

A sponsor may be a UAE National or a company fully owned by UAE Nationals. The choice of a sponsor can be of significant importance, particularly for a larger company. Appointing a sponsor who is considered prominent and influential can open many doors that might otherwise be extremely difficult to access. Local sponsors may be paid a lump sum and/or a percentage of the profits or turnover.

A foreign national looking to establish a business in Dubai must place a lot of trust in this system – before choosing an agent, it is highly advisable to first investigate his reputation in the market, and agree on each party's rights and responsibilities. Once established, it is very difficult to break an agency agreement, except in the case of cessation of activity.

Commercial Agent

If a foreign company wants to supply goods and/or services from abroad without establishing a physical presence in Dubai, it can appoint a commercial agent as a distributor for its goods and/or services in the UAE. The agent is entitled to exclusive rights to distribute and market specific products and services within a specific territory. The company is not allowed to distribute these products in that territory. If the company does assist in a sale, its commercial agent is entitled to a commission.

Such a commercial agency also covers franchises, distributorships and commission arrangements. The agent must register the agency agreement with the Ministry of Economy.

Disputes

The UAE legal system has its roots in French and Egyptian law. In the event of a dispute, it is highly advisable that you undertake good legal counsel. Generally, you can measure the '*wasta*' a consultant has by the cases he handles (wasta – a very important term in business here; essentially means 'influence' that one has over the powers that be).

Financial Issues

The primary dispute that you will encounter in the UAE is the flow of payments for goods and services. At present, there is no credit measurement system in the UAE that helps determine creditworthiness. This leads to fearlessness of paying late! Credit granting decisions are taken on history, reputation and legacy (bad criteria at times for judging creditworthiness!).

Be wary of extending credit and be sure to ask around in the banking community where your industry tends to gravitate on potential customers. Additionally, run the gamut in your industry and collect information on your potential customer. You'll be able to find a semblance of their reputation (rumours filtered out).

Legal Consultants

Afridi & Angell	331 0900
Al Tamimi & Company	331 7090
Clifford Chance	331 4333
Clyde & Company	331 1102
Denton Wilde Sapte	331 0220
James Berry & Assosiates	351 1020
Stockwell & Assosiates	228 3194
Towry Law Group	335 3137
Trench & Associates	355 3146
Towers & Hamlins	351 9201

Lastly, talk to your competitors and see what you can get from them (difficult, but you may find a sympathetic ear from those who've been burned before).

A solid way to measure the depth of your customer is to get an understanding of how willing they are to put up deposits or provide post dated cheques. Post dated cheques are the securest form of payment here, as there is criminal recourse for not clearing them. Some banks are willing to offer you a discount for payments prior to maturity (also depending upon company and reputation). The key here is not to wave the legal flag too quickly. Be patient and work with your customers; it's a vicious circle and, quite possibly, on their end the money could be held up by their own customers. Additionally, the chance of legally seeing a quick return on your dues is slim. Courts here pass judgement on the ability to pay; not amounts owed (ie, a Dhs.1 million debt could be settled for Dhs.1,000 a month, as long as the defendant can prove inability to pay).

Labour Law

Other options → **Banning [p.76]**

The UAE Labour Law is very employer friendly. The Federal Ministry of Labour & Social Affairs administers labour issues. The law is loosely based on the International Labour Organisation's model and deals with employer/employee relations such as working hours, termination rights, benefits and repatriation. Little recourse for employees exists and exploitation does occur, particularly amongst blue collar workers and labourers. Trade unions do not exist and strikes are forbidden.

Government workers and employees of quasi government institutions are not necessarily subject to the UAE Labour Law. Some free zones, including the Jebel Ali Free Zone Authority, have their own labour rules and the Authority settles disputes without recourse to the Federal Ministry. A copy of the UAE Labour Law can be obtained from the Dubai offices of the Ministry of Labour (269 1666). The law applies to all staff and employees working in the United Arab Emirates, whether UAE National or expatriate, barring a few exempt categories. The law also deals with all aspects of employee-employer relationships: the contracts, employment restrictions on women and children, salaries, working hours, leave, employee protection, medical care, benefits and compensation.

Legal Eagle

If you are working with intellectual property (ie, music, publishing, software etc), be sure to register your trademarks and copyrights with the Dubai Chamber of Commerce & Industry. This ensures you have legal recourse in case there are any illegal attempts to resell your material. Without this registration, you will not be recognised as the owner!

Copyright Law

Introduced in 1993, the UAE Copyright Law was most recently updated in 2002 with the development of Federal Copyright Law No.7. This law, which is overseen by the Ministry of Information and Culture, protects the rights of creators, performers, producers of audio recordings as well as broadcasting and recording corporations.

Trademark Law

The UAE Federal Government first introduced its trademark law in 1974, then updated it in 1993. Throughout, the government has continually improved its efforts to protect registered trademark owners. Trademark registration in the UAE is done through the Ministry of Economy and Commerce. The entire registration process can take anywhere from 12 to 18 months. Under the UAE trademark law, trademark owners can now protect their marks and count on government assistance to penalise those infringing upon their trademark.

Setting Up

It is difficult to provide 'hard and fast' rules for those wishing to set up a company in Dubai. The main difficulty in providing this information arises from the amount of variables involved. Rules depend on nationality, business activity, capital amounts, partners, products etc, and the laws and/or

regulations change on a regular basis. Check with the relevant government department(s) before proceeding.

After obtaining a trade license, there are generally five set up options for non GCC nationals. These are: setting up a branch of a foreign company, a limited liability company (LLC), a sole proprietorship, a professional company, and setting up in a free zone.

Trade Licence

Grab a copy of the *Zappy Explorer (Dubai)* to sufficiently arm yourself with knowledge of the procedure involved. Next, visit the Department for Corporate Relations and the Investment Promotion Centre at the Dubai Economic Department (DED). In an effort to promote investment, and in particular, foreign investment, this friendly and efficient department will assist with the paperwork involved in obtaining a trade license, which is the first step in setting up. The Dhs.200 - 500 fee is worthwhile, and will save numerous headaches. The office is located in the DED head office on the first floor.

Getting a Trade License

Once you've decided on your line of business, and type of licence (ie, branch or representative office, limited liability company, sole proprietorship, professional company, distributorship etc), the typical steps to follow would be:

If the business is to be located outside a free zone, find a reliable UAE National.

Then visit a reputable 'documents typing and photo copy' centre, preferably one near the Economic Department. All relevant forms are available with them. Alternatively, you can opt for companies who, for a fee, take care of all formalities, even that of finding a local sponsor/partner. However, finding a local sponsor/partner through personal contacts is highly recommended.

This local sponsor/partner will charge an annual fee, which is based on the size of the operation and personal contact (anywhere from Dhs.6,000 to Dhs. 40,000).

Also, a combination of the agreement and power of attorney is required between the investor/owner and the local sponsor/partner, which is to be attested by the notary public's office (charges around Dhs.55).

If the company is an LLC (see p.[148]), approximately Dhs.250,000 must be shown as bank guarantee to the Economic Department. In the case of sole proprietorship, around Dhs.150,000 is needed.

Branch or Representative Office

Established foreign companies may set up a branch or a representative office of their firm in Dubai. The branch will be considered a part of the parent company and not a separate legal entity. A representative office, unlike a branch office, is permitted to practice promotional services for the company and products and also facilitate contacting potential customers.

Be wise... get a PRO

Although laws exist, there is always some preferential treatment for a special segment of the population. Again, it is strongly advised to hire a Public Relations Officer (PRO), preferably an Arabic speaker. Selection of a PRO should be done carefully to avoid misdealing (selection of a PRO by referral is recommended).

For the complete branch or representative office setting up procedure, including costs, timing, tips and advice, refer to the *Zappy Explorer (Dubai)*.

Limited Liability Company (LLC)

An LLC is a business structure that is a hybrid of a partnership and a corporation. Its owners are shielded from personal liability; the liability of the shareholders is limited to their shares in the company's capital.

This company type suits organisations interested in developing a long term relationship in the local market. Responsibility for the management of an LLC can be vested in either the National or foreign partners, or in a third party.

Refer to the *Zappy Explorer (Dubai)* for the complete LLC setting up procedure, including costs, timing, tips and advice.

Sole Proprietorship

A sole proprietorship, by definition, means 'one owner'. This is the most basic company form where the owner has a trade license in his name and is personally held liable for his accounts, ie, he is responsible for the company's financial and legal obligations. The proprietor can conduct business in the commercial, professional, industrial or agricultural industries.

Nationals and GCC nationals are permitted to set up a sole proprietorship with few restrictions. Stricter conditions apply for non GCC nationals.

A non GCC national setting up a sole proprietorship is restricted in the type of activities he may perform. The company should be in a service or knowledge based industry.

For the complete sole proprietorship setting up procedure, including costs, timing, tips and advice, refer to the *Zappy Explorer (Dubai)*.

Professional Company

Also referred to as a business partnership, professional business company, or consultancy business, this company type falls under the civil code rather than under commercial law. This differentiation is unique to the UAE. Such firms may engage in professional or artisan activities, but the number of staff members that may be employed is limited and a UAE National must be appointed as a local service agent.

An important part in applying for the license is showing evidence of the credentials and qualifications of the employees and partners.

Check out the *Zappy Explorer (Dubai)* for the complete professional company setting up procedure, including costs, timing, tips and advice.

Free Zones

Other options → **Free Zones [p.149]**

Jebel Ali Free Zone Authority (JAFZA), established in 1985 at an estimated cost of over US$2 billion, has become a runaway success and today is home to almost 2,500 companies from about 100 different countries. The signboards dotting the free zone are a who's who of both Fortune 500 companies and local business houses. The original area between the port and Sheikh Zayed Road is almost full, and massive efforts are underway to develop the desert on the other side of the road. JAFZA offers investors 100% control of their business, duty free import of products (for manufacturing/transit/export), leasehold land ownership and guaranteed freedom from corporate taxation.

Dubai Internet City

The success of JAFZA has spawned competing facilities in Sharjah, Ajman, Fujairah and Ras al Khaimah. Although these other free zones offer lower fees, JAFZA still remains the preferred choice for many companies due to the excellent infrastructure and relatively easy administrative procedures. Dubai's other innovative free zones are Dubai Internet City (DIC) and Dubai Media City (DMC), the Dubai Airport Free Zone and the newly announced Dubai International Financial Centre among many other upcoming ventures. Each of these free zones offers investors 100% control of their business.

Other upcoming developments in Dubai include the Dubai HealthCare City (www.dhcc.ae), Dubai Maritime City, a state of the art development that will provide every element of infrastructure required by key marine and maritime related industries (www.dubaimaritimecity.com), Techno Park, Dubai Silicon Oasis (www.dso.ae), Dubai Business Park (www.unionproperties.com) and Dubai Investments Park (www.dip.ae).

For details on setting up in any of the UAE's free zones, have a look at their respective Websites. For the setting up procedure for JAFZA, DIC or DMC, pick up a copy of the *Zappy Explorer (Dubai)*.

UAE Free Zones	
Ajman Free Zone	06 742 5444
Dubai Airport Free Zone	04 299 5555
Dubai Healthcare City	04 324 5555
Dubai International Financial Centre	04 330 0100
Dubai Internet City	04 391 1111
Dubai Maritime City	04 390 3820
Dubai Media City	04 391 4615
Fujairah Free Zone	09 222 8000
Hamriyah Free Zone	06 526 3333
Jebel Ali Free Zone (JAFZA)	04 881 5000
RAK Free Zone	07 228 0889
Sharjah Airport Free Zone Authority	06 557 0000
UAQ Ahmed Bin Rashid Free Zone	06 765 5882

Dubai Internet City

This hub of technology, situated amidst scenic grounds, offers foreign companies 100% tax free ownership, 100% repatriation of capital and profits, no currency restrictions, easy registration and licensing, stringent cyber regulations and protection of intellectual property. The ICT companies housed here offer software development, business services, web based & e-commerce, consultancy, education & training, sales & marketing and back office operations. For more information, check out their Website (www.dubaiinternetcity.com).

Dubai Media City

Quite the venue for all media activities, the Media City has become a local media hub, providing the right infrastructure and environment for any media related business. Companies in this free zone are not subject to censorship within the broad guidelines of the country's moral code. The rapidly growing list of names housed here covers broadcasting, publishing, advertising, public relations, research, music, production and new media. Names such as CNN, Reuters, Sony and MBC are among the 550 plus media companies. Also popular here is the interdependent media community with over 170 freelance media professionals offering a range of creative skills. Benefits of creating a company base here include 100% company ownership along with a 50 year tax exemption from personal, income and corporate taxes. Their Website (www.dubaimediacity.com) keeps you abreast of the current and future activities within this hub, and is nicely packed with information on services offered.

Selecting an Office or Warehouse

When applying for a trade licence, the rent agreement is normally required as part of the documentation. Ensure you select a location for your premises in an area in which you are permitted to perform your business activity. Dubai has strict zoning rules, which restrict where a company may open an office or warehouse. Approval must be gained from the Dubai Municipality and will depend on the business activity.

Don't sign a tenancy agreement for a warehouse or office before the Dubai Economic Department (DED) has contacted the Municipality and approved it. If the property is leased from or granted by the Government of Dubai, you will also need a sub lease no objection letter from the Real Estate Department.

In the last year, Dubai has announced freehold offices in the Dubai Marina and other areas allocated for freehold properties. You can monitor this through the real estate classifieds in the local newspapers or through real estate brokers who specialise in commercial space.

Dubai Media City

The Banks in Dubai

Office Rents

Office rents in Dubai compare with those of most international cities. Rents are usually calculated by the square foot and vary depending on location. Certain areas, such as Sheikh Zayed Road and Dubai Internet & Media Cities tend to have much higher rents than other areas due to their prime location and high demand. Building facilities vary from none to those including a health club, restaurants, retail outlets and assigned parking. Leases are on an annual basis and must be paid up front or with up to four postdated cheques.

Serviced Offices

As an alternative to the hassle and expense involved in finding and leasing office space, fully serviced offices are now being offered by a number of companies in Dubai. This is a good option if you are starting up a small business, for normally, the facilities and services offered are of top quality. Serviced offices are fully furnished and come equipped with a high speed Internet connection, telephone lines, business support services etc.

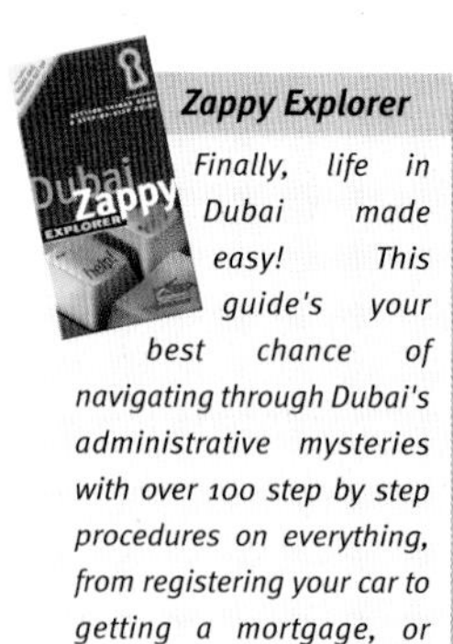

The Gulf Business Centre (332 8850) offers fully serviced apartments within the Crowne Plaza complex on Sheikh Zayed Road. The international corporation, Regus, (211 5100) has serviced offices plus gym facilities in the Union House Building across from the Deira City Centre shopping mall. The Signature Business Club (332 8990) also offers fully serviced offices at the Fairmont Hotel for a single monthly charge.

Land Ownership

Currently, foreign companies and non nationals are not permitted to own commercial land in the UAE other than in free zones, where leasehold ownership is offered. Commercial property must be either rented or leased, and rates are high.

The year 2002 witnessed significant changes in land ownership rules for residential properties, where leasehold and freehold ownership opportunities emerged for non Nationals (see, 'Selecting an office or warehouse [p.50]).

Work Permits

Other options → **Visas [p.21]**
Residence Visa [p.64]
Labour Card [p.65]

The employer is responsible for all work permits and related immigration procedures; this can be quite a tedious endeavour, so be warned and start the process early. If setting up in a free zone, the free zone authority will handle all immigration related procedures, which simplifies the process dramatically but costs slightly more. The company must cover all costs (visa, medical test etc) involved in hiring an employee. Costs for family members are the employee's responsibility unless otherwise stated in the employment contract.

Labour Contracts

Other options → **Employment Contracts [p.76]**

When applying for a work permit, the Ministry of Labour provides a model labour contract in Arabic. It is advisable to draft an additional contract with further employment and benefit details, particularly for senior staff. The employment contract is enforceable in a court of law (except in the case of some free zones) as long as it does not contravene the Labour Law. In a court of law, the Arabic version of the contract will prevail.

Staffing

Other options → **Finding Work [p.74]**

For companies operating outside the free zones, the Ministry of Labour will set a maximum number of expatriate staff that may be hired, according to the size of the business and the business activity. In some cases, such as banks, the Ministry will state the minimum percentage of employees that must be UAE Nationals.

Recruitment of staff is an entirely separate challenge. Various agencies can assist with the recruitment of labourers from overseas, while other local recruiters specialise in searches for professional and managerial positions. In reality, many positions are filled through word of mouth between friends and business colleagues, and also through 'wasta' (connections).

Customs

Other options → **Customs [p.23]**

Imports to Dubai (and the UAE) are subject to 4% customs duty, which is applied at the time of delivery at the port or airport; there are no duties on the import of personal effects. No customs duties are payable on goods that do not leave the various free zones.

The Gulf Co-operation Council (GCC) announced plans for a GCC Customs Union, which took effect in 2003. Under the terms of this agreement, all six GCC countries apply a rate of 5% to imports.

Taxation

Although UAE law provides for taxation, no personal income taxes or corporate taxes are actually levied and collected, either in the city or the free zones; the free zones offer additional guarantees to companies concerning their future tax free status. The UAE has double taxation treaties with various countries, although the effectiveness of these treaties is limited, given that the effective tax rates in the UAE are nil. The only corporations subject to income taxes in the UAE are courier companies, oil companies and branches of foreign banks.

Exchange Controls

Other options → **Money [p.42]**
Banks [p.44]

The UAE dirham (AED or Dhs.) is pegged to the US Dollar at the rate of about 3.67 dirhams per dollar, and never fluctuates significantly from this level. Due to the strength of the local economy, the large foreign currency reserves, the lack of advanced financial currency products, and restrictions on foreign share ownership, the dirham has not been attacked by foreign speculators and is perceived to be a safe currency.

There are no foreign exchange controls, and there are generally no restrictions on repatriating capital and/or earnings. In an attempt to control problems of money laundering, banks are supposed to report all transactions in excess of Dhs.40,000 to the government, although pre-approval is not required. September 11 changed things considerably, and now the Central Bank keeps an eye on all kinds of bank transactions. Now, even when opening a bank account, background checks are conducted.

White Collar Crime

Like everywhere in the world, here too there are instances of white collar crime, so companies must establish proper audit controls. However, companies exert a greater level of control over their employees because most are expatriates.

In the UAE, it is considered a crime to issue a cheque for which insufficient funds exist in the bank account – penalties for this offence range from a fine to imprisonment. The authorities tend to favour the more extreme punishment for this crime – be warned!

Sheikh Zayed Road

Exploring EXPLORER

Exploring

What's new?

Visitors' Checklist

Page 162

Toothbrush... check! Sun-cream... check! Underpants... check! Well that wasn't quite what we had in mind when lovingly providing this fab checklist, but what you will see, is an easy to use list of Explorer recommended unique ways in which to cherish your stay in Dubai – other than shopping of course...

Will You Or Won't You?

Page 158

To make your life a little easier, and as a quick reference to the different areas in Dubai, turn to Highlights for a summary of each area in Dubai. The main points of interest are listed out, that may (or may not) inspire you to jump in a cab and check things out for yourself.

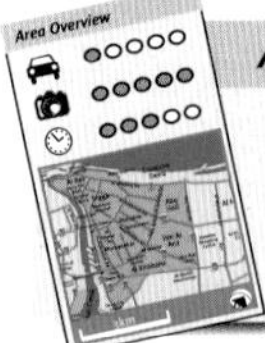

Area Overview Maps

Page 158

A car icon denotes accessibility; whether it's possible to drive there, how easy is it to get a parking spot, or would it be wiser to just cab it. A camera icon indicates its 'tourist' value, and a clock icon depicts the length of time that can be easily spent in exploring your surroundings.

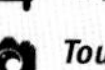

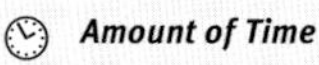

Car/Traffic
Touristic Value
Amount of Time

Dubai Areas

Exploring

Known as the City of Gold or the City of Lights, Dubai is simply unique and for many travellers it's where 'East meets West'. The following section is aimed at everyone, whether you have chosen Dubai for a holiday, or find yourself here on a long flight stopover, or if you work/live here, and think you know it all. As well as being voted the safest holiday destination by Conde Nast Traveller magazine for the past two years, Dubai has many reasons to be proud. From the highest hotel standards, including the famous Burj Al Arab and many other top hotels, to chic shopping malls, beach resorts, amazing night life and a variety of sporting activities, pretty much everything is covered. There are also numerous photographic opportunities; mosques, palaces, dhows, camel and horse racing, sunsets, architecture, windtowers, to name a few. However, in addition to all the modern conveniences, it is interesting to explore the places where old meets new.

This cosmopolitan city has something for everyone and just when you think you have heard it all, Dubai comes up with something fresh; whether it's the world's tallest building, the world's largest shopping mall, the first underwater luxury hotel or a ski slope in the desert! To see what you can cram into a one or two day stopover, refer to the Visitors Checklist [p.162], while for a leisurely week or two, refer to the Guide Checklist or to explore it all, read on!

Also covered are places out of Dubai, although for more information on Abu Dhabi, the Sultanate of Oman and off the beaten track in the UAE, refer to the *Abu Dhabi Explorer*, the *Oman Explorer* and the *Off-Road Explorer (UAE)*, all by Explorer Publishing.

Dubai's heart is still considered to be the Creek, where early settlers built their mud and palm frond huts – difficult to imagine now, when you see the Creek lined with skyscrapers. However, the modern city is developing into a linear coastal settlement, mainly spreading southwest towards Abu Dhabi. The 15 km long Creek is about 500 metres wide, and has three main crossing points; the Al Shindagha Tunnel nearest the sea, then the Al Maktoum Bridge and furthest inland, the Al Garhoud Bridge. For each of the main geographical areas of Dubai, we have described the key activities and landmarks. Dubai Creek divides the city into two areas – to the south is known as Bur Dubai and to the north as Deira. On the Bur Dubai side of the city are Oud Metha (a recreational and commercial area), Satwa and Karama (both original suburbs of old Dubai), plus Jumeira and Umm Suqeim (originally fishing settlements) further along the coast away from the Creek. Further past Umm Suqeim on the way to Abu Dhabi, is Jebel Ali, which is the most southerly point of the city, and famous for its port and free zone (these can be seen from space). The road leading to Jebel Ali and Abu Dhabi is the Sheikh Zayed Road, an eight lane highway lined with skyscrapers. Areas north of the Creek include Al Garhoud, the district close to the airport, and the newer residential development of Mirdif. Wherever you go, don't forget to take along the best guide available – your pull-out map from the back of this book.

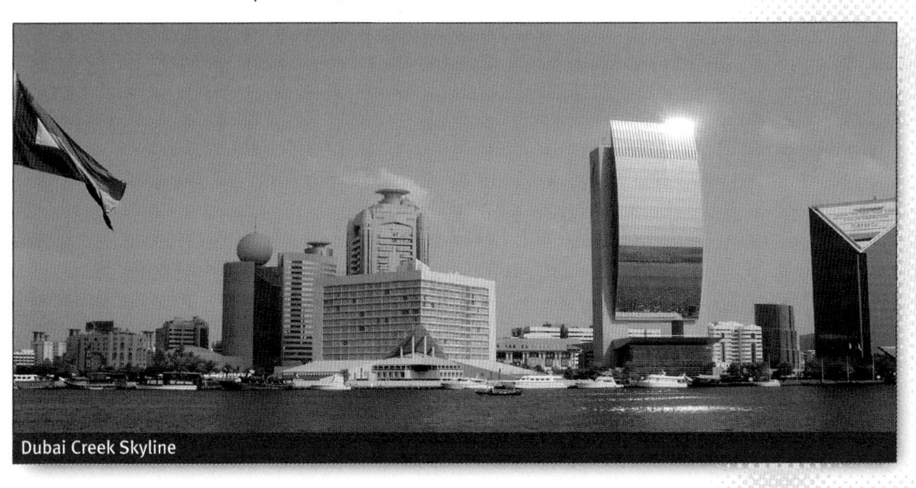
Dubai Creek Skyline

Dubai – Main Areas

Dubai Creek

The Creek has played a pivotal role in the development of Dubai, and it neatly divides the modern city into two distinct areas (Bur Dubai to the south and Deira to the north). In Arabia, like anywhere in the world, a creek or waterway made a natural environment to build a community around. The earliest Dubai settlement was near the mouth of the Creek, but when it was dredged to create a larger anchorage and encourage trade, the growing town gradually crept further inland.

Dubai Creek has three main crossing points – Al Shindagha Tunnel nearest to the sea, then Al Maktoum Bridge and furthest inland, Al Garhoud Bridge. Both bridges can be raised to allow boats through to the boatyard inland, but this usually only happens late at night. There is also a pedestrian foot tunnel near Al Shindagha.

The layout of the roads and the heat, especially in summer, do not make Dubai the easiest city to explore on foot, however, some parts are well worth the effort of walking around. In particular, these include the souks and the corniche areas on both sides of the Creek, which can be combined with an atmospheric 'abra' (water taxi) crossing. The word 'corniche' refers to any walkway by a stretch of water – in the UAE this can be along the seafront or around one of the creeks or lagoons.

A useful guide is the *Dubai Town Walk Explorer* (Dhs.10), which outlines two routes through the most interesting parts of the city. It is available from all good bookshops or directly from Explorer Publishing.

Whilst there are three main crossing points of the Creek, a more exciting way of crossing it is by boat. Known locally as abras, these water taxis ply between the two banks as they have done for decades. The abra crossing takes about ten minutes and can be made in either direction from the dhow wharfage area on the Deira side or Al Seef Road in Bur Dubai. The basic wooden boats seat about 30 people and are used as a convenient and cheap method of transport. For visitors, they are a great way to see the modern towers of Deira, the older Arabic architecture of Bur Dubai and to get a real feel of the city. At 50 fils, it's probably the cheapest tour in the world! The steps down to the Creek are steep and can be slippery, so be careful when stepping across to your boat.

Alternatively, for Dhs.40 - 50, you can hire a boat and driver for a private river tour for half an hour.

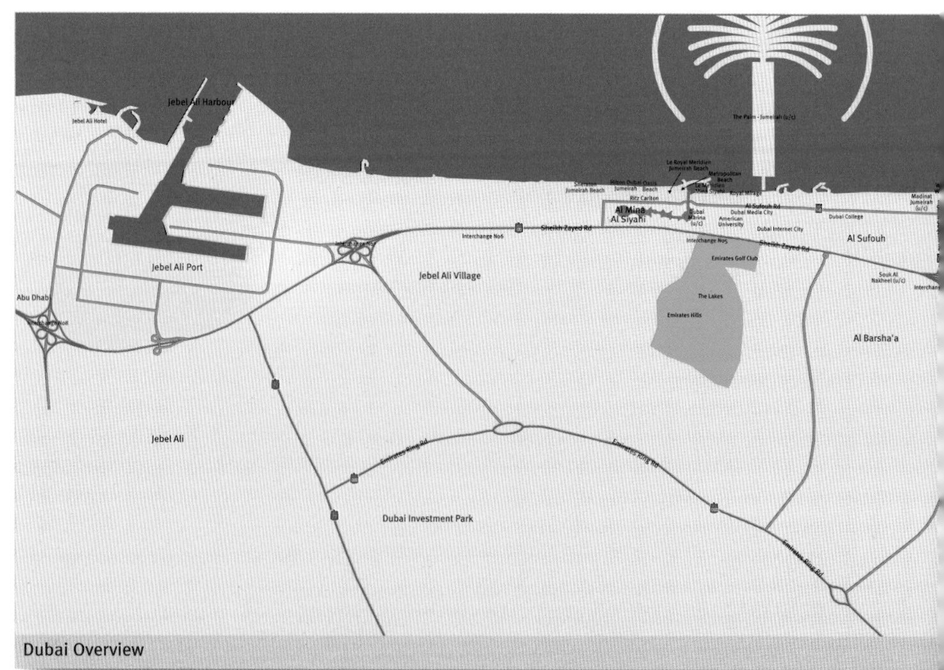

Dubai Overview

A View of the Creek

For a more luxurious tour of the Creek, consider an organised boat trip. For further details, refer to the Creek Tours table.

Creek Tours

For a more luxurious tour of the Creek than by abra, an organised Creek tour is a wonderful way to see new and old Dubai side by side, while enjoying a peaceful and relaxing journey. Prices per adult range from about Dhs.35 for a daytime trip to Dhs.260 for an evening cruise with dinner. Many of the tours are in a traditional wooden dhow (often with air conditioned decks to avoid the heat in summer).

Creek Tours	
Bateaux Dubai	337 1919
Creekside Leisure	336 8406
Danat Dubai Cruises	351 1117
Royal Tours	na

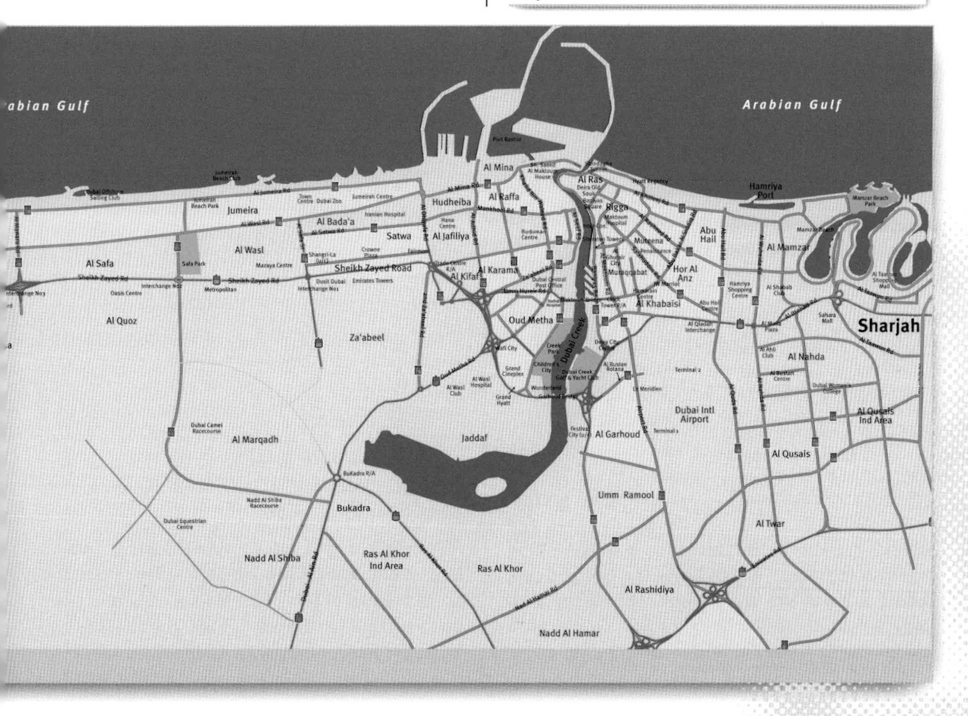

Deira

Arrive at the Deira side of the Creek by abra for an atmospheric feel of the place, or arrive by road for a more hair-raising experience! Narrow convoluted streets bustle with residential and commercial activity, and gold, spices, perfumes and general goods beckon from the numerous souks. Rents are generally less expensive on this side of the Creek and the streets are full of people in the evenings.

Area Overview

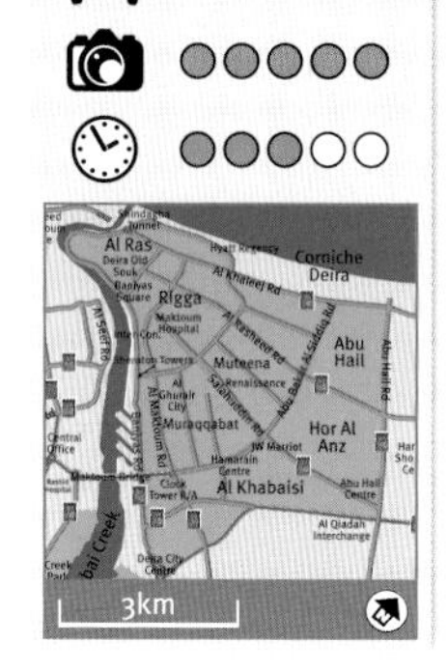

Take a stroll along the dhow wharfage to experience the hustle and bustle of wooden dhows being unloaded – excellent for a feel of old and new Dubai, side by side. Marvel at the trust that is evident from the piles of goods left on the wharf and take in the incongruous sight of fruit, vegetables, electronics and even cars being offloaded from the same vessel. This is a real visual treat and an excellent photo opportunity.

Bordering the Creek are some wonderful buildings; the large golf ball on top of a high rise pinpoints the Etisalat telecommunications building – you can't miss it! The glass building housing the National Bank of Dubai (known locally as the 'pregnant lady') is an amazing feat of engineering and has an almost sculptural feel. For the best view of the contrast of ancient trading dhows moored in front of modern Dubai, try to be on the opposite side of the Creek at dusk (near the British Embassy). As the sun goes down behind you, it creates dramatic reflections in both the glass and water.

Area Hightlights

Souks, souks, souks! Gold, spices, electronics – it's all here. Walk along the streets and discover the various souks that imitate the unspoilt authentic trading methods of the Arab world.

Dhow Wharfage

Magnificent wooden dhows lazily docked by the water's edge provide excellent photo opportunities for the happy snappers. Often you will find a stack of electrical goods trustingly left on the wharfage – a sight rarely seen elsewhere.

Take the pedestrian underpass to the left of the abra station steps to enter the oldest market in Dubai, now mainly selling household items. Close by is the Spice Souk, where a lot of the stores look half closed with only a few items in the window. That's all a trader needs to see to order dozens, hundreds or tons of the goods on offer. Produce such as loose frankincense and other perfumed oils are available, along with dried herbs, which are sold for medicinal purposes. The souk spreads over a large area between Al Nasr Square and the Gold Souk.

If you are interested in carpets, Deira Tower on Al Nasr Square is the place to go. About 40 shops offer a colourful profusion of carpets from Iran, Pakistan, Turkey and Afghanistan to suit everyone's taste and pocket.

Dubai, 'City of Gold', is famed for its gold shopping and one of the most popular places to shop for it is the Gold Souk. Here there are streets and streets of shops with windows laden with 22 or 24 carat gold – the volume is so overwhelming that a second, or even third visit may be required before making a final purchase. Bargaining is expected, and discounts depend on the season and the international gold rate. Dubai Shopping Festival and Dubai Summer Surprises are the main periods for low prices; at these times huge discounts attract gold lovers from around the world. Be sure to haggle hard to get the 'best price'. Individual pieces can be made or copies to your own specifications done within a few days. Take time to look up at the beautiful wooden structure, erected to make shopping more bearable under the hot sun. Even if you aren't buying, an evening stroll through the gold souk in Deira is one of Dubai's unique, not to be missed experiences.

In this part of town, the earliest school in the city, Al Ahmadiya School, has been turned into the Museum of Education and is located next to the Heritage House. For further information on Al Ahmadiya School, refer to Museums, Heritage & culture [p.174].

Dubai Municipality has also reconstructed Murabba'at Umm Rayool (the name derives from the Arabic word for 'leg' as the building stands on seven pillars/legs). This was originally used as a weapons store and was located on Baniyas Street, although the new building is on Union Square near the Deira taxi stand. This building style dates from 1894 - 1906.

Also worth a visit for its atmosphere is Dubai's largest and busiest fish market. A fish museum is being created at Deira Fish Market as part of a two and a half million dirham facelift. The aim is to give shoppers and tourists alike a better idea about fish

Deira Sights

in the Arabian Gulf, the history of the fishing trade in the UAE in general and Dubai in particular, and the types of fishing boats and equipment used by fishermen.

The Fruit & Vegetable Market is another visual treat, but rather less smelly (note: this is moving to Al Awir in April, 2004). You'll find an astonishing range of shapes and colours and produce from many countries. As in the Fish Market, you can pay a 'wheelbarrow man' to follow you around; while you buy, he carries your shopping. Prices are quite cheap – you can end up paying the same for a box of fruit or vegetables as you'd pay for a small bag in the supermarket. However, be prepared to work for it – as in any souk, haggling is the name of the game!

Nearby, the weekly Friday Market operates between September and April. Stalls sell everything from food, such as Yemeni spices and honey, to traditional crafts, pets, plants and household items. Children can enjoy donkey and cart rides, adding to the family day out feel. Look for the road signs to the Hamriya fruit and vegetable markets.

Being Dubai, development plans are in the offing to reclaim land from the sea and transform the Deira seafront by building residential and commercial units, as well as public utilities and tourist attractions. The aim is to complete these by 2005. For further information on carpets and gold, refer to the Shopping section of the book [p.207].

Dubai's Visitors' Check List

The following is our list of 'must do's' for you to make the most of your stay in Dubai. This checklist will help you plan a schedule, tell you where to go, and what to see and do. While this city isn't steeped in culture and heritage, there are still plenty of options other than shopping or lounging by the hotel pool. So while you're topping up on your tan, sit back, read on and tailor your own memorable tour of this fascinating city. If you're an extreme adventure buff, pop down to the beach and try an alternative crazy sport ie, kite surfing. For the kids, there's hours of endless fun at the Wild Wadi, while those with an artistic streak can get their creative juices flowing at the Camel Caravan – you paint a camel (not a real one!) and have it displayed on the streets of Dubai for all to see.

Camel Caravan

Wildlife invades art in Dubai! Artists have unleashed their talent on life size camel sculptures that are scattered around the city till May, when they are auctioned off. Proceeds go to children's charities and the development of art in the region. (www.camelcaravan.ae)

Tee Off [p.281]

Hire a bike, play a round of 18 hole mini golf or enjoy a panoramic view of the Creek in these scenic surroundings.

Bastakiya [p.175]

Learn ancient facts at the Dubai museum, stroll through historical streets and stop for a coffee at the Basta Art Café. Traditional wind towers, courtyard houses, museums and galleries accentuate this more traditional part of the city.

Burj Al Arab [p.28]

Indulge in the glamour and luxury of the Burj. Order pre-dinner drinks and watch the sunset from the Juna Lounge. Next, take the two minute submarine ride to the Al Mahara seafood restaurant for a delicious and hearty meal.

Jumeirah Mosque [p.171]

Learn more about the local culture through organised tours held here on Thursdays and Sundays (10:00 sharp). You don't need to book, but it would be wise to call beforehand, just to confirm and adhere to the dress code.

Open Top Bus [p.181]

Jump on the bus for a whistle stop tour of Dubai's main attractions. Starting and finishing at Wafi City, the hop on and hop off tour includes traditional points of interest, such as the Dubai Museum and the Heritage & Diving Village.

Wonder Bus [p.182]

This amphibious bus offers a different way of experiencing Dubai. Each trip costs Dhs.95 (per adult) and Dhs.65 (per child). Dhs.290 gets a family package, which allows two adults and two kids.

Shop Till You Drop [p.207]

Keep fresh and cool this summer at one of the many malls. Skim through the Shopping section for detailed descriptions and choose the one that best suits your retail indulgence moods.

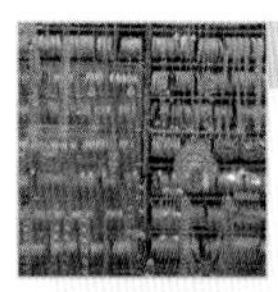

Souks [p.254]

Visit the gold souk to understand why Dubai is called the City of Gold. But gold isn't the only thing for sale in this Aladdin's cave. Diamonds, pearls and most other precious stones can also be found here. Better still, spoil yourself by designing your own piece of jewellery.

Dhows Unloading [p.160]

Visit an unloading site, only to be amazed by the trusting way in which boxes of electrical goods are unloaded and left on the pavement. This practice has been going on for decades, only now, instead of the traditional pile of material and food, you'll see televisions and DVD players.

Scenic Flying [p.183]

Catch an aerial view of Dubai. Book a scenic flight with a tour operator [p.187] and see the city's new developments underway. Prices start from Dhs.250 for a 45 minute to one hour flight. The helicopter can be an alternative, but the price will be dearer.

Water Delights [p.259]

Parasailing, snorkelling, diving, and surfing – there's lots to do at the beach. Hotels run various in-house activities, but also check with tour operators [p.187] or flip to the Activities section [p.259] for independent facilities.

Water Taxi [p.158]

Soak up the panoramic views of the Creek in traditional abras. If you've already seen the sights of Bastakiya, visited the Dubai Museum and perused the textile souk, then catch an abra for Fils.50, cross the Creek and start exploring the gold souk.

Wild Wadi [p.307]

Next door to the Burj Al Arab, this 12 acre water park has 23 rides in all. Dhs.100 (for kids aged 4 - 12) and Dhs.120 (for adults) will give you full access for the day. Be sure to check the opening times as these do vary from month to month.

A Day at the Races [p.53]

The Dubai World Cup will be held on the 27th of March 2004. This annual event is an expensive day out but an internationally distinguished event. An alternative is camel racing, popular during Oct - April. Dhs.2 for adults and Dhs.1 for children.

Ice Skating [p.288]

Al Nasr Leisureland allows you to take a breather from the hot outdoor sun and show off your balancing skills (or not) on the ice rink [p.288] also. An indoor Go-Karting rink next to the Jebel Ali hotel is quite popular with kids, costing Dhs.150 for the whole day.

Cable Car [p.186]

Take an exciting trip in a cable car at the Creekside Park. Suspended 30 feet in the air, this 45 minute ride travels the full length of the park, and is not advisable for those suffering from acrophobia.

Desert Safari [p.187]

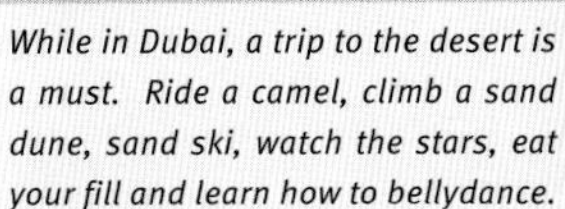

While in Dubai, a trip to the desert is a must. Ride a camel, climb a sand dune, sand ski, watch the stars, eat your fill and learn how to bellydance. Plenty of tour operators offer various excursions at competitive prices, so be sure to shop around first.

Shawarma [p.20]

Grab a tasty shawarma at any time of the day or night. Or, take a break from sightseeing with a thirst quenching fruit cocktail. If you're a health freak, you will know that watermelon juice is a great digestive tonic containing Vitamin A, B Complex and Vitamin C.

Dine Al Fresco [p.341]

Choose a sightseeing cruise and experience a memorable evening in Dubai. Dining options vary from lunch and sunset and dinner cruises, and on board entertainment is included. (Don't forget your camera.)

Dhow Building

Grab a taxi and ask the driver to take you to the dhow building yard by Garhoud bridge. Watch the mesmerising procedures of dhows being constructed without the aid of drawings or modern equipment.

Shisha [p.20]

Join in the social tradition of hanging out at a shisha café. A widely favoured pastime with the locals, shisha consists of tobacco, mixed with molasses and flavouring, and smoked from a water pipe. Choose from a variety of yummy tasting options, sit back and chill.

Bur Dubai

Once a flat, sandy area with a sprinkling of palm trees and barasti (palm) houses, this area of the city is now very much the bustling business hub of Dubai, with modern buildings and plenty of shops selling textiles and electronics. It is also a heavily residential part of the city, and popular with expats of all nationalities. Most live in eight storey apartment blocks in an area known as Golden Sands (between Al Mankhool Road and Trade Centre Road), which seems very popular, despite the concrete jungle feel and high rents. This district is not great for exploring on foot since there's not much to see, except for near the Creek.

Area Overview

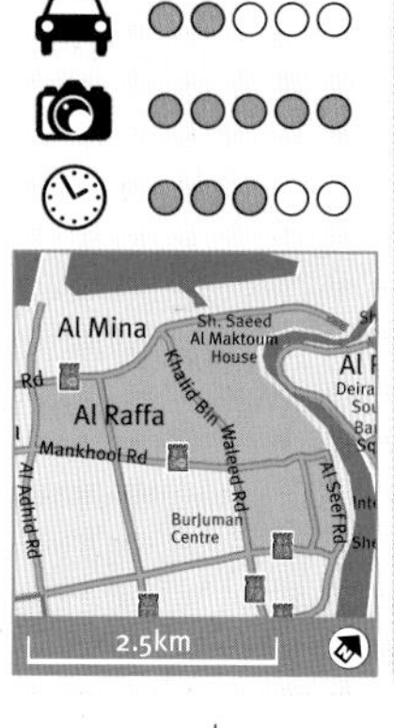

South of the Creek mouth is Port Rashid. The Dubai Ports Authority building (a large glass and chrome construction imaginatively designed like a paddle steamer) indicates its proximity, and all the paraphernalia of a port can be glimpsed over the surrounding fence.

The area near the mouth of the Creek, known as Al Shindagha, is a good starting point to explore Bur Dubai. Here you can visit Sheikh Saeed Al Maktoum's House and the Heritage & Diving Village (a two minute walk from each other), before following the Creek inland to Dubai Museum. For further information, see Museums, Heritage & Culture [p.174].

Area Hightlights

BurJuman Shopping Centre

Another Dubai venue not content with its present status, this mall is currently undergoing massive expansion to make it even bigger and better.

Textile Souk

Located just off the Creek, hours can be killed browsing the myriad of stalls. Fashion victims can stock up on enough cheap material to start their own garment store.

Water Taxi (Abra)

Stroll down to the Creek and catch an abra. This traditional wooden boat will take you to the other side of the Creek for a criminally low fare, and the scenic route provides a bird's eye view of the magnificent structures aligning the Creek.

Near the Astoria Hotel is the busy Al Faheidi Street, see [p.252]. Its narrow, bustling streets are a paradise for electrical goods. Close by, underneath wooden shaded walkways, every type of fabric imaginable can be bought at the Textile Souk.

Facing Dubai Museum is the Diwan, the Ruler's office, where the business of Dubai emirate's administration is undertaken. The Diwan is the highest administrative body of the Dubai government. Built in 1990, the low white building is surrounded by black railings and combines modern materials with a traditional design, including examples of traditional windtowers.

Located near the Diwan, the Grand Mosque was recently renovated at an estimated cost of fifteen and a half million dirhams. It can accommodate 1,200 worshippers, and has 54 domes and a 70 metre minaret – presently the tallest in the city.

It is possible to walk inland along the edge of the Creek past the Diwan to the Bastakiya district of the city. The relaxed atmosphere of this walkway is popular with residents and tourists in the know. Refer to the *Dubai Town Walk Explorer* for further details. An outdoor restaurant in this area is a great place to enjoy Arabic fare and shisha pipes while watching the river traffic.

Near to the Diwan, the Bastakiya (also Bastakia) district is one of the oldest heritage sites in the city. Originally known as Bastakia Chok (square), this intriguing neighbourhood dates back to the early 1900s when traders from Bastak in southern Iran were granted tax concessions by the then ruler of Dubai and encouraged to settle there. Here you can view one of the earliest forms of air conditioning in the shape of windtowers ('barajeel' in Arabic), which are distinctive rectangular structures on top of the traditional flat roofed buildings. These were built to catch the slightest of breezes and funnel them down into the rooms below. Amble down alleyways, step into a converted house, which is now an art gallery, and picture yourself living in a bygone era. Next to the gallery in another restored building, the Basta Art cafe is a good point for a break before continuing to explore. Bastakiya is gradually being reconstructed by the Dubai Municipality to give a feel of 'old' Dubai with small winding alleys leading to over 50 houses. These include a guesthouse, a new gallery and café.

Nearby, Bait Al Wakeel was built in 1934 as Dubai's first office building. It currently houses the fishing museum. Numerous embassies are located in this area, and further inland from the Creek is the popular BurJuman Shopping Centre, see [p.245]. Located near Golden Sands, on a busy crossroads on Khalid bin Waleed Road (or Bank Street, as it is popularly known), this already huge mall has recently been extended and has almost tripled in size.

Bur Dubai Sights

Al Garhoud

The area known as Al Garhoud lies to the north of the Al Garhoud Bridge between the Creek and Deira and bordered by the airport. It is primarily a commercial district, which quietens down at night, although there are residential pockets.

There are places by the Creek that offer escape – near the bridge is a popular spot for fishing. Close to the bridge is space allocated for **Dubai Festival City,** one of the city's latest shopping and entertainment extravaganzas. It is being developed at an estimated cost of six billion dirhams over the next three years. The first phase, which is due to open in 2005, will include a marina, a 3.2 km waterfront promenade, 40 water view restaurants and an amphitheatre. Subsequent phases will include hotels, restaurants, family entertainment venues, a 'global village', residential and office space, plus indoor and outdoor shopping.

Area Overview

In the middle of Garhoud is **Dubai Tennis Stadium**, which doubles as a concert venue since Dubai presently has no other public stadium. Concerts seem to take place more frequently than sporting events. A couple of locations in Garhoud have al fresco licensed bars and restaurants overlooking pleasant landscaped courtyards. Two are Century Village and the Irish Village, which are built into the side of the tennis stadium, and another is The Meridien Village at Le Meridien Dubai hotel near the airport.

Area Hightlights

Century Village

Lets you chill out with friends at your choice of indoor/ outdoor restaurants in quaint surroundings, and then carry on the festivities at the authentic Irish Village pub next door.

Dubai Creek Golf & Yacht Club

A prime spot to enjoy panoramic views of the Creek. The vistas, coupled with the architectural splendour of the club puts it on the must do list for avid photographers.

One of the more visually interesting buildings in Garhoud is shaped like the front half of an airplane, which rather appropriately is the training centre for the national airline, Emirates (unfortunately, and rather alarmingly, viewed from the air it looks rather like a crashed plane).

The main shopping centre in Garhoud is **Deira City Centre Mall.** This is not just a humongous shopping centre, but entertainment in its own right, complete with an 11 screen cinema. Usually referred to as City Centre, it is always busy and gets particularly crowded at weekends and in the evenings. It is a linear mall with a light airy feel and plenty of underground parking, plus two adjacent multi storey car parks. Recent expansion has created 20 more outlets, and it is probably the most popular mall with visitors and residents alike.

Opposite City Centre and bordering the Creek for 1½ km is an enticing stretch of carefully landscaped greenery, home to the **Dubai Creek Golf & Yacht Club**. The club boasts an imaginative clubhouse based on the shape of dhow sails – the image of the famous buildings is found on the Dhs.20 note. This peaceful retreat from the bustle of the city offers night golf, a gym and swimming pool, plus excellent restaurants that are open to non members.

Located to the North East, Dubai Airport has been voted Airport of the Year several times, and is once again undergoing extensive expansion. Currently work is in process for Terminal 3 and two additional concourses, which are expected to be completed by 2006.

Dubai Tennis Stadium

Oud Metha

The Oud Metha Road cuts diagonally through this part of Dubai and is bordered by the Creek to the north, Umm Hureir and Za'abeel roads to the west and Al Quta'eyat Road to the south. Within this residential area, you'll find recreational, social and educational facilities, as well as Lamcy Plaza, another of Dubai's enormous shopping malls, with a maze like layout that virtually forces you around the whole store. Just off Oud Metha Road are various countries' social clubs and two of Dubai's churches. Close by are Rashid Hospital, the American Hospital and Al Nasr Leisureland. This leisure complex offers a variety of facilities, including bowling and an indoor ice rink.

Area Overview

Near Al Maktoum Bridge are the Dubai Courts and Creekside Park. The manicured lawns of the park run for 2.5 km alongside the Creek to Garhoud Bridge. An entrance fee is charged and facilities include an amphitheatre, mini 'falaj' (traditional irrigation system), children's play area, plus you can roller blade or hire 2 seater bicycles. For an aerial view of your surroundings, travel high above in one of the silver cable cars. The latest attraction at Creekside Park is Children's City, the world's fifth largest 'infotainment' facility, comprising 77,000 square metres. Exhibits target children between the ages of 5 - 15 and are science and learning focused. There is also a planetarium inside.

Area Hightlights

Wafi City

An Egyptian themed health spa, a plush shopping mall, nightclubs, restaurants... did we miss anything out?

Lamcy Plaza

One of the many malls in Dubai, and a particular favourite with kids. Front door valet parking makes it easier for the mums!

Creekside Park

Great family venue overlooking Dubai Creek with numerous leisure activities in finely manicured gardens. The early birds can start the day with a relaxing yoga session in this peaceful scenic environment.

WonderLand Theme & Water Park is at the Garhoud Bridge end of Creekside Park, and is a popular amusement park offering various rides, from bumper cars to a hot air balloon. There's even a roller coaster and a log flume ride. Between WonderLand and the park is Paintball, an entertaining (and painful) way to de-stress and 'kill your enemies' with powerful paintball sub-machine guns. For further details see Activities, Sports, Paintballing [p.295].

Near Garhoud Bridge is Al Boom Tourist Village, which is mainly popular with local couples who hire the hall for wedding functions. Tourists visit to sample the local cuisine and to enjoy an evening cruise of the Creek on one of the beautifully illuminated dhows.

Opposite Al Boom Tourist Village is a patch of land where, if you are lucky, you can glimpse a traditional wooden dhow being built. Mainly used for trade, these distinctive high bowed vessels take months to construct, but their lifespan is reckoned to be over a century.

Wafi City consists of several complexes, including a shopping mall, numerous popular restaurants, a nightclub and a health club and spa with an ancient Egyptian theme. The health club and mall exteriors are impressive, with huge mock Egyptian statues and a row of crouching sphinxes guarding the entrances. Wafi Mall specialises in upmarket quality items from established names. This site is also home to Planet Hollywood (hard to miss, as it is housed in a giant blue globe).

Near Wafi City are the Grand Cineplex, an 11 screen cinema, and the Grand Hyatt Hotel with its impressive lobby resembling a beautiful, lush tropical garden, which opened in 2003.

The Pyramid at Wafi Mall

Al Karama

Al Karama is primarily a residential area, consisting of 3 - 4 storey apartment blocks and street level shops. It is very built up, but unusually for Dubai, the layout of the pavements and streets encourages pedestrians.

Area Overview

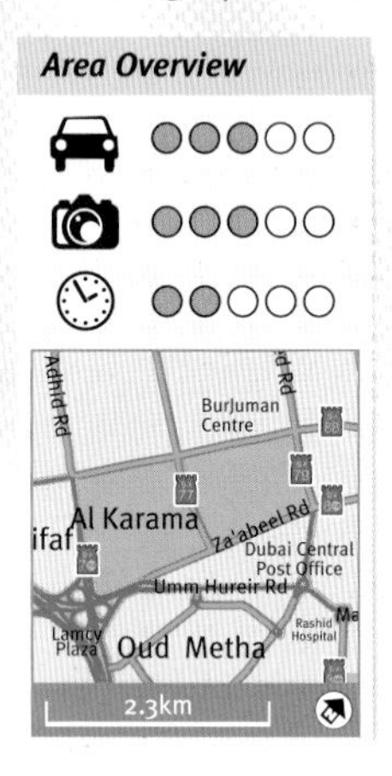

The heart of Karama is an open air shopping centre consisting of two central streets lined with lots of small shops, all with their goods spilling out onto the pavements. This is a great area for buying anything from cheap and cheerful items such as funky clothes or suitcases to kitsch fluffy camels and Omani silver jewellery and boxes. It is also great for watching the cosmopolitan hotchpotch of nationalities that comes to shop here. Many of the goods are cheap imitations, if not counterfeit copies, of designer labels (usually easy to spot, although some of the fakes aren't too bad). Dubai Municipality has been strict in clamping down on the sale of such items, but that said, you're still likely to have a guy sidle up to you asking if you want to buy a 'Rolex'!

If all this shopping makes you hungry, there are numerous cafes offering shawarma, fruit juices, etc, or try one of the many Indian, Pakistani or Filipino restaurants.

The renovated fish and vegetable markets are also worth a visit for the atmosphere and some good cheap produce. If you are looking for second hand or inexpensive furniture, a street virtually devoted to furniture can be found near the Fruit and Vegetable Market, parallel to the main shopping drag. More expensive furniture can be found in the upmarket interior design showrooms that line the busy Za'abeel Road.

Karama is overall cheap and cheerful, but with something for everyone!

Area Hightlights

Al Karama Shopping Centre

This open air shopping area is famous for its stock of good fake designer brands. A myriad of shops sells everything, from bags to shoes, sunglasses and clothes.

Fruit & Vegetable Market

This busy and very atmospheric marketplace is great for purchasing or for just taking in the sights and sounds.

Cheap Furniture!

Parallel to the main shopping drag is a street entirely devoted to selling cheap or second hand furniture, and an ideal choice for decorating fans on a tight budget.

Karama Souk

Sheikh Zayed Road

Another important area in Dubai stretches southwest from Trade Centre roundabout towards Abu Dhabi, parallel with the coast along the infamous eight lane Sheikh Zayed Road (known for its numerous accidents, total lack of lane etiquette and crazy drivers!). The initial stretch after the roundabout is lined with modern high rise office and apartment blocks, hotels and shopping malls – a truly amazing forest of stunning buildings in various architectural styles.

Area Overview

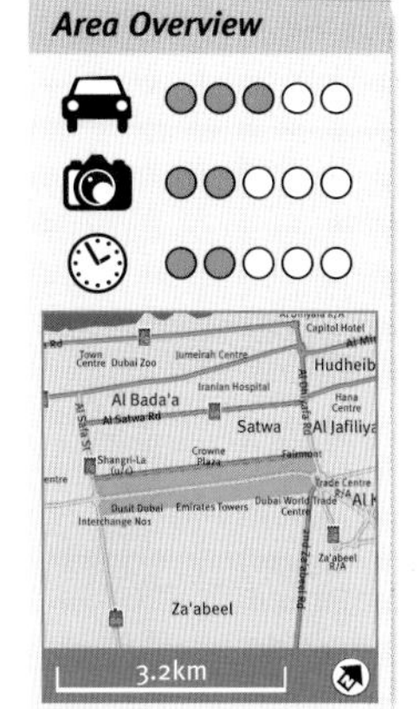

At the start of the Sheikh Zayed Road 'business district' is the landmark Dubai World Trade Centre and exhibition halls (illustrated on Dhs.100 banknotes). The 39 storey tower was once the tallest building in Dubai and remains an instantly recognisable point on the skyline, although it has now been surpassed in terms of size and grandeur by several other buildings in the city. For a great view, especially in winter when it is less hazy, try the guided tour to the observation deck (timings: 09:30 and 16:00 from the information desk in the lobby; cost: Dhs.5). At the top is an Arabic restaurant offering typical Lebanese /Arabic food, but with a gorgeous view over the city. The new conference and exhibition centre successfully accommodated the IMF Conference in late 2003.

Area Hightlights

World Trade Centre

This landmark is housed in the busy central business district of Dubai and is a popular venue for exhibitions; GITEX is one, taking place yearly and attracting a fair amount of international visitors.

Emirates Towers

These two magnificent towers are a favourite with photographers. Venture inside for a drink or a bite at one of the many restaurants and bars, or indulge in some retail therapy at the Emirates Shopping Boulevard.

Architectural Marvels

There is no shortage of architectural monuments on this visually artistic highway. Its location just 10 minutes away from the beach and other major city attractions makes this a hip place to stay.

Nearby, and towering above most other buildings in the city (but not for long), the Emirates Towers is an impressive address for international business in Dubai. At 355 metres, the tower housing offices is the tallest building in the Middle East. The smaller tower, at 305 metres and with 'only' 53 storeys, houses the Emirates Towers five star hotel.

At the end of 2003, work on Burj Dubai will start, with completion due in 2008. This aims to be the world's tallest building, although the actual height is presently being kept secret. The building will reflect the UAE's heritage, and the three leaf design will ensure visitors have the ultimate view over Dubai. The budget, apparently, is a mere US$1 billion!

Interchange One is often known locally as Defence Roundabout, and near here is another interesting skyscraper with a missing central piece. Apparently, the design of the Dusit Dubai Hotel is based on the image of hands praying, but to some it looks like a pair of trousers.

The area to the north of the Sheikh Zayed Road is mainly residential with a mix of villas and apartment towers. Between Sheikh Zayed Road and Al Wasl Road you can find Safa Park [p.187]. To the south of the road, off Interchange Two, is Al Quoz Industrial Estate and tucked away here is the Courtyard. This building is home to a variety of retail outlets, and art exhibitions are held on a regular basis; however, the main attraction is the imaginatively designed courtyard itself, which reflects a variety of building styles from around the world.

Even further south on the Sheikh Zayed Road between Interchanges 3 and 7 there is a number of large projects evolving, one of which will have the largest indoor ski slope, see [p.135].

Inland from Interchange Two for about 5 km, is the Dubai Camel Racecourse. Here, first thing in the morning, it's possible to watch racing camels and their young riders being put through their paces. A large floral roundabout proclaims the entrance to Nad Al Sheba, which has a golf course (excellent night golf available), but is mainly known for horseracing, including the richest horse race in the world, the Dubai World Cup.

Sheikh Zayed Road at Night

Al Satwa

One of the more atmospheric and 'Arabic feeling' areas of Dubai, Satwa has plenty of low 4 - 5 storey apartment blocks with small shops on the ground floor. In Arabic, Satwa means 'hold up' referring to its more adventurous past. The focal point of Satwa is Al Diyafah Street where residents can dodge the traffic and wander up the broad palm lined street checking out the shops, inexpensive restaurants and cafés.

Area Overview

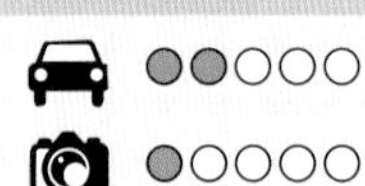

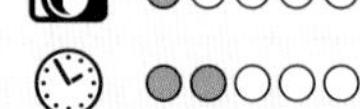

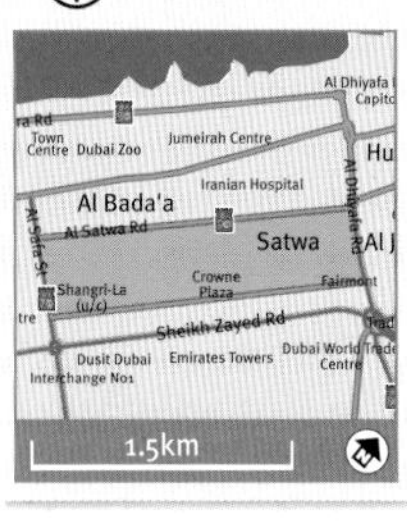

At the western end of Al Diyafah Street, nearest the sea, is the Dar Al Ittehad (Union House) building. This is where the treaty to create the Arab world's first federation of states, the United Arab Emirates, was signed on 2 December 1971. It is also the site of the UAE's largest flag at 40 x 20 metres on top of a 120 metre reinforced column. This is floodlit at night and is noticeable from quite a distance.

Area Hightlights

Al Diyafah Street

Meander down this popular street to experience a myriad of shopping areas, outdoor cafes and restaurants (the traffic noise level can be a little distracting though).

Plant Street

Experience a more down to earth way of trading amongst the hustle and bustle of this colourful street. Plants are strewn across the pavement to attract shoppers and you'll find bargains galore.

Tailors & Textiles Area

The choice of material shops is never ending, and a wide variety of fabrics are on display. Pick your choice of fabric and pop into one of the many tailor shops. These crafty devils can conjure up a designer outfit for you at criminally low costs.

At the other end of Al Diyafah Street (near the Rydges Plaza Hotel) is the permanently busy Al Satwa Road. Along here are numerous small shops selling mainly textiles, inexpensive clothes and general household items. You will also find tailors here who have a good reputation for copying designs very inexpensively. There is also a small area full of car repair shops. If you need a tyre change, new battery, etc, and your car is more than five years old or no longer on the dealer's warranty, this place is worth a visit – they can fix just about anything and everything.

Between Al Satwa Road and Al Wasl Road is a street with wider pavements and shops selling plants and flowers. The aptly named Plant Street is where you can buy fir trees in December, unusual artificial trees all year round and all sorts of fresh flowers. It also has numerous pet shops, selling exotic birds, fish and animals. Near this mini 'jungle' are art shops selling original paintings, drawings and prints. Many offer framing facilities at very reasonable rates.

On Al Wasl Road is the beautiful and intricate Iranian Mosque, with distinctive blue tiles, arches and pillars mirroring the similarly patterned Iranian Hospital opposite.

The Largest Flag in the UAE

Jumeira

On the Bur Dubai side of the city, stretching south for about 10 km along the coast from Satwa's borders towards Umm Suqeim, is the area known as Jumeira. In English, it translates as 'burning embers'. This was once a fishing village, but is now a desirable residential area. The expression, 'Jumeira Jane', has even entered the local lingo, referring to a stereotyped well heeled female resident of this district.

Area Overview

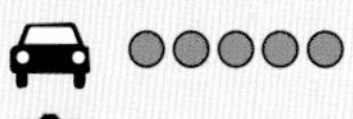

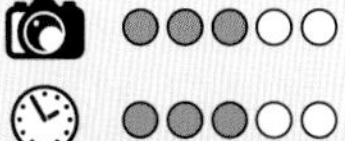

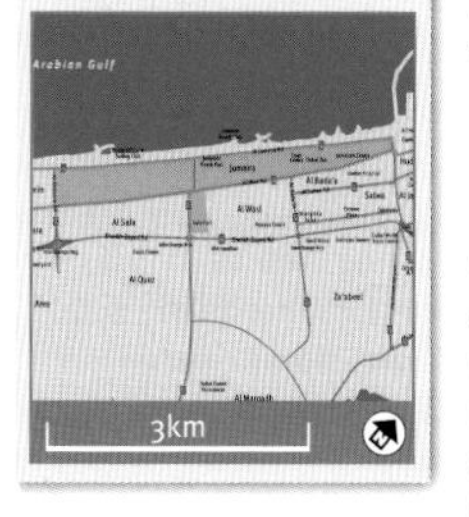

There are lots of medical practices, beauty salons, etc, catering to the needs of the local population along the two main roads in the district – Jumeira Beach Road (also known as the Beach Road) and Al Wasl Road. Jumeira Beach Road is fast becoming a shopping mall alley, along with exclusive beauty salons, several flower shops and numerous cafes and restaurants (such as the ever popular Lime Tree, Japengo and Starbucks).

However, there is a small town feel to the shopping strip on either side of the road near the Jumeirah Mosque. This is easily the most beautiful mosque in the city, as well as the best known, and it features on the Dhs.500 bank note. Constructed from a distinctive creamy/pink stone, it is especially lovely at night when it is lit up.

Between Al Wasl Road and Sheikh Zayed Road is the green oasis of Safa Park. Facilities here include a big wheel, various games pitches and plenty of barbecue sites. The tennis courts are generally busy and it's a popular place in the early evening with joggers who trot around the perimeter and avoid paying the entrance fee.

The public beach, Jumeira Beach Corniche, quickly fills with tourists and people gawping at other people – if you want some peace, try one of the beach parks. The nearest is Jumeira Beach Park, which is off the Beach Road in a beautiful tropical paradise setting.

Along Beach Road a poignant sight can sometimes be seen – the head of a giraffe peeking over the perimeter wall of Dubai Zoo. This was originally a private collection of animals housed in a large private garden, but it is now owned by the Municipality. The animals are in small, limiting cages, and although some of them have been sent to other zoos around the world to increase space for the remaining inmates, those of you with a more 'modern' approach to animal welfare may prefer to pass on a visit here. The zoo is due to be relocated to Mirdif [p.88].

Jumeirah Mosque

Area Hightlights

Jumeirah Mosque

This beautiful landmark is a visual delight, particularly in the evenings when lit up. Although sightseeing in mosques is usually prohibited, the Jumeirah Mosque opens its doors to organised tours.

Jumeirah Beach Park

Sections of the park are open to the public for an entrance fee (Dhs.20 per car or Dhs.5 per person) and Saturdays are set aside for the ladies. Public beaches can be found past the park but are not very popular with the ladies, who may feel a bit uncomfortable and exposed.

Shopping Malls

There is no shortage of shopping areas on the Jumeira strip; scores of retail outlets are found here. This is however, not a place for the bargain hunter.

Umm Suqeim

Umm Suqeim is mostly residential, stretching from Jumeira towards Al Mina Al Seyahi (Al Sufouh). The area was hit by the plague at the beginning of the 20th century and most of the people who resided there passed away, hence the name Umm Suqeim, which, when translated, means 'mother of sickness'.

Today, Umm Suqeim is a pleasant family neighbourhood and boasts some of Dubai's most prominent attractions. The summer residence of the late Sheikh Rashid bin Saeed Al Maktoum is now the Majlis Ghorfat Um Al Sheef – a small park with an excellent museum reflecting Arabic tradition.

Dubai's international landmark, the Burj Al Arab, stands 280 metres off the coast; the atrium alone is large enough to fit the Dubai World Trade Centre inside. The Jumeirah Beach Hotel, dwarfed in the Burj's shadow, complements the famous sail with its own shape of a breaking wave. The ever popular water adventure park, Wild Wadi, is also located here. Currently under construction is the exclusive hotel and residential complex, Madinat Jumeirah, which is due for completion in 2004 and will border Umm Suqeim and Al Sufouh.

Al Sufouh

Al Sufouh is the coastline area that stretches from Black Palace Beach (named after one of the palaces visible from the road), to the borders of Jebel Ali Port.

The coast is home to a number of exclusive five star hotels, such as The Ritz-Carlton, Sheraton Jumeirah, One&Only Royal Mirage and Le Meridien Mina Seyahi, all of which align the coast. With the entrance to the manmade Palm Island (which is visible from space!) added to this address, and with Dubai Marina and Madinat Jumeirah as neighbouring developments, this area will continue to be regarded as a high prestige residential locale.

Emirates Hill

A number of luxurious residential complexes has been constructed around the Emirates Golf Club (before the Jebel Ali Interchange). These are part of the massive Emaar project, Emirates Living, which consists of The Lakes, The Greens, The Meadows, The Springs and, of course, the very opulent Emirates Hills. This mixture of apartments, villas, townhouses and some freehold properties has luxurious family residential areas, landscaped gardens, parks and water features. The first class Montgomerie Golf Estate is perhaps the most prestigious address here.

Across the highway, Nakheel Properties have launched another residential development: fifty islands will accommodate villas, apartments and townhouses, all surrounded by unique waterways in the form of landscaped canals, waterfalls, gardens and marinas. Two Brazilian style islands will be the main feature of this complex. Eventually, Jumeirah Islands Village will complete this visionary self contained environment with retail and leisure facilities.

Jumeirah Lake Towers is another exceptional project underway nearby. Located just off Sheikh Zayed Road (between Interchanges 5 and 6), residential, office and retail spaces will be surrounded by attractive water features.

Marsa Dubai

Formerly known as Dubai Marina, Marsa Dubai is located past Al Sufouh on the Jumeira beach side. This area is going through some extensive construction. Offering panoramic views of the ocean, the Dubai Marina project by Emaar is aiming to be a residential community for 40,000 people, with five star hotels, residential apartments, townhouses, villas and shopping malls, all enhanced by the beautiful and blissful surrounding marina.

Jebel Ali

Situated south of the city, this area is chiefly known for its free zone and port. Jebel Ali was the first free zone in Dubai and an extremely attractive one for foreign investors with the luring temptations of 100% business ownership exempt of all tax and customs duties.

Jebel means 'mountain' in English, which seems to be a rather dramatic reference to this slight rise in the land (it's barely even a hill!). Contrary to its reputation of being a busy industrial area, it is not all factories and workers. Many residential and scenic developments are coming up, including the Palm Island Jebel Ali project, due to start this year. Jebel Ali also boasts its own quaint village with beautiful residential apartment complexes aptly named 'The Gardens'. With seemingly natural floral surroundings and The Gardens shopping mall underway, this area is fast evolving into a pleasant family neighbourhood.

Art Galleries

While there's nothing like the Tate Gallery or the Louvre in Dubai, there is a number of art galleries that have interesting exhibitions of art and traditional Arabic artefacts. Most simply operate as a shop and a gallery, but some also provide studios for artists and are involved in the promotion of art within the emirates. The Majlis Gallery, The Courtyard and the newly opened, XVA Gallery, are all worth visiting in their own right as examples of traditional or unusual architecture. They provide striking locations in which you can enjoy a wide range of art, both local and international.

Creative Art Centre

Location → Nr Choithrams · Beach Rd, Jumeira | 344 4394
Hours → 08:00 - 18:00
Web/email → arabian@arts.com | Map Ref → 5-E2

Previously a centre for art classes, the Creative Art Centre is now a large art gallery with eight showrooms set in two villas. The gallery has a wide range of fine art, Arabian antiques and gifts, and a team of in-house framers, artists and restorers work on-site. The gallery provides art for hotels, offices and interior designers, as well as for the general public. The range of antiques includes Omani chests, old doors, weapons and silver. Lynda Shephard, the managing partner, is a well known artist in both Oman and Dubai. Location: in two villas set back from Jumeira Beach Road. Take the turning inland between Choithram supermarket and Town Centre shopping mall.

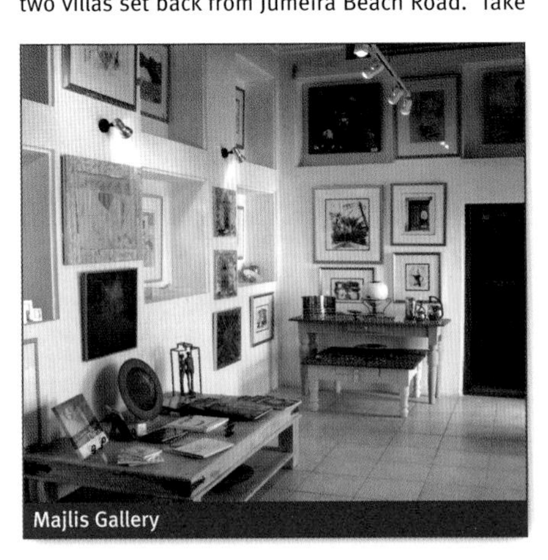

Majlis Gallery

Four Seasons Ramesh Gallery

Location → Al Karama Shopping Complex | 334 9090
Hours → 10:00 - 22:00
Web/email → www.fourseasonsgallery.com | Map Ref → 10-D2

This large gallery, previously situated in the BurJuman shopping centre, has moved to Karama, near the main post office. Opened in 1970, it is one of the larger galleries in Dubai, exhibiting and selling a mixture of work by local and international artists. There are different exhibitions of art throughout the year, and it's a great place to purchase a gift that will leave a lasting impression. Their range has also been expanded to include furniture now, making this a one stop home decorating shop; purchase your favourite artwork, have it framed, then find the furniture to match!

Green Art Gallery

Location → Villa 23, St 51, Beh Dubai Zoo · Jumeira | 344 9888
Hours → 09:30 - 13:30 16:30 - 20:30
Web/email → www.gagallery.com | Map Ref → 6-A2

The Green Art Gallery features original art, limited edition prints and handcrafted work by artists from all over the world. In particular, the gallery draws on those influenced and inspired by the heritage, culture and environment of the Arab world and its people. The gallery also encourages local artists by guiding them through the process of exhibiting and promoting themselves. Seasonal exhibitions are held from October to May.

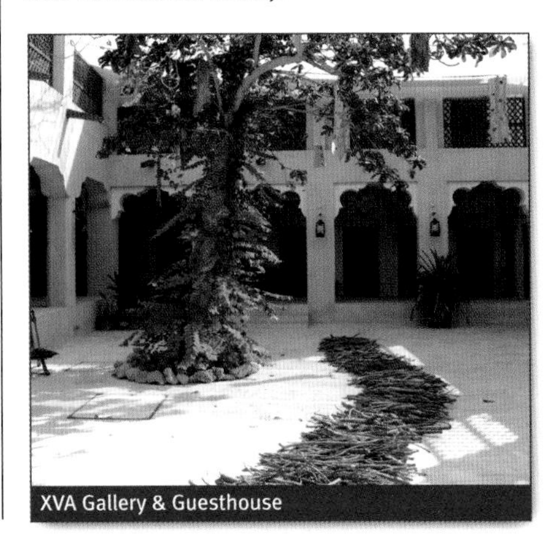

XVA Gallery & Guesthouse

Hunar Art Gallery

Location → Villa 6, Street 49 · Al Rashidiya | 286 2224
Hours → 09:00 - 13:00 16:00 - 20:00
Web/email → hunarart@emirates.net.ae | Map Ref → 15-A4

This gallery exhibits fine art by international artists. Beautifully decorated Japanese tiles, Belgian pewter and glass pieces fill the spaces between traditional Persian paintings and contemporary art. Often on display is work by the well known artists Rima Farah and Abdul Quadir Al Rais.

Majlis Gallery

Location → Al Faheidi Street · Bur Dubai | 353 6233
Hours → 09:30 - 13:30 16:00 - 19:30
Web/email → majlisga@emirates.net.ae | Map Ref → 8-A2

In the quaintest of surroundings in the old Bastakiya area of the city, the Majlis Gallery is situated in an old Arabic house, complete with windtowers and courtyard. Small whitewashed rooms lead off the central garden area and host a variety of exhibitions by contemporary artists. In addition to the fine art collection, there's an extensive range of handmade glass, pottery, fabrics, frames, unusual pieces of furniture and bits and bobs. The gallery hosts, on average, ten exhibitions a year, but is worth visiting year round for both the artwork and the atmospheric surroundings.

Total Arts

Location → Courtyard, The · Al Quoz | 228 2888
Hours → 10:00 - 13:00 16:00 - 20:00
Web/email → www.courtyard-uae.com | Map Ref → 4-D4

Operating since 1996, Total Arts is one of the galleries located in this unique courtyard. The gallery generally exhibits works of art from a variety of cultures and continents, however, there is a bias towards Middle Eastern artists, or to works that have somehow been influenced by Arabian culture. Total Arts occupies two floors of The Courtyard, with over 10,000 square feet of gallery space. It has over 300 paintings on permanent display, and there are regular shows of traditional handicrafts and antique furniture. One of the main attractions here must be the cobbled courtyard itself, which is surrounded by different façades combining a variety of building styles from around the world. All provide great photo opportunities and make it well worth the trek from the centre of town. Other outlets here include furniture and antiques, artist studios, photo studios, and a coffee shop.

Heritage Sites – City

Other options → Art

Bastakiya

Location → Nr Diwan & Al Faheidi R/A · Bur Dubai | na
Hours → n/a
Web/email → n/a | Map Ref → 8-B3

The Bastakiya (also spelt Bastakia) area is one of the oldest heritage sites in Dubai. This intriguing neighbourhood dates back to the early 1900's when traders from Bastak in southern Iran, encouraged by the tax concessions granted by the then ruler of Dubai, settled there. Here you can view one of the earliest forms of air conditioning in the shape of windtowers ('barajeel' in Arabic), which are distinctive rectangular structures on top of the traditional flat roofed buildings. These were built to catch the slightest of breezes and funnel them down into the rooms and courtyards of the houses below.

Amble down alleyways, step into a converted house, which is now an art gallery, and picture yourself living in a bygone era. An ongoing reconstruction project is gradually turning the area into a pedestrian conservation area, with over 50 houses due for restoration by early 2005. Eventually there will be a museum, a cultural centre and a restaurant.

See also: *The Majlis Gallery [p.175].*

Heritage & Diving Village

Location → Nr Al Shindagha Tunnel · Al Shindagha | 393 7151
Hours → 07:30 - 14:30 16:00 - 22:00 Fri 16:00 to 22:00
Web/email → www.dubaitourism.ae | Map Ref → 8-B1

Located near the Creek mouth, the Heritage & Diving Village focuses on Dubai's maritime past, pearl diving traditions and architecture. Plans are underway to rebuild some of the traditional windtower houses and narrow 'sikkas' (alleyways) of Al Shindagha, as well as to create a modern promenade along the Creek with cafés and souks.

Ideal for family visits (camel and pony rides are available some afternoons), the village is close to Sheikh Saeed Al Maktoum's House and houses several shops and a cafeteria.

Majlis Ghorfat Um Al Sheef

Location → Beach Rd, Jumeira | 394 6343
Hours → 07:30 - 14:30
Web/email → www.dubaitourism.co.ae | Map Ref → 5-A2

Constructed in 1955, this simple building was used by the late Sheikh Rashid bin Saeed Al Maktoum as a summer residence. The ground floor is an open veranda (called 'leewan' or 'rewaaq'), while on the second floor, the majlis (Arabic for 'meeting place') is decorated with carpets, lanterns and rifles. The roof terrace was used for sleeping – ideal to catch the slightest breeze – and it originally offered an uninterrupted view right to the sea. Dubai Municipality has added a garden, which includes the traditional 'falaj' irrigation system.

Location: look for the brown Municipality historical places signposts for Majlis Al Ghoraifa, off Jumeira Beach Road, past Jumeira Beach Park, next to Valuemart supermarket and Al Hamur Marine Sports.

Sheikh Saeed Maktoum's House

Location → Nr Al Shindagha Tunnel · Al Shindagha | 393 7139
Hours → 08:00 - 20:30 Fri 15:00 - 21:00
Web/email → www.dubaitourism.ae | Map Ref → 8-A1

The modest home of Dubai's much loved former ruler was once strategically located at the mouth of Dubai's lifeline, the Creek, but now lies close to the Bur Dubai entrance to Al Shindagha Tunnel. Dating from 1896, this carefully restored house turned museum is built in the traditional manner of the Gulf coast, from coral covered in lime and sand coloured plaster. The interesting displays include rare and wonderful photographs of Dubai pre-oil, plus an old currency and stamp collection. Worth combining with a visit to the nearby Heritage & Diving Village.

Entrance fees: *Dhs.2 adults; Dhs.1 children; under 5's free.*

Heritage Sites – Out of City

Other options → **Tours & Sightseeing**

Al Hisn Kalba

Location → Kalba, Nr Fujairah · East Coast | na
Hours → 09:00 - 13:00 17:00 - 21:00
Web/email → www.shjmuseum.gov.ae | Map Ref → UAE-E2

As you drive along the coast road in Kalba town, you come to the restored house of Sheikh Sayed Al Qassimi, overlooking the sea. It's located at the end of a large grassy expanse with swings and small rides for children. On the opposite side of the road is Kalba's Al Hisn Fort, which houses the town's museum. It includes a limited display of weapons and admission is free. Note: Wednesday afternoon it's open to ladies and children only.

Fujairah Heritage Village

Location → Nr Fujairah Fort · Fujairah | 09 222 7000
Hours → 07:00 - 13:30
Web/email → n/a | Map Ref → UAE-E2

Opened in 1996, this 6,000 square metre heritage village depicts life in the UAE pre-oil, with displays of fishing boats, simple dhows, clay, stone and bronze implements and pots, and hunting and agricultural tools. The heritage village is close to Ain Al Madhab Gardens, which are situated in the foothills of the Hajar Mountains just outside Fujairah City. The gardens are fed by mineral springs and this warm sulphur laden water is used in two swimming pools (separate for men and women). Private chalets with large wooded gardens can be hired and on public holidays an outdoor theatre is used for festivals that include traditional singing and folklore dances. Entrance fee: Dhs.5.

Hatta Heritage Village

Location → Hatta town · On road to Hatta Pools | na
Hours → 08:00 - 19:30 Fri 15:00 to 21:00
Web/email → n/a | Map Ref → UAE-D3

Opened to the public in early 2001, Hatta Heritage Village is located an hour's drive south east of Dubai City and a few kilometres from the Hatta Fort Hotel. It is constructed around an old settlement and was restored as a creation of a traditional mountain village. Explore the tranquil oasis, the narrow alleyways and discover traditional life in the mud and barasti houses. Hatta's history goes back over 3,000 years and the area includes a 200 year old mosque and the fortress built by Sheikh Maktoum bin Hasher Al

Maktoum in 1896, which is now used as a weapons museum.

Sharjah Heritage Area

Location → Nr Corniche Rd · Sharjah | 06 569 3999
Hours → 09:00 - 13:00 17:00 - 20:00 Fri 17:00 - 20:00
Web/email → www.tourath.ae | Map Ref → UAE-C2

The beautifully restored heritage area in Sharjah is a great place for individuals with an interest in local history. The area includes a number of old buildings: Al Hisn Fort (Sharjah Fort); Sharjah Islamic Museum; Sharjah Heritage Museum (Bait Al Naboodah); the Majlis of Ibrahim Mohammed Al Midfa and the Old Souk (Souk Al Arsah). Here you will see traditional local architecture and home life depicted as it was over 150 years ago. Be prepared to park your car and walk – the round trip is less than 1½ km. Toilets can be found at each venue and there's an Arabic coffee shop in the shady courtyard of Souk Al Arsah. The Majlis of Ibrahim Mohammed Al Midfa is situated between the souk and the waterfront. This peaceful majlis is famous for its round windtower, the only one of its kind in the UAE. The owner, Mr Al Midfa, was secretary to four rulers of Sharjah until he died in 1983. One of the first writers in the UAE, he also initiated the beginnings of a library in Sharjah. See also: Museums – Out of the City section.

Museums – City

For residents and visitors alike, a visit to one of the museums or heritage sites is a great opportunity to discover something more about the culture and history of the UAE, as well as to catch a glimpse of a fast disappearing way of life. Dubai Municipality has an active role in preserving Dubai's past and is currently overseeing a huge renovation project on over 230 of Dubai's old buildings. Completion is expected sometime in 2009. As of the end of 2003, renovation has finished on more than 90 buildings, including six mosques: Al Shoyookh, Al Mulla, Bin Zaywed, Abdul Qader, Al Mur bin Hiraiz and Al Otaibat. Entrance fees are minimal and information is given in both Arabic and English. Note that opening times often change during the summer months, Ramadan, Eid, and public holidays, so check before leaving home to avoid disappointment. Refer also to Dubai Areas [p.157] for further information on what there is to do in these areas.

Al Ahmadiya School

Location → Al Khor St, Al Ras · Deira | 226 0286
Hours → 08:00 - 19:30 Fri 14:00 - 19:30
Web/email → www.dubaitourism.ae | Map Ref → 8-C2

Al Ahmadiya School, or the Museum of Education, was the earliest regular school in the city and a visit here is an excellent opportunity to see the history of education in Dubai. It was established in 1912 by Mr Ahmadiya for Dubai's elite. It closed in 1962, until its restoration and conversion into a museum in March 2000. The school is located next to the Heritage House, the former home of Mr Ahmadiya, which dates back to 1890. Touch screens take you on a guided tour of the two museums. Admission is free.

Dubai Museum

Location → Al Faheidi Fort · Bastakiya, Bur Dubai | 353 1862
Hours → 08:00 - 20:30 Fri 14:30 - 20:30
Web/email → www.dubaitourism.ae | Map Ref → 8-B3

This is no stuffy museum and is well worth a visit, even if the museum 'thing' isn't your scene. Built in 1787 for sea defence and residence of the ruler of Dubai, Al Faheidi Fort was renovated in 1970 to house the museum. The site has been expanded to include a large area under the courtyard of the old fort. Everything is represented in a highly creative way: spy on a typical bride preparation scene, step off a dhow unloading its wares to enter a souk of the 1950s and walk through a labyrinth of shops... you can even peek into an Islamic school. Then enter the world of an oasis, a tribute to the sea and archaeological finds from

A Dhow – Up Close & Personal

the area. Tour guides are available and there's also a restaurant and children's playground. Highly recommended. Entrance fees: adults Dhs.3; children under 10 Dhs.1.

Godolphin Gallery

Location → Nad Al Sheba Racecourse · Nad Al Sheba | 336 3031
Hours → 09:00 - 17:00 Race nights 09:00 - 20:00
Web/email → www.godolphin.com Map Ref → 17-A3

A great location for horse racing fans, the Godolphin Gallery celebrates the Maktoum family's private racing stable, and houses the world's finest collection of horse racing trophies. The gallery was refurbished in 2002 and incorporates interactive touch screen consoles, photographs, video presentations and memorabilia from the first nine years of the Godolphin racing stable. Adjacent to the Nad Al Sheba Club, the gallery is open during horse racing season till April 30.

Gold & Diamond Museum

Location → Jct 4, Shk Zayed Rd | 347 7788
Hours → 10:00 - 22:00 Fri 16:00 - 22:00
Web/email → www.goldanddiamondpark.com Map Ref → 4-B4

An interesting feature of the Gold & Diamond Park is the visitors' centre, which includes a museum and a themed café. Showcases display traditional Arabian jewellery and give its history, and there are guided tours of the manufacturing plant to see how jewellery is made. Then of course, there's the chance to flex your plastic and buy from the numerous retail outlets in the complex. Alternatively, watch your own design being made on the spot. The tour takes approximately 30 minutes. Entrance is free.

Museums – Out of City

Other options → **Tours & Sightseeing**

Ajman Museum

Location → Opp Etisalat · Ajman Town Centre | 06 742 3824
Hours → 09:00 - 13:00 16:00 - 19:00 Fri 16:00 - 19:00
Web/email → ajmuseum@emirates.net.ae Map Ref → UAE-C2

Ajman Museum, like most museums in the Emirates, is interesting and well arranged, with displays described in both English and Arabic. The fort guide is well worth the Dhs.4 charged. The museum has a variety of exhibits, including a collection of passports (Ajman used to issue its own). It is housed in a former residence of the ruler of Ajman – a fortress dating back to around 1775. In 1970, it became the main police station, before becoming the museum in the early 1980s.

Entrance fees: *Adults Dhs.4; children under 6 years Dhs.2; students Dhs.1. Evening timings: 17:00 - 20:00 summer; 16:00 - 19:00 winter.*

Al Hisn Fort/Heritage Museum

Location → Al Hisn Ave, Bank St · Sharjah | 06 568 5500
Hours → 09:00 - 13:00 17:00 - 20:00
Web/email → sdci@sdci.gov.ae Map Ref → UAE-C2

Built in 1820, this fort was originally the home of Sharjah's ruling family, the Al Qassimi. It was renovated in 1996 - 97 and includes an interesting display of old photographs and an introductory video (English and Arabic) covering Sharjah's history. The fort is built in the traditional courtyard style with three towers on the surrounding walls. Enclosed by modern buildings, it's hard to imagine it as it once was – a more isolated building on the edge of the Creek. The fort links Sharjah's main heritage and arts areas. Timings: 09:00 - 13:00 & 17:00 - 20:00; Closed Mon, Fri am.

Discovery Centre

Location → Opp Sharjah Airport · Al Dhaid Rd | 06 558 6577
Hours → See timings below
Web/email → www.shjmuseum.gov.ae Map Ref → UAE-C2

This colourful scientific centre offers everything toddlers to under 13s love to see and do in safe, supervised surroundings. Based on themed areas, children can touch, experiment, run and have fun. Of course, the underlying aim is to teach youngsters about the biological, physical and technological worlds in a practical way. A soft play area is available for the very young. Pushchair access is good and the centre has a café and a shop, as well as ample parking. Costs: children under 2 years free; ages 2 - 12 mornings Dhs.4, evenings Dhs.7; 13+ years mornings Dhs.5, evenings Dhs.10. For families (maximum two adults, three children) mornings Dhs.15, evenings Dhs.30.

Timings: *Sat - Tue 09:00 - 14:00, Wed - Fri 15:30 - 20:30; School groups: Sat - Wed 09:00 - 14:00. Public holidays: open morning and afternoon.*

Fujairah Museum

Location → Opp Ruler''s Palace · Fujairah | 09 222 9085
Hours → 08:30 - 13:30 16:30 - 18:30 Fri 14:00 - 18:30
Web/email → na | Map Ref → UAE-E2

Situated near Fujairah Fort, this museum offers an insight into Fujairah's history and heritage. It has displays of the traditional way of life and artefacts found in archaeological excavations throughout the emirate. Work by local and foreign archaeologists has yielded items dating back over 4,500 years, including Bronze and Iron Age weapons, finely painted pottery, delicately carved soapstone vessels and pre-Islamic silver coins. The museum was enlarged during the summer of 1998 to permit more finds to be displayed. **Entry fee:** adults Dhs.3; children Dhs.1.

Fujairah Fort

Fujairah Fort has been going through a major renovation programme over the past few years and once complete, it is expected that the Municipality will use it as a museum. Carbon dating estimates the main part of the fort to be over 500 years old, with other sections being built about 150 years later. Several buildings nearby are also being renovated.

National Museum of Ras Al Khaimah

Location → Beh Police HQ · Ras Al Khaimah | 07 233 3411
Hours → 10:00 - 17:00
Web/email → www.rakmuseum.gov.ae | Map Ref → UAE-D1

Located in a fort, and former home of the present ruler of Ras Al Khaimah, this museum mainly has local natural history and archaeological displays, plus a variety of paraphernalia from life pre-oil. Upstairs you can see an account of the British expedition against Ras Al Khaimah in 1809, as well as a model of a 'baggala', a typical craft used in the early 1800s. Look out for fossils set in the rock strata of the walls of the fort – these date back 190 million years!

Entrance fees: *Adults Dhs.2; children Dhs.1. T o enter with your camera, it's Dhs.5.*

Location: *Behind Police Headquarters in the old town close to the bridge. From Dubai, turn left at the second roundabout after the Clock roundabout and the museum is 100 metres on your right.*

Sharjah Archaeological Museum

Location → Nr Cultural R/A · Sharjah | 06 566 5466
Hours → 09:00 - 13:00 17:00 - 20:00
Web/email → /www.archaeology.gov.ae | Map Ref → UAE-C2

This hi-tech museum offers an interesting display of antiquities from the region. Linked to a conference centre and used as an educational venue for local schoolchildren, the museum has installed computers in each hall to provide in-depth information on the exhibits. One area displays the latest discoveries from excavation sites in the Emirates. Well worth a visit for archaeology and history lovers. Wednesday afternoons are for ladies and children only. There is no entry fee.

Sharjah Art Museum

Location → Sharjah Arts Plaza Area · Sharjah | 06 568 8222
Hours → 09:00 - 13:00 17:00 - 20:00 Fri 17:00 - 20:00
Web/email → www.sharjah-welcom.com | Map Ref → UAE-C2

Opened in April 1997, Sharjah Art Museum dominates the arts plaza area. It was purpose built in a traditional style, chiefly to house the personal collection of over 300 paintings and maps of the ruler, HH Dr Sheikh Sultan. Permanent displays include the work of 18th century artists, with oil

Dubai Museum

paintings and watercolours depicting life from all over the Arab world, while other exhibits in the 72 small galleries change frequently. There's also an art reference library, bookshop and coffee shop, and the museum hosts various cultural activities. Wednesday afternoons are for ladies and children only. There is no entry fee.

Sharjah Heritage Museum

Location → Sharjah Arts Plaza Area · Sharjah | 06 569 3999
Hours → 09:00 - 13:00 16:00 - 20:00 Fri 16:30 - 20:30
Web/email → www.sharjah-welcom.com | Map Ref → UAE-C2

This two storey building was once owned by the late Obaid bin Eesa Al Shamsi, nicknamed Al Naboodah, and is a reconstruction of a typical family home (bait) about 150 years ago. Originally home to the Al Naboodah family (three generations of the family lived here until 1972), it is built around a traditional courtyard. The various rooms display items such as clothing, weapons, cooking pots and goatskin water bags. A visit here includes a short documentary film, and in true Arabic style, coffee and sweets are offered. Wednesday afternoons are for ladies and children only. There is no entry fee.

Sharjah Islamic Museum

Location → Nr Cultural R/A · Sharjah | 06 568 3334
Hours → 09:00 - 13:00 16:30 - 20:30 Fri am
Web/email → www.shjmuseum.gov.ae | Map Ref → UAE-C2

Sharjah Islamic Museum is home to an unrivalled collection of Islamic masterpieces and manuscripts, representing the cultural history of Muslims over 1,400 years. On display are examples of Islamic crafts such as ceramics, jewellery and textiles. There's also an impressive collection of gold plated Korans and a replica of the curtain that covers the Ka'aba Stone at Mecca. Housed in a 200 year old building, the display is from HH Dr Sheikh Sultan's private collection. The museum is open during holy days and public holidays. Wednesday afternoons are for ladies and children only. There is no entry fee.

Sharjah Natural History Museum

Location → Jct 8 - Sharjah - Al Dhaid Rd · Sharjah | 06 531 1411
Hours → 09:00 - 17:30 11:00 - 17:30 Fri 14:00 - 17:30
Web/email → www.shjmuseum.gov.ae | Map Ref → UAE-C2

Combining entertainment and learning in the most dynamic of atmospheres, this fascinating museum unfolds through five exhibition halls to expose you to the earth's secrets. Exhibits include a 35 metre diorama of the UAE's natural habitat and wildlife; a stunning geological UV light display; a hall showing the interaction between man and his environment – including the museum's best known exhibit... a mechanical camel; plus a botanical hall, and the marine hall, where replicas of Gulf and Indian Ocean sea creatures can be viewed as if from the bottom of the sea.

The site also incorporates the Arabian Wildlife Centre (06 531 1999), which is a breeding centre for endangered species; most famously, the Arabian leopard (note: photography is forbidden – if you are caught taking photos, your camera will be confiscated).

There is also a Children's Farm (06 531 1127) where animals, such as donkeys, camels and goats, can be fed and petted. The facilities are state of the art and offer an enjoyable, interactive and educational day out. Picnic areas are available, plus cafés and shops. Great fun for all ages, and a place that you will want to visit again and again.

Entrance fees: *Adults Dhs.5; children Dhs.2. School classes by appointment. Timings: Sat - Wed 09:00 - 17:30; Thu 11:00 - 17:30; Fri 14:00 - 17:30. Location: about 28 km outside Sharjah on the Al Dhaid highway.*

Sharjah Science Museum

Location → Halwan, Nr TV station · Sharjah | 06 566 8777
Hours → 09:00 - 14:00 15:30 - 20:30
Web/email → www.shjmuseum.gov.ae | Map Ref → UAE-C2

Opened in 1996, this museum offers visitors hands on exhibits and demonstrations, covering subjects such as aerodynamics, cryogenics, electricity and colour. There's also a children's area where the under fives and their parents can learn together. Those who are inspired to learn more can visit the Learning Centre, which offers more in-depth programmes on many of the subjects covered in the museum. There is also a café and gift shop. School groups are more than welcome.

Timings: *Sat & Mon 09:00 - 14:00 for boys and girls; Sun & Tue 09:00 - 14:00 for girls only. Wed - Fri and public holidays 15:30 - 20:30. June, July, August evenings from 16:30 onwards. Entrance fees: Under 5's free. Ages 6 - 12 morning Dhs.2, ages 12+ Dhs.5; families (two adults and four kids) morning Dhs.8, afternoon Dhs.15; groups of 15+ are given a 20% discount.*

Zoos

Arabia's Wildlife Centre

Location → Shj Natural History Museum · Sharjah | 06 531 1411
Hours → 09:00 - 17:30 Thu 11:00 - 17:30 Fri 14:00 - 17:30
Web/email → www.shjmuseum.gov.ae Map Ref → UAE-C2

Please see the review under the 'Sharjah Natural History Museum'.

Children's Farm

Location → Shj Natural History Museum · Sharjah | 06 531 1127
Hours → 09:00 - 18:30 Thu 11:00 - 18:00 Fri 14:00 - 17:30
Web/email → n/a Map Ref → UAE-C2

Please see the review under 'Sharjah Natural History Museum'.

Dubai Zoo

Location → Jumeira Beach Rd · Jumeira | 349 6444
Hours → 10:00 - 17:00
Web/email → n/a Map Ref → 6-A2

Dubai Zoo was created from a private collection of animals housed in a large private garden, but it is now owned by the Municipality. This is an old fashioned type of zoo with caged lions, tigers, giraffe, monkeys, deer, snakes, bears, flamingos, giant tortoise and other animals that are well cared for by Dr Rezi Khan, the dedicated manager, and his staff. Space is tight for the animals, although attempts have been made to send some to other zoos around the world to increase the space for the remaining inmates. Over recent years there has been much talk about building an entirely new zoo at Mushrif Park near the airport. At the moment it seems that this is just talk and those with a more 'modern' approach to animals may prefer to pass on a visit here. Cost: Dhs.3 per person.

Other Attractions

Birdwatching

As a destination for birdwatchers, Dubai's reputation has grown considerably over the years. The increasing lushness of the area attracts birds in growing numbers, many of which are not easily found in Europe or in the rest of the Middle East. Over 80 species breed locally, and during the spring and autumn months, over 400 species have been recorded on their migration between Africa and Central Asia. Within the city, the best bird watching sites would be the many parks and golf clubs, where parakeets, Indian rollers, little green bee eaters and hoopoe can easily be spotted.

The Khor Dubai Wildlife Sanctuary at the end of the Creek is the only nature reserve within the city and a great place to see flamingos and other shore birds and waders. Entrance to the reserve is prohibited but you can easily spot the flamingos from the road as you drive from Bu Kidra roundabout to the Wafi junction, or as you drive towards Al Awir from Ras Al Khor Road or Bu Kidra interchange.

Other species that are found in the Emirates include the Socotra cormorant, striated scops owl, chestnut bellied sandgrouse, crab plover, Saunders' little tern and Hume's wheatear. Some good places for birdwatching include the mangrove swamps in Umm al Quwain and Khor Kalba on the East Coast. Khor Kalba is the only place in the world where you can spot the rare white collared kingfisher. Birdwatching tours to the mangroves in a canoe can be arranged through Desert Rangers.

In addition, falconry, the sport of sheikhs, has a deep rooted tradition here. The best opportunity for enjoying these beautiful and powerful birds is on an organised tour, where you can see the birds in flight.

Bus Tours

Other options → **Walking Tours**

Big Bus Company, The

Location → Wafi City · Umm Hurair (2) | 324 4187
Hours → Various timings
Web/email → www.bigbus.co.uk Map Ref → 13-D2

It's not a mirage, there really are eight open air London double decker buses roaming the streets of Dubai! Operating since May 2002, the buses leave from Wafi City on the hour and half hour. There's a live commentary in English, with little known facts such as in 1968 there were only 13 cars in Dubai! It's wise to break the tour at their recommended stops (the seats aren't very comfortable) and then hop on the following bus once you've finished exploring. Overall, visually very interesting and informative. Prices: adults Dhs.75; children Dhs.45 (ages 5 - 15); free for under 5s; families Dhs.195 (two adults and two children).

Wonder Bus Tours

Location → BurJuman Centre · Dubai | 359 5656
Hours → na
Web/email → www.wonderbusdubai.com Map Ref → 11-A1

Another first in Dubai is the Wonder Bus, an amphibious bus that is capable of doing 120 kph on the road and seven knots on water (life jackets supplied, if you're nervous)! The trips are two hour mini tours of Dubai, concentrating on the Creek, and covering Creekside Park and Dubai Creek Golf Club, under Maktoum Bridge towards Garhoud Bridge, then up the boat ramp and back to BurJuman, where the tours start and end. The bus is air conditioned and can take 44 passengers. Prices: adults Dhs.95; children Dhs.65 (ages 2 - 12).

Camel Racing

Camel racing followed by a freshly cooked campfire breakfast... is there a better way to start the day? For the young and old alike, a morning at the races is a memorable experience. This extraordinary sport involves large numbers of camels, the owners and their families, and the young jockeys, all congregated to form an atmosphere of intense anticipation and excitement.

For visitors, this is an opportunity to see a truly traditional local sport and to visit the 'shops' selling camel paraphernalia (blankets, rugs, beads etc). Races take place during the winter months, usually on a Thursday and Friday morning, at the tracks in Dubai, Ras Al Khaimah, Umm Al Quwain, Al Ain and Abu Dhabi. Often, additional races are held on National Day and certain other public holidays. Races start very early (by about 07:30) and are usually over by 08:30, and admission is free.

Ras Al Khaimah has one of the best racetracks in the country at Digdagga, situated on a plain between the dunes and the mountains, about 10 km south of the town. There are some beautiful campsites in the big red dunes that overlook the racetrack, just five minutes away.

Camel rides are available at various heritage sites, and also within the city of Dubai during the Dubai Shopping Festival. Call the Camel Racing Club (04 342 2208) for details. The local press also has information on dates and times. Also check with tour operators [p.189] who organise camel rides in the desert, very often at their desert camps.

Horseracing

Other options → Annual Events

Dubai Racing Club

Location → Nad Al Sheba Racecourse · Nad Al Sheba | 332 2277
Hours → 19:00 - 22:00
Web/email → www.dubairacingclub.com Map Ref → 17-A3

A visit to Dubai during the winter months is not complete without experiencing Race Night at the Nad al Sheba Racecourse. This racecourse is one of the world's leading racing facilities, with top jockeys from Australia, Europe and the USA regularly competing throughout the season (November - April). Racing takes place at night under floodlights and there are usually 6 - 7 races each evening, held at 30 minute intervals. The start time is 19:00 (except during Ramadan when it is 21:00). The clubhouse charges day membership on race nights of Dhs.85, which allows access to the Members Box. Everyone can take part in various free competitions to select the winning horses, with the ultimate aim of taking home prizes or cash. Hospitality suites, with catering organised on request, can be hired by companies or private individuals. The dress code to the public enclosures is casual, while race goers are encouraged to dress smart/casual in the clubhouse and private viewing boxes. General admission and parking are free and the public has access to most areas with a reserved area for badge holders and members.

Location: *Nad Al Sheba is approximately 5 km south east of Dubai, signposted from Sheikh Zayed Road at the Metropolitan Hotel junction and then from the roundabout close to the Dubai Polo Club and Country Club.*

Horseracing

Mosque Tours

Other options → **Museums – City**

Shk Mohd. Centre for Cultural Understanding

Location → Beach Centre, The · Beach Rd, Jumeira | 353 6666
Hours → 09:00 - 17:00
Web/email → smccu@emirates.net.ae | Map Ref → 6-B2

This non profit making organisation was established to bring down the barriers between different nationalities and to help visitors and residents understand the customs and traditions of the UAE through various activities. These include visits to a mosque, usually Jumeira Mosque (Thursday morning, limited numbers only. Remember to cover up/dress conservatively). There are also opportunities to visit the home of a UAE National for a traditional lunch. Arabic courses are offered, usually during the Shopping Festival, and visits by school groups can be arranged.

Powerboat Racing

Powerboat Racing

Other options → **Annual Events**

DIMC

Location → DIMC · Al Sufouh | 399 5777
Hours → 08:30 - 17:30
Web/email → dimcdxb@emirates.net.ae | Map Ref → 3-A2

The UAE is well established on the world championship powerboat racing circuit; in Abu Dhabi with Formula I (inshore) and in Dubai and Fujairah with Class I (offshore). These events make a great spectacle – take a picnic, family and friends and settle in to be an armchair sports fan for the day. The Dubai Creek also provides a stunning setting for national events in Formulas 2 and 4, which become more competitive every year. The local Victory Team of Dubai continues to compete in Class I and is ranked amongst the best in the world.

Scenic Flights

What better way to view the sights of Dubai than from the air? Just book a helicopter, soar above the skies and be introduced to a fresh new perspective of the city. Within a short sightseeing tour, you have the chance to get an aerial view of the impressive parks, traditional dhows, the Creek, beaches and much more. For more information, refer to Flying [p.280] in the Activities section.

Stable Tours

Other options → **Horse Riding**

Nad Al Sheba Club

Location → Nr Bu Kidra Interchange · Nad Al Sheba | 336 3666
Hours → 06:30 - 01:00
Web/email → www.nadalshebaclub.com | Map Ref → 17-A3

An early morning visit to the world's top racehorse training facilities at Nad Al Sheba is inclusive of a cooked breakfast, a behind the scenes glimpse of the jockey's facilities and a view over the racecourse from the Millennium Grandstand, plus the chance to see horses training. The tour ends with a visit to the Godolphin Gallery where the Dubai World Cup is on display. Call for timings and prices.

Parks & Beaches

Beaches

Lovers of the seaside who want to swim or enjoy the beach will find a number of options in Dubai. Choose between the public beaches which usually have limited facilities but no entrance charge, and the beach parks which charge for entrance, but have a variety of facilities, including changing rooms and play areas. If none of these appeal, try the beach clubs, which are normally part of a hotel or resort (refer to [p.32]). If you want to explore by yourself, map pages 1-6 clearly show Dubai's

southwestern coastline where there are several beaches, although access to the public is restricted in some areas.

Options for public beaches include the lagoon at Al Mamzar (Map Ref 12-E2), which has a roped off swimming area, chalets and jet skis for hire. Travelling south, you'll come to Jumeira Beach Corniche (Map Ref 5-C1) (known locally as Russian Beach), which is a great favourite with tourists for soaking up the sun, swimming and people watching. Facilities include shaded picnic tables, small play areas, showers and sheltered swimming areas. A tree planting programme will eventually screen the beach from the road and provide more shade. The jetty here is a popular spot for fishing. Moving further south brings you to the small beaches near the Dubai Offshore Sailing Club (Map Ref 4-E2), Wollongong University (immensely popular with the kite surfers) and the Jumeirah Beach Hotel (Map Ref 4-B2).

Die hard beach lovers frequent the beach past the Jebel Ali Hotel, where there is a 10 km expanse of beach (Map Ref 1-A1). This is a great spot for barbecues and camping, with occasional shade and showers that never seem to work!

Regulations for the public beaches are gradually becoming stricter. Currently dog owners are banned from walking their dogs on the beaches. There is also a ban on 4 wheel driving on the beach, but this is often ignored. Dubai Police and Municipality patrol units roam the beaches looking for any sort of offender. Officially, other banned beach activities include barbecues on sand, camping and holding large parties. Contact the Public Parks and Recreation Section (336 7633) for clarification. Regulations don't appear to be strictly enforced on the more open beaches, such as at Jebel Ali. New regulations with far more restrictions on what you can and cannot wear operate in Sharjah; so if you are planning a trip there, ensure that you are aware of the latest rules. Refer to the Decency Law [p.195].

Warning!

Although the waters off the coast of Dubai generally look calm and unchallenging, very strong rip tides can carry the most confident swimmer away from the shore very quickly. Fatalities have occurred in the past. Take extra care when swimming off the public beaches where there are no lifeguards.

Beach Parks

A visit to one of Dubai's beach parks is an enjoyable way to spend the day and a perfect break from city life. Here you can enjoy that tropical paradise experience, with an oasis of lush greenery and stretches of sandy beach and palm trees!

Both of Dubai's beach parks are very busy at weekends, especially in the cooler months, although Al Mamzar Park covers such a large area that it rarely feels overcrowded. They both have a ladies day when men are not admitted (except for young boys with their family). Dress wise, it is fine to wear swimsuits, bikinis (top and bottom halves please!). Like the green parks, the beach parks open at 08:00 and close over 12 hours later (opening and closing times change during Ramadan). Al Mamzar has an amphitheatre and often stages concerts on special occasions or public holidays – look out for details in the newspapers 2 - 3 days in advance.

Both of the beach parks have lifeguards on duty during the day. A raised red flag means that it is unsafe to swim, and you are strongly advised to heed the warning. Although the waters off Dubai's coast generally look calm and unchallenging, rip tides can carry swimmers away from the shore very quickly. Fatalities have occurred in the past.

Jebel Ali Beach

Jumeira Beach Park

Location → Beach Rd, Jumeira | 349 2555
Hours → 08:00 - 22:30 Sat ladies & children only
Web/email → www.dm.gov.ae | Map Ref → 5-C2

With azure seas, palm trees and a long, narrow, shady stretch of beach, this is a popular and well used park and there are plenty of grassy areas for all ages to run around on. Barbecue pits are available for public use, as well as a volleyball area for ball games. Lifeguards are on duty along the beach between 08:00 to sunset and swimming is not permitted after sunset. No adult bicycles or rollerblades are allowed in the park. Entrance fee: Dhs.5 per person; Dhs.20 per car. Saturdays are for women and children only, including boys up to the age of about five years, unless Saturday falls on a public holiday, then the park is open to all.

Mamzar Park

Location → Past Al Hamriya Port · Al Hamriya | 296 6201
Hours → 08:00 - 22:30 Thu & Fri 08:00 - 23:30
Web/email → www.dm.gov.ae | Map Ref → 12-E2

Four beaches, open grassy spaces and plenty of greenery create a tranquil haven. A large amphitheatre is located near the entrance and paths wind through picnic areas and children's playgrounds. The well maintained beaches have sheltered areas for swimming and changing rooms with showers. Kiosks sell food and other small necessities you may have left at home. Chalets complete with a barbecue area can be hired for Dhs.150 - 200. There are also two swimming pools and lifeguards patrol the beaches and pool areas.

Entrance fees: *Dhs.5 per person; Dhs.30 per car, including all occupants.*

Pool fees: *Dhs.10 per adult; Dhs.5 per child. Under 12's must be accompanied by an adult.*

Timings: *Wednesdays are for women and children only (boys up to eight years are allowed).*

Parks

Dubai has a number of excellent parks, and visitors are certain to be pleasantly surprised by the expanses of green lawns and the variety of trees and shrubs – a perfect escape from the concrete jungle of the city. In the winter months, the more popular green parks are very busy at weekends. Most have a kiosk or café selling snacks and drinks; alternatively take a picnic or use the barbecue pits that many provide (remember to take your own wood or charcoal, and food!). Creekside Park has an amphitheatre and often holds concerts on public holidays or special occasions (details are announced in the newspapers 2 - 3 days before).

Regulations among the parks vary, with some banning bikes and rollerblades, or limiting ball games to specific areas. Pets are not permitted and you should not take plant cuttings. Most have a ladies day, when entry is restricted to women, girls and young boys (check the individual entries). All parks open at 08:00 and close at varying times over 12 hours later. During Ramadan park timings change, usually opening and closing later in the day. Entrance to the smaller parks is free, while the larger ones charge Dhs.5 per person, except for Safa and Mushrif parks, which cost Dhs.3 per person.

Creekside Park

Location → Nr Wonderland · Umm Hurair (2) | 336 7633
Hours → 08:00 - 23:00
Web/email → www.dm.gov.ae | Map Ref → 14-A1

Here you can enjoy a 'day in the country' with acres of gardens, as well as fishing piers, jogging tracks, BBQ sites, children's play areas, restaurants and kiosks. There's also a mini falaj and a large amphitheatre. Running along the park's 2.5 km stretch of Creek frontage is a cable

Jumeira Beach

car system allowing visitors an unrestricted view from 30 metres in the air. Alternatively, near gate 1, visit the amazing Children's City, a new interactive museum for children. From gate 2, four wheel cycles can be hired (Dhs.20 per hour; you can't use your own bike in the park. Rollerblading is allowed. Wednesdays are for women and children only (boys up to the age of six). Entrance fee: Dhs.5. Cable car: adults Dhs.25; children Dhs.15. Children's City: adults Dhs.15; children Dhs.10.

Mushrif Park

Location → 9 km past Dxb Airport · Al Khawaneej Rd | 288 3624
Hours → 08:00 - 23:00
Web/email → www.dm.gov.ae Map Ref → 16-D4

The largest park in Dubai, Mushrif Park is a little out of town, but popular with families owing to its unusual features and extensive grounds (you may prefer to take your car in to get around!). Wander around miniature houses or take the train, which tours the park in the afternoons (Dhs.2 a ride), then visit the camel and pony areas (afternoon rides cost Dhs.2). Separate swimming pools are available for men and women. No bikes or rollerblades are allowed and there are no ladies only days.

Entrance fees: *Dhs.3 per person; Dhs.10 per car. Swimming pools: Dhs.10 per adult; Dhs.5 per child (a membership scheme is available).*

Rashidiya Park

Location → Past the Dubai Intl. Airport · Rashidiya | 285 1208
Hours → 07:30 - 23:00 Thu & Fri 08:00 - 23:00
Web/email → www.dm.gov.ae Map Ref → 16-A2

This is a surprisingly clean and pretty park with attractive flowerbeds and brightly coloured children's play areas. It is mainly used by local residents, although it would also suit mothers with pre-school children. Shaded grassy areas are ideal for picnics. Saturdays to Wednesdays are for ladies and children only.

Safa Park

Location → Nr Union Co-op & Choithrams · Al Wasl Rd | 349 2111
Hours → 08:00 - 23:00
Web/email → www.dm.gov.ae Map Ref → 5-C3

Spot the giant Ferris wheel opposite Jumeira Library and you've found Safa Park. Artistically divided, this large park offers electronic games for teenagers, plus bumper cars and the big wheel (at weekends). It also has volleyball, basketball and football pitches, tennis courts, obstacle course, barbecue sites and expanses of grassy areas. Bicycles can be hired inside (the use of personal bikes is not allowed). Rollerblading is allowed and Tuesday is ladies day (boys aged up to about seven admitted).

Entrance fee: *Dhs.3 per person, free for children under three years. Bike hire: Dhs.100 deposit; Dhs.20 - 30 for one hour.*

Organised Tours

Tours & Sightseeing

There are many companies in Dubai offering an exciting variety of city and safari tours. An organised tour can be a great way to discover the UAE, especially if you are only here for a short time or do not have ready access to a vehicle. The following information is not exhaustive, but covers the most popular tours given by the main operators. Refer to Tour Operators [p.189] for a the largest and most respectable companies operating out of Dubai.

Tours range from a half day city tour to an overnight safari visiting the desert or mountains and camping in tents. On a full day, evening or overnight tour, meals are generally provided, while on a half day city tour you will usually return in time for lunch. Check what is included when you book, as sometimes there may be an extra charge for meals. Generally, all tours include soft drinks and water as part of the package. Expect to pay anything from Dhs.50 for a half hour tour of the Creek to Dhs.110 for a half day city tour, and about Dhs.350 for an overnight desert safari.

Most trips require a minimum of four people for the tour to run. Companies usually take couples or individuals if there is a group already booked that they can join. If you want a tour or car to yourself, you will probably have to pay for four people, even if there are less of you. It is advisable to book three or four days in advance, although in some cases less notice is not a problem. A deposit of up to 50% is normal, with the balance payable when you are collected. Cancellation usually means loss of your deposit, unless appropriate notice is given; this differs from company to company.

On the day of the tour you can be collected from either your hotel, residence, or from a common meeting point if you are part of a large group. Tours usually leave on time – no shows do not get a refund, so don't be late!

It's advisable to wear cool, comfortable clothing, plus a hat and sunglasses. Desert or mountain tours require strong, flat soled shoes if there is the possibility of walking. The temperature can drop considerably in the desert after sunset, especially in winter, so take warm clothing. Other necessities include suncream and camera with spare films and batteries.

The desert safaris are a must for anyone who hasn't experienced dune driving before, especially good for friends and relatives visiting the Emirates. Most companies will take an easier route if there are young children, the elderly, or anybody who doesn't want to experience extreme dunes. Most companies have excellent safety records, but there is an element of risk involved when driving off-road. Remember, you are the client and if the driver is going too fast for your group, tell him to slow down – there shouldn't be any wheels leaving the ground! Accidents have happened in the past, but with a good driver you should have total confidence and you'll be in for a thrilling ride.

The following descriptions of the main tours are intended simply to give an idea of what's most commonly included. Obviously each tour operator has their own style, so the content and general quality may differ from one company to another. Refer also to the Visitors' Checklist for suggestions of half, one, two or three day tours.

City Tours – Dubai

Dubai by Night

This is a tour around the palaces, mosques and souks of the city, whilst enjoying the early evening lights. See the multitude of shoppers in their national costumes, and streets heaving with character, then enjoy dinner at one of Dubai's many restaurants. (half day)

Dubai City Tour

This is an overview of the old and new of Dubai. The souks, the fish market, mosques, abras, Bastakiya windtower houses and thriving commercial areas with striking modern buildings are some of the usual inclusions. (half day)

City Tours – Out of Dubai

Abu Dhabi Tour

The route from Dubai passes Jebel Ali Port, the world's largest manmade seaport, on the way to Abu Dhabi, capital of the United Arab Emirates. Founded in 1761, the city is built on an island. Visit the Women's Handicraft Centre, Heritage Village, Petroleum Exhibition and Abu Dhabi's famous landmark – the Corniche. (full day)

Ajman & Sharjah Tour

Ajman is the place to visit if you want to see wooden dhows being built today just as they were hundreds of years ago. Take in the museum before driving to the neighbouring emirate of Sharjah, where you can visit the numerous souks. Finish with a wander around the restored Bait Al Naboodah house to see how people lived before the discovery of oil. (half day)

Al Ain Tour

Known as the 'Garden City', Al Ain was once a vital oasis on the caravan route from the Emirates to Oman. Here there are many historical attractions, from one of the first forts to be built by the Al Nahyan family over 175 years ago, to prehistoric tombs at Hili, said to be over 5,000 years old. Other attractions include Al Ain Museum, the camel market, the falaj irrigation system, which is still in use, and the quaint souk. (full day)

Ras Al Khaimah Tour

Drive up country along the so called Pirate Coast through Ajman and Umm Al Quwain. Explore ancient sites and discover the old town of Ras Al Khaimah and its museum. The return journey passes natural hot springs and date groves at Khatt, via the starkly beautiful Hajar Mountains. (full day)

Shopping Tour

Known as the 'shopping capital of the Middle East', Dubai is a shopper's paradise! From almost designer clothes at incredibly low prices to electronics, watches or dazzling bolts of cloth in the Textile Souk, everything is available at prices to suit every budget – don't forget to bargain your way through the day! Then there are the malls... ultra modern and air conditioned, and selling everything you'd expect, plus a lot more! (half day) See also: Bargaining [p.210], Shopping Malls [p.244].

Safari Tours

Dune Dinners

Late afternoons are ideal for enjoying the thrill of driving over golden sand dunes in a 4 wheel drive vehicle. Departing at around 16:00, the route passes camel farms and fascinating scenery, which provide great photo opportunities. At an Arabic campsite, enjoy a sumptuous dinner and the calm of a starlit desert night, then return around 22:00. (half day)

East Coast

Journey east to Al Dhaid, a small oasis town known for its fruit and vegetable plantations. Catch glimpses of dramatic mountain gorges before arriving at Dibba and Khor Fakkan on the East Coast. Have a refreshing swim, then visit the oldest mosque in the UAE nestling below the ruins of a watchtower. This tour usually visits the Friday Market for a browse through carpets, clay pots and fresh local produce. (full day)

Full Day Safari

This day long tour usually passes traditional Bedouin villages and camel farms in the desert, with a drive through sand dunes of varying colours and heights. Most tours also visit Fossil Rock and the striking Hajar Mountains, the highest mountains in the UAE. A cold buffet lunch may be provided in the mountains before the drive home. (full day)

Hatta Pools Safari

Modern highways, soft undulating sand dunes and a kaleidoscope of colours lead the way to Hatta, in the foothills of the Hajar Mountains. Swim in the Hatta Pools and see the hidden waterfall inside a gorge. The trip generally includes a stop at the Hatta Fort Hotel, where you can relax and enjoy the swimming pool, landscaped gardens, archery, clay pigeon shooting and 9 hole golf course. Not every tour has lunch at the hotel; some have it in the mountains, especially in the cooler winter months. (full day)

Mountain Safari

Travelling north along the coast and heading inland at Ras Al Khaimah, the oldest seaport in the region, you enter the spectacular Hajar Mountains at Wadi Bih. Rumble through rugged canyons onto steep winding tracks, past terraced mountainsides and old stone houses at over 1,200 metres above sea level. It leads to Dibba where a highway quickly returns you to Dubai, stopping at Masafi Market on the way. Some tours operate in reverse, starting from Dibba. (full day)

Overnight Safari

This 24 hour tour starts at about 15:00 with a drive through the dunes to a Bedouin style campsite. Dine under the stars, sleep in the fresh air and wake to the smell of freshly brewed coffee, then head for the mountains. The drive takes you through spectacular rugged scenery, along wadis (dry riverbeds), before stopping for a buffet lunch and then back to Dubai. (overnight)

Travel Agents

Other options → Tour Operators (see below)

Travel Agencies	
Airlink	282 1050
Al Futaim Travel	228 5470
Al Naboodah Travel	294 5717
Al Tayer Travel Agency LLC	223 6000
Belhasa Tourism Travel & Cargo Co.	391 1050
DNATA	295 1111
Emirates Holidays	800 5252
Kanoo Travel	393 5428
MMI Travel	209 5527
SNTTA Travel & Tours (L.L.C.)	282 9000
Thomas Cook Al Rostamani	295 6777
Turner Travel & Tourism	345 4504

Tours & Sightseeing

Activity Tours

In addition to the city and safari tours, some companies offer more specialised activities. From the adrenaline buzz of a desert driving course, a dune buggy desert safari, mountain biking or hiking to a peaceful canoe tour of Khor Kalba, these tours combine fun and adventure. Note that a basic level of fitness may be required. Refer to the Activities section of the book for other activities that you can enjoy in the Emirates.

Arabian Adventures

Location → Emirates Holiday Bld · Shk Zayed Rd | 303 4888
Hours → 09:00 - 18:00
Web/email → www.arabian-adventures.com | Map Ref → 5-C4

Arabian Adventures offers the chance to venture into the desert or to explore the rugged Hajar Mountains with experienced guides. Their tours cover the whole of the UAE and are a perfect opportunity to discover the richness of Arabian culture. The company also arranges sporting activities, such as golf, fishing or scuba diving, and will create an itinerary just for you. In addition, they organise overland trips to Bahrain, Iran, Oman, Qatar and Yemen. Call the above number or Abu Dhabi (02 633 8111).

Desert Rangers

Location → Dubai Garden Centre · Shk Zayed Rd | 340 2408
Hours → 09:00 - 18:00
Web/email → www.desertrangers.com | Map Ref → 4-B4

Desert Rangers are one of only a few companies in the country offering outdoor adventure activities. In addition to the standard range of desert and mountain tours, they offer something a little different, visiting locations that you are unlikely to see with another company. With camel riding, sand boarding, canoeing, raft building, initiative tests and team building, camping, hiking, mountain biking, desert driving courses or dune buggying to choose from, your weekends should never be dull! They also specialise in multi-activity trips for children, especially schools and youth groups. Timings: most tours start around 08:00; afternoon tours start around 14:00; evening tours start around 16:00.

East Adventure Tours

Location → In Pyramid Centre · Al Karama | 335 5530
Hours → 10:00 - 19:00
Web/email → www.holidayindubai.com | Map Ref → 10-E1

If you're new to Dubai and would like to discover the city and its surroundings, East Adventure Tours can provide a personal guide/driver as an escort. Trips can include a Bedouin desert safari, a dhow dinner cruise and camel safari, as well as activities such as horse riding and golf, and the service extends to after dark. This unique chauffeur/escort service is available 24 hours a day. For further information, visit the website or contact Mr Ali (050 644 8820).

Voyagers Xtreme

Location → Dune Centre · Al Satwa | 345 4504
Hours → 09:00 - 18:00
Web/email → www.turnertraveldubai.com | Map Ref → 6-E3

To help people make the most of their leisure time, Voyagers Xtreme (VX) provides a range of adventurous activities over land, air and sea. On offer is everything from hot air ballooning, dune driving, a Mussandam cruise, dive charters, skydiving, sailing, rock climbing, plus outdoor team building programmes. They also offer a two day self drive desert expedition to the Empty Quarter – the world's largest sand desert. VX also offer a selection of overseas adventure holidays – from easy to xtreme!

Out of Dubai

If you have access to a car, it's worth spending time exploring places outside the city. To the east of Dubai lies the town of Hatta; just over an hour's drive away. It is the only town of any notable size in the emirate of Dubai, apart from the capital itself. South of Dubai is Abu Dhabi, the largest of all the emirates, covering 87% of the total area of the country and with a population close to one million. The capital is Abu Dhabi, which is also the capital of the UAE. Al Ain is the second most important city in this emirate.

To the north are the other emirates which form the northern part of the UAE; as you travel north of Dubai, these are Sharjah, Ajman, Umm Al Quwain and Ras Al Khaimah. Also covered in this section is Fujairah, which is the only emirate located entirely on the East Coast of the peninsula. This region is a mix of rugged mountains and golden beaches, and is one of the most interesting areas in the country to explore. For further information on exploring the UAE's 'outback', refer to the *Off-Road Explorer (UAE)*, published by Explorer Publishing.

Hatta

About 100 km from Dubai and 10 km from the border with Oman, but within the emirate of Dubai, is the town of Hatta. Nestling at the foot of the Hajar Mountains, the town is the site of the oldest fort in the emirate (built in 1790), and there are several watchtowers on the surrounding hills. The town has a sleepy, relaxed feel about it and beyond the ruins and the Heritage Village, there is little to see or do here. However, past the village and into the mountains are the Hatta Pools, where you can see deep, strangely shaped canyons carved out by rushing floodwater.

As you come to Hatta, left at the fort roundabout on the main Dubai - Oman road, is the Hatta Fort Hotel. This is an ideal weekend destination, either for a meal, to enjoy the range of activities or for a longer stay.

On the way to Hatta, just off the main Dubai - Hatta road is the 100+ metres high Big Red sand dune. It's a popular spot for practising dune driving in 4 wheel drives or dune buggies, as well as trying sand skiing. Alternatively, take a walk to the top (it takes about 20 minutes), for a sense of achievement and a great view. For further information on the area around Hatta, refer to the *Off-Road Explorer (UAE)* by Explorer Publishing. See also: Dune Buggies [p.277]; Sand Skiing [p.299]; Tour Operators [p.189].

Hatta Fort Hotel

Abu Dhabi Emirate

Only 50 years ago, Abu Dhabi consisted of little more than a fort, surrounded by a modest village of just a few hundred date palm huts. However, with the discovery of oil in 1958 and with exports starting five years later, the situation changed dramatically. The income enabled the growth of a modern infrastructure – visitors will find a city of highrise buildings, a large port, numerous hotels, hospitals and all the latest facilities.

Abu Dhabi From the Air

The airport is located on the mainland, 35 km from the city. The city lies on an island, which became home to the Bani Yas Bedouin tribe in 1761 when they left the Liwa oasis in the interior. Being an island, it offered security, but the tribe also found excellent grazing, fishing and fresh water supplies. The descendants of this tribe have, in alliance with other important families in the region, governed the emirate ever since.

Liwa Oasis

If you have access to a car, it's worth spending some time exploring places outside the city. To the south of Abu Dhabi lies the Liwa Oasis situated on the edge of the infamous Rub Al Khali desert, also known as the Empty Quarter. This region stretches from Oman, through the southern UAE into Saudi Arabia, and was regarded as the edge of civilisation by the ancients.

Al Ain

Al Ain is the second most important city in the Abu Dhabi emirate and birthplace of the ruler of the UAE, HH Sheikh Zayed bin Sultan Al Nahyan. It lies on the border with Oman and shares the Buraimi Oasis with the Sultanate. The shady oasis is a pleasant stretch of greenery amidst the harsh surroundings, and the palm plantations have plenty of examples of the ancient 'falaj' irrigation system. Al Ain has a variety of sights to interest visitors, including a museum, fort and livestock and camel souks, while visits to the nearby Jebel Hafeet and Hili Fun City and archaeological site are also worthwhile. If you are a fan of off-road driving and would like to explore this area further, the *Off-Road Explorer (UAE)* gives details of four stunning trips around Al Ain/Buraimi. For detailed information on the emirate of Abu Dhabi, refer to the *Abu Dhabi Explorer*, published by Explorer Publishing.

Ajman

The smallest of the seven emirates is Ajman, the centre of which lies about 10 km from Sharjah, although the buildings of the two towns merge along the beachfront. Ajman is not merely a coastal emirate, but also has two inland enclaves, one at Masfut on the edge of the Hajar Mountains and one at Manama in the interior between Sharjah and Fujairah. Ajman has one of the largest dhow building centres in the UAE, which offers a fascinating insight into this traditional skill.

Investment in this small emirate is growing, with the opening of the Ajman Kempinski Hotel & Resort and a popular shopping complex, Ajman City Centre, sister to the busy Dubai mall. Outlets include Carrefour hypermarket, Magic Planet amusement centre, as well as many small shops and a six screen CineStar cinema complex.

Ras Al Khaimah

The most northerly of the seven emirates, Ras Al Khaimah (RAK) is one of the most fertile and green areas in the UAE, with possibly the best scenery of any city in the country. It lies at the foot of the Hajar Mountains, which can be seen rising into the sky just outside the city. Some areas of the town are even built on slightly elevated land with a view – rare when compared to other cities in the UAE, which are as flat as the proverbial pancake! Like all coastal towns in the region, it traditionally relied on a seafaring existence and had an important port for pearling, trading and fishing. It is really two towns; the old town (Ras Al Khaimah proper) and across the creek, the newer business district (Al Nakheel).

Visit the souk in the old town and the National Museum of Ras Al Khaimah, which is housed in an old fort, a former residence of the Sheikh. The RAK Free Trade Zone is a five year development plan designed to accelerate economic growth in the emirate. A large shopping and leisure complex known as Manar Mall provides a one stop shop for everyday needs, a cinema complex, family entertainment centre and water sports area.

The town is quite quiet and relaxing, and it is a good starting point for exploring the surrounding countryside and visiting the ancient sites of Ghalilah and Shimal. Alternatively, visit the hot springs at Khatt or the camel racetrack at Digdagga. One town in the emirate, Masafi, is home of the country's favourite bottled spring water; the UAE's (far superior!) answer to Evian. RAK is the starting or finishing point for a spectacular trip through the mountains via Wadi Bih to Dibba on the East Coast and is also the entry point to the Mussandam Peninsula, Oman. Refer to the *Off-Road Explorer (UAE)* for further information on the trip through Wadi Bih and for exploring the Mussandam. See also: Wadi & Dune Bashing [p.306].

Sharjah

Historically, Sharjah was one of the wealthiest towns in the region, with settlers earning their livelihood from fishing, pearling and trade, and to a lesser extent, from agriculture and hunting. It is believed that the earliest settlements date back over 5,000 years. Today Sharjah is still a centre for trade and commerce, although its importance in this respect has been overshadowed by Dubai. The city grew around the creek or lagoon, which is still a prominent landmark in the modern city. Sharjah is only a 20 minute drive from Dubai (depending on the infamous Dubai to Sharjah highway which in rush hour can delay your journey by anything up to two hours!).

The emirate is definitely worth a visit, mainly for its various museums. In 1998, UNESCO named Sharjah the cultural capital of the Arab world due to its commitment to art, culture and preserving its traditional heritage. Opposite Sharjah Natural History Museum, on the Al Dhaid road, past Sharjah Airport, a monument has been built to commemorate this award.

Sharjah is the only emirate with a coastline on both the Arabian Gulf and the Gulf of Oman. A visit from the city of Sharjah to its territory on the East Coast heads through the spectacular Hajar Mountains and takes 1½ - 2 hours (obviously depending on whether you're a speed demon). The towns of Dibba, Khor Fakkan and Kalba are all part of Sharjah.

A useful guidebook to refer to for further information on this emirate is Sharjah The Guide.

Sharjah Creek

Sharjah is built around Khalid Lagoon, which is popularly called the Creek or Al Buheirah Creek, with a walkway around it known as the Corniche. The Corniche is a popular spot for a stroll in the cool of the evening, especially with families, and there are various places for coffee along the way. In the middle of the lagoon is a huge fountain, or jet of water, allegedly the second highest in the world. From three points on the lagoon, small dhows can be hired for a trip around the Creek to see the lights of the city from the water. It is also a great photo opportunity during daylight hours. Prices for these dhows are fixed and cost Dhs.30 for a 15 minute trip for a party of ten, while a tour of the lagoon to the bridge and back takes about 30 minutes and costs Dhs.60.

Decency Law

Visitors should be aware that a decency law has been implemented in Sharjah. Leaflets have been distributed in all public places to make people aware of the codes of moral behaviour and dress sense that are expected. This essentially means that there is now little freedom in this emirate for men and women who are not related or married to interrelate, or even be in a car together. In addition, to avoid offence (and attracting the interest of the police) you should dress much more conservatively than in Dubai. Basically, avoid wearing tight or revealing clothing in Sharjah (and that goes for guys as well as ladies!).

Sharjah Heritage Site

Majaz Canal

An eighty million dirham project links Khalid Lagoon with the Al Khan Lagoons and the Mamzar Park area via the new 1,000 metre long Majaz Canal. The aim is to create a 'Little Italy' tourist attraction along the canal, complete with boat rides between the two lagoons, although the Venice like touches might not seem quite as impressive as the original. The development is in keeping with the Sharjah government's desire to develop the tourism industry on a cultural and educational basis. Three bridges have been built over the canal near Khalid Lagoon, on Al Khan Road, and near Al Khan Lagoon as part of the project. For the past couple of years, it's been complete, but largely sitting deserted – shame!

Al Dhaid

Al Dhaid is a green oasis town on the road from Sharjah to the East Coast. It is the second most important town in the Sharjah emirate and was once a favourite retreat from the deserts and coasts during the scorching summer months. Years ago, an extensive falaj (irrigation system) was built, both above and below ground to irrigate the land. The area is fertile, and agricultural produce includes a wide range of fruit and vegetables from strawberries to broccoli and, of course, a large date crop. On the outskirts of Al Dhaid, shoppers will find roadside stalls selling pottery, carpets, fruit and vegetables. During the winter camel racing is held at the racetrack on the road to Mileiha.

Sharjah New Souk

Location → Nr Corniche · Sharjah | na
Hours → 09:00 - 13:00 16:00 - 22:00
Web/email → n/a | Map Ref → UAE-C2

Consisting of two long, low buildings running parallel to each other and connected by footbridges, Sharjah New Souk (or Blue Souk) is a haven for bargain hunters. The inside is functional and new, but the outside is intricately decorated and imaginatively built in an 'Arabian' style. Each building is covered and air conditioned to protect shoppers from the hot sun. The site has about 600 shops that sell everything from furniture and carved wood to clothing, jewellery and souvenirs, plus a fabulous range of carpets.

Souk Al Arsah

Location → Nr Bank St · Sharjah | na
Hours → 09:00 - 13:00 16:30 - 21:00
Web/email → n/a | Map Ref → UAE C2

This is probably Sharjah's oldest souk, and has been renovated in the style of a traditional market place using shells, coral, African wood and palm leaves. There are almost 100 small shops set in a maze of peaceful alleyways and selling goods such as traditional silver jewellery, perfumes, spices, coffee pots and wedding chests, plus numerous other items, old and new. There is also a small coffee shop selling Arabic tea, coffee and sweets.

Umm Al Quwain

Lying further north along the coast from Dubai, between Ajman and Ras Al Khaimah, is the emirate of Umm Al Quwain. The town is based around a large lagoon or creek and has a long seafaring tradition of pearling and fishing. On a superficial level, not much has changed here over the years and it gives an idea of life in the UAE in earlier times. The emirate has six forts that are still standing and there are a few old watchtowers around the town, but otherwise there is not a lot to see or do in the town itself.

However, the lagoon, with its mangroves and birdlife, is a popular weekend spot for boat trips, windsurfing and other water sports, since it is sheltered and free of dangerous currents. Just north of Umm Al Quwain, near the Barracuda Hotel (and grey market liquor store) is a growing fun park, Dreamland Aqua Park. There are also various clubs, UAQ Flying Club, UAQ Shooting Club, UAQ Equestrian Centre and the opportunity to try karting and paintballing. All of which make this the 'activity centre' of the Northern Emirates. With more resorts and facilities planned, this area can only get better!

East Coast

A trip to the East Coast of the Emirates is well worth making, even if you are only in the UAE for a short time. The coast can be reached in under two hours, and the drive takes you through the rugged Hajar Mountains and down to the Gulf of Oman. Take the road through the desert to Al Dhaid (an important agricultural town famous for its strawberries) and Masafi (source of the local bottled water). Just before Masafi, you will pass the Friday Market selling carpets, pottery, fruit and plants. On reaching Masafi, you can do a loop round, either driving north to Dibba and then along the coast to Fujairah and Kalba and back to Masafi, or the other way round.

The mountains and East Coast are popular for camping, barbecues and weekend breaks, as well as various sporting activities. Snorkelling is excellent, even near the shore, and locations such as Snoopy Rock are always popular. In addition, the diving on this coastline is usually excellent, with plenty of flora and fauna to be seen on the coral reefs. Check out the *Underwater Explorer (UAE)* for further information.

For off-road driving fans, the route to the East Coast has a number of interesting diversions, check out the *Off-Road Explorer (UAE)*. Both titles are published by Explorer Publishing. See also: Camping [p.268]; Diving [p.274]; Snorkelling [p.301].

In Dibba, the Holiday Beach Motel is an ideal place to stay and is situated opposite Dibba Island, which is good for diving and snorkelling [p.301]. Immediately opposite is Northstar Adventures, a company that specifically offers activities for kids. Close by, and almost next to the Holiday Beach Motel, is Al-Fujairah Royal Beach, which will offer bungalow chalets when it is completed in mid 2004. Another five star hotel, Le Meridien, was built in December 2002 in the small village of Al Aqqah. Rising more than 20 storeys high, it creates a rather bizarre sight against the backdrop of the wonderful mountain range. The East Coast is fast catching up with the West Coast in the constructions takes, and the beach road has been closed off at various intervals between Dibba and Sharm, although a new road, running parallel but further inland has been built.

Badiyah

Probably best known as the site of the oldest mosque in the UAE, Badiyah is located roughly half way down the East Coast, north of Khor Fakkan. The mosque is made from gypsum, stone and mud bricks finished off with white washed plaster, and the design of four domes supported by a central pillar is considered unique. It was restored in March 2003 and is officially called Al Masjid Al Othmani. It is thought to date back 1,400 years, having been built in the year 20 Hijra in the Islamic calendar or 1446 AD in the Roman calendar. Surrounded by a 1½ metre wall, the mosque is still used for prayer, so non Muslim visitors have to satisfy themselves with a photo from the outside. The mosque is built into a low hillside with several recently restored watchtowers on the hills behind, and the area is now lit up at night with lovely sodium coloured lighting. The village of Badiyah itself is one of the oldest settlements on the East Coast and is believed to have been inhabited since 3000 BC.

Bithna

Set in the mountains about 12 km from Fujairah, the village of Bithna is notable chiefly for its fort and archaeological site. The fort once controlled the main pass through the mountains from east to west and is still impressive; however, even more impressive is the man that still lives there, guarding it (he's said to be aged over 90)! The village can be reached from the Fujairah - Sharjah road and the fort is through the village and wadi. There are rumours that the fort will be renovated, but nothing has started in 2003. The archaeological site is known as the Long Chambered Tomb or the T-Shaped Tomb, and was probably once a communal burial site. It was excavated in 1988 and its main period of use is thought to date from between 1350 and 300 BC, although the tomb itself is older. Fujairah Museum has a detailed display of the tomb that is worth seeing since the site itself is fenced off and covered against the elements. The tomb can be found by taking a right, then left hand turn before the village, near the radio tower.

Dibba

Located at the northern most point of the East Coast, on the border with the Mussandam, Dibba is made up of three fishing villages. Unusually, each part comes under a different jurisdiction: Dibba al Hisn is Sharjah, Dibba Muhallab is Fujairah and Dibba Bayah is Oman! However, there is no sign of this when you visit the town, which is relaxed and friendly (perhaps what is most noticeable is a distinguishing lack of blue plastic bag trees!). The Hajar Mountains provide a wonderful backdrop to the village, rising in places to over 1,800 metres. Dibba is the starting or finishing point for the stunning drive to the West Coast through the mountains via Wadi Bih. Various burial sites litter this historical region. In particular, rumour has it that a vast cemetery with over 10,000 headstones can still be seen (although we have yet to hear of anyone actually finding it!). This is the legacy of a great battle fought in 633 AD, when the Muslim armies of Caliph Abu Baker were sent to suppress a local rebellion and to re-conquer the Arabian Peninsula for Islam. See also: Khasab Dhow Charters – Dhow Charters [p.273].

Wadi Bih Closed...

For some months now (Dec 2003) the wadi has been closed on the UAE side. Access is still possible from the Dibba side, but not as a round trip. For the journey through Wadi Bih, a 4 wheel drive is essential, since the route is often blocked by boulders carried by the floods... be prepared to rebuild the road, or to turn back.

Fujairah

Fujairah often seems to be best known as the youngest of the seven emirates, since it was part of Sharjah until 1952. However, there is a lot more to the only emirate located entirely on the East Coast. It is in a lovely area with golden beaches bordered by the Gulf of Oman on one side and the Hajar Mountains on the other. The town is a mix of old and new; overlooking the atmospheric old town is the fort, which is reportedly about 300 years old. It is currently being renovated and is not yet reopened to the public, although it looks complete. The surrounding hillsides are dotted with ancient forts and watchtowers, which add an air of mystery and charm. Most of these also appear to be undergoing restoration work. Off the coast, the seas and coral reefs make it a great spot for fishing, diving and water sports. It is also a good place for birdwatching during the spring and autumn migrations since it is on the route from Africa to Central Asia. The emirate has started to encourage more tourism by opening new hotels and providing more recreational facilities. Since Fujairah is close to the mountains and many areas of natural beauty, it makes an excellent base to explore the countryside and see wadis, forts, waterfalls and even natural hot springs. An excellent tourist map has been produced by the

Municipality (09 222 7000) and Fujairah Tourism Bureau (09 223 1436). It includes superb hill shading, roads, graded tracks, 4 WD tracks, a decent co-ordinate system and places of interest. On the reverse side is a brief overview of each place of interest, combined with an overview of the city. During the winter months late on a Friday afternoon, between the Hilton Hotel and Khor Kalba area, you may see pick up trucks on the right hand side of the road and a crowd of people gathered to watch bullfighting. This isn't bullfighting in the Spanish sense, but an unusual Arabic version. It consists of two huge bulls facing each other for several rounds, until after a few head nudges and a bit of hoof bashing, they somehow determine a winner. If you decide to watch, take care; some of the bulls get rather agitated (unsurprisingly) and take their owner for a walk, bash into a few vehicles or even get totally out of control and run riot down the street.

Kalba

If you go on an outing to the East Coast, don't turn back at Fujairah, for just to the south lies the tip of the UAE's Indian Ocean coastline. Here you will find Kalba, which is part of the emirate of Sharjah and renowned for its mangrove forest and golden beaches. The village is a pretty, but modern, fishing village that retains much of its charm. A road through the mountains linking Kalba to Hatta has recently been completed, creating an interesting alternative to returning to Dubai on the Al Dhaid - Sharjah road.

Khor Kalba

South of the village of Kalba is Khor Kalba, set in a beautiful tidal estuary (khor is the Arabic word for creek). This is the most northerly mangrove forest in the world, the oldest in Arabia and is a 'biological treasure', home to a variety of plant, marine and birdlife not found anywhere else in the UAE. If you are a birdwatcher or nature lover, try to spend a few days in this surprising and beautiful region of Arabia. Although it has been proposed to make this a fully protected nature reserve, it is still waiting for Federal protection. The mangroves grow in this area due to the mix of saltwater from the sea and freshwater from the mountains, but they are receding due to the excessive use of water from inland wells. For birdwatchers, the area is especially good during the spring and autumn migrations, and special species of bird include the reef heron and the booted warbler. It is also home to the rare white collared kingfisher, which breeds here and nowhere else in the world. There are believed to be only 55 pairs of these birds still in existence. A canoe tour by Desert Rangers is an ideal opportunity to reach the heart of the reserve and you can regularly see over a dozen kingfishers on a trip. There is also the possibility of seeing one of the region's endangered turtles. The reserve is a unique area so treat it with respect – leave it as you would wish to find it –undisturbed! See also: Desert Rangers – Canoeing [p.269]; Birdwatching [p.321].

Khor Fakkan

Khor Fakkan lies at the foot of the Hajar Mountains halfway down the East Coast between Dibba and Fujairah. It is a popular and charming town, set in a bay and flanked on either side by two headlands, hence its alternative name 'Creek of the Two Jaws'. It is a favourite place for weekend breaks or day trips and has an attractive corniche (waterfront) and beach. A new souk sells the usual range of the exotic and the ordinary. There are plenty of things

Oman

to do including fishing, water sports or a trip to Shark Island; alternatively, sit in the shade with a fruit juice and people watch. Part of the emirate of Sharjah, it has an important modern port; ships discharging their cargo here can save a further 48 hour journey through the Strait of Hormuz to the West Coast. Nearby is the old harbour, which is an interesting contrast to the modern port. Set in the mountains inland is the Rifaisa Dam. Local legend has it that when the water is clear, a lost village can be seen at the bottom of the dam

Wahala

This site is inland from Khor Kalba and is notable for a fort, which archaeologists judge to be over 3,000 years old. It is believed that the fort once protected the resources of the mangrove forests for the local population. A complete renovation program started in late 2003 and may be completed by the end of 2004.

Mussandam

The Mussandam Peninsula is the Omani enclave located to the north of the UAE. It has only been opened to tourists relatively recently and is a beautiful, unspoilt region of Arabia. The capital is Khasab, a quaint fishing port largely unchanged by the modern world. The area is of great strategic importance since its coastline gives control of the main navigable stretch of the Strait of Hormuz, with Iran only 45 km across the water at the narrowest point. To the west is the Arabian Gulf and to the east, the Gulf of Oman. The region is dominated by the Hajar Mountains, which run through the UAE and the rest of Oman. The views along the coast roads are stunning. Inland, the scenery is equally as breathtaking, although to explore properly, a 4 wheel drive and a good head for heights are pretty indispensable! It is sometimes called the 'Norway of the Middle East', since the jagged mountain cliffs plunge directly into the sea and the coastline is littered with inlets and fjords. Just metres off the shore are beautiful coral beds with an amazing variety of sea life, including tropical fish, turtles, dolphins, occasionally sharks, and even whales on the eastern side.

To reach the Mussandam from Dubai, follow the coast road north through Ras Al Khaimah. At the roundabout for Shaam take the exit right and follow the road to the UAE exit post. The Omani entry point is at Tibat, then basically follow the road until it runs out. Note that by car, non GCC nationals can only enter and exit the Mussandam on the Ras Al Khaimah side of the peninsula, not at Dibba on the East Coast. There are UAE and Omani border posts here, so the correct visas are required.

Refer to the *Off-Road Explorer (UAE)* and the *Oman Explorer* for further information on this fascinating part of Arabia.

Sultanate of Oman

The Sultanate of Oman is a friendly, laid back and very beautiful place to visit, especially after the hustle and bustle of Dubai. Visitors have two options – either go east and into Oman proper or north to visit the Omani enclave known as the Mussandam. Both areas can be visited either by plane or car. If you are driving into Oman, there are two main border crossing points; at Hatta (if you want to travel to Muscat) or through the Buraimi Oasis, near Al Ain (if you are driving towards Ibb, Nizwa or Al Salalah). At both places your vehicle will be searched, so it's advisable not to include prohibited items (alcohol, for instance) in your luggage. The journey from Dubai to Muscat by car takes 4 - 5 hours, although crossing the border at the start or end of a public holiday can sometimes be tediously slow, with a 1 - 2 hour wait.

Flying takes about 45 minutes to Muscat. There are flights daily by Emirates and Oman Air, which cost between Dhs.400 - 600, depending on the season. Regular flights direct to Salalah from Dubai are a new service. Salalah, in the south of Oman, is a 'must do' location for visitors.

The local currency is the Omani Riyal (referred to as RO), which is divided into 1,000 baisa (or baiza). The exchange rate is usually about Dhs.10 = RO.1.

Note that talking on hand held mobile telephones whilst driving is illegal in Oman, as is driving a dirty car (yes, seriously)! For further information on what Oman has to offer both visitors and residents, refer to the *Oman Explorer*.

Omani Visas

Visas for Oman are required for most nationalities, whether entering by air or road, and different regulations apply depending on your nationality and how long you want to stay in Oman. In general, a visit visa can be obtained on arrival at the airport or on reaching the border crossing for between Dhs.33 - 50. Remember that regulations in this part of the world often change virtually overnight, so check details before you leave to avoid disappointment. Note that special clearance is required if you have 'journalist' or

'photographer' as a profession in your passport. It is a straightforward procedure to apply at the consulate in Dubai for a visit visa, though this will cost more than just arriving at the border. Alternatively, let your sponsor (hotel, tour operator, Omani company) do the paperwork for you. Certain nationalities in the UAE on a tourist visa may obtain an Omani tourist visa (without sponsorship) on arrival at Seeb International Airport for Dhs.50. If you wish to return to the UAE after your visit to Oman, you will need a new visa. If you are a UAE resident, a visa can be obtained on arrival at the border for Dhs.33. British and American citizens with UAE residency may consider applying for a two year multiple entry visa (Dhs.100). If you are travelling to the Mussandam from Dibba port, the tour company will arrange a special pass for the day, usually for no additional cost. However, if you are travelling to the Mussandam from Ras Al Khaimah to visit the Khasab side, the standard visit visa is needed, either from the consulate or by applying at the border (if you fulfil the criteria).

Weekend Breaks

A great way to escape the hassles of city and work is to go away for the weekend. This can either be a 'do it yourself' break within the UAE or to Oman, or a special deal arranged through a travel agent to a destination such as Jordan, the Seychelles or Kish Island. With distances in the UAE being relatively small, it's easy to get well away from home without having to drive for hours – you can even check into a beach hotel minutes from home and feel that you have entered another world! The alternative to staying in a hotel is to camp, and this is a very popular, well established pastime in the UAE.

The main travel agents in Dubai often have special offers for people wanting something a little different – how about a trip to Zanzibar, Bahrain or India? These offers are generally only available to GCC residents. The travel agents listed in the table are some of those that meet the needs of people living in Dubai, who want good advice, exciting itineraries and holidays that will not cost the earth. Last minute deals can often be found on the Internet (eg, www.mytravelchannel.com, www.emirates.com, www.dnata.com, www.arabia.msn.com).

If you decide to stay in a hotel and are booking with them directly, remember that (if asked) they will often give a discount on their 'rack' rate or published price. There are also often special promotions running, particularly in the quieter summer months when there are some incredible bargains available at five star hotels. The cost of breakfast may or may not be included, so check when you book. Typically, for a weekend in the peak season or for corporate rates, expect a 30% discount off the rack rate. Off peak this can be as much as 60% lower.

For a list of places to stay, check out the Weekend Break table. This has a guide to the room costs at the hotels, however, as explained above, these may be discounted further. Before choosing a destination, you may like to refer to the information on the other emirates under Out of Dubai or the Sultanate of Oman.

For more detailed information on Abu Dhabi and the Sultanate of Oman, refer to the *Abu Dhabi Explorer* and the *Oman Explorer*; both books are part of the Explorer series of guidebooks. For camping options, see the *Off-Road Explorer (UAE)*, while if you're a fan of the marine world, refer to the *Underwater Explorer (UAE)*.

The Rugged Mountains of the UAE

Weekend Break Summary

United Arab Emirates (+971)

Abu Dhabi Emirate		Hotel	Phone	Email	Rate
Abu Dhabi	180km	Abu Dhabi Hilton	02 681 1900	auhhitw@emirates.net.ae	900 (+16%)
		InterContinental	02 666 6888	abudhabi@interconti.com	950(+16%,B)
		Khalidia Palace	02 666 2470	kphauh@emirates.net.ae	550
		Le Meridien	02 644 6666	meridien@emirates.net.ae	1300(+16%)
		Mafraq Hotel	02 582 2666	mafraq@emirates.net.ae	450 (+16%)
		Sheraton Abu Dhabi	02 677 3333	sheraton@emirates.net.ae	950(+16%)
Al Ain	130km	Al Ain Hilton	03 768 6666	alhilton@emirates.net.ae	400(+16%)
		InterContinental	03 768 6686	alain@interconti.com	650(+16%)
		Mercure Grand Hotel	03 783 8888	mgjh@mercure.alain.com	320
Jazira	60km	Al Diar Jazira Beach	02 562 9100	reservations@jaziraresort.com	350(+16%)
Liwa	365km	Liwa Resthouse	02 882 2075	-	165(B)
Ajman Emirate					
Ajman	20km	Ajman Kempinski	06 745 1555	ajman.kempinski@kemp-aj.com	950
Dubai Emirate					
Dubai		Jumeirah Beach	04 348 0000	info@thejumeirahbeachhotel.com	1,600(+20%)
		Ritz-Carlton Dubai, The	04 399 4000	rcdubai@emirates.net.ae	1,290
		Royal Mirage (Palace)	04 399 9999	royalmirage@royalmiragedubai.com	1,460 (+20%)
		Royal Mirage (Courts)	04 399 9999	royalmirage@royalmiragedubai.com	1,670 (+20%)
		Royal Mirage (Residence)	04 399 9999	royalmirage@royalmiragedubai.com	1,900 (+20%)
Hatta	110km	Hatta Fort	04 852 3211	hfh@jaihotels.com	780 (+20%)
Jebel Ali	50km	Jebel Ali Resort	04 883 6000	jagrs@jaihotels.com	1,200 (+20%)
East Coast					
Fujairah	130km	Al Diar Siji	09 223 2000	sijihotl@emirates.net.ae	650 (15%)
		Le Meridien Al Aqqah	09 244 9000	info@lemeridien-alaqqah.com	900
		Fujairah Hilton	09 222 2411	shjhitwres@hilton.com	425 (15%)
		Sandy Beach Motel	09 244 5555	sandybm@emirates.net.ae	385 (10%)
Khorfakkan	160km	Oceanic Hotel	09 238 5111	oceanic2@emirates.net.ae	575
Ras Al Khaimah					
RAK	75km	Al Hamra Fort	07 244 6666	hamfort@emirates.net.ae	700
		Ras Al Khaimah Hotel	07 236 2999	rakhotel@emirates.net.ae	250
		RAK Hilton	07 228 8888	ras-al-khaimah@hilton.com	550
Umm Al Quwain					
UAQ	50km	Flamingo Beach Resort	06 765 1185	fbruaq@hotmail.com	450 (B)

Sultanate of Oman (+968)

		Hotel	Phone	Email	Rate
Barka	250km	Al Sawadi Resort	+968 895 545	sales@alsawadibeach.com	230(+17%)
Khasab	150km	Golden Tulip Khasab	+968 830 777	info@goldentulipkhasab.com	459
		Khasab	+968 830 271	–	340
Muscat	450km	Al Bustan Palace	+968 799 666	albustan@interconti.com	1,290(+17%)
		Crowne Plaza	+968 560 100	cpmct@omantel.net.om	580(+17%)
		Grand Hyatt Muscat	+968 602 888	hyattmct@omantel.net.om	880(+17.4%)
		Holiday Inn Muscat	+968 687 123	mcthinn@omantel.net.om	590(+17%)
		Chedi Muscat, The	+968 505035	chedimuscat@ghmhotels.com	823(+17%)
		InterContinental	+968 600 500	muscat@interconti.com	700(+17%)
		Mercure Al Falaj	+968 702 311	accorsales@omanhotels.com	420(+17%)
		Radisson SAS	+968 685 381	sales@mcdzh.rdsas.com	550(+17%)
		Sheraton Oman	+968 799 899	sheraton@omantel.net.om	650(+17%)
Nizwa	350km	Falaj Daris	+968 410 500	fdhnizwa@omantel.net.om	295
Salalah	1,450km	Holiday Inn Salalah	+968 235 333	hinnsll@omantel.netcom	574 (+17%)
		Salalah Hilton Resort	+968 211 234	sllbc@omantel.net.om	660(+17%)
Sohar	250km	Sohar Beach	+968 841 111	soharhtl@omantel.net.om	350(+17%)
Sur	650km	Sur Mercure	+968 443 777	reservationssur@omanhotels.com	430(+17%)

Note Rack Rate = Price in dirhams of one double room; +xx% = plus tax; B = Inclusive of breakfast.
The above prices are the hotel's peak season rack rates. Remember many hotels will offer a discount off the rack rate if asked!
Distances are measured from Dubai.

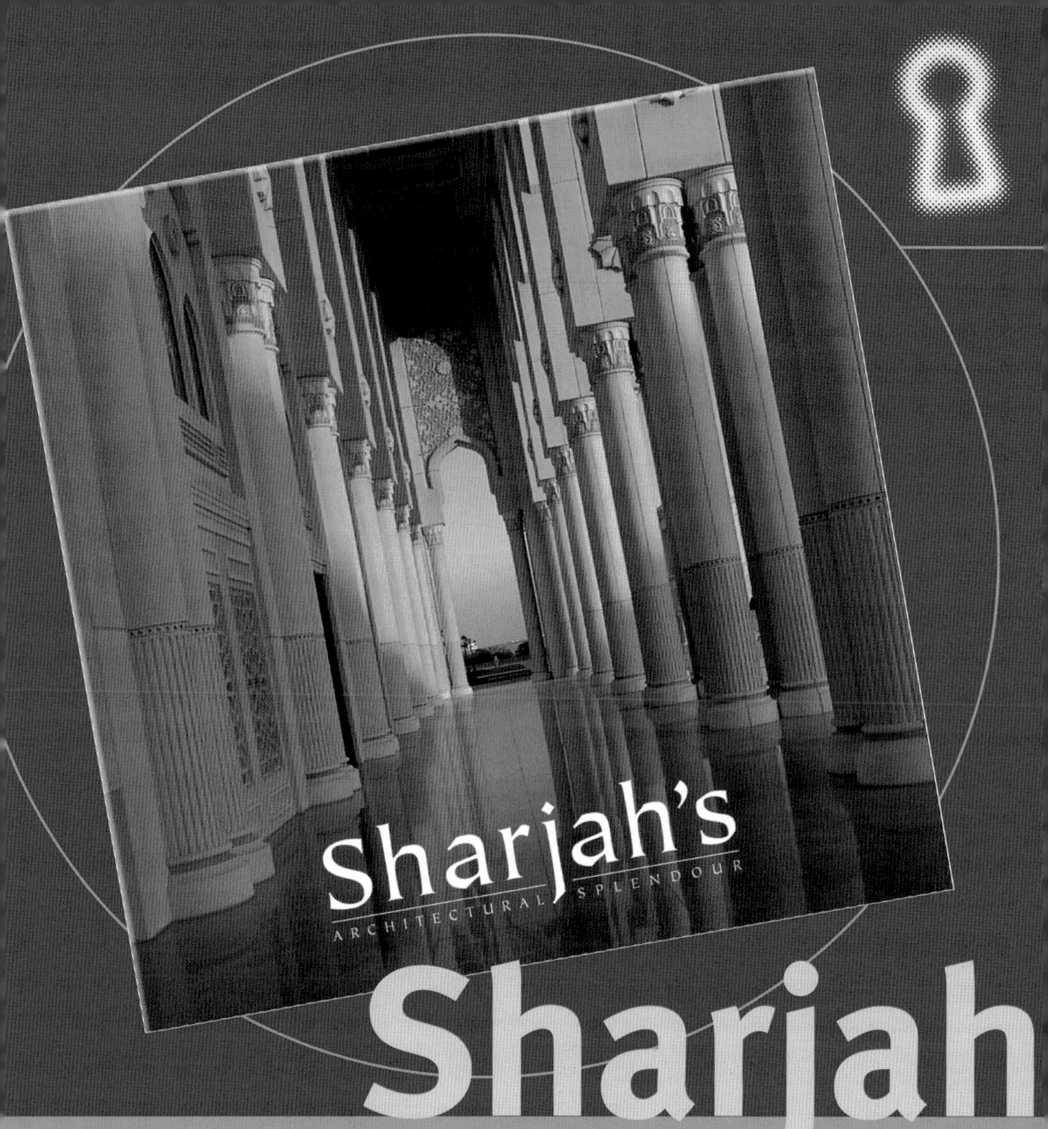
Sharjah's
ARCHITECTURAL SPLENDOUR
Sharjah

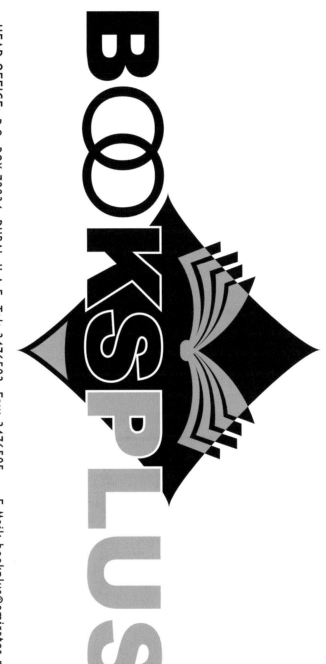

8

Shopping
EXPLORER

Shopping

What's new?

Hubba, hubba, hubba

Page 132

Dubai is the shopping hub of the Middle East and intends to make sure that it always will be, judging by the rapid increase of shopping malls and never ending expansions on the existing buildings. Developers are furiously competing to create the crème de la crème of retail architecture with the Emirates Mall and Dubai Mall on the horizon, to name only two. Flick back to the Business section [p.132] for details on the latest developments.

Calling all home owners

Page 226

Just bought a palace and itching to turn the garden into a landscaped wonder? Swot up on the emerging garden centres [p.226] and make use of those green fingers. If the creative (or destructive) streaks are fighting to emerge, DIY and Hardware [p.228] won't explain how to hammer a nail into a wall without ruining the plaster, but it will tell you where to buy the hammer and nail. Get the rest of the advice from the salesperson.

Clothing Sizes

Women's Clothing						
Aust/NZ	8	10	12	14	16	18
Europe	36	38	40	42	44	46
Japan	5	7	9	11	13	15
UK	8	10	12	14	16	18
USA	6	8	10	12	14	16

Women's Shoes						
Aust/NZ	5	6	7	8	9	10
Europe	35	36	37	38	39	40
France only	35	36	38	39	40	42
Japan	22	23	24	25	26	27
UK	3.5	4.5	5.5	6.5	7.5	8.5
USA	5	6	7	8	9	10

Men's Clothing						
Aust/NZ	92	96	100	104	108	112
Europe	46	48	50	52	54	56
Japan	S	-	M	M	-	L
UK	35	36	37	38	39	40
USA	35	36	37	38	39	40

Men's Shoes						
Aust/NZ	7	8	9	10	11	12
Europe	41	42	43	44.5	46	47
Japan	26	27	27.5	28	29	30
UK	7	8	9	10	11	12
USA	7.5	8.5	9.5	10.5	11.5	12.5

Measurements are approximate only; try before you buy

Shopping

Other options → Exploring [p.156]

There's no doubt that shopping has been elevated to an art form in Dubai and the city basks in its reputation as the 'Shopping Capital of the Middle East'. However, despite its tax-free status, visitors are often surprised, not to mention a little disappointed, to realise that the accolade doesn't necessarily translate into bargains galore in every store. Although prices on certain speciality items, such as carpets, textiles and gold, are extremely competitive, many imported goods are generally similar in price to any other major city in the world. The key to shopping like a pro in Dubai is to bargain where possible and the best deals are to be found in and amongst the souks.

What this city does afford avid shoppers, however, is choice and a thousand ways to flex their plastic. The following section provides information on all that is relevant for shoppers – from what to buy to where to buy it, plus a few tips on how to stretch the mighty dirham.

Dubai's glitzy shopping centres, replete with world-renowned shops and ample parking, are covered in detail. The modern malls are a pivotal social setting for many residents and visitors, offering air conditioned entertainment for a hotchpotch of nationalities and an unrivalled selection of shops and activities to pass the time.

Check out the coloured boxes; these list the most popular brand names of goods and cover where you can buy them. However, don't forget the streets and areas for shopping; they're worth braving the heat for, and the intrepid shopper can track down some genuine bargains. The same applies to Dubai's souks (also covered in the Exploring section).

Buyer Beware!

Note: Traps for the unwary shopper exist in Dubai, as elsewhere. Some of the international stores sell items at prices that are far more expensive than in their country of origin (you can even still see the original price tags!). This can be as much as 30% higher - beware!

Consumers will quickly become aware of the numerous (and endless) promotions and raffles on offer by local radio and TV shows, Dubai International Airport and the smallest, most insignificant of shopping malls. The majority don't even require you to buy a ticket, but will simply hand them over with your till receipt. Great fun – especially if you win that Lexus!

Dubai Chamber of Commerce & Industry (228 0000) publishes a useful book: The Dubai Commercial Directory, which lists products and services available, and the companies that sell them. All international brands including department stores, designer shops and car dealerships are offered in the UAE on an agency basis, mostly run by a few large national families such as Al Futtaim, Al Ghurair, Al Tayer and Al Nabooda.

Refunds & Exchanges

In general, faulty goods are more easily exchanged than refunded at the shop of purchase. If, however, you have simply changed your mind about a recently purchased item, many retailers are not so obliging. Most will only exchange or give credit notes; very few will refund. You may also find that their policy changes for different items.

To be successful returning unwanted items, make sure that they are unworn, unused and in their original packaging. Always check the refund and exchange policy when buying something, always keep your receipt, and if there is a problem ask to see the manager. Most retailers will get hot under the collar if you persist; just let them know that the customer is always right! As a last resort, appeal to their need for ongoing patronage by their customers. If you really think you've been duped, see the following.

Consumer Rights

There are no laws, codes or regulations in Dubai that protect consumers as such – rendered into another language this means that stores can do what they please. However, there is an excerpt in the UAE Civil and Commercial code, which states that the customer is entitled to recover the price paid for faulty goods (although unless you are prepared to take the shop to court, an exchange will have to do).

Dubai Chamber of Commerce & Industry is, however, negotiating to introduce a federal arbitration law that will cater for such commercial disputes. In the meantime, any complaints are best dealt with by the Commercial Protection division of the Department of Economic Development. You can send your complaint by email, fax or visit the department in person, but make sure you can produce your receipt. The department will in turn commence proceedings based on the complaint.

Always check a shop's returns policy before purchasing. You will find that many of the

international department stores are more proactive when it comes to customer service, so for products that are more expensive it may be best to stick with what you know. For more information, contact the Department of Economic Development, Consumer Protection Division (202 0200 or 222 9922) or visit www.dubaided.gov.ae.

Shipping

Getting purchases home can be a tedious business, but a welter of shipping and cargo agencies will ease the experience and lessen the pain. The best plan is to contact an agency directly – look under 'Shipping' in the Dubai Yellow Pages. Most companies operate globally and are quite reliable.

Prices can vary considerably, but to give an indication, the average cost per kilo to Australia is Dhs.95, to the UK around Dhs.85, and to North America, from Dhs.180. These prices are inclusive of handling and packing... taking care of all those tiresome custom clearance papers, careful packing, door to door delivery (on request) and generally allowing the customer more time to shop to fill up their next shipment crate! Items can be sent by sea freight (cheapest), airfreight or by courier.

To send possessions by air, DNATA Sky Cargo based in Cargo Village at Dubai Airport, is the sole handler in the region. It's advisable to shop around for prices or you can deal directly with Sky Cargo. They offer immediate quotes by phone (211 1111) and prices vary daily depending on route, airline and the space available. All you need to provide is the weight of your package and the destination airport. If required, Sky Cargo will also handle sea freight.

During the Dubai Shopping Festival and Dubai Summer Surprises, some courier and shipping companies offer special rates; check them out if you're planning to export the results of your shopping frenzy.

See also: *Moving Services [p.90].*

How to Pay

You will have no problems exchanging or withdrawing money or paying for goods in Dubai. ATMs (otherwise known as automatic teller machines, service tills or cash points) are readily accessible. Most cards are accepted by the plethora of banks in Dubai, which offer international access through CIRRUS or PLUS ATMs.

Credit cards are widely accepted, the exception being small traders in the souks and local convenience stores. Accepted international credit cards include American Express, Visa, MasterCard and Diners Club. Discounting the high rates of interest you will have to pay, local banks reward their credit card users with a number of promotions, competitions and discounts.

US currency is also widely accepted, even by the ubiquitous 'corner shops', and since the dirham is pegged to the US dollar, the exchange rate is broadly the same throughout Dubai. However, for the astute shopper, the best bargains are had by using the local currency. There are numerous money exchange bureaus in major shopping areas and the souks, and being equipped with dirhams makes shopping a whole lot quicker and hassle free. It can also, potentially, translate into some cash discounts.

See also: *Money (General Information) [p.3].*

Bargaining

Other options → Souks [p.254]

Although for many bargaining is an alien way of doing business, it is a time-honoured tradition in this part of the world. Vendors will often drop the price quite substantially for a cash sale, especially in the souks. So, relax, think 'something for nothing' and take your time – this can be fun!

The key to bargaining is to decide what you are happy paying for the item and to walk away if you don't get it for that. Always be polite and amiable, and never use rudeness or aggression as bargaining tools. Start with a customary greeting and know the value of the item beforehand; you can learn this by scouting other shops. Ask the shop assistant how much, and when he tells you, look shocked or indifferent. In the souks, a common rule is to initially offer half the quoted price.

Once you've agreed to a price, that's it – it's a verbal contract and you are expected to buy. Remember, storekeepers are old pros at this and have an instinct for a moment's weakness! Remember also that you don't have to buy if the price isn't right for you. You can always walk away (it's not uncommon for shop assistants to chase you out of the store to secure a purchase). The

consumer is the one with the power here, so use it or lose it!

Away from the souks, bargaining is not common practice, although many stores operate a set discount system, saying that the price shown is 'before discount'. Offering to pay cash can be beneficial, so it won't hurt to ask for a further discount. Even pharmacies have a last price system whereby they will reduce what is shown on the price tag, normally by ten percent.

What & Where to Buy

Dubai's stores sell an abundance of goods and you should have few problems finding what you need. The following section covers the main categories of products that can be bought in the city, from carpets to cars, electronics to gold, and where to buy them.

Alcohol

Other options → Liquor Licence [p.69]
On the Town Section

Anyone aged over 21 years can buy alcohol at licensed bars, restaurants and some clubs for consumption on the premises. However, to buy alcohol for consumption at home requires a liquor licence – it's not just a case of popping into your local supermarket. Only non Muslim residents can apply for a liquor licence. For information on how to obtain a licence and the restrictions that apply, refer to the Residents section.

Note that residents who have a liquor licence from another emirate are not permitted to use it in Dubai (except for old Sharjah licences, which are no longer valid in Sharjah, but can be endorsed by Dubai Police).

Once you have gone to the trouble of acquiring a licence, it's easy enough to purchase alcohol from the special stores that are strategically scattered around Dubai. Especially useful are those located near supermarkets, so you can do all your shopping in one trip. When you do get your licence, you may find that friends you never knew you had are angling to help you out on shopping trips! There is one catch to be aware of; when you get to the checkout, expect to pay 30% more than the sale price in tax.

However, there are ways of jumping the gun... the UAE has a few 'hole in the wall' stores selling tax free alcohol to unlicensed patrons. These stores are easy to buy from if you don't mind the trek. The Barracuda Beach Motel next to Dreamland Aqua Park near Umm Al Quwain is one of those most frequented by Dubai residents. Another store is opposite the Ajman Kempinski, which literally is a hole in the wall. Although this sounds like the easy option, you will find the selection less comprehensive than the licensed outlets scattered throughout the city. Bear in mind that it is illegal to transport alcohol over the border of an emirate, and in particular, through Sharjah. Police often turn a blind eye to this practice, but if you get busted with booze in your car, don't say you weren't warned!

Alcohol

African & Eastern Ltd		
Al Karama	334 8056	Map 9-C3
Al Wasl	394 2676	Map 5-A3
Bur Dubai	352 4521	Map 7-A3
Deira	222 2666	Map 10-D2
Jumeira	344 0327	Map 5-C2

Maritime & Mercantile Int'l LLC		
Al Karama	335 1722	Map 9-C2
Al Wasl	394 1678	Map 4-A3
Bur Dubai	393 5738	Map 10-D2
Deira	294 0390	Map 10-D2
Jumeira	344 0223	Map 5-C2
Shk Zayed Rd	321 1223	Map 9-C2
Trade Center	352 3090	Map 10-E1

Timings: 10:00 - 14:00 & 17:00 - 21:00; 10:00 - 21:00 Thursdays and Saturdays. Closed Friday.

Arabian Souvenirs

Other options → Carpets [p.218]

For visitors and residents alike, many items from this part of the world make novel souvenirs, gifts or ornaments for the home. Historically, this was a Bedouin culture and possessions had to be practical and transportable, reflecting the nomadic lifestyle. The price and quality of traditional items vary enormously and the souks usually offer the best bargains, although there is something to suit all budgets here. These days many of the items are manufactured in India or Oman.

Shopping malls have many stores specialising in Arabic artefacts; the wooden wedding chest is popular and has been widely copied. Traditional wooden doors are also sought after. These can be used as intended or hung against the wall as a piece of art. Alternatively, it's popular to have them turned into furniture, usually tables with a glass top so the carving can still be seen. Carpets are a favourite buy. Don't forget to take your time and see as many choices as possible, plus build up a rapport with the carpet seller and haggle, haggle, haggle!

The symbol of Arabic hospitality, the coffee pot and cups (usually beaten copper), is widely available. The coffee itself can be bought from many supermarkets and really is worth trying. The traditional method of preparing it is still practiced today; coffee beans are roasted, ground and boiled, then cardamon, rosewater, saffron and cloves are added to create a wonderful aroma. The final coffee is quite refreshing when served with dates. Another favourite is the 'khanjar', which is the traditional dagger, a short curved knife in an elaborately wrought sheath. It is often displayed in picture frames and the effect is striking. However, travellers beware, you will not be allowed to take it on an airplane as hand luggage because it is still considered a dangerous item.

Traditional wedding jewellery made of heavy silver and crafted into simply engraved (and extremely heavy) necklaces, bracelets, earrings and rings are coveted forms of historical art, especially as many of the larger pieces make excellent pictures if they are mounted behind glass in a frame. Alternatively, you are in the right city if gold is more to your taste – there is an amazing choice in Dubai. The Gold Souk (see [p.254]) is well worth a visit and because there are no taxes on top of the international gold rate, it is very reasonably priced. The cost of workmanship is also very competitive, and if you are feeling artistic, you can create your own design.

You will either love or hate the smell of incense and the heavy local perfumes, but they make great gifts. Take a walk among the many stalls in the Perfume Souk (between the gold and Deira souks) for the smell of frankincense and myrrh. In the Middle East, frankincense has been traded for centuries and was at one time considered more desirable than gold.

Shisha or hubbly bubbly pipes are a fun item to have and can be bought with variously flavoured tobacco, such as apple or strawberry. Both working or ornamental ones are available and some stores sell a protective carrying case – handy if you are taking it to the desert or beach. Foodwise, look out for delicious Lebanese sweets, often made from pastry, honey, ground nuts and dates, or fresh dates supplied by the main producers from around the world. Iranian caviar is widely available and very good value, and is sold without import duty or a valued added tax.

Arabian Souvenirs

Al Jaber Gallery	City Centre	295 4114
	Opp Hamarain Centre	266 7700
Creative Art Centre	Nr Choithrams	344 4394
Falcon Gallery	Nr. G.P.O, Bur Dubai	337 5877
Showcase Antiques	Nr. Dubai Municipality Umm Suqueim	348 8797

Finally, the jokers out there should try the 'I ♥ Dubai' items, fluffy camels (snoring variety optional) and sand pictures with glass panels that contain the seven different coloured sands of the seven different emirates (it's a wonder that there's any sand left in the UAE). A particular favourite is the tackiest of tackiest, award winning alarm clock in the shape of a mosque, which comes in a variety of attractive colours. The wailing sound of the 'azzan' (prayer call) is sure to get those endorphins going first thing in the morning... they are generally found in the local supermarkets at the bargain price of Dhs.20 - 30, though hurry, stocks won't last.

However, if you're tired of cliches and looking for a more upmarket, easily transported souvenir of the UAE, pick up a good coffee table book such as *Images of Dubai & the United Arab Emirates*.

Arabian Souvenirs

Art

Other options → Art Classes [p.320]
Art Galleries [p.174]

A growing and avid interest in art is being displayed in the region, and many local and international artists are setting up base here. Most shops selling art also double up as gallery space, so, flick back to Art Galleries [p.174] in the Exploring section of the book for a listing of the best options.

Art	
Aquarius	349 7251
Artworks Gallery	332 8277
Hotel Inter-Continental	222 7171
Profile Gallery	349 1147
Sharjah Art Museum	06 568 8222

Art Supplies

Other options → Art [p.214]
Art Galleries [p.174]

Creative types who like to dabble in arts and crafts can find tools of the trade at any of the following stores. If you're looking for anything in particular, try contacting each individual store before embarking on a wild goose chase. The stores are sprawled throughout the city and you could find yourself shop-hopping if you don't plan ahead.

Art Supplies	
Al Hathboor General Trading	286 5965
Art Source	285 6972
Art Stop	349 0627
Chinese Trading	266 3384
Crafters Home	343 3045
Dubai International Art Centre	344 4398
Elves & Fairies	344 9485
Emirates Trading Establishment	337 5050
Talent Stationery	343 2734

Beach Wear

Other options → Clothes [p.219]

Since many Dubai residents spend their weekends basking by the pool or catching some sporting action on the beach, it's not perhaps surprising that some people spend as much money on a pukka set of swimming togs as on a suit for work!

Generally, prices are extremely high in the specialist beach wear boutiques that stock everything from French and Italian designer wear to achingly hip Californian and Australian surfing labels. Since there is no real 'off' season, these shops often have sales at strange times of the year – so if labels are crucial for you, it's worth asking to be added to their mailing list so you can be first to snap up the bargains.

Dubai's many sports shops also stock a decent range of swimwear, but these veer towards no-nonsense styles for competitive swimmers rather than teeny weeny bikinis for die-hard beach babes. For those less bothered about making a fashion statement when they peel off on the beach, head for the department stores in the larger malls such as City Centre and Bur Jurman.

BHS, Woolworth's, Debenhams and Marks & Spencer all sell a good range of fashionable beach wear, plus all the related paraphernalia like hats and beach bags, and at prices that won't break the bank.

Beach Wear		
Al Boom Marine	Ras Al Khor, nr Coca Cola	289 4858
Bare Essentials	Jumeirah Centre	344 0552
Beyond the Beach	Palm Strip	346 1780
Heat Waves	Le Meridien, Dubai	399 3161
Oceano	Palm Strip	346 1961
Westwood	City Centre	295 5900

Books

Other options → Libraries [p.332]

A reasonable selection of English language books is sold in Dubai, covering a broad range of subjects, from travel or computing to children's books, the latest bestsellers and coffee table books about the emirates. Most of the larger

Bookstores

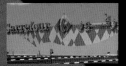

hotels have small bookshops offering a limited choice, including the latest fiction and travel books on the UAE. However, you are unlikely to find as extensive a range of books and bookshops as in your home country, although the number and size of outlets are increasing.

Foreign newspapers and magazines are flown in regularly, but are always more expensive than at home. While for all males out there who enjoy perusing racy blokes' mags, be warned: due to censorship laws, pictures of semi-naked women are always disguised by a giant black pen mark.

Good chains with wide-ranging selections are Book Corner, Books Plus and Magrudy's. Carrefour, Choithrams, Park'nShop and Spinneys supermarkets also carry a very reasonable selection of books and magazines.

There are several second-hand bookshops (good for buying cheap novels or selling unwanted books at a decent price). If you wish to buy used books from them, they offer a fifty percent refund, but remember to keep your receipt.

Alternatively there are plenty of charities that appreciate book donations, while Medecins Sans Frontieres holds an annual second-hand book bazaar. For more information on such events, visit www.msfuae.ae.

Books		
Al Jabre Al El Miah	BurJuman Centre	351 6740
Book Corner	Al Ghurair City	228 2835
	City Centre	295 3266
	Dune Centre	324 2442
Book Worm	Behind Park 'n Shop	394 5770
Books Plus	Oasis Centre	339 4080
	Lamcy Plaza	336 6362
	Spinneys (Umm Suqeim)	394 0278
Carrefour	City Centre	295 1600
	Al Shindagha	393 9395
House of Prose	Jumeirah Plaza	344 9021
Kids Plus	Town Centre	344 2008
Magrudy Book Shop	BurJuman Centre	359 3332
	City Centre	295 7744
	Magrudy Shopping Mall	344 4193
	Spinneys - Trade Centre	351 1777
Spinneys	Nr Ramada Htl	355 5250
	Nr. Bur Juman Centre	351 1777
	Mercato Mall	349 6900
	Umm Suqeim	394 1657
Titan Book Shop	Holiday Centre	331 8671
	Intercontinental Hotel	227 1372
White Star	Beach Centre, The	344 6628
Virgin Megastore	Mercato	344 6971

Camera Equipment

Other options → Electronics & Home Appliances [p.222]

For those who enjoy photography as a hobby, the latest cameras are widely available in Dubai. Prices from the agents are usually fixed and reasonable. However, many famous brands can be found for less on Al Faheidi Street and the surrounding area in Bur Dubai. Here prices can be negotiated, but watch out for 'parallel' imports. UAE agents will not honour the warranty on parallel import items and you'll have to send your camera overseas for warranty repairs.

Opinion is divided as to whether it's cheaper to buy cameras in Dubai than elsewhere. Due to low import costs, cameras here are less expensive than in the UK for instance, but that doesn't mean Dubai is the cheapest place in the world; Hong Kong and Singapore are both cheaper, if you know what you are looking for. However, the cheapest price doesn't always make it a bargain. There are several issues to be aware of before purchasing a camera. If you need advice, try on the Web first.

If you are purchasing in Dubai to take back home, check out the tax implications of the importing country. It may be that the 'bargain' price plus the added import tax, matches or is greater than the price in your own country. It is also important to get a stamped and dated international warranty otherwise the agent in your home country will not honour any future defects. Sony UK refuses to honour any of their products bought outside the UK claiming that they are not an international company.

Salam Studios & Stores in Wafi Mall and Grand Stores in BurJuman and Emirates Towers are the two main shops for photographers; Grand sells Nikon, Fuji and Mamiya, while Salam sells Pentax, Leica, Minolta, Bronica and Noblex. If you are looking for Canon, then JK National Stores is the agent.

Film is available in supermarkets, local shops and hotel foyer shops. UCF stocks Kodak, while Grand Stores supply Fuji and Ilford. Both outlets refrigerate the film; vital in Dubai's climate.

Camera Equipment	
Grand Stores	282 3700
Jacky's Electronics	881 9933
M.K. Trading Co.	222 5745
Salam Studios & Stores	282 4945
UCF	336 9399

For serious photographers, Salam and Grand have the best selection for everything from darkroom equipment and filters to tripods and studio equipment. However, purchasing professional equipment in Dubai is expensive. One cheaper alternative is to buy online from the US; in New York, B&H Photo is a reputable company with prices that are often a great deal cheaper than in the UAE, even including shipping costs.

Cards & Stationery

Other options → Art Supplies [p.214]
Books [p.214]

Most supermarkets carry an ample supply of greeting cards, wrapping paper and stationery. However, there is a number of speciality stores amid the weaving and winding corridors of Dubai's streets and malls. It is here that you will find the best variety in Dubai, especially for cards, where they offer everything from Christmas and Easter to Mother's Day and Eid cards.

However, if you are usually found in the naughty card section, you will be disappointed. The more daring cards do not slip through Dubai's censorship, although if you look hard enough the odd one may be found. Failing that you will just have to stock up next time you are away from the UAE.

While postcards are a bargain, greeting cards tend to be expensive, especially those celebrating special occasions or holidays. Locally produced cards are much cheaper, more original, and often better quality – they can be found in most card shops and usually feature local artists' work. Wrapping paper? THE One (home furnishings) and Bayti in Woolworths have some of the most unique and certainly the most reasonable. Similarly, IKEA sells gift wrapping paraphernalia at a fraction of the price of the more established card and gift wrap stores.

Cards & Stationery

Al Fahidi Stationery	Al Fahidi Street	353 5861
	Opp Al Khaleej Hotel	222 8641
Bayti (Woolworth's)	City Centre	295 7536
	Town Centre	342 2345
Carlton Cards	City Centre	294 8707
	Lamcy Plaza	336 6879
Carrefour	City Centre	295 1600
Emirates Trading	Nr Al Nasr Cinema	337 5050
Farook International Stationary	Meena Bazaar	352 1997
Gulf Greetings	Al Bustan Centre	263 2771
	BurJuman Centre	351 9613
	City Centre	295 0079
	Oasis Centre	339 5459
	Spinneys (Umm Suqeim)	394 0397
	Wafi Mall	324 5618
IKEA	City Centre	295 0423
Office 1	Zabeel Rd	335 9929
THE One	Jumeira	342 2499
Titan Book Shop	Holiday Centre	331 8671

Carpets

Other options → Arabian Souvenirs [p.212]
Bargaining [p.210]

Whether you are a regular buyer or just a novice, carpet shopping can be a fascinating experience. In Dubai, countries of origin range from Iran and Pakistan to China and Central Asia, and there is a truly exquisite array of designs and colours.

To ensure that you are buying the genuine article at a good price, it's advisable to find out a bit about carpets before making the final decision. Information can be found on the Internet; try www.persiancarpetskingdom.com or www.persiancarpethouse.com. However, while you can buy over the Internet, it is better to visit a number of shops to get a feel for price, quality and traditional designs, as well as the range available.

As with most goods, carpets differ in quality, and this is reflected in the price. For nearly 3,000 years, some of the finest carpets have been considered great investments and have strong links with tradition. Silk is more expensive than wool, and rugs from Iran are generally more valuable than the equivalent from Turkey or Kashmir. Check if it is machine or handmade (handmade ones are never quite perfect and the pile is slightly uneven).

A good tip is to decide in advance the maximum you are prepared to spend, and to begin the bargaining by offering half that. Bargaining is expected in most shops; prices vary from a few hundred to many thousand dirhams, but are always negotiable. If you are new to the haggling game, check our guide to Bargaining (p.210).

Deira Tower shopping mall in Al Nasr Square has the largest number of carpet outlets under one roof – the majority of traders are from Iran. As part of the Dubai Shopping Festival, a carpet souk is set up in a large air conditioned tent at the Airport Exhibition Centre. Here you can find a mind boggling choice of carpets at excellent prices.

See also: *Dubai Shopping Festival [p.132].*

Carpets

Afghan Carpets	Airport Road	286 9661
	Oasis Centre	339 5786
Al Orooba Oriental	BurJuman Centre	351 0919
Carpetland	Near Lamcy Plaza	337 7677
Feshwari	Nr Oasis Center	344 5426
Kashmir Gallery	Al Ghurair City	222 5271
Khyber Carpets	Galleria Shopping Mall	272 0112
Persian Carpet House	Crowne Plaza	332 1161
Quem Persian Carpets	Sheraton Htl & Towers	228 1848
Red Sea Exhibition	Beach Centre, The	344 3949

Cars

Other options → Buying a Vehicle [p.122]

New residents are often pleasantly surprised to find that cars here are much cheaper than in their own country, and with competitive interest rates offered by banks and dealers, buying a new car isn't necessarily for an elite few. All the major car manufacturers are represented and give good discounts towards the end of the year (when next year's model is due in the showroom) and during the Shopping Festival.

Alternatively, the second-hand market thrives with an abundance of used car dealerships all over town. Here you'll find everything from barely used Porsches and Ferraris to 4x4s – ideal for thrashing around in the desert. Prices are never final so stand your ground if you're determined to clinch a deal; remember the dealer has paid the previous owner a fraction of the price he's trying to sell it to you for.

It is quite common to find adverts offering cars for sale that are described as 'unwanted gifts'. Keep an eye out for such things particularly after the Shopping Festival and similar events. These 'unwanted gifts' are often advertised privately in the Classifieds section of the newspapers, a beneficial result of Dubai's competition mania.

For other good deals, check the newspapers, supermarket noticeboards or websites such as www.valueonwheels.com. It's a good idea to have the vehicle checked out by a reputable garage before you take the plunge and buy.

Clothes

Other options → Beach Wear [p.214]
Kids' Items [p.234]
Lingerie [p.232]
Shoes [p.236]

Dubai is fashion lovers' heaven – here you will find everything from the priciest designer shops or up-to-the-minute boutiques to 'pile it high, sell it cheap' bargain basement stores. Most malls have a good selection of inexpensive quality clothing and there is an increasing trend for 'global' stores that sell the same clothing the world over, turning over their stock every four to six weeks. Handily, they show the retail price in each country on the tag, so you can easily check whether you're being ripped off.

Upmarket stores dedicated to designer names are mainly found in the shopping malls and hotel arcades, although many designer names are still located on Al Maktoum Street in Deira. For further information on Deira, see the Exploring section. For smart men's suits, jackets and casuals, there is a number of shops along the Creek in Deira, especially around the Twin Towers area. Many offer permanent sales on 'designer' suits. The shopping areas of Satwa and Karama offer a heady mixture of cheap clothing outlets of wildly varying quality. On a good day, you can easily kit yourself for a night on the town for the price of a few fruit cocktails; but on a not so good

Authentic Treasures

Clothes

Amichi	Mercato	349 0999
Armani Jeans	Mercato	344 4161
	Palm Strip	345 9944
Bebe	Al Ghurair City	223 2333
Benetton	Al Ghurair City	221 1593
	BurJuman Centre	351 1331
	City Centre	295 2450
	Jumeirah Centre	349 3613
	Lamcy Plaza	334 7353
Bershka	City Centre	295 4545
	Mercato	344 4161
Bhs	Al Ghurair City	227 6969
	BurJuman Centre	352 5150
	Lamcy Plaza	305 9208
Bossini	Al Ghurair City	221 5917
	Beach Centre, The	349 0749
	BurJuman Centre	351 6917
	Lamcy Plaza	305 9313
	Meena Bazaar	352 4817
Burberry	City Centre	295 0347
Calvin Klein	BurJuman Centre	352 5244
	City Centre	295 0194
Cartoon Fashion	Al Ghurair City	221 6461
Cerruti	Twin Towers	227 2789
Chanel	Wafi Mall	324 0464
Christian Lacroix	BurJuman Centre	351 7133
	Wafi Mall	324 0465
Debenhams	City Centre	294 0011
Diesel	City Centre	295 0792
DKNY	BurJuman Centre	351 3788
	City Centre	295 2953
DKNY Jeans	Town Centre	349 7693
Dolce & Gabana	City Centre	295 0790
Donna Karan	BurJuman Centre	351 6794
Escada	BurJuman Centre	352 9253
Esprit	BurJuman Centre	355 3324
Etoile	Wafi Mall	324 0465
Evans	City Centre	294 0011
G2000	BurJuman Centre	355 2942
Gasoline	Palm Strip	345 0543
Gerry Webber	City Centre	295 4914
	Wafi Mall	324 3899
Giordano	Al Ghurair City	223 7904
	BurJuman Centre	351 3866
	City Centre	295 0959
	Karama Centre	336 8312
	Wafi Mall	324 2852
Givenchy	Wafi Mall	324 2266
Guess	City Centre	295 2577
Hang Ten	BurJuman Centre	351 9285
	City Centre	295 3702
Hyphen	City Centre	295 2110
Hugo Boss	City Centre	295 5281
In Wear	BurJuman Centre	355 4007
	City Centre	295 0261
Jaeger	Wafi Mall	324 9838
Jenyfer	Lamcy Plaza	337 2924
JC Penney (Liwa)	BurJuman Centre	351 5353
Karen Millen	City Centre	295 5007
Kookai	Al Rigga Street	223 8500
	City Centre	295 2598
	Wafi Mall	324 9936
Lacoste	City Centre	295 4429
Levis	BurJuman Centre	351 6728
	City Centre	295 9943
Mango	BurJuman Centre	355 5770
	City Centre	295 0182
	Palm Strip	346 1826
Marks & Spencer	Al Futtaim Centre	222 2000
	Salah Al Din Rd	222 2000
Massimo Dutti	BurJuman Centre	351 5750
	City Centre	295 4788
	Mercato	344 7124
Max Mara	BurJuman Centre	352 2162
Mexx	BurJuman Centre	355 1881
	City Centre	295 4873
	Lamcy Plaza	334 0182
Miss Sixty	Mercato	349 9199
	Wafi Mall	324 1998
Monsoon	City Centre	295 0725
MTV Fashions	Palm Strip	345 2991
Next	BurJuman Centre	351 0026
	City Centre	295 2280
Oasis	Nr Emirates Exchange	334 4227
	Wafi Mall	324 9074
Oui	City Centre	295 3906
Part Two	City Centre	295 0261
Polo Ralph Lauren	BurJuman Centre	352 5311
	City Centre	294 1200
Pull & Bear	City Centre	295 3525
River Island	City Centre	295 4413
Rodeo Drive	Al Bustan Hotel	282 4006
	Galleria Shopping Mall	343 4000
Sana Fashion	Karama	337 7726
Splash	Nr Maktoum Bridge	335 0525
	Oasis Centre	339 0511
Truworths	City Centre	295 1010
Westwood	City Centre	294 9292
Woolworths	City Centre	295 5900
XOXO	BurJuman Centre	355 3324
Zara	BurJuman Centre	351 3332
	City Centre	294 0839

day, forget it, unless there's a bad taste party in the offing. If you are confused about the sizing system here, the shop assistants usually know each country's sizing equivalent, or they will have a conversion chart for ready reference. Failing that, why not take along your *Dubai Explorer* and refer to the conversion table [p.208] that the Explorer team has lovingly provided.

An alternative to buying clothes off the rack is to have them made by a tailor, and there are many places around the city offering this service. They will make an item from a drawing or photograph, and can copy outfits purchased elsewhere if you can leave the original for a few days. If necessary, they will also advise on the amount of material you should buy. The finished results can be excellent and prices are very reasonable. Word of mouth is the best method of finding a reliable, switched-on tailor; otherwise, trial and error is the only answer.

See also: Tailoring [p.237].

For sales, the period around the Dubai Shopping Festival isn't bad, but the best times are August/September and January when everywhere is getting rid of the old and bringing in the new. If you can bear to rummage, discounts of 70% aren't uncommon. Another excellent time for bargains is the end of Ramadan when the Eid sales begin. However, beware; if the stock in many of the international stores looks like it's been made and shipped in especially to satisfy sales fever – you're right, it has.

Designer label fans should refer to the table in this section. Here you will find those favourite brands and their respective locations, yet again making the task of clothes shopping that little bit easier.

Women's Fashions

Computers

Other options → Electronics & Home Appliances [p.222]

You should have few problems finding the right hardware and software to submerge yourself in the latest technology. Numerous outlets sell the latest merchandise – there are even specialist shopping malls devoted to computers and computer products. Try the Al Ain Centre next to Spinneys Ramada or the Al Khaleej Centre across the road. These two malls mainly cater to IT types, selling everything and anything associated with computer gadgets. There is also 'Computer Street', at the Shindagha end of Bank Street, which has many small stores that specialise in selling in bulk. The price quoted is often a cash price only.

The UAE government, together with the BSA (Business Software Alliance) is clamping down heavily on the sale of pirated software. As a result, most computer shops are reputable and offer the usual international guarantees. However, if you have a legitimate problem with sub-standard computer equipment, and cannot gain a satisfactory outcome after complaining directly to the shop, the Consumer Protection Cell (222 9922) in the Department of Economic Development should be able to give practical assistance to gain a fair outcome.

Each October, GITEX Shopper (the retail sister of GITEX) is held at the Airport Expo. You will be charged an entrance fee of around Dhs.15 simply for the honour of attending. Although there are attractive looking discounts, be warned that many are nothing more than a good marketing ploy. You may end up paying more and toting around a free printer or mobile phone you didn't really need. Just remember, you rarely get something for nothing and shop or call around before you buy.

Computers		
Aptec Gulf LLC	Oud Mehta	336 6885
Compu-Me	Al Garhoud	282 8555
Emirates Computers	Al Garhoud	282 5800
Explorer Computers	Bur Dubai	393 4080
GBM Distribution	Jebel Ali	883 5652
Interdev Info Systems	Computer Street	351 4153
Jumbo Electronics	Opp. Spinneys (Ramada)	352 3555
EVO (Mac)	Media City	390 8745
Plug-ins	City Centre	295 0358
Seven Seas Computers	Opp. Al Nasr Cinema	308 3555
SMB Computers	Al Musallah Towers	397 4799

Electronics & Home Appliances

Other options → Computers [p.221]

From well known to not so instantly recognisable brands, Dubai's stores stock a reasonable selection of electronics and home appliances. Prices are often hyped as being lower than in many parts of the world, but it is worth checking things out before leaving home, especially if you are buying a major item. Shops here are generally competitive due to the number of places offering the same or similar items (especially Carrefour; check there first!). Bargaining in some stores may reduce the price further (often apparently to the level of destroying the store's profit margin!).

Electronics & Home Appliances		
Aftron	Al Futtaim Electronics	211 9111
	Deira City Centre	295 4545
Aiwa	Al Sayegh Bros	227 4142
Bang & Olufsen	Music Centre	262 2700
Black & Decker	Jashanmal	269 3659
Bosch	Mohd Hareb Al Otaiba	269 1575
Bose	G & M International LLC	266 9000
Braun	The New Store LLC	353 4506
Elekta	Elekta Gulf	883 7108
General Electronics	Juma Al Majid	266 0640
Grundig	Agiv (Gulf)	223 2228
Hitachi	Eros Electricals	266 6216
Ignis	Universal Electricals	282 3443
Jashanmal	Wafi Mall	324 4800
JVC	Oasis Enterprises (LLC)	282 1375
Kenwood	Jashanmal	266 5964
Lenox	Eros Electricals	266 6216
Minolta	Viking Electronics	223 8167
National	Al Zubaidi Electronics	226 3688
	Jumbo Electronics	352 3555
Palm	Axiom - City Centre	295 1888
	Plug-ins	295 0404
	Jumbo	352 3555
Panasonic	Jumbo Electronics	352 3555
	Viking Electronics	223 8167
Phillips	Agiv (Gulf)	223 2228
	Al Ghandi Electronics	337 6600
Pioneer	Agiv (Gulf)	223 2228
Popular Brands	Carrefour	295 1600
	Jacky's Electronics	282 1822
	Plug-ins	295 0404
	Radio Shack	295 2127
Russel Hobbs	Jashanmal National	266 5964
Samsung	Al Ghurair City	223 2333
	Eros Electricals	266 6216
	Juma Al Majid	266 2340
	Samsung Electronics	222 5747
Sanyo	Agiv (Gulf)	223 2228
	Al Futtaim Electronics	359 9979
Sharp	Agiv (Gulf)	223 2228
	Cosmos	352 1155
Siemens	Scientechnic	266 6000
Simpson	Universal Electrical	282 3443
Sony	Jumbo Electronics	352 3555
Thomson	G & M International	266 9000
Toshiba	Al Futtaim Electronics	211 9111
Whirlpool	Al Ghandi Electronics	337 6600
Yamaha	Agiv (Gulf)	223 2228

Warranties, after-sales service, delivery and installation should be finalised before making any purchase. If you intend on returning to your home country with an item, check that you are buying a model that will operate there (for example, manufacturers set the sound frequency on televisions differently in different parts of the world, so what works in Dubai won't necessarily work at home, and vice versa).

Alternatively, if you are happy buying second-hand, check out the Classifieds sections of the daily newspapers (Gulf News and Khaleej Times); some items are virtually as good as new. It can also be worth going to some of the garage sales advertised by people who are returning to their home country and are selling off unwanted possessions. You can buy something for nothing from leaving expats; they usually sell at ridiculously low prices since their priority is to get rid of everything as quickly as possible, regardless of how much money they lose. Remember, it's a buyer's market, and some great bargains can be found, making these options excellent for people who do not want to part with their hard earned cash.

Eyewear

The strength of the sun in the Gulf means that for many people, sunglasses are their most important accessory. Consumers will find just about every brand of normal glasses and sunglasses imaginable, from designer names to designer ripoffs and much more in between. While prices range from a few dirhams to many hundreds, it is best to buy sunglasses with a good quality lens. Make sure that they give 100% UVA and UVB protection, and are dark enough (and large enough) to protect the eye from the sun's glare.

Most of the larger shopping malls have an opticians that will make prescription lenses, offer a good range of glasses and contact lenses, and also give eye tests. These are free of charge in most optical shops, as long as you order your glasses there or specify that the glasses are for driving. However, some places charge Dhs.20 - 50 for an eye test.

Eyewear		
Al Adasat Opticals	Lamcy Plaza	335 4006
Al Jaber Optical Centre	City Centre	295 4400
Al Sham Optic	Oasis Centre	339 1193
Barakat Opticals	Beach Centre	329 1913
City Optic	City Centre	295 1400
Dubai Opticals	BurJuman Centre	351 0051
	City Centre	295 4303
Fashion Optics	Palm Strip	348 6559
Grand Optics	Carrefour	393 6133
	City Centre	295 4699
Grand Sunglasses	City Centre	295 5334
Lunettes	Jumeirah Centre	349 2270
Lutfi Opticals Centre	Wafi Mall	324 1865
Optic Art	BurJuman Centre	352 8171
Optic Gallery	City Centre	295 4545
Sunglass Hut	Wafi Mall	324 4277
Yateem Optician	Al Ghurair Centre	228 1787
	BurJuman Centre	352 0222
	Emirates Towers	330 3301

Flowers

Other options → Garden Centres [p.226]
Plants & Trees [p.235]

For those special occasions or for that special someone (or as a desperate last minute present), flowers make a beautiful gift. There is a reasonable selection of florists all over the city, offering superb arrangements at decent prices. Many sell dried flowers as well as fresh. Excellent arrangements can also be bought from Spinneys and Carrefour in Deira City Centre Mall, plus Lifco supermarkets have their own in-house florist. Prices vary according to the type of arrangement and flowers you choose, but the minimum order for local delivery is usually Dhs.100 per bouquet.

If you are looking for florists who deliver internationally, refer to the Dubai Yellow Pages. Interflora signs adorn many of the windows of local shops. Alternatively, try your luck on the Internet. Browse through various designs and choose just as if you were in the shop itself. The price is dearer to send internationally, starting at around Dhs.200, but you can pay with major credit cards online and specify time and date of arrival. A great quick 'fix' for that forgotten birthday!

Flowers		
Blooms	Near Dubai Zoo	344 0912
City of Flowers	Jaddaf	324 3525
Desert Flowers	Nr Iranian Hospital	349 7318
Dubai Garden Centre	Shk Zayed Rd	340 0006
Flower Box Intl.	DIC, Bldg # 13	390 1144
Gift Express	Jumeirah Centre	344 0405
	Magrudy Centre	342 0568
Intraflora	Sheikh Zayed Road	332 5333
Planters	Opp Hamrain Centre	266 6427
Sentiments	Al Quoz	295 9850

Flowers

Food

Other options → Health Food [p.226]

Foodwise, Dubai has a good range of stores and supermarkets that cater more than adequately to the city's multi-national inhabitants. While there may be some speciality foods you can't buy, most items are available somewhere. Prices vary dramatically; produce is imported from all over the world and some items are double what they would cost in their country of origin. However, fresh foods, such as fruit and vegetables, can be amazingly cheap, especially if bought from places like the Fruit and Vegetable Market near Hamriya Port, or Karama.

There are plenty of 'corner shops' in residential areas, good for a pint of milk and more. Many accept phone orders for local home deliveries, saving you the walk. Popular food shops include Spinneys and Choithrams (both have branches all over the city), and Park'nShop. Lifco caters mainly for residents of the Sheikh Zayed Road and Al Garhoud areas. Carrefour, a huge French hypermarket sells everything from cheap shoes to toothpaste, as well as a good selection of fruit, vegetables and seafood.

Add a little
colour
to someone's life...
Intraflora

If you are looking for a certain type of food, try Choithrams, Safestway or Park'nShop for American, Lal's for Asian/Japanese, Spinneys for British and European and Carrefour for French. High quality but expensive pork is sold in a limited number of shops around town.

Health Food/Supplements

The health food trend is slowly arriving in Dubai, giving more options to those who take extra care of their diet. Specialist stores and pharmacies selling a range of supplements are popping up on a regular basis.

Larger supermarkets sell an ever-increasing (but still very limited) range of organic and allergy-inducing ingredient-free products as well.

Vitamins, minerals, supplements, organic and health foods are expensive compared to back home, and the selection of brands, while improving, is still limited, so bring speciality vitamins and supplements with you, if possible.

Health Food/Supplements

Diet & Delight	Al Hana Centre	398 3826
GNC	BurJuman	352 6771
Healthy Eating	Nr Princeton Hotel	286 5777
Healthy Living	Mazaya Centre	343 8668
Nutrition Centre	Jumeirah Centre	344 7464
Nutrition Palace	Crowne Plaza	332 8118
Nutrition World	Palm Strip	345 0652
Nutrition Zone	Jumeirah Town Centre	344 5888
Planet Nutrition	Bur Dubai	355 3338

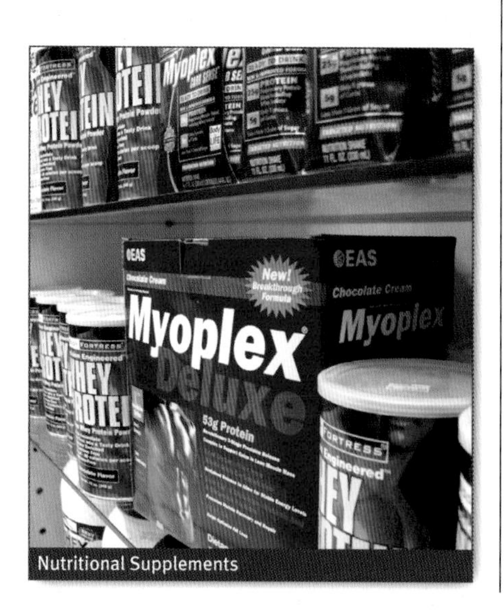

Nutritional Supplements

Garden Centres

Other options → Flowers [p.224]
Plants & Trees [p.235]

For the green fingered among us, gardening is slowly becoming more than just having someone to cut the grass and trim the bushes every week. Perhaps, with people beginning to purchase their own properties, there now comes a certain amount of pride in maintaining one's castle (aka villa and garden). Greenery is quickly replacing the dust that was termed 'the backyard' by many.

The all glass Dubai Garden Centre overlooking Sheikh Zayed Road is currently the only indoor gardening centre. Despite it being hard to miss visually, it's not that easy to get to. Inside, garden furniture, barbecues, pots, fountains, indoor plant life and other garden accessories are displayed beautifully, but the pure magic of the centre is the 2,000 square metres of canopied outdoors overflowing with outdoor plants and display gardens. Prices are higher than the Dubai Municipality garden centre, but it's a more pleasant shopping experience with better quality and selection of accessories.

For those who don't mind a little dirt under their fingernails, Dubai Municipality Nursery, located just before the Al Garhoud bridge towards Sharjah, is worth a visit. Individual nurseries are tightly packed in one big area, making it difficult to figure out where to start. But if you've fought the traffic and made it there, you may as well muster up the energy to visit all the nurseries and stock up. Although they all offer pretty much the same variety of plants, the quality can vary on a day to day basis. The sellers enjoy bargaining and are keen to offer free advice on how to handle your plants, be it indoors where the persistence of air conditioning strives to eradicate all innocent plant life, or outdoors, where the odd sandstorm endeavours to confuse and ruthlessly disrobe the bashful plant of all its foliage.

For garden accessories (tiles, ornaments etc), try Royal Gardenscape, located off Interchange 4 (340 0648).

Hardware & DIY

Other options → Outdoor Goods [p.234]

While it is often easier and cheaper in Dubai to get 'a man who can' to tackle all those niggling domestic jobs, many people still prefer to do it themselves. As a result, stores such as Ace Hardware, with branches around Dubai, have

become better stocked with each passing year. Customised paints, glazes, special paint effect materials, electronic tools and hardware materials are all easily obtained in Ace, but also check out the smaller stores in downtown Satwa where prices may be cheaper and the choice surprisingly varied.

Hardware & DIY

Ace Hardware	BurJuman Centre	355 0698
	Sh Zayed Rd	338 1416
Carrefour	Al Shindaga	393 9395
	City Centre	295 1600
Speedex	Sh Zayed Rd	339 2616

Home Furnishings & Accessories

Other options → Furnishing Accomodation [p.90]

As the construction boom continues in Dubai and new shopping malls, hotels, villas and apartments appear magically overnight, the interior design industry celebrates in style. Whether you need kitchenware, linen, towels, curtain rods, lampshades or furniture, you will find goods to suit every taste and budget. Besides well-known international retailers such as IKEA, Debenhams, and Woolworths, Dubai overflows with some excellent home furnishing outlets and independent furniture stores. Prices vary hugely, but the cosmopolitan environment ensures that every taste is catered for, from contemporary designs to colonial styles or Arabic glamour.

Opened in January 2002, Indian Village in Al Barsha specialises in both genuine and reproduction antique Indian furniture. Visit their website for more information and a much needed map of their location (www.indianvillagegroup.com). While you are in Al Barsha, it's worth a cruise around the industrial area to spot the many outlets hidden away.

In addition to all the shops that have sprung up in Dubai offering 'antique' Indian furniture, the originals in Sharjah are still going strong: Khans, Pinkies and Luckys sell an excellent range of Indian teak and wrought iron items at very reasonable prices. However, if you would rather design your own, Feshwari will custom make lounge suites; the hard part is deciding what style you like (www.feshwari.com).

As well as the following list, many supermarkets sell kitchenware and linen; Carrefour (Deira City Centre Mall) has a great selection and prices are criminally low. A number of upmarket stores sell the latest styles; THE One, Home Centre and IKEA are just a few of the options. THE One (345 6687) has recently started a wedding gift registry; all you have to do is make a list of presents and THE One will do the rest. Debenhams in Deira City Centre Mall is also keen to attract customers to its home section by offering the service of a personal shopper (the service is free, but it's advisable to book in advance, 294 0011).

Home Furnishings & Accessories

2Xl	Sharjah Mega Mall	06 574 4313
Aati	Za'abeel Road	337 7825
Al Jaber Gallery	City Centre	295 4114
	Opp Hamarain Centre	266 7700
Apollo Furniture	Sh Zayed Rd	339 1358
Bafco	Karama	335 0045
Bhs	BurJuman Centre	352 5150
	Lamcy Plaza	305 9208
Carpe Diem	Town Centre	344 3629
Carre Blanc	City Centre	295 3992
Chen One	Century Plaza	342 2441
Cottage Furniture	Behind Gold & Diamond Park	347 8228
Ethan Allen	Jumeira	342 1616
Fauchar	Wafi Mall	324 6769
Feshwari	Nr Oasis Center	344 5426
Grand Stores	Garhoud	282 3700
Guess Home	BurJuman Centre	355 3324
Harvest Home Trading	Jumeirah Centre	342 0225
Home Centre	Oasis Centre	339 5218
	Mercato	344 2266
Homes R us	Mazaya	321 3444
ID Design	Sharjah Road	266 6751
IKEA	City Centre	295 0434
Indian Village	4th interchange	347 8335
JC Penney (Liwa)	BurJuman Centre	351 5353
Lalique	Wafi Mall	324 2556
Laura Ashley	City Centre	295 1804
Living Zone, The	Mercato	344 5994
Liwa	City Centre	295 3988
Loft, The	Al Quoz	347 4255
Marina Gulf Trading	Al Barsha Road	347 8940
MFI Bedrooms & Kitchens	Oasis Centre	339 3503
Pan Emirates	Nr Oasis Centre	339 1910
Pier Import	Bin Sougat Centre	286 0030
	Mazaya Centre	343 2002
Sara - Villeroy & Boch	Wafi Mall	324 4555
	City Centre	295 0408
Showcase Antiques	Umm Suqueim	348 8797
Tanagra	Al Ghurair City	223 4302
	City Centre	295 0293
	Wafi Mall	324 2340
THE One	Nr Jumeira Mosque	342 2499
	Sahara Centre	06 531 2233
	Wafi Mall	324 1224
Westwood/Bayti	City Centre	295 5900

If your budget won't stretch to that antique coffee table, then stick your nose in the Classifieds section of the local newspapers for second-hand items and start dialling. The expat community in Dubai is enormous, and those leaving often prefer to sell their furniture rather than take it with them. Supermarket noticeboards are another good option – in addition to a three piece suite, you can pick up anything from a dog or a cat to a used car.

Indian Village

Jewellery, Watches & Gold

Other options → Souks [p.254]

When it comes to watches and jewellery, Dubai is almost guaranteed to be able to supply whatever you are looking for. Prices range from a few dirhams to diamond studded watches costing many thousands of dirhams. Don't forget to check out the souks – here you can find all kinds of designs, for all ages and tastes.

Appropriately for the City of Gold, jewellery comes in many forms, from Japanese cultured pearls to classic, ethnic creations from India. The standards of workmanship vary, so if you are spending a lot of money, it is worth going to a more reputable store.

Dubai is famous in this part of the world as the 'City of Gold', as it sells and imports/re-exports a vast amount of this beautiful metal. Priced according to the international daily gold rate, it is available in 18, 21, 22 or 24 carats, in every form imaginable, from bracelets, rings and necklaces to gold ingots.

In addition to the weight price, a charge is added for craftsmanship, which varies according to the intricacy of the design. Dubai's Gold Souk is famed the world over for its low prices and the sheer variety on offer – just remember to bargain hard. If you don't see the particular piece you're looking for, bring in a photo or drawing and the craftsman will make it for you – usually on approval, so even if you don't like the finished product, you are not obliged to buy.

Jewellery, Watches & Gold		
Al Fardan Jewellers	City Centre	295 4238
	Hamarain Centre	269 9997
Al Futtaim Jewellery	City Centre	295 2906
Al Liali	Mercato	344 5055
Breitling Watches	City Centre	295 4109
Cartier	Emirates Towers	330 0333
Chopard	Wafi Mall	324 1010
Citizen	Al Ghurair City	222 5222
Damas Jewellery	BurJuman	352 5566
	City Centre	295 3848
	Gold Centre Bldg	226 6036
Fossil	BurJuman Centre	351 9794
	City Centre	295 0108
Gold Souk	Nr Hyatt Regency Htl	na
Golden Ring	City Centre	295 0373
Guess	City Centre	295 2577
Mahallti Jewellery	Mercato	344 4771
Mansoor Jewellery	BurJuman Centre	355 2110
Paris Gallery	City Centre	295 5550
Philippe Charriol	BurJuman Centre	351 1112
Prima Gold	BurJuman Centre	355 1988
	City Centre	295 0497
Pure Gold	Mercato	349 2400
Raymond Weil	City Centre	295 3254
Rivoli	BurJuman Centre	351 2279
Rossini	City Centre	295 4977
	Wafi Mall	324 0402
Seiko	Al Ghurair City	227 8036
Silver Art	City Centre	295 2414
Swarovski	Wafi Mall	324 4555
Swatch	BurJuman Centre	359 6109
	City Centre	295 3932
Tag Heuer	Wafi Mall	324 3030
Tiffany & Co	BurJuman Centre	359 0101
Watch House, The	City Centre	295 0108

Kids' Items

Other options → Clothes [p.219]
Family Explorer

A variety of goods can be found in Dubai for children of all ages, from nursery equipment or the latest computer games to mini designer fashions. For younger children, it's even possible to hire specialised items, such as car seats or cots. Virtually every conceivable toy or game is available

somewhere in Dubai, and you should have few problems buying the more old fashioned games or the latest fashionable 'must have' toys. You may prefer to buy toys, especially for very young children, from more reputable shops that are less likely to sell sub-standard items.

Kids' Items

Adams 0 - 10	Bur Juman	355 2205
Baby Shop 0 - 9	Karama	335 0212
Baby Shop, The	Deira & Oasis Centre	266 1519
Early Learning Centre	City Centre	295 1548
Kids R Us	Oasis Centre	339 1817
Little Me	Palm Strip	345 6424
Mothercare	Al Ghurair City	223 8176
	BurJuman Centre	352 8916
	City Centre	295 2543
	Spinneys (Umm Suqeim)	394 0228
Mummy & Me	Al Maktoum St	228 2029
Ovo Kids	City Centre	295 0885
Prémaman	Bur Juman Centre	351 5353
Toys 'R' Us	Al Futtaim Centre	222 5859

One novel idea is The Bear Factory, Deira City Centre Mall (295 9751), where kids can create their own teddy bear and then select an outfit for it from the costume wardrobe, complete with accessories such as glasses should teddy be a little short-sighted. Be warned, if you go to have a look with your child in tow, you're unlikely to leave empty handed!

For a fuller picture on all that Dubai and the Northern Emirates have to offer families with children up to the age of 14 years, refer to the *Family Explorer* published by Explorer Publishing. This offers invaluable information on everything from education and medical care to top venues for a birthday party, and both outdoor and indoor activities – perfect for when the temperatures soar.

Lingerie

Other options → Clothes [p.219

Emirati ladies have a reputation for being one of the highest consumers of luxury lingerie in the world and, as testament to that, almost every mall houses a proliferation of frilly, frighteningly expensive lingerie boutiques!

Every designer name in lingerie is healthily represented in Dubai (there's even one lingerie boutique in the Mazaya Centre that is better known elsewhere for its boudoir 'accessories' but, in this store at least, it sells underwear only). So, if you are on the lookout for a few decent additions to a bridal trousseau, and money is no object, there surely can be few better places to shop.

However, if you veer towards function rather than glamour, there are several noteworthy alternatives. In the past year or so, lingerie chain La Senza has been opening branches in shopping malls throughout the Emirates, offering decent underwear and nightwear at affordable prices. Woolworth's (South Africa's equivalent of the UK's Marks & Spencer) in City Centre stocks a good range of lingerie at excellent value. Marks & Spencer itself in Deira and the newly opened branch in Sharjah's Sahara Centre, has a staunch following for its lingerie lines, but expect to pay heavily inflated prices for the privilege of buying the UK's favourite underwear in Dubai.

Fluffly Camels

Lastly, as long as you don't mind standing at the cash till with your smalls nestled among the weekly shop, well-regarded European labels Sloggi and Dim are available in many supermarkets. Larger branches of Choithram's and Park'n'Shop offer a range of styles and great value for money.

Lingerie		
Bare Essentials	Jumeirah Centre	344 0552
Carrefour	City Centre	295 1600
Inner Lines	City Centre	294 0011
La Belleamie	Beach Centre, The	349 3928
La Perla	BurJuman Centre	355 1251
La Senza	BurJuman Centre	352 0222
	Palm Strip	344 0552
Marks & Spencer	Al Futtaim Centre	222 2000
My Time	BurJuman Centre	352 0222
Outfit	BurJuman Centre	295 4545
Triumph	City Centre	295 1010
	Mercato	344 4161
Womens Secret	City Centre	295 1010

Luggage & Leather

Like the memories of Dubai, good leather lasts forever. Imagination and artistry combine in a wide range of fine leather goods, from gloves or wallets to handbags, shoes, suitcases, etc.

With the warm climate, leather clothing is not exactly in demand, but Dubai is a retail oasis and attracts international designer brands selling leather accessories. The more expensive malls, such as Wafi, house specialised leather shops such as ST Dupont (324 2340) a Parisian boutique with exclusive prices. Louis Vuitton (359 2535) and Tod's (355 4417) are both found in the Bur Juman Centre and other expensive brand names can be found scattered in this shopping paradise as well, although prices are similar to the rest of the world.

Less exclusive, more functional luggage can be found in Carrefour. A vast selection of luggage is available here and at reasonable prices.

If you've got the cash to spend, hit the designer stores and be prepared to part with lots of your hard earned money. However, as Dubai is a crossroads of trade and nearby countries known for excellent quality and dirt cheap deals supply the market as well, you can check out places like Karama for some decent leather and luggage from Pakistan or Thailand.

Designer copies can be found in some stores, which make great Christmas presents, although the quality can vary. Always check the inside as well as the outside of the product for tears or snags and remember, the chances of an exchange or refund at a later date are pretty slim.

Luggage & Leather		
Aigner	BurJuman Centre	351 5133
	Wafi Mall	324 0893
Aristocrat	BurJuman Centre	355 2395
Chanel	Wafi Mall	324 0464
Francesco Biasia	Mercato	349 9622
La Valise	City Centre	295 5509
Leather Palace	Al Ghurair City	222 6770
	BurJuman Centre	351 5251
Louis Vuitton	BurJuman Centre	359 2535
Mohd Shareif	BurJuman Centre	355 3377
Porsche Design	City Centre	295 7652
Sacoche	City Centre	295 0233

Medicine

Other options → General Medical Care [p.102]

There's no shortage of pharmacies or chemists in Dubai – these are indicated on shop signs by what looks like a snake wrapped around a cocktail glass. Remember to check the expiry date of medicine before purchasing it. Most pharmacies also carry a variety of beauty products, baby care items, sunscreens, perfumes etc.

In the UAE you are able to buy prescription drugs over the counter. If you are certain what drug or antibiotic you need it can save the expense and hassle of a doctor, and pharmacists themselves are always willing to listen to symptoms and suggest a remedy.

Each emirate has at least one pharmacy open 24 hours a day – the location and phone numbers are listed in the daily newspapers. In addition, a Municipality emergency number (223 2323) gives the name and location of 24-hour pharmacies.

Music, DVD's & Videos

Other options → Music Lessons [p.333]
Musical Instruments [p.234]

Although the selection isn't as large or as up to date as in Asia, Europe or North America, there are now Virgin 'megastores' in Dubai selling the latest current releases on CD, DVD and video. From famous international bands, Arabic or classical music to Bollywood and Hollywood releases, Dubai caters for a variety of styles and tastes. However, CDs, DVDs and videos are only released once they have been

Music, DVD's & Videos		
Al Mansoor	BurJuman Centre	351 3388
	Wafi Mall	324 4141
Carrefour	Al Shindagha	393 9395
	City Centre	295 1600
Diamond Palace	BurJuman Centre	352 7671
Music Box	Al Ghurair City	221 0344
Music Master	Palm Strip	345 1753
Music Room, The	Beach Centre, The	344 8883
Plug-ins	City Centre	295 0358
Thomsun	Al Ghurair City	222 9370
Virgin Megastore	Deira City Centre	295 4545
	Mercato	344 6971

screened (and censored, if appropriate) to ensure that they do not offend the country's moral code.

Videos are in the PAL format, so before you buy or rent a VCR make sure it has a multiformat capability. There are numerous video rental stores around the city – check out one in your area. Blank audio and videotapes are for sale at major grocery stores. Rental prices range from Dhs.4 - 10 per video and around Dhs.10 per DVD (plus a hefty deposit sometimes).

Copies of the latest released movies can often be found circulating the streets, although piracy is frowned upon in the UAE. The copies are usually of good quality, although occasionally you may find that you are sharing your living room with a whole cinema audience coughing and sneezing, their silhouettes wandering past the screen mid film!

Musical Instruments

Other options → Music Lessons [p.333]

Music lovers will find only a limited number of places to buy instruments in Dubai, and if you want to buy a larger instrument, such as a piano, you will have to place an order. Sheet music is not widely available; your best bet is probably to order it over the Internet – check out the main search engines and see where they take you.

Musical Instruments		
Fann Al Sout Music	Nr Fish R/A	271 9471
Galleria Music	Wafi Mall	324 2626
Golden Guitar	Hamriya	269 0681
House of Guitar	Karama	334 9968
Melody House Musical Instruments	Opp. Hamarain Centre	227 5336
Mozart Musical Instruments	Karama	337 7007
Sound of Guitar	Naif Rd	222 1508
Thomsun Music	Nr. Mashreq Bank	266 8181
Zak Electronics	Zabeel Rd	336 8857

Outdoor Goods

Other options → Camping [p.268]
Hardware & DIY [p.226]

Aside from the humidity, sand and a few creepy crawlies, the UAE offers a wonderful outdoor existence, and off-roading and camping are revered pastimes for many. A weekend away is a peaceful escape from the chaos of city and there are virtually no limits on where you can pitch your tent and light your fire. For most people, the lack of heat and humidity make the winter months the best time to go. However, if you choose your location carefully – at altitude or by the sea – the summer months aren't always completely unbearable. To kit yourself out with the basics for a night under the stars or just some gear to enjoy a few hours in the great outdoors, check out the following list of stores. However, if you prefer to use more specialised equipment, you'll have to either order it online or bring it from home.

Those that enjoy the great outdoors, but limit it to the exterior of the house, will find that many of the stores listed in the Home Furnishings section [p.228] supply garden furniture. For more expensive tastes check out the individual stores. Dubai Garden Centre offers a stylish range of colonial garden furniture, but if you are looking for versatile, cheap, plastic versions then try Carrefour in Deira City Centre – great for bargain barbecues!

Outdoor Goods		
Ace Hardware	BurJuman Centre	355 0698
	Shk Zayed Road	338 1416
Carrefour	City Centre	295 1600
	Al Shindagha	393 9395
Harley-Davidson	Shk Zayed Road	339 1909
Picnico General Trdg	Beach Rd (Jumeira)	394 1653
ULO Systems Ltd	Sharjah	06 531 4036

Party Accessories

Other options → Party Organisers [p.235]

Most major supermarkets and stationery stores sell the basic party paraphernalia, and if you go to the more specialised shops, you'll find an even wider range. From cards, balloons, candles, table settings and room decorations to gift wrapping and fancy dress outfits, bouncy castles and entertainers, the choice for both children and adult parties is comprehensive.

Party Accessories

Balloon Lady, The	Jumeirah Plaza	344 1062
Card Shop	Al Diyafah St	398 7047
Elves & Fairies	Jumeirah Centre	344 9485
Flying Elephant	Interchange Two	347 9170
Gulf Greetings	BurJuman Centre	351 9613
In Disguise	Satwa	342 2752
Magrudy Book Shop	Magrudy Shopping Mall	344 4193
Papermoon	Mina Rd, off Diyafah St	345 4888
Toys 'R' Us	Al Futtaim Centre	222 5859

Party Services (MMI)

Everything you need to get your party going! Wine or pint glasses, ice buckets, coasters, etc, are available from Maritime & Mercantile International LLC (MMI), which offers this service free of charge (no liquor licence required). Leave a Dhs.500 refundable deposit to use all the items listed below. A minimal breakage charge of Dhs.5 per glass will be deducted from the deposit and the balance refunded. Items must be returned within five days of the deposit being paid. A party pack includes 24 pint beer glasses; 24 wine glasses, 2 ice buckets, 2 waiter trays, 3 bar towels and 24 coasters.

Costumes/Fancy Dress

Although Dubai is an established party place, it's still relatively new to such things as costume or fancy dress shops, hence they are quite hard to find. In Disguise, Satwa (342 2752) and Too Much Fun, Jumeira Plaza (344 1062), specialise in costumes and accessories, but why not make the most of Dubai's wonderfully skilled tailors? Let those artistic juices flow and design your own costume; you never know, it may be the start of your fashion designer catwalk to success!

Perfumes & Cosmetics

Other options → Souks [p.254]

Beauty in Dubai is big business, and whether the temperature goes up or down, there's always a busy trade in perfumes and cosmetics. You will find the latest additions to the market available in most main shopping malls.

For a personalised fragrance, look out for the local perfumeries that are in every shopping area. Beware, however, many of these scents are rather powerful: if applied too generously you may find you spend the following week very much alone. You have been warned.

Perfumes & Cosmetics

Ajmal Perfumes	Al Ghurair City	222 7991
	BurJuman Centre	351 5505
	City Centre	295 3580
	Emirates Towers	330 0000
	Hamarain Centre	269 0102
Areej	BurJuman Centre	352 2977
	Emirates Towers	330 3340
	Atrium Centre	201 1111
	Mercato	344 6894
	Oasis Centre	339 1224
Body Shop	City Centre	294 5101
	Jumeirah Centre	344 4042
Crabtree & Evelyn	BurJuman Centre	352 5425
Debenhams	City Centre	294 0011
Faces	Al Ghurair City	223 4302
Jashanmal	Wafi Mall	324 4800
Lush	BurJuman Centre	352 0222
	City Centre	295 1010
MAC	City Centre	295 7704
	Mercato	324 4555
	Wafi Mall	324 4555
Make Up Forever	Wafi Mall	324 4426
Nature Shop, The	City Centre	295 4181
Paris Gallery	BurJuman Centre	351 7704
	City Centre	295 5550
	Hamarain Centre	268 8122
	Lamcy Plaza	336 2000
	Town Centre	342 2555
	Wafi Mall	324 2121
Rasasi	Al Ghurair City	222 5222
	BurJuman Centre	351 2757
Red Earth	Al Ghurair City	227 9696
	City Centre	295 1887
	Mercato	344 9439

Plants & Trees

Other options → Flowers [p.224]
Garden Centres [p.222]

If you're lucky enough to have a garden, or even a balcony, it is definitely worth planting a few shrubs, trees or bedding plants in pots which are all very good value for money.

Having a garden full of foliage is great for keeping the sand at bay and it's surprising how many varieties of plants can thrive in such arid conditions, although constant watering is vital. Be aware that the extra water used may add substantially to your water bills, but the plus side is that if you decide to hire a gardener, it will probably be a great deal cheaper than you imagined. If you can't be bothered to traipse around a nursery, all the larger supermarkets stock

a good selection of indoor and outdoor plants, but expect to pay a few dirhams more for convenience.

Plants & Trees		
Dubai Garden Centre	Shk Zayed Rd	340 0006
DM Nursery	Jaddaf	n/a

Second-hand Items

Other options → Books [p.214]
Cars [p.219]

Rather than throwing out your unwanted clothes, shoes, books, kitchen equipment etc, why not take them to one of the second-hand shops in Dubai? Some of these shops operate on a charity basis, so you are doing a good turn, as well as not being wasteful.

For buying or selling second-hand items, such as furniture, cookers etc, remember to check out the Classifieds section of the newspapers, or the notice boards at the various supermarkets as well as referring to the following table. For clothes, Dubai Charity Shop and notable newcomer In Disguise are worth a visit for their abundant selection of designer items for sale – most in excellent condition and at bargain basement prices.

Second-hand Items	
Al Noor Charity Shop	397 9989
Dubai Charity Association	268 2000
Holy Trinity Thrift Shop	337 0247
House of Prose	344 9021
In Disguise	342 2752

Shoes

Other options → Beach Wear [p.214]
Clothes [p.219]

Dubai: Tomorrow's City Today

A photography book that sheds light on the beauty and functionality of contemporary Dubai. Pages and pages of stunning images showcase the city's historical highlights, municipal successes and civic triumphs, making you wonder of the grandeur in store for the future.

Whether your penchant is for Doc Martins, flip-flops or kitten-heeled mules, shoes come in as many shapes and sizes as there are feet.

Training shoes tend to be more reasonably priced in Dubai than elsewhere, although fashion addicts (victims?) may find that the styles are one season behind. All major brands are available at decent prices, but be warned; if you're shoe shopping in Karama and think you've just stumbled on the deal of a lifetime, remember this is the area for fakes.

Shoes		
ALDO	Al Ghurair City	223 8851
	City Centre	295 1010
	Mercato	344 7995
Aqua Shoes	Al Ghurair City	221 3340
Bally	BurJuman Centre	351 8129
	City Centre	295 0240
Cesare Paccioti	Wafi Mall	324 3227
Domino	Al Ghurair City	221 0298
	BurJuman Centre	351 2321
	Mercato	344 4161
Ecco	Al Ghurair City	222 5222
	Mercato	344 4161
Escada	BurJuman Centre	352 9253
Florsheim	BurJuman Centre	351 5353
	City Centre	295 3988
Marelli	Al Ghurair City	227 0933
Mario Bologna	BurJuman	552 9726
Milano	Al Ghurair City	222 8545
	City Centre	295 7492
	Mercato	344 9517
Nine West	Al Ghurair City	221 1484
	BurJuman Centre	351 6214
	City Centre	295 6887
	Lamcy Plaza	336 5994
	Mercato	349 1336
	Oasis Centre	339 1779
	Town Centre	344 0038
Philippe Charriol	BurJuman Centre	351 1112
Rockport	City Centre	295 0261
Shoe Bazaar	Bur Dubai	353 0444
Shoe City	City Centre	295 0437
Shoe Mart	Lamcy Plaza	337 9811
	Near Jumbo Showroom	351 9560
	Oasis Centre	338 0440
Valencia	City Centre	295 0990
	Jumeirah Centre	344 2032

Sporting Goods

Other options → *Off-Road Explorer* [
Sports [p.259]
Underwater Explorer

Dubai is a great location for a variety of sports, from the popular activities such as tennis, sailing, golf or football to more unusual ones like sand skiing. Try the general sports shops listed below for items like squash racquets or sports clothing. Alternatively, there's a range of specialist sports shops around

the city. Unless yours is an unusual sport in the emirates or you require a more specialised piece of equipment, you should have little difficulty in finding what you require.

See also: ***Canoeing*** *(ULO Sharjah);* ***Cycling*** *(Carrefour, Future Bikes, Magrudy's, Pascal's, Trek, Wheels, Wolfi's);* ***Diving*** *(see dive centres);* ***Ice Skating*** *(ice rinks sell some equipment);* ***Jet Skiing*** *(Al Boom Marine, ULO Sharjah);* ***Motor Sports*** *(various shops on Al Awir Road);* ***Sailing*** *(Dubai Offshore Sailing Club, Jebel Ali Sailing Club, ULO Sharjah);* ***Snorkelling*** *(dive centres, Carrefour);* ***Water skiing*** *(Al Boom Marine);* ***Windsurfing*** *(Al Boom Marine, ULO Sharjah).*

Sporting Goods		
360 Sports	BurJuman Centre	352 0106
Adidas	Deira City Centre	295 4151
Al Boom Marine	Ras Al Khor	289 4858
Alpha Sports	City Centre	295 4087
Body Glove	Oasis Centre	352 0222
Carrefour	City Centre	295 1600
	Al Shindagha	393 9395
Emirates Sports	Jumeirah Plaza	344 7456
	Wafi Mall	324 2208
Future Bike	Al Sharafi Centre	396 6015
Golf House	BurJuman Centre	351 9012
	City Centre	295 0501
	Lamcy Plaza	334 5945
Magrudy's	Jumeira	344 4192
Sketchers	BurJuman Centre	352 0106
Sport One Trading	BurJuman Centre	351 6033
Studio R	City Centre	295 0261
Sun & Sand Sports	BurJuman Centre	351 5376
	City Centre	295 5551
	Jumeirah Centre	349 5820
	Al Gurg Bldg	352 9666
	Al Ghurair City	222 7107
ULO Systems Ltd	Sharjah	06 531 4036
Wolfi's	Sheikh Zayed Rd	339 4453

Sports Shop

Tailoring

Other options → Al Satwa [p.88]
Arabian Souvenirs [p.212]
Textiles [p.238]

With the vast number of textile shops in Dubai, it's well worth buying some fabric and having something made to your specification; whether it's curtains, cushions or an almost designer suit, most items are possible.

Many tailors also provide an alteration service (sometimes while you wait, depending on how busy they are), and some textile shops can arrange a tailor for you (if you buy their material of course). Unless you are a veteran and have a budding relationship with a particular tailor, then this service is great for first timers.

Tailors will follow a pattern or copy an original item if you can leave it for a few days. Most have a range of pattern books and magazines in-house that you can browse through; alternatively check out a bookstore for pattern books.

When trying a tailor for the first time, it's advisable to order only one piece to check the quality of the work. They will advise on how many metres of material are needed (buy a little extra to be on the safe side), and most provide the extras such as buttons, linings and zips. Confirm the price (obviously the more complex the pattern, the pricier it is), before committing to have it made, and make sure that it includes the cost of the lining, if appropriate.

A good tailor should tack it all together so that you can have a trying on session before the final stitching. When it is finished, try it on again. Don't be bashful about asking them to put something right if you are not completely happy.

Tailoring		
Ali Eid Al Muree	Jumeirah Beach Rd	348 7176
Couture	Deira	269 9522
Dream Girl	Meena Bazaar	352 6463
Eves	Nasr Square	228 1070
First Lady	Bur Dubai	352 7019
Garasheeb	Karama	396 8900
La Donna	Al Wahida Rd	266 6596
Ma Belle	Nr. Hamrian Centre	269 6500
Monte Carlo	Behind York Hotel	352 0225
Oasis	Nr Emirates Exchange	334 4227
Regency Tailors	Bur Dubai	352 4732
Sheema	Nr Astoria Hotel	353 5142
Tailorworks	Satwa	344 1736
Vanucci Fashions	Al Ghusais	263 2626

Tailored Dresses

Textiles

Other options → Arabian Souvenirs [p.212]
Carpets [p.218]
Tailoring [p.237]

On both sides of the Creek you can find plenty of fabric shops selling everything from the cheapest to the finest quality textiles. In particular, Cosmos Lane and the Al Faheidi Street area in Bur Dubai have an excellent choice of shops. However, if you can't face busy, non air conditioned areas of the city, most of the shopping malls have textile shops, although prices here are generally higher.

Textiles		
Abdulla Hussain	Al Ghurair City	221 7310
Al Masroor (Gents)	City Centre	295 0832
Damas (Ladies)	Al Ghurair City	221 6700
Deepak's	Satwa	344 8836
Yasmine (Ladies)	Al Diyafa Street	398 8476

Places to Shop

The following section on places to shop has been split into two. It covers shopping malls or centres and their main outlets, and the main shopping streets or areas in the city.

Shopping Malls

The attractive, and often imaginatively designed, modern shopping malls in Dubai are one of the highlights of shopping here. They are generally spacious and air conditioned, offering a great escape from the often searing heat of the city. Here you will find virtually every kind of store that you can imagine, from supermarkets or card shops, to clothes emporiums and specialist perfume shops. However, the popular malls are more than just a place to buy goods; in the evenings and on weekends especially, a lively, social buzz ensues as people window shop, meet friends, eat out and people watch as they sip coffee.

During the Dubai Shopping Festival and Dubai Summer Surprises, the larger malls are venues for special events such as dancing or magic shows. These performances are always popular and involve acts from all around the world. The malls also feature numerous raffles during these months – the prize for the lucky few is usually a car.

Most malls have a foodcourt, which generally offer a wonderful variety of cuisine, from the ubiquitous hamburger to Arabic mezze, Japanese or Mexican food. Some malls also have children's play areas, arcade games, cinemas and most have convenient, extensive and free parking. The following are the largest and more popular malls in town.

Check out what Dubai's malls have to say about themselves at: www.dubaishoppingmalls.com.

Jumeirah Centre

iP
DECOPACK
INTERPLAST CO. LTD.

Complete Range of
Paper & Plastic
Luxury Shopping Bags
Tel: + 971 6 5324404, Fax: + 971 6 5322821
P.O.Box: 4679, Sharjah, U.A.E.
E - mail: decopack@emirates.net.ae
www.decopack.com
FRENCH BAKERY
DUBAI
بردیات
BARDIAAT
POWER
TO
PERFORM
peltier
MALDINI
VIA ROSSI
SHOES & BAGS
ETISALAT
YOUR SMART CHOICE
Amélie
Lingerie · Prêt-à-Porter
Jameela
Marquise

Beach Centre, The

Location → Nr Dubai Zoo · Beach Rd, Jumeira | 344 9045
Hours → 09:30 - 13:00 16:30 - 21:30
Web/email → n/a | Map Ref → 6-B2

This is a large, airy mall with spacious restaurants lining the Beach Road. Over 50 outlets sell goods ranging from books and furniture to jewellery, knick knacks and carpets, plus there is a pharmacy and an optician. There is also an Internet corner called Cyber Cafe – Training Zone (surfing and playing games cost Dhs.7.50 per hour).

The Beach Centre is a good place to meet friends, shop and then sit and chat in the central coffee shop area, where the atmosphere is pleasantly sociable. Look for the blue glass building, to distinguish it from the 'pink' plaza (Jumeira Plaza) and Jumeirah Centre further along the road.

Other outlets include: Baskin Robbins, Bossini, Crystal Gallery, Dubai Desert Extreme, Hobby Land, Jenny Rose, Kids to Teens, Kuts 4 Kids, La Femme Saloon, Luxury International, Music Room, Party Zone, Photo Magic, Queen's Laundry, Sports House, Touch of Class, Vertigio Boutique, White Star, World of Art, Yateem Opticians.

Bin Sougat Centre

Location → Airport Rd · Rashidiya | 286 3000
Hours → 10:00 - 22:00 16:00 - 22:00 Fri
Web/email → n/a | Map Ref → n/a

This modest mall mainly caters for its local community, priding itself on a family atmosphere. However, it is also a regular attraction for Middle Eastern families from neighbouring countries. It hosts many children's activities during the evenings, which enhance the family concept.

Bin Sougat is in the process of expanding with the construction of a Spinneys supermarket and there are also plans for an ice rink and two cinemas due to open in January 2004. This is great news for the residents in Rashidiya and Mirdif as it is the first of its kind in the local area.

Emirates Towers

Location → Emirates Towers · Shk Zayed Rd | 319 8999
Hours → 10:00 - 22:00 Fri 16:00 - 22:00
Web/email → www.jumeirahinternational.com | Map Ref → 9-C2

Emirates Towers Shopping Boulevard certainly has the number 1 address in the city; linking two of Dubai's most imposing buildings, the Emirates Towers Hotel and Emirates Towers Offices. This exclusive, spacious and striking mall is home to over forty quality retail outlets, from expensive international jewellery stores to exclusive fashion boutiques. However, if you are intimidated by the grandeur of it all, try the relaxed coffee shop, Bytes, which offers great snacks and cheap Internet facilities.

The evenings are more crowded with the novelty of licensed restaurants such as Scarlett's and The Noodle House, while The Agency is a definite after work hangout for the suave 'suited and booted', and the sophisticated Tapas lounge a favourite meeting place for girlies on weekend nights. In fact, there are so many great sources of entertainment, mainly focusing on food and drink, that it is easy to forget that this is a shopping mall!

Other outlets include: Ajmal, Areej, Bottega Veneta, Bvlgari, Cartier, Damas, Ermenegildo Zegna, Europcar, Flowers the Towers, Flying Colours, Galerie Hamadan, Giorgio Armani, Grand Stores, Gucci, Janet Reger, Jimmy Choo, La Casa del Habano, Lanvin, My Fair Lady, N-Bar, Persian Carpet House, Rivoli, Rodeo Drive, Safari Gems, Telefonika, T Junction, Villa Moda, Yateem Opticians, Yves Saint Laurent.

Jumeirah Centre

Location → Nr Jumeira Mosque · Beach Rd, Jumeira | 349 9702
Hours → 09:00 - 21:00 Fri 16:00 - 21:00
Web/email → www.dubaishoppingmalls.com | Map Ref → 6-C2

Formerly known as Markaz Al Jumeira, this mall has exclusive ladies boutiques side by side with The Body Shop and Baskin Robbins ice-cream parlour. It's popular with Jumeira residents. Stationery Stores are well stocked and toyshops keep youngsters occupied, while adults can check out the latest watch design, get their camera repaired or choose Persian rugs and unusual art.

For those interested in natural healing, Essensuals on the first floor offers professional advice on aromatherapy. Elves & Fairies, a craft and hobbies shop, is also located here and the Coffee Bean is great for a coffee and to relax after all that shopping.

Other outlets include: Baskin Robbins, Benetton, Blue Cactus, Camera Repairs, Caviar Classic, Cut Above, Elves & Fairies, Flower Box, Lunnettes, Mother Care, Nutrition Centre, Photo Magic, Rivoli, Sun & Sands Sports, Sunny Days, Sweet Station, The Barber Shop, Thomas Cook, Toy Magic.

Jumeirah Plaza

Location → Nr Jumeira Mosque · Beach Rd, Jumeira | 349 7111
Hours → 09:30 - 13:00 16:30 - 21:30 Fri 16:30 - 21:30
Web/email → www.dubaishoppingmalls.com Map Ref → 6-C2

Easily spotted alongside the Beach Road, this pink stone and glass building is a delight to browse around. The shops are full of items for the home. There is also a second-hand bookshop House of Prose and a kids' play area, Safe Play.

The cascading fountains, fish and tropical vegetation under the glass-roofed atrium are a perfect foil for art exhibitions and Dubai International Arts Centre has an outlet here. You can also arrange licence renewals or pay fines to Dubai Police (avoid the queues at this little known branch).

Other outlets include: Aquarius, Art Shop, Balloon Lady, Benedetti, Brush N Bisque IT, Fantasy Games Trading, FGE - The Warehouse, Girls Talk Beauty Centre, Heatwaves, Kashmir Craft, Perfect Selection Stationery, Remera Boutique, Safeplay,

Oasis Centre

Location → Nr Ace Hardware · Jct 2, Shk Zayed Rd | 339 5459
Hours → 10:00 - 22:00 Fri 16:00 - 22:00
Web/email → www.landmarkgroupco.com Map Ref → 5-A4

One of the calmer malls in terms of parking and shopping, the Oasis Centre nevertheless offers a good range of shops in its compact design. It has a number of bright, good-value superstores, but is probably best known for Home Centre, Lifestyle (a fantastically-priced giftware store) and a large Shoemart, which is guaranteed to tempt the 'shoe-aholic' with designer brands at unbeatable prices. Petland is one of the few good pet shops in Dubai and there's also a pet grooming service.

The mall is a good family venue with two excellent children's areas; Fun City for youngsters and Cyborg – a migraine-inducing, cave-like area that boasts a ten-pin bowling alley and several karaoke booths among its neon attractions. If you're peckish, choose between the small Jungle Foodcourt or the great Italian restaurant, La Fontana, which is open plan and ideal for those that prefer people watching while enjoying the Arabic style décor.

Other outlets include: Afghan Carpet Palace, Baby Shop, Book Plus, Dar Al Zain Perfumes, Gulf Greetings, Himat Jewellers, Kids R Us, Nine West, Splash, Sun & Sand Sports.

Palm Strip

Location → Opp Jumeira Mosque · Beach Rd, Jumeira | 346 1462
Hours → 10:00 - 22:00 Fri 13:30 - 22:00
Web/email → www.dubaishoppingmalls.com Map Ref → 6-D2

Located just off the beach, this open fronted mall is a pleasant place for a stroll around the shops or for a coffee and to catch up on emails at FI Net Café. The shady frontage has easy access to a range of upmarket shops, which primarily include designer labels and other familiar names like Mango and Music Master. It also features N-Bar, Dubai's first slick, groovily kitted-out nail bar (no appointment necessary).

Although the front car park is frequently busy, it's a mystery where the owners are as the mall is

Palm Strip

generally quiet (if there's no space at the front, try the underground car park; entrance around the side). However, the Strip is generally lively in the cooler evenings when Japengo Cafe becomes an ideal location to sit outside and enjoy a relaxed meal while taking in the magnificent sight of Jumeirah Mosque opposite.

Other outlets include: Barcelona Shoes, Bashar Trading Lingerie, Beyond the Beach, Elite Models, Escada Sport, Fashion Optics, Gasoline, Gian Franco Ferre Studio, Gulf Pharmacy, Karen Millen, Little Me, MTV Fashions, Nutrirition World, Oceano, The Young Designers Emporium.

Town Centre

Location → Jumeirah Beach Road · Beach Rd, Jumeira | 344 0111
Hours → 10:00 - 22:00 Fri 17:00 - 22:00
Web/email → www.towncentrejumeirah.com Map Ref → 5-E1

This well-planned mall offers a variety of stores selling everything from clothes to jewellery. Since opening a little over four years ago, it has earned the hospitable reputation of being a 'community mall'.

A novel concept is Café Ceramique where adults can enjoy a coffee, while kids concentrate on painting their own piece of pottery (the glass of water you are given on arrival is for the paintbrushes!).

On a practical level, there's an Empost for posting mail, an electronic Etisalat machine for paying phone bills, plus a payment machine for traffic fines... a great way to avoid any embarrassment.

Other outlets include: Al Jaber Optical, Bang & Olufsen, Being Negotiated, Books Plus, Cafe Moka, Carpe Diem, Damas Jewellery, DKNY Fashion, Dunkin Donuts/Baskin Robbins, Empost, Kaya Beauty Centre, Marie Claire, Nail Station, Nine West, Nutrition Zone, Oasis Fashion, Papermoon, Paris Gallery, SOS Salon, World of Pens.

Twin Towers

Location → Nr Htl Inter-Continental · Deira | 221 8833
Hours → 10:00 - 13:00 17:00 - 22:00 Fri 17:00 - 22:00
Web/email → www.twintowersdubai.com Map Ref → 8-C4

One of Dubai's most spectacular malls in terms of location, Twin Towers stands proudly on the edge of the Creek and the refined surroundings offer a relaxing and congenial shopping experience.

The Towers are home to the more desirable designer outlets, such as Pierre Cardin and Cartier. Jewellery, perfumes, watches and children's clothes round out the shopping selection and generally attract local residents and a business clientele. There is a variety of cafés and restaurants on the third floor, and the building also has residences, offices and a health club. Free underground parking is available for shoppers, but only after 18:00. Not a place for bargain hunters generally, but great at sale time as discounts tend to be hefty.

Other outlets include: Armani, Baumier, Boss, Brioni, Cerruti 1881, Italian Jewellery LLC, Marco Borocco, Mini Man, Verri.

Shopping Malls		
Al Ain Centre	Nr Ramada Hotel	351 6914
Al Ghurair City	Al Rigga Rd	222 5222
Al Hana Centre	Al Mankhool Rd	398 2229
Al Khaleej Centre	Opp Ramada Htl	355 5550
Al Rais Center	Opp Ramada Htl	352 7755
Al Twar Mall	-	263 6566
Beach Centre	Nr Dubai Zoo	344 9045
Bin Sougat Centre	Airport Rd	286 3000
BurJuman Centre	Trade Centre Rd	352 0222
Center, The	Nr JW Marriott Htl	269 3155
Century Mall	Dubai-Sharjah Rd	296 6188
Century Plaza	Jumeirah	349 8062
Deira City Centre	Al Garhoud	295 4545
Emirates Towers	Shk Zayed Rd	319 8999
Galleria	Hyatt Regency	209 6000
Gold & Diamond Park	Shk Zayed Rd	347 7788
Hamarain Centre	Nr JW Marriott Htl	262 1110
Holiday Centre	Shk Zayed Rd	331 7755
Jumeirah Centre	Nr Jumeira Mosque	349 9702
Jumeirah Plaza	Nr Jumeira Mosque	349 7111
Lamcy Plaza	Nr Eppco HQ	335 9999
Mamzar Mall	Al Mamzar	297 6666
Mazaya Centre	Shk Zayed Rd	343 8333
Mercato	Jumeirah Beach Road	344 4161
Oasis Centre	Nr, Ace Hardware	339 5459
Palm Strip	Opp Jumeira Mosque	346 1462
Spinneys	Umm Suqeim	394 1657
Town Centre	Jumeirah Beach Road	344 0111
Twin Towers	Nr Htl Inter-Continental	221 8833
Wafi Mall	Oud Metha	324 4555

Sharjah Malls		
Sahara Centre	Sharjah	06 531 3666
Sharjah City Centre	Sharjah	06 532 7700
Sharjah Mega Mall	Sharjah	06 574 6666

Shopping Malls - Main

Al Ghurair City

Location → Al Rigga Rd · Deira | 222 5222
Hours → 10:00 - 22:00 Fri 14:00 - 22:00
Web/email → www.alghuraircity.com | Map Ref → 11-D1

When this first purpose built mall to Dubai was built in 1981, little did we know that it would set a shopping trend that would be followed at such a furious pace.

In keeping with the retail development boom, the mall was revamped in 2003 with an eight screen cinema, Spinneys, a huge range of shops, many designer brands and four new restaurants amongst the many new additions.

Seafood, Arabic, international and Oriental dining options are there to give you much needed respite after an intense spree. Entertainment options also include huge Fun Corner for the kids. A multi storey indoor car park has a capacity of 2,000 cars and boasts wider spaces with the widest ramps. This mall may be modern but retains a good feel of the traditional.

Al Ghurair City

Books, Cards & Gifts

Book Corner
Gulf Greetings
Lifestyle

Clothes

Bebe
Benetton
Bossini
Cartoon
Esprit
Evans
French Connection (FCUK)
G2000
Guess
Mexx
Pierre Cardin
Springfield
United Colours Of Benneton

Department Stores

Bhs
Mohd Sharief & Bros

Electronics

Samsung Digital

Eyewear

Al Jaber Opticals
Yateem Opticians

Food

Al Safeer (Lebanese)
Chinese Palace (Chinese)
McDonald's
Mrs. Vanellis (Italian)
Nawab (Indian)
Seattle's Best Coffee & Cinnabon
Starbucks

Jewellery & Gold

Al Haseena Jewellery
Damas Jewellery

Kids' Stuff

Funland

Leather & Luggage

Leather Palace

Lingerie

La Senza
Lujean Lingerie
Triumph

Medicine

Sultan Pharmacy

Music & Videos

Music Box
Plug-Ins

Perfumes & Cosmetics

Faces
Paris Gallery
Rassasi
Red Earth

Services

Al Ghurair International Exchange
Baby Strollers
Free Gift Wrapping (Information Desk)
Postage Stamps (Information Desk)
Rainbow Photolab
Wheel Chairs for the Handicapped (Information Desk)

Shoes

Aldo
Ecco
Nine West

Sporting Goods

Sun & Sand Sports

Supermarkets

Spinneys

Watches

Citizen
Hour Choice
Popley La Classique
Rivoli
Swatch
Watch House

BurJuman Centre

Location → Trade Centre Rd · Bur Dubai | 352 0222
Hours → 10:00 - 22:00 Fri 16:00 - 22:00
Web/email → www.burjuman.com | Map Ref → 11-A1

This stylish mall is undergoing massive expansion (nearly four times its original size). Five new buildings will not only double the retail space but also include offices, conference space, apartments, a theatre, a health club and a multi screen cineplex.

Already, the mall has a reputation for being a superior host to many designer shops. Joining the list will be the likes of Hugo Boss, Christian Dior and Tommy Hilfiger to name a few. Don't be disheartened by all the designer outlets though, as there are shops of a more relaxed nature too, such as BHS, Giordano and Mango. A good selection of electronics, furnishings and lifestyle shops keeps every shopper happy. A well populated foodcourt offers diverse eating options and the kids' area (Fun City) keeps the little ones happily occupied. The Dome on the ground floor is a popular hangout for both residents and tourists and also presents a good people watching option for cars waiting at the traffic lights. Two basement levels provide plenty of underground parking.

BurJuman Centre

Books, Cards & Gifts

Al Jabre Al Elmiah Bookshop
Gulf Greetings
Magrudy's Bookshop

Clothes

Benetton
Bossini
Calvin Klein
Christian Lacroix
DKNY
Donna Karan
Elle
Escada
Esprit
G2000
Giordano
Guess
In Wear
Kenzo Homme
Levis
Liz Claiborne
Mango
Massimo Dutti
Max Mara
Mexx
Next
Paul Smith
Polo Ralph Lauren
XOXO
Zara

Department Stores

Ace Hardware
Bhs
Grand Stores
Mohd Sharief & Bros

Electronics

Jumbo
Oman National Electronics

Eyewear

Optic Art
Optics
Yateem Optician

Food

A & W
Al Baiq (Lebanese)
Chinese Palace (Chinese)
Dome Cafe
Fujiyama (Japanese)
Gloria Jeans
La Gaufrette
Mrs. Fields
Sala (Thai)
Shamiana (Indian)
Starbucks

Jewellery & Gold

Damas Jewellery
Mansour Jewellery
Tiffany & Co.

Kids' items

Early Learning Centre
Guess
Mothercare

Leather & Luggage

Aigner
Aristocrat
Leather Palace
Louis Vuitton

Lingerie

Ines de la Fressange
La Perla
La Senza

Medicine

BurJuman Pharmacy

Music & Videos

Al Mansoor
Diamond Audio Visuals
Virgin

Perfumes & Cosmetics

Ajmal Perfumes
Areej
Crabtree & Evelyn
Liwa store
Lush
Paris Gallery

Services

Al Ghurair International Exchange
Champion Cleaners (Laundry Service)
DNATA (Travel Agent)
Glamour Shots
Mashreq Bank
Seconds (Key Cutting)
Xerox Emirates

Shoes

Bally
Bruno Magli
Domino Shoes
Nine West
Opera Shoes
Tods

Sporting Goods

Golf House
Nike
Sport One Trading
Sportslines
Sun & Sand

Supermarkets

Lals

Watches

Cartier
Fossil
Rivoli
Swatch
The Watch House

Deira City Centre

Location ➜ Opp Dubai Creek Golf Club · Al Garhoud | 295 4545
Hours ➜ 10:00 - 22:00 Fri 14:00 - 22:00
Web/email ➜ www.deiracitycentre.com Map Ref ➜ 14-D1

This mall is a major stop on every tourist bus list and attracts shoppers of all nationalities, also satisfying the culture hungry tourists eager for a more Arabic shopping experience (Arabian Treasures is well stocked with Arabic perfumes, knick knacks, carpets and more).

Debenhams is at one end; a massive Carrefour spreads through the centre and the other end houses IKEA and an eleven screen cinema complex with a host of restaurants to tempt you on the way. Compacted into this structure are numerous shops, many recognisable around the world. The Jewellery Court is a mixture of the more expensive brand names with some cheaper options; some shops will gladly re-string those pearls while you wait. Magic Planet is an exciting escape for the kids, and is surrounded by an ever busy foodcourt.

With the latest expansion, the new ground floor focuses on electronic goods, a great shoe shiner (for the lazy ones) and a key cutting stall, which also cobbles shoes! Be prepared though, for the weekend crowd of relentless shoppers.

Deira City Centre – Dubai's Tourist Hub!

Books, Cards & Gifts
Book Corner
Carlton Cards
Gulf Greetings
Magrudy's
Sara
Tanagra

Cinema
Cinestar

Clothes
Benetton
Bershka
Burberry
Calvin Klein
Diesel
DKNY
Dolce & Gabbana
Evans
Gerry Webber
Giordano
Guess
Hang Ten
In Wear
Karen Millen
Kookai
Lacoste
Levis
Mango
Massimo Dutti
Mexx
Monsoon
Next
Pull & Bear
River Island
Truworths
Zara

Department Stores
Debenhams
Westwood
Woolworths

Electronics
Aftron
Al Falak
Plug-Ins
Radio Shack

Eyewear
Al Jaber Optical
City Optic
Dubai Opticals
Grand Optics
Grand Sunglasses

Food
Al Safeer (Lebanese)
Cactus Cabana (Tex-Mex)
Chilis (American)
China Times (Chinese)
Cinnabon
Coco's (American)
Costa Coffee
Fujiyama (Japanese)
Hatam (Persian)
Mrs. Vanelis
Panda Chinese
Pizzeria Uno
Shamiana (Indian)
Subway

Furniture & Household
Al Jaber Gallery
Carre Blanc
Carrefour
IKEA
Marina Gulf Trading

Hypermarket
Carrefour

Jewellery & Gold
Al Futtaim Jewellery
Bin Hendi
Damas Jewellery

Kids' Stuff
Early Learning Centre
Magic Planet
Mothercare

Leather & Luggage
Aigner
Aristocrat
La Valise
Porsche Design
Sacoche

Lingerie
Inner Lines
Triumph
Womans' Secret

Medicine
New Ibn Sina Pharmacy

Music & Videos
Plug-Ins
Virgin Megastore

Perfumes & Cosmetics
Ajmal Perfumes
Body Shop
Debenhams
Lush
MAC
Nature Shop, The
Paris Gallery
Red Earth

Services
Al Futtaim Travel
Al Ghurair Exchange
National Bank Of Dubai

Shoes
Aldo
Bally
Branato
Clarks
Milano
Rockport
Shoe City
Valencia

Sporting Goods
Adidas
Golf House
Quicksilver
Studio R

Watches
Breitling
Raymond Weil
Rivoli
Rossini
Swatch

Lamcy Plaza

Location → Nr EPPCO HQ · Oud Metha | 335 9999
Hours → 10:00 - 22:00 Fri 10:00 - 22:30
Web/email → na | Map Ref → 10-D4

When it opened its doors in 1997, Lamcy's aim was to sell anything and everything under the same roof, and judging by the recent expansion it has proved very successful.

Located a stone's throw from the Wafi Centre, it's a huge five-storey mall with open plan shops that offer a multitude of fashions, shoes and home wear. It's particularly good for sports goods, children's toys and clothing and the children's play area is always a hit with youngsters.

They've even got an in-house radio station, aptly named Radio Lamcy, which plays the latest hits and updates shoppers on any sales events about to hit the shops.

Paris Gallery sells a good selection of perfumes and cosmetics, and the department store BHS is a reasonably priced place for fashion and home wear

However, Lamcy can become very cramped and confusing (probably because of the vast range of goods); just don't be in a rush to dash in, buy what you want and dash out – it's not that simple!

Finding parking can be your first challenge, but they've introduced a valet service to alleviate parking headaches.

With sales galore during Eid and the shopping festivals, Lamcy is ideal for bargain hunting for the whole family. However, if you're not keen on sharing your shopping space with several hundred people, then avoid the weekends or go early morning.

Lamcy Plaza

Books, Cards & Gifts
Books Plus
Carlton Cards

Clothes
Benetton
Bhs
Bossini
G2000
Hang Ten
Indigo Nation
Jenyfer
Mexx for less
Mr. Price

Eyewear
Al Adasat Opticals

Food
Arrabiatta (Italian)
Bombay Chowpatty (Indian)
China Grill (Chinese)
Hardees
KFC
Kwality (Indian)
Mongolian BBQ
Pizza Hut
Starbucks
Taste Buds

Kids' Stuff
Loulou Al Dugong's
Mothercare

Lingerie
Bhs
La Senza

Medicine
Lamcy Pharmacy

Music & Videos
Al Mansoor Video

Perfumes & Cosmetics
Paris Gallery

Services
Al Ansari Exchange
ATM Machines
Emirates Driving Institute
Empost (Postal Services)
Etisalat Bill Payment Machine
Flower Shop
Gift Wrap & Balloon Shop
Traffic Fine payment Machine

Shoes
Aldo
Hush Puppies
Nine West
Shoe Mart

Sporting Goods
City Sports
Golf House

Supermarkets
Lamcy Supermarket

Watches
Rivoli
Swatch

Mercato

Location → Jumeirah Beach Road · Jumeira | 344 4161
Hours → 10:00 - 22:00 Fri 14:00 - 22:00
Web/email → n/a | Map Ref → 5-E1

This candy-coloured confection of a mall certainly brightens up the Beach Road and all that colour brings to mind Disneyland – and that's just from the outside! With an ever present festive atmosphere, this is yet another experience for Dubai's ever restless shopping junkies.

Built in Italian renaissance style, Mercato (which means 'market' in Italian) has upped the shopping experience several gears in the Jumeira area. With over 90 upmarket outlets, including a Spinneys supermarket and several food and coffee pit stops, it is an overwhelming success. Novel concepts include every little girl's dream – a store devoted to Barbie. At weekends there is always some form of entertainment to amuse visitors, plus there's a multi-screen cinema complex (although with its over the top décor and many new to Dubai stores, a couple of hours wandering around Mercato is actually enough visual entertainment in itself!).

Mercato Mall

Automotive Accessories
BMW Lifestyle

Books, Cards & Gifts
Hallmark
Magrudy's

Cinema
Century Cinemas

Clothes
Amichi
Armani Jeans
Bershka
Diesel Jeans
Energie
Gianfranco Ferre
Hip Hop
Maestro
Mango
Massimo Dutti
Miss Sixty
Next
Polo Jeans Co.
Promod
Pull & Bear
Top Shop
Trussardi

Electronics
G&M International

Food
Castanea
Chinese Palace (Chinese)
Cinnabon
Dolce Antico (Italian)
Paul Rustic & Specialty Breads
Starbucks

Home Accessories
Home Centre
KAZ Australia
Susan Walpole
The Zone

Jewellery & Gold
Al Liali
Damas
Mahallati
Pure Gold

Kids' Stuff
Adams
Armani Junior
Early Learning Centre

Leather & Luggage
Francesco Biasia

Lingerie
Beyond the Beach
Nayomi
Triumph

Music & Videos
Virgin Megastore

Perfumes & Cosmetics
MAC
Red Earth

Services
The Nail Spa

Shoes
Aldo
Domino
Ecco
Milano
Nine West

Supermarkets
Spinneys

Wafi Mall

Location → Umm Hurair (2) | 324 4555
Hours → 10:00 - 22:00 Fri 16:30 - 22:00
Web/email → www.waficity.com | Map Ref → 13-D2

Possibly the most exclusive mall in Dubai, Wafi's four floors and maze of walkways are packed with trendy boutiques, luxury gift shops, coffee shops, designer food stores, home furnishings and many other smart retail outlets.

The large complex is topped by three distinctive glass pyramids and one wall frames a stunning stained glass window. The size of the mall can be a bit daunting, but there are plenty of location charts, so take your time. It can also be a little quiet, but possibly because there are so many other attractions just around the corner in Wafi City, such as restaurants, nightclubs, a health spa and a cinema. For the kids, there's the popular Encounter Zone offering excellent activities, and children are well looked after if you want to leave them while you browse. Christmas is a particular favourite with shoppers as the decorations are spectacular and well worth a visit in their own right.

Wafi Mall

Books, Cards & Gifts
Aloha
Gulf Greetings
Patchi
Petals
Sara - Villeroy & Boch
Swarovski
Tanagra

Clothes
Betty Barclay
Chanel
Gerry Weber
Giordano
Givenchy
Jaeger
Kookai
Marina Rinaldi
Miss Sixty

Department Stores
Salam Studio & Stores
Tanagra

Electronics
Jumbo Electronics

Eyewear
Lutfi Optical Centre
Rivoli

Food
Biella Caffé Pizzeria Ristorante
Elements
Renoir
Square, The
Starbucks

Furniture & Household
Petals
THE One

Jewellery & Gold
Al Mansour Jewellers
Chopard
Damas Jewellery
Mont Blanc

Kids Stuff
Early Learning Centre
Fun City
Miki House
Osh Kosh B'gosh

Lingerie
Caresse
Charisma

Medicine
Al Sham Pharmacy

Music & Videos
Al Mansoor
Popular Music Institute

Perfumes & Cosmetics
MAC
Make Up Forever
Paris Gallery

Services
Al Ansari Exchange
Encounter Zone
Photo Magic

Sporting Goods
Emirates Sports

Supermarkets
Goodies

Watches
Casa Marakesh
Givenchy
Jashanmal
Rossini
Swatch
Tag Heuer

Streets/Areas to Shop

Other options → Satwa [p.88]
Bur Dubai [p.86]
Al Karama [p.88]

Al Diyafah Street

Location → Nr Jumeira Rotana Htl · Al Satwa | na
Hours → 09:00 - 14:00 16:00 - 21:30
Web/email → n/a Map Ref → 7-A3

Al Diyafah Street is fondly known as 'uptown Satwa' to residents, as opposed to the cheaper shopping area around the corner ('downtown Satwa'). With many shops facing the street and in the Dune Centre, this is the place to buy everything from silk carpets to drinks cabinets in the shape of a globe. Be prepared though, this area has a high shop turnover and what was there yesterday may not be there today.

If you've been invited to a last minute black-tie event and there's no time for a tailor to whip you up a tuxedo, you can hire one at Elegance or Formal Wear. However, if there is time to have a tux made, visit 'downtown Satwa' with its material shops and tailors all in close proximity. While you wait for that suit, pay a visit to Ravi's,the atmospheric Pakistani restaurant that serves great food at amazing prices.

Cooler evenings are a good time to visit this busy area for a quick shop and a bite to eat. Enjoy a sundowner espresso at the pavement tables of one of the numerous cafés or an ice cream at the Haagen-Dazs Café. There are also Lebanese, Persian and Chinese restaurants, as well as one of the best shawarma restaurants in Dubai, Al Mallah. Weekend evenings are great for people watching, especially if you enjoy observing testosterone-pumped young men cruising the strip and revving the engines of their flashy cars in the hopes of attracting even more attention.

Al Faheidi Street

Location → Nr Astoria Htl · Bur Dubai | na
Hours → 08:00 - 13:30 16:00 - 21:30
Web/email → n/a Map Ref → 8-A2

This busy street in Bur Dubai is definitely the place to visit when you're in the market for electronic goods. The multitude of electrical shops offers brand names such as Sony, Panasonic, JVC, Sharp, Phillips, Grundig, GEC, etc, at negotiable prices. Don't make your purchase at the first shop you come to; take time to look around and discover the best range and price. It gets busy in the evenings, so you may have difficulty parking.

The Thomson shop has a large choice of cheap original cassettes and inexpensive CD's. Thomas Cook Al Rostamani is the place to go to change your currency or travellers cheques at a favourable rate, and plenty of restaurants are on hand to replenish you after a hectic session of haggling. These include Talk of the Town for Chinese and Indian food, and Bananas for a decent pizza, as well as the various outlets at the nearby Astoria and Ambassador hotels.

Al Karama Shopping Complex

Location → Shopping Area · Al Karama | na
Hours → 08:30 - 14:00 16:00 - 22:00
Web/email → n/a Map Ref → 10-D2

This long street running through the middle of Karama has veranda covered shops on both sides enticing you to 'buy, buy, buy' cheap goods at below average prices. Browse through mix n' match ideas direct from the Far East – there's sports apparel, t-shirts, shorts, sunglasses, shoes, gifts and all the usual souvenirs (fluffy camels, shisha pipes etc). Or dive into a sea of fake designer accessories – stores are packed to the gills with Gucci, Prada and Chanel copies. And remember, the best lines are tucked away in the back, so ask for entry to the inner sanctum and bargain hard.

Several small restaurants in the area offer Indian, Pakistani, Filipino and Arabic cuisine – it's good food at amazingly cheap prices. For the daring, the fish market offers fresh hammour, prawns, crabs etc, or choose from a variety of regular and not so easily available supplies at the fruit and vegetable shops.

Interesting knick knacks

Souks

Other options → Bur Dubai [p.86]

Souks are the Arabic markets where all kinds of goods are bought, sold and exchanged. Traditionally, dhows from the Far East, China, Ceylon and India would discharge their cargoes, and the goods would be haggled over in the souks adjacent to the docks. Over the years, the items on sale have changed dramatically from spices, silks and perfumes to include electronic goods and the latest kitsch consumer trends.

Although Dubai's souks aren't as fascinating as others in the Arab world, such as Marrakech in Morocco or Mutrah in Oman, they are worth a visit for their bustling atmosphere, the eclectic variety of goods and the traditional way of doing business.

Deira Souk

The myriad of souks are located on both banks of the Creek, but predominantly in Deira (it's worth exploring both sides if you have the time). You can cross between the two banks of the Creek in about ten minutes on one of the many abras (small wooden dhows) that line the Creek; it only costs 50 fils. Alternatively, most taxi drivers know where to go if you ask for a specific souk and the fares are reasonable. If you have the time, why not brave the public transport. Bus numbers 5, 16, 19 and 20 run frequently throughout the day and stop at all of the souks, both sides of the Creek.

It is wise to visit when the weather is a little cooler in the late afternoon, but for early birds the souks open 07:00 - 12:00. They then re-open between 17:00 - 19:00, every day except Friday, when they only open in the afternoon. Thursday and Friday evenings are the busiest times as this is the weekend for many people. This is a great time to witness the souk trading at full throttle, but if you are more interested in exploring at a leisurely place, then these evenings are best avoided.

Fish Market

Location → Nr Shindagha Tunnel · Deira | na
Hours → 07:00 - 23:00
Web/email → na | Map Ref → 8-C2

Smelly... but just the spot for the non squeamish seafood fanatics. The fish market is worth a trip for a few snapshots to show the folks at home. The variety of fresh fish is amazing and you will most likely come across some species that you've never seen before. It isn't just the display of fish; the cleaning and gutting activity and the bargaining process is quite fascinating too. The market has undergone a revamp in the bid to accentuate the fishing heritage of the region and also to educate tourists. Besides a seafood restaurant, a museum explains the history of this past fishing village. The Al Hamriya fruit and vegetable market opposite offers tropical fruit; the variety is bountiful and the prices are ridiculously low, especially for the huge quantities you leave with.

Gold Souk

Location → Nr Hyatt Regency Htl · Deira | na
Hours → 09:30 - 13:00 16:00 - 22:00
Web/email → n/a | Map Ref → 8-C2

This is what many people around the world primarily recognise Dubai for – The City of Gold. As

Shisha Pipes

people race straight from the plane to the Gold Souk, they are not disappointed (take your sunglasses the greeting glare is bound to be retina damaging!). Streets and streets of shops are aligned with sparkling windows and the choice is impressive, as are the prices. The downfall could only be the difficulty in deciding where to start. For the mere window shopper, the plan is simple – start from one end and walk to the other (set aside a whole day). For the shopper with a purpose as well as those who've conned their partners into taking a cultural walk (but with ulterior motives), there really is no constructive strategy to tackling the souk. Just close your eyes, point your finger and turn around in a circle five times to come to your starting point!

Besides gold, diamonds, rubies, emeralds, opals and amethysts line the windows in decorative displays, and pearls are extremely cheap compared to Western prices.

Spice Souk

Location → Deira · Deira | na
Hours → 09:00 - 13:00 16:00 - 22:00
Web/email → na | Map Ref → 8-C2

A wonderfully different experience, the Spice Souk has narrow streets and an aroma so unique, it's like walking into another era. The place seems to have downsized in the past year and the rows of stalls displaying spice laden sacks are fast diminishing. Although spices are available, a Far Eastern influence seems to be setting in, with integrated shops of cheap electronic goods and wholesale shoes. Perhaps the slow demise is due to more and more supermarkets supplying a wider range of spices.

Carrefour in Deira City Centre has a separate section with colourful spices on show. The choice is great but the experience is a secondary alternative to that of the souk. The sellers at the souk are only too happy to chat endlessly, advising you on the various spices and herbs. Although most of the stalls have more or less similar stocks, expensive spices such as saffron are much cheaper here than anywhere else in the world.

Arabian Souvenirs

Textile Souk

Location → Nr Creekside · Bur Dubai | na
Hours → 09:00 - 13:00 16:00 - 22:00
Web/email → n/a | Map Ref → 8-A2

The shops in Bur Dubai's Textile Souk are a treasure trove of textiles, colours, textures and weaves from around the world. Shimmering threads adorn thin voile, broderie anglaise, satin and silk tempt, and velvets jostle with peach skin, although good drill cottons are still hard to find. Shop around as the choice is virtually unlimited and prices are negotiable. Sales occur quite frequently in this area, particularly around major holidays and the Dubai Shopping Festival.

Spice Shop

Activities

EXPLORER

Activities

What's new?

Gym Mania!

Page 315

Dubai has gone fitness mad. With so many wonderful and diverse restaurants constantly popping up, a counter movement is very kindly combating the potential calorie invasion and matching the myriad of restaurants with an influx of health clubs. Check out [p.318] for a list of clubs, details on facilities, prices, venues and more.

Activities

It might not seem readily apparent, but life in Dubai is not all shopping malls, restaurants, and 5 star hotels. No matter what season, visitors and residents alike will discover a variety of engaging activities to fulfil almost any interest or hobby. Warm winters provide the perfect environment for a variety of outdoor activities, while a host of diversions are available to take your mind off the extreme heat and humidity of the summer. From rock climbing on an indoor training wall to flower arranging or yoga classes, the fun doesn't have to stop when the tarmac starts melting! However, it's surprising what can actually be done in the heat of the summer, and even in the hottest months you can find dedicated enthusiasts sailing or playing golf when it's 48° C.

Land access is far less of a problem than in many expats' home countries; it's quite easy to travel into the mountainous wilderness or onto remote beaches.

Sometimes word of mouth is the best way to learn about your favourite hobby, so if it's not listed here, ask around and you may well find that trainspotting really does go on.

As usual, we welcome your suggestions as to what to include or change in the book next year. If you belong to any club, organisation, or group; however, small, large, official or unofficial – we'd like to hear from you. See the Reader Profile Survey on our Website (www.Explorer-Publishing.com) and give us your comments and details.

For information on where to buy sports equipment, refer to Sporting Goods [p.236].

Sports

When the weather starts to cool, Dubai and the surrounding emirates are ideal for athletes and outdoor enthusiasts. It seems there isn't a sport or activity that isn't being practised at some point in the year. Traditional favourites such as tennis, golf (on beautifully manicured courses), aerobics, rugby, cricket and hashing abound, while for the more adventurous, skydiving, rock climbing, mountain biking, and caving are available.

With its stunning beaches, clear water and world-class water parks, it's no surprise that a variety of water sports is represented in Dubai. Scuba diving is probably the most popular, while other ways to have fun getting wet include sailing, surfing, water skiing, and a rising interest in the eccentric sport of kiteboarding. Keep in mind that while the Gulf waters often seem tranquil, dangers such as stingrays, jellyfish, strong currents and rip tides are lurking, so always be wary. At beach parks, pay attention to the lifeguard's flag (if it's red, stay on the beach), but if you're at one of the public beaches, always take a little more care.

One of the original pastimes, and still one of the most popular, is getting out into the wilderness. As you spend more time in the area, and the weather starts to cool, you too will feel the lure of the open desert, the dramatic wadis, and the rustic mountains. Whether you decide to partake in camping, hiking, wadi and dune bashing, or some combination of these, grab a copy of the *Off-Road Explorer*, published by Explorer Publishing. Included in the guide are stunning photographs and detailed satellite imagery of many routes and hikes. The guide is ideal for discovering the best of the UAE's scenery, which is reminiscent, in places, of the Australian outback or African savannah. Apart from detailed satellite images, the handy guide also has GPS co-ordinates, information and photos of flora and fauna, and twenty off-road routes to explore. It really is the UAE's definitive outdoor guide!

Basketball

Aerobics

Whether it's to shed unwanted bulk or just keep in shape, aerobics is great exercise. Be it step, pump, aqua or straight aerobics, most of the health, beach and sports clubs offer exercise classes on a regular basis. For a complete list of up to date classes, timings and instructors, check with individual clubs and book in advance for the more popular sessions. Prices per class are usually Dhs.20 - 25 for club members and Dhs.25 - 30 for non members.

Al Majaz

Location → Trade Centre Rd · Al Karama | 335 3563
Hours → 09:00 - 14:00 16:00 - 21:00
Web/email → www.goldenfistkarate.com | Map Ref → 10-D1

For more information on Al Majaz, please refer to their entry under Yoga [p.314].

Ballet Centre, The

Location → Beh Jumeira Plaza · Jumeira | 344 9776
Hours → 09:00 - 12:30 15:00 - 18:30
Web/email → n/a | Map Ref → 6-C3

The Ballet Centre is a long established dance and fitness centre, offering a wide range of classes in a relaxed and attractive environment. For aerobics fans, there are a variety of sessions at different times and plenty of choice for different levels of fitness. The well equipped studios and coffee shop are popular, and the instructors are friendly and professional.

Aikido

A Japanese martial art founded by Morihei Ueshiba, Aikido takes joint locks and throws from jujitsu and combines them with the body movements of sword and spear fighting. Please see Martial Arts [p.291].

Amusement Centres

Other options → Amusement Parks [p.262]

Adventureland

Location → Sahara Centre · Sharjah | 06 531 6363
Hours → 10:00 - 22:30
Web/email → www.adventureland-sharjah.com Map Ref → UAE-C2

The unique distinction of Adventureland as an entertainment centre is its ideal size and balanced mix of ride offerings. It covers 70,000 square feet of fun space indoors and caters to all ages, from unique rides for the toddlers and kids to teenage videogames and adult thrill rides, truly living up to its name as the ultimate family entertainment destination.

Costs: *Buy a card and put in credits; the more credits you buy, the better the discount. Any leftover credits can be used on your next visit. T he rides vary from Dhs.3 - 7. Membership is Dhs.50 and allows Dhs.30 worth of rides, discounts in the mall and a host of other benefits.*

City 2000

Location → Hamarain Centre · Deira | 266 7855
Hours → 10:00 - 23:00 Fri 16:30- 23:00
Web/email → city2000@emirates.net.ae | Map Ref → 12-A4

City 2000 offers video games and rides in an air conditioned environment. From racing on a track or bombing in a fighter plane, young or old can enjoy the simulators and find an outlet for the adventurous spirit! For little ones there are funny videos and the latest rides. City 2000 claims to eliminate the more violent machines that are available in many adult amusement centres. Entrance is free and food is supplied by the nearby foodcourt. Machines are operated by Dhs.1 tokens and all machines take two tokens, except for adult simulator games, which take three.

Encounter Zone

Location → Wafi Mall · Umm Hurair (2) | 324 7747
Hours → 10:00 - 22:00 Fri 13:30 - 22:00
Web/email → n/a | Map Ref → 13-D2

Divided into two sections, Encounter Zone offers a range of action packed fun for all ages; Galactica for teenagers and adults, and Lunarland for kids aged 1 - 8. Galactica is based on interactive attractions and The Chamber, a 'living house of horror'. Features include Galactica Express, a themed inline skates/skateboarding park. Lunarland hosts a galaxy of games and activities especially designed for younger children, such as Crater Challenge, Lunar Express or the Komet. Encounter Zone also offers packages for special occasions. Costs: All attractions have individual rates and can be played separately. Prices range from Dhs.5 to Dhs.25; day pass packages cost Dhs.45 which include access to all major attractions plus a selection of video games; an hour pass costs Dhs.25 and includes access to all attractions plus selected video games.

ADVENTUROUS
EARTHLINGS THERE
ARE 19 MORE RIDES.
ADVENTURELAND
at Sahara Centre
Asteroids
Surf to space you out with unexpected twists and turns, it's one
of the most thrilling rides you'll find at Adventureland. Or on Earth.
20 thrilling rides and attractions • Billiards • Bowling • Arcade Games • Sports Café • Internet
Sahara Centre, Sharjah • Tel 06-5316363 • www.adventureland-sharjah.com

Fantasy Kingdom

Location → Al Bustan Centre · Al Twar | 263 2774
Hours → 10:00 - 23:00 Fri 14:00 - 23:00
Web/email → www.al-bustan.com Map Ref → 15-C2

Themed as a medieval castle, Fantasy Kingdom offers adventure, fun and excitement for the little ones. The centre is located in the comfort of a 24,000 square foot indoor play area, which is divided into sections for different age groups. While younger children enjoy the soft play area and merry-go-around, or learn in the relaxed atmosphere of the learning corner, older ones can opt for the latest redemption, video, sports and interactive games, bumper cars, pool or air hockey. The centre also caters for birthday parties. Cost: Dhs.2 per token with no entrance fee (tokens become cheaper the more you buy).

Magic Planet

Location → City Centre · Al Garhoud | 295 4333
Hours → 10:00 - 24:00 Fri 12:00 - 24:00
Web/email → www.deiracitycentre.com Map Ref → 14-D1

Magic Planet is one of Dubai's favourite family entertainment centres. Ride the carousel or ferris wheel, swing through Clarence Camel's adventure zone, or test your skills on the bumper cars and latest video games. If you prefer a more leisurely route, watch the world pass from the City Express train or take a trip in a safari car. When you need a break, stop at the foodcourt where you can choose from over a dozen outlets. Entrance is free – you pay as you play, using Dhs.2 cards (they become cheaper the more you buy). Alternatively, for unlimited entertainment buy a Planet All Day Special. For Dhs.50 you can play and play and play...

Amusement Parks

Other options → Amusement Centres [p.260]

Fruit & Garden Luna Park

Location → Al Nasr Leisureland · Oud Metha | 337 1234
Hours → 09:00 - 22:30
Web/email → www.alnasrleisureland.ae Map Ref → 10-E4

This park offers some great rides, suitable for everyone from four years to 60 years old, ideal for a child's birthday party. Rides include go-karts, bumper cars, helicopter, mini bumper and a roller coaster. Entrance fees: Adults Dhs.10; children under five Dhs.5.

WonderLand Theme & Water Park

Location → Nr Creekside Park · Umm Hurair (2) | 324 3222
Hours → 15:00 - 21:00 Thu & Fri 17:00 - 24:00
Web/email → www.wonderlanduae.com Map Ref → 14-A3

This is the only theme and water park in the Middle East. There is a huge variety of indoor and outdoor rides for all ages, from the 130 kph Space Shot, which shoots you 210 feet into the air in less than 2½ seconds, to their two new thrilling rides 'Freefall' and 'Action Arm'. Alternatively, just enjoy the tropical landscape, relax by the pool or visit the food outlets. Parties and events can be catered for and there's also paintballing and go-karting. See their entry under Water Parks [p.307] also.

Parks Abound in Dubai

Aqua Aerobics

Other options → Aerobics [p.260]

Jumeirah Beach Club

Location → Jumeirah Beach Club · Jumeira | 344 5333
Hours → Sat & Wed 08:00
Web/email → www.jumeirahbeachclub.com Map Ref → 5-D1

Aqua Aerobics is a form of exercise that's great for cardiovascular fitness, as well as for toning the body. In particular, it's a good workout for people who suffer from knee to lower back injuries, as the water acts as a cushion around the joints and reduces impact. It has also been known to help slow down the advance of osteoporosis, and is an excellent exercise for pregnant women. Weights

WESLO
HUFFY SPORTS
Etonic
arena
SPALDING
STRATA
DUNLOP SPORT
GAMMA
TOP-FLITE XL 2000
MAXFLI
loubsol
IMAGE
Ben Hogan
ICON
REEF
Timberland
unicorn
KETTLER
Power Sport
POWERJOG
Slazenger
GoldToeGear
TYR
PENN REELS
weider
SUN & SAND SPORTS

can be used to increase the intensity of the workout, which last 45 - 60 minutes.

Archery

Dubai Archery Group

Location → Dubai College · Al Sufouh | 344 2591
Hours → Thu 15:00
Web/email → linton@emirates.net.ae | Map Ref → 3-C2

Small, friendly and informal, the Dubai Archery Group gathers at the Dubai Country Club on Thursday and Friday afternoons (from approximately 15:00 until dark). Coaching is available and there is club equipment that novices can use. While no great physical strength is required, archery is not really a sport for children under the age of ten. Targets up to 90 metres are available and they hope to introduce a Field Archery Course in the near future. For further information contact either Richard Arbuthnot on 050 624 7982 or Simon Linton on 221 5839. There's a target charge of Dhs.10 per session for adults and Dhs.5 for under 18's.

Hatta Fort Hotel

Location → Hatta Fort Hotel · Hatta | 852 3211
Hours → Timings on request
Web/email → www.jebelali-international.com | Map Ref → UAE-D3

Hatta Fort Hotel's archery range is 25 metres long and has eight standard target stands. The recurve bow, which is curved forward at the ends and straightens out when the bow is drawn, is suitable for adults and children over the age of ten. Archery fans can enter the hotel's annual archery competition and the Dubai Archery Club also holds its annual archery tournament here. Professional assistance is available for this surprisingly challenging sport. Hotel residents can try archery for a nominal fee of Dhs.10, while visitors are charged Dhs.30 per 30 minute session.

Basketball

Where are all you bouncers, dribblers and dunkers? Courts for this fun American sport can be rented at the Aviation Club and Dubai Country Club, plus there is a public court at Safa Park (349 2111). However, at this stage no teams seem to be around, so it looks like lone net practice for the time being. Let us know if you get a team off the ground so that we can provide details to other interested folks.

Billiards

Other options → Snooker [p.300]

Boat & Yacht Charters

Other options → Dhow Charters [p.273]

Bateaux Dubai

Location → Nr British Embassy · Bur Dubai | 337 1919
Hours → 12:30 - 15:00 20:30 - 23:00
Web/email → www.bateauxdubai.com | Map Ref → 8-C4

Built in 2003, the Al Minsaf ensures parties of up to 300 unobstructed sightseeing from all seats. It encompasses state of the art technology, and offers charters for everything

Sunset over Dubai International Marine Club

FLYING
ELEPHANT
...We put the FUN in function.

from corporate events to private festivities. The Al Minsaf is a perfect setting for product launches, press conferences, seminars, conventions, fashion shows, birthday parties or breakfast cruises. Al Minsaf can be chartered daily with advance booking (weekends and official holidays as per request). See their review under Eating Out for further information, or call for timings, charter costs etc.

Charlotte Anne Charters

Location → Dibba · Fujairah | 09 222 3508
Hours → Timings on request
Web/email → www.charlotteannecharters.com Map Ref → UAE E1

Charlotte Anne is a twin-masted Baltic Trader rigged in a traditional schooner style. Charters, which range from a day (up to 33 passengers) to up to seven days (minimum six people, maximum eleven), leave from Dibba Port on the East Coast and cruise the coast of the Musandam. For divers, a trip aboard the Charlotte Anne is ideal, but snorkelling and swimming are also a great way to enjoy the ocean. The vessel is fully air conditioned and all meals are provided. Omani visas are not required.

Danat Dubai Cruises

Location → Nr British Embassy · Bur Dubai | 351 1117
Hours → Timings on request
Web/email → www.danatdubaicruises.com Map Ref → 8-C4

Boasting a top speed of 18 knots, this 34 metre catamaran is available for group charters, product launches, wedding receptions... the options are endless. Danat Dubai has a capacity of 300 passengers (or 170 people for sit down functions). Onboard facilities include a dance floor, music system, video monitors, sun deck and two enclosed air conditioned decks. Catering, live entertainment or a DJ can be provided as part of the charter.

El Mundo

Location → DIMC · Al Sufouh | 343 4870
Hours → Timings on request
Web/email → www.elmundodubai.com Map Ref → 3-A2

El Mundo is an exciting 60 ft catamaran that's available for charter for anywhere between two and fifty people. The company caters to most requests, from watching the dhows and abras on Dubai's Creek to business lunch cruises or dinner cruises around Palm Island. Alternatively, why not enjoy a two or three day sail to snorkel, dolphin watch and hike in the Mussandam? Live entertainment, DJs and bellydancers can be arranged, or try their 'Friday Fun in the Sun' cruise.

Le Meridien Mina Seyahi Beach Resort & Marina

Location → Le Meridien Mina · Al Sufouh | 399 3333
Hours → Timings on request
Web/email → www.lemeridien-minaseyahi.com Map Ref → 3-A2

Le Meridien Mina Seyahi operates a variety of charters from their marina. A number of boats is available for trips of different lengths, numbers of people and for a variety of activities, such as deep sea fishing, trawling, sightseeing or full day cruises. Prices are available on request and depend on the package required (all rates include a skipper and equipment).

Yacht Solutions

Location → Jumeirah Beach Htl · Umm Suqeim | 348 6838
Hours → Timings on request
Web/email → www.yacht-solutions.com Map Ref → 4-B2

Yacht Solutions promises to arrange anything from a short exciting blast aboard a high speed sports rib to an exclusive overnight stay on their 20 metre Princess motor yacht. A myriad of cruising options is available, and they provide full catering options. Corporate enquiries are especially welcome.

Bowling

Al Nasr Leisureland

Location → Beh American Hospital · Oud Metha | 337 1234
Hours → 09:00 - 24:00
Web/email → www.alnasrleisureland.ae Map Ref → 10-E4

One of Dubai's original leisure venues, Al Nasr Leisureland is popular with all. The modern eight lane bowling alley is synthetic and thus smarter looking and faster. Shoes, etc can be hired as usual. Sustenance is provided by various fast food outlets and alcohol is served at the bar. Booking is recommended, since there are regular leagues during the week when the whole alley is busy. Check before you go! Entrance fees: Dhs.10; plus Dhs.7 per game and free shoe rental.

Thunder Bowl

Location → Nr Defence R/A, · Trade Centre 1&2 | 343 1000
Hours → 09:00 - 24:00
Web/email → tb@emirates.net.ae | Map Ref → 5-E3

Thunder Bowl is a complete entertainment experience and the first bowling alley of its kind in the Middle East! It operates 20 computerised Brunswick lanes, a pool and snooker hall, and three food outlets. Various leagues operate including one for junior league (ages 6 - 16) every Thursday from 10:00, and a ladies league every Monday and Wednesday morning. The centre also has a hall for parties, with packages that include bowling time and the usual party paraphernalia. Prices: weekdays Dhs.10 per game; weekends Dhs.15; shoe rental Dhs.2; lane rental per hour Dhs.80. There is no entrance fee.

Bungee Jumping

For those adrenaline junkies and lovers of bungee, throwing yourself at the ground from high altitudes is not possible all year round. However, during the Dubai Shopping Festival, it is one of the attractions of the Bur Dubai side of the Creek, offered by an organisation from Australia. For more information, keep a lookout when DSF approaches and check the daily press for details.

Camel Rides

A visit to Arabia is hardly complete without a close up experience with the 'ship of the desert', the camel. Many tour operators incorporate a short camel ride on their desert safaris, alternatively for a unique adventure, try a camel ride into the spectacular sand dunes. Your guide will lead you to a Bedouin camp, where you can enjoy a rest and some refreshments. Along the way there are stops for photos, so you can remember this unique experience long after the aches subside! Prices are from Dhs.200 per person.

Al Ain Golden Sands Camel Safaris

Location → Hilton Al Ain · Al Ain | 03 768 8006
Hours → 09:00 - 13:00 17:30 - 20:00
Web/email → n/a | Map Ref → UAE-D4

For something a bit more adventurous, Al Ain Golden Sands Camel Safaris offers a selection of tours that include a camel ride over the dunes of Bida Bint Saud. The rides usually last 1 - 2½ hours, and all the tours include transfers from Al Ain, as well as Arabic coffee and dates.

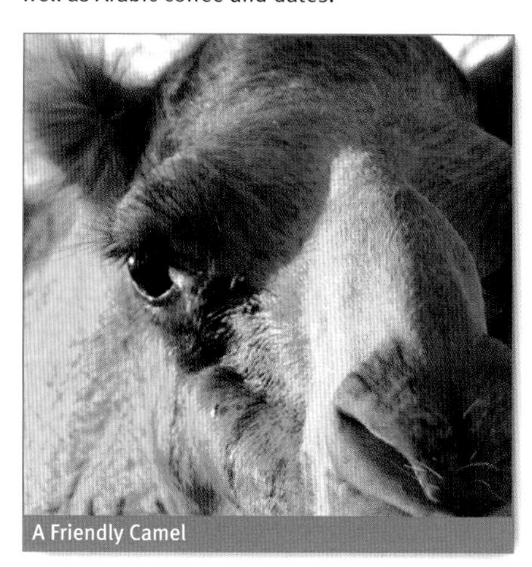

A Friendly Camel

Camping

For happy campers and city slickers alike, the UAE has something to offer everybody. Many spectacular locations are easily accessible and the sun is always shining – literally! Good campsites can be found only short distances away from tarmac roads, so a 4 WD is not necessarily required. Choose between the peace and stillness of the desert, or camp amongst the wadis and mountains, next to trickling streams in picturesque oases.

In general, very little rain and warm temperatures mean you can camp with much less equipment and preparation than in other countries. This can be the perfect introduction for first timers or families with children of any age, although a certain amount of care is needed to avoid the occasional insect. For most, the best time to go is between October and April, as in the summer, it can get unbearably hot sleeping outside.

Although the UAE has low rainfall, care should be taken in and near wadis during the winter months for flash floods (remember, it may be raining in the mountains miles from where you are and when it rains, boy, does it rain!).

For most people, a basic amount of equipment will suffice. This may include:

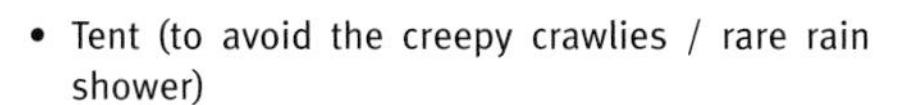

- Tent (to avoid the creepy crawlies / rare rain shower)
- Lightweight sleeping bag (or light blankets and sheets)
- Thin mattress (or air bed)
- Torches and spare batteries (a head torch looks silly, but is a useful investment)
- Cool box (to avoid food spoiling / keep food from insects)
- Water (always take too much)
- Food and drink
- Camping stove, firewood or BBQ and charcoal (if preferred)
- Matches!
- Insect repellent and antihistamine cream
- First aid kit (including any personal medication)
- Sun protection (hats, sunglasses, sunscreen)
- Jumper / warm clothing for cooler evenings
- Spade
- Toilet rolls
- Rubbish bags (ensure you leave nothing behind!)
- Navigation equipment (maps, compass, Global Positioning System (GPS))

Don't Forget Water When Camping!

For the adventurous with a 4 WD, there are endless possibilities for camping in remote locations amongst some of the best scenery in the UAE. The many locations in the Hajar Mountains (in the north near Ras Al Khaimah or east and south near Hatta or Al Ain), and the huge sand dunes of Liwa in the south provide very different areas, each requiring some serious off-road driving to reach, but offering the real wilderness camping experience. For more information on places to visit, refer to the *Off-Road Explorer (UAE)*.

Canoeing

With very few shark or crocodile attacks in the UAE, canoeing is a great way to get up close to the local marine and bird life, and access hidden places of natural beauty. Areas for good canoeing include the Khor Kalba Nature Reserve, the coastal lagoons of Umm Al Quwain, between the new and old towns of Ras Al Khaimah, north of Ras Al Khaimah before Ramsis, and through the mangrove covered islands off the north coast of Abu Dhabi.

Off-Road Explorer

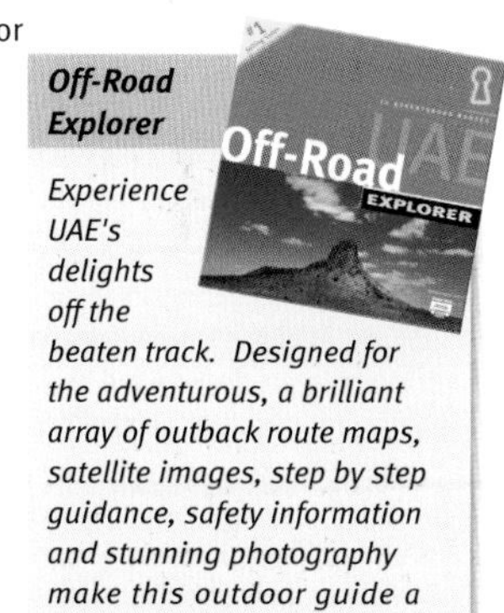

Experience UAE's delights off the beaten track. Designed for the adventurous, a brilliant array of outback route maps, satellite images, step by step guidance, safety information and stunning photography make this outdoor guide a perfect addition to your four wheeler.

Many of these areas are on their way to becoming protected reserves, so treat them with respect. Some adventurous kayakers occasionally visit the Mussandam in sea touring canoes. Here it is possible to visit secluded bays and view the spectacular rocky coastline, with its fjord like inlets and towering 1,000 metre cliffs.

For further information, refer to the Hatta to Kalba route in the *Off-Road Explorer*. See also: Khor Kalba [p.198].

Desert Rangers

Location → Jct 3, Shk Zayed Rd | 340 2408
Hours → Timings on request
Web/email → www.desertrangers.com | Map Ref → 4-B4

Desert Rangers offers trips through the mangroves of the UAE's unique nature reserve at Khor Kalba. Initial instruction is followed by hands-on practice to develop skills and

confidence, then paddle through the mangrove lagoon and experience the unique scenery and abundant wildlife. Enjoy the tranquillity and beauty; all you can hear is the lap of the water and the clicking of crabs' claws. Only a basic level of fitness is needed and it is suitable for all ages. A guide accompanies you and the cost per person is Dhs.300, or you can make your own way to Khor Kalba and rent a canoe on the spot. Please check with their office for availability and timing.

Caving

The caving network in the Hajar Mountains is extensive, and much of it is yet to be explored and mapped. As in any region, caving varies from the fairly safe to the extremely dangerous. Even with an experienced leader, it is not for the casual tourist or the poorly equipped.

Some of the best caves are near Al Ain, the Jebel Hafeet area and in the Hajar Mountains just past Buraimi, near the Omani border. The underground passages and caves have spectacular displays of curtains, stalagmites and stalactites, as well as pretty gypsum flowers and wool sparkling – all unimaginably fragile, so don't touch!

Unfortunately, there are no companies offering guided tours; caving is limited to unofficial groups of dedicated cavers who plumb the depths on a regular basis.

The Hajar Mountain range continues into the Sultanate of Oman, where it is higher and even more impressive. In Oman, the range includes what is believed to be the second largest cave system in the world, as well as the Majlis Al Jinn Cave – the second largest known chamber in the world.

It is important to understand the dangers of going underground and the precautions that must be taken. Take at least two torches each and enough spare batteries and bulbs – someone will always drop a torch, or one may fail. Other equipment should include: minimum two litres of water, a hard hat and long sleeved overalls to protect you from sharp rocks, or knee and elbow pads, a basic first aid kit and twine to mark less obvious parts of the route (remember to take it, and any other rubbish, with you when you leave).

In addition, never wander off alone and don't break any of the rock formations to take away as souvenirs. Check the weather forecasts or the local meteorological office to find out about recent rainfalls. Flash floods occur regularly at certain times of the year.

Warning: No mountain rescue services exist, therefore anyone venturing out into mountains should be reasonably experienced, or be with someone who knows the area. Tell someone who is not going with you where you are going and when you will be back. Tragedies have occurred in the past.

Climbing

For those who feel at home on vertical cliff faces or hanging from rocky precipices, excellent climbing can be found in a number of locations in the UAE. Particular areas to explore include Ras Al Khaimah, Dibba, Hatta and the Al Ain/Buraimi region. By choosing venues carefully, it is possible to climb all year round – even in summer when daytime air temperatures approach 50°C.

The earliest recorded rock climbs were made in the south east near Al Ain/Buraimi in the late 1970s and, apart from some climbing in the Ras Al Khaimah area, little seems to have been recorded until the mid-1990s. Since then, a small group of climbers has been pioneering new routes and discovering a number of major new climbing areas. To date, more than 200 routes have been climbed and named. These vary from short outcrop routes to difficult and sustained mountain routes of alpine proportions. New routes are generally climbed 'on sight', with traditional protection.

Beginners' Climbing in Wadi Bih

Most routes are in the higher grades – ranging from (British) Very Severe, up to extreme grades (E5). Due to the nature of the rock, some climbs can feel more difficult than their technical grade would suggest. However, there are some excellent easier routes for new climbers, especially in Wadi Bih and Wadi Khab Al Shamis. Many routes, even in the easier grades, are serious propositions with loose rock, poor belays and difficult descents, often by abseil, making them unsuitable for total novices.

Several areas are being developed for sport climbing with a growing number of routes being bolted where protection would otherwise be a problem. Some of the hardest routes in the country (up to French Grade 7c) have been pioneered in Wadi Bih and Wadi Khab Al Shamis by serious climbers from Dubai and Abu Dhabi.

If you want to meet up with like-minded people, you're sure to find some rope-clad individuals in Wadi Bih every weekend! For further information on rock climbing in the UAE, refer to the *Off-Road Explorer*, published by Explorer Publishing.

For further information on climbs around Buraimi and in the Hajar Mountains in Oman, refer to the guidebook Rock Climbing in Oman by RA McDonald (Apex Publishing 1993, London/Oman). Despite being several years old, it still gives a comprehensive overview of the most frequented climbing sites within easy reach of Muscat and in the more remote areas, and provides plenty of practical information. Few new routes have been opened or documented in these areas since the book was published.

Pharaohs' Club

Location → Pyramids · Umm Hurair (2) | 324 0000
Hours → 07:00 - 22:00 Fri 09:00 - 21:00
Web/email → www.waficity.com | Map Ref → 13-D2

Dubai's first and only indoor climbing wall at Pharaohs' Club lets climbing enthusiasts polish their skills under a trained instructor or on their own. The wall comprises a varied set of walls for climbing routes and bouldering, with crash mats for safety during low level climbs, and ropes in place on all routes. During the winter, there are climbing trips to Ras Al Khaimah (some training is needed before going into the mountains). Bi-monthly competitions are also held. Charges for the climbing wall are Dhs.40 per hour. Book in advance, as numbers are limited.

Rock Climbing

Location → Various locations | 050 647 7120
Hours → Timings on request
Web/email → arabex@emirates.net.ae | Map Ref → n/a

No formal climbing or mountaineering club currently exists in the Emirates, however unofficial meetings at Dubai's indoor climbing wall at the Pharaohs' Club do take place. While new climbers are welcomed, this group does not run courses for beginners. Since there are no mountain rescue services available, it is expected that anyone venturing into the mountains is basically competent. If you are interested in learning to climb, refer to the review for the Pharaohs' Club on [p.271]. For more information, contact John Gregory on the above details.

Crab Hunting

Lama Desert Tours

Location → Al Khaleej Rd · Deira | 273 2240
Hours → Timings on request
Web/email → www.lamadubai.com | Map Ref → 12-A2

This is a more unusual tour for the Emirates. Leaving at 17:00 by coach, you head to Umm Al Quwain, where it will then take approximately one hour and 45 minutes before reaching the site. Upon arrival, you will be served light snacks before heading out by boat to hunt crabs. This is followed by a BBQ buffet dinner, where your catch of the day is served as per your choice, then at 24:00 you head back to Dubai. Cost: Dhs.220 per person (minimum of six people required) and includes a return transfer, water, soft drinks, light snacks and traditional buffet dinner. For further information, call the above number, 273 1007 or 050 453 3168.

Cricket

What do Dubai expats from the Indian sub-continent, the antipodeans and the United Kingdom have in common? Cricket!

Cricket is a passion shared across the community in Dubai. Carparks, rough land and grassy parks all sprout stumps at weekends and evenings as a mix of ages comes out to play. Many organisations field their own cricket teams for inter-company competitions and it is also popular in schools. Coaching is widely available.

International matches are held regularly in the Emirates, especially at the grounds in Sharjah, where it's possible to see some of the world's best teams and cheer your own side on.

Cycling

Darjeeling Cricket Club

Location → Nr Dubai Country Club · Al Awir Rd | 333 1746
Hours → Timings on request
Web/email → coxoil@emirates.net.ae | Map Ref → 17-B3

Formed in 1969 by a group of expats, the name comes from the Darjeeling Sports Shop in Bahrain which provided the first playing kit. Matches of 25 overs start at 09:00 and 13:30 every Friday, while net practice takes place under floodlights on Tuesday evenings. In early March, there's a six-a-side Gulf tournament and the rest of the year sees matches against visiting test sides when they are competing in Sharjah. Hockey is played at the same ground, and the clubhouse, complete with bar, is open Tuesday to Sunday. The club is available for private functions. Membership costs Dhs.650 per playing member; Dhs.250 per social member. A non member match fee of Dhs.20 is levied.

Croquet

I say old chap, fancy a game of croquet? A classic croquet lawn is available for a game in the grounds of the Jebel Ali Hotel. For more information, call Club Joumana (283 6000).

Cycling

Bicycle! Bicycle! I want to ride my bicycle...I want to ride my bike! Dubai, and the Emirates in general, are not the most bike-friendly of places, but there are plenty of areas to ride and it can be a great way to get out there exploring the city. Riding in traffic requires a lot of care and attention in any country, but in the Middle East you need to be particularly vigilant! Drivers vastly underestimate the speed cyclists are capable of and don't allow enough room, or time for them – be especially careful at junctions and roundabouts.

There are, however, some quieter areas with fewer cars, and some roads have wide footpaths providing traffic free routes for biking around town. Although bikes are not allowed in most of Dubai's parks, you can hire 2 or 4 wheel bikes, which can be a lot of fun at Safa Park and Creekside Park.

The pedestrian areas on both sides of the Creek are pleasant places to ride, especially in the evening. Although helmets are not legally required, you'd be silly not to wear one considering the dangers of Dubai traffic.

Outside the city, the roads are fairly flat and boring until you near the mountains. Jebel Hafeet near Al Ain, the Hatta area of the Hajar Mountains and the central area in the mountains near Masafi down to the coast at either Fujairah or Dibba offer interesting paved roads with better views. The new road from Hatta through the mountains to Kalba on the East Coast, is probably one of the most scenic routes in the country.

Clubs and groups of cyclists generally ride on weekends, early mornings and evenings when the roads are slightly quieter.

Dubai Roadsters

Location → Various locations | 339 4453
Hours → Timings on request
Web/email → wolfisbs@emirates.net.ae | Map Ref → n/a

Dubai Roadsters was born out of a passion for cycling shared by a number of individuals. The only

criteria for joining are a safe bike, cycling helmet, pump and spare tubes. The average distance covered on a Friday ride is 65 - 100 km, depending on the weather and heat, while weekly rides are about 30 km. The average speed is a comfortable 30 km/h. There are no membership fees and Mario Cippolini wannabees are most welcome! For further details contact Wolfgang Hohmann.

Dhow Charters

Travelling up and down the Creek or along the coast by traditional wooden dhow can be a wonderfully atmospheric and memorable experience. For charters, contact one of the following companies. Alternatively, large independent groups can charter a dhow from the fishermen at Dibba to travel up the coast of the Mussandam. Be prepared to haggle hard – knowing a bit of Arabic may smooth things along. Expect to pay around Dhs.2,500 per day for a dhow large enough to take 20 - 25 people, or Dhs.100 per hour for a smaller one. You'll need to take your own food and water, etc, as nothing is supplied except ice lockers that are suitable for storing supplies. Conditions are basic. However, you will have freedom to plan your own route and to see the beautiful fjord-like scenery of the Mussandam from a traditional wooden dhow. If you leave from Dibba (or Dabba), Omani visas are not required, even though you enter Omani waters. It is also possible to arrange stops along the coast and it's probably best to take camping equipment for the night, although you can sleep on board. The waters are beautifully clear, although the weather can seriously reduce visibility for divers, and turtles and dolphins can be seen from the boat. It's ideal for diving, but hire everything before reaching Dibba (refer to the *Underwater Explorer* for dive shop rentals or Diving [p.274]). Alternatively, spend the day swimming, snorkelling and lazing, and for an extra Dhs.500 hire a speedboat.

Al Boom Tourist Village

Location → Nr Al Garhoud Bridge · Umm Hurair (2) | 324 3000
Hours → 20:00 - 22:30
Web/email → www.alboom.co.ae | Map Ref → 14-A3

Al Boom Tourist Village is the biggest operator of dhow boats on the Creek. They currently have seven dhows, ranging in capacity from 20 - 280 passengers. Along with each private charter, they offer a range of enticing international menus. Another highlight of this location is Al Areesh Restaurant. Situated on the bank of the Creek, it offers an Arabic and international buffet in five banqueting halls that can also be used for weddings, exhibitions, etc. Prices range from Dhs.500 per hour for Al Taweel (single deck, 20 passenger capacity), to Dhs.3,000 for Kashti (double deck, 150 passenger capacity). For private parties with catering there is no hire charge for the dhow. 'Open' boats are sometimes available where you can book for Dhs.100 per person.

Al Marsa Charters

Location → East Coast | +968 836 550
Hours → Timings on request
Web/email → www.musandemdiving.com | Map Ref → UAE-E1

Al Marsa has two luxurious, purpose-built dhows that are suitable for divers and overnight visitors. Operating out of Daba Al-Mina (Daba is the Omani side of Dibba) fishing harbour on the East Coast, they can cruise some of the most fascinating coastline of the Musandam. Relax on the spacious sundeck for a one day trip and discover fishing

Dhow Dinner Cruises on Dubai Creek

villages that are only accessible from the sea. Alternatively, on an overnight voyage, explore the sheltered 'dawhat' (fjords) by day and enjoy the tranquillity of a secluded 'khawr' (bay) anchorage by night.

Creek Cruises

Location → Nr DCCI · Creekside, Deira | 393 9860
Hours → 20:30 - 22:30
Web/email → www.creekcruises.com | Map Ref → 11-C2

The magnificent dhows Malika Al Khor and Zomorrodah are the largest of their kind on the Creek. They can be chartered for any occasion and are suitable for groups of 20 to 200 people. Facilities include an air conditioned deck, majlis, sound system and dance floor. A DJ or magician, etc, can also be arranged. Alternatively, join the air conditioned dhow Jamila for a two hour dinner cruise of the Creek (boarding 20:00; disembarkation 22:30). Charter prices are Dhs.1,500 per hour (minimum two hours). Catering can be provided from Dhs.80 per person.

Creekside Leisure

Location → Opp Dubai Municipality HQ · Deira | 336 8406
Hours → Timings on request
Web/email → www.tour-dubai.com | Map Ref → 11-C1

Creekside Leisure was one of the first companies to be established on the Creek. They have two boats for charter for any occasion, from a romantic dinner for two to corporate hospitality for up to 50 guests. The dhows are licensed and have a professional sound system. Catering, live entertainment and business facilities can also be arranged. The company also offers a two hour dinner cruise on Saturdays and Wednesdays, with a bellydancer. Cost per person is Dhs.150 (children aged 5 - 12, half price).

Khasab Travel & Tours

Location → Mezzanine, Warba Centre · Deira | 266 9950
Hours → Timings on request
Web/email → www.khasab-tours.com | Map Ref → n/a

Visit the spectacular Mussandam Peninsula on a dhow, with the chance of seeing dolphins, going swimming and snorkelling or just enjoying the scenery of the area known locally as the 'Norway of Arabia'. Sailing north from Dibba on the East Coast, the cruise follows the stunning coastline where rocky cliffs rise straight out of the sea, and pass small fishing villages accessible only by boat. The company can also arrange flights to the Mussandam, weekend breaks or longer breaks in Khasab (Omani visas required, see [p.200]). Costs range from Dhs.150/adult for a half day, four hour cruise with refreshments; Dhs.250 for a full day, including lunch. At some times of the year children under 12 are free and there are special rates for groups. Cruises depart from Dibba harbour and there is no minimum number per trip. Although the Mussandam is part of Oman, no visas are required for this trip.

Diving

The coastal waters around the UAE are rich in a variety of marine and coral life as well as shipwrecks, which make diving here a fascinating sport. It's possible to dive all year round in the warm seas. As well as exotic fish, such as clownfish and seahorses, you might just see spotted eagle rays, moray eels, small sharks, barracuda, sea snakes, stingrays and much more.

The UAE is fortunate to have two coastlines – to the west, covering Abu Dhabi, Dubai and Sharjah, and on the East Coast, covering Fujairah, Khor Fakkan and Dibba. Most of the wrecks are on the western coast, while the beautiful flora and fauna of coral reefs can be seen on the eastern coast.

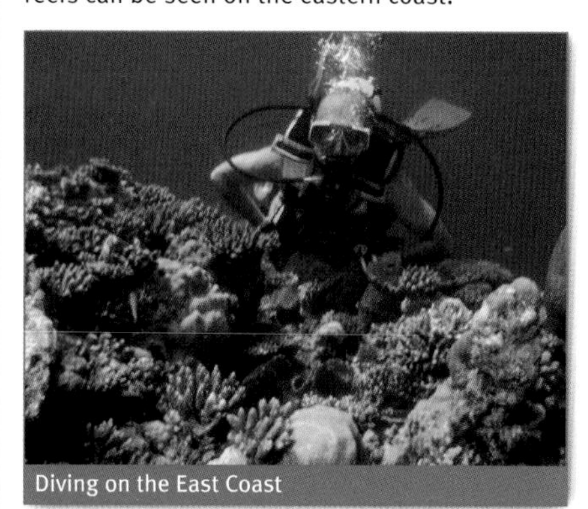
Diving on the East Coast

There are many dive sites that are easily accessible from Dubai and provide some great diving opportunities. Visibility ranges from 5 - 20 metres. Some of the more popular sites include:

MV Sarraf – Three. About seven nautical miles offshore, this 42 metre long barge lies upright in 22 metres of water; a car barge complete with various vehicles and a tugboat rest close by, providing a good opportunity for a limited penetration dive. The wrecks abound with a multitude of fish including barracuda, guitar sharks and spotted eagle rays.

Cement Barge – this 25 metre long vessel sits upright in ten metres of water, about 12 minutes off Dubai's coast. It is a relatively easy dive and ideal for newly qualified divers or those seeking the first time thrill of diving. This is an opportunity to see a mixture of reef creatures such as clownfish and parrotfish, together with stingrays.

MV Dara – this is perhaps the most historic of the West Coast wrecks. Sunk as the result of an Omani rebel mine, the MV Dara constituted the greatest loss of life at sea during peacetime (with 238 lives lost), since the Titanic. The vessel lies on her side in 20 metres of water. This dive is classified as an advanced dive due to tidal influences. Sunk in 1961, it provides an excellent dive if the conditions are favourable as the marine life is well established.

Port Rashid Wrecks – the breakwater at Dubai Dry Dock is the final resting place for a number of wrecks, including the LC Beauty Judy, an 8½ metre landing craft, the MV Nasser and the MV Ant, a tug boat. These vessels lie in 12 - 15 metres of water and provide an opportunity for some interesting exploration.

Sheikh Mohammed Barge – this is a former working barge that was deliberately sunk approximately 12 nautical miles offshore by order of Sheikh Mohammed bin Rashid Al Maktoum to establish an artificial reef. Close to the barge is another boat and a lifting crane. For advanced divers this site provides an excellent wreck dive among an abundance of large marine life.

Off the East Coast, dive sites include **Martini Rock**, which is a small underwater mountain covered with colourful soft coral, with a depth range of 3 - 19 metres. North of Khor Fakkan lies the **Car Cemetery**, a reef that has thrived on a number of vehicles placed in 16 metres of water. Visibility off the East Coast ranges from 5 - 20 metres.

In addition, dive trips are available to the area north of the UAE, known as the Mussandam, which is part of the Sultanate of Oman. Often described as the 'Norway of the Middle East' due to the numerous inlets and the way the sheer cliffs plunge directly into the sea, it offers some of the most spectacular and virgin dive sites in the region. Here, sheer wall dives with strong currents and clear waters make it a thrilling experience for advanced divers, while the huge bays, calm waters and shallow reefs offer easier dives for the less experienced. Visibility ranges from 10 - 35 metres.

Note that if you travel to Khasab, the capital of the Mussandam, you are sometimes not allowed to take your own tanks across the border, but must rent from one of the dive centres there. Omani visas are required. Alternatively, from Dibba on the East Coast of the UAE, fast dive boats take divers up the coast for a distance of between 5 - 75 km. The cost, for what is normally a two dive trip, ranges between Dhs.150 - 500. During the winter, whale sharks are sometimes sighted and dolphins normally ride the bow waves of boats.

Experienced divers, intermediates and people wishing to learn how to dive are all well catered for by a plethora of companies in the UAE. These offer all levels of courses, starting from an introductory dive to instructor level and technical diving, under the different international training organisations, such as CMAS, PADI, NAUI, IANTD, HAS, etc. For further details on diving in the UAE and the Mussandam, refer to the *Underwater Explorer*. For more general information on Abu Dhabi and the Sultanate of Oman refer to the *Abu Dhabi Explorer* and the *Muscat Explorer*. All these books are published by Explorer Publishing.

See also: *The Mussandam – Sultanate of Oman [p.200].*

7 Seas Divers

Location → Nr Khorfakkan Souk · Khorfakkan | 09 238 7400
Hours → 08:00 - 20:00
Web/email → www.7seasdivers.com | Map Ref → UAE-E2

This PADI (Professional Association of Diving Instructors) 5 star IDC dive centre offers daily day and night diving trips to a variety of sites in Khor Fakkan, the Mussandam in Oman and to Lima Rock. Training is given from beginner to instructor level and lessons can be given in Arabic, English, or Russian. Facilities include three boats and the centre also arranges equipment sale, rental and servicing. The company can also arrange accommodation, transport and visas for visitors to the UAE.

Al Boom Diving

Location → Nr. Iranian Hospital · Al Wasl Rd | 342 2993
Hours → 10:00 - 20:00
Web/email → www.alboommarine.com | Map Ref → 6-C3

Pleasure dives and courses are run daily out of their Dive Center at DIMC (399 2278). Their Aqua Centre on Al Wasl Rd (342 2993) is a purpose built school with a diving retail shop offering a complete range of dive equipment, and wide selection of accessories and clothing. Their PADI Gold Palm Resort based at the Le Meridien Al Aqah Beach Resort (09 204 4912) runs daily pleasure dives, has a full retail shop and offers the complete range of PADI courses. For any enquiries contact Simon on 050 457 7427.

Prices: *Open Water Course Dhs.1,700; Advanced Open Water Course Dhs.1,000. A two two tank dive with full equipment will cost Dhs.280.*

Emirates Diving Association

Location → Heritage & Diving Village · Al Shindagha | 393 9390
Hours → 08:30 - 13:00 17:00 - 21:00
Web/email → www.emiratesdiving.com | Map Ref → 8-B1

The main aim of this group is to conserve, protect and restore the UAE's marine resources by understanding and promoting the importance of the marine environment and environmental diving. They do this by promoting research on the marine environment and by holding the annual 'clean-up dive' and 'beach clean-up' campaigns. The association also looks after the well-being of UAE corals, with their unique Coral Monitoring Project. In the future, they hope to establish a marine park using the artificial reefs technique, which attempts to create coral reefs.

Pavilion Dive Centre

Location → Jumeirah Beach Htl · Umm Suqeim | 406 8827
Hours → 09:00 - 18:00
Web/email → www.jumeirahinternational.com | Map Ref → 4-B2

This PADI Gold Palm IDC Centre is run by qualified PADI instructors, offering an extensive range of courses from Discover Scuba Diving for beginners through to instructor development courses. Daily dive trips for certified divers leave the hotel marina at 10:00, weather permitting. This is generally a two dive trip, and returns to the marina between 13:00 - 15:00. Trips to the Musandam are also organised. MARES equipment is available from the retail centre, together with Bodyglove wetsuits and a range of accessories. Costs: Discover Scuba Diving Dhs.320; Open Water Dhs.1,750; Adventures in Diving Dhs.1,000; two dive full equipment Dhs.250; two dive tank only Dhs.190. NITROX available on request.

Sandy Beach Diving Centre

Location → Sandy Beach Motel · East Coast | 09 244 5555
Hours → 08:00 - 18:00
Web/email → sandybm@emirates.net.ae | Map Ref → n/a

This dive centre is now managed by the Sandy Beach Hotel and offers a qualified and dynamic team of dive instructors and support staff. It's open year round for diving, accommodation and a retail outlet that stocks the latest diving gear (Scubapro, Ikelite, Uwatec, etc). Their famous 'house reef', Snoopy Island, is alive with hard corals and marine life and is excellent for both snorkelling and scuba diving. The more adventurous can take a trip on one of their dive boats that depart daily to sites around Fujeirah and Khor Fakkan. Trips to the Mussandam offer fascinating dives for the more experienced.

Boat timings: *09:30, 12:00, 14:30. Location: Al Aqqah, Fujeirah – halfway between Dibba and Khor Fakkan.*

Scuba 2000

Location → Al Badiyah Beach · Fujairah | 09 238 8477
Hours → 09:00 - 19:00
Web/email → www.scubauae.com | Map Ref → UAE-E2

This East Coast dive centre is open all year and provides daily trips to dive sites on both the Dibba and Khor Fakkan sides. All sites are easily accessible by boat from the centre; in particular Snoopy and Sharque islands provide excellent diving and snorkelling. The standard courses are available for everyone from beginners to advanced divers. The centre has one fully qualified PADI instructor, and an experienced diver is on hand if a buddy is needed. Costs range from Dhs.250 for Discover Scuba; Dhs.1,500 for Open Water; Dhs.800 for Advanced. Three air conditioned twin bedrooms with refrigerator and satellite TV are also available for divers and 'snorkellers' for Dhs.150 per night. Directions: After Le Meridien and Sandy Beach, 15 minutes drive to Scuba 2000.

Scuba International

Location → Fujairah Int Marine Club · Fujairah | 09 222 0060
Hours → 10:00 - 19:00
Web/email → www.scubaInternational.net | Map Ref → UAE-E2

The first diving college in Arabia, Scuba International offers facilities for both divers and

non divers from recreational dive charters and diver training (PADI, DSAT and TDI), to RYA sanctioned boat handling courses; chamber operating courses; instructor courses; water sports and dive vacation bookings. As well as over 20 reef sites in the area, two wrecks provide the ideal opportunity for first time and experienced divers. The 'discover scuba' dive costs Dhs.250. The college is purpose-built to cater to divers' needs, and offers nearby accommodation in Fujairah's hotels, plus an on-site restaurant, bar and pool. A recompression chamber with on-call chamber staff to treat any diving emergency 24 hours a day will be available from January 2004.

Scubatec

Location → Sana Bld · Trade Centre Rd, Al Karama | 334 8988
Hours → 09:00 - 13:30 16:00 - 20:30
Web/email → www.scubatec.net | Map Ref → 10-C1

Scubatec is a 5 star IDC centre licensed by the Professional Association of Diving Instructors (PADI) and Technical Diving Instructors (TDI), who make the transition from above to below the water a safe and enjoyable one. Instruction can be in Arabic, English, German or Urdu. The company offers a full range of courses from beginner to instructor and will schedule a course to fit your schedule. Dubai and East Coast dive trips are available. Including hire of full gear, the cost is Dhs.200 for two wreck dives at a site 10 km offshore from Dubai.

Sharjah Wanderers Dive Club

Location → Shj Wanderers · Sharjah | 050 636 6802
Hours → See timings below
Web/email → www.sharjahwanderers.com | Map Ref → UAE-C2

Sharjah Wanderers Dive Club is a main member section of the Sharjah Wanderers Sports Club (SWSC). Hence, in addition to an energetic and friendly diving club, members get the benefit of the sports and social activities of SWSC. The diving club is a full member of the British Sub Aqua Club (BSAC branch number 406), and follows its training, certification and diving practices. The clubhouse facilities include a training room, social area, equipment room, compressors, dive gear for hire, two dive boats and on-site pool facilities. Club night is every Tuesday from 20:30 until late, with diving every Thursday and Friday, weather permitting.

Dune Buggy Riding

If bouncing over dunes with the sand in your hair is your bag, dune buggy riding is exhilarating and totally addictive, though not particularly environmentally sound. In particular, every Friday, the area around the 'Big Red' sand dune on the Dubai – Hatta Road is transformed into a circus arena for off-road lovers. Future Motor Sports, along with about four other companies, rent out off-road quad bikes and karts, which are available to drive (without a licence) in fenced off areas. Alternatively, if you're in the area on a Friday, hang around to be entertained by the sight of locals driving their Nissan Patrols on two wheels!

Buggy addicts can also contact the tour operators [p.189], since many of them offer the chance to try dune buggies as part of their desert safaris. Remember, these things are heavy if you roll them, but don't fret... Dubai has some of the best hospitals in the region!

Dune Buggies on Big Red

Al Badayer Motorcycles Rental

Location → Hatta Rd | 050 636 1787
Hours → Timings on request
Web/email → n/a | Map Ref → UAE-D3

Also called quad bikes, dune buggies are great fun and extremely exhilarating. Al Badayer Motorcycles Rental has buggies that range in power from 50 or 80cc to 250cc (watch out for the 250 if it's your first

time!) Prices vary from Dhs.80 - 200 per hour. Group discounts are available. For further details, contact Mohamed on 050 736 55 33.

Desert Rangers

Location → Jct 3, Shk Zayed Rd | 340 2408
Hours → Timings on request
Web/email → www.desertrangers.com | Map Ref → 4-B4

This is your chance to experience an exhilarating ride first hand with Desert Rangers' fleet of single or two seater buggies, especially designed for the desert. After a brief safety talk, having been given a helmet and strapped in, you will be led on a dedicated roller coaster route through the dunes. Only with Desert Rangers will you be able to experience the thrill of genuine buggies – not to be mistaken for quad bikes! Safaris can be combined with a BBQ dinner. Cost: Dhs.350 per person.

Fencing

Dubai Fencing Club

Location → Jumeirah Beach Club · Jumeira | 050 794 4190
Hours → See timings below
Web/email → www.dubaifencingclub.com | Map Ref → 5-D1

Applying coaching techniques of the Bulgarian National Sports Academy, the Dubai Fencing Club was established in October 2002 and is located in the Jumeirah Beach Club. They provide individual and group training sessions mainly in Epee and Foil, for juniors and adults. All beginners receive the necessary basic equipment such as masks, gloves and weapons. For the advanced fencers, the club offers two fencing paths with an electrical scoring system, electrical weapons – Epee and Foil – as well as a fencing costumes and masks. A service facility for maintaining equipment is also available. Cost: members Dhs.30; non members Dhs.45.

Training Schedule: *Advanced Sat 17:30 - 19:00; Beginners Mon 18:30 - 20:00; Advanced & Beginners mixed Thurs 19:30 - 21:00; Juniors (7-14 years) Fri 09:00 - 10:00; Advanced Fri 18:30 - 20:00.*

Fishing

The fishing season runs from September/October through to April, although it is still possible to catch sailfish and queenfish in the hot summer months. Fish commonly caught in the waters off Dubai includes king mackerel, barracuda, tuna, trevally, bonito, kingfish, cobia, and dorado or jacks. Beach or surf fishing is popular all along the coast of the UAE — even barracuda can be caught from the shore in season. As well as the numerous beaches lining Dubai's coast, the Jumeira Beach Corniche is a good place — try the end of the promenade. The Creek front in Creekside Park is also a popular spot, though you might not want to put these fish on the barbie!

Alternatively, on Friday, hire an abra for the morning (either at the Bur Dubai or Deira landing steps) and ask to be taken out to the mouth of the Creek to fish; be sure to agree on a price before you leave.

The more adventurous, with lots of cash to spare, may consider deep sea fishing with one of the charter companies listed below.

Bounty Charters

Location → Various locations | 348 3042
Hours → Timings on request
Web/email → n/a | Map Ref → n/a

Bounty Charters is a fully equipped 36 ft Yamaha Sea Spirit game fishing boat captained by Richard Forrester, an experienced game fisherman from South Africa. Fishing charters can be tailor made to your needs, whether you want a full day trying for challenging sailfish, or a half day trawling or bottom fishing for the wide variety of fish found in the Gulf. There is also night fishing or charters of 3 - 5 days to the Mussandam Peninsula (book in advance, since planning takes 7 - 10 days). For prices and more details contact Richard on the above number or on 050 658 8951.

Club Joumana

Location → Jebel Ali Htl · Jebel Ali | 804 8058
Hours → Timings on request
Web/email → www.jebelali-international.com | Map Ref → 1-A1

Departing from one of Dubai's most beautiful marinas, deep sea fishing trips are arranged into

the Arabian Gulf twice daily. Four hour and eight hour fishing trips are available for up to seven people per boat. The captain, all tackle and equipment, soft drinks and snacks are included while the opportunity exists to catch sailfish, barracuda, lemonfish, trevally, hammour (groupers) and kingfish. Prices: Dhs.2,200 to Dhs.2,600 for a day trip and Dhs.1,200 to Dhs.1,400 for a four hour trip.

Dubai Creek Golf & Yacht Club

Location → Opp Deira City Centre Mall · Al Garhoud | 295 6000
Hours → 06:30 - 19:00
Web/email → www.dubaigolf.com | Map Ref → 14-C2

Take a trip on the club's own yacht 'Sneakaway' into the Arabian Gulf waters and experience the adrenaline rush of big game sports fishing for yourself! The fully equipped 32' Hatteras comfortably carries up to six passengers and rates include tackle, bait, ice, soft drinks, fuel and a friendly crew who know how to give you a fishing trip (and tips) to remember! Rates: four hours Dhs.1,875; five hours Dhs.2,125; six hours Dhs.2,375; eight hours Dhs.2,850 (each additional hour is Dhs.250). For further information and reservations, contact the marina directly on 205 4646, fax 295 6081 or email mshop@dubaigolf.com.

Fun Sports

Location → Various locations, see below | 399 5976
Hours → 09:00 - 17:00
Web/email → www.funsport-dubai.com | Map Ref → n/a

Fun Sports offers fishing, sailing, windsurfing, water skiing, wakeboarding, jet skiing, knee boarding, banana rides, kayaking, power boat rides, parasailing and sunset cruising. Their facilities are available at some of Dubai's main beach hotels, however, you don't have to be a beach club member to use Fun Sports' equipment. Tuition is available for all levels of ability, with courses in sailing, windsurfing, water skiing and kite surfing. They have a team of professional instructors, and safety is always a priority. For bookings contact Suzette on the above number or 050 453 4828. Locations: Dubai Marine Beach Resort & Spa, Hilton Dubai Jumeirah, Metropolitan Resort & Beach Club, Oasis Beach Hotel, Ritz-Carlton Beach Club, Royal Mirage, Le Meridien Mina Seyahi and Jumeira Beach Park.

Le Meridien Mina Seyahi Beach Resort & Marina

Location → Le Meridien Mina · Al Sufouh | 399 3333
Hours → Timings on request
Web/email → www.lemeridien-minaseyahi.com | Map Ref → 3-A2

Enjoy a full or half day fishing trip in one of the best fishing grounds of the Arabian Gulf. Sailfish are the main prize, and Le Meridien Mina Seyahi supports the tag and release scheme. Trips are made on the custom built Ocean Explorer and Ocean Luhr. While you are welcome to take your own gear, the boats are fully equipped with 20, 30 and 50 lb class tackle, as well as fly fishing equipment. Charters can be tailored to suit your requirements.

Oceanic Hotel

Location → Beach Rd, Khorfakkan · East Coast | 09 238 5111
Hours → Timings on request
Web/email → www.oceanichotel.com | Map Ref → UAE-E2

Round off a trip to the East Coast with a sunset fishing trip. Set off in a speedboat to the local fishermens' favourite fishing spot (apparently a catch is virtually guaranteed!). Then watch the sunset as you return to the hotel. The catch can be cooked by the hotel chef, who will prepare it according to your taste. All equipment is supplied. Cost: Dhs.100 per person, minimum six people per boat, for about four hours.

Yacht Solutions

Location → Jumeirah Beach Htl · Umm Suqeim | 348 6838
Hours → Timings on request
Web/email → www.yacht-solutions.com | Map Ref → 4-B2

Yacht Solutions offers the opportunity to experience the thrill of fishing on board one of their sports fishing vessels. With modern tackle and some luck you may even catch one of the prized Gulf sailfish (a tag and release scheme is in operation), while other catch includes kingfish, tuna, and barracuda. Experienced skippers guide you to the best fishing grounds, and for the less experienced, there is plenty of advice to make your fishing experience a memorable one. Shorter charters are available. For further information, please contact Chris on the above number.

Flying

Other options → Helicopter Flights [p.285]

Dubai Flying Association

Location → Dubai International Airport · Al Garhoud | 351 9691
Hours → Timings on request
Web/email → www.dfadxb.com Map Ref → 14-D3

In 1987 a group of private pilots formed Dubai Flying Association (DFA) by selling Dhs.10,000 debentures to 18 individuals. They raised enough money to buy their first aircraft and within a year had bought a second. Today, DFA is a registered flying association of qualified pilots and is well known in aviation circles throughout the region. The club is non profit making, aiming to provide flying to members at cost. In addition to the DFA's activities out of Dubai International Airport, the association has recently also taken up operations at Umm Al Quwain Airfield. 2002 saw the inauguration of the 'UAE Pilot of the Year Competition' which is now an established and treasured feature in GA circles. Call Evelyn Brey for details.

Membership: *Dhs.500 per annum. All holders of UAE private pilot's licences are welcome, and the association can assist in licence conversion from any ICAO recognised licence.*

Emirates Flying School

Location → Terminal 2, Dubai Int Airport · Al Twar | 299 5155
Hours → 08:30 - 17:30
Web/email → www.emiratesaviationservices.com Map Ref → 15-B2

Emirates Flying School, the only approved flight training institution in Dubai, operates six US built Piper aircraft and has been training pilots of all nationalities since 1989. The school offers the basic private pilot's licence and the commercial pilot's licence for those who want to make flying a career, while the instrument rating course allows pilots to fly in restricted visibility. The school offers conversion of international licences to a UAE licence. Gift vouchers costing Dhs.500 are available for those interested in experiencing flying for the first time.

Fujairah Aviation Centre

Location → Fujairah Int'l Airport · Fujairah | 09 222 4747
Hours → Timings on request
Web/email → www.fujairah-aviation.ae Map Ref → UAE-E2

This company grew from a hobby into a business: the Fujairah National Group's chairman is a keen aviator and set up the centre. With its high calibre instructors, the centre quickly received accreditation as a flying school from the Civil Aviation Authorities in the UAE and UK. Facilities include twin and single engine training aircraft, an instrument flight simulator and workshop for repairs. Training is offered for private pilot's licence, commercial pilot's licence, instrument rating and multi-engine rating. All ages are welcome, but students must be aged 17+ to fly solo and 18 when a licence is issued. Trial lessons and gift vouchers are available. Students must be conversant in written and oral English. Trial flying lessons cost Dhs.250 per half hour; Dhs.500 per hour. Ground training costs Dhs.50 per hour; flight training Dhs.500 per hour. Flight training for the new Cessna 172S is Dhs.500 per hour; the Cessna 172P is also Dhs.500 per hour; and twin engine is Dhs.1,200 per hour.

Umm Al Quwain Aeroclub

Location → 17km north of UAQ on RAK Rd · UAQ | 06 768 1447
Hours → See timings below
Web/email → www.uaqaeroclub.com Map Ref → UAE-C1

This was the first sports aviation club in the Middle East, providing opportunities for aviation enthusiasts to fly and train throughout the year at excellent rates. Activities include flying, skydiving, skydive boogies, paramotors and helicopter training. The modern facilities include a variety of small aircraft, two runways, eight spacious hangars with engineering services, pilot's shop and a briefing room. Sightseeing tours are also offered. Timings: 08:30 - 17:30 winter; 09:00 - 19:00 summer.

Prices: *Sightseeing tours by Cessna aircraft (Dhs.300 per 30 minutes for three people plus pilot; 10 minute tours for Dhs.50 per person). For longer flights, a plane with a professional pilot can be hired for Dhs.600 per hour.*

Location: *16 km along the road from UAQ roundabout heading in the direction of Ras Al Khaimah, before Dreamland Aqua Park and opposite UAQ Shooting Club, on the left hand side of the road... just look for the big aeroplane by the sea.*

Football

Like most places on the planet, you don't have to travel far to have a game of football in the Emirates. On evenings and at weekends, parks, beaches and any open areas seem to attract a game, generally with a mix of nationalities taking part. Even villages in the countryside usually have a group knocking a ball around on the local sand and rock pitch — see if you can join in, or join a more formal club. Both outdoor and indoor pitches exist in

Dubai, while coaching, mainly for kids, is offered at a number of sports centres and health clubs.

Dubai Celts GAA

Location → Dubai Exiles Rugby Club · Al Awir Rd | na
Hours → 20:00 - 22:00
Web/email → www.dubaicelts.com | Map Ref → 17-B3

Dubai Celts GAA Club (Gaelic Athletic Association) holds games and organises training in the sports of men's and ladies' Gaelic football, hurling and camogie. In addition to monthly matches within the UAE, international tournaments are held in Bahrain (November) and Dubai (March) each year. The season runs from September to June and everyone is welcome to join in, regardless of whether they've played the sports before. Social members are also welcome and there is at least one social gathering every month. Training sessions are held every Saturday and Tuesday at 18:30 at the Dubai Exiles Rugby Club. Contact them through their Website.

Emirates Golf Club

Location → Emirates Hill | 380 2222
Hours → 06:00 - 23:00
Web/email → www.dubaigolf.com | Map Ref → 3-A3

Emirates Golf Club is home to the Reebok Soccer Academy, which was established in September 2000. With 140 juniors enrolled, the academy is aiming for bigger and better things this year with the opening of two polyurethane pitches. These will complement the existing grass pitches that are arguably the best five-a-side pitches in Dubai. The academy operates regular squad coaching, as well as camps during school holidays and half terms.

Football at Safa Park

Golf

Golf in the desert? Strange, but true... the UAE is known as the premier golf destination in the Gulf, with excellent year round facilities and many important tournaments being held here. Dubai has a range of international courses that are fully grassed, as well as brown (sand) courses, and courses that are a mixture of both. In an area of the world where rain is so scarce, the green golf courses appear as oases of colour in the middle of the desert!

The Montgomerie Dubai is the most recent addition to the Dubai golf scene. Designed by champion golfer, Colin Montgomerie and course architect, Desmond Muirhead, it comprises 72 bunkers, 14 lakes and the largest single green in the world.

The Dubai Creek Golf & Yacht Club and Emirates Golf Club are the home of the Dubai Desert Classic, which is part of the European PGA (Professional Golf Association) Tour. There are also monthly local tournaments and annual competitions that are open to all, such as the Emirates Mixed Amateur Open, the Emirates Ladies' Amateur Open (handicap of 21 or less) and the Emirates Men's Amateur Open (handicap of 5 or less).

Dubai Golf operates a central reservation system for individuals or groups who wish to book a round of golf in Dubai. They currently represent Emirates Golf Club, Dubai Creek Golf & Yacht Club and Dubai Golf & Racing Club. For further information check out their website at www.dubaigolf.com, or contact booking@dubaigolf.com, or 347 5201 (fax 347 5377).

Emirates Golf Club

Location → Emirates Hill | 380 2222
Hours → 06:00 - 23:00
Web/email → www.dubaigolf.com | Map Ref → 3-A3

The unique clubhouse and buildings are immediately recognisable by their Bedouin tent design, which disguises modern, air conditioned interiors. This club was the first grass course in the Middle East and is a former and future host of the European PGA Dubai Desert Classic. Standards throughout are high, with two 18 hole championship courses to choose from; the Majlis and the Wadi. The club also offers the perfect learning environment at the Emirates Academy of

Golf, two driving ranges (one floodlit) and dedicated practice areas. Other facilities include restaurants and a large swimming pool and patio (often the site of concerts and shows). Fees: Majlis course Dhs.475; Wadi course Dhs.330 - 365. Cart hire Dhs.50; club hire Dhs.80. Facilities are open to members and non members alike, although all players must produce a valid handicap certificate (28 men / 45 women).

Montgomerie Golf Club

Location → In Emirates Hills Estate · Emirates Hill | 380 1333
Hours → 05:30 - 20:00
Web/email → www.themontgomerie.com | Map Ref → 2-E4

The first thing you notice about The Montgomerie is the scale of the course; set in 200 acres and designed by Colin Montgomerie in association with Desmond Muirhead, the 18 hole par 72 course has some unique characteristics, including the world's largest green in the shape of the UAE! Practice facilities include a driving range, short game areas, putting practice greens, a 9 hole par 3 Academy course, plus an extensive golf teaching academy complete with swing studio and state-of-the-art swing analysis software.

Nad Al Sheba Club

Location → Nad Al Sheba | 336 3666
Hours → 07:00 - 01:00
Web/email → www.nadalshebaclub.com | Map Ref → 17-A3

This Scottish links style golf course with its undulating fairways and pot bunkers is the only floodlit 18 hole golf course in the UAE, with golf being possible until midnight year round. The newly reopened back nine are situated inside the track of the famous Nad Al Sheba racecourse, home of the Dubai World Cup, the world's richest race meeting. The Club has a fully stocked pro shop and a 50 bay floodlit driving range. Individual, group and junior coaching is available from a team of five British PGA professionals. One of the most popular coaching programmes is 'Learn Golf in a Week.' A variety of memberships is available on an annual or monthly basis.

Resort Golf Course, The

Location → Jebel Ali Htl · Jebel Ali | 804 8058
Hours → 06:30 - nightfall
Web/email → www.jebelali-international.com | Map Ref → 1-A1

Situated in beautifully landscaped grounds, this 9 hole par 36 course offers golfers the opportunity to play in the company of peacocks and with panoramic views of the Arabian Gulf. The course has a selection of four tee boxes on each hole, giving the opportunity to play either a 9 hole or an 18 hole round. The course is also home to the Challenge Match, curtain raiser to the annual Dubai Desert Classic. Past participants include Tiger Woods and Ernie Els. Timings: 07:00 till nightfall. Location: approximately 30 minutes from Dubai. Costs: Visitors are welcome on a 'pay as you play' basis and although no handicap certificates are necessary, they must have a sound knowledge of golfing etiquette, rules and course experience. Appropriate golfing attire is required and the course is spikeless.

UAE Golf Association

Location → Creek Golf Club · Al Garhoud | 295 6440
Hours → 09:00 - 17:00
Web/email → www.ugagolf.com | Map Ref → 14-C2

This non profit organisation is the governing body for amateur golf in the UAE. It is overseen by the General Authority of Youth & Education and is

Golf at the Jebel Ali Hotel

affiliated to the Royal and Ancient Golf Club of St Andrews in the United Kingdom. Its aims are to make golf more affordable and accessible in the UAE, with a programme to support junior players and the development of the national team. Affiliate membership starts at Dhs.200 per year. UGA membership runs from 1 January to 31 December. Members can attain a handicap according to CONGU (Council of National Union of Golf) or LGU (Ladies Golf Union) rules (Dhs.400).

Hang Gliding

For those of you without wings who have the desire to fly like a bird, hang gliding is one of the most exciting and affordable solutions. Please see Flying [p.280] for more.

Hashing

Sometimes described as drinking clubs with a running problem, the Hash House Harriers are a worldwide family of social running clubs, the aim being not to win (which is actually frowned upon), but to be there and take part. It was started in Kuala Lumpur in 1938 and is now the largest running organisation in the world, with members of approximately 1,600 chapters in over 180 countries.

Hashing consists of following a course laid out by a couple of 'hares'. Running, jogging or walking is acceptable, and courses are varied and often cross country. Hashing is a fun way to keep fit and to meet new people, since clubs are invariably very sociable and the running is not competitive.

While it was in Malaysia that the sport first took off, its roots can be traced to the British cross country sport of 'hare and hounds'. In the 1930s, British servicemen in Malaysia were stationed in the Royal Selonger Club, which was known as the 'hash house' due to the quality of its food. After a particularly festive weekend, a hare and hound paper chase was suggested, and so the hash began. After World War II the hash continued, but it wasn't until 1962 that a second chapter was permanently formed in Singapore, and from there the sport has spread worldwide.

Barbie Hash House

Location → Various locations | 348 4210
Hours → See Website
Web/email → www.deserthash.net | Map Ref → n/a

Meeting on the first Tuesday of every month, this is a girls' only gathering with a Barbie theme – the dress code is pink with a tiara. It helps to be blond and champagne is the drink of the evening. About 20 to 25 members meet all year round for a fun social evening that also involves a bit of hashing/walking, a meal and singing their Barbie song. It's open to women of all ages for a monthly fee of Dhs.10. Contact can be made through the Website address or call the above number.

Creek Hash House Harriers

Location → Various locations | 050 451 5847
Hours → Timings on request
Web/email → www.creekhash.net | Map Ref → n/a

This is a men only hash that meets at different locations each Tuesday throughout the year. Start times are normally 45 minutes before sunset, with runs lasting 40 - 50 minutes. The concept of hashing is not to race but to follow pre marked trails and false trails, with the keen runners covering more ground than the social members, who jog and walk their way round at the rear of the pack. Further information can be obtained from Ian Browning on the above number or Richard Holmes (050 644 4285). Information for the weekly run can be obtained on the Website : www.creekhash.net.

Desert Hash House Harriers

Location → Various locations | 050 454 2635
Hours → Sunday evenings
Web/email → www.deserthash.net | Map Ref → n/a

The Desert Hash House Harriers (DH3) is a social running group for men and women. It meets every Sunday evening throughout the year at various locations in Dubai. Runs start an hour before sunset and last about 50 minutes. For more information, contact the GM Stuart Wakeham (050 454 2635) or Alan Permain (050 457 1603). For details of where they meet see the Gulf News Classifieds on Sunday under the Dubai personals column, or visit their Website. Cost per run: Dhs.50 per person, inclusive of food and beverages.

Moonshine Hash House Harriers

Location → Various locations | 050 774 1580
Hours → Timings on request
Web/email → www.deserthash.net | Map Ref → n/a

Moonshine Hash House Harriers run once a month on the night of the full moon. A mixed hash that meets throughout Dubai in local taverns, the Moonshine Hash was set up as more of a 'runner's run' and the runs last approximately one hour. The

run/walk creates a thirst, which is then quenched upon return to the aforementioned alehouse for the traditional hash ceremonies. The Moonshine is a small friendly hash with the emphasis on being sociable, not competitive runners. Cost: Dhs.10 per hash. Contact: Maria Cottam on the above number.

Helicopter Flights

Other options → Flying [p.280]

Aerogulf Services Company

Location → Dubai Int'l Airport · Al Garhoud | 220 0331
Hours → 07:00 - 19:00
Web/email → aerogulf@emirates.net.ae | Map Ref → 15-A2

What better way to view the sights of Dubai than from the air? This is an ideal opportunity for residents and visitors alike to experience the UAE from a unique perspective – see traditional dhows, the impressive parks, the Creek, beaches and much more. Aerogulf offers short sightseeing tours by helicopter, as well as transport to selected hotels. Flights can be anytime between 10:30 and before sunset, around 17:00.

Flight location: *Oilfields Supply Centre, near Al Maktoum Bridge, opposite Deira City Centre Mall.*

Hiking

The UAE is much more than just the flat sandpit one might expect; spectacular locations ideal for hiking can be found just an hour's drive from Dubai. This can be a perfect way to get away from it all to vastly different surroundings.

One of the nearest, and easiest, places to reach from the city is the foothills of the Hajar Mountains on the Hatta road, about 100 km from Dubai and near the border with Oman. After passing through the desert and the flat savannah-like plains, you will notice stark, rugged outcrops transforming the landscape on either side of the road. Explore turnings you like the look of, or take the road to the right signposted 'Mahdah 64 km', along which are numerous paths, wadis and scaleable hills.

Further into the Hajar Mountains (Hajar is Arabic for rock), the multi-coloured mountains and large wadis provide peace and tranquillity, as well as the famous Hatta Pools. Here there are plenty of excellent walks, with a surprising amount of greenery and refreshing, cool pools. Explore further to find the less popular pools in this area; those which are easiest accessed are now polluted with environmentally unfriendly picnickers' trash.

Off-Road Explorer

Experience UAE's delights off the beaten track. Designed for the adventurous, a brilliant array of outback route maps, satellite images, step by step guidance, safety information and stunning photography make this outdoor guide a perfect addition to your four wheeler.

Other great areas for hiking and exploring in the Hajar Mountains include anywhere near Al Ain, many places in Wadi Bih (the mountainous route from Ras Al Khaimah to Dibba), or the mountains near the East Coast. The mountains here do not disappoint, and the further off the beaten track you get, the more likely you are to find interesting villages where residents still live much as they have for centuries.

As with any trip into the UAE 'outback', take sensible precautions. Tell someone where you're

Hiking in the Wadis

going and when you should be back, take a map and compass or GPS, and stout walking boots (for the loose rock). Don't underestimate the strength of the sun, take food for energy, sunscreen, and most importantly, loads of water. For most people, the cooler and less humid winter months are the best season for hiking. One of the most important warnings – be especially careful in wadis (dry riverbeds) during the wet season, as dangerous flash floods can flood a wadi in seconds.

Refer also to the *Off-Road Explorer* published by Explorer Publishing. Apart from striking satellite images of routes to explore, there are details of interesting hikes with tracks superimposed on photographs. This is a handy manual and includes information on health and safety, flora and fauna, GPS co-ordinates, etc.

***Contacts:** Useful contacts willing to advise like-minded people are: Alistair MacKenzie (Alistair@Explorer-Publishing.com) - Dubai, John Gregory (050 647 7120) - Ras Al Khaimah.*

Desert Rangers

Location → Dubai Garden Centre · Jct 3, Shk Zayed Rd | 340 2408
Hours → Timings on request
Web/email → www.desertrangers.com Map Ref → 4-B4

Guided by experienced Rangers, walk among the majestic mountains of the UAE, ascend rocky summits and enjoy the freedom of rough mountain country with its dramatic sun-baked features. Desert Rangers can easily handle up to 100 people at once by dividing them into smaller groups and taking different tracks to the summit. A variety of routes can be taken to suit the group's age and level of fitness. Locations include Fujairah, Dibba, Masafi, Ras Al Khaimah and Al Ain. Cost: Dhs.275 per person.

Hiking Frontiers

Location → Various locations | na
Hours → See timings below
Web/email → n/a Map Ref → n/a

A sister club to Biking Frontiers with pretty much the same outdoor loving members, this group is involved in hiking around the UAE and Oman. This is a diverse bunch of active hikers and bikers, both male and female. The typical hiking season is from November through to March. Either meet on Friday morning, or head out camping on Thursday evening and hike Friday. Main requirements are that you are enthusiastic, have proper walking boots, carry enough water and are reasonably fit. You are responsible for your own safety and ensuring that you don't exceed your own capabilities. If you are interested in meeting a fun bunch of like-minded people, or in knowing a bit more, email Alistair on Alistair@Explorer-Publishing.com.

Hockey

Other options → Ice Hockey [p.288]

Darjeeling Hockey Club

Location → Darjeeling Cricket Club · Al Awir Rd | 333 1746
Hours → 20:00 - 22:00
Web/email → darjeelinghockey@hotmail.com Map Ref → 17-B3

The hockey club shares facilities with the Darjeeling Cricket Club, which was formed over 30 years ago by a group of British expats. The club also enters many local tournaments and arranges home tournaments including the annual Darjeeling weekend festival, the Dubai schools tournament and other hockey events. The English style clubhouse bar is open throughout the week, except Mondays. Games and practices are usually held on Sundays and Wednesdays. The floodlight field is also available for hire. Annual membership as a playing member of the hockey or cricket section or both is Dhs.650 per member; Dhs.250 per social member. For more information contact Freddie, the clubhouse steward.

Sharjah Wanderers Hockey Club

Location → Shj Wanderers · Sharjah | 06 566 2105
Hours → Timings on request
Web/email → www.sharjahwanderers.com Map Ref → UAE-C2

This club began as a small part of the Sharjah Contracts Club in 1976 and from its inception has been very successful. The hockey section became the first mixed side in the Gulf and has always retained a strong mixed club atmosphere. With an age range of 16 - 45, it's also a family club. The main principle here is to play sport within a friendly atmosphere, without losing the competitive challenge. Changing facilities are available at the clubhouse and all are welcome. For further information on timings, contact Cormac on 06 566 0864 or the Sharjah Wanderers Club.

Horse Riding

Other options → Annual Events [p.50]

Club Joumana

Location → Jebel Ali Htl · Jebel Ali | 804 8058
Hours → Timings on request
Web/email → www.jebelali-international.com | Map Ref → 1-A1

Approximately 30 minutes drive from central Dubai and set in the beautiful grounds of the Jebel Ali Golf Resort & Spa, the riding centre has five horses, an outdoor arena and keeps livery on request. Keith Brown, the riding instructor, is available for lessons Tuesday to Sunday from 1st October to 1st June each year. Horse riding is not available during the summer months (June to September). Individual half hour lessons and one hour desert rides are also available at competitive rates.

Emirates Riding Centre

Location → Nr Camel Race Track · Nad Al Sheba | 336 1394
Hours → See timings below
Web/email → emrc@emirates.net.ae | Map Ref → 17-A3

The Emirates Riding Centre (ERC) originally known as the Dubai Equestrian Centre, was formed in 1983. The centre has 147 horses, and facilities include an international sized floodlit arena, riding school arenas, dressage arenas and lunging ring. ERC holds at least two competitions and three riding school shows per month, as well as gymkhanas from October to early May. Training is also offered in showjumping and dressage. Trail rides and hacks are also available. The centre holds regular clinics/stable management courses. Riding school timings are from 07:00 - 10:00 & 17:00 - 20:00.

Jebel Ali Equestrian Club

Location → Jebel Ali Village · Jebel Ali | 884 5485
Hours → Timings on request
Web/email → n/a | Map Ref → 1-E3

'Just like stables back home' describes the comfortable atmosphere of the Jebel Ali Equestrian Club. Fully qualified BHS instructors are on hand to teach both children and adults from beginners through to advanced levels. For the more experienced, dressage, jumping and hacking are options. Gymkhana games, dressage & jumping competitions are held on a regular basis. Children can also join 'stable management' courses. The club is an approved branch of the British Pony Club. A full livery service is available. There is a registration fee of Dhs.120 per rider or Dhs.300 per family. Packages for ten lessons start from Dhs.450 for a child and Dhs.700 per adult. Location: Adjacent to the Al Muntazah Complex at Jebel Ali Village.

Sharjah Equestrian & Racing Club

Location → Jct 6 · Al Dhaid Rd | 06 531 1155
Hours → Timings on request
Web/email → www.forsanuae.org.ae | Map Ref → UAE-C2

Located about 20 minutes drive from the centre of Sharjah, the riding centre was built in 1984 under the supervision of HH Sheikh Sultan Bin Mohammed Al Qassimi, member of Supreme Council and Ruler of Sharjah. Facilities include a big floodlit sand arena and paddock, a grass showjumping arena and hacking trails into the desert. The centre keeps 250 horses and regular riders number about 200, with occasional riders for dressage, showjumping and hacks. Riding here is by prior appointment and approval. Note: Summer timings may differ; call first.

Horse Racing at Nad Al Sheba

Hot Air Ballooning

Other options → Flying [p.280]

Voyagers Xtreme

Location → Dune Centre · Al Satwa | 345 4504
Hours → Timings on request
Web/email → www.turnertraveldubai.com | Map Ref → 6-E3

The adventure that takes you higher than the rest! This is a great way to celebrate anything from a birthday or anniversary to a product launch. Daily flights for up to 12 people operate every morning from Fossil Rock with a fully certified pilot. Enjoy breakfast as the balloon is prepared, although you're more than welcome to give the setup team a hand. Once the balloon is ready, it's up, up and away! You'll enjoy a one hour flight over the desert and mountains that will take your breath away (don't forget your camera).

Hot Air Ballooning At Fossil Rock

Ice Hockey

Dubai Mighty Camels Ice Hockey Club

Location → Al Nasr Leisureland · Oud Metha | 337 1234
Hours → Sat & Tue 09:00 - 11:00
Web/email → www.dubaimightycamels.com | Map Ref → 10-E4

Ice hockey has been a fixture on the local sports scene ever since Al Nasr Leisureland opened in 1979. The club's purpose is to provide adult recreational ice hockey with no upper age limit. Currently membership stands at over 80 players, of more than a dozen nationalities. If you have your own equipment, give them a call. There are social get-togethers and barbecues from September to May. The club hosts an annual tournament in April, which in 2004 will be attended by 12 - 15 teams from the Gulf, Europe and the Far East. For more information, contact Ron Murphy (050 450 0180) or visit the Website for the latest news and scores.

Dubai Sandstorms Ice Hockey Club

Location → Al Nasr Leisureland · Oud Metha | 344 1885
Hours → Sat 16:30 - 21:00
Web/email → rproctor@emirates.net.ae | Map Ref → 10-E4

This club was established to provide boys and girls (6 - 18 years) with the opportunity to learn ice hockey. The emphasis is on participation, teamwork and sportsmanship. No previous experience is necessary since participants are placed in teams based on their age. The season runs from mid September to mid May, with practices held twice a week. Throughout the season, matches are played against Dubai, Abu Dhabi, Al Ain and Oman teams. There is a registration fee which covers all practices and games during the season. Ice hockey jersey and socks are extra.

Ice Skating

Other options → Ice Hockey [p.288]

Al Nasr Leisureland

Location → Beh American Hospital · Oud Metha | 337 1234
Hours → 09:00 - 24:00
Web/email → www.alnasrleisureland.ae | Map Ref → 10-E4

If it's large enough to hold an ice hockey tournament, then it's large enough for an energetic youngster's birthday party, or to just skate around to your heart's content. Open to the public, except when rented by clubs, the rink is part of the Leisureland complex, which also houses a bowling alley, fast food outlets, arcade amusements and small shops. Occasionally the rink is used in the evening as a concert venue. The rink is open for two hour sessions starting at 10:00, 13:00, 16:00 and 19:30. Skating costs Dhs.10 for two hours, including boot hire.

Galleria Ice Rink

Location → Hyatt Regency · Deira | 209 6550
Hours → See timings below
Web/email → apadgett@hyattintl.com | Map Ref → 8-D2

Located in the centre of the shopping mall (which makes the environment a bit chilly!) and next to the Galleria cinema, this is a popular and usually busy ice rink. Fees for public sessions are Dhs.25 per person, including skate hire, or Dhs.15, using your own skates. The use of socks is mandatory in rental boots, so take your own, or buy them for Dhs.5. Membership rates start at Dhs.300 per month or Dhs.1,200 per year and members are entitled to unlimited skating. Lessons are available for non members, and cost from Dhs.80 per half hour. Timings: Sat - Thu 10:00 - 13:30, 14:00 - 17:30 & 18:00 - 21:00. On Fridays and public holidays the rink closes at 20:00.

Ice Skating at Al Nasr Leisureland

Jet Skiing

Every afternoon sees trailer loads of jet skis parked at the first lagoon between Dubai and Sharjah near Al Mamzar Beach Park, or near Al Garhoud Bridge, on the opposite side of the bridge to Dubai Creek Golf & Yacht Club. Most jet skis are available for hire at approximately Dhs.100 for half an hour. A new area to hire jet skis is between the Ritz-Carlton and Le Royal Meridien Beach Resort & Spa, where locals turn up everyday with trailers carrying 4 - 10 jet skis. Likewise, the beach near the Jumeirah Beach Hotel is a good place to try, and many of the beach clubs offer them for rent.

Jet Skis on Jumiera Beach

Note that a 1998 law limits jet skiers to within a 500 metre boundary from the shore, with the threat of legal action for exceeding this limit. With all the aquatic traffic, you may find the waters of Dubai Creek a little murky; other locations offer a cleaner environment, as well as stricter controls and better safety records. Recently a Russian man died when his jet ski accidentally collided with that of a British woman on Dubai Creek. The charges against the woman were eventually dropped and she was allowed home, but only after spending time in prison.

In addition, it may be worth checking that your medical insurance covers you for this potentially dangerous sport – apparently broken legs are not all that uncommon!

Judo

Not just about throwing others on their back and armlocking them, Judo is a recreational sport and discipline, as well as a means of self defence. Founded by Dr. Jigoro Kano in 1882, it is a refinement of the ancient Japanese martial art of Jujitsu. See Marial Arts [p.291].

Karate

Please see Martial Arts [p.291].

Karting

Other options → Moto-Cross [p.292]

Emirates Kart Centre

Location → Nr Jebel Ali Htl · Jebel Ali | 282 7111
Hours → 14:00 - 19:00
Web/email → www.emsf.ae | Map Ref → 1-A1

Dubai Kart Club runs the 12 round UAE championship at their purpose built international standard FIA licensed circuit, just 20 minutes from Dubai. Founded over 25 years ago, the circuit has four different configurations with the longest being just under one kilometre. The UAE championship runs from January to April and September to December. Four classes of kart are raced: International 16 years and above, National 12 years and above, Rotax Max Seniors, Cadets 8 - 12 years. Entrance is free. Facilities include a grandstand and catering by the Jebel Ali Hotel. Membership is under discussion.

Formula One Dubai

Location → WonderLand · Umm Hurair (2) | 338 8828
Hours → 10:00 - 22:00
Web/email → f1dubai@emirates.net.ae | Map Ref → 14-A3

Formula One Dubai offers a range of racing opportunities for individuals, groups or corporate entities . They no longer have any indoor circuits but they have an outdoor circuit. They also cater for corporate entertainment, children's parties, individual practice sessions and specialised outdoor functions. No experience is necessary to take part in this exhilarating and entertaining activity. For information on costs, please contact the office on the above number.

Kayaking

Other options → Canoeing [p.269]

Beach Hut, The

Location → Sandy Beach Motel · East Coast | 09 244 5555
Hours → Timings on request
Web/email → www.sandybm.com | Map Ref → n/a

The Beach Hut offers a variety of water sports equipment. For those who just want to paddle out to Snoopy Island and explore, there are kayaks for hire at Dhs.30 an hour. You can also try your hand at windsurfing. Diving and snorkelling equipment is available for rent or sale.

Kitesurfing

Kitesurfing is a fast growing new sport that's gaining loads of publicity, partly because it's so extreme. It's not windsurfing, it's not wakeboarding, it's not surfing and it's not kite flying, but instead is a fusion of all these disciplines with other influences to create the wildest new water sport for years.

Fitness Help!

Can't seem to take out time for the gym? Why not hire a personal trainer. There are plenty of fitness gurus advertising privately. They will pop over and set you on the road to body sculpting success with your very own tailor made fitness programme. For information and contacts, check out the classifieds of the daily newspapers, or refer to any of Dubai's monthly magazines.

Dubai Kite Club, The

Location → Various locations | 884 5912
Hours → Timings on request
Web/email → www.fatimasport.com | Map Ref → n/a

The Dubai Kite Club regulates the sports of kitesurfing, mountain board kiting, power kiting, display kiting and kite buggys. A popular meeting place for Dubai kitesurfers is the beach between the University of Wollongong and Umm Suqeim Clinic, off Jumeira Beach Road. Equipment sale and training courses are available and the club recommends equipment by Naish, Flexifoil and Peter Lynn for use in Arabian Gulf conditions, though other brands are also available in the UAE. For further details, contact Fatima Sports (050 455 5216).

Fun Sports

Location → Various locations | 399 5976
Hours → 09:00 - 17:00
Web/email → www.funsport-dubai.com | Map Ref → n/a

A little bit of knowledge of wake boarding and/or windsurfing is helpful to get a handle on this sport. It deals with tackling the forces of nature – specifically the wind. It's even suitable for children above the age of eight, as safety is ensured and stressed upon. For those who are taking this sport up for the first time, there's a one hour session on the sand before you actually face the real thing. Sessions are booked according to your convenience.

Martial Arts

Al Majaz

Location → Trade Centre Rd · Al Karama | 335 3563
Hours → 09:00 - 14:00 16:00 - 21:00
Web/email → www.goldenfistkarate.com | Map Ref → 10-D1

For more information on Al Majaz, please refer to their entry under Yoga [p.314].

Ballet Centre, The

Location → Ballet Centre, The · Jumeira | 344 9776
Hours → Sat - Thu 09:00 - 13:30 15:30 - 18:30
Web/email → www.balletcentre.com | Map Ref → 6-C3

The Ballet Centre has Abdurahiman (7th Dan black belt) teaching taekwondo. This form of martial art teaches children mental calmness, courage, strength and humility, courtesy, integrity, perseverance, self control and indomitable spirit!

Dubai Aikido Club

Location → Dubai Karate Centre · Al Satwa | 344 4156
Hours → See timings below
Web/email → www.aikido-uae.net | Map Ref → 6-A4

Aikido is an effective martial art for self defence, not only because it teaches how to defend against an attack, but also because it trains the mind. Enthusiasts believe that it makes you a stronger and more complete human being, being better able to diffuse or defend oneself against negative situations. Dubai Aikido Club was established in 1995 and is affiliated to the Aikido Association International, USA with the Aikikai Aikido world headquarters in Japan. For further information contact John Rutnam, Chief Instructor. Location: Dubai Karate Centre, Al Wasl Road, Jumeira. Classes are held on Sun and Tue 17:30 - 18:30 for children and families and 19:30 - 21:30 for the general public.

Dubai Karate Centre

Location → Al Wasl Rd, Nr Emirates Bank · Al Satwa | 344 7797
Hours → See timings below
Web/email → n/a | Map Ref → 6-A4

At Dubai Karate Centre, a team of black belt, JKA qualified instructors teach a style of karate called shotokan, the oldest and most popular form of karate, as well as aikido and judo. The club is a member of the Japanese Karate Association (JKA), and has been established in Dubai since 1985. It offers tuition from beginner to black belt for anyone aged six years and above. Courses are held on Saturday, Monday and Wednesday evenings between 17:00 - 19:00, depending on experience, and the fees include three sessions a week. Costs: Dhs.100 initial registration fee, then Dhs.200 monthly membership fee. Uniforms cost Dhs.100 from the club. For further information please call the number above.

Golden Falcon Karate Centre

Location → Beh Sony Jumbo · Al Karama | 336 0243
Hours → 08:30 - 12:00 16:30 - 22:30
Web/email → www.goldenfalconkarate.com | Map Ref → 10-C3

Established in 1990, this karate centre is affiliated to the Karate Budokan International and the UAE Judo, Taekwondo and Karate Federation. The Karate Centre is open throughout the week, morning and evening. Students can choose class timings according to their convenience. Official certificates are issued from International Headquarters to successful upgrade test candidates. Call instructors Suresh and Sathian for further details.

House of Chi & House of Healing

Location → Musalla Towers · Bank St, Bur Dubai | 397 4446
Hours → 10:00 - 22:00 Fri 16:00 - 22:00
Web/email → www.hofchi.com | Map Ref → 8-A4

Shotokan karate; Kung Fu and Aikido are some of the martial arts on offer. Shotokan karate is an unarmed combat system that employs kicking, striking & defense blocking with arms and legs. Kung Fu means 'progress achieved through discipline' and originates from the Shaolin temple in China while Aikido is a traditional Japanese martial art based on the blend of ancient sword, staff and body techniques. For information on House of Chi & House of Healing, refer to the review under Pilates [p.314].

Microlights

Other options → Flying [p.280]

They might look unwieldy, and are not a particularly practical means of getting to and from work, but microlight aircraft can carry two people for 400 miles on just a single tank of fuel!

Mini Golf

Other options → Golf [p.281]

Aviation Club, The

Location → Nr Tennis Stadium · Al Garhoud | 282 4122
Hours → 06:00 - 23:00
Web/email → www.aviationclubonline.com | Map Ref → 14-C3

This 9 hole, par 3 pitch and putt course is set in picture postcard surroundings between the tennis stadium and the clubhouse. With manicured fairways and greens, each hole is a reasonable challenge for beginners as well as more accomplished golfers. The course offers great variation with the holes differing in distance from 40 to 82 yards. Open to members only; for further details contact the sports reception.

Hatta Fort Hotel

Location → Hatta Fort Hotel · Hatta | 852 3211
Hours → Timings on request
Web/email → www.jebelali-international.com | Map Ref → UAE-D3

With a background of lovely views of the Hajar Mountains, the Hatta Fort offers a choice of mini golf or a 9 hole cross country fun golf course. The mini course is American style crazy golf and lies mostly in the shade of the trees below the hotel. The charge for two people is Dhs.25. The 9 hole course can be played for Dhs.35 per person, per round (including clubs and balls). Each hole is par 3, ranging from 68 to 173 yards. Golf instruction and lessons are available. Day visitors on Fridays and public holidays must purchase a voucher at the entry gate (Dhs.40 for adults, Dhs.20 for children), which is redeemable against hotel facilities.

Hyatt Golf Park

Location → Hyatt Regency · Deira | 209 6741
Hours → 15:30 - 23:00
Web/email → www.dubai.hyatt.com | Map Ref → 8-D2

Adjacent to the Hyatt's side car park is a 9 hole pitch and putt grass golf course for the avid golfer to improve his or her short game. There is also an 18 hole crazy golf course. Clubs are provided and golf balls can be purchased for Dhs.8 each. The park is floodlit in the evenings and the clubhouse in the centre of the park overlooks a small lagoon. Go for golf or simply enjoy a drink at the 19th hole. Prices: 9 hole pitch and putt – one round Dhs.15, two rounds Dhs.25; 18 hole crazy golf – Dhs.10 per person (ball and club included).

Moto-Cross

Other options → Karting [p.290]

Dubai Youth Moto-Cross Club

Location → Various locations | 050 452 7844
Hours → Timings on request
Web/email → www.dubaimotocross.ae | Map Ref → n/a

The DYMXC bids a final farewell to the Al Awir Track, which closes on February 28th, 2004 after 20+ years of highly addictive fun. The Club is actively negotiating for a new home; for updates on the current situation, contact Jonathan (050 452 7844) or Ivan (050 644 3990) or visit the Website.

Motorcycling

Al Ramool Motorcycle Rental

Location → Big Red Dune Area · Hatta Rd | 050 453 4401
Hours → Timings on request
Web/email → n/a | Map Ref → UAE-D3

Al Ramool offers LT50, LT80, 125cc, 350cc and 620cc motorcycles for rent, as well as dune buggies and two and four seater safari cars. Crash helmets are provided for safety and, as an additional service, transport from Dubai is available on request. The company offers a variety of tailormade packages; camel rides, falcon hunting and baby camel feeding can also be organised.

Contact: Mohamed (050 453 3033) or Mr Balam on the above number)

Cost: *Dhs.20 - 100 for 30 minutes*

UAE Motorcycle Club

Location → Al Muragabat Street · Deira | 266 9002
Hours → 09:00 - 17:00 Fri 09:00 - 13:00
Web/email → www.uaedesertchallenge.com | Map Ref → 11-E2

Now in its sixth season, the UAE Motorcycle Club is officially sanctioned by the International Motorcycle Federation, the world governing body of the sport. The club runs a five round off-road endurance championship series, leading to an overall UAE champion. Interest has grown considerably, with an average of 70 competitors per race and an overall membership of 175. The

E BEST REASON YET TO
IDE RED
61
It's the many years of experience, advanced 4-stroke technology and unparalleled reliability that have made Honda off-road bikes the finest on earth! Choose from one of the widest range of off-road bikes and ATVs, including the class leading CRF450R3 and TRX400EX.
Experience a piece of the action - visit your local Trading Enterprises - Honda showroom and 'Ride Red'.

HONDA
PERFORMANCE FIRST

Chairman is Middle East Rally Champion, Mohammed bin Sulayem. The club is used as a launching ground for competitors to race in the UAE Desert Challenge. Membership: Any riders over the age of 18 who have their own motorcycle and UAE driving licence, are welcome. Races are on Friday mornings, starting in January 2004, and then every four weeks, until early May.

Mountain Biking

Contrary to a first glance of the Emirates, the interior has a lot to offer outdoor enthusiasts, especially mountain bikers. The 'outback' is rarely visited, but on a mountain bike it is possible to see the most remote places that are inaccessible even in 4 wheel drive.

For hardcore mountain bikers there is a good range of terrain, from super technical rocky trails, in areas like Fili and Siji, to mountain routes like Wadi Bih, which climb to over 1,000 metres and can be descended in minutes. The riding is mainly rocky, technical and challenging. There are many tracks to follow and, if you look hard, some interesting singletrack can be found.

However, be prepared and be sensible – the sun is strong, you will need far more water than you think and it's easy to get lost. Plus, falling off on this rocky terrain can be extremely painful!

For further information on mountain biking in the UAE, including details of possible routes, refer to the *Off-Road Explorer*, published by Explorer Publishing.

Extreme Mountain Biking

Biking Frontiers

Location → Various locations | na
Hours → See timings below
Web/email → www.bikingfrontiers.com | Map Ref → n/a

So, you're a mountain biking fan? If you don't mind thrashing yourself over seriously rocky trails, up and down big mountains, through wadis and like getting lost once in a while... then give Biking Frontiers a call! All competent mountain bikers are welcome. Your own bike, helmets and proper gear are essential. The group also enjoys camping, hiking and barbecues – there's always something going on. Rides are every Friday, and sometimes Saturdays, as well as city rides in the evenings during the week. Contact: Paul on the above number or Pete (050 450 9401).

Desert Rangers

Location → Jct 3, Shk Zayed Rd | 340 2408
Hours → Timings on request
Web/email → www.desertrangers.com | Map Ref → 4-B4

Whether you're a fanatical biker craving challenging terrain, or a complete beginner preferring a gentler introduction to the delights of off-road biking, Desert Rangers will determine a suitable route depending on your requirements and group size. The company is one of only a few outward bound leisure companies to specialise in more unusual activities in the UAE. The cost of Dhs.300 per person includes a bike, helmet, guide, pick up and drop off, and soft drinks.

Mountaineering

Although the area immediately surrounding Dubai is mostly flat with sandy desert and sabkha (salt flats), there are areas inland that are a paradise for the more adventurous mountain walker. To the north, the Ru'us Al Jibal Mountains contain the highest peaks in the area, at over 2,000 metres. To the east, the impressive Hajar Mountains form the border between the UAE and Oman; stretching from the Mussandam Peninsula north of Ras Al Khaimah, to the Empty Quarter desert, several hundred kilometres to the south.

The terrain is heavily eroded and shattered due to the harsh climate, and trips range from short easy walks leading to spectacular viewpoints, to all day treks over difficult terrain, with some major mountaineering routes on faces of alpine

proportions. Many of the routes follow centuries old Bedouin and Shihuh trails through the mountains, and a few are still used today as a means of access to the more remote settlements. Some of the terrain is incredible and one can only wonder at the skills of the hardy mountain people who have pioneered these trails.

Battered photocopies of a guide written in the mid-1980s exist, and this may form the basis of a dedicated climbing and mountaineering book at some point.

Prohibitive heat and humidity mean that serious mountain walking is best between the months of November and April.

For further information on possible routes for mountaineering in the UAE, refer to the *Off-Road Explorer*, published by Explorer Publishing.

Warning: No mountain rescue services exist, therefore anyone venturing out into the mountains should be reasonably experienced, or be with someone who knows the area. Tragedies have occurred in the past.

Contacts: Useful contacts willing to advise like-minded people are: Alistair MacKenzie (Alistair@Explorer-Publishing.com) - Dubai, John Gregory (050 647 7120) - Ras Al Khaimah.

Netball

Dubai Netball League

Location → Country Club · Al Awir Rd | 050 352 5871
Hours → Wed 18:30 - 22:30
Web/email → na | Map Ref → 17-B3

Established in the mid-1970s, there are over 15 teams divided into three divisions. Players range from teenagers to grandmothers, and beginners to experts. Games are played from September to May on Wednesday nights on the two courts at the Dubai Exiles Rugby ground. During the season, players are selected for the InterGulf Netball Championships; a competition that brings together teams from Abu Dhabi, Bahrain, Dubai, Kuwait, Oman and Saudi Arabia. For further information, contact Mercedes Sheen on the above mobile number or by email at mercedessheen@hotmail.com

Paintballing

Other options → Shooting [p.299]

Pursuit Games

Location → WonderLand · Umm Hurair (2) | 324 1222
Hours → Any time
Web/email → wonderld@emirates.net.ae | Map Ref → 14-A3

This is a fun fighting game for teenagers and adults where the bullets are balls of paint! Get a crowd together and they will soon be divided into two teams by the experts, who give a thorough safety demonstration before equipping you with overalls, facemasks and special guns equipped with paintballs. This is a strategy game played by shooting balls of paint at your opponent, thus marking and eliminating them. Stalk your enemies and get them before they get you! For further information contact Kaz (050 651 4583). Cost: Dhs.70 for a typical two hour game with 100 paintballs, gun and gas. An extra 100 paintballs cost Dhs.50.

Paintballing

If you want to maintain a great work environment, why not take your office mates on a team building exercise? Paintballing [p.295] is sure to improve, boost or destroy relations in the office. Find out if you're brave enough to smoke out the 'silent but deadly' types.

Note of caution: It is advisable for the boss to wear extra padding.

Paragliding

For details, refer to Sky Diving [p.300] and Flying [p.280].

Parasailing

Experience the thrill of parasailing in the Gulf. It's worth a try, if only to experience the wonderful views of the coast from a different perspective. Pop down to any of the major resort hotels, and you will find parasailing among many other water activities being offered. Flights last for about eight minutes, and there's no need to run down the beach for take off or landing – it all happens off the back of the boat. Availability is subject to weather conditions.

Plane Tours

Other options → Flying [p.280]

Fujairah Aviation Centre

Location → Fujairah Int Airport · Fujairah | 09 222 4747
Hours → Timings on request
Web/email → www.fujairah-aviation.ae | Map Ref → UAE-E2

A bird's eye view of the mixture of coastline, rugged mountains, villages and date plantations is available from the Fujairah Aviation Centre. Flights can last from 30 minutes (at Dhs.100 per person) to four hours, which will enable you to see almost the entire UAE. A longer tour for 1 - 3 people costs Dhs.480 per hour. The following are some suggested itineraries, although the pilots can prepare other routes especially for you.

Scenic Flight 1: Fujairah – Dibba – Masafi – Fujairah; **Scenic Flight 2:** Fujairah – Hatta – Al Dhaid – Masafi – Fujairah; **Scenic Flight 3:** Fujairah – Al Ain – Abu Dhabi – Dubai – Sharjah – Ajman – Umm Al Quwain – Ras Al Khaimah – Dibba – Fujairah.

Polo

Other options → Horse Riding [p.287]

Ghantoot Polo & Racing Club

Location → Dubai - Abu Dhabi Road · Jazira | 02 562 9050
Hours → Timings on request
Web/email → n/a | Map Ref → UAE-A4

With six polo fields, and two stick and ball fields built to international standards, three of which are floodlit, three tennis courts, swimming pool, gym, sauna and restaurant, this club has first class facilities for the entire family to enjoy. Non members are welcome to dine at the restaurant or to watch the regular polo matches. The polo season starts in October and continues until the end of April. The calendar is full of regular chukka tournaments and high profile international games. Ghantoot is located half way between Dubai and Abu Dhabi, near Jazira Hotel, about thirty minutes from Dubai by car.

Quad Bikes

For further information, refer to Dune Buggy Riding [p.277].

Rally Driving

Other options → Annual Events [p.50]

Emirates Motor Sports Federation

Location → Nr Aviation Club · Al Garhoud | 282 7111
Hours → Timings on request
Web/email → www.emsf.ae | Map Ref → 14-D4

For rally enthusiasts in the UAE, the Federation organises a variety of events throughout the year, from the 4 WD 1000 Dunes Rally to the Champions Rally for saloon cars. Other Federation events include road safety awareness campaigns and classic car exhibitions. The driving skill competitions are open to all (separate category for ladies), the only prerequisite being a valid UAE driving licence. This is the official motor sport authority in the UAE and is a non profit government organisation.

__Membership Fees:__ Federation membership for rally enthusiasts is Dhs.750 and a professional competition licence is required to participate.

Dune Buggy Riding

Rappeling

For more on ropes, rocks and hanging from high places, see Climbing [p.270].

Rollerblading

Strap on the rollerblades and get wired for sound! Although the experts make it look easy, rollerblading is a good challenge and great exercise, as well as being lots of fun. Dubai's many parks provide some excellent locations: try the Creekside Park and Safa Park for smooth, wide pathways, fewer people and enough slopes and turns to make it interesting. Alternatively, check out the seafront near the Hyatt Regency Hotel or the promenade at the Jumeira Beach Corniche, where the view is an added bonus.

Rugby

Other options → Annual Events [p.50]

Dubai Exiles Rugby Club

Location → Nr Dubai Country Club · Al Awir Rd | 333 1198
Hours → 08:00 - 22:00
Web/email → www.dubaiexiles.com | Map Ref → 17-B3

Definitely Dubai's serious rugby club, the Exiles is the Emirates' oldest and best established bastion of the sport. Training sessions are scheduled throughout the week with the 1st and 2nd XVs meeting on Sundays and Wednesdays, and veterans on Tuesdays and Saturdays. There's also training for children (mini's) on Sundays and Mondays. The Exiles also host the annual Dubai International Rugby Sevens tournament, which attracts international teams from all the major rugby playing nations. Clubhouse facilities are available for hire.

Dubai Hurricanes

Location → Country Club · Al Awir Rd | 333 1198
Hours → See timings below
Web/email → hurricanepaul@hotmail.com | Map Ref → 17-B3

Dubai Hurricanes are the latest exciting arrival on the Gulf rugby scene. Originally formed in 1999 as a purely social outfit, the club has competed in the annual Dubai Sevens tournament and its success on both the rugby and social fronts, enabled their entry into the Arabian Gulf League for the 2001/02 season. They also have a ladies team. All new players (whatever their ability) are welcome... go on, dust off those boots! Training sessions are held on Sun and Tue evenings from 19:30 at the Dubai Country Club. Contacts: Club Captain Paul Manders (050 457 0321); Sarah Barrett (050 658 8370); Cecile (050 694 7938).

Running

Running is one of the few ways to avoid extra expat kilos in Dubai. For over half the year, the weather couldn't be better for running, whilst in the summer, despite the high temperatures and humidity, you'll find dedicated runners out pounding the miles all over the UAE. In the hottest months, the evenings, and the early mornings especially, are the best times to be out.

Clubs and informal groups meet regularly to run together, with some runs being competitive or training for the variety of events organised throughout the year. Regular, short distance races are held, as well as a variety of biathlons, triathlons, duathlons and hashes, which provide a reasonably full and varied schedule.

Two of the favourite competitions are the 'Round the Creek' relay race and the epic 'Wadi Bih Run'. For the latter, teams of five run the 70 km from Ras Al Khaimah on the west coast to Dibba on the east, over mountains topping out at over 1,000 metres. Runners take turns to run different stages with a support vehicle, and this event, held annually, attracts up to 300 participants. Note: at time of print, the border post on the Ras al Khaimah side of Wadi Bih was closed. If it remains closed, this popular event may, sadly, be history.

A relatively new event is the Dubai Marathon, which will be held early 2004.

Contacts: Wadi Bih race: John Gregory (050 647 7120) or arabex@emirates.net.ae. Round the Creek Hash Relay: Ian Colton (050 658 4153) or sukka@emirates.net.ae.

Dubai Creek Striders

Location → Exhib. hall car park · Trade Centre 1&2 | 321 1999
Hours → Fri 06:00
Web/email → malcolmm@murrob.co.ae | Map Ref → 9-E2

This medium to long distance running club was established in 1995 and organises weekly runs on Friday mornings. Distances and routes differ each week, but normally consist of shorter 10 km runs during the summer, up to winter marathon training runs of about 32 km, ready for the annual 42.2 km Dubai Marathon in early January. Scenic running is guaranteed, with most runs visiting the Creek at some stage. It's wise to confirm the start time and place, as special runs are held during the year. There are no joining fees, but take Dhs.5 - 10 for drinks. Contact Malcolm Murphy for further details.

Dubai Road Runners

Location → Safa Park · Al Wasl Rd | 394 1996
Hours → Sat 18:30
Web/email → www.dubai-road-runners.com | Map Ref → 5-C3

Come rain or shine, 100% humidity and 50°C temperatures, Dubai Road Runners meet every Saturday at 18:30 at Safa Park in the car park by gate number 4. The objective of the meeting is to run either a 3½ km or 7 km track around the park. A Dhs.5 entrance fee is charged, and most people try to run this standard course against the clock. The club also organises competitions and social events throughout the year. All standards, all ages and all nationalities are welcome. Contact Graham Rafferty on 050 624 3213 for more information, or visit the Website.

Sailing

Ship ahoy! Temperatures here in winter are perfect for sailing and water sports, which also serve as an escape from the scorching heat in summer that prohibits some land based sports. Sailing is a popular pastime in Dubai and many people are members of the sailing clubs on Jumeira Beach and Mina Seyahi. Membership allows you to participate in club activities and rent sailing and water sports equipment. You can also use the leisure facilities and the club's beach, and moor or store your boat (which is always an extra cost!). There's quite a healthy racing scene for a variety of boat types, and there's also the occasional long distance race, such as the annual Dubai to Muscat race, held in March. The traditional dhow races are also a sight to see. Many companies will take you out on a cruise for pleasure or for fishing. The time can range from a couple of hours to a full day. You can also charter your own boat for periods ranging from one morning to several weeks!

See also: *Dhow Racing – Annual Events [p.50].*

Dubai Offshore Sailing Club

Location → · Beach Rd, Jumeira | 394 1669
Hours → See timings below
Web/email → www.dosc.org | Map Ref → 4-E2

This is a friendly club that welcomes sailors of all abilities. It's recognised by the Royal Yachting Association (RYA) and runs dinghy, keelboat and windsurfing courses throughout the year. The Thursday and Friday Cadet Club is great for younger sailors. The club provides mooring, storage, launch facilities, sail training and a full yachting and social calendar. The clubhouse has full catering facilities. This is a non profit making organisation, and its success depends on the active support of its members. For further information contact Senior Sailing Instructor Carolyn Honeybun, Club Administrator Alison Maynard, or Club Manager Alfred Hunteron on the above number. Timings: 09:00 - 24:00 members only; 09:30 - 17:30 public sailing.

Fun Sports

Location → Various locations, see below | 399 5976
Hours → 09:00 - 17:00
Web/email → www.funsport-dubai.com | Map Ref → n/a

Fun Sports offers multi-hull sailing courses to anyone who has been bitten by the sailing bug, with professional sailing instructors available to teach beginners and improvers. Membership with one of the beach clubs is not necessary to sail with Fun Sports. For bookings contact Suzette on the above number, fax (399 5796) or (050 453 4828). The company operates at the following beach clubs: Dubai Marine Beach Resort & Spa, Hilton Dubai Jumeirah, Metropolitan Resort & Beach Club, Oasis Beach Hotel, Ritz-Carlton Beach Club Royal Mirage, Le Meridien Mina Seyahi and Jumeira Beach Park.

Hobies on Jumeira Beach

Jebel Ali Sailing Club

Location → Nr Le Meridian Mina Seyahi · Al Sufouh | 399 5444
Hours → See timings below
Web/email → www.jebelalisailingclub.com | Map Ref → 2-E2

This club is fully recognised by the RYA to teach and certify sailing, windsurfing and powerboat licences and instruct in kayaking. Races are held most Fridays for toppers, lasers, catamarans and cruisers. Topper coaching takes place every Wednesday afternoon at 15:30, while cadet club takes place from 10:00 - 13:00 on Thursday mornings and laser 4.7 training and novice racing on Thursday afternoons at 14:30. There's a pool to chill in with an outside barasti bar for refreshment. The main clubhouse and restaurant are open 09:00 - 20:00 Sat to Wed, and 09:00 - 22:00 Thurs and Fri. Contact: Sharon Allison or Colin Slowey on h2osport@emirates.net.ae for more information.

Oops?

Did we miss anything out? If you have any thoughts, ideas or comments for us to include in the Activities section, do drop us a line. (Any weird fetishes can be limited to you.) If there is an activity that you and at least one other person may be interested in, please inform us and we'll share it with our readers.

Sand Boarding/Skiing

Ok, so it's rather like skiing through sludge... but it can be great fun! Head into the desert (especially easy if you have a 4 wheel drive, although not essential), find yourself some big dunes, and feel the wind rush (?) past you as you take a slow, jerky ride down sandy slopes. A popular sand boarding spot is the huge dune on the left of the main road halfway to Hatta, affectionately known as 'Big Red'.

The boards are usually standard snowboards, but as the sand wears them down quite a bit, they often end up good for nothing else. Some sports stores sell 'sand boards', which are really the cheaper and more basic snowboards. As an alternative for children, a plastic sledge or something similar can be quite fun.

All major tour companies offer sand boarding on the highest dunes, giving basic instruction on how to stay up, how to surf – and how to fall properly. Sand boarding can be done either as part of another tour, or as a dedicated sand boarding tour. A half day sand boarding tour costs around Dhs.175 - 200.

Shooting

Other options → Paintballing [p.295]

Hatta Fort Hotel

Location → Hatta Fort Hotel · Hatta | 852 3211
Hours → Timings on request
Web/email → www.jebelali-international.com | Map Ref → UAE-D3

Clay pigeon shooting is one of the many activities offered at the Hatta Fort Hotel, which is less than an hour's drive from Dubai. More frequently visited as an overnight retreat from the hustle and bustle of Dubai, the Hatta Fort is a sports fan's playground with the added attraction of superb food and beverage facilities. The hotel has a newly opened rock pool, and offers a Friday barbie for Dhs.85 net, including complimentary pool entry. Cost: Dhs.95 for 25 shots. Day visitors on Friday and public holidays purchase a voucher at the entry gate (Dhs.40 for adults, Dhs.20 for children), which is redeemable against hotel facilities.

Jebel Ali Shooting Club

Location → Nr Jebel Ali Htl · Jebel Ali | 883 6555
Hours → See timings below
Web/email → www.jebelali-international.com | Map Ref → 1-A2

The Jebel Ali Shooting Club has five floodlit clay shooting layouts that consist of skeet, trap and sporting. Additional to these there are also two fully computerised indoor pistol ranges of ten, 25m long lanes (open shortly). Professional shooting instructors give comprehensive lessons on clay shooting as well as pistols, and experienced shooters are welcome to try their hand at pistol shooting (variety of calibres available) or engage in clay shooting. Members and non members are welcome. Prices: Non member lessons: Dhs.100 (clay shooting); Dhs.75 (pistol shooting). Member lessons: Dhs.75 (clay shooting); Dhs.50 (pistol shooting). The club is open Wed to Mon (closed on Tue) and operates from 13:00 to 22:00.

Ras Al Khaimah Shooting Club

Location → Al Dehes · 20 min from RAK Airport | 07 236 3622
Hours → 15:00 - 20:00
Web/email → n/a | Map Ref → UAE-D1

This club welcomes anyone interested in learning to shoot any type of gun, from 9mm pistols to shotguns and long rifles. There is a variety of ranges, some air conditioned and indoors such as the 50 metre rifle range, while others are outdoors, like the 200 metre rifle range. Archery is also available. A canteen sells snacks and soft drinks, and the club is open on Mondays for women and children only.

Skydiving

Other options → Hang Gliding [p.284]

Umm Al Quwain Aeroclub

Location → 17km North of UAQ on RAK Rd · UAQ | 06 768 1447
Hours → 09:00 - 17:30
Web/email → www.uaqaeroclub.com | Map Ref → UAE-C1

In addition to pilot training, helicopter flying, hangar/aircraft rental, paramotors and microlights, the club operates as a skydive school and boogie centre. You can enjoy an eight level accelerated free fall parachute course (price Dhs.5,200, the Dhs.200 is refundable) and train for your international parachute licence. Alternatively, try a tandem jump with an instructor from 12,000 feet for Dhs.720. Special rates are available for practice jumps for professional teams, and skydivers from all around the world are welcome.

Location: 16 km along the road from UAQ roundabout heading in the direction of Ras Al Khaimah, before Dreamland Aqua Park and opposite UAQ Shooting Club, on the left hand side of the road... just look for the hangars and the big plane by the sea.

Snooker

Other options → Billiards [p.264]

Dubai Snooker Club

Location → Nr Post Office · Al Karama | 337 5338
Hours → 09:00 - 02:00 Fri 15:00 - 02:00
Web/email → www.dubaisnooker.com | Map Ref → 10-E2

Snooker and pool for everyone, and you don't need to be a member to have a game. Dubai Snooker Club has 15 snooker tables and eight pool tables, plus three private snooker rooms for families and groups. Five tournaments a year are organised, which anyone can enter. Cost: Dhs.20 per hour per table. Location: On the small street joining the road connecting Zabeel Road with Maktoum Bridge road, opposite the main Post Office. The entrance is on the right side of the building.

Millennium Avenue

Location → Al Safiya Bld, nr Galadari R/A · Deira | 266 6844
Hours → 10:00 - 03:30 Fri 14:00 - 03:30
Web/email → www.uaebilliard.com | Map Ref → 12-B4

Opened in July 2000, Millennium Avenue has 18 billiard tables in spacious surroundings and two private snooker tables. The club organises annual interclub leagues as well as international tournaments. They are also the official organiser of the Billiards Championships in Dubai. Other facilities include computer games and an Internet café.

Snooker Point

Location → Nr Al Nasr Cinema · Al Karama | 334 1551
Hours → 10:00 - 03:00 Fri 14:00 - 03:00
Web/email → n/a | Map Ref → 10-D3

Not your regular pool hall, but a smart venue set in surprisingly salubrious surroundings! Play at one of the eight full size snooker tables or nine pool tables and relax inbetween shots at the bar in the pool room, which offers fruit cocktails, coffees and teas. Alternatively use one of the 99 computers

Snooker

available in their Internet café. The fast food chain Hardees are set to take over the restaurant, so lip-smacking burgers will be available soon. Price: Dhs.4 per 15 minutes per table.

Location: *Pass the main entrance of Lamcy Plaza then follow the signs to Snooker Point. Just before you join the slip road onto Umm Hureir Road heading towards Maktoum Bridge, it's on the right, just past Italian Connection restaurant.*

Other Snooker Venues	
VIP Gym	345 2208

Snorkelling

A mask and snorkel is a great way to see the varied underwater life of the Gulf (the East Coast is especially good for this). On the Gulf of Oman coast, popular places include Snoopy Island, near the Sandy Beach Motel, Dibba. There are also good spots further north, such as the beach north of Dibba village, where the coast is rocky and corals can be found close to the shore. For somewhere closer to home, the sea off Jumeira Beach has a fair amount of marine life. Most hotels or dive centres rent equipment – snorkel, mask and fins. Costs vary greatly, so shop around. Check out the *Underwater Explorer (UAE)* for further information on where and how to go snorkelling in the UAE.

Beach Hut, The

Location → Sandy Beach Motel · East Coast | 09 244 5555
Hours → Timings on request
Web/email → www.sandybm.com | Map Ref → n/a

For those who want an exhilarating snorkelling experience, the Beach Hut is the only way to go! Snoopy Island, the 'house' reef, is just off their private beach and is an excellent site to enjoy the underwater world. Equipment is available for sale; alternatively rent a full set for the day for Dhs.50. You can also try your hand at kayaking or windsurfing.

Oceanic Hotel

Location → Beach Rd, Khorfakkan · East Coast | 09 238 5111
Hours → Timings on request
Web/email → www.oceanichotel.com | Map Ref → UAE-E2

An ideal place for snorkelling, the East Coast boasts beautiful clear waters and plenty of fish and coral. The Oceanic Hotel offers a boat ride to Shark Island and provides snorkelling gear for Dhs.60; alternatively snorkel and swim from the hotel beach to Hidden Beach. Equipment hire is Dhs.30 for one hour. These prices apply to hotel residents; visitors will also have to pay an entrance fee of Dhs.45 per adult and Dhs.25 per child.

Scuba 2000

Location → Al Badiyah Beach · Fujairah | 09 238 8477
Hours → 09:00 - 19:00
Web/email → www.scubauae.com | Map Ref → UAE-E2

This East Coast centre offers snorkelling either directly from the beach or with a boat ride, usually to Snoopy and Sharque Islands, or Al Badiyah Rock. Snorkelling trips to these destinations cost Dhs.50, inclusive of fins, mask, snorkel and boots. The centre also has other water sports facilities, including diving; jet skis; pedal boats and canoes. They also have accommodation for divers and snorkellers – three air conditioned twin bedrooms with refrigerator and satellite TV for Dhs.150 per night.

Scuba Dubai

Location → Trade Centre Apts · Trade Centre 1&2 | 331 7433
Hours → 09:00 - 13:00 16:00 - 20:30 Thu 09:00 - 19:00
Web/email → www.scubadubai.com | Map Ref → 9-D2

For those wishing to arrange their own snorkelling trips, diving and snorkelling equipment can be rented from Scuba Dubai on a 24 hour basis, collecting one day and returning the next. Rates for Thursday, Friday and Saturday are the same as renting for one day as the shop is closed on Fridays. Rental of mask and snorkel is Dhs.10 for 24 hours, boots and fins are an additional Dhs.10.

Scuba Diving

Softball

Dubai Softball League

Location → Metropolitan Htl · Shk Zayed Rd | 050 650 2743
Hours → Wed & Sat 19:00 - 23:00
Web/email → www.dubaisoftballleague.com | Map Ref → 5-C4

The Dubai Softball league runs from mid September until the beginning of December, and again from mid January to the end of May. The only criteria to play is that you must be aged 16 or over. Dubai is host to the bi-annual Middle East Softball Championships (MESC). Generally held in November and April, MESC attracts about 30 teams with over 500 players from around the Gulf. Everyone is welcome to watch, entrance is free and food and beverages are available. The next MESC will be April 13th - 16th, 2004. For further information, call Garth Gregory (050 650 2743) or check out the Website.

Speedboating

Other options → Boat & Yacht Charters [p.264]

Fun Sports

Location → Various locations | 399 5976
Hours → 09:00 - 17:00
Web/email → www.funsport-dubai.com | Map Ref → n/a

For those of you who wish to take a break and let your hair down, or just venture out into the vast blue waters of the Gulf, speed boating will be right up your alley. You can hire a boat that comes along with a captain and go wherever you please, even up close to the Burj al Arab. Trips are based on prior bookings as well as weather conditions.

Squash

Other options → Beach, Health & Sports Clubs [p.315]

Dubai Squash League

Location → Dubai & Sharjah | 343 5672
Hours → Timings on request
Web/email → meshrakh@emirates.net.ae | Map Ref → n/a

The squash league has been active in Dubai and Sharjah since the mid 1970s and is run by the UAE Squash Rackets Association. Approximately 300 competitors play three 10 week seasons at over 30 clubs each year. The league meets every Monday evening and this involves five divisions with each team fielding four players, and having eight to ten players registered to join in the competition. For more information, please contact Shavan Kumar (343 5672), Chris Wind (333 1155) or Andy Staines (339 1331).

Surfing

Surf's up, so wax those boards quick! Surprisingly, Dubai is a respectable surfing location. While it certainly doesn't compare to the hot spots in Indonesia or Hawaii, and you probably wouldn't come here on a surfin' safari, there is a dedicated group of surfers watching the weather and tides from November to June, to satisfy their cravings with a couple of days' worth of rideable waves a month.

Swells are generally on the smaller side (2 - 4 feet), but every now and then, conditions are right and bigger stuff comes through. The sport's popularity has increased in the last few years with more boards becoming available on the market.

Check out the Surfers of Dubai Website (www.surfersofdubai.com) for information on the best surf locations, current conditions, where to buy boards, and when to meet to watch surf videos.

Swimming

Dubai's location on the Arabian Gulf means that you can swim to Iran if you're really enthusiastic (and with an upcoming underwater hotel, you never know what else you may find!) The other advantage is easy access to water that's relatively clean with pleasant temperatures most of the year. During the three hottest months of summer, the water at the beach is often hotter than a bath!

Most hotels have swimming pools that are open for use by the public for a day entrance fee. This charge varies, starting from Dhs.60 on weekdays and more on the weekends. Swimming lessons are widely available from health and beach clubs, as well as from dedicated swimming coaches. Pools are usually cooled for the summer months.

Dubai's white sandy beaches make for great swimming spots, whether it's a public beach, a beach club or one of the beach parks. Do keep an eye out for jellyfish etc, especially on the east coast, and ogling men at the public beaches. Remember to be modest in your choice of costume.

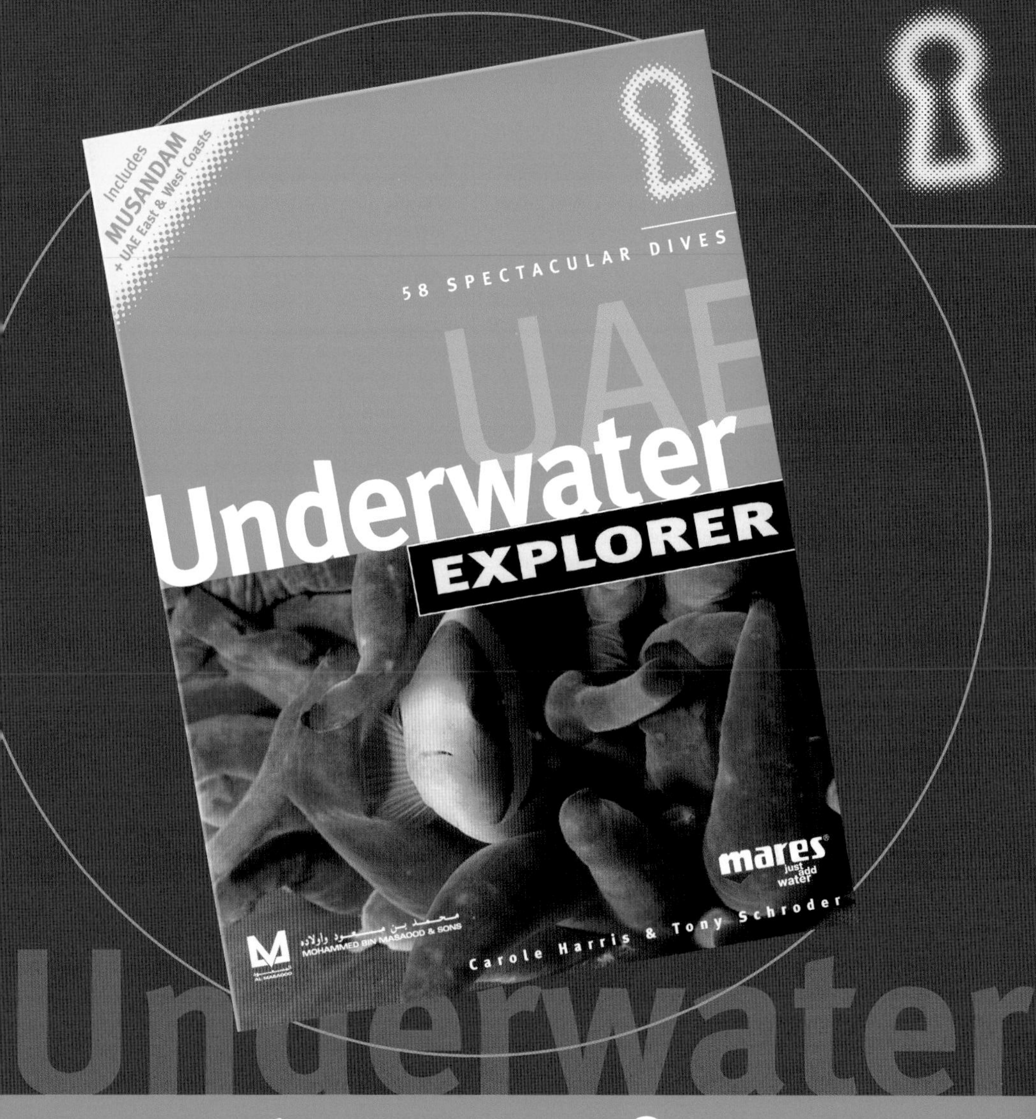
Includes
MUSANDAM
+ UAE East & West Coasts
58 SPECTACULAR DIVES
UAE
Underwater
EXPLORER
mares
just add water
MOHAMMED BIN MASAOOD & SONS
Carole Harris & Tony Schroder
Underwater

Warning: when swimming in the sea, do not underestimate the strength of the tides and currents. Even on the safest looking beaches, rip tides have been known to carry people out to sea. A few years ago, 100 people drowned in one year off the UAE's coast, due in part to the combination of strong rip tides and lack of swimming ability.

Table Tennis

Ping pong! Please see the list of beach, health and sports clubs. Most offer at least one table tennis table!

Tennis

Dubai has firmly established itself on the international tennis circuit with the $1,000,000 Dubai Duty Free Tennis Open, held each year in the middle of February. However, if the centre court is a little out of your league, you'll find plenty of other opportunities to enjoy this popular game.

For the budding Pete Sampras', outdoor courts are available at most of the health and beach clubs. Many courts are floodlit, allowing play in the cool of the evening – in the summer, this is about the only time you'd want to play outside! The indoor courts at InSportz (347 5833) are a bonus for the summer months, and are for public use at reasonable rates.

Prices for hiring courts vary between Dhs.25 - 50 weekdays, but you may be charged as much as Dhs.100 on the weekend. Group or individual coaching is also widely available.

Aviation Club, The

Location → Nr Tennis Stadium · Al Garhoud | 282 4122
Hours → 06:00 - 23:00
Web/email → www.aviationclubonline.com | Map Ref → 14-C3

The Clark Francis Tennis Academy at The Aviation Club offers a variety of courses, lessons and activities for all ages and abilities. The club boasts a range of excellent facilities, including six floodlit Decoturf tennis courts. It also hosts The Aviation Cup (Dhs.78,000) and the annual ATP, WTA and Dubai Duty Free Tennis Open each February (the latter is an event that's firmly established on the international tennis circuit).

Prices: *Individual classes start at Dhs.150 per person (Dhs.600 for five lessons).*

Dubai Tennis Academy

Location → American University · Al Sufouh | 397 5828
Hours → Timings on request
Web/email → n/a | Map Ref → 3-A3

The Academy offers world class, up to the minute training with experienced international coaching year round for aspiring players of all ages and abilities. All coaches are internationally qualified professionals. The Academy's full time adult and junior programmes include private lessons, group clinics, competitions, ladies tennis mornings and school holiday sports camps for children. At the end of each term, players will receive an Academy T-shirt and a certificate of achievement. A personal progress report and video analysis are also available. For further information please call Strath on 050 655 6152.

Emirates Golf Club

Location → · Emirates Hill | 380 2222
Hours → 06:00 - 23:00
Web/email → www.dubaigolf.com | Map Ref → 3-A3

The Emirates Tennis Academy in the Emirates Golf Club is open to members and non members alike, and offers coaching for all ages and levels of ability. The centre has six courts, and coaching is taught by qualified LTA (Lawn Tennis Association) and USPTR (United States Professional Tennis Registry) professionals. The programme for

Mamzar Beach

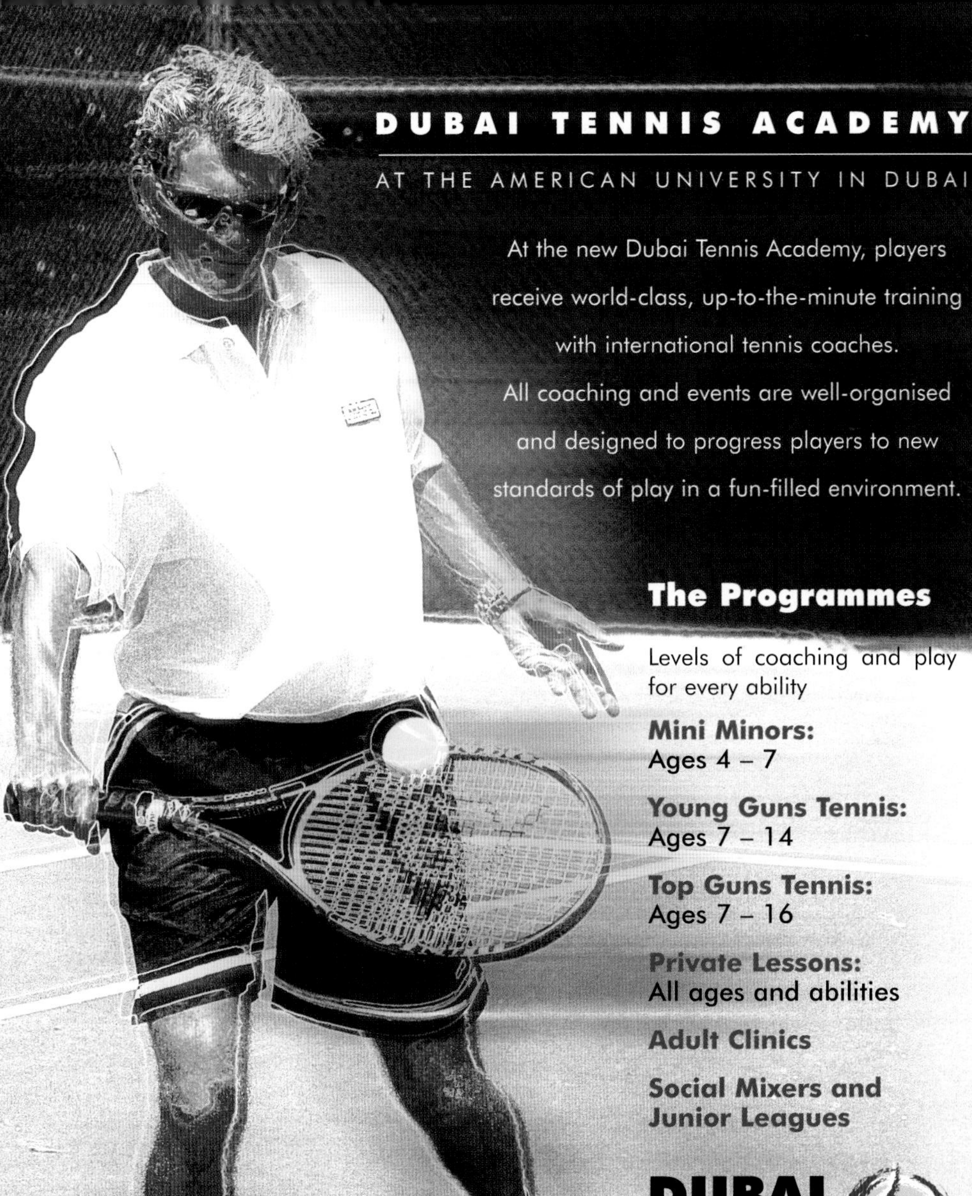
DUBAI TENNIS ACADEMY
AT THE AMERICAN UNIVERSITY IN DUBAI
At the new Dubai Tennis Academy, players receive world-class, up-to-the-minute training with international tennis coaches.
All coaching and events are well-organised and designed to progress players to new standards of play in a fun-filled environment.
The Programmes
Levels of coaching and play for every ability
Mini Minors:
Ages 4 – 7
Young Guns Tennis:
Ages 7 – 14
Top Guns Tennis:
Ages 7 – 16
Private Lessons:
All ages and abilities
Adult Clinics
Social Mixers and Junior Leagues

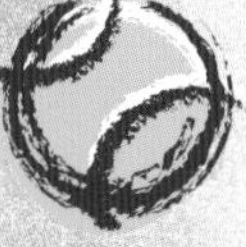
DUBAI
TENNIS
ACADEMY
Contact Strath Sherriff
Tel 04 397 5828
sherriff@emirates.net.ae
COACHING EXCELLENCE AT SUPERB, CONVENIENTLY SITUATED FACILITIES

SHERRIFF
INTERNATIONAL
MANAGEMENT

OASIS

AUD

QUICK PRINT

7DAYS

DUNLOP

adults provides group clinics, individual lessons and club nights, as well as ladies social tennis mornings. The academy has two teams in the ladies Spinneys League and one in the men's Prince League. Every few years, a junior academy trip is planned to the UK to play against London clubs and to the Wimbledon Championships to watch the world's top players in action at the world's most famous tennis tournament.

Boxing at Colosseum

Thai Boxing

Other options → Martial Arts [p.291]

Colosseum

Location → Montana Centre Bld, Za'abeel Rd | 337 2755
Hours → 06:00 - 22:00
Web/email → n/a | Map Ref → 10-E3

This health and fitness club is the first to introduce the martial art of Muay Thai (Thai Boxing) to the UAE. Safety foremost in mind, state of the art training equipment is a welcome asset. The studio is based on a traditional Thai training camp, with highly respected teachers from Northern Thailand coaching you on everything from overall fitness improvement to training on a competitive level. Evening classes are held daily, especially for the whipper snappers.

Triathlon

Dubai Triathlon Club

Location → Various locations | 050 654 7924
Hours → Timings on request
Web/email → www.dubaitriclub.com | Map Ref → n/a

There is a large and growing number of triathlon enthusiasts of all ages in the Emirates, and during the winter season (October to April) the Dubai Tri Club committee organises the Dubai Triathlon Series comprising three or four triathlons, aquathons or duathlons. Weekly training sessions take place Thursday mornings from 07:00 – 08:00 at Umm Suqeim Beach. No membership is required, just turn up at to the training sessions and the events. All enthusiasts are also invited to register on the UAE database via email. For further information see the Website or contact Rory McRae on 050 654 7924 or Adrian Hayes on 050 622 4191.

Wadi & Dune Bashing

With vast areas of rarely visited wilderness to explore, wadi and dune 'bashing' are two of the most popular pastimes in the Emirates, offering a variety of challenging driving. Dune or desert driving is possibly the toughest challenge for car and driver, but probably the most fun, while in the mountains and wadis, the driving is relatively straightforward. Wadis are (usually dry) gullies, carved through the rock by rushing floodwater, that follow the course of seasonal rivers.

One point about the word 'bashing' – while a popular term for this form of entertainment, it can be misleading. Most, if not all, of your journey off-road should be on existing tracks to protect the environment from further damage. Try to avoid the temptation to create new tracks across virgin countryside. Although much of the UAE 'outback' may look devoid of life, there is a surprising variety of flora and fauna that exists in a delicate balance.

For further information and tips on driving off-road, including stunning satellite imagery with 20 tip and driving instruction superimposed routes, detailed route descriptions and striking photos, refer to the *Off-Road Explorer* guidebook, published by Explorer Publishing. This book also includes a useful off-road directory.

If you want to venture into the wilderness, but don't want to organise it yourself, contact the

tour companies; all offer a range of desert and mountain safaris. See Tour Operators [p.189]. If you don't have a 4 wheel drive, one can be hired from most car hire companies.

See also: Car Hire [p.39].

Wakeboarding

Other options → Beaches [p.183]

Dubai Water Sports Association

Location → Jadaf · End of Dubai Creek | 324 1031
Hours → 08:00 - 18:00
Web/email → dwsa@emirates.net.ae | Map Ref → n/a

Wakeboarding was pioneered by the Dubai Water Sports Association (DWSA) who 'bred' one of the top junior wakeboarders in the world. This is the aquatic equivalent of snow boarding; basically, you strap your feet onto one large board, weigh the back of the boat down to create a bigger wake and then jump over it! Sounds simple? To have a go at this fun, flamboyant and still relatively new sport in the UAE, contact DWSA on the above number.

Water Parks

Other options → Amusement Parks [p.262]

Dreamland Aqua Park

Location → 17km North of UAQ on RAK Rd · UAQ | 06 768 1888
Hours → 10:00 - 18:00 Thu & Fri 10:00 - 20:00
Web/email → www.dreamlanduae.com | Map Ref → UAE-C1

Dreamland Aqua Park brings you the excitement of four million gallons of fresh water and over 60 acres of intense fun! Easily accessible from Dubai and Sharjah, Dreamland is one of the largest aqua parks in the world – a truly unique experience for any resident or visitor to the Middle East. Food stalls and restaurants offer a variety of cuisines as well as a jacuzzi bar. Dreamland recently launched a water attraction called the 'Aqua Play' that includes 12 different water games. A visit here is excellent value for money: adults Dhs.40; children Dhs.20. Opening hours vary according to the season. Fri and public holidays are for families, season pass holders or pre-booked groups only.

SplashLand

Location → WonderLand · Umm Hurair (2) | 324 1222
Hours → 10:00 - 19:00
Web/email → www.wonderlanduae.com | Map Ref → 14-A3

Try any of the nine water rides, relax by the pool and sunbathe, or eat at one of the restaurants. Rides include 'lazy river' (relax on an inner tube on a meandering river), 'shoot the rapids' (slide down a 35 foot ramp on a sled and skip across the water like a pebble), or try the 'speed slides' and 'twister'. There's an adult swimming pool and a children's activity pool, with slides, bridges and water cannons. Lockers and changing rooms are available. Timings change seasonally, so check to avoid disappointment.

See also: WonderLand Theme & Water Park [p.262].

Wild Wadi Water Park

Location → Wild Wadi · Umm Suqeim | 348 4444
Hours → See timings below
Web/email → www.jumeirahinternational.com | Map Ref → 4-A2

Wild Wadi is one of the world's most advanced water adventure theme parks. The park is created around the adventures of Juha, a mythical friend of Sinbad. Spread over 12 acres, it offers a variety of water rides, including Jumeirah Sceirah (the tallest

Wild Wadi

and fastest free fall slide outside North America), where speeds of up to 80 km per hour are possible! For pure relaxation, Juha's Journey allows you to float serenely through a changing landscape, while younger visitors can enjoy Juha's Dhow and Lagoon. Timings: June – Aug 13:00 - 21:00; Nov – Feb 11:00 - 18:00, Sep – Oct and Mar – May 11:00 - 19:00. Adult all day admission is Dhs.120; child all day admission is Dhs.100. Lifeguards patrol all water areas and rides are regulated by height restrictions for those under 1.1 metres. To safeguard your wallet, you are given a wrist credit card – what you don't spend is refunded when you leave.

Water Skiing

Other options → Beach Clubs [p.315]

Dubai Water Sports Association

Location → Jadaf · End of Dubai Creek | 324 1031
Hours → 08:00 - 18:00
Web/email → dwsa@emirates.net.ae | Map Ref → n/a

Set along Dubai's Creek, Dubai Water Sports Association is devoted to the promotion of water sports, primarily water skiing and wakeboarding. The association has two tournament ski boats, a slalom course and a full sized jump for hire. The club organises occasional wakeboarding competitions for all levels of ability. Clubhouse facilities include a lawn with sun loungers, swimming pool, children's playground, barbecue area and jacuzzi. There's no skiing on Sundays, but the club is still open. Monday is for kids coaching from 15:30 until dusk. Yearly and monthly memberships are available, and annual members receive a discount on the ski tow. Daily entrance fees for non members: Dhs.15 weekdays; Dhs.25 Fri and public holidays (free entrance for your first visit). Ski tow: Dhs.45 for 10 - 15 minutes for non members.

Water Sports

Club Joumana

Location → Jebel Ali Htl · Jebel Ali | 804 8058
Hours → 06:30 - 22:00
Web/email → www.jebelali-international.com | Map Ref → 1-A1

Located on the hotel's pristine beach and part of Club Joumana, the Aqua Hut offers several types of water sports, from motorised activities such as water skiing and banana boat rides, to non motorised activities such as windsurfing, catamaran and laser sailing as well as kayaking. Waterskiing costs Dhs.80 for half an hour, with lessons an extra Dhs.40. Non residents of the hotel are charged an additional fee for day access to the beach and pools.

Windsurfing

Other options → Water Sports [p.308]

Fun Sports

Location → Various locations | 399 5976
Hours → 09:00 - 17:00
Web/email → www.funsport-dubai.com | Map Ref → n/a

Fun Sports is one of the leading water sports companies in Dubai – for information, refer to their review under Fishing.

Well-Being

For lovers of leisure, Dubai's booming tourist trade combined with its vast and vibrant expat community make it a natural centre for abundant leisure activities. These can range from the gentle pampering of a beauty salon or health spa to a more energetic Pilates session, a relaxing day at a beach club, or a concert or play. You may even want to take the option of participating in a drama group, dance lessons, or chill to the core with a little meditation guidance. Whichever your leisure pleasure, there's a good chance someone in town is willing to provide it.

Beauty Salons

Beauty is big business in Dubai! There is a huge variety of salons to visit, offering every type of treatment imaginable. Shoppers can find a range of products including everything from Paul Bryan to KMS to Toni & Guy. Services ranging from manicures, to pedicures, waxing to henna, to the latest cuts, styles and colours.

Salons here tend to be very popular, and especially busy at night for weddings and special occasions or functions. As is expected, the quality and range of treatments vary greatly, so trial and error or word of mouth are probably the best way of finding a good salon.

WILD WADI

All salons are filled with a multitude of cultures. Or, as some prefer, have the stylist come to your home. In hotels you'll find both male and female stylists working alongside one another, but outside hotels, only female stylists are permitted to work in salons. These independent salons are good for privacy; men are not permitted inside and the windows are blocked out for those nosy pedestrians.

There are also numerous small salons aimed primarily at Arab ladies. In particular, they offer henna designs – look out for a decorated hand on the signboards in shop windows. The traditional practice of painting henna on the hands and feet, especially for weddings or special occasions, is still very popular with the National population. The intricate brown patterns fade after 2 - 3 weeks. For visitors to the Emirates, a design on the ankle or shoulder can make a great memento of a visit here and costs only about Dhs.30.

Salons

Female Salons		
Franck Provost	Burj Al Arab	301 7249
	Ritz Carlton	318 6141
Jacques Dessange	Jumeira	344 6776
Maria Dowling	Satwa	345 4225
Paul Bryan	Airport Hotel	282 9949
Pretty Lady	Satwa	398 5255
Toni & Guy	Emirates Tower Htl	330 3345

Male Salons		
Beverly Hills	BurJuman Centre	355 6567

Franck Provost at the Burj Al Arab

Health Spas

Other options → Beach, Health & Sports Clubs [p.315]

Ayoma Spa

Location → Taj Palace Hotel · Deira | 223 2222
Hours → 10:00 - 22:00
Web/email → www.tajpalacehotel.co.ae | Map Ref → 11-D2

With a focus on Ayurvedic therapy and treatments, Ayoma Spa promises 'total relaxation of the mind, body and soul'. A divine foot therapy at the start of your treatment sets the tone for the rest of your unforgettable experience. Facilities include separate saunas and steam rooms, a swimming pool and jacuzzi. A recommended treatment is the Abyanga, an all over body massage performed with a combination of strokes, using oils specifically suited for mind and body constitution – a unique and addictive experience.

Chi Spa

Location → Shangri-La Hotel · Shk Zayed Rd | 343 8888
Hours → 06:00 - 24:00
Web/email → www.shangri-la.com | Map Ref → 9-A2

Check all anxiety at the door as you enter this (very slick!) haven of peace and tranquillity. The Chi spa aims to impress with understated elegance and luxurious facilities. Embracing a holistic approach to physical and spiritual well being, their healing philosophies and treatments are based on the principal of restoring balance and harmony to the mind and body. Hence, the Chi balance massage is the obvious choice here. A cosy shop filled with fragrant oils, aromatic herbs and spices, indulges the addicts who haven't had their fill of relaxation. LM

Cleopatra's Spa

Location → Pyramids · Umm Hurair (2) | 324 7700
Hours → 09:00 - 20:00 Fri 10:00 - 20:00
Web/email → www.waficity.com | Map Ref → 13-D2

Cleopatra's Spa offers the ultimate relaxation and pampering experience for weary Dubai souls. Tranquillity and friendly staff greet you the moment you step through the doors; staff are discreetly on hand throughout your stay to ensure you have the best experience possible. Treatments range from Ayurvedic to Balinese, aromatherapy to reflexology, facials to pedicures, rubs and wraps to flower baths, and from what we've experienced, they all do wonders! Arrive early to make the most of the opulent

FRANCK PROVOST
PARIS
air Service
tyling
olor
erming
traightening
reatment
xtension
ake up Service
pplication
essons
attoo
ridal Packages
ail Service
anicure
edicure
Coiffure at
Burj Al Arab
04.301.7249
The Ritz-Carlton
04.318.6141
Customer Care:
Tel: 04 - 351.1100
email: customercare@franckprovost-dubai.com
web: www.franckprovost-dubai.com

ancient Egyptian-style facilities, particularly the 'wet area' – a sauna, jacuzzi and steam heaven; linger afterwards in the relaxation area with a cup of herbal tea. Special offers change monthly, offering you the opportunity to try various treatments and combination packages, many of which are suited to the season. Men's spa timings: 10:00 - 22:00; Sun 10:00 - 19:00.

Dubai Marine Spa

Location → Dubai Marine Hotel · Beach Rd, Jumeira | 346 1111
Hours → 10:00 - 19:00
Web/email → www.dxbmarine.com | Map Ref → 6-D2

Opened in late 1998, this spa specialises in Guinot and Espa products, with a good selection of packages for both men and woman. Treatments are designed to combat the environmental, physical and mental stresses of modern living, as well as making you look and feel great. The spa has five qualified therapists and five treatment rooms. Programmes include facials, massages, reflexology, seaweed wraps, manicures and pedicures. For full day programmes, a light lunch and use of the facilities at the resort are included.

Givenchy Spa

Location → One&Only Residence & Spa · Al Sufouh | 399 9999
Hours → See timings below
Web/email → www.royalmiragedubai.com | Map Ref → 3-A2

Located within such opulent confines, the Givenchy Spa could not be more indulgent. The tranquil backdrop and tasteful decor instantly switches you off from the outside world before professionals whisk you off to one of a range of heavenly treatments. There is no 'gimmicky theme' or 'concept' to this spa - just a quiet efficiency and a team who are obvious experts in their field. From a vast range of treatments and therapies, their deep cleansing facial has to be one of the best in Dubai. They say diamonds are a girl's best friend, but a morning at The Givenchy Spa is a close second.

Timings: *Daily 09:30 - 20:00; Ladies only 09:30 - 13:00; Ladies and Gentlemen 14:30 - 20:00. Last treatment booking 19:00.*

See also: *Royal Mirage Residence & Spa – Health Spas [p.310].*

Oxygen Parlour

Location → Sh Rashid Bldg, 307 · Satwa | 354 2387
Hours → 10:00 - 22:00 Fri 16:00 - 22:00
Web/email → www.fourwayshealthworld.com | Map Ref → 8-A4

O2World is the region's first oxygen parlour and the world's first oxygen sauna where you can fill your lungs with fresh pure oxygen infused with essential oils to have an all natural healthy feeling. Aromatherapy and electronic massages are offered as well. o2World suggests a minimum of two sessions per week, continuously for three months for 'optimum results'. Costs: 20 minutes of 95% pure oxygen along with aromatherapy is Dhs.60; 15 minutes of electronic massage (body, leg or eye) is Dhs.15. The combined package of oxygen and aromatherapy and full electronic massage is Dhs.100 for 65 minutes. To learn more, visit their Website.

Ritz-Carlton Spa

Location → Ritz-Carlton Dubai · Marsa Dubai | 399 4000
Hours → 06:00 - 20:00
Web/email → spa.dubai@ritz-carlton.com | Map Ref → 2-E2

This very busy spa reflects a Balinese theme throughout – from the treatments to the décor, with much of the wooden furniture and artwork coming from this Indonesian island. The subterranean facilities include eight treatment rooms, a hair and beauty salon, jacuzzi, sauna, steam room and a ladies' gym, complete with toning tables. The most popular treatment – the Balinese massage – is luxury (tell your masseur how much or how little pressure you'd like). Treatments are deluxe, and this is reflected in the prices. With easy access between the spa and the health and beach club, the Ritz's extensive facilities ensure that any visit will be one of exquisite pampering.

Royal Waters Health Spa

Location → Al Mamzar Centre · Deira | 297 2053
Hours → 09:00 - 17:00 Fri 10:00 - 24:00
Web/email → therwspa@emirates.net.ae | Map Ref → 12-C4

This spa offers a gym, rooftop swimming pool, café, sauna and steam. The focus is on holistic healing and they pride themselves on being 'a haven of

Flower Petal Bath Spa Treatment

Family Explorer

Written by Mums and Dads residing in the Emirates, this guidebook is the only essential resource for families with kids, providing you a multitude of indoor and outdoor activity options with your little ones. Make your life easier by following tips on practical topics, such as education and medical care.

peace and tranquillity'. The spa offers different memberships and programmes, from stress management to nutrition, Reiki, Pilates, a range of spa and beauty treatments, and consultations with their in-house doctor. Italian Comfortzone and Lillian Terry complexes products are used.

Timings: *ladies only: gym 09:00 - 17:00; spa 10:00 - 19:00; men only: gym 07:00 - 09:00 and 17:00 - 24:00; mixed ladies and men: spa 19:00 - 24:00.*

Satori Spa

Location → Jumeirah Beach Club · Jumeira | 344 5333
Hours → 09:00 - 21:00
Web/email → www.jumeirahinternational.com | Map Ref → 5-D1

Tucked away within the lush foliage and undulating paths of the Jumeirah Beach Club, Satori Spa is a serene surprise. A tranquil indoor garden, an exotic outdoor shower, a spread out 'resort style' structure, wind chimes and soothing shades on hand finished walls create an instantly calming atmosphere. All sorts of treatments are offered to relax and revive the individual, but the Satori Signature Treatments should not be missed. Blending age old practices with modern techniques, these treatments pamper and spoil with a complete package of massages, showers, flower baths and facials topped with a warm cup of herbal tea. The spa is exclusive to The Jumeirah Beach Club members and guests.

Spa Thira

Location → Opp Jumeira Beach Park · Jumeira | 344 2055
Hours → 09:00 - 18:00 Thu 09:00 - 14:00
Web/email → amalchachaa@hotamil.com | Map Ref → 5-C2

The ultimate one stop beauty shop, Spa Thira is located in a converted double storey villa. Music filters through the rooms and a sense of peace and well being pervades. A full range of beauty therapies is on offer including facials, manicures, semi permanent makeup, Moroccan baths and Chinese massages. The most outstanding treatment is the soft light laser, for safe and lasting hair removal. It's only open to women during normal hours, but men are welcome to make appointments outside these times.

Willow Stream Spa

Location → Fairmont Hotel · Shk Zayed Rd | 332 5555
Hours → 06:00 - 24:00
Web/email → www.fairmont.com | Map Ref → 9-E1

Set in the busy business district of Sheikh Zayed Road, the Fairmont houses this luxurious health club and spa. Decorated like a Roman bath, the club wraps around the hotel's light rectangular centre. On the east side, there's the sunrise pool and jacuzzi for early birds, while for some afternoon sun, move to the sunset pool on the west side. The gym has state of the art Technogym equipment and a good cardio area, but the free weights section is a little more limited. Half and full day tailor made programs in the spa make an ideal gift for that special someone.

Massage

In the eclectic, multicultural community that is Dubai, there are numerous massage types available to the individual with a need to pamper and unwind. Soothing for the body, mind and soul, it could be a weekly treat, a gift to someone special or a relaxation technique to get through a trying time at work. Prices and standards vary, so shop around until you find someone that suits you. The cost for a full body massage ranges from Dhs.100 - 300 for one hour of heaven! Massages, in addition to variety of other treatments well worth a try, are available at Dubai's excellent spas; for further details refer to [p.310].

Meditation & Reiki

Learning how to levitate may not be your bag, but Reiki and meditation are excellent for creating a sense of calm and well being. While meditation can be performed at home with only basic knowledge, Reiki is a healing technique based on the belief that energy can be channelled into the patient by means of touch. Translated as 'universal life force energy', Reiki can, like meditation, emotionally cleanse, physically invigorate and leave you more focused.

Archie Sharma Reiki

Location → Al Garhoud Residential Area · Al Garhoud | 282 4468
Hours → 10:00 - 17:00
Web/email → - Map Ref → 14-D4

Archie Sharma is a reiki master who has been practising for over six years and is involved in both teaching and healing. She also conducts Zen meditation, is a qualified herbalist and reflexologist, and when time permits, advises on feng shui, the Chinese art of placement.

Pookat Suresh Reiki

Location → Various locations | 285 9128
Hours → 08:00 - 13:00 16:00 - 19:00
Web/email → esbipookat@yahoo.com Map Ref → n/a

Reiki is one of the simplest forms of natural healing, needing only one or two days to learn its main feature, which is to heal the self and others. The Pookat Suresh Reiki centre offers various degrees of attunement. In the first degree seminar, which also covers theoretical and practical aspects of Reiki, a series of four attunements are given by a traditional master to channel a higher amount of universal life force energy. The second degree level teaches powerful absentee healing and the tremendous flexibility of Reiki. For further details, contact Reiki master Pookat Suresh Babu on 050 453 9643.

Pilates

Other options → Yoga [p.314]

House of Chi & House of Healing

Location → Musalla Towers · Bank St, Bur Dubai | 397 4446
Hours → See timings below
Web/email → www.hofchi.com Map Ref → 8-A4

In perfect balance... mind, body and spirit is the maxim of this alternative therapies outlet. The surroundings inspire peace and well being, while the team of practitioners include professionals in the fields of traditional Chinese medicine, martial arts, yoga, Tai Chi, Karate, Kung Fu, Aikido, Pilates and meditation. A variety of methods is offered to alleviate health problems and promote inner harmony. Services include the treatment of physical ailments, stress, weight loss and physical therapy to improve your mind and spirit. Timings: House of Chi 08:00 - 21:30; House of Healing 10:30 - 22:30.

Pilates Studio, The

Location → Nr Thunder Bowl · Trade Centre 1&2 | 343 8252
Hours → 08:00 - 20:00 Thu 08:00 - 16:00
Web/email → pilates@emirates.net.ae Map Ref → 5-E3

Pilates is an effective and safe way to tone up and strengthen core muscles. The technique was developed over 70 years ago by German Joseph Pilates and has since been refined and updated in the light of modern anatomical knowledge. Using over 500 controlled movements, it is a form of exercise for everyone – young, old, fit, not so slim, and especially those in rehabilitation (post illness or injury). Pilates was introduced to the UAE in 1998 by Catherine Lehmann, a physiologist with many years' experience of teaching the Pilates method. The current studio space opened in September 2000 and offers both mat and reformer classes for absolute beginners through to advanced.

Stress Management

Other options → Support Groups [p.112]

Holistic Healing & Life Source Energy

Location → Nr Al Wasl Park · Jumeira | 344 9880
Hours → 09:00 - 18:00
Web/email → n/a Map Ref → 4-D3

Karen Meyer-Reumann is a counsellor, holistic healer and family display practitioner whose aim is to help you 'break your pattern'. With 27 years' experience of meditation/monasteries, teaching meditation and being a 'zero point antenna', licensed to produce Life Source Energy products, she creates individual grids – a combination of forms and colours (wisdom of the Maya) downloaded into your aura, so you will attract new options into your life. She gives you the tools to lift your energy levels through healing, balancing emotion and mind.

Yoga

Other options → Pilates [p.314]

Al Karama Ayurvedic Centre

Location → 109 Karama Centre · Al Karama | 337 8921
Hours → 08:30 - 23:30 Fri 08:30 - 14:00
Web/email → almadxb@emirates.net.ae Map Ref → 10-D2

Operating for over 18 years, this centre (previously known as the Karama Natural Massage & Yoga

Centre is run by qualified professionals with expertise in the traditional systems of Ayurveda, herbal beauty care, yoga and meditation. This is a one stop institution with all the facilities that are necessary for a natural system of healing, rejuvenation and beauty care. Separate areas are available for men and women.

Al Majaz

Location → Trade Centre Rd · Al Karama | 335 3563
Hours → 09:00 - 14:00 16:00 - 21:00
Web/email → www.goldenfistkarate.com | Map Ref → 10-D1

Al Majaz offers a variety of self improvement and fitness classes as well as swimming lessons. For ladies and girls above the age of ten, there's yoga – the natural way to keep body and mind together – as well as aerobics and self defence classes (Al Majaz Ladies Fitness Centre in Karama). In addition, separate classes for adults, girls and boys are available in karate, kung fu, taekwondo and jiu-jitsu (Golden Fist Karate Club in Bur Dubai 3551029). Transport can be provided.

Gems of Yoga

Location → Wht. Crown Bld · Trade Centre 1&2 | 331 5161
Hours → 06:30 - 13:30 15:00 - 22:00 Fri 16:00 - 22:00
Web/email → www.gemsofyogadubai.com | Map Ref → 9-D2

Gems of Yoga integrates yoga and art, bringing increased fitness to an individual's lifestyle. Yogasanas, mudras, pranayam, meditation and various stress release techniques are built into the programmes. On a mental level, yoga helps to focus and increase concentration, bringing increased harmony and balance to life. The centre offers classes such as weight-watchers desktop yoga, prenatal and postnatal yoga, therapeutic yoga and animal yoga for children. Nutritional consultations and naturopathy consultations are available. Packages range from Dhs.550 to Dhs.1,500, yoga at home packages Dhs.2,500. Free beach yoga classes are held the last Thu of the month at Umm Suqeim beach from 17:00 - 18:00.

House of Chi & House of Healing

Location → Musalla Towers · Bank St, Bur Dubai | 397 4446
Hours → 10:00 - 22:00 Fri 16:00 - 22:00
Web/email → www.hofchi.com | Map Ref → 8-A4

Hatha yoga, can teach you to get your stress under control – not only on a physical, but on a mental and spiritual level as well. Most of our diseases are a result of accumulation of toxins in our body. Yoga asanas help in the elimination of these toxins from the body, and at the same time keep the body fit while pranayama plays a vital role in learning how to control the life force through breathing exercises. For more information on the House of Chi & House of Healing, refer to the review under Pilates [p.314].

Beach, Health & Sports Clubs

Beach Clubs

Other options → Beaches [p.183]

Beach, Health & Sports Clubs

Keep fit fans should have no problem finding facilities that suit them among Dubai's excellent range of health clubs, beach clubs and sports facilities. To help distinguish among the various types of facilities available, we have categorised them as follows:

- Health clubs generally offer workout facilities: machines, weights etc, plus classes varying from aerobics to yoga
- Beach clubs are similar to health clubs, but with the added bonus of beach access
- Sports clubs have similar facilities to health clubs, and also offer additional activities such as swimming, tennis, squash and/or golf.

VIP Gym

Neighbourhood gyms also exist in Dubai. Many of these are filled with 'serious' workout fanatics (mostly beefy men) and the facilities tend to be older and dated. Prices, however, are generally a fraction of health club membership fees.

Refer to the Club Facilities table on [p.318] for full details of the various clubs in Dubai, including their membership rates and all amenities offered.

Health Clubs

Other options → Annual Events [p.50]

Cardio Equipment

Sports Clubs

The following clubs offer a range of sporting activities and a variety of facilities, from swimming pools to tennis or squash courts and golf courses. However, for details of individual sports refer to that particular listing in this section of the book.

Dubai Country Club

Location → Nr Bu Kidra Interchange · Al Awir Rd | 333 1155
Hours → 08:00 - 22:00
Web/email → www.dubaicountryclub.com Map Ref → 17-B3

Dubai Country Club is a club that caters to all your family needs. Sports facilities are excellent and include amongst others, tennis, squash, badminton and football, as well as a sand golf course and a fully equipped gym. There's a large pool area, plus shaded children's play areas. All activities are available to members, however, the two restaurants (the Windtower and the Oasis) and certain activities are open to all, upon reservation. Entrance fees depend on the activity.

India Club

Location → Nr Indian High School · Oud Metha | 337 1112
Hours → 06:00 - 24:00
Web/email → www.indiaclubdubai.com Map Ref → 10-E4

Opened in 1964, this club currently has 6,500 members and its objective is to provide facilities for sports, entertainment and recreation, and to promote business. Facilities include a gym, with a separate steam and sauna for men and women, badminton, squash and tennis courts, snooker, table tennis, basketball, a swimming pool, and a variety of indoor games. The India Club has become the first club anywhere to be awarded ISO 9001:2000 accreditation by Lloyds Register Quality Assurance.

LG InSportz

Location → Jct 3, Shk Zayed Rd | 347 5833
Hours → 09:00 - 22:00
Web/email → www.insportzclub.com Map Ref → 4-C4

LG InSportz Club is Dubai's first indoor sports centre – it makes the idea of participating in sport all year a reality! Facilities include five multi-purpose playing courts, a cricket coaching net, changing room and cafeteria, all within the comfort of air conditioned surroundings. Sports available include cricket, football, basketball, hockey and there's a complete coaching programme for juniors. Individuals and teams can hire the courts too. InSportz also caters for birthday parties, corporate events, event management, children's holiday sports programmes and summer camps. Prices start from Dhs.20 per child or Dhs.25 per adult inclusive of equipment.

Sharjah Wanderers Sports Club

Location → Nr Sharjah English School · Sharjah | 06 566 2105
Hours → 08:00 - 24:00
Web/email → www.sharjahwanderers.com Map Ref → UAE-C2

This is a popular and sociable club that's well used by the expat community in Sharjah, Dubai and the Northern Emirates. Facilities include floodlit tennis courts, squash courts, floodlit football, rugby and hockey pitches, a swimming pool, gym, library, snooker, darts, aerobic classes, yoga for adults and kids, dancing for kids, girls' netball and a kids play area. There's a good restaurant, and the club holds regular social events, such as a twice monthly quiz night.

V.I.P
HEALTH CLUB
& NOW ... !
NEW MANAGEMENT
NEW COACH
NEW EQUIPMENT
EW PRICES
itness
ody Building
aining & Losing Weight
rivate Instruction with
Guarantee
(Men & Women)
04-3451575,3452209, 3452207, Fax : 04-3452208 , P.O.Box : 74822
Near Capitol Hotel, VIP GYM, Mina Road Bur Dubai - U.A.E.
E-mail : vipgym_fsgari@yahoo.com

Club Membership Rates & Facilities

Club Name	Location	Area	Map	Tel. no.
Beach Clubs				
Caracalla Spa & Health Club	Le Royal Meridien Beach Resort & Spa	Al Sufouh	2-E2	399 5555
Club Joumana	Jebel Ali Hotel & Golf Resort	Jebel Ali	1-A1	804 8058
Club Mina	Le Meridien Mina Seyahi	Al Sufouh	3-A2	399 3333
Dubai Marine Beach Resort & Spa	Dubai Marine Beach Resort & Spa	Jumeira	6-D2	346 1111
Jumeirah Beach Club	Jumeirah Beach Club	Beach Rd, Jumeira	5-D1	344 5333
Jumeira Health & Beach Club	Sheraton Jumeirah Beach Resort & Towers	Al Sufouh	2-D2	399 5533
Metropolitan Beach Club	Metropolitan Resort & Beach Club Htl	Marsa Dubai	2-E2	399 5000
Oasis Beach Club	Oasis Beach Hotel	Al Sufouh	2-D2	315 4029
Pavilion Marina & Sports Club	Jumeirah Beach Hotel	Umm Suqeim	4-B2	406 8800
Ritz-Carlton Health Club & Spa	The Ritz-Carlton, Dubai	Marsa Dubai	2-E2	399 4000
Health Clubs				
Al Nasr Fitness Centre (m/f separate)	Al Nasr Leisureland	Oud Metha	10-E4	337 1234
Assawan Health Club	Burj Al Arab	Umm Suqeim	4-A1	301 7338
Aviation Club	Aviation Club	Al Garhoud	14-C3	282 4122
Ayoma Health Club	Taj Palace Hotel	Deira	11-D2	223 2222
Big Apple, The	Emirates Towers Boulevard	Trade Centre 1&2	9-C2	330 0000
Body Connection Health Club	Rydges Plaza Hotel	Al Satwa	7-A4	398 2222
Bodylines Jumeira	Jumeira Rotana Hotel	Al Satwa	6-E3	345 5888
Bodylines Leisure & Fitness	Towers Rotana Hotel	Trade Centre 1&2	9-B2	343 8000
Bodylines Leisure & Fitness	Al Bustan Rotana Hotel	Al Garhoud	14-E3	705 4571
Club Olympus	Hyatt Regency Hotel	Deira	8-D2	209 6802
Club, The	Dubai International Hotel Apartments	Trade Centre 1&2	9-D2	306 5050
Colosseum	Zabeel Road, Montana Building	Zabeel, Karama	10-E3	337 2755
Creek Health Club	Sheraton Dubai Hotel & Towers	Creekside, Deira	11-C1	207 1711
Dimensions Health & Fitness Center	Metropolitan Hotel	Jct 2, Shk Zayed Rd	5-C4	407 6704
Fitness Centre	World Trade Centre Hotel	Trade Centre 1&2	10-A2	306 1139
Fitness Planet (mixed & ladies)	Al Hana Centre	Al Satwa	7-A4	398 9030
Griffins Health Club	JW Marriott	Deira	12-A3	607 7755
Gym 2000 (9 months)	Dubai Creek Golf & Yacht Club	Al Garhoud	14-C2	205 4567
Health Club, The	Emirates Towers Hotel	Trade Centre 1&2	9-C2	330 0000
Hiltonia Health Club	Hilton Dubai Jumeirah	Al Sofouh	2-D2	399 1111
Inter Fitness Dubai	Hotel Inter-Continental Dubai	Deira	8-C4	222 7171
Le Mirage Dubai	Le Meridien Dubai	Al Garhoud	14-E3	702 2430
Lifestyle Health Club	City Centre Residence	Deira	14-D1	603 8825
Nautilus Fitness Centre	Crowne Plaza	Trade Centre 1&2	9-D2	331 4055
Nautilus Health Centre	Metropolitan Palace Hotel	Deira	11-D2	227 0000
Pharoahs (mixed & ladies)	Pyramids	Umm Hurair (2)	13-D2	324 0000
Platinum Club	Atrium Suites	Hor Al Anz	12-C4	266 9990
VIP Gym	Near Capitol Hotel	Satwa	7-A2	345 2208
Willow Stream	Fairmont Hotel	Trade Centre 1&2	9-E1	332 5555
Golf Clubs				
Dubai Country Club		Al Awir Rd	17-B3	333 1155
Dubai Creek Golf & Yacht Club		Al Garhoud	14-C2	295 6000
Emirates Golf Club		Emirates Hill	3-A3	380 2222
Montgomerie Golf Club		Emirates Hill	2-E4	380 1333
Nad Al Sheba Golf & Racing Club		Nad Al Sheba	17-A3	336 3666
Jebel Ali Golf Course	Jebel Ali Hotel & Golf Resort	Jebel Ali	1-A1	804 8058

Membership Rates					Gym						Activity				Relaxation				
Male	Female	Couple	Family	Non-Members (peak)	Treadmills	Exercise bikes	Step machines	Rowing machines	Free weights	Resistance machines	Tennis courts	Swimming Pool	Squash courts	Aerobics/Dance Exercise	Massage	Sauna	Jacuzzi	Plunge pool	Steam room
8,000	8,000	11,000	12,500	–	8	6	6	3	✔	16	4FL	✔	2	✔	✔	✔	✔	✔	✔
3,300	2,200	5,500	5,500+	80	1	1	1	1	✔	✔	4FL	✔	2	–	✔	✔	✔	–	✔
6,000	6,000	9,000	9,000	–	8	3	1	1	✔	18	4FL	✔	–	✔	✔	✔	✔	✔	✔
5,000	3,500	–	6,750	–	5	5	2	1	✔	13	2FL	✔	✔	✔	✔	–	–	✔	✔
8,250	8,250	11,250	13,800	150	8	9	3	2	✔	12	7FL	✔	3	✔	✔	✔	✔	✔	✔
4,800	4,800	6,500	On req.	80	3	4	3	2	✔	11	2FL	✔	2	✔	✔	✔	–	✔	✔
5,000	4,000	6,000	6,500	–	3	2	1	1	✔	✔	2FL	✔	0		✔		✔	✔	
3,800	3,800	4,500	5,500	80	2	2	2	1	✔	✔	1FL	✔	–	–	✔	✔	✔	✔	✔
7,000	7,000	9,200	10,800	200	9	8	2	3	✔	23	7FL	✔	3	✔	✔	✔	✔	✔	✔
10,700	10,700	13,500	16,000	–	3	6	3	2	✔	10	4FL	✔	2		✔	✔	✔	✔	✔
1,150	920	–	–	–	4	5	–	–	✔	4	✔	✔	✔	–	–	✔	–	–	–
On req.	On req.	On req.	On req.	–	5	8	3	2	✔	15	–	✔	1	✔	✔	✔	✔	✔	✔
5,000	3,750	6,500	7,500	–	10	4	3	2	✔	14	6FL	✔	2	✔	✔	✔	✔	✔	✔
3,500	3,000	5,250	–	85	5	3	1	1	✔	7	–	✔	–	✔	✔	✔	✔	✔	✔
2,600	2,600	3,900	–	25	8	3	4	2	✔	11	–	✔	–	✔	–	–	–	–	✔
2,500	2,500	3,800	4,000	–	2	2	2	2	✔	9	–	✔	–	–	✔	✔	✔	✔	✔
1,900	1,600	2,500	2,850	50	1	1	–	–	✔	2	–	✔		–	–	✔		✔	–
2,600	2,000	3,600	4,000	55	2	1	2	1	✔	6	–	✔	–	✔	✔	✔	✔	✔	✔
3,250	2,750	4,250	4,750	75	6	6	2	2	✔	9	3	✔	2	✔	✔	✔	✔	✔	✔
3,000	1,800	3,900	On req.	60	7	4	2	2	✔	10	3	✔	2	✔	✔	✔	✔	✔	✔
3,500	3,000	4,500	5,700	35	6	3	2	2	✔	12	4FL	✔	3	✔	–	✔	✔	✔	✔
On req.	On req.	On req.	On req.	–	5	3	–	–	✔	10	–	✔	–	–	✔	✔	✔	✔	✔
2,500	2,500	3,400	4,500	50	2	2	2	–	✔	1	1	✔	–	–	✔	✔	–	✔	✔
2,400	2,000	3,500	4,000	55	6	4	2	2	✔	19	1	✔	–	✔	✔	✔	✔	✔	✔
2,100	2,100	3,000	–	25	5	6	4	4	✔	10	–	✔	1	–	✔	✔	–	–	✔
2,350	2,350	–	–	30	7	7	5	2	✔	25	–	–	–	✔	✔	✔	✔	✔	✔
3,575	2,530	5,060	On req.	80	7	6	4	2	✔	4	–	✔	2	✔	✔	✔	✔	✔	✔
2,000	2,000	2,750	3,750	70	4	3	2	3	✔	13	7 FL	✔	3	✔	✔	✔	✔	✔	✔
4,000	4,000	6,500	On req.	100	8	3	2	2	✔	11	–	✔	–	–	✔	✔	✔	✔	✔
4,500	4,500	6,000		100	4	2	2	2	✔	2	–	✔	–		✔	✔	–	–	✔
4,300	3,500	5,800	–	80	5	3	2	2	✔	10	1FL	✔	2	✔	✔	✔	✔	✔	✔
4,750	3,600	6,250	7,250	100	10	4	2	3	✔	22	3FL	✔	2	✔	✔	✔	✔	✔	✔
2,600	2,600	4,160	4,160	50	6	5	2	1	✔	14	1FL	✔	2	✔	✔	✔	–	✔	✔
3,200	3,200	4,600	On req.	50	2	4	1	2	✔	15	–	✔	2	✔	✔	✔	✔	✔	✔
3,750	2,750	5,000	–	–	4	2	2	2	✔	13	–	✔			✔	✔	✔	✔	✔
5,500	5,500	8,000	10,000	–	7	8	4	2	✔	18	3	✔	2	✔	✔	✔	✔	✔	✔
3,000	3,000	5,000	–	–	10	9	2	2	✔	36	–		–	✔	✔	✔	✔	–	✔
On req.	On req.	On req.	On req.	–	5	11	1	1	✔	38	–	–	–	–	–	✔	✔	–	–
4,500	4,500	7,500	–	150	5	4	2	2	✔	13	–	✔	–	✔	✔	✔	✔	✔	✔
3,350	2,200	–	5,350	60	4	3	2	2	✔	✔	7FL	✔	3	✔	–	–	–	–	
4,500	4,500	6,500	6,500	–	4	3	2	2	✔	13	–	✔	–	–	✔	–	–	✔	✔
13,000	10,000	On Req.	17,500	–	4	4	3	2	✔	10	4	✔	2	✔	✔	–	–	–	–
12,500	12,500	16,500	16,500	–	–	–	–	–	–	–	–	–	–	–	–	–	–	–	–
On Req.	On Req.	On Req.	On Req.	–	–	–	–	–	–	–	–	–	–	–	–	–	–	–	–
On Req.	On Req.	On Req.	On Req.	–	–	–	–	–	–	–	–	–	–	–	–	–	–	–	–

Expand Your Horizons

Now that you actually have the time to do it, why not take that painting or flower arranging class you've always dreamed of? Or, since you've come all this way, think about taking a course in Arabic or one of the many other languages available. Dubai has a surprising range of extracurricular activities for eternal students. From workshops or month long courses to special interest groups, learning opportunities are abundant and flexible enough to fit your schedule.

Art Classes

Other options → Art Galleries [p.174]

Café Ceramique

Location → Town Centre · Beach Rd, Jumeira | 344 7331
Hours → 08:00 - 24:00
Web/email → www.cafeceramique.com | Map Ref → 5-E1

Please refer to the Café Ceramique review under Cafes & Coffee Shops – Going Out Section.

Creative Modern Center

Location → Opp Audio Workshop · Al Rashidiya | 285 9925
Hours → 08:30 - 13:00 16:00 - 19:30
Web/email → mdrnart@emirates.net.ae | Map Ref → n/a

Previously known as the Modern Art Centre, the Creative Modern Centre offers mothers and children the chance to be creative in an arty atmosphere. The centre has a variety of courses, including painting, drawing, calligraphy, sculpture, fabric painting, flower arranging, ceramic flower making and cookery. Mums can also join aerobics, aqua aerobics or karate classes. For children, the centre offers activities for different age groups. Contact the above number for details on prices and class timings.

Dubai International Art Centre

Location → Beach Rd · Jumeira | 344 4398
Hours → 08:30 - 19:00 Thu 8:30 - 16:00
Web/email → artdubai@emirates.net.ae | Map Ref → 6-C2

Fondly known as the 'Arts Centre', this hub of arty-crafty types is a haven of tranquillity. The arty ones are busy doing, while other visitors are looking at displays, using the excellent art shop or library, or just enjoying a drink in the small garden. Classes are offered in over 70 subjects, including all types of painting and drawing, Arabic, dressmaking, etching, pottery, photography, and much more. Each course lasts for six or eight weeks and prices vary according to the materials required. Exhibitions of members' work are held twice a year and there are also regular lectures and demonstrations. Annual membership fees: Dhs.250 but all classes are open to non members for a 30% higher class fee. Family membership Dhs.350; student membership Dhs.60.

Emirates Hobbies Ass'n Art and Crafts

Location → Street 51, Villa 16, beh zoo · Jumeira | 398 0500
Hours → 09:00 - 13:30 16:00 - 21:30
Web/email → helenart@emirates.net.ae | Map Ref → 5-B2

Emirates Hobbies Association Art & Crafts offers a variety of classes/workshops for adults and children (some classes with babysitting facility). Students and artists are offered a full range of art

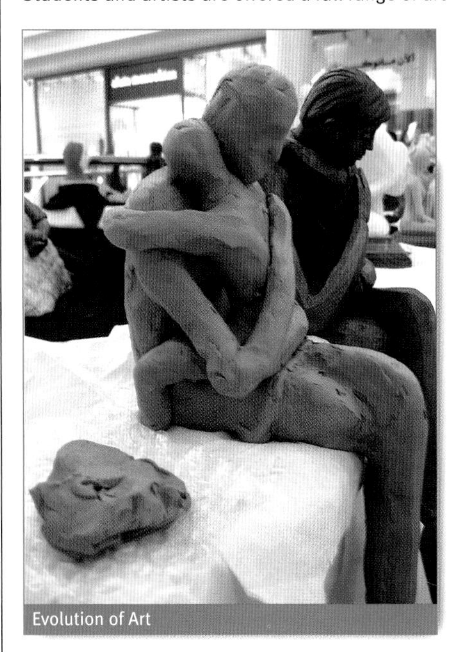

Evolution of Art

supplies, as well as knowledgeable staff to guide them with their art projects and purchases. Schedules are available on request, or visit their centre for further information and advice. First class art/craft products are also on sale to students and members of the public in a helpful and relaxed atmosphere.

Ballet Classes

Other options → Dance Classes [p.324]

Ballet Centre, The

Location → Beh Jumeira Plaza · Jumeira | 344 9776
Hours → Sat - Thu 09:00 - 13:30 15:30 - 18:30
Web/email → n/a | Map Ref → 6-C3

Located in central Jumeira, this dance and exercise centre offers plenty of classes for adults and children. There is a coffee shop and dance wear shop on the premises, but more importantly, five of the dance rooms have wooden sprung floors – vital for this activity. Adult fitness covers step aerobics, aerobics, pilates, yoga and jazzercise. For those interested in dance, you have a choice of ballet, tap, jazz, Irish, salsa, Spanish, ballroom and belly dancing! The centre also offers taekwondo, gymnastics, wing-tsun, guitar, piano and singing lessons, plus specialist classes for expectant mothers, such as antenatal fitness, yoga and baby massage. Contact the centre for a timetable – there's bound to be something that suits your schedule.

Beauty Training

Other options → Beauty Salons [p.308]

Cleopatra & Steiner Beauty Training Centre

Location → Wafi Residence · Umm Hurair (2) | 324 0250
Hours → 08:30 - 20:00
Web/email → www.cleopatrasteiner.com | Map Ref → 13-D2

This is the Middle East's first internationally endorsed beauty and holistic training centre. Courses vary from basic make up and teenage grooming, to advanced facial treatments and aromatherapy. Opportunities are provided for beginners or those pursuing their hobby, as well as individuals wishing to build on existing qualifications. Lasting from 12 to 250 hours, the courses can help develop career opportunities in beauty salons, sales and consultancy, marketing and/or management and assist self-employed therapists. On completion, participants are awarded an internationally recognised diploma.

Belly Dancing

To learn more about the ancient art of belly button wiggling, please see Dance Classes [p.324].

Birdwatching Groups

Other options → Birdwatching [p.181]

Birdwatching Tours

Location → Various locations | 050 650 3398
Hours → Timings on request
Web/email → www.birding-arabia.com | Map Ref → n/a

Colin Richardson, author of 'The Birds of the United Arab Emirates', has been organising birdwatching trips since 1993. Tours include a visit to Khor Dubai, where thousands of Arctic shore birds and flamingos winter; Umm Al Quwain with its crab plovers and Socotra cormorants; Khor Kalba, where the rare and threatened white-collared kingfisher is found, and irrigated fields where Indian rollers, bee-eaters and migrants are abundant. Trips are easy going and can be custom-made. Some previous birdwatching experience is an advantage. Prices start at Dhs.250 per person.

Bird Watching in the Emirates

Emirates Bird Records Committee

Location → N/a | 050 642 4358
Hours → Timings on request
Web/email → www.uaeinteract.com | Map Ref → UAE-A4

The Emirates Bird Records Committee collates information about the country's birds and maintains the UAE checklist. A weekly round up of sightings and a monthly bird report are available via email. For further details, contact the Committee Chairman, Simon Aspinall on the above number.

Bridge

Country Club Bridge

Location → Country Club · Al Awir Rd | 333 1155
Hours → 20:00 - 23:00
Web/email → n/a | Map Ref → 17-B3

This group plays on the last Saturday of the month at Dubai Country Club and at a different location every Monday, from 20:00 - 23:00. You don't have to be a member of the club to play bridge here, and newcomers are always welcome. For more information, contact jeffann@sahmnet.ae.

Dubai Bridge Club

Location → Country Club · Al Awir Rd | 050 658 6985
Hours → Mon 20:00 - 23:30
Web/email → olavo786bridge@yahoo.com | Map Ref → 17-B3

The Dubai Bridge Club was formed in 1977 with the main objective of promoting the game in the UAE. It has no clubhouse or premises and operates on a non profit making basis, with committee members serving in an honorary capacity. The club has a multitude of nationalities, with members from the UAE, Poland, Iran, France, India, Syria and the UK, to name a few. Tournaments are monthly. For more information contact Olavo D'Sousa on 050 658 6985.

Dubai Ladies Bridge Club

Location → Nad al Sheba · Nad Al Sheba | 395 4070
Hours → See timings below
Web/email → n/a | Map Ref → 17-A3

Ladies only bridge mornings are held at 09:00 on Sundays and Wednesdays at the Nad Al Sheba Millennium stand. For further details, contact Marzie Polad or Jan Irvine (398 0727).

Chess

Other options → Scrabble [p.335]

Dubai Chess & Culture Club

Location → Nr Al Shabab Club · Hor Al Anz | 296 6664
Hours → 10:00 - 13:00 16:00 - 22:00 Fri 17:00 - 23:00
Web/email → www.dubaichess.com | Map Ref → 12-C3

As its name suggests, this club is involved in all aspects of chess and cultural programmes. Members can play chess at the club seven nights a week and competitions are organised on a regular basis. International competitions are also promoted including the Dubai International Open, Emirates Open and Dubai Junior Open, attracting representatives from Asia, Arabia and Europe. Members can take classes with the professional chess school. Facilities at the club include an Internet room, cafeteria and a snooker/billiard room.

Costs: *Annual membership: Dhs100 for Nationals; Dhs200 for expats.*

Chess

Cookery Classes

Avid cooking fans, fret not, because cooking classes do exist... you just need to know where to find them. There seems to be little information on regular classes, however, check out the hotels. Many of them offer specialist classes throughout the year. Keep yourself up to date with weekly/monthly publications. Alternatively, surf the net and you will find plenty of online options, some with entertaining video footage.

Dance Classes

Whether it's the Polka, Salsa or Bharatnatyam, all tastes are catered for in Dubai, so grab your dancing shoes and move those hips! Dance has a universal appeal that breaks down barriers and inhibitions, as well as being great exercise for all ages and standards. In addition to the following organisations that are dedicated to dance, some health clubs, restaurants and bars hold weekly sessions in flamenco, salsa, samba, jazz dance, ballroom, and so on. Some health clubs also offer dance based aerobic classes that are good fun, surprisingly energetic and totally exhausting!

Al Naadi Club

Location → Al Ghurair City · Deira | 205 5229
Hours → See timings below
Web/email → www.alghuraircentre.com | Map Ref → 11-D1

Ballet lessons leading to Royal Academy of Dancing examinations are taught by Sally Bigland, who also teaches Latin American dance to adults at 20:00 on Saturdays. Saraswathi Pathy teaches Indian dance on Mondays and Wednesdays from 17:00 - 19:00. Taekwondo is taught by Munir Gharwi every Thursday from 13:30 - 14:30 for boys and girls aged six and older, while karate is held for an hour at 17:00 every Sunday and Tuesday. Tennis and squash is available 7 days a week.

Costs: *Latin American dance and ballet: Dhs.400 per term of 12 sessions. Indian dance: Dhs.200 per month. Taekwondo: Dhs.240 per term of eight classes. Karate: Dhs.200 per month.*

Ceroc Dubai

Location → Various locations | 050 428 3061
Hours → Timings on request
Web/email → www.cerocdubai.com | Map Ref → n/a

Ceroc is an exiting modern dance from the UK and is a great way to socialise and keep fit. It can be danced to a wide range of music, from the latest club hits to the sounds of yesteryear, and footwork is kept to a minimum, so it's easy to learn. The evening starts with a beginners' class led by a UK champion instructor, followed by intermediates and finally the freestyle section where you can practice all your moves. It's pure dance addiction! There's no need to bring a partner, since everyone rotates to dance with everyone else, and no special footwear or clothing is required. Call Des for further information.

Dance Centre, The

Location → Various locations | 286 8775
Hours → 09:00 - 17:00
Web/email → www.dance-centre-dubai.com | Map Ref → n/a

The Dance Centre offers classes in ballet, ISTD tap, jazz, modern and Irish dance to children from the age of three years and up, as well as GCSE dancing for ages 14 years and upwards. Studios and classes run in several locations around Dubai. The centre is affiliated to the Royal Academy of Dance in London and hence is able to enter students for their RAD graded examinations each year. For further information contact the above number or 050 624 2956.

Indian Classical Dances

Location → Nr MMI & Pioneer Bld · Al Karama | 335 4311
Hours → 16:30 - 20:00
Web/email → www.nrityaupadesh.com | Map Ref → 10-C3

Indian classical dances have their own unique style, with fast rhythmic footwork and facial expressions. Mrs Geetha Krishnan, a reputed Bharatnatyam and Kuchipudi teacher, holds classes for anyone aged six years and up. On completion of the course, which takes around four years, the pupil performs her Arangetam – a presentation in front of reputed maestros and critics. Mrs Krishnan also choreographs classical and folk dances, plus fashion shows, when her students get a chance to exhibit their talents. She is available for event organising on a freelance basis. A short term workshop will be conducted regularly. Advanced individual classes for only expressions (abhinaya) are also conducted.

Leaders Dance Club

Location → Btn Mazaya & Safestway · Shk Zayed Rd | 343 3288
Hours → 10:00 - 22:00
Web/email → leadclub@emirates.net.ae | Map Ref → 5-D3

This ballroom and Latin dance club offers a stylish choice of 15 kinds of dance for everyone and for all ages from five and above. Everything from tango or waltz to rumba, cha-cha, salsa, merengue, paso doble, jive, samba, quick step or belly dancing is covered, as well as a new exercise called 'dance fitness'. Courses can be in groups or privately according to timings and your choice of dance.

Savage Garden

Location → Capitol Hotel · Al Satwa | 346 0111
Hours → 18:00 - 03:00
Web/email → caphotel@emirates.net.ae | Map Ref → 7-A2

Savage Garden is the venue for salsa and merengue dance classes, run by Leonardo and Andrea, to the sounds of the live Colombian band and DJ. The classes are offered daily from 20:00 - 21:00 for beginners and 21:00 - 22:00 for more advanced salseros. Afterwards you can stay behind and practice your moves. The charge is Dhs.35 per hour, with a package of ten classes offered at a discounted rate of Dhs.300.

Desert Driving Courses

Gliding over rolling sand dunes can feel a bit like flying on air, but getting stuck on a dune will feel rather sandy and sweaty. For those who want to master the art of driving a 4 wheel drive in the desert without getting stuck (and getting yourself out when you do!), several organisations offer desert driving courses with instruction from professional drivers. Both individual and group tuition per vehicle is available. Vehicles are provided on some courses, while others require participants to take their own means of transport. Alternatively, you may be able to hire a vehicle for an additional cost. Courses vary widely, but expect to pay around Dhs.250 - 300 for the day. Picnic lunches and soft drinks may be included.

Al Futtaim Training Centre

Location → Nr Dubai Municipality Garage · Rashidiya | 285 0455
Hours → Fri 08:00 - 17:00
Web/email → training@alfuttaim.ae | Map Ref → n/a

The desert campus training course gives off-road driving enthusiasts knowledge of and experience venturing into the desert. It starts with a three hour classroom session covering the basics of your vehicle, with tips on protecting it from breaking down, overheating, changing tyres in the sand, negotiating sand dunes and other driving techniques. This is followed by five hours of supervised off-road driving where you take your own 4 WD up and down the dunes. (Also known as the Jeep UAE Off-Road Driving Academy.)

Cost: *Dhs.300 per person, and Dhs.450 for two people in one car, which includes an off-road driving manual and snacks.*

Desert Rangers

Location → Jct 3, Shk Zayed Rd | 340 2408
Hours → 09:00 - 18:00
Web/email → www.desertrangers.com | Map Ref → 4-B4

Desert Rangers offers lessons for anyone wanting to learn how to handle a car in the desert. If you are just starting, introductory days teach you the basics of venturing off-road, including how to negotiate easy dunes, how to avoid getting stuck and how to get out of it if you do! Advanced days involve guided drives to more challenging areas of the desert where you can learn how to get yourself out of bigger trouble. Courses are available for individuals or groups, and since programmes are flexible, they can be combined with barbecues and other activities to make your ideal day.

Emirates Driving Institute

Location → Beh Al Bustan Centre · Al Qusais | 263 1100
Hours → 09:00 - 16:00 (desert) 09:00 - 17:00 (defensive)
Web/email → www.edi-uae.com | Map Ref → 15-D2

The Emirates Driving Institute offers a one day desert driving course for Dhs.175 from Sat to Thurs and Dhs.200 on a Friday, which includes lunch. Equipment can be supplied, if required. The institute also offers a one day defensive driving course for Dhs.300 from Sat to Thurs and Dhs.350 on a Friday. Participants receive certificates on completion of all courses. Training is conducted on all kinds of light and heavy vehicles, trucks, buses and motorcycles. Branches: Al Aweer (320 0989); Satwa (331 3200); Lamcy (334 1442); Al Quoz (340 0449).

Off-Road Adventures

Location → Metropolitan Htl · Jct 2, Shk Zayed Rd | 343 2288
Hours → 08:00 - 20:00
Web/email → www.arabiantours.com | Map Ref → 5-C4

The great outdoors is an environment that suits Karim Rushdy, the owner of Off-Road Adventures. With 16 years off-road experience in the UAE, he is well equipped to handle the portfolio of thrills generated by his safari tours, and focuses on three factors; safety, exclusivity and personnel expertise. The company caters to individuals and small groups, and the range of activities can be stretched even wider, as Karim believes that it is possible to tailor make a tour to suit any requirement (within reason!). In addition to off-road driving courses, the company arranges weekly fun drives, treasure hunts, camping and trekking tours, camel safaris and sand boarding.

Voyagers Xtreme

Location → Dune Centre · Al Satwa | 345 4504
Hours → 09:00 - 18:00
Web/email → www.turnertraveldubai.com | Map Ref → 6-E3

Under the expert guidance of Jochen Neugebauer, Voyagers Xtreme offers lessons for anyone wishing to handle a 4 WD in the desert. The one day introductory course covers all the basic skills required for off-roading; the dos and don'ts, negotiating dunes, how to avoid getting stuck and what to do when you are (recovery techniques). You're given a walkie-talkie to enable you to learn as you drive (don't worry, you won't be the only one saying 'I'm stuck'!). If, like many clients, you're bitten by the off-roading bug, more advanced courses can be arranged. Courses are available for individuals or groups. Take your own vehicle or hire from Voyagers Xtreme.

Drama Groups

Dubai Drama Group

Location → Country Club · Al Awir Rd | 333 1155
Hours → Timings on request
Web/email → www.dubaidramagroup.org | Map Ref → 17-B3

The Dubai Drama Group has been entertaining Dubai for twenty years, and is still going strong. Members range from those on the stage (actors, singers, dancers) to those behind the scenes (directors, costumiers, painters, gaffers, etc.). This amateur dramatic society stages four productions each year: the infamous pantomime at Christmas and three other plays which may be anything from farce to thrillers and one act plays. Everyone is welcome at rehearsals and they always need help in all areas of stagecraft. Visit the Webpage or contact the Secretary on the above email for timings.

Annual membership: *Dhs.100, which entitles you to a monthly newsletter and a lot of hard work and fun.*

Environmental Groups

People don't generally chain themselves to palms or dunes here, but over the last few years, environmental issues have gradually become more important in the UAE. However, as is always the case, far more needs to be done by all sections of the community.

Leading the way, HH Sheikh Mohammed bin Rashid Al Maktoum, Crown Prince of Dubai, has established a prestigious international environmental award in honour of HH Sheikh Zayed bin Sultan Al Nahyan, President of the UAE. The award, which was first presented in 1998, goes to an individual or organisation for distinguished work carried out on behalf of the environment.

On an everyday level, there are increasing numbers of glass and plastic recycling points around the city. The Khaleej Times sponsors bins for collecting newspapers for recycling; these are easily spotted at a variety of locations, but mainly outside shopping centres.

Camel Racing

If you decide to go and watch a camel race, don't be surprised to see underage jockeys at the helm. Children from Pakistan, Sri Lanka, India and Bangladesh, who are as young as four, are often sold by their parents into this trade. Strapped into saddles by ropes or velcro, the lightest boys are the hot favourites, as they have the most chances of winning. In 1993, the UAE banned children under eleven from the circuit, but sadly, this law remains largely ignored to date.

In addition, the government of Dubai is gradually taking action with school educational programmes and general awareness campaigns. However, overall, there seems to be very little done to persuade the average person to be more active environmentally, for instance, by encouraging the reduction of littering.

If you want to do something more active, contact one of the environmental groups that operate in the Emirates. These range from the Emirates Environmental Group to the flagship Arabian Leopard Trust. They always need volunteers and funds; go on, do your bit!

Dubai Natural History Group

Location → Jumeira English Speaking Sch · Jumeira | 349 4816
Hours → Timings on request
Web/email → na | Map Ref → 5-B3

Dubai Natural History Group (DNHG) was formed in 1986 to further knowledge and interest in the flora, fauna, geology, archaeology and natural environment of the Emirates. Meetings are held on the first Sunday of each month and are free of charge. These usually take the form of lectures by local or visiting speakers on a range of natural history topics, mostly involving the UAE. Regular field trips are arranged and the group maintains a modest library of natural history publications, which are available for members to use. Members receive a monthly newsletter, The Gazelle, which

covers news, articles, future activities and those of related groups in Abu Dhabi and Al Ain. Annual membership is Dhs.100 per family; Dhs.50 for individuals. Contact: Valerie Chalmers, Vice Chairman and Secretary on the above number; Gary Feulner, Chairman (330 3600); or write to PO Box 9234, Dubai.

Emirates Environmental Group

Location → Crowne Plaza Htl, 7th flr · Shk Zayed Rd | 331 8100
Hours → 09:00 - 18:00 Thu 09:00 - 14:00
Web/email → www.eeg-uae.org | Map Ref → 9-D2

This is a voluntary, non governmental organisation devoted to protecting the environment through education, action programmes and community involvement. The group started in September 1991 and has since grown considerably. Its membership includes everyone from individuals to corporate members, schools and government organisations. Activities include regular free evening lectures on environmental topics, and special events such as recycling collections and cleanup campaigns. Volunteers are always needed and everyone is welcome. Join the Emirates Environmental group in its journey towards sustainable development! Annual membership: adults Dhs.50; students Dhs.15 - 30. Corporate membership is also available. For further information, phone, fax (332 8500), visit their Website, or email.

Flower Arranging

Other options → Flowers [p.224]

Ikebana Sogetsu Flower Arranging Classes

Location → Hamriya, Opp Syrian Consulate · Deira | 262 0282
Hours → Timings on request
Web/email → fujikozarouni@hotmail.com | Map Ref → 12-C3

Ikebana means the art of Japanese flower arranging. It is seen as a way of life; an artistic way to enrich our lives and the environment with all the glories of plant life. There are numerous schools of Ikebana, each following a particular set of rules and arrangement techniques, but without losing sight of the fundamentals of the art. Classes in Dubai are held by Fujiko Zarouni, a qualified teacher from Japan. In addition to creating wonderful displays for the home, teachers and students who form the Ikebana Sogetsu group do demonstrations, displays, open days, and so on.

Gardening

Gardening

Other options → Garden Centres [p.226]

Dubai Gardening Group

Location → Jumeira | 344 5999
Hours → See timings below
Web/email → bomi@emirates.net.ae | Map Ref → 5-C2

The Dubai Gardening Group was established in October 2000, taking over from The Gardening Group. Members of the group aim to share their love and knowledge of gardening in a friendly and informal atmosphere. During the cooler months, trips to greenhouses, nurseries and member's gardens are arranged. Speakers, who are experts in various fields, address the meetings and, where possible, give practical demonstrations. Meetings are generally held on a Monday at 16:00. For further information, contact Deena Motiwalla on the above number.

Kids' Museums

Kiddly-winks have plenty to keep them occupied in Dubai, even in the summer months when outside activities are a little too hot to handle. There are numerous play sites and activities devoted specifically to children. From the thrill of 'discovering' dinosaur bones in the sand to visiting a planetarium or the just plain goofy fun of a bouncy castle, amusement for the little ones is never far away.

For further details of what there is for kids in Dubai and the Northern Emirates to do, refer to the *Family Explorer* (formerly *Kids' Explorer*). This handbook offers a wealth of information for the whole family, not only on what there is to do in the area, but also on 'how' to live here. Covering everything from medical care, education and birthday parties to eating out and activities divided into indoor and outdoor sections to make the most of facilities during the hot summer months, the *Family Explorer* has all the answers.

Children's City

Location → Creekside Park · Umm Hurair (2) | 334 0808
Hours → 09:00 - 22:00 Fri 16:00 - 22:00
Web/email → www.childrencity.ae | Map Ref → 14-A1

Opened in 2002, Children's City is an educational project providing kids with their own learning zone and amusement facilities by providing hands-on experiences of the theoretical subjects that they learn at school. Children's City is aimed at 5 - 12 year olds, although items of interest are included for toddlers and teenagers. Highlights include a planetarium with a 180 degree screen. A mockup of the front of an aircraft is found in the Flying Gallery, plus there are natural and cultural galleries nearby.

The Colourful Children's City

Sharjah Science Museum

Location → Halwan, Nr TV station · Sharjah | 06 566 8777
Hours → 09:00 - 14:00 15:30 - 20:30
Web/email → www.shjmuseum.gov.ae | Map Ref → UAE-C2

See the review under Museums – Out of Town [p.331].

Language Schools

Alliance Française

Location → Opp American Hospital · Umm Hurair (2) | 335 8712
Hours → 09:00 - 13:00 16:00 - 20:00
Web/email → afdxb@emirates.net.ae | Map Ref → 13-E1

Founded in Paris in 1883, the Alliance Française is a non profit organisation supported by the French Government, with the goal of promoting French language and culture. Established in Dubai in 1982, it is the ideal place to learn the French language. Special morning classes are available for ladies, afternoon classes for children and evening classes for everybody. Adult classes are also held in the evenings in Sharjah at the French School, Lycée Georges Pompidou.

Term: *September – June. However, an intensive course is held during the summer for both adults and children.*

Arabic Language Centre

Location → Trade Centre · Trade Centre 1&2 | 308 6036
Hours → 08:30 - 18:30
Web/email → alc@dwtc.com | Map Ref → 10-A2

A division of the Dubai World Trade Centre, this language school was established in 1980 to teach Arabic as a foreign language. Courses, from beginner to advanced levels, are held five times a year and each course lasts 30 hours. Specialist courses can be designed to meet the requirements of the hotel, banking, hospital, motor and electronic industries, while private courses offer individual tuition and flexible timings.

Location: *Hall 4, Level 1 of the DWTC exhibition complex.*

Hours: *Sessions are held at 09:00 - 11:00, 13:30 - 15:30 and 18:15 - 20:15.*

Fees: *Dhs.1,600 (inclusive of all materials, which are provided by the centre).*

Berlitz

Location → Nr Dubai Zoo · Beach Rd, Jumeira | 344 0034
Hours → 08:00 - 20:00 Thu 08:00 - 14:00
Web/email → www.berlitz.co.ae | Map Ref → 6-B2

For more than a century Berlitz has been operating worldwide and the Berlitz Method has helped more than 41 million people acquire a new language. A variety of courses is offered and they can be customised to fit specific requirements, such as 'English for banking' or 'technical English'. Instruction is in private or small groups, with

morning classes for women and special children's classes (minimum age four years) on Thursdays. Additional training includes translation and interpretation, self-teaching audio and videotapes, books and interactive CD-ROM. Contact the above number for additional information or 06 572 1115 for the Sharjah branch.

British Council

Location → Nr Maktoum Bridge · Umm Hurair (2) | 337 0109
Hours → 08:00 - 20:00
Web/email → www.britishcouncil.org-uae | Map Ref → 11-A3

The British Council has teaching centres in Dubai, Abu Dhabi, Sharjah and Ras Al Khaimah, offering English language courses for adults, children (3 - 16 year olds) and company groups. There are also business English courses aimed at professionals who need to improve their language skills for the workplace. In addition, the Council offers a range of exam preparation courses for IELTS, Cambridge English exams, Preliminary English Test (PET), First Certificate in English (FCE) and Business English Certificates.

Classes: *Held daily (during the summer or Ramadan), or two or three times a week, depending on ability. Fees: English courses (36 hours) Dhs.1,650. For more details call the above number or toll free 800 4066.*

Dar El Ilm School of Languages

Location → Exhibitn Hall 4 · Trade Centre 1&2 | 331 0221
Hours → 09:00 - 19:00 Thu 09:00 - 13:00
Web/email → darelilm@emirates.net.ae | Map Ref → 9-A2

Now entering its fifteenth year, Dar El Ilm offers language courses to students of all ages and abilities, with the emphasis on making learning fun. The company strives to provide a professional yet personal approach. Adult and child tuition is offered in English, French, German, Italian and Spanish as well as Arabic for kids. Courses last 21 hours and are run six times during the academic year. Extra tuition is available for help with schoolwork, etc. There is also a summer school. Fees start at Dhs.1,200.

Location: *World Trade Centre, Exhibition Hall 4, First floor.*

Polyglot Language Institute

Location → Al Masaeed Bld, beh Inter-Con · Deira | 222 3429
Hours → 09:00 - 13:00 16:30 - 21:00
Web/email → www.polyglot.co.ae | Map Ref → 8-C4

Opened in 1969, the Polyglot Language Institute offers year round courses in modern languages, secretarial and computer skills for individuals and companies. Courses offered include: Arabic, general English, business English, TOEFL preparation, French, German, office skills, typing, secretarial and computer studies. There's also a high quality translation service in four languages. Each course lasts 6 - 10 weeks and consists of classes three times a week in the mornings or evenings. All books and materials are provided. Contact the above number or 222 2596 for further information. Location: Fourth floor, Al Masaeed building, above the Iran Insurance Company.

Costs: *Courses are either Dhs.1,350 or Dhs.1,500.*

Libraries

Other options → Books [p.214]

Alliance Française

Location → Opp American Hospital · Umm Hurair (2) | 335 8712
Hours → 09:00 - 13:00 16:00 - 20:00
Web/email → afdxb@emirates.net.ae | Map Ref → 13-E1

The Alliance Française multimedia library has over 10,000 books (including a children's section), plus 50 daily, weekly and monthly French newspapers and magazines, 1,800 videos, 100 CD-ROMs and, very soon, a collection of DVDs.

Archie's Library

Location → Pyramid Bld, Nr Burjuman · Al Karama | 396 7924
Hours → 10:00 - 13:30 17:00 - 22:00
Web/email → abcl180@hotmail.com | Map Ref → 10-E1

Forty-five thousand books, all in English, and you don't have to buy a single one! Archie's Library is stocked up on fiction, non fiction, classics, cookery, health and fitness and management. A vast selection of children's books and comics are also available, plus an array of the latest magazines. The annual membership fee of Dhs.75 (and a Dhs.100 refundable deposit) entitles you to borrow any four books for ten days, and the renewal fee is Dhs.50. The reading charge varies between Dhs.1 - 4. There is also a branch in Sharjah (06 572 5716).

British Council Library

Location → Nr Maktoum Bridge · Umm Hurair (2) | 337 0109
Hours → 09:00 - 20:00
Web/email → www.britishcouncil.org-uae | Map Ref → 11-A3

The British Council is well known for its English courses and for being the centre for UK-based

examinations and assessments. The library is used by students who attend the courses, but is also open to the public; non members may use the reference collection. The service includes a lending library with a wide selection of fiction and non fiction materials, as well as videos and CD-ROMs, a self-access centre for students of English and an education information unit for those wishing to study in the UK. An Internet unit is open to the public.

Membership fees: *the annual adult membership fee of Dhs.350 entitles you to borrow two books for two weeks, plus one CD-ROM and two videos for one week.*

Juma Al Majid Cultural & Heritage Centre

Location → Nr Dubai Cinema · Deira | 262 4999
Hours → 08:00 - 19:30
Web/email → n/a | Map Ref → 12-A4

Established in 1991, this is a non profit reference library and research institute. With an emphasis on Islam, the collection includes 500,000 items of cultural media with topics ranging from heritage to current world issues, plus 3,000 periodicals and out of print publications. These are mainly in Arabic, but there are also some items in English, French, German, Persian and other languages. The library and private collections are open to anyone interested in social and human sciences. Books cannot be taken home, but you are able to use the reading room. There's no fee to use the library.

Old Library, The

Location → Int Art Centre · Beach Rd, Jumeira | 344 6480
Hours → 10:00 - 12:00 16:00 - 18:00
Web/email → orford@emirates.net.ae | Map Ref → 6-C2

The Old Library is the oldest English language library serving the expatriate community in Dubai (established 1969). It is non profit organisation run entirely by volunteers. The library has a collection of over 13,000 adult fiction and reference books including specialist sections on Science Fiction, Romance, Biographies and the Middle East. The library also boasts an extremely well stocked children's section. A German language collection has also been added recently. Volunteers and donations of books are always welcome. The library is located in the grounds of the Dubai International Art Centre (Street 35a – off Jumeira Beach Rd near Jumeira Plaza). Annual subscriptions: Family Dhs.100 (may borrow five books at a time); Single Dhs.60 (may borrow two books at a time); Child Dhs.30 (may borrow three children's books at a time).

Public Library

Location → Nr St George Htl · Bur Dubai | 226 2788
Hours → 07:30 - 21:30 Thu 07:30 - 14:30
Web/email → www.dpl.gov.ae | Map Ref → 8-B2

This library was established in 1963, which makes it one of the oldest in the Gulf. It has an English and an Arabic lending section, plus a reading room for magazines and newspapers. Books can be borrowed for two weeks at a time, with a limit of three books per person. For the application form you'll need one passport sized photo and a copy of your passport and visa.

Fees: *Dhs.200 adults (Dhs.150 refundable), with no lending fee.*

Music Lessons

Other options → Dance Classes [p.324]

Crystal Music Institute

Location → Opp Karama Municipal · Al Karama | 396 3224
Hours → 08:30 - 12:00 15:30 - 21:00
Web/email → www.crystalmusicdubai.com | Map Ref → 10-E2

Recognised by the UAE Ministry of Education, the Crystal Music Institute aims to promote fine arts and enhance the cultural horizon of individuals. Courses are mainly for children and are available for a variety of instruments. Classical Indian singing, Bharatnatyam and Western dance, as well as arts and crafts are also offered. Children take periodic examinations, which are conducted by the Trinity College of Music (London), in Dubai. Transport can be provided.

Dubai Music School

Location → Stalco Bld, Zabeel Rd · Al Karama | 396 4834
Hours → 09:00 - 13:00 15:00 - 20:00
Web/email → www.glennperry.net | Map Ref → 10-D3

Dubai Music School (DMS) was founded in 1980 by pop star and producer Glenn Perry to encourage the artistic potential of aspiring musicians. One to one classes are offered in guitar, piano, organ, violin, brass, drums, singing and composing for beginners and serious amateurs. Students take the Trinity College of London examination (there's a 100% pass rate!). The school has a recording studio and will arrange songs for singers and help them to appear on MTV. Lessons last for one hour and students are expected to attend two classes a week. DMS also has centres in Deira and Sharjah.

Transport can be arranged. Costs: monthly prices range from Dhs.200 - 395, plus a Dhs.50 registration fee.

Gymboree Play & Music

Location → Al Mina Rd · Satwa | 345 4422
Hours → 08:00 - 18:00
Web/email → www.gymboree.com | Map Ref → 7-A2

Gymboree offers play and music classes, which combine age appropriate parent or carer interaction, for newborn babies to the under fives. Set in a colourful area, filled with state-of-the-art child-safe gym equipment, classes are designed to build confidence, imagination, social skill and physical abilities. The music classes combine rhythm, movement and use of basic musical instruments while exploring styles of music that change every three weeks.

Gymboree is also a new name for parties and events, hosting everything from birthdays or baby showers to theme parties.

Sruthi Music & Dance Training Center

Location → No 14, Sana Fashion Bld · Al Karama | 337 7398
Hours → 08:00 - 12:00 16:00 - 21:00
Web/email → www.crystalmusicdubai.com | Map Ref → 10-C1

Coaching is available for a variety of instruments including piano, electric organ, guitar, drums, violin (Carnatic), accordion and tabla. Students can enter the Trinity College of Music (London) examinations held in Dubai. Lessons are also offered in Carnatic and Hindustani vocals, as well as dance, from Indian styles such as Bharatnatyam or Kathak to Western dance styles, like disco and jive. Within the arts and crafts programme are sketching, watercolours, oils, pastels and pottery painting. Transport can be provided. For further information visit their Website.

Vocal Studio

Location → Al Rostamani Bld. · Trade Centre 1&2 | 332 9880
Hours → Timings on request
Web/email → doremivs@emirates.net.ae | Map Ref → 9-B2

The Vocal Studio offers vocal instruction and a range of singing related activities for adults and youngsters. The centre offers exam preparation for the ABRSM and Trinity College London syllabuses; grades range from beginner to advanced. Students are also encouraged to take part in performances, such as recitals and concerts, and are also featured in full musical productions with visiting international guest artists under the banner of 'Working with Children for Children' wherein all proceeds go towards various charities in aid of children.

Orchestras/Bands

Other options → Music Lessons [p.333]

Dubai Chamber Orchestra

Location → Various locations | 349 0423
Hours → Timings on request
Web/email → dubaichamberorchestra@hotmail.com | Map Ref → n/a

The Dubai Chamber Orchestra was founded in the summer of 2002 by a group of musicians and music lovers, all residing in the UAE. The players comprise a variety of nationalities, from varied professions, who meet regularly to rehearse in their free time. Their aim is to give at least two public performances a year, and to include works featuring different soloists from within the orchestra. New members are always welcome. For more information, phone 050 625 2936.

Dubai Singers & Orchestra

Location → Various locations | 349 1896
Hours → Timings on request
Web/email → www.dubaisingers.tripod.com | Map Ref → 11-A3

This is a well established group of amateur musicians who meet regularly to make music in a variety of styles, from requiems and serious choral works to Christmas carols, musicals or variety shows. Membership is open to all and no audition is required, except for solo parts – tenors are especially welcome! Members pay Dhs.50 per year and enjoy subsidised music, regular social events and after show parties. The choir meets once, sometimes twice a week; venues and days may vary.

Dubai Wind Band

Location → American High School · Jumeira | 394 1011
Hours → Tue 19:30 - 21:00
Web/email → www.geocities.com/dubaiwindband2002 | Map Ref → 6-A3

This is a group of over 50 woodwind and brass musicians. Abilities range from beginners to Grade 8 plus, and all levels and ages are welcome. The band is in popular demand during December for seasonal singing and music engagements at clubs, malls and hotels. For further information,

contact Peter Hatherley-Greene on the above number or 050 651 8902.

Salsa Dancing

Other options → Belly Dancing [p.321

Salsa Dubai

Location → Various locations | 050 450 7427
Hours → See timings below
Web/email → www.salsanight.com | Map Ref → n/a

Salsa Dubai introduces the worldwide craze of salsa to Dubai. It's fronted by Phil, who has over ten years of salsa experience, including Cuban, New York and Spanish styles. Classes are tailored to the individual, so everyone can progress at their own speed. Members also have the opportunity to learn the famous La Rueda Cuban Dance. Classes are fun and present an excellent mix of dance, music, fitness and socialising, and afterwards members often stay on to dance for fun. Nights out are organised at local Latin venues to enjoy live Latin bands and dance music.

Classes:

- *Ballet Centre: Monday 19:30 - 20:30 (beginners/ intermediates)*
- *Cactus Cantina: Saturday 20:15 - 22:15 (intermediates/ advanced), Sunday 20:15 - 22:15 (beginners/advanced)*
- *Pharaohs Club: Tuesday 20:15 - 22:15 (beginners/ intermediate). For more information, view their Website www.salsanight.com*

Scouts

Scouts Association (British Groups Abroad)

Location → Various locations | na
Hours → See timings below
Web/email → n/a | Map Ref → n/a

The Scout Association aims to encourage the balanced development of youngsters through weekly activities and outings. Different groups are for different ages: Beavers 6 - 8 years; Cubs 8 - 10 ½; Scouts 10½ - 14; Explorer Scouts 14 - 18; and the Scout Network 18 - 25. Activities for the younger groups include games, badge activities, sports, competitions, outings, etc. Leader and assistant positions are voluntary; new recruits are welcome! Three groups operate in Dubai: the 1st Dubai Scout Group (one Cub pack), meets Tues 16:30 - 18:00 at DESS (contact dbcubs@yahoo.com). The 2nd Dubai Scout Group has a Cub pack that meets Sun 17:30 - 19:00 at JESS, and a Beaver colony that meets Mon 15:30 - 16:30 at JESS (contact madscot@emirates.net.ae). Contact dawnltate@hotmail.com for the 3rd Dubai Scout Group (two Beaver colonies, two Cub packs and a Scout troop) meeting times and locations. In Sharjah, the 1st Sharjah Scout Group (one Cub pack), meets Mon 17:00 - 18:30 at Sharjah English School (contact jddymock@emirates.net.ae). For any general enquiries contact UAE District Commissioner Susan Jalili (349 3982).

Scrabble

Other options → Chess [p.322]

Dubai Scrabble League

Location → Al Karama | 050 653 7992
Hours → Mon 19:00
Web/email → alicoabr@emirates.net.ae | Map Ref → 10-D2

If you're looking for a game of scrabble, then this club meets once a week for friendly games between all levels of players. Members include everyone from beginners to world cup players! Regular competitions are held and players also attend competitions as far afield as Bahrain, Singapore and Bangkok. The UAE Open Tournament, held every year in March/April, is the qualifier for the Gulf Open in Bahrain, from which the top ranked UAE player goes to represent the country in the World Cup. For more information, contact Selwyn Lobo.

Singing Lessons

Other options → Music Lessons [p.333]

Dubai Harmony Chorus

Location → Various locations | 348 9395
Hours → Tue 19:30 - 22:00
Web/email → holmqvis@emirates.net.ae | Map Ref → n/a

Imagine creating exciting choral music and being part of a harmonious blending of female voices, barbershop style... and then do it! Barbershop harmonising is different from other kinds of group singing. Finding the right part for your voice is the initial step, but this is simple as any woman of average singing ability, with or without music or vocal training, will find a part that fits her range. Dubai Harmony Chorus boasts a membership of 50 women from many different countries who share a

love of singing. Rehearsals are held weekly. Call Phyllis Holmqvist or Kathy Young for details.

Social Groups

With its cosmopolitan population, it's hardly surprising that Dubai has a large number of social and cultural groups. These are sometimes linked to an embassy or business group and can be an excellent way of meeting likeminded people. However, if your particular interest or background is not covered, now is the perfect opportunity to challenge your organisational skills and start something new – there'll always be someone out there who'll join in! Refer to the Business Section [p.131].

Dubai Adventure Mums

Location → Various locations | 390 4053
Hours → Timings on request
Web/email → www.dubaiadventuremums.com | Map Ref → n/a

This group of women (34 nationalities) from all over Dubai value the excitement of life and the opportunity to meet new people. Once a month they set off without their children or partners to test themselves in new, challenging and fun ways. The aim of this non profit group is to offer women (ages range from 17 to 70) a wide range of recreational activities that they may not have tried before. Instructors offer advice and teach everyone the safest way to enjoy these activities, which all start at beginners' level. Contact Debbie Magee for further information. The group also meets for a monthly coffee morning.

Dubai Manx Society

Location → Various locations | 394 3185
Hours → Timings on request
Web/email → www.dubaimanxsociety.com | Map Ref → n/a

Formed in July 2000 by Gil Costain Salway, the Dubai Manx Society provides a focal point for expats from the Isle of Man and promotes both business and social links between the island and Dubai through its contacts, culture, history and traditions. Membership is primarily for those born on the island or of Manx origin, but the group also welcomes those who have the interests of the island at heart. The society issues an annual newsletter and has traditional Manx/Viking gatherings (Cooish) throughout the year.

Dubai Round Table

Location → Country Club · Al Awir Rd | 050 456 1068
Hours → 1st Mon every month 20:00
Web/email → www.dubaicountryclub.com | Map Ref → 17-B3

Round Table has been around for over 75 years. It is a descendant of Rotary and is now present in over 60 countries, and is further extending this year to three new countries around the world. In the Arabian Gulf there are 11 Tables with a membership that represents a broad cross section of professions within your locality. Also active are Dubai Creek (Indian) Ladies Circle and 41 Club. For further information, please contact Mr. Richard Miles on the above number.

Toastmasters International

Location → Al Futtaim Training Centre · Rashidiya | 507 2383
Hours → Alternate Mondays 19:15 - 21:30
Web/email → www.toastmasters.org | Map Ref → n/a

Toastmasters International is the leading movement devoted to making effective oral communication a worldwide reality. Through member clubs, it helps men and women learn the arts of listening, thinking and speaking – vital skills that enhance leadership potential and foster human understanding. The clubs provide a supportive and positive learning environment, which in turn foster self confidence and personal growth. They have a variety of clubs in the UAE. For further information contact Ms Saira Ranjith on 050 535 7435.

Summer Camps & Courses

Alliance Française

Location → Opp American Hospital · Umm Hurair (2) | 335 8712
Hours → 09:00 - 13:00 16:00 - 20:00
Web/email → afdxb@emirates.net.ae | Map Ref → 13-E1

EduFrance was founded to promote training in France as well as international, educational and scientific exchanges with France. It enhances the French educational system by coordinating with French universities and grandes écoles, and also provides international students with assistance for admission, enrolment, registration, rental, housing, medical, civil liability and repatriation insurance. EduFrance offers a personal welcome at Paris airport and, if required, transfers you to your desired destination on one of France's world class trains.

Going Out

EXPLORER

Going Out

What's new?

Explorer Top Picks
Page 344

You don't have to pore through 400 reviews for the one that offers a breathtaking sunset. And you may as well go easy on your hair, blown dry to a frizz from maniacally flipping through pages to find a sushi joint. The genius souls at Explorer have made your life easier by categorising eateries under cuisines and moods. Go to the table at the beginning of this section and look under romantic for the best spot to woo your sweetheart, business dinners for those important power meetings, and the list goes on...

Eat Out Speak Out
Page 346

Ticked off that your top nosh wasn't top notch? Peeved that your pasta wasn't perfect? Or delighted that your dinner was divine? The Restaurant Review Revolution has arrived! Log on to www.EatOutSpeakOut.com - the UAE's first forum for restaurant reviews. We publish your views online, and we pass them on. Check the Website for details.

Going Out

If you're out and about in Dubai, you will soon find there is a surprising variety of places to go and things to do. It may not be quite the buzzing city found in other parts of the world, but Dubai is without doubt the 'Party Capital of the Gulf', with enough choice to amuse even the most passionate pleasure seeker. The following section has been divided into two; the city's numerous restaurants are listed under Eating Out, while cafés, bars, pubs, nightclubs and 'cultural' entertainment such as theatre, cinema and comedy clubs, are under On the Town.

Eating Out

Cosmopolitan and vibrant, Dubai has an excellent variety of restaurants. From Austrian to Thai, Indian to Italian and everything in between, there really is something to suit every taste and budget, and eating out is extremely popular with all segments of the Dubai community. As well as offering the chance to enjoy cuisine from all over the world, it gives the opportunity to exchange news and argue the merits of anything from a foreign leader to the latest movie.

Most places open early in the evening at around 18:00, but generally aren't busy until about 21:00. As well as dining out, dining in with a takeaway is very popular – it sometimes seems as though no one in Dubai knows how to cook! Many of Dubai's most popular restaurants are in hotels, and these are virtually the only outlets that can serve alcohol with your meal (if you want booze, check for the Alcohol Available icon in individual reviews). However, remember that there are many superb independent restaurants around town that shouldn't be ignored just because they are unlicensed.

Many restaurants specialise in more than one style of cuisine; for instance, an Indian restaurant may also serve Thai and Chinese food. In addition, many places promote theme nights with different types of cuisine or ingredients, such as Italian or seafood. The choice of what you can eat is dramatically increased by these speciality nights, allowing you to sample some truly international cuisine. Many restaurants also have weekly buffet nights when you can eat, and sometimes drink, as much as you like for a great value, all inclusive price.

Drinks

Although Dubai is about the most liberal state in the GCC, alcohol is only available in licensed restaurants and bars that are within hotels, plus a few non hotel outlets, such as golf clubs and some government owned establishments. The mark up can often be considerable – it's not unknown for a Dhs.11 bottle of indifferent wine to be charged at Dhs.90 plus. While most independent restaurants are unable to serve alcohol, don't let it put you off, since the food is often just as good, sometimes better.

Like alcohol, a bottle of house water can also be outrageously marked up, especially for premium brands. Imported water can be charged at up to Dhs.30 a bottle and if you object to this, we suggest you send it back and ask for a local bottled water (but not tap water). A standard one litre bottle of water usually costs Dhs.1.50 in a supermarket and is in no way inferior to imported brands.

See also: *Alcohol [p.212].*

Hygiene

Outlets are regularly checked by Dubai Municipality for hygiene, and they are strict on warning places to improve and, when necessary, closing them down. Bear this in mind when you consider eating at the 'tatty' little shawarma shop by the side of the road or a small independent restaurant. It is safe to eat there and you're unlikely to get food poisoning. Indeed, you'll probably have an excellent cheap and atmospheric meal.

Tax & Service Charge

On top of the basic bill, there can be a 10% municipality tax and a 15 - 16% service charge. The municipality tax apparently only applies to 'rated' hotels. These taxes are required to be incorporated into the customers' bill, but they are often indicated as being in addition to a price by ++. This information has to be clearly indicated somewhere on the menu. It's unclear whether the latter charge is actually passed on to staff or whether it can be withheld for poor service. When in doubt, give your servers a break.

Chevrolet Menu

2004

CHEVROLET CORVETTE — 5.7 L / V8

The only sports car that matters.

CHEVROLET LUMINA COUPE — 3.8 L / V6; 5.7 L / V8

Game over.

CHEVROLET TRAILBLAZER — 4.2 L / 6 cyl.

Rock solid, this is one unbeatable 4x4.

CHEVROLET TAHOE — 5.3 L / V8

The class-beating 4x4 that spells fun for all the family.

CHEVROLET VENTURE — 3.4 L / V6

Venture out. Venture in safety.

CHEVROLET SUBURBAN — 5.3 L / V8; 6.0 L / V8; 8.1 L / V8

The ultimate family vehicle.

Explorer Top Picks

Not sure what's hot and what's not in the city? Don't make your dining experience a 'hit and miss' with a random option. Guarantee yourself a fabulous time with a choice from our discerning top picks.

Alfresco

Al Muna	384
Beach Bar, Al Hadiqa Tent, The	444
Boardwalk	386
Fatafeet	367
St Tropez Bistro	375
Wharf, The	418

American

Go West	350
La Parrilla	363
Maria Bonita	408
Pachanga	405

Arabic Experience

Al Boom Tourist Village	426
Al Hadiqa Tent	356
Awafi	360

Business Dinners

Al Muntaha	370
Casa Mia	393
Exchange, The	388
M's Beef Bistro	421
Miyako	402
Ossigeno	397
Sakura	403
Verre	372
Vu's	408

Cheap Chow

Al Mallah	438
Karachi Darbar	412
Mr. Chow	365
Ravi's	412

Cocktail Lounges

Boudoir	446
Ginseng	446
Tangerine	461
Trader Vic`s	447
Uptown	450
Vu's	450

Deliciously Unpretentious

BiCE	393
Der Keller	376

Family Oriented

Go West	350
India Palace	379
Planet Hollywood	352
Shabestan	413

Far Eastern

Blue Elephant	424
Hoi An	426
Noodle House, The	369
Peppercrab	418
Sakura	403
Thai Chi	425
Yakitori	404

Hidden Away Gems

Al Safadi	358
Basta Art Café	428
Elements	430
Maria Bonita	408
More!	432

Indian

Asha's	377
Ashiana	377
Coconut Grove	378
Gazebo	379
Handi	379
India Palace	379
Nina	381

Italian

BiCE	393
Casa Mia	393
Il Rustico	396
Ossigeno	397

Japanese

Creekside	400
Kiku	400
Miyako	402
Sakura	403
Yakitori	404

Live Music

BiCE	393
Go West	350
Seville's	454
Jimmy Dix	458

Merry Zoos

Alamo, The	448
Hard Rock Café	350
Jimmy Dix	458
Lodge, The	460
Rock Bottom Cafe	443
Spice Island	391

Posh

Al Muntaha	370
Fusion	405
Marrakech	410
Tagine	410
Verre	372

Romantic

Al Muna	384
Apartment, The	374
Medzo	406
Prasino's	408
Retro	372
Rooftop Lounge	447

Seafood

Al Mahara	416
Beach Bar & Grill, The	416
Fish Market, The	417
Peppercrab	418

Smokin'!

Cigar Bar	446
Cubar	367
Exchange, The	388
MIX	460
Shahrzad	413

Steakhouses

Grill Room, The	420
JW's Steakhouse	420
M's Beef Bistro	421
Prime Rib	421
Rodeo Grill	422
Western Steak House	422

Sunsets

Barasti Bar	444
Eauzone	369
Marina Seafood Market	417
Rooftop Lounge	447
Sunset Bar	444
Wharf, The	418

Trendy/Terminally Hip

Boudoir	446
Glasshouse - Brasserie	368
M-Level	999
Noodle House, The	369

Wine Cellars

Agency, The	454
Apartment, The	374
Cellar, The	368
Spectrum On One	450
Verre	372
Vinoteca	9999
Vintage	454

Plate smashing is a form of expression, culturally acceptable only in Greek restaurants. You can now get your point across for all other eateries and still avoid costly lawsuits. Just log on to ***Eat Out Speak Out****, UAE's first online restaurant review forum and freely spill all thoughts about the dining experience.*

www.EatOutSpeakOut.com

Area Top Picks

Feeling lazy? Want to tumble out of bed and roll into a nearby joint? Just choose your area from the list below and relish in the listed dining and drinking options in the vicinity.

Eat Out Speak Out

www.EAT OUT SPEAK OUT.com

Explorer Publishing is quite proud to be a bit of a 'people's publisher'. We understand your hangovers, your need for excitement, your boredom thresholds and your desire to be heard, and we're always striving to make our publications as interactive with our loyal readership as possible. In the past, our Food Correspondent's telephone has been ringing constantly with people wanting to add their two pennies' worth to the reviews in our guidebooks.

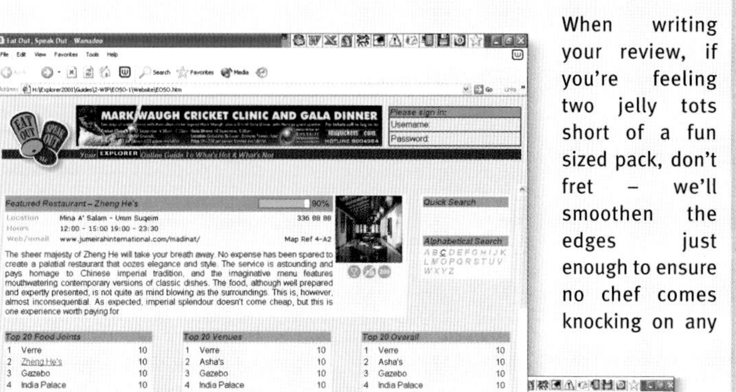

Hence, our most ingenious solution for a satisfied diner, accurate food reporting and lower decibels in the work place, is **EAT OUT SPEAK OUT**.

This Website provides the opportunity to pen down all of your comments, frustrations, tips and tantrums about specific dining experiences at any of the restaurants listed in our guide. Not only will we publish your thoughts online, we'll also pass on your review (anonymously, of course) to the outlet concerned and take your views into consideration for next year's edition of our guidebook.

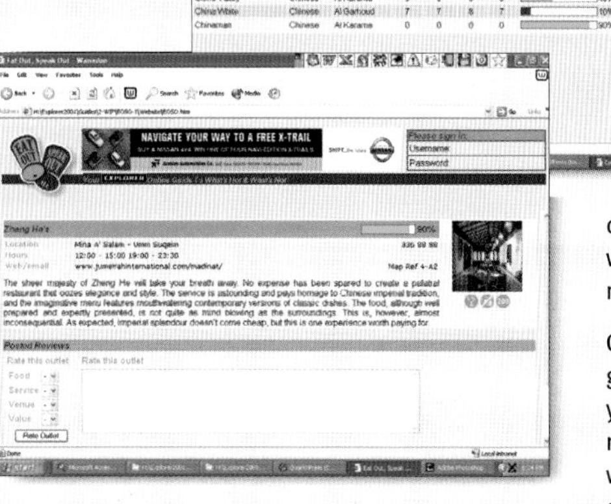

Now that you know what it's all about, we will restrain you no longer...

Once logged on to **www.EatOutSpeakOut.com**, select the restaurant you wish to review by typing in the outlet name. Alternatively, you can search for your restaurant alphabetically, by cuisine or area/location.

Once you've found the object of your wrath or praise, simply scroll through people's previously penned prose and then enter your own. Don't forget to put in those all important ratings too.

When writing your review, if you're feeling two jelly tots short of a fun sized pack, don't fret – we'll smoothen the edges just enough to ensure no chef comes knocking on any doors wielding a meat cleaver.

Once you've got it all off your chest, relax and read what everyone else has to say about your favourite joint. See the restaurant rated by 'Venue' and also skim through the 'Best Overall' category.

Come on, lets hear what you have to say to improve, or reward the service here!

All You Can Eat & Drink Nights Out

Day	Name	Location	Phone	Cost (Dhs)	Promotion/Theme
Thu	Bamboo Lagoon	JW Marriott	262 4444	160/-	Far East
	Bella Vista	Jum. Rotana Htl	345 5888	79/-	Curry
	Fontana	Al Bustan Rotana Htl	282 0000	89/-	Mexican
	Garden Café	World Trade Centre Htl	331 4000	95/-	Pasta & International
	Gardinia	Towers Rotana Htl	343 8000	85/-	Italian
	Gozo Garden	Millennium Airport Htl	282 3464	79/-	Hawaiian
	Market Place	JW Marriott	262 4444	160/-	International
	Spice Island	Renaissance Htl	262 5555	130/-	Seafood
	Tahiti	Metropolitan Palace Htl	227 0000	125/-	Teppanyaki & Hot Pot
Fri	Bamboo Lagoon	JW Marriott	262 4444	160/-	Far East
	Gozo Garden	Millennium Airport Htl	282 3464	79/-	BBQ & Seafood
	Market Place	JW Marriott	262 4444	160/-	International
	Masala	World Trade Centre Htl	331 4000	89/-	Indian
	Spice Island	Renaissance Htl	262 5555	130/-	Mongolian
Sat	Benihana	Al Bustan Rotana Htl	282 0000	95/-	Sushi
	Market Place	JW Marriott	262 4444	160/-	International
	Masala	World Trade Centre Htl	331 4000	89/-	Indian
	Tahiti	Metropolitan Palace Htl	227 0000	139/-	Seafood
Sun	Bella Vista	Jum. Rotana Htl	345 5888	79/-	Carvery
	Benihana	Al Bustan Rotana Htl	282 0000	95/-	Teppanyaki
	Fontana	Al Bustan Rotana Htl	282 0000	119/-	Seafood
	Garden Café	World Trade Centre Htl	331 4000	95/-	Sates
	Gardinia	Towers Rotana Htl	343 8000	85/-	Spit Roast
	Market Place	JW Marriott	262 4444	160/-	International
	Spice Island	Renaissance Htl	262 5555	130/-	Steak & BBQ
	Tahiti	Metropolitan Palace Htl	227 0000	139/-	Seafood
Mon	Bamboo Lagoon	JW Marriott	262 4444	160/-	Far East
	Bella Vista	Jum. Rotana Htl	345 5888	79/-	Pasta
	Fontana	Al Bustan Rotana Htl	282 0000	89/-	Arabian
	Gardinia	Towers Rotana Htl	343 8000	85/-	Asian
	Gozo Garden	Millennium Airport Htl	282 3464	79/-	Curry
	Market Place	JW Marriott	262 4444	160/-	International
	Spice Island	Renaissance Htl	262 5555	130/-	Seafood
	Tahiti	Metropolitan Palace Htl	227 0000	125/-	Sushi
Tue	Benihana	Al Bustan Rotana Htl	282 0000	95/-	Sushi
	Brahaus	Jumeira Rotana Htl	345 5888	79/-	Traditional German
	Garden Café	World Trade Centre Htl	331 4000	95/-	Fajitas
	Gardinia	Towers Rotana Htl	343 8000	85/-	British
	Gozo Garden	Millennium Airport Htl	282 3464	79/-	European
	Market Place	JW Marriott	262 4444	160/-	International
	Spice Island	Renaissance Htl	262 5555	130/-	Spice
	Tahiti	Metropolitan Palace Htl	227 0000	125/-	Teppanyaki
Wed	Bella Vista	Jum. Rotana Htl	345 5888	79/-	Asian
	Come Prima	Al Bustan Rotana Htl	282 0000	95/-	Italian
	Fontana	Al Bustan Rotana Htl	282 0000	79/-	Curry
	Gardinia	Towers Rotana Htl	343 8000	85/-	Seafood
	Gozo Garden	Millennium Airport Htl	282 3464	79/-	Chinese
	Market Place	JW Marriott	262 4444	160/-	International
	Spice Island	Renaissance Htl	262 5555	130/-	Asian
	Tahiti	Metropolitan Palace Htl	227 0000	125/-	Mongolian

Tipping

Tipping is another grey area, but following the standard rule of 10% will not be out of line. It's not necessarily expected, but will be appreciated. Few waiters seem to realise that there's a direct correlation between good service and the size of the tip!

Independent Reviews

We undertake independent reviews of all restaurants and bars that we include in this book. The following outlets have been visited by our freelance reporters and the views expressed are our own. The aim is to give a clear, realistic and, as far as possible, unbiased view (that we are permitted to print!). However, if we have unwittingly led you astray, please do let us know. We appreciate all feedback, positive, negative and otherwise. Please log on to *www.Explorer-Publishing.com* and share your views. Your comments are never ignored.

Restaurant Listing Structure

With over 400 outlets serving food and drink listed in the *Dubai Explorer*, the choice can seem daunting. Listed alphabetically by region, then country, or commonly known style of cuisine, this section aims to add to the variety of your dining experience by giving as much information as possible on the individual outlets. For an 'at a glance' clarification of this listing, refer to the index at the beginning of this section.

As with all good, simple rules, there are exceptions. Restaurants in the international category usually serve such a variety of food that it is impossible to pin them down to one section. While a restaurant that specialises in cooking seafood in styles from all over the world will be found in Seafood, a Thai restaurant that cooks a lot of fish Thai style will still be listed under Thai! Makes sense? We hope so! Where a restaurant specialises in more than one type of cuisine, the review appears under the main category.

In order to avoid any confusion concerning a particular restaurant's listing, as a rule, any non English names retain their prefix (ie, Al, Le, La and El) in their alphabetical placement, while English names are listed by actual titles, ignoring prefixes such as 'The'. Bon appetit!

Privilege Cards

The table shows a list of privilege or discount cards for use at various establishments. These cards are basically offered to encourage you to return as often as possible. Generally, they can be used at a number of restaurants, so you won't get bored, and most offer incredible discounts and other added benefits, making them excellent value for money.

Ratings

Rating restaurants is always a highly subjective business. We asked our reviewers to summarise their experiences (see the bottom of each entry) in terms of Food, Service, Venue, and Value. They were also asked to consider their restaurant as compared to other venues in the category and in the same price range. In other words, you may notice that a local cafe has the same summary rating as a premium gourmet restaurant. This is not to say that they are equal to one other. Instead,

Privilege Cards

Hotel / Company	Includes	Phone	Cost
Entertainer	-	390 2866	195
Hilton Hotels	Hilton Dubai Creek, Hilton Jumeirah Beach	399 1111	800
Hyatt Regency Hotel	-	209 1234	610
Jumeirah International	-	314 3500	Free
JW Mariott	-	262 4444	444
Le Meridien Hotels	Le Meridien Dubai, Le Meridien Mina Seyahi, Le Royal Meridien	282 4040	750
Metropolitan Hotels	Metropolitan Beach, Metropolitan Deira, Metropolitan Hotel, Metropolitan Palace	343 0000	500
Ramada Hotel	-	351 9999	350
Rotana Hotels	Al Bustan Rotana, Jumeirah Rotana, Rihab Rotana, Rimal Rotana, Towers Rotana	343 8000	630
Sheraton Hotels	Four Points, Sheraton Deira, Sheraton Dubai Creek, Sheraton Jumeirah Beach	268 8888	595
DNATA	n/a	316 6767	500
Dining Club, The	n/a	335 5656	395
Landmark Group	n/a	338 3683	25

this is a way of comparing restaurants that are similarly styled and priced to each other. We hope this will help you to make informed choices regardless of your taste or budget.

Each rating is out of five – one dot means poor, two and a half means acceptable, whereas five means fab:

Food ●●●◐○ Serv ●◐○○○ Venue ●●●●● Value ●●●●○

Venues scheduled to open later in 2004 received 'n/a' ratings:

Food - n/a Service - n/a Venue - n/a Value - n/a

Table Icons – Quick Reference

For an explanation of the various symbols or icons listed against the individual reviews, refer to the Quick Reference Symbols below.

Quick Reference ICONS

The prices indicated are calculated as the cost of a starter, main course and dessert for one person. This includes any relevant taxes, but excludes the cost of drinks. Another good cost indication is whether the outlet is licensed, the restaurant location (in a hotel or not), type of cuisine, etc. The Dhs.150 icon indicates that an average meal should cost anywhere between Dhs.100 to Dhs.200, ie Dhs.150 ± 50.

Quick Reference Explorer Icons

 Explorer Recommended!

 Average price ± Dhs.25 (3 courses per person, including Tax & Service)

 NO Credit Cards Accepted

 Live Band

 Alcohol Available

 Have a Happy Hour

 Will Deliver

 Kids Welcome

Reservations Recommended

 Dress Smartly

 Outside Terrace

 Vegetarian Dishes

Vegetarian Food

Vegetarians may be pleasantly surprised by the range and variety of veggie cuisine that can be found in restaurants in Dubai. Although the main course of Arabic food is dominated by meat, the staggering range of meze, which are often vegetarian, and the general affection for fresh vegetables should offer enough variety to satisfy even the most ravenous herbivore.

Nowadays, most outlets offer at least one or two veggie dishes. However, if you want a little more variety, choices include the numerous Indian vegetarian restaurants, which cater for the large number of Indians who are vegetarian by religion. These offer so many styles of cooking and such a range of tasty dishes, that Indian cuisine is hard to beat for vegetarians. Other highlights include loads of excellent Italian, Mexican, Far Eastern and International restaurants all over the city.

A word of warning: if you are a strict veggie, confirm that your meal is completely meat free. Some restaurants cook their 'vegetarian' selection with animal fat or on the same grill as the meat dishes.

Restaurants

American

Other options → **American Bars [p.442]**

Billy Blues

Location → Rydges Plaza Hotel · Al Satwa | 398 2272
Hours → 18:00 - 23:00
Web/email → n/a | Map Ref → 7-A4

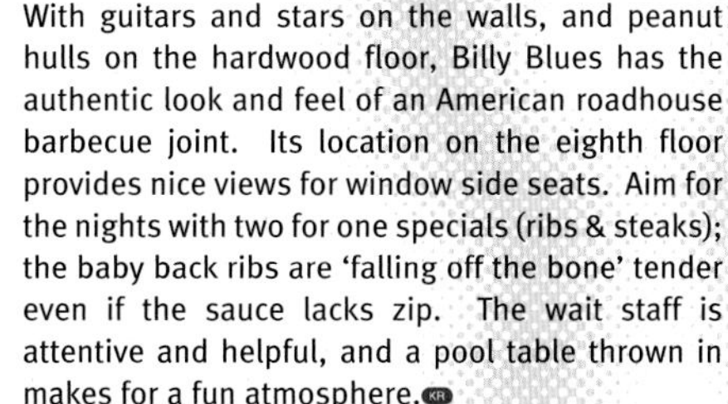

With guitars and stars on the walls, and peanut hulls on the hardwood floor, Billy Blues has the authentic look and feel of an American roadhouse barbecue joint. Its location on the eighth floor provides nice views for window side seats. Aim for the nights with two for one specials (ribs & steaks); the baby back ribs are 'falling off the bone' tender even if the sauce lacks zip. The wait staff is attentive and helpful, and a pool table thrown in makes for a fun atmosphere.

Food ●●●○○ Serv ●●●◐○ Venue ●●●●○ Value ●●●●○

Chili's

Location → Merdian Fairways · Al Garhoud | 282 8484
Hours → 11:00 - 23:00 Thu 11:00 - 24:00 Fri 13:00 - 23:00
Web/email → chilisg@emirates.net.ae Map Ref → 14-D2

Catch a wave of 'flavour' at this American themed family fun restaurant. The menu caters to all tastes including a number of 'be good to yourself' recipes for those counting calories. The burgers are famous but try the steak and fish recipes (they really get taste buds going). With roaring trade during lunchtime, soup and salad combos are popular. The service is pleasant and children are well catered for, with activities (such as colouring pencils and sheets) to keep them occupied and very happy.

Other Locations: *City Tower II, Sheikh Zayed Road (331 2499); Deira City Centre (294 0833); DNATA Airline Centre, Sheikh Zayed Road (321 0975); Internet City (391 8896); Spectrum Building, next to Lamcy Plaza (335 0814).*

Food ●●●●○ Serv ●●●◐○ Venue ●●●◐○ Value ●●●●○

Chili's

Fuddruckers

Location → Beh Al Tayer Motors · Al Garhoud | 282 7771
Hours → 07:30 - 24:00 Fri 08:00 - 22:00
Web/email → fuddubaigar@emirates.net.ae Map Ref → 14-D2

Everything at this restaurant seems bigger (and better) than its fast food competitors. Large portions, 'baked on the premises' buns, bottomless beverages (coffee, tea, iced tea and soft drinks) and a large, well organised dining area, bags Fuddruckers a spot in the favourites list of many families. Although their burgers and fries are already popular with the 'simple and reasonable meal' fans, their pancake breakfast shouldn't be missed. This is one fast food restaurant people go out of their way to visit.

Other locations: *Town Centre (342 9693).*

Food ●●●○○ Serv ●●●◐○ Venue ●●●○○ Value ●●●◐○

Go West

Go West

Location → Jumeirah Beach Htl · Umm Suqeim | 406 8181
Hours → 18:00 - 23:30 Thu, Fri 12:30 - 15:00
Web/email → www.jumeirahinternational.com Map Ref → 4-B2

Reminiscent of a kitsch Colorado steak joint with saddles, wagons and servers in plaid shirts, Go West completes the Western experience with great North American chowder. For starters, the buffalo wings are enough for two, chicken fajitas arrive sizzling with all the trimmings, and the BBQ ribs are rich and tender. Children get their own menu and colouring book, and mum and dad get a great live band, an impressive range of beers and half price happy hour from 18:00 - 19:00.

Food ●●●●○ Serv ●●●●○ Venue ●●●●○ Value ●●●●○

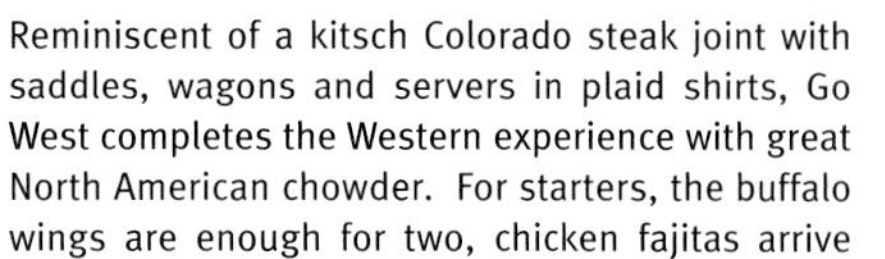

Hard Rock Café

Location → Hard Rock Café · Jct 5, Shk Zayed Rd | 399 2888
Hours → 12:00 - 02:00
Web/email → www.hardrock.com Map Ref → 3-A3

Packed to the rafters most nights with families, tourists and work parties, this café serves an American style menu of burgers, Tex Mex, pasta and salads complemented by hip cocktails and live music. Energetic wait staff pump up the party, offering their HRC trademark consistent dining experience time after time. Ideal for mixed get togethers where there's something for everyone, or for a late night drink in a jazz club atmosphere.

Food ●●●◐○ Serv ●●●●○ Venue ●●●◐○ Value ●●●●◐

Coca-Cola
Fajita Trio,
hree times the Flavor!
our tempting three-way combination of grilled **beef**, **chicken** and spicy
imp served on a sizzling hot skillet with grilled bell peppers and onions.
rm flour tortillas, guacamole, pico de gallo, shredded cheese and sour
am complete this tasty treat. **Only at Chili's!**

chili's
Fun.Fresh.Flavorful.

Harry's Place

Location → Renaissance Hotel · Hor Al Anz | 262 5555
Hours → 12:00 - 15:00 19:00 - 00:30
Web/email → rendubai@emirates.net.ae | Map Ref → 12-A3

Harry's Place is going through a mid life crisis. Gone are the jazz band and Cuban cigar room, and in their place are Top 40 tunes and a pool table. The place looks dreary and tired, but Harry's still has one saving grace – the food. Meals are well prepared and delicious, and come in good pub sized portions. The cocktails also deserve attention. Still, it is time for old Uncle Harry to go in search of his true identity, get a makeover and invest in a new wardrobe. JK

Food Serv Venue Value

Johnny Rockets

Location → Opp Jumeirah Centre · Jumeira | 344 7859
Hours → 12:00 - 24:00
Web/email → www.johnnyrockets.com | Map Ref → 6-C2

Give McDonald's a miss and head to Johnny Rockets instead. This themed diner will rock and roll you into the past and satisfy your craving for hamburgers, french fries and malts in a 50s atmosphere, complete with juke boxes, bright lights and red vinyl. The menu is simple but good value and includes various hamburger combinations and grilled cheese sandwiches. The restaurant attracts a steady stream of customers. With limited seating, it is advisable that you go early. MML

Food Serv Venue Value

Planet Hollywood

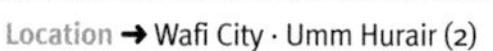

Location → Wafi City · Umm Hurair (2) | 324 4777
Hours → 12:00 - 24:00
Web/email → www.planethollywood-dubai.com | Map Ref → 13-D2

Planet Hollywood is a good place for a 'fun' meal out. Movie memorabilia covers the walls and ceilings in this buzzing venue that caters to families, tourists, and kids birthday parties. The menu includes a wide range of American dishes and caters to both veggies and meat lovers. However, be warned – in keeping with the Hollywood theme, portions are larger than life, and if you overindulge yourself early on, you'll miss out on some decadent desserts. Family Friday brunch is very popular here – book ahead. S

Food Serv Venue Value

Rattle Snake

Location → Metropolitan · Jct 2, Shk Zayed Rd | 343 0000
Hours → 19:00 - 02:30
Web/email → www.methotels.com | Map Ref → 5-C4

Walk past a county jail and enter the wild town of Rattle Snake. This American themed restaurant, with a separate bar and dance area, is designed around an old Western movie town. Each corner maintains a private and intimate feel, creating a mellow, relaxed mood early on that complements the surrounding activity. The food is good, the portions (not surprisingly) are large, and the staff is friendly. A Filipino band offers a tuneful selection of very lively numbers, and is the probable cause of your late departure from the restaurant. AR

Food Serv Venue Value

Planet Hollywood

PLANET HOLLYWOOD
The perfect Hollywood setting...
fun, exciting and absolutely delicious.
GREAT AMERICAN FOOD, AUTHENTIC HOLLYWOOD MEMORABILIA AND THE BIGGEST STARS PERFORMING FOR YOU ON THE BIG SCREEN.
TONS OF FUN FOR KIDS WITH EXCITING ACTIVITIES EVERY MONTH AND AN AWESOME WILD BRUNCH EVERY FRIDAY.
WHAT'S MORE... BRING THIS COUPON WITH YOU AND GET 20% OFF YOUR FOOD BILL. THIS OFFER IS FOR A ONE-TIME USE ONLY AND CANNOT BE USED IN CONJUNCTION WITH ANY OTHER OFFER OR PROMOTION. VALID UP TO 31ST DECEMBER, 2004.
PLANET HOLLYWOOD
LOCATED AT WAFI CITY. FOR RESERVATIONS, PLEASE CALL: 3244777
20% OFF
FOOD ONLY
PLANET HOLLYWOOD

Scarlett's

Location → Emirates Towers · Shk Zayed Rd | 319 8768
Hours → 12:00 - 15:00
Web/email → www.jumeirahinternational.com | Map Ref → 9-C2

The decadence of the Deep South lives on in the club section of Scarlett's. A festive mood and consistent crowds testify to the popularity of the venue. This is a place to see and be seen. A dining area downstairs gives way to a well used dance floor stocked bar upstairs. Arrive late and stay until early to experience its full effect. Music tends to be top 40 and a strict dress code is in effect. Tuesdays and Sundays are ladies nights.

Please also see Scarlett's under American Bars – On the Town [p.442].

Food Serv Venue Value

TGI Friday's

Location → Holiday Centre · Trade Centre 1&2 | 331 8010
Hours → 11:00 - 02:00
Web/email → tgifdxb@emirates.net.ae | Map Ref → 9-D2

This famous chain has typical American offerings in most of its outlets: loud music, a bar, a dance floor and Hollywood memorabilia. The menu of enormous burgers, sizzling Tex Mex fajitas, speciality salads, appetisers, pasta and ribs, are more than generous in size. The sinful dessert of Oreo cookies and vanilla ice cream is a calorie watcher's nightmare. Extremely helpful – if sometimes manic – staff keep the pace moving. TGI Friday's appeals to many despite the lack of alcohol, and is a particular treat for the kids.

Food Serv Venue Value

Americas

Lumping together Central, North and South America may seem strange, but there is method to the madness! Generally speaking, this cuisine is especially good for meat lovers. Many of the steakhouses and American joints, for example, offer prime quality meat especially flown in from the States to be cooked to your preference. Desserts vary widely in this category, but often the old favourites like Mississippi mud pie, apple pie or chocolate cake with lashings of ice-cream can be found somewhere on the menu - to the delight of those who like to finish with a dish that is sweet, filling and calorie laden! In general, this is hearty fare with the emphasis on portion size: steaks, ribs and burgers in such restaurants usually make dainty eaters cringe with disbelief. Often main courses in this category come with chips, but most restaurants will offer alternatives, such as baked potato or salad, if you show some concern for your arteries.

Moving south, the cuisine is still meat based - in particular, Argentinean cooking is noted for serving high quality steaks, but Caribbean dishes show a little more familiarity with fruit, vegetables and chicken. The hotter and spicier Mexican and Tex-Mex cooking usually has a wider choice for vegetarians. Some of the options include refried beans, guacamole, salsa, nachos (small, hard tortillas topped with melted cheese, peppers and chilli), fajitas (a soft tortilla, wrapped around sizzling vegetables and cheese or meat) and enchiladas (a tortilla filled with meat or cheese and served under a rich sauce), plus some great salads. Great if you have the appetite of a bear, but be careful if you like to have room for dessert.

Scarlett's

Arabic/Lebanese

Other options → **Nightclubs [p.458]**

Al Dar

Location → Above McDonald's · Jumeira | 342 0990
Hours → 11:00 - 24:00
Web/email → n/a | Map Ref → 6-C2

From Jumeira Beach Road, McDonalds is what you see before glimpsing the name, Al Dar, above it. With skilled cooks using fresh ingredients, it deserves that elevation. It does not, however, deserve its look of a school cafeteria disguised with Middle Eastern furniture. Nonetheless, the huge clean dining room offers big chairs, cloth napkins and a delicious mixed grill accompanied by the usual Arabic suspects, all neatly turned out. Fish at Al Dar, too, enjoys a fine reputation. AP

Food ●●●●○ Serv ●●●○○ Venue ●●○○○ Value ●●●●○

Al Diwan

Location → Metropolitan Palace · Deira | 227 0000
Hours → 19:30 - 03:00
Web/email → www.methotels.com | Map Ref → 11-D2

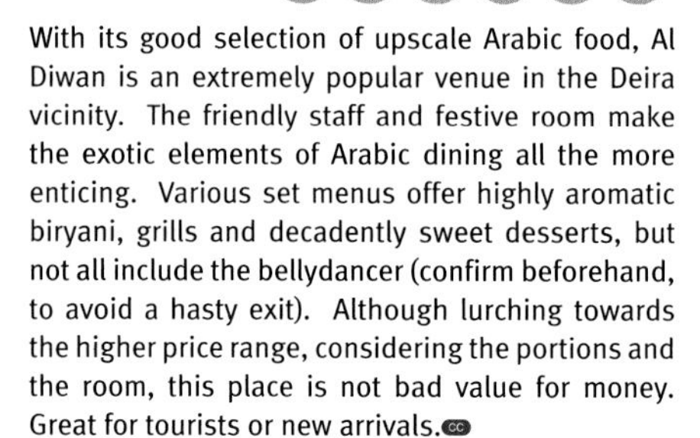

With its good selection of upscale Arabic food, Al Diwan is an extremely popular venue in the Deira vicinity. The friendly staff and festive room make the exotic elements of Arabic dining all the more enticing. Various set menus offer highly aromatic biryani, grills and decadently sweet desserts, but not all include the bellydancer (confirm beforehand, to avoid a hasty exit). Although lurching towards the higher price range, considering the portions and the room, this place is not bad value for money. Great for tourists or new arrivals. CC

Food ●●●◐○ Serv ●●●○○ Venue ●●●●○ Value ●●●○○

Al Fardous

Location → Sheraton Deira · Hor Al Anz | 268 8888
Hours → 11:00 - 03:00
Web/email → www.starwood.com | Map Ref → 12-A3

Cosy and dimly lit, this venue offers a flexible menu that is bound to please. The usual suspects are served up with the usual good cheer and playfulness. Live music, bellydancing, and a sociable atmosphere make this a loud restaurant. As expected in this category, things start late and continue on until early. Very popular on weekends, so reservations are recommended. Not the cheapest option, but the extra price is reflected in the quality of the venue. Closed during Ramadan. CC

Food ●●◐○○ Serv ●●●○○ Venue ●●●◐○ Value ●●◐○○

Al Hadiqa Tent

Location → Sheraton Jumeirah Beach · Marsa Dubai | 399 5533
Hours → 18:00 - 03:00
Web/email → www.starwood.com | Map Ref → 2-D2

An excellent Arabic experience for out of town visitors, the newly renovated Al Hadiqa Tent serves up a solid selection of Arabic food in comfortable seating with traditional Arabic décor to set the mood. A range of appetisers is on offer followed by mostly grilled meats for the main courses; the shawarma is excellent. Desserts include predominantly Arabic sweets, and aromatic shisha puts a soothing end to a hearty meal. Parched souls can avail the Beach Bar's full drinks menu. CG

Food ●●●◐○ Serv ●●●○○ Venue ●●●◐○ Value ●●●○○

Al Khayal

Location → Jumeirah Beach Htl · Umm Suqeim | 406 8181
Hours → 12:30 - 15:00 20:00 - 03:00
Web/email → www.jumeirahinternational.com | Map Ref → 4-B2

 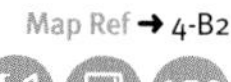

The spices of Arabia run past your senses on the Jumeira sea breeze as you enjoy sizzling meats and scrumptious salads. The belly dancing and music are a nice backdrop to the traditional Arabic foods offered. This place can fill up with a sophisticated late night Arabic crowd, especially during the Ramadan tent season, sending wafts of sweet smelling tobacco your way. Go for the experience and stay late to enjoy a cappuccino, strawberry or coconut flavoured shisha. LA

Food ●●◐○○ Serv ●●●◐○ Venue ●●●●○ Value ●●●◐○

Al Khayma

Location → Dubai Marine Beach · Jumeira | 346 1111
Hours → 19:30 - 02:00
Web/email → www.dxbmarine.com | Map Ref → 6-D2

Located in the heart of Jumeira, the Al Khaimah offers upscale Arabic cuisine, various flavours of

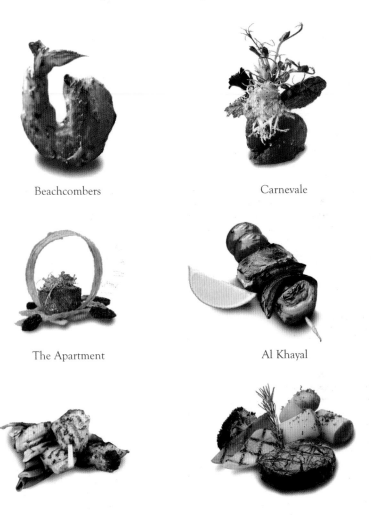

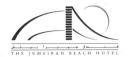

shisha, and live Arabic music. As the name suggests, the decor revolves around the khaimah seating with a variety of couches and low chairs. The lively atmosphere is friendly, and the service adequate. In terms of food, no particular surprises: grills, meze, biryanis, etc that are generally well prepared and tasty. The venue itself, however, pushes the restaurant into the more interesting category of options. CC

Food Serv Venue Value

Al Koufa

Location → Nr Cyclone · Oud Metha | 335 1511
Hours → 18:30 - 02:00
Web/email → n/a | Map Ref → 10-D4

Al Koufa offers good Arabic food (including Emirati dishes), great people watching and pretty decent shisha. The 'look' has evolved over the years from a temporary looking tent into something of a building complete with polystyrene walls and now proper tables for seating. In comparison to the decor, the food and service are better. Before 23:00, the place is almost deserted. After that, the band starts up and people pack in. An authentic Emirati experience you won't find here, but definitely a glimpse into Dubai's 'prowling' culture. CC

Food Serv Venue Value

Go Arabic

Surrounded by strong competition, seeing as Dubai is a haven for a variety of international cuisines, a common mistake is to categorise Arabic food into one general category. Break this myth and sample the different delights, from Lebanese and Moroccan to the local Emirati flavours.

Al Mijana

Location → Le Meridien Dubai · Al Garhoud | 282 4040
Hours → 12:30 - 14:45 20:00 - 23:45
Web/email → reservation@le-meridien-dubai.com | Map Ref → 14-E3

This quality Middle Eastern restaurant serves good Lebanese food in an upscale outdoor setting. The restaurant is part of the Le Meridien Village complex with its courtyard and water features, and has a roomy, if minimalist, interior. There is the usual extensive selection of dishes from both set menus as well as a la carte; the standard of food is high and the portions are large. Starve yourself all day if you want to do justice to this five star menu. SB

Food Serv Venue Value

Al Nafoorah

Location → Emirates Towers · Shk Zayed Rd | 319 8760
Hours → 12:30 - 15:00 20:00 - 23:30
Web/email → www.jumeirahinternational.com | Map Ref → 9-C2

Another authentic Lebanese restaurant with an exhaustive menu; Al Nafoorah starts early and excels in food and presentation. The décor is warm without being over the top, and efficient service keeps things moving and helping out the rare few struggling with the menu. Start with fish kibbeh, continue with the mixed grill and know that the tantalising desserts are complimentary. The terrace offers a welcome continuation of the evening where gentle puffs of shisha ensure that any remaining stress goes up in smoke. JK

Food Serv Venue Value

Al Qasr

Location → Dubai Marine Beach · Jumeira | 346 1111
Hours → 12:30 - 15:30 18:30 - 02:30
Web/email → www.dxbmarine.com | Map Ref → 6-D2

Al Qasr offers two dining experiences: a lunch, or a late night meal accompanied by an Arabic show. The menu includes many Lebanese favourites; the meze and grilled prawns are especially good. However, come 22:30, and the audience is merry and mesmerised by the bellydancer and the live music. This festive mood can be mellowed out with shisha in the majlis. Service is generally good, but waiters can be hard to find once the show starts. CC

Food Serv Venue Value

Al Safadi

Location → Al Rigga Rd · Deira | 227 9922
Hours → 08:00 - 12:00 13:00 - 02:00 Fri 08:00 - 02:00
Web/email → n/a | Map Ref → 11-D2

Like most restaurants in this category, the service is good, the food copious and tasty, and the value for money, fantastic. Perhaps the menu is not so vast here, but the payback is that what's listed is likely to be very nicely prepared. A meat selection in full view is prepared in front of you; don't miss

Announcing a beach resort with everything under the sun.

finz

Seafood Restaurant & Oyster Bar

BAY VIEW

RESTAURANT

t the Beach Rotana Hotel & Towers.

Enjoy weekend luxuries. Superior room for Dhs 275* and Premier room for Dhs 425*.

Relax at the soothing Beach Club, complete with gym and health spa facilities.

Ten exciting Food & Beverage outlets to enjoy and dine in style; with theme nights and events.

Conditions Apply

THERE'S ONE FOR YOU

reservations and more information please call 02-6443000

www.rotana.com

the chopped wings, which are grilled to perfection and a must try. The lights are bright and the customer turnover is high with a mainly Lebanese clientele, so don't plan to linger. A new location is set to open early 2004 on Sheikh Zayed Road.

Food●●●●◐Serv●●●◐○Venue●●●○○Value●●●●◐

Al Shami

Location → Nr Travel Centre · Deira | 269 5558
Hours → 07:00 - 04:00 Fri 15:00 - 03:00
Web/email → n/a | Map Ref → 11-E3

Run by a Syrian team, this Arabic restaurant is a very traditional affair, not only in terms of ambience but also in taste. Usually very busy, Al Shami has excellent value lunch buffets everyday for Dhs.22. Choose from over 25 Arabic starters or opt for the daily specials (which are not listed on the menu, so don't forget to ask!).

Food●●◐○○Serv●●●◐○Venue●●◐○○Value●●●●○

Al Tannour

Location → Crowne Plaza · Trade Centre 1&2 | 331 1111
Hours → 23:00 - 03:00 20:00 - 03:00
Web/email → www.dubaicrowneplaza.com | Map Ref → 9-D2

This very large and very good restaurant is sure to please serious diners. What the ambience lacks in authenticity is amply made up by the excellent food and gracious service. The extensive menu offers standard Lebanese fare, but it is the selection of meze that is dazzling. For a party of two or more, a blend of the set menu and the mains will not disappoint. The set menu includes meze an army couldn't finish and the delicious main courses give the meal a hearty touch.

Food●●●●◐Serv●●●●◐Venue●●●●○Value●●●●○

Amazeena

Location → Ritz Carlton · Marsa Dubai | 399 4000
Hours → 19:30 - 00:30 Thu 19:30-01:30
Web/email → rcdubai@emirates.net.ae | Map Ref → 2-E2

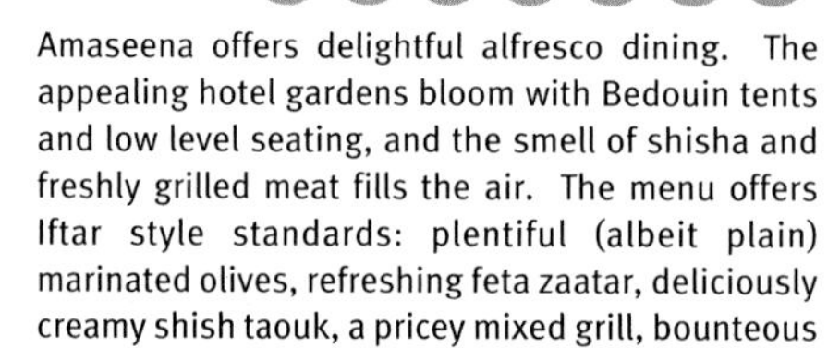

Amaseena offers delightful alfresco dining. The appealing hotel gardens bloom with Bedouin tents and low level seating, and the smell of shisha and freshly grilled meat fills the air. The menu offers Iftar style standards: plentiful (albeit plain) marinated olives, refreshing feta zaatar, deliciously creamy shish taouk, a pricey mixed grill, bounteous baklawa and, during Ramadan, exotic seasonal drinks, such as the rosewater and pine nut jallab. Open till July, Amaseena's welcoming service and holiday ambience provides a perfect escape from the working week.

Food●●●●◐Serv●●●●◐Venue●●●●○Value●●●●○

ARZ Lebanon

Location → Trade Centre Rd · Al Karama | 396 4466
Hours → 08:00 - 01:00 Fri 12:00- 01:00
Web/email → abci1@emirates.net.ae | Map Ref → 10-E1

This beautifully decorated (Danish run) Lebanese restaurant has seating for about 70, including a romantic little alcove outside. The menu has so much to offer that you'll welcome the help of your friendly waiter in making your choice. If you're not in the mood for Lebanese, ARZ also offers a small range of Italian pastas and continental dishes. The highlight is the piping hot Lebanese bread, freshly baked in an open oven while you watch.

Food●●●◐○Serv●●●◐○Venue●●●◐○Value●●●◐○

Automatic

Location → Beach Centre, The · Jumeira | 349 4888
Hours → 12:00 - 01:00
Web/email → n/a | Map Ref → 6-B2

A perennial favourite place to introduce visiting relatives and friends to Arabic food. Big, fresh portions, a lively cafeteria ambience and delightfully affordable prices make this a winner. The extensive menu includes excellent fish, a standard selection of meze, a mixed grill (a scrumptious selection of expertly grilled meats and fish), tempting daily specials and an excellent Friday buffet. There are vegetarian items available, but this is essentially a carnivore's carnival.

Food●●●●○Serv●●●◐○Venue●◐○○○Value●●●●○

Awafi

Location → JW Marriott Hotel · Deira | 262 4444
Hours → 20:00 - 24:00
Web/email → www.marriott.com | Map Ref → 12-A3

Located at the very top, this charming Arabic style restaurant has an open plan dining area wrapped around a swimming pool, Arabic sofas and a live band that sets the mood. Apart from the regular hot and cold meze, main courses offer

quite a few meat and fish options. The speciality mixed grill, however, gets the thumbs up. You can also purchase your very own shisha from the market. Overall a pleasant dining experience, but the cost, considering the other choices in Dubai, is a little high. EAT

Food Serv Venue Value

Awtar

Location → Grand Hyatt Dubai · Umm Hurair (2) | 317 2222
Hours → 12:00 - 15:00 19:00 - 03:00 Closed Saturdays
Web/email → www.dubai.grand.hyatt.com Map Ref → 13-E3

Whether you're looking for a 'taste of Arabia', a venue for overseas guests, live entertainment within the warmth of a Bedouin styled restaurant or just friendly waiters, this is the place to come. Seating styles range from tables to comfy plush sofas, accommodating a variety of dining moods. The menu boasts an excellent choice of meze, and both seafood and mixed grills can be found, albeit rather expensive for the size of portion. EAT

Food Serv Venue Value

Ayam Zaman

Location → Ascot Hotel · Bur Dubai | 352 0900
Hours → 19:30 - 03:00
Web/email → www.ascothoteldubai.com Map Ref → 7-E3

150

This is definitely a late night venue, so don't come before eleven or you're likely to be there by your lonesome. An uncomplicated yet delicious selection of meze and mixed grills are served amidst authentic Lebanese entertainment. Indulge in a wine from the extensive (albeit pricey) list, which includes some Lebanese reds and whites, for as soon as the singer comes out, the crowd rolls in and the place takes on a warm and satisfying feel. DM

Food Serv Venue Value

Beach Café Restaurant

Location → Beach Centre, The · Jumeira | 344 6066
Hours → 09:00 - 02:00
Web/email → n/a Map Ref → 6-B2

This little gem of a restaurant is a welcoming oasis after a long, hot morning on the beach. The menu combines Arabic and Italian dishes, all freshly and expertly prepared, well presented, and delivered to your table with a friendly smile. It's worth straying off the beaten track to find this venue, tucked away on the first floor of the Beach Centre. Good food, good service and a cool, welcoming environment will reward your efforts, and you will certainly return. CC

Food Serv Venue Value

Fakhreldine

Location → Mövenpick Hotel Bur Dubai · Oud Metha | 335 0505
Hours → 12:30 - 15:00 20:00 - 03:00
Web/email → hiburdxb@emirates.net.ae Map Ref → 10-D4

Tickle those tastebuds with the popular Lebanese cuisine at Fakhreldine. The richly coloured interior sets a cheerful Arabic mood. Be sure to dress in elasticated slacks as the menu of fresh breads and meat is never ending. Eat to your heart's content, then relax on the terrace with the stars and sample the local shisha. A great social place for friends to meet and catch up on the week's gossip. Excellent food is what sets this restaurant apart from the rest in this very full category. FA

Food Serv Venue Value

Fakhreldine

Grand Café

Location → Al Ain Centre, Al Mankhool Rd · Bur Dubai | 352 5155
Hours → 11:00 - 02:00 14:00- 02:00 Fri
Web/email → n/a Map Ref → 8-A4

Perhaps a shopping centre is not the ideal spot for tasting traditional Arabic food, but with the Grand

Café, we can make an exception. A diverse menu includes starters, main courses and speciality Moroccan sweets, all very reasonably priced and within an equally traditional Egyptian setting. Certainly worth mentioning is their selection of shisha, which includes the somewhat rare banana flavour!

Food ●●●○○ Serv ●●●○○ Venue ●●◐○○ Value ●●●○○

Kan Zaman Restaurant

Location → Heritage & Diving Village · Al Shindagha | 393 9913
Hours → 11:00 - 03:00
Web/email → www.dubaitourism.ae | Map Ref → 8-B1

  50

Kan Zaman offers patrons one of Dubai's best night time views of the Creek. Located at the turning point for boats, this Arabic restaurant with a large terrace is part of the Heritage and Diving Village. They also offer a good selection of meze, with both portions and value for money in the above average slot. Service is fast and efficient, and unlike most venues located on the Creek, this one has plentiful parking too. Iranian, Chinese and continental dishes are also available, but stick to the Arabic and local dishes for a more 'authentic' experience. CC

Food ●●●◐○ Serv ●●●◐○ Venue ●●●●○ Value ●●●◐○

> **Indulge in Goodies**
>
> *Goodies (324 4433) in Wafi City is a haven for Arabic food, selling a wide variety of foods from humous to tabouleh, stuffed vine leaves, spices and olives. New to the cuisine? You can sample the food, before dishing out the dough.*

L'Auberge

Location → City Centre · Deira | 295 0201
Hours → 12:00 - 24:00 Fri 13:00 - 24:00
Web/email → www.deiracitycentre.com | Map Ref → 14-D1

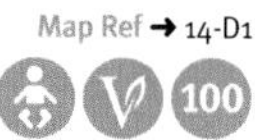

L'Auberge offers decent Arabic food within the mall. Seating options include social booths, open tables or small alcoves that can be curtained off for private dining, and the service is good and not too rushed. Like most Lebanese restaurants, Arabic bread and a huge garden salad arrive at your table first, with which you can enjoy a selection of meze or other starters, and main meals consist mostly of grills. Overall, this a surprisingly pleasant restaurant, particularly suited for an escape from consumer mania.. CC

See also: *Hamarain Centre (262 6965)*

Food ●●●○○ Serv ●●●○○ Venue ●●○○○ Value ●●●○○

Mays El Reem

Location → JW Marriott Hotel · Deira | 607 7823
Hours → 18:00 - 03:00
Web/email → www.marriott.com | Map Ref → 12-A3

Out of towners will enjoy the lively entertainment and tasty Middle Eastern cuisine at this renowned Lebanese venue. Share a few hot and cold meze for starters, and then tuck in to a feast of grilled meats, chicken or seafood; set menus and lunch specials reduce the overall prices. Complete the mood with live music, shisha and bellydancing. However, gear up for a late night when you come here – the action only starts at around 20:00, and before that, Mays El Reem has little atmosphere to offer. JLR

Food ●●●○○ Serv ●●●●○ Venue ●●◐○○ Value ●●○○○

Mazaj

Location → Century Village · Al Garhoud | 282 9952
Hours → 12:00 - 03:00
Web/email → n/a | Map Ref → 14-C3

If you crave the fruity aroma of shisha pipes on the night air, then Mazaj is the place to go. This authentic venue offers alfresco Arabic cuisine among the fairy lit palms of Century Village. The menu comprises an attractive range, but since the staff's English skills are a bit lacking, newcomers to Lebanese cuisine could face difficulties when ordering. Stick to the starters (which are wonderful) and the shisha; the main courses (although generous) are average kebab house fare. Also, take a Lebanese friend. JAW

Food ●●●○○ Serv ●●○○○ Venue ●●●●○ Value ●●●◐○

Orchestra, The

Location → Al Itthiad Rd · Deira | 295 8010
Hours → 10:00 - 02:00 Fri 13:00 - 02:00
Web/email → na | Map Ref → 11-E4

Located in a quiet area is a cosy and dimly lit outlet mirroring the social and relaxed life of Arabic tradition. Grab a place on the terrace in the cooler evenings and try the fragrant fruit flavoured shisha. A television provides modest entertainment for the locals to chill out and catch up on the news. Although the area is lacking in panoramic value, this is a great place to chat with friends and escape the bustling city for a more tranquil environment.

Food ○○○○○ Serv ●●●◐○ Venue ●●●○○ Value ●●●◐○

Reem Al Bawadi

Location → Nr HSBC · Jumeira | 394 7444
Hours → 08:00 - 03:00
Web/email → aymanshj@emirates.net.ae | Map Ref → 5-B2

With its Levantine décor and curtained majlises, the Reem Al Bawadi has a definite Arabian buzz, attracting Arabs as well as expats looking for a taste of local culture. Customers linger over Turkish coffee, Arabic sweets and shisha, or sample the tasty meze and mains from the menu. Leafy salads, dips, kibbehs and koftas are on offer, and the international entrees range from the seafood platter to the Moroccan chicken. Service is good (despite the bustle), the portions are generous, and the prices typical of this type of restaurant. AB

Food ●●●●○ Serv ●●●●○ Venue ●●●●○ Value ●●●●○

Saj Express

Location → Oasis Tower · Trade Centre 1&2 | 321 1191
Hours → 09:00 - 02:00
Web/email → sajxpress@emirates.net.ae | Map Ref → 9-B2

Better for a takeaway than eating in. Amidst shockingly bright lighting and disinterested service, Saj Express offers quite a menu, ranging from their speciality saj (thin bread filled with savoury or sweet ingredients baked on a metal dome), to a selection of hot and cold dishes – from humous to grilled meats. Meat lovers are better cared for than veggies; regardless, both will appreciate the humous beiruti and divine 'chocoba extra' – saj filled with chocolate sauce, fruits and nuts. PG

Food ●●●●○ Serv ●●◐○○ Venue ●●◐○○ Value ●●●●○

La Parrilla

Argentinean

La Parrilla

Location → Jumeirah Beach Htl · Umm Suqeim | 406 8181
Hours → 12:30 - 16:00 19:00 - 02:00
Web/email → www.jumeirahinternational.com | Map Ref → 4-B2

As any successful restaurant, La Parrilla too, offers wonderful décor, food and service. But add some Argentinean spice, lively entertainment and a sensational view of Dubai's sparkly night lights, and you have a venue that's a 'must do' on the city's fine dining circuit. Steak lovers should not miss the signature meaty treats on the menu, which also offers vegetarian and seafood options. Overall delicious, you would be enticed into becoming a regular, were it not for the prices that relegate this to a 'special occasion' restaurant. JJR

Food ●●●●○ Serv ●●●●○ Venue ●●●●○ Value ●●●○○

www.EAT OUT SPEAK OUT.com

About time your favourite waiter got a pat on the posterior for good service? Prompt a pay raise or promotion by shouting 'good service' from the rooftops! Eat Out Speak Out is the perfect way to get your 'pat' across. Not only will we publish your 'pat' online, we'll also make sure that it is transported straight from your hands to the 'back' of the establishment.

Chinese

Other options → **Filipino [p.370]**

China Club, The

Location → Hotel InterContinental · Deira | 222 7171
Hours → 13:00 - 15:00 20:00 - 23:00
Web/email → n/a | Map Ref → 8-C4

The China Club offers authentic Chinese cuisine in intimate, serene surroundings. A reasonably short yet diverse menu offers classics such as crispy hot spring rolls and tender cold lamb marinated in chilli. The main courses here are the real winner: succulent, freshly cooked and bursting with flavour. Service is genuine, if a little over attentive, and the overall meal is good value – a relatively inexpensive yet quality escape from the hustle and bustle of the world outside. VB

Food ●●●◐○ Serv ●●●◐○ Venue ●●●●○ Value ●●●◐○

China Valley

Location → Nr Sana, Trade Centre Rd · Al Karama | 336 4364
Hours → 12:00 - 15:00 19:00 - 23:30
Web/email → n/a | Map Ref → 10-C1

Gilded Chinese lions guard the entrance to China Valley, a popular local hangout. The illustrated eight page menu is enough to make your mouth water, but that's where the mysticism ends. Meals, although large, fresh and colourful, are disappointingly bland. A notable exception, however, are the wrapped prawns 'valley style', which are exquisite. The dining room is grubby and jaded, and the service is patchy but earnest. Not the best choice for an Emperor, but neither for a peasant.

Food ●●◐○○ Serv ●●◐○○ Venue ●◐○○○ Value ●●◐○○

China White

Location → Century Village · Al Garhoud | 282 5377
Hours → 12:00 - 01:00
Web/email → n/a | Map Ref → 14-C3

Nestled within Century Village, the restaurant offers an attractive outdoor terrace and a Chinese themed indoor section. A large selection of dishes will appeal to both meat eaters and vegetarians, and non MSG fare can be requested. Cantonese and Szechwan styles dominate, but at times the resulting food does not quite match the description on the menu. Nevertheless, China White will certainly satisfy any cravings for Chinese cuisine, and the relaxing outdoor atmosphere will more than compensate for the missing ingredients.

Food ●●●◐○ Serv ●●●◐○ Venue ●●●●○ Value ●●●◐○

Chinaman

Location → Hamdan Colony · Al Karama | 396 9685
Hours → 12:00 - 15:00 19:00 - 23:30
Web/email → n/a | Map Ref → 10-E1

As good as or better than most, this tiny and inexpensive venue is a handy secret. No Chinese lanterns or stone dragons clutter the space – there's simply no room in this 15 person space! The menu has all the usual choices at a cheaper price than elsewhere, and dishes are promptly served by the manager. The quantity and quality are good; try the Cantonese roast chicken or the spicy duck in plum sauce. Take away is available, but can be slow as the restaurant is usually busy.

Food ●●●○○ Serv ●●●○○ Venue ●●◐○○ Value ●●●◐○

Chinese Kitchen

Location → Nr Union Co-op · Jumeira | 394 3864
Hours → 12:00 - 15:00 18:00 - 24:00
Web/email → n/a | Map Ref → 5-B2

This creative kitchen offers tasty, inventive Chinese cooking. The décor is bright and colourful with authentic touches, and the food on offer is inspired chiefly from the Szechwan and Canton regions. Favourites include lemon chicken, garlic prawns and Shanghai rice, all fresh and perfectly cooked. The chef prides himself on his homemade sauces and individually made spring rolls and wontons; don't give the duck with pineapple a miss either. Outside catering and free delivery is also available.

Other Locations: Al Wasl Road, Jumeira (394 3864)

Food ●●●●◐ Serv ●●●●◐ Venue ●●●●◐ Value ●●●●●

Chinese Pavilion

Location → Beach Centre, The · Jumeira | 344 4432
Hours → 12:30 - 15:00 19:00 - 23:30
Web/email → n/a | Map Ref → 6-B2

This small, friendly restaurant, tucked away in a far corner of the Beach Centre, is simply and tastefully decorated with wicker furniture and dim lighting. The menu offers a good selection, with specialities ranging from Singapore chicken to chilli dishes with crispy vegetables. The restaurant is not licensed to sell alcohol, so try the hot jasmine tea, which complements the food. On Fridays, Chinese Pavilion has special offers for lunch, which are very popular with families – rice or noodles are on the house with any dish.

Food ●●◐○○ Serv ●●●○○ Venue ●●◐○○ Value ●●●◐○

Dynasty

Location → Ramada Hotel · Bur Dubai | 351 9999
Hours → 12:30 - 14:30 19:00 - 23:30
Web/email → rhdfmb@emirates.net.ae | Map Ref → 7-E3

Dynasty offers an authentic Chinese food experience in the heart of Bur Dubai. An intriguing

mix of Sichuan, Cantonese and Beijing cuisines are offered (but not categorised as such on the menu). Spicy fried prawns are a great way to kick start the meal, the Gungpao chicken can a bit heavy, stir fried lamb in Mongolian sauce is popular and a variety of duck and vegetarian dishes are on offer. Chinese tea and, of course, fortune cookies, make an excellent end to an enjoyable evening out.

Food●●●○○ Serv●●●●○ Venue●●◐○○ Value●●●○○

Four Seasons

Location → Rydges Plaza Hotel · Al Satwa | 398 2222
Hours → 12:00 - 15:00 19:00 - 24:00
Web/email → rhrdxb@emirates.net.ae | Map Ref → 7-A4

100

The location (on the ninth flour of the Rydges Plaza) grants diners at the Four Seasons pretty views of the city. The menu offers standard Chinese fare, from soups and spring rolls to crispy duck and sweet and sour chicken, as well as banquets for the starving. The service is attentive and pleasant, and the food is quite tasty, but not nearly special enough for the relatively high price.

Food●●●◐○ Serv●●●●○ Venue●●●◐○ Value●●●◐○

Golden Dragon

Location → Trade Centre Rd · Al Karama | 396 7788
Hours → 12:00 - 14:45 19:00 - 23:45
Web/email → n/a | Map Ref → 10-D1

100

This popular Chinese restaurant beckons you with neon flashing dragons and promising aromas from within. Much bigger than expected (on two floors with 'private dining rooms' upstairs), this restaurant is spacious and welcoming. A huge menu offers all the old favourites, accommodating even those choices that aren't listed. Not quite the venue for a romantic sojourn, Golden Dragon fits those just craving authentic Chinese food from 'real' Chinese people at good prices.

Food●●●○○ Serv●●●○○ Venue●◐○○○ Value●●●○○

Long Yin

Location → Le Meridien Dubai · Al Garhoud | 282 4040
Hours → 12:30 - 14:45 19:30 - 23:45
Web/email → longyin@lemeridien-dubai.com | Map Ref → 14-E3

150

Expanses of shiny black lacquer amplify the sound of 'dirham confident' diners, as well as Long Yin's insistence that it is Chinese. The dim sum verifies the accuracy of one's culinary GPS, but roaming the territory provides little excitement. Cantonese and Szechwan dishes place an emphasis on fish, as does the prominent tank holding other potential main courses. The broccoli with black mushrooms and oyster sauce is quite good, and speaks well for the other vegetable prospects.

Food●●●○○ Serv●●◐○○ Venue●●◐○○ Value●●○○○

Mini Chinese

Location → Al Diyafah Street · Al Satwa | 345 9976
Hours → 12:00 - 24:00
Web/email → www.binhendi.com | Map Ref → 7-A3

This bright beacon of fresh, quick Chinese cuisine literally lights up the Satwa strip. The large windows are bursting with hungry patrons till late, every night of the week, and you can reliably expect giant servings and speedy service at a modest price. With modern wall prints, loud colours to liven the mood and an open glassed kitchen, you can do both: keep an eye on your chef as well as people watch. Quite a good stop off in a group outing.

Food●●●○○ Serv●●◐○○ Venue●●●●○ Value●●●●○

Mr. Chow

Location → Imperial Suites Rd · Bur Dubai | 351 0099
Hours → 11:00 - 02:30
Web/email → openhouse_rest@yahoo.com | Map Ref → 7-E3

100

Whether you want to eat out, get a takeaway or cater for a party, Mr. Chow is happy to be of service. The small restaurant on the edge of Satwa is bedecked in red and black with an array of Chinese artefacts. There's a large selection of traditional Chinese dishes plus some Thai fare, and the gargantuan portions mean that most people leave with half their meal in a 'doggie bag'. Do check out the lunchtime specials. For cheap 'Chow' you can't go wrong.

Food●●●◐○ Serv●●●●○ Venue●●●◐○ Value●●●●◐

Nanking Chinese

Location → Beh Regent Palace Htl · Al Karama | 396 6388
Hours → 12:00 - 24:00
Web/email → n/a | Map Ref → 11-A1

Run by the enthusiastic Mr Errol, this modest looking restaurant offers excellent food. A comprehensive Chinese menu emphasises healthy

eating; garlic chicken with plum sauce wrapped in crispy iceberg lettuce is light and crispy and the spicy tofu is a wonderful vegetarian option. Portions are just right, allowing you to try a range of dishes without feeling that you've overeaten or burnt a hole in your wallet. A rare example of genuine concern for food and hospitality.

Food●●●○○Serv●●●◐○Venue●●◐○○Value●●◐○○

Open House

Location → Nr Pyramid Bld · Al Karama | 396 5481
Hours → 12:00 - 02:30
Web/email → n/a | Map Ref → 10-E1

100

Enter here, and you're assaulted by the maddest decor you could shake a paint roller at. Piped water runs down the windows while inside, the ultraviolet and green strip lights tinge the red colour scheme. Once the novelty wears off, it's an agreeable little place to chew the naan. Welcoming waiters gently serve a largely familiar menu, where fragrant curries beat the so so Chinese dishes. Tuck in and watch the 'rain' outside, then re-emerge (surprised) to Dubai's heat.

Food●●●◐○Serv●●●○○Venue●●◐○○Value●●●◐○

Peacock, The

Location → Sheraton Jumeirah Beach · Marsa Dubai | 399 5533
Hours → 12:00 - 15:00 19:00 - 23:30
Web/email → www.starwood.com | Map Ref → 2-D2

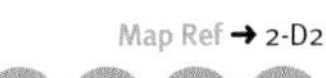

200

Although minimalist in concept, there is nothing minimalist about the food at the Peacock. Refurbished not so long ago and situated with a great view overlooking the lobby, the menu offers old favourites as well as exotic alternatives – the fish and shellfish are excellent. Although the wait staff is adept at pointing out the spicier meat dishes, be warned... a so called 'mild' soup might result in throat fireworks. Overall, this is an ideal spot for a reasonably priced meal in a low key and sedate atmosphere.

Food●●●●○Serv●●●◐○Venue●●●◐○Value●●●●○

Shang Palace

Location → Shangri-La Hotel · Trade Centre 1&2 | 343 8888
Hours → 12:30 - 15:00 20:00 - 24:00
Web/email → www.shangri-la.com | Map Ref → 9-A2

100

Here's one to tempt your taste buds. The menu provides a varied and intriguing range of dishes; the meat and fish are succulent and tender with distinctive flavours, the honey barbecued chicken and giant prawns are delicious, and a dedicated dim sum menu widens choice. The enthusiastic staff is eager to assist with your selection. This restaurant is ideal for small groups with diverse tastes to sample a variety of dishes.

Food●●●●○Serv●●●◐○Venue●●●◐○Value●●●●○

Summer Place, The

Location → Metropolitan · Jct 2, Shk Zayed Rd | 343 0000
Hours → 12:30 - 15:30 19:00 - 23:00
Web/email → www.methotels.com | Map Ref → 5-C4

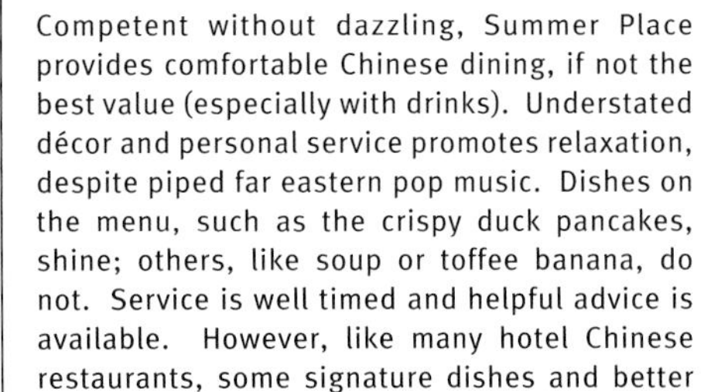

150

Competent without dazzling, Summer Place provides comfortable Chinese dining, if not the best value (especially with drinks). Understated décor and personal service promotes relaxation, despite piped far eastern pop music. Dishes on the menu, such as the crispy duck pancakes, shine; others, like soup or toffee banana, do not. Service is well timed and helpful advice is available. However, like many hotel Chinese restaurants, some signature dishes and better service do not justify the higher prices – in this respect, the independent restaurant competition wins.

Food●●●◐○Serv●●●●○Venue●●◐○○Value●●◐○○

Zheng He's

Chinese

Going Out

Zheng He's

Location → Mina A'Salam · Umm Suqeim | 366 8888
Hours → 12:00 - 15:00 19:00 - 23:30
Web/email → reservations@jumeirahinternational.com Map Ref → 4-A2

The sheer majesty of Zheng He will take your breath away. No expense has been spared to create a palatial restaurant that oozes elegance and style. The service is astounding and pays homage to Chinese imperial tradition, and the imaginative menu features mouthwatering contemporary versions of classic dishes. The food, although well prepared and expertly presented, is not quite as mind blowing as the surroundings. This is, however, almost inconsequential. As expected, imperial splendour doesn't come cheap, but this is one experience worth paying for. JK

Food ●●●◐○ Serv ●●●●● Venue ●●●●● Value ●●●◐○

Cuban

Other options → **Cigar Bars [p.446]**

Cubar

Location → Hilton Jumeirah · Marsa Dubai | 399 1111
Hours → 18:00 - 24:00
Web/email → www.hilton.com Map Ref → 2-D2

With immaculately polished parquet floors, slowly rotating ceiling fans and deep leather armchairs, Cubar reflects the gracious living of a gentler era. Listen to the evocative Latino music drifting through the night air and relax with your favourite cocktail, a plate of tapas and possibly a cigar. This place is an ideal prelude or finale to an evening at Pachanga or any of the other excellent restaurants here. However, with a Caipirinha, a plate of potato salad and some shrimp in saffron butter, who needs to go anywhere else? LS

Food ●●●●○ Serv ●●●●○ Venue ●●●●◐ Value ●●●○○

El Malecon

Location → Dubai Marine Beach · Jumeira | 346 1111
Hours → 19:30 - 03:00
Web/email → www.dxbmarine.com Map Ref → 6-D2

This venue remains popular for extended evenings of drinks and salsa dancing (lessons offered on certain days). A fun activity for sure, and the food does not disappoint either. The duck with polenta is divine and the Cuban inspired dishes are bursting with bright flavours and spice. As with any busy venue, the service may feel at times harried but they do a good job of trying to appease everyone. Later, as the band gets going, the place becomes decidedly festive. CC

Food ●●●◐○ Serv ●●●◐○ Venue ●●●◐○ Value ●●●◐○

Egyptian

Other options → **Arabic/Lebanese [p.356]**

Fatafeet

Location → Nr British Embassy · Bur Dubai | 397 9222
Hours → 10:30 - 24:00
Web/email → na Map Ref → 8-C4

Shisha, Arabic coffee and a wonderfully atmospheric view of the Creek is what this cafe has to offer. Additional offerings are the usual batch: fruit juices, meze, salads and so forth, plus some

Fatafeet

good Egyptian dishes. The service can be extremely leisurely (consider it part of the 'cultural' experience) and, although parking seems ample, it does fill up quickly. Alternatively, park further along the Creek and enjoy the stroll. This venue is ideal in the cooler months as the setting is delightful. Evenings are recommended over a daytime visit for a better overall experience. PG

Food Serv Venue Value

Emirati

Other options → Arabic/Lebanese [p.356]

Al Areesh

Location → Al Boom Tourist Village · Umm Hurair (2) | 324 3000
Hours → 12:00 - 16:00 19:00 - 24:00
Web/email → abt@emirates.net.ae | Map Ref → 14-A3

This venue offers alfresco dining right next to the Creek in a setting of traditional Gulf Arab sailing style. An extensive buffet of local fare is offered for a very reasonable price indeed. However, Al Areesh's speciality is catering to large parties, including weddings and local sheikhs, so you may feel a little out of place if there for an intimate dinner for two. For dabbling in local culture and tastes, Al Areesh is a safe bet. DM

Food Serv Venue Value

Hidden Charges

When the bill arrives, subtly check out the dreaded small print (slyly lurking at the bottom of the bill) that says 'INCLUSIVE +15% +5%'. Be careful what you touch, as you may find that even the most innocent eye contact with a nut bowl can result in surplus charges.

Local House

Location → Bastakiya · Bur Dubai | 353 9997
Hours → See timings below
Web/email → n/a | Map Ref → 8-B3

50

Emirati cuisine seems to be sadly overshadowed by the hub of international flavours rife in Dubai. Ideally located in vintage Bastakiya, Local House fills the gap with a dedicated Emirati menu. Sit inside or outside on padded platforms, and feast away. Harees, magly and amouesh are among the authentic dishes served, and if you want to find out more... you'll just have to go and see for yourself. CC

***Contact:** For further information, call Maria on 050 774 6207.*

European

Cellar, The

Location → Aviation Club, The · Al Garhoud | 282 9333
Hours → 12:00 - 15:30 19:00 - 23:30
Web/email → www.aviationclubonline.com | Map Ref → 14-C3

With a Gothic meets contemporary décor and a globe hopping menu, The Cellar is a post modern shrine with an eclectic yet sophisticated feel. The extensive wine selection works well with the innovative menu offerings, which range from Thai curries and Portobello mushrooms stuffed with mashed potatoes and mange-tout, to uncomplicated grilled salmon. The sesame coated fried camembert with gooseberry marmalade is decadent. For more casual dining, try the Friday brunch or terrace BBQ. Well priced lunch specials, a happy hour and fine service make this a smart choice. ABH

Food Serv Venue Value

European

European cuisine is as varied as the number of languages spoken. From German sausages (wurst) or Greek moussaka to Spanish tapas or English beef Wellington, there really is a style to suit every preference and mood. Most European restaurants are located in hotels with an upmarket ambience, a liquor licence and commensurate prices. In Dubai, the most dominant of the European cuisines is Italian. Numerous independent restaurants are springing up around the city, offering good value for money, but sadly, no chance to indulge in a glass of Chianti with your cannelloni.

Dubai truly offers diners a handful of genuinely world class restaurants that match - in terms of food, wine, décor, service and price - anything that the European capitals have to offer.

Glasshouse - Brasserie

Location → Hilton Creek · Deira | 227 1111
Hours → 12:30 - 15:30 19:00 - 23:30
Web/email → www.hilton.com | Map Ref → 11-C2

From London's signature chef, Gordon Ramsey, this is one of the trendiest and most tasteful restaurants in Dubai. With fantastic food set in a funky backdrop, Glasshouse continues to rival

fashionable eateries anywhere in the world. The food is clever and imaginative, while a carefully contrived menu ranges from homey classics to fusion extravaganzas. Well balanced cocktails complement an extensive wine list. With top service and great ambience, Glasshouse is perfect for a lazy liquid lunch (with a bit of class) or a special night out. HK

Food ●●●●◐ Serv ●●●●◐ Venue ●●●●◐ Value ●●●●◐

Far Eastern

Eauzone

Location → One&Only Arabian Court · Al Sufouh | 399 9999
Hours → 19:30 - 24:00
Web/email → www.oneandonlyresort.com | Map Ref → 3-A2

'By the swimming pool' orients one to Eauzone. Its romantic location is reached by wooden causeways crossing tranquil pools to tented tables. Vegetable wontons in red curry sauce with snow peas announce the Asian touch and general excellence of the menu. Impeccably cooked fish entrees are especially appealing and most likely to distract fantasists from dreams of dessert. Fanciful sorbets, such as raspberry with red chillies or creations such as sesame crust packed with ginger ice cream, are mirages materialised. AP

Food ●●●●○ Serv ●●●●● Venue ●●●●● Value ●●●●○

Yum!

Location → Hotel InterContinental · Deira | 205 7333
Hours → 12:00 - 01:00 12:00 - 01:00
Web/email → n/a | Map Ref → 8-C4

This is fast food designer style. Yum offers a fusion of oriental cuisine for those looking to eat and run. The décor, like the clientele, is modern, trendy and casual. Tables are arranged around a glass and stainless steel enclosed kitchen, where six chefs prepare specialities from all over the East. Skip the alcohol and enjoy the zing of real lemonade. However, not the place for an intimate dinner – most tables seat six, so expect company! Yum offers tasty, affordable food for people with no time to waste. LS

Food ●●●●○ Serv ●●◐○○ Venue ●●●○○ Value ●●●●○

Noodle House, The

Location → Emirates Towers · Shk Zayed Rd | 319 8757
Hours → 12:00 - 23:30
Web/email → www.jumeirahinternational.com | Map Ref → 9-C2

On a busy night (and they're all busy here), you'll be at a long communal table sitting cheek to jowl with strangers, while friendly staff will serve you extremely tasty Chinese and Thai dishes. The posh stainless steel and redwood decor (this is after all, the Emirates Towers!) is sharp and simple, and more New York trendy Chinese than Hong Kong. As long as you don't have an intimate meal in mind or

Far Eastern

For lovers of light, generally healthy food with an emphasis on steamed or stir-fried cooking methods, Far Eastern cuisine is an excellent option either for dining out or takeaway. Seafood and vegetables dominate the menu, but the staples are rice and noodles, with dishes enhanced by the use of delicate and fragrant herbs and spices like ginger and lemon grass, and coconut milk. The food can be spicy, but generally less so than a fiery, denture melting Vindaloo curry.

The décor of Thai, Malaysian and Polynesian restaurants often reflects a stereotypically exotic view of the Far East, with bamboo, beach huts and 'demure' oriental waitresses. Sometimes this combines to create a tasteful, relaxing and classy ambience, and sometimes it doesn't quite make it. With the exception of Chinese outlets, Far Eastern restaurants are generally located in hotels in more upmarket surroundings, with prices that match. Japanese restaurants generally offer a choice of seating options, from teppanyaki tables where the entertainment is provided by the chefs as they juggle, dice and slice, to private tatami rooms, or the sushi option, where dishes pass before your eyes on a conveyor belt. Any way you like it, the standard of Japanese food in Dubai is high, but, again, with prices to match.

Dubai also has a great number of Chinese restaurants, and standards vary greatly from monosodium glutamate-laden, taste killing dishes to light and delicious cuisine. Many of the independents (ie, those not linked to a hotel or club) offer good value for money, with large portions of quality food. As with Indian outlets, many Chinese restaurants offer tasty takeaway and home delivery, giving Dubai residents even less incentive to learn how to use their wok.

a personal space fetish, the quick fire service, quasi fast food dining and closeness to humanity make for an entertaining change.

Food Serv Venue Value

Noodle Kitchen

Location → Millennium Airport Hotel · Al Garhoud | 282 3464
Hours → 12:00 - 15:00 19:00 - 12:00
Web/email → apothotl@emirates.net.ae | Map Ref → 14-D3

Picture eating a home cooked meal on the kitchen table of a close Chinese friend – this great little restaurant is reminiscent of that image. The décor is so spartan, it must be trendy, and the food matches perfectly: no frills, no fuss and no pretension. After ticking your preferences on the menu sheet provided, the delicious, mainly noodle based dishes, come quickly, which may not suit dawdling diners. Definitely worth a visit, especially if you're after tasty food in a hurry.

Food Serv Venue Value

Zinc

Location → Crowne Plaza · Trade Centre 1&2 | 331 1111
Hours → 19:00 - 03:00
Web/email → sean@crowneplaza.co.ae | Map Ref → 9-D2

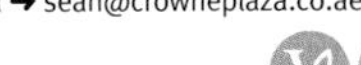

Chemistry just got exciting! This is not the metal Zinc. It is a fusion of bar, restaurant and club, and the perfect 'element' for a night on the town. The surprisingly large venue plays host to three bar counters, a dining area and large dance floor.

Al Muntaha

Entertainment alternates between a seven piece Canadian band and DJ Greg Stainer. If you do manage to 'iron' out the strict, if sometimes confusing, entrance policies, you're guaranteed a fun filled evening.

Food Serv Venue Value

Filipino

Other options → Chinese [p.363]

Tagpuan

Location → Karama Shopping Centre · Al Karama | 337 3959
Hours → 10:00 - 24:00
Web/email → n/a | Map Ref → 10-D2

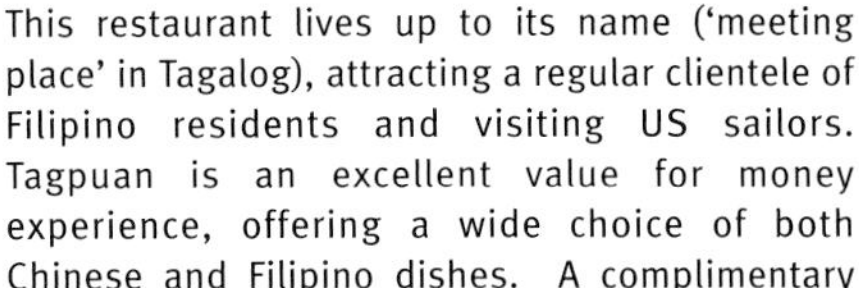

This restaurant lives up to its name ('meeting place' in Tagalog), attracting a regular clientele of Filipino residents and visiting US sailors. Tagpuan is an excellent value for money experience, offering a wide choice of both Chinese and Filipino dishes. A complimentary bowl of soup arrives with each main, and portions are generous. The Formica tables, TVs and free karaoke give this workingman's diner an unpretentious and happy atmosphere that genuinely welcomes visitors.

Food Serv Venue Value

Fine Dining

Al Muntaha

Location → Burj Al Arab · Umm Suqeim | 301 7600
Hours → 12:30 - 15:00 19:00 - 24:00
Web/email → www.jumeirahinternational.com | Map Ref → 4-A1

Al Muntaha is a great experience: its panoramic daytime view and modern techno décor become even more dramatic at night. Much thought has gone into the sophisticated menu that lists a dazzling choice of enticingly described dishes, and the wine list is encyclopaedic. Presentation is beautiful, and most dishes live up to expectations, but one or two are somewhat lacking in flavour. Al Muntaha pampers its guests with an exceptional venue and professional service, but at these prices, needs greater consistency in the food quality.

Food Serv Venue Value

Café Chic

Location → Le Meridien Dubai · Al Garhoud | 282 4040
Hours → 12:30 - 14:45 20:00 - 23:45
Web/email → cafechic@lemeridien-dubai.com Map Ref → 14-E3

This is a classic French restaurant with a modern twist. Overseen by internationally renowned chef Michel Rostang, the menu is an interesting mix of traditional dishes (Dover sole, foie gras and fillet mignon) and contemporary fare (sea bream and duck carpaccio); the star of the show is the legendary chocolate soufflé. The elegant and stylish decor is also reflected in the excellent presentation of the food, and this, coupled with attentive service ensures a delightful evening. SC

Food ●●●●○ Serv ●●●●○ Venue ●●●●○ Value ●●●◐○

Verre

Retro

Location → Le Meridien Mina · Al Sufouh | 399 3333
Hours → 11:00 - 21:00 19:00 - 21:00
Web/email → retro@lemeridien-minaseyahi.com Map Ref → 3-A2

Retro serves up consistently high quality food, thanks to the passion and expertise of the manager, Giles, and the chef's extraordinary culinary craft. The portions are healthy, the ingredients fresh, the presentation classic and the service impeccable, but it's the simple yet delicious food that will have you returning. Despite the open plan and minimalist décor, Retro feels intimate. The service is pleasant and the atmosphere relatively unpretentious. Book a table for special occasions. PG

Food ●●●●● Serv ●●●●◐ Venue ●●●●○ Value ●●●◐○

Verre

Location → Hilton Creek · Deira | 212 7551
Hours → 19:00 - 24:00
Web/email → www.hiton.com Map Ref → 11-C2

If you've been looking for a confident, elegant and sophisticated restaurant, Verre will end your search. Polite, knowledgeable staff guide you through an extensive wine list and on to a varied, mouth watering menu. Nouvelle cuisine as it was meant to be; the surroundings and staff put you at ease and let you enjoy some of the finest European dining in Dubai. More affordable than expected (especially for non drinkers), Verre is a fantastic place to celebrate and to impress. CG

Food ●●●●● Serv ●●●●● Venue ●●●●○ Value ●●●○○

Fish & Chips

Chippy, The

Location → Nr Defence R/A · Trade Centre 1&2 | 343 3114
Hours → 17:00 - 24:00
Web/email → n/a Map Ref → 9-A2

If you need a fish and chips fix, then this shop is ideal. Resembling a local UK chippy with plastic

Cascades

formica tables and chairs, The Chippy feels and looks authentic. Order the popular haddock and chips or try the haggis, white pudding (very tasty), or macaroni pie. The chips are golden and plump but the mushy peas could be mushier. If you have room for dessert try the pineapple and banana fritters or decadent battered Mars bars – if you dare! CC

Food Serv Venue Value

Fryer Tuck

Location → Opp Jumeirah Centre · Jumeira | 344 4228
Hours → 12:00 - 15:00 17:00 - 22:30
Web/email → n/a | Map Ref → 6-C2

Fancy good old English fish and chips, served with mushy peas and pickled onions – or how about steak and kidney pie? Eat in the bright, airy, though rather clinical, 50 seat restaurant, or take it away. The standard menu includes sausage in batter, cod, hammour, pies and other easily recognised fare, all deliciously cooked. Since opening in 1976, they have offered authentic chip shop food, and certainly know how to wrap a mean paper package of chips. The real thing, although arteries beware! CC

Food Serv Venue Value

Plaice, The

Location → Century Village · Al Garhoud | 286 8233
Hours → 11:00 - 01:00
Web/email → n/a | Map Ref → 14-C3

The Plaice offers a casual and relatively inexpensive dining experience with seating limited to a few tables inside and out (in the cooler months). While fish & chips is the main staple, diners can also choose from pies, prawns, chicken, fish fingers or even haggis. The dessert menu is limited and unexciting, and the beverage menu is concise. Service is, nevertheless, enthusiastic and attentive. Takeaway as well as home delivery is available to those in the restaurant's vicinity. NC

Plate smashing is a form of expression, culturally acceptable only in Greek restaurants. You can now get your point across for all other eateries and still avoid costly lawsuits. Just log on to Eat Out Speak Out, UAE's first online restaurant review forum and freely spill all thoughts about the dining experience.

Food Serv Venue Value

French

Apartment, The

Location → Jumeirah Beach Htl · Umm Suqeim | 406 8181
Hours → 19:00 - 23:30
Web/email → www.jumeirahinternational.com | Map Ref → 4-B2

Tucked away in a cosy corner of this magnanimous hotel, the Apartment offers fine French dining from a menu that changes monthly. Patrick Lenôtre has established the highest quality cuisine amid a friendly atmosphere sans the snobbish maitre d'. Guests are invited by the attentive staff to begin with complimentary wine and cheese. The braised foie gras appetiser and filet mignon are highly recommended. Great food, varied wine selection, hovering service (and even a small disco thrown in) rank the Apartment amongst the best in Dubai. AC

Food Serv Venue Value

The Apartment

Le Classique

Location → Emirates Golf Club · Emirates Hill | 380 2222
Hours → 12:00 - 14:30 19:00 - 22:30
Web/email → egc@dubaigolf.com | Map Ref → 3-A3

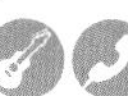

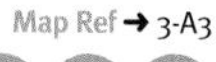

Le Classique lives up to its name, both in terms of décor as well as in the variety and quality of food. The menu exemplifies a good balance of meat, fish and fowl, but caters for vegetarians as well. The live pianist/singer does not intrude upon conversation, and the service is efficient. If you're looking to celebrate a special occasion or just want to pamper yourself, head to this place and you will not be disappointed. A note of caution: strict dress code applies.

Food Serv Venue Value

St Tropez Bistro

Location → Century Village · Al Garhoud | 286 9029
Hours → 12:30 - 23:30 00:30 - 00:00
Web/email → n/a | Map Ref → 14-C3

This quaint and intimate restaurant has the ambience of a small French bistro. The inside is cosy and friendly; alfresco dining is available in the Century Village courtyard, which is especially pleasant and relaxing in the winter months. On offer is a variety of grilled meats, such as juicy lamb rack or fillet. Steak, either prime beef or veal, is the house speciality. This is the type of place where you go for a quick bite – only to return home several hours later!

Food Serv Venue Value

Fusion

Other options → Fine Dining [p.370]

La Baie

Location → Ritz-Carlton Dubai · Marsa Dubai | 399 4000
Hours → 19:00 - 23:00
Web/email → rcdubai@emirates.net.ae | Map Ref → 2-E2

A pungent sea breeze and glimpses of the beach from over treetops give the outdoor terrace a more relaxed, tropical dining atmosphere, pulling away from the pretentious fine dining image. Simon Barber's innovative signature dishes, with a focus on seafood, blend modern and traditional styles, for example, oyster lemongrass ravioli in vanilla and lobster broth. An impressive wine list boasts plenty of New World offerings, however, some may find the single vegetarian option limiting. Warm, interactive table service resists the hotel like sterility of the décor.

Food Serv Venue Value

Mystizo

Location → Hotel InterContinental · Deira | 222 7171
Hours → 19:00 - 23:30
Web/email → intercon_bc@ihcdubai.co.ae | Map Ref → 8-C4

Mystizo gives a whole new meaning to fusion, mixing African, Arabian, Oriental and Spanish flavours. The ambience is modern and exotic, the food adequate. You're best off with one of their specialities – lamb shanks, the seafood combination or their signature dessert, the Strawberry Kilimanjaro. After your meal, head over to the Mystizo bar/club and dance the calories away. A special deal of unlimited beverages for Dhs.69 (ladies) and Dhs.99 (men) attracts a decent crowd. Good as a place to see and be seen.

Food Serv Venue Value

> **DUI**
>
> *Drinking and driving is illegal in Dubai, and although it's tempting to jump in the car after just one beer - don't! You may find yourself locked up for a couple of months. Be responsible when it comes to drinking and driving. Remember that you're in a Moslem country and must adhere to the rules here.*

Sphinx

Location → Pyramids · Umm Hurair (2) | 324 4100
Hours → 12:30 - 15:00 19:30 - 23:30
Web/email → www.pyramidsdubai.com | Map Ref → 13-D2

For an evening of great food and exotic ambience, the Sphinx is a must. From the excellent service to the scrumptious offerings on the menu, this venue continues to rate highly. The décor is unusual but beautiful, and the ambience, exotic (and very romantic). Try the bresola ham and cherantie melon starter, served with a sour berry dressing with slices of brie and parmesan (luscious!). The hot double chocolate sponge on a banana fritter with butterscotch sauce is a gastronomic delight.

Food Serv Venue Value

Teatro

Location → Towers Rotana · Trade Centre 1&2 | 343 8000
Hours → 11:30 - 15:00 18:00 - 02:00
Web/email → www.rotana.com | Map Ref → 9-B2

You are the leading player in the theatrically themed, buzzing Teatro. The extensive, cosmopolitan menu has offerings from Europe, Asia and India. Three samplers within the main menu, each in four acts (courses), provide decorative presentations from these regions. The main menu starter samplers, the dal dip and Thai style seafood, are the winners. When the curtain falls, try the dessert platter – a choice of cream laden mini Tiramisu, sorbets, chocolates and fruits. Well paced courses are served by friendly, attentive and helpful staff.

Food Serv Venue Value

German

Brauhaus

Location → Jumeira Rotana · Al Satwa | 345 5888
Hours → 18:00 - 01:00 Thu & Fri 12:00 - 24:00
Web/email → www.rotana.com
Map Ref → 6-E3

150

Devoid of pretense, this hidden venue delivers heavy German food with good cheer. The rustic authenticity begins with the music (cringe!), and continues through the gigantic portions and rich combinations. No-nonsense menu includes sausages aplenty, horseradish salmon (very nice), peppersteak (excellent), goulash soup, perfect Spätzle, apple strudel, and cheesecake. Vegetarian options are sparse. If you manage dessert, God bless; we couldn't. Unlike many joints in town, this one feels genuine. CC

Food Serv Venue Value

Der Keller

Location → Jumeirah Beach Htl · Umm Suqeim | 406 8181
Hours → 18:00 - 23:30
Web/email → www.jumeirahinternational.com
Map Ref → 4-B2

    150

Der Keller, meaning the cellar, gives you a warm welcome and hearty food along with an unexpected but fantastic view of the sea. The red bricked walls, carefully planned lighting and soft background music create a relaxed family atmosphere, regardless of whether you sit at the restaurant or sip at the bar. Do try the speciality veal dishes and the sauerkraut, not to mention the fondue to share. Service here, is always with a smile, but beware the Germanic sized portions – this is not a place for light eaters. EAT

Food Serv Venue Value

Der Keller

Hofbrauhaus

Location → JW Marriott Hotel · Deira | 262 4444
Hours → 19:30 - 24:30 19:30 - 24:30
Web/email → www.marriott.com
Map Ref → 12-A3

150

Doubling as both, a bar and a restaurant, this Bavarian style keller's specialities include a variety of German beers alongside an extensive selection of typical hearty south German dishes. The long list of German sausages, wiener schnitzel, sauerkraut, potato dumplings and soups will delight carnivores, while the Dunkelgold and Münchner Weissbier will have beer lovers in ecstasy. Get a group together and take over one of the 'Stuben' (private rooms) for a great alternative to the standard bar experience found elsewhere in Dubai. HP

Food Serv Venue Value

Indian

Other options → Pakistani [p.412]

Al Tandoor

Location → Opp Century Htl · Bur Dubai | 393 3349
Hours → 12:30 - 15:00 19:00 - 24:00
Web/email → n/a
Map Ref → 7-E2

100

In the heart of Indian restaurant land, Al Tandoor attracts a mixed crowd of happy eaters. The menu, offering no pork or beef, is extensive and the food is unusually subtle and delicate without being bland. Service can be spotty, but is always friendly. As expected, the value for money is good. If you're also looking for Indian furniture and wall coverings, Samuel will happily take you to his shop to continue your patronage! CC

Food Serv Venue Value

Antique Bazaar

Location → Four Points Sheraton · Bur Dubai | 397 7444
Hours → 12:30 - 15:30 19:30 - 03:00
Web/email → www.starwood.com
Map Ref → 8-A4

Perfectly adequate Indian food complements the pleasing scene at Antique Bazaar. Though not for

sale, antique seats – silver, heavily carved, or ivory inlaid chairs – define the beautifully decorated bazaar. A large troupe of musicians arrive at 21:00 to add authentic sound to sight. Bring out of town visitors to this lively, popular venue. Seek the security of thali (two meats, three vegetables, rice, naan and dessert) served on silver trays, and pretend that your intimate knowledge of Mughal cuisine created the memorable evening. CC

Food Serv Venue Value

Asha's

Location → Pyramids · Umm Hurair (2) | 324 4100
Hours → 12:30 - 15:30 19:30 - 02:00
Web/email → www.asharestaurants.com | Map Ref → 13-D2

Billed as contemporary Indian cuisine, Asha's offers flavoursome foods in a modern yet cosy atmosphere. The menu is a mix of Indian fusion and traditional Indian, and rich dishes are served by friendly and attentive staff. Diners can order from the chefs' favourites or choose from a wide selection of kebabs, meats, biryani, vegetarian and breads, all complemented by an extensive drinks list. Regardless of whether or not you're craving Indian food, Asha's deserves a visit. MML

Food Serv Venue Value

Ashiana

Location → Sheraton Hotel & Towers · Deira | 228 1707
Hours → 12:30 - 15:00 19:30 - 00:30
Web/email → www.starwood.com | Map Ref → 11-C1

Enjoy the diverse tastes of Indian in the intimate and upscale Ashiana. Jumpstart your taste buds with a bowl of cinnamon and pink lentil soup before taking on the house speciality main courses. Veggie lovers will find more than just the usual choices. Save room for the beautifully presented mango mascarpone dessert. The live music may not suit every taste but is non intrusive. A long time favourite, Ashiana's quality, service and value have built a loyal following. ABH

Food Serv Venue Value

Ashiana

Bikanervala

Location → Beh Bombay Chowpatty · Al Karama | 396 3666
Hours → 09:00 - 24:00
Web/email → bikanodb@emirates.net.ae | Map Ref → 10-E1

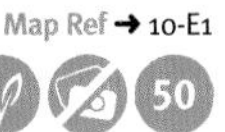

This fast food joint is famous for its Indian sweets and namkeens (salty snacks). Notorious for authenticity and bargain prices, the restaurant prides itself on traditional Rajasthani recipes passed down through the generations. Pani Puri (a savoury dish) and Ras Malai (a sweet dish) are two of the many mouthwatering delights on offer. Simply grab a voucher and move towards the cooking stations to watch your order come to life. Banquet tables as well as smaller settings satisfy all customers. Couch potatoes have the option of takeaway. CC

Food Serv Venue Value

Bombay Brasserie

Location → Marco Polo Hotel · Hor Al Anz | 272 0000
Hours → 24:00 - 24:00 19:30 - 03:00 none
Web/email → marcohot@emirates.net.ae | Map Ref → 8-E4

The Bombay Brasserie combines the best of hotel Indian with neighbourhood Indian. Low key service, an upscale setting, coherent decor, a variety of beverages and moderate decibel music give credit to the Marco Polo Hotel. The wonderfully prepared food served in generous quantities (with superb naan) parallels that of the best neighbourhood establishments. The inevitable price differential seems justified here because the crispy paneer, the fish curry, the perfectly cooked bindi and the many splendid companion dishes could simply not be better. AP

Food Serv Venue Value

Bombay Chowpatty

Location → Trade Centre Rd · Al Karama | 396 4937
Hours → 08:00 - 13:30 17:00 - 24:00
Web/email → n/a | Map Ref → 11-A1

Good, convenient Indian food makes this pair of casual eateries worth knowing. Bombay Chowpatty's main restaurant is located opposite the BurJuman Centre; its sister is in Lamcy Plaza. To help break the burger habit, consider this Indian alternative. The usual dishes – sometimes inscrutable on the menu – are fresh and tasty. Some preparations are quite spicy, but there is always a cool fruit juice or an iced lassi to put out the fire. Great value for money.

Food Serv Venue Value

Chhappan Bhog

Location → Trade Centre Rd · Al Karama | 396 8176
Hours → 09:00 - 24:00 Fri 09:00 - 11:00, 13:30-24:00
Web/email → n/a | Map Ref → 10-E1

One of the more refined vegetarian restaurants in town, Chhappan Bhog is a Karama favourite. Uniformed waiters competently present colourful, filling meals, and the tastefully decorated dining room is clean and bright. The chef clearly has a penchant for overdosing on oil, butter and cream, but judging by the popularity of the place, this is what people come for. Health conscious individuals can choose from the limited 'Weight Watchers' section, but be prepared for a calorie overdose, as there's ultimately no escape from the delicious lard.

Food Serv Venue Value

Chicken Tikka Inn

Location → · Various locations | 396 4600
Hours → 12:00 - 15:00 18:30 - 01:00
Web/email → na | Map Ref → n/a

Still going strong after 30 years, the original outlet has expanded into a small chain of restaurants. Popular favourites include chicken and mutton dishes, kebabs, grills, curries and biryani, plus a variety of vegetable dishes and a few seafood items. The restaurants are clean but fairly basic with ample seating and family rooms. Catering is also available and worth considering. Reasonably priced, friendly, and probably in your neighbourhood, this is an above average cheap eats joint. Other branches in Deira 222 5683, Jumeira 344 5524, Karama and Qusais 263 0677.

Food Serv Venue Value

Coconut Groove

Location → Rydges Plaza Hotel · Al Satwa | 398 3800
Hours → 12:00 - 15:00 19:00 - 24:30
Web/email → coconut@emirates.net.ae | Map Ref → 7-A4

This is as close as it gets when sampling authentic Indian cuisine in Dubai. Vibrant colours and taste combine to form wonderful flavours, and the mixture of Indian and Sri Lankan palates bring the best from Kerala, Tamil Nadu, Goa and Old Ceylon. An intimate setting with servers in ethnic garb make for a memorable setting. Wooden artefacts and palm trees modestly transform this restaurant into a time honoured dining experience.

Food Serv Venue Value

Delhi Darbar

Location → Opp Post Office · Al Karama | 334 7171
Hours → 11:30 - 15:30 18:30 - 00:30
Web/email → na | Map Ref → 10-E2

Delhi Darbar excels at Mughlai food, despite the extensive Chinese options. Subtle colours and simple decor contribute to the pleasant atmosphere. From reshmi paratha or biryani to fish fingers or golden fried prawns, plenty of delicious options are on offer. Free home delivery and takeaway are available. Business sorts frequent the restaurant for lunch because it's light on the stomach and the wallet. Due to its popularity, service can be slow; just enjoy the paintings on the wall and exercise patience.

Food Serv Venue Value

Foodlands

Location → Opp Ramada Continental Htl · Bur Dubai | 268 3311
Hours → 12:30 - 15:30 19:00 - 24:00
Web/email → n/a | Map Ref → 7-E3

Despite its supermarket style name, Foodlands provides a tasty range of Indian, Persian and Arabic dishes in comfortable, family friendly surroundings. After being presented a menu displaying a massive array of choices, your attention will most likely be

drawn to the buffet – excellent value at Dhs.29. The veggie offerings are the strongest of a broad selection, and all are served with fresh baked naan (bread). In addition, South Indian breakfast and lunch buffets make Foodlands the perfect stop for good cheap eats at any time. DK

Food ●●●●○ Serv ●●●●○ Venue ●●●◐○ Value ●●●●◐

Gazebo

Location → · Al Karama | 397 9930
Hours → 12:00 - 15:30 19:00 - 24:00
Web/email → n/a | Map Ref → 10-E1

100

An unusual name for an unusually great place. Indian food just doesn't get better than this as Gazebo impresses with spicy, authentic cuisine that is low on lard and high on flavour. Charcoal grilled specialities, such as the chunky chicken kebabs and mouthwatering marinated leg of lamb are second to none, and the salads and side dishes are bursting with zingy freshness. Try and leave room for a fresh fruit kulfi – it's exquisite. The staff here is genuinely friendly and service is top notch. JK

Food ●●●●● Serv ●●●●● Venue ●●◐○○ Value ●●●●●

Handi

Location → Taj Palace Hotel · Deira | 223 2222
Hours → 12:00 - 15:00 19:00 - 23:30
Web/email → tajdubai@emirates.net.ae | Map Ref → 11-D2

150

Great food, good service and a welcoming atmosphere describes an evening at Handi. Helpful staff keenly explain dishes on the menu and give recommendations. A delicious Hyderabadi chicken curry and an eye watering bhuna gosht are some of the star dishes. The vegetable biryani, a house speciality, is a soothing and tasty accompaniment. Alcohol is not served, however, exotically named mocktails are a worthy alternative. And your bill will end up to be a lot less than the food actually deserves. VB

Food ●●●●◐ Serv ●●●●◐ Venue ●●●●○ Value ●●●●○

India Palace

Location → Opp Sofitel City Cen. Htl · Al Garhoud | 286 9600
Hours → 12:00 - 16:00 19:00 - 01:00
Web/email → n/a | Map Ref → 14-D2

50

Walk through the doors and enter into a virtual India. The culinary experience, from start to finish, is close to perfection, and it only gets better when the bill arrives (you'll be pleasantly surprised at just how far your dirhams have stretched). The cuisine is yummy and authentic; chefs are handpicked right from the Indian subcontinent. The atmosphere nicely balances the adults and the kids. A booth upstairs provides the option of a more intimate experience, and a band downstairs makes for a livelier evening. AR

Food ●●●●◐ Serv ●●●●● Venue ●●●●◐ Value ●●●●●

Indian Pavilion, The

Location → Spinneys · Umm Suqeim | 394 1483
Hours → 12:30 - 15:00 18:45 - 23:15
Web/email → pavillion@emirates.net.ae | Map Ref → 5-A3

The Indian Pavilion brings you a taste of contemporary Indian cooking with traditional flavours and cooking styles, but an unconventional use of ingredients. Popular in Jumeira for takeaway and party catering, its food is a harmonious blend of India's diverse regional cuisines and ingredients, with tandoori kebabs from the northern frontier to curries from central India and seafood specialities from the southern coastal regions. Notable favourites are 'Omar Khayyam', tender marinated chicken kebabs, 'Karwari prawns', fried and tossed in masala and curry leaves, or 'daal pavilion', a quintessentially Indian creamy black lentil dish simmered overnight. CC

Food ●●●●◐ Serv ●●●◐○ Venue ●●●○○ Value ●●●◐○

Kamat

Location → Opp Bur Juman · Al Karama | 396 7288
Hours → 10:30 - 15:30 19:00 - 24:00
Web/email → n/a | Map Ref → 10-E1

50

Kamat, serving only veggie food, is quite well known and not without reason. If you're craving delicious curry and garlic naan at unbelievably reasonable prices, this is the place to go. The interior and the atmosphere do not drip Indian elegance; moreover, this always crowded joint is not the place for an intimate conversation (the next table is barely five inches away). It is, nevertheless, cheap, tasty and convenient dining. Good crispy papad is the king of the starters, to be followed by one of the best dosas in town. The South Indian selections are absolutely yummy. FA

Food ●●●○○ Serv ●●◐○○ Venue ●◐○○○ Value ●●●○○

Kitchen

Location → Beh Hardees · Satwa | 398 5043
Hours → 12:00 - 02:30
Web/email → openhouse_rest@yahoo.com | Map Ref → 7-A3

Just off the hustle and bustle of Diyafah Street, lies the real spice of India. They serve up flavourful kormas, kebabs and biryanis at reasonable prices. Once you're tucked into your corner of red tapestries and Maharaja paintings, let the fast service and Bollywood tunes consume your mood. Soon you'll be grooving to your own unrecognisable beat and eating up a storm. If you're looking for a late night spot to service your gulab jamun tooth, this is the place, where the kitchen doesn't close until 02:30! LA

Food Serv Venue Value

Kohinoor

Location → Sea View Hotel · Bur Dubai | 355 8080
Hours → 12:00 - 15:00 20:00 - 03:00
Web/email → www.seaviewhotel.co.ae | Map Ref → 7-E2

The Kohinoor certainly lives up to its name as the 'Star of India' amongst the Bur Dubai hotel restaurants. The real strength of the place is the quality and quantity of food on offer – a wide range of melt in the mouth kebabs, and other Mughlai style delicacies, are cooked and presented to perfection. Come with a strong appetite, as the menu rightly warns of a 'high satiety value' for some of the courses. The excellent food and good service are only marred by the high prices. LG

Food Serv Venue Value

Kwality

Location → Opp Ascot Htl · Bur Dubai | 393 6563
Hours → 13:00 - 15:00 20:00 - 23:45
Web/email → n/a | Map Ref → 7-E2

In spite of the orthographic nightmare of its name, this Indian restaurant is better than highly competent. Popular for many years, Kwality offers a bewildering array of dishes in a friendly setting. Downstairs is for bachelor diners and takeaway clients, but upstairs is where family customers sit and savour. Big portions, very reasonable prices, good service and endless options attract hoards. Novice Indian food aficionados will appreciate somewhat westernised flavours. The restaurant is busiest from 21:30 onwards and it is advisable to book on weekends and holidays. CC

Food Serv Venue Value

Masala

Location → Trade Centre Hotel · Trade Centre 1&2 | 331 4000
Hours → 12:30 - 15:00 19:30 - 23:30
Web/email → www.jumeirahinternational.com | Map Ref → 10-A2

Dark wood and soft furnishings set the scene for this mid scale Indian restaurant. A gimmicky wooden menu lists a good range of curries and tandoori dishes, with extensive vegetarian and health food options. Low key Indian music plays live in the background as smartly dressed waiters take your order, introducing you to their country's cuisine with touching enthusiasm. If the food disappoints, it's only a little, and the bill is quite moderate for an eatery of this level. GS

Food Serv Venue Value

Masala

Mohanlal's Taste Buds

Location → Nr Fish Market · Al Karama | 336 2001
Hours → 12:30 - 15:00 19:00 - 24:00
Web/email → tastbuds@emirates.net.ae | Map Ref → 10-D2

  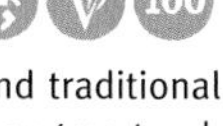

Escape to a world of friendly faces and traditional ambience. Soft ethnic music, a Banyan tree trunk supporting the roof and rustic wooden décor tastefully add to the charm. The menu warmly proposes a variety of Keralite dishes and a limited

range of Mughlai and Far Eastern delicacies, either a la carte or in a buffet. Value for money encourages families to flock here and courteous service and consistent warmth define this as a venue that feels like home away from home. CC

Food ●●◐○○ Serv ●●◐○○ Venue ●●●◐○ Value ●●●●○

Nawab

Location → Computer Plaza · Bur Dubai | 359 9884
Hours → 12:30 - 15:00 18:30 - 24:00
Web/email → nawabs@emirates.net.ae | Map Ref → 7-E4

 50

Nawab continues to dish up tasty and economical Indian food from the corner of the Al Ain Centre. The somewhat authentic dining area is cosy but rarely crowded. A picture menu guides diners through an assortment of veggie, tandoori and other favourites, spanning the range of Indian cuisine. Food is always reliable but not spectacular, and can be seasoned to taste. Best bets include masala fries, tawa veggies, the chilli garlic chicken, the spinach and the methi dishes. Finish with a mint tea to cap an enjoyably low key dining experience. DK

Just had a disastrous dining experience at a top nosh spot? Was your knickerbocker glory less than glorious, or your pizza a bit pathetic? Don't bottle it all up. Explode online with Eat Out Speak Out; we'll publish your pain, advertise your agony and forward your constructive criticism to the restaurant itself.

Food ●●●◐○ Serv ●●●◐○ Venue ●●●○○ Value ●●●●○

Nina

Location → One&Only Arabian Court · Al Sufouh | 399 9999
Hours → 19:00 - 23:30
Web/email → www.oneandonlyresort.com | Map Ref → 3-A2

    150

In keeping with the Royal Mirage, the décor is immersed in Arabic opulence. Dining here is akin to an evening in an Arabic palace, where the smallest detail warrants attention. The food is presented in novel tradition, and is a fusion of European and Indian ingredients. Friendly and knowledgeable staff value the customer, and extensively discuss the menu. The range of food caters to a variety of tastes, and the portions are small but adequate. Definitely a choice for a special occasion. AR

Food ●●●○○ Serv ●●●●◐ Venue ●●●●● Value ●●●●○

Tamasha

Location → Ramada Continental · Hor Al Anz | 266 2666
Hours → 20:00 - 03:00
Web/email → ramadadb@emirates.net.ae | Map Ref → 12-B4

    100

Closely packed tables set at different levels offer a good view of the entertainment in this late night venue. Geetmala specialises in live singing, Indian style. The tatty surroundings disguise attentive, smiling staff serving a wide variety of Indian specialities ranging from tandoori to prawn masala. A longish, if entertaining, wait is richly rewarded with fragrant, freshly cooked dishes with a blend of flavours, which complement but never overpower. A snack menu is popular with patrons arriving after 22:00 to enjoy the live music. CC

Food ●●◐○○ Serv ●●●◐○ Venue ●●●○○ Value ●●◐○○

Yoko Sizzlers

Location → Opp Bur Juman Centre · Al Karama | 396 8558
Hours → 12:00 - 15:00 19:00 - 24:00
Web/email → zaki206@hotmail.com | Map Ref → 11-A1

No, it's not a Japanese restaurant; it's a Bombay chain. Yoko is what the management prefers to describe as a 'sizzler' and the food does sizzle, with hot plates of beef, chicken, mutton or seafood steaks. Gigantic portions of Indian (and some Chinese) food are served quickly and efficiently. The décor is reminiscent of a fast food joint, with a few comfortable seats in the corners. A good place to take the kids or to pop in for a quick meal if you're in the neighbourhood.

Food ●●○○○ Serv ●●●○○ Venue ●●◐○○ Value ●●◐○○

Thai Chi

International

Aeroplane

Location ➜ Golden Tulip Aeroplane Hotel · Deira | 272 2999
Hours ➜ 13:00 - 15:00 19:30 - 23:30
Web/email ➜ www.goldentulip.com Map Ref ➜ 8-E3

100

Upon boarding, it may appear that you've stumbled into the first class section of an Emirates aircraft. Comfortable plane seats, complete with attendant call lights, are contained within an aircraft cabin of sorts. The menu includes a diverse and very reasonably priced selection of good quality food. The service, sadly, is anything but first class. Travellers should also note that the flight is dry. This is a unique dining concept that may appeal to some, (particularly families with kids) but not a place for business dinners or first dates. NQ

Food ●●●●○ Serv ●●○○○ Venue ●●●◐○ Value ●●●◐○

Al Dana

Location ➜ Crowne Plaza · Trade Centre 1&2 | 331 1111
Hours ➜ 24 hours
Web/email ➜ hicpdxb@emirates.net.ae Map Ref ➜ 9-D2

Crowne Plaza has a variety of interesting places to dine in. And with so much choice, there is actually little reason to choose Al Dana, unless it's for breakfast. A buffet only restaurant, the typical array of Arabic meze and a good sprinkling of antipasti can cause you to overfill on the starters – no bad thing since the main courses leave a lot to be desired. The ambience and décor do not reflect the Arabic name and the overall effect is more cafeteria than restaurant. LG

Food ●●○○○ Serv ●●◐○○ Venue ●◐○○○ Value ●●◐○○

Al Dana

Location ➜ Riviera Hotel · Deira | 222 2131
Hours ➜ 12:00 - 15:00 18:00 - 24:00
Web/email ➜ riviera@emirates.net.ae Map Ref ➜ 8-C3

50

Located in the Riviera Hotel along the Creek, Al Dana offers good value for simple fare and an opportunity for an evening stroll along the wharf after dinner. Small, quiet, and unpretentious, the restaurant's international buffet menu changes daily and includes soups, salads, a variety of meats and fish, and homemade desserts. The service is excellent, the wait staff attentive. The unlicensed status can mean a quiet atmosphere, but although this is not a destination in itself, it's a worthwhile option if in the neighbourhood. SC

Food ●●●◐○ Serv ●●●○○ Venue ●○○○○ Value ●●●●○

Al Dawaar

Location ➜ Hyatt Regency · Deira | 209 1100
Hours ➜ 12:30 - 15:30 19:00 - 23:30
Web/email ➜ www.dubai.regency.hyatt.com Map Ref ➜ 8-D2

 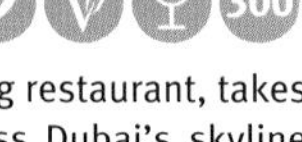

Al Dawaar, Dubai's only revolving restaurant, takes you on a panoramic spin across Dubai's skyline whilst offering excellent international cuisine. The lunch/dinner buffet is extensive and quite creative, and prices veer towards the higher side with drinks costing extra. Candles flicker at sunset and giant windows provide diners with a magical scape of the Arabian Gulf, Creek and quick paced city below.

Al Dawaar

Service is polite and friendly and children are heartily welcomed. This is sky dining at its best!

Food●●●●◐Serv●●●●○Venue●●●●◐Value●●●◐○

Al Muna

Location → Mina A'Salam · Umm Suqeim | 366 8888
Hours → 06:00 - 11:00 12:30 - 15:00 19:00 - 23:30
Web/email → www.jumeirahinternational.com Map Ref → 4-A2

Immersed in good company (given the Burj Al Arab is literally a stone's throw away), the atmosphere/ambience within this restaurant is subtle and unpretentious. But happen upon the terrace and the surrounding environment conjures up a fusion of paradise and romance. Serving international cuisine, a menu plus buffet option caters to all. The staff are extremely friendly and eager to please, but do choose your company carefully – many words would need to fill the extended gaps between courses. Top off the meal with some deserts, which are particularly tasty.

Food●●●○○Serv●●●◐○Venue●●●●◐Value●●●●○

Al Muna

Al Riqa Restaurant

Location → Metropolitan Deira · Deira | 295 9171
Hours → 06:30 - 15:30 19:30 - 22:30
Web/email → www.methotels.com Map Ref → 11-D3

This is a bright and uncomplicated restaurant, serving basic and simple food that is well produced and presented. The menu seems to cater mainly for German visitors and the choice is therefore small but reasonably diverse. Vegetarian food is also available and service is warm and friendly. Tucked away in the back streets of Deira you are unlikely to stumble on Al Riqa Restaurant by accident. As a result ,it seems to be similar to the other outlets in the hotel, practical and designed for the hotel guest, as opposed to the local resident or Dubai visitor staying elsewhere.

Food●◐○○○Serv●●○○○Venue●○○○○Value●◐○○○

Amby's

Location → Ambassador Hotel · Bur Dubai | 393 9444
Hours → 12:00 - 14:30 19:00 - 23:30
Web/email → ambhotel@astamb.com Map Ref → 8-A2

Situated in the heart of Bur Dubai, Amby's proximity to the George and Dragon allows it a wider than average range of well priced draught beers. Being the only formal restaurant in the Ambassador, the menu is broad by default, covering English, Indian and Italian classics. The service is friendly and efficient; the architecture and décor, however, are more than a little dated. Although not a destination venue, the restaurant's convenient location makes for a decent well priced meal.

Food●●●○○Serv●●●◐○Venue●○○○○Value●●●●○

Antigo

Location → Le Meridien Dubai · Al Garhoud | 282 4040
Hours → 12:30 - 15:30 19:00 - 23:30
Web/email → antigo@le-meridien-dubai.com Map Ref → 14-E3

Arabic eclectic? Matisse-ish? The décor may be hard to classify, but is definitely colourful and fun to discuss. Theme nights offer a range of possibilities; the generous buffet includes forty cold and twenty hot items, some prepared while you wait by a most helpful and attentive chef. Be sure to ask the staff for any deals, especially ones that might include alcohol.

Food●●●●○Serv●●○○○Venue●●◐○○Value●●◐○○

Bella Vista

Location → Jumeira Rotana · Al Satwa | 345 5888
Hours → 11:00 - 15:30 19:00 - 23:00
Web/email → www.rotana.com Map Ref → 6-E3

Visitors and residents alike flock to the Bella Vista to enjoy its dinner buffet theme nights. A wide range of

food is offered and quickly replenished by the chef, and the quality rarely differs. Function rooms dot the restaurant's entrance, giving it a slightly confused look, but this gives way to a beautiful view and a casual Mediterranean layout at the back. Moreover, the number of patrons that the restaurant attracts endorses the excellent value of the buffet. VML

Food ●●●○○ Serv ●●●●○ Venue ●●●○○ Value ●●●●○

Boardwalk

Location ➔ Creek Golf Club · Al Garhoud | 295 6000
Hours ➔ 09:00 - 24:00
Web/email ➔ creekfnb@dubaigolf.com | Map Ref ➔ 14-C2

Arguably the most scenic alfresco eating area in town, the Boardwalk offers panoramic views of the Creek from each of its three decks and from the indoor bar area. With European, Arabic and Asian cuisine, the menu boasts an exotic range of appetisers and entrées, from a Middle Eastern platter to a prime fillet of beef. Although the food itself is unpredictable, ranging from delicious to bland, the service is efficient and pleasant – and anyway, you go to the Boardwalk for the stunning view. AB

Food ●●●○○ Serv ●●●●○ Venue ●●●●● Value ●●●●○

Cascades

Location ➔ Fairmont Hotel · Trade Centre 1&2 | 332 5555
Hours ➔ 00:00 - 23:45 00:00 - 23:45 24 hrs
Web/email ➔ www.fairmont.com | Map Ref ➔ 9-E1

Bathed in an electric blue aura, it's hard not to be mesmerised by the slick, artsy look and feel of this 24/7 restaurant. Once you do manage to lift your jaw, soft spoken waitresses offer you the choice of dining a la carte or diving straight into an extensive buffet. Cuisines range from European, Mediterranean, Arabic and seafood, with perfect portions geared to fill, not bloat, your appetite. Skipping dessert can be a punishable offence, as it is the perfect end to your overall Cascades experience. DP

Food ●●●●○ Serv ●●●●○ Venue ●●●●◐ Value ●●●●○

Celebrities

Location ➔ One&Only Palace · Al Sufouh | 399 9999
Hours ➔ 08:00 - 10:30 19:00 - 23:30
Web/email ➔ www.oneandonlyresort.com | Map Ref ➔ 3-A2

Celebrities offers contemporary fine dining with elegance and quality. The sumptuous dining room is a quirky candlelit retreat with hypnotic views, and is perfect for those in search of a romantic idyll. Ramsay protégé Chef Frederick presents dainty, delectable dishes with quasi Persian influences, which are a triumph of quality over quantity. As with the food, the service can be inconsistent, but is at times inspired. Celebrities, like any major star, clearly has a lot of talent, even if it doesn't always produce an Oscar winner. JK

Food ●●●◐○ Serv ●●●◐○ Venue ●●●●● Value ●●●○○

Clubhouse, The

Location ➔ Jumeirah Beach Club · Jumeira | 344 5333
Hours ➔ 07:00 - 23:00
Web/email ➔ www.jumeirahinternational.com | Map Ref ➔ 5-D1

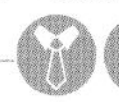     

Verdant landscaping, salty air and the soothing sound of waves frame the Clubhouse's casual

Boardwalk

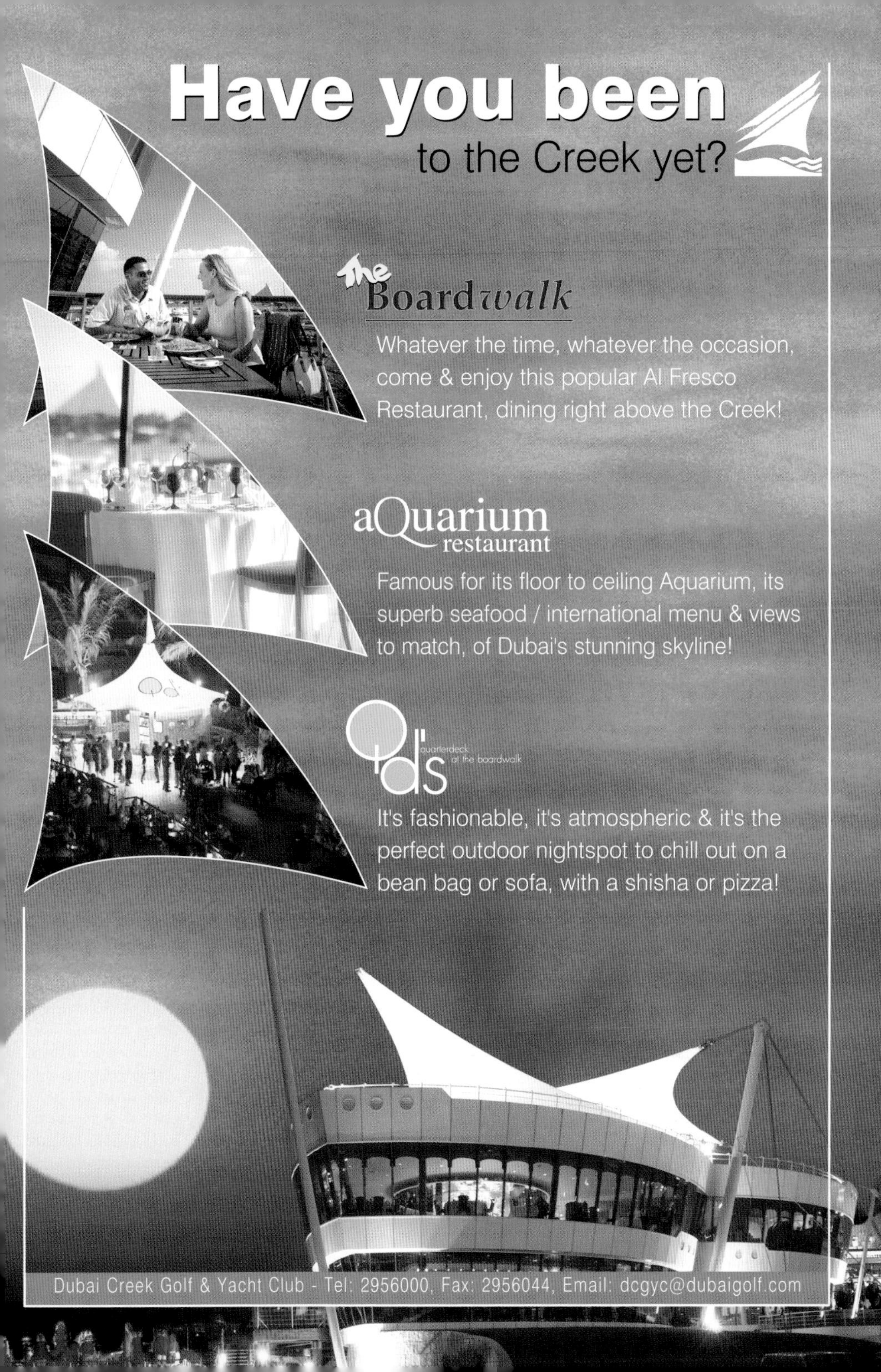
Have you been
to the Creek yet?
The Boardwalk
Whatever the time, whatever the occasion, come & enjoy this popular Al Fresco Restaurant, dining right above the Creek!
aQuarium restaurant
Famous for its floor to ceiling Aquarium, its superb seafood / international menu & views to match, of Dubai's stunning skyline!
QD's quarterdeck at the boardwalk
It's fashionable, it's atmospheric & it's the perfect outdoor nightspot to chill out on a bean bag or sofa, with a shisha or pizza!
Dubai Creek Golf & Yacht Club - Tel: 2956000, Fax: 2956044, Email: dcgyc@dubaigolf.com

ambience. After an ocean swim or a game of tennis, you can relax with a breakfast, lunch or dinner on the patio. A dinner menu offers a trendy mix of salads, sandwiches, Asian dishes, pasta, and Arabian meze, although the best value is the grilled fish and meat. Efficient service, good food and a relaxed setting make this an ideal option for comfortable outdoor dining during the cooler months. (SC)

Food ●●●●○ Serv ●●●◐○ Venue ●●●●○ Value ●●●◐○

Colonnade, The

Location → Jumeirah Beach Htl · Umm Suqeim | 406 8181
Hours → 06:00 - 00:00
Web/email → www.jumeirahinternationa.com | Map Ref → 4-B2

Stylishly set in the Jumeirah Beach Hotel, variety defines this venue. The profitable strategy of alternating daily themes attracts the buffet boffin as well as the hotel guests. If you want to sample some local food, be sure to try the Arabic buffet, which has an excellent range of starters, including hot and cold meze and Shorbat Dijaj (chicken, tomato and coriander soup). With the added attraction of an outside terrace, The Colonnade is ideal for a casual family brunch. (TP)

Food ●●◐○○ Serv ●●○○○ Venue ●●○○○ Value ●●○○○

Exchange, The

Entre Nous

Location → Novotel World Trade Centre · Shk Zayed Rd | 332 0000
Hours → 06:00 - 01:00
Web/email → www.novotel.com | Map Ref → 9-E3

An above average international restaurant in a hotel geared more towards serving business clientele than holiday makers, Entre Nous serves as a great place for a tasty lunch or an intimate dinner. The menu has a mix of healthy and indulgent choices, and the chef is confident enough to advise against well done steaks (and he's right!) If you like a good meal in a dining atmosphere with a more contemporary feel, this place is right up your alley. (AH)

Food ●●●○○ Serv ●●●○○ Venue ●●◐○○ Value ●●◐○○

Exchange, The

Location → Fairmont Hotel · Trade Centre 1&2 | 311 8000
Hours → 19:00 - 01:00
Web/email → www.fairmont.com | Map Ref → 9-E1

Succulent US Angus beef cooked to absolute perfection, and stringently trained staff (who really know their stuff!) make this a winning entry in the list of top Dubai steakhouses. Tailored primarily to business clientele, the decor is rich, simple and masculine and yet, families and couples look equally at home. Choose one of the three private dining rooms to really impress guests and if you can drag yourself from the heady comforts of the leather armchairs, slip next door to the Cigar Bar for a fitting finale. (KM)

Food ●●●●◐ Serv ●●●●● Venue ●●●●○ Value ●●●◐○

Fontana

Location → Al Bustan Hotel · Al Garhoud | 705 4650
Hours → 12:30 - 15:00 19:00 - 23:30
Web/email → www.rotana.com | Map Ref → 14-E3

200

Variety sure is the spice of life at Fontana's theme nights. Sunday is seafood night; Monday, Spanish night; Wednesday, curry night and Thursday, Tex Mex (all theme nights include unlimited select beverages). The décor tunes in to each particular theme with colour and zest. The food lacks pizzazz but is, nevertheless, good value for money. Open for the early birds, they serve a breakfast, lunch and dinner, both buffet and la carte. Service is friendly and attentive, but at times, can be rather spotty. (AD)

Food ●●●○○ Serv ●●●○○ Venue ●●●●○ Value ●●●●○

> **Cultural Meals**
>
> *Bastakiya is a great place to eat and simultaneously soak up local culture. This traditional part of the city is best experienced by strolling in the streets, visiting the museums and dining at one of many art cafés. A cultural and fuel boost injection rolled into one.*

Garden Café, The

Location → Trade Centre Hotel · Trade Centre 1&2 | 331 4000
Hours → 06:30 - 23:00
Web/email → www.jumeirahinternational.com Map Ref → 10-A2

The Garden Café has satisfied patrons for many years in this relatively old and even venerable hotel. Trying to be all things to all visitors, the café must satisfy a number of tastes (British, Russian, French etc) and, in doing so, rarely reaches gastronomical heights. The food is, nevertheless, dependable. The buffet, perhaps, is better value than the a la carte, but it is the desserts – cakes, tortes, puddings, mousses, cookies, candies and more – that declare their quality, allowing diners to enjoy the best of this place. AP

Food Serv Venue Value

Japengo Café

Location → Oasis Tower · Trade Centre 1&2 | 343 5028
Hours → 07:30 - 24:30
Web/email → www.binhendi.com Map Ref → 9-B2

As the fusion sounding name suggests, this is a fresh Japanese Western hybrid diner that impresses with top notch food and drink in a bright, minimalist setting. The meals are excellent here and include sushi, salads, sandwiches, hot dishes and fresh juices. Crab cakes and chicken dumplings are a treat and the assorted yakitori is superb – even better washed down with a fresh Kiwi juice. The portions are generous and the prices reasonable, although drinks and water border on steep. JK

Food Serv Venue Value

La Cité

Location → Sofitel City Centre · Al Garhoud | 603 8200
Hours → 12:00 - 15:00 19:30 - 23:30
Web/email → cityhotl@emirates.net.ae Map Ref → 14-D1

Typical of catch-all hotel restaurants, La Cite piles on standard international fare, both á la carte and in a daily changing theme. Multitudinous choices can please or disappoint against midrange hotel prices. Sunny Mediterranean decor bounces blue tinged lighting off pale yellow furnishings and a black wrought iron central cooking station. Food and service are both, generally ever present and amenable, but not altogether crisp. Although handy for the amenities of the Deira City Centre, few would seek La Cite out. DW

Food Serv Venue Value

Lakeview

Location → Creek Golf Club · Al Garhoud | 295 6000
Hours → 06:30 - 23:00
Web/email → creekfnb@dubaigolf.com Map Ref → 14-C2

Lounge by the Creek, watch the boats go by, and indulge in elegant pub food. This is Lakeview, one of the lesser expensive spots at the Club, with food that is just as good. Sections of the menu are infused with Asian flavour; the rest is above average pub fare and pastas. Nevertheless, the venue encourages an intimate evening with a loved one, or a quiet catch up with an old friend over a seafood salad and a chocolate orange layered cake. The house wine (both red and white) is recommended.

Note: *The restaurant will re-open in September.(LA)*

Food Serv Venue Value

Entre Nous

Market Café, The

Location → Grand Hyatt Dubai · Umm Hurair (2) | 317 2222
Hours → 12:30 - 15:30 19:00 - 23:30 Breakfast - 06:00 till 11:30
Web/email → www.dubai.grand.hyatt.com Map Ref → 13-E3

  100

Situated in the lower lobby of the opulent Grand Hyatt, this glorified food court offers Italian, Indian and Japanese cuisine, a limited Arabic selection and a grill station. Diners are obliged to walk around the food stations to 'shop' for their meal, using personal swipe cards. The general atmosphere is too casual to be categorised as a relaxing social venue, but probably works well if you're an individual, out in the market for a quick bite. JT

Food Serv Venue Value

Market Place, The

Location → JW Marriott Hotel · Deira | 262 4444
Hours → 12:30 - 15:00 19:30 - 23:30
Web/email → www.marriott.com Map Ref → 12-A3

  200

A good 'all you can eat' concept with a range of cuisine, from Italian to Chinese to BBQ grill plus beverages (and at a very reasonable price). The venue has a marketplace feel with strategically placed 'shop shelves' of goodies and fare piled high. The ambience is perfect for lunch and just intimate enough for a cosy dinner. A diverse buffet suits every taste; the unusual and delicious hors d'oeuvres are highly recommended. The staff is jovial and helpful, making for a relaxed atmosphere and a leisurely bite. AH

Food Serv Venue Value

Market Café, The

Meridien Village Terrace

Location → Le Meridien Dubai · Al Garhoud | 282 4040
Hours → 20:00 - 24:00
Web/email → julesbar@le-meridien-dubai.com Map Ref → 14-E3

   100

Buffeted senseless by Dubai's buffets, diners can rejuvenate at the hotel's terrace (during the cooler evenings of course). Amidst soothing greenery and flowing water, eight inviting stations (six with their own cooks) offer salmon with ginger, lamb roast, fish thermidor, roasted quail, grilled vegetables and more, with the return of each on East meets West night (themes change nightly). Cheerful staff ceaselessly replenish beverages – all for Dhs.99, but obviously not without reservations. AP

Food Serv Venue Value

Midnight Cafeteria

Location → Opp Municipality · Al Karama | 396 7899
Hours → 10:30 - 15:00 17:00 - 24:45
Web/email → www.midnightcafeteria.com Map Ref → 10-E2

    50

Rightfully claiming to be 'The Little Café with a Lot', Midnight Café comprises two tables and four chairs on the pavement, but offers a great Indian meets Western fast food menu bursting with flavour. The majority of their business is delivery within Deira, Karama and Bur Dubai. Specialties include Frankeez, (rolled chapattis filled with spicy chicken tikka, vegetable or mutton), 'Chicken Looks Good', garlic bread that literally melts in your mouth and dates with banana in cream. Control the drool and order now! CH

Food Serv Venue Value

Oceana

Location → Hilton Jumeirah · Marsa Dubai | 399 1111
Hours → 12:00 - 15:00 18:30 - 23:00
Web/email → www.hilton.com Map Ref → 2-D2

Although mostly frequented by hotel guests, Oceana is an option worth considering if you're looking for a quiet relaxed brunch, lunch or dinner buffet with family or friends. An a la carte menu is on offer, but the buffet is the draw, with a variety of themed nights, ranging from Arabic to New Orleans and Italian. Veggies can have a feast on the selection of salads on offer, and meat lovers will

drool at the live cooking station where the daily special is prepared before their eyes. HK

Food Serv Venue Value

Oxygen

Location → Al Bustan Hotel · Al Garhoud | 282 0000
Hours → 18:00 - 03:00
Web/email → www.rotana.com | Map Ref → 14-E3

All that dancing built up your appetite? Take a break from strutting your stuff in this stylish nightclub, and dine in their restaurant. A basket of fries and a greasy burger is the expected norm in most clubs, but Oxygen clearly shrugs off this stereotype with innovative dishes and chic presentation. With sushi on the menu and the 'vegilicious' burger, a variety of tastes are catered for. The tempting desserts are worth the indulgence and don't fret those calories – just shed 'em off back at the dance floor. PR

Food Serv Venue Value

Palm Garden

Location → Sheraton Jumeirah Beach · Marsa Dubai | 399 5533
Hours → 06:00 - 24:00
Web/email → www.starwood.com | Map Ref → 2-D2

After a recent refurb, Palm Garden offers a serene dining environment in – you've guessed it – an indoor garden of palms. A la carte is available, but the focus is on the buffet. The choice is standard fare; the dishes, though, are well executed – fresh, hot and tasty. Braised lamb shank falls from the bone and the beef in black beans is full of flavour. A sinful crème brulee is a worthy temptation. The Palm Garden is nothing innovative – just your average good hotel buffet. VB

Food Serv Venue Value

Seasons

Location → Century Village · Al Garhoud | 286 9216
Hours → 08:00 - 13:00 22:00 - 01:00
Web/email → www.mmidubai.com | Map Ref → 14-C3

Nestled under the tennis stadium at the well landscaped Aviation Club, Seasons takes its spirit from a steady baseline game played swiftly and surely. After a gently satisfying warm up volley of chicken soup, you encounter salads, pastas, sandwiches with splendid fries, and unpretentious main courses – the core of the Seasons game. Beverages of all sorts, breakfast at eight, and lunch specials give it the unique spin. Never to be a singles star, Seasons is nonetheless a reliable partner that is not to be overlooked.

Other Locations: Dubai Internet City (391 8711) AP

Food Serv Venue Value

Spectrum On One

Location → Fairmont Hotel · Trade Centre 1&2 | 311 8101
Hours → 17:30 - 19:00
Web/email → www.fairmont.com | Map Ref → 9-E1

Eight kitchens, corresponding décors, authentic, flavourful dishes and delightful service (on most nights) barely sum up an otherwise 'enormous' dining experience. Just turn the menu to be transported to Normandy for seafood, Thailand for curries, Japan for teppanyaki and yakitori, Europe for modern classic, India for tandoori delights and China for dim sum, or visit the Raw Bar for everything... well... raw. Cap the night with house prepared chocolates from their gourmet retail boutique (yes, they have that too!).

Please see review under On the Town – General Bar Section [p.450]. LM

Food Serv Venue Value

Spice Island

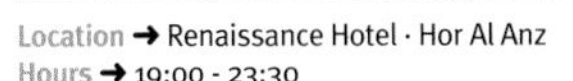

Location → Renaissance Hotel · Hor Al Anz | 262 5555
Hours → 19:00 - 23:30
Web/email → rendubai@emirates.net.ae | Map Ref → 12-A3

A fixed price for Tex Mex, Middle and Far Eastern food plus drinks work out well for a big night out or

Spice Island

a party. The extensive buffet and live cooking stations, and plentiful drink options attract hoards of revellers. On the weekends, they spill out into the chillier foyer cafe. Food themes are spread out in different alcoves along the restaurant. The wood and bamboo décor adapts with each section, while varied seating areas keep the place relatively intimate for such a large, popular venue.

Food ●●●●○ Serv ●●●●○ Venue ●●●●◐ Value ●●●●◐

TIMES

Location → Dubai Media City · Al Sufouh | 391 0199
Hours → 09:00 - 23:00
Web/email → www.dubaimediacity.com | Map Ref → 3-A2

What better way to maximise use of a large floor space than to convert it into a salsa tutorium? Weekly classes are given by South American Latin dance champions, and the Wednesday's Dhs.70 'dine and dance' option is a novel idea. Keep an eye out for the regular promotions each week. The menu is diverse, tasty and healthy; Friday is 'Family Fun Day', while regular special discounts, late night hours and free coffee refills draw in the local Media City crowd on a daily basis.

Food ●●●○○ Serv ●●●◐○ Venue ●●●◐○ Value ●●●●○

> **www.EAT OUT SPEAK OUT.com**
>
> *Just had a disastrous dining experience at a top nosh spot? Was your knickerbocker glory less than glorious, or your pizza a bit pathetic? Don't bottle it all up. Explode online with Eat Out Speak Out; we'll publish your pain, advertise your agony and forward your constructive criticism to the restaurant itself.*

Villa Beach Restaurant

Location → Jumeirah Beach Htl · Umm Suqeim | 406 8181
Hours → 12:00 - 18:00 19:00 - 23:00
Web/email → www.jumeirahinternational.com | Map Ref → 4-B2

Follow the signs to perhaps the most romantic and isolated of all the restaurants at the Jumeirah Beach Hotel – a truly outstanding dining experience awaits you. While the view of the Burj with its changing colours is unparalleled, the fine service and excellent food at Villa Beach will soon capture all your attention. Don't miss the lobster starter and be sure to save room for dessert. In between, don't forget to go slow and savour the beautifully presented and exquisitely prepared international cuisine.

Food ●●●●● Serv ●●●●● Venue ●●●●◐ Value ●●●●●

Wavebreaker

Location → Hilton Jumeirah · Marsa Dubai | 399 1111
Hours → 10:00 - 22:00
Web/email → www.hilton.com | Map Ref → 2-D2

Spend a lazy afternoon in the sun at Wavebreaker. Set on a spacious deck, indulge in alcoholic beverages and snacks, such as fish and chips, sandwiches and salads. Theme night buffets include seafood on Mondays, Polynesian on Wednesdays and Arabic on Fridays. Happy hour is a real treat, at two drinks for the price of one every evening from 17.00 to 19.00. Whilst the food and service here are perfectly fine, it is the view and ambience of a beachside bar that are the attraction.

Food ●●●○○ Serv ●●●○○ Venue ●●●●○ Value ●●●○○

Italian

Other options → **Mediterranean [p.405]**

Al Fresco

Location → Crowne Plaza · Trade Centre 1&2 | 331 1111
Hours → 12:00 - 15:30 19:00 - 23:00
Web/email → www.dubaicrowneplaza.com | Map Ref → 9-D2

This captivating trattoria brings in quite a bit of business, so make reservations before you go. Dinner is a relaxing experience, and lunch, rejuvenating (sunshine and honey kissed skylights boost declining afternoon energy levels). In an open plan kitchen, the chef spins out a delectable variety of truly Italian pastas and pizzas, and the service is quick and helpful. A perfect venue for a business lunch or an intimate tête à tête.

Food ●●●◐○ Serv ●●●◐○ Venue ●●●◐○ Value ●●●◐○

Andiamo!

Location → Grand Hyatt Dubai · Umm Hurair (2) | 317 2222
Hours → 12:30 - 15:00 18:00 - 23:30
Web/email → www.dubai.grand.hyatt.com | Map Ref → 13-E3

Off the atrium of the impressive Grand Hyatt is Andiamo! – a modern Italian restaurant with a colourful decor and simply huge lava lamps that threaten to distract you from everything (maybe even your date). Andiamo! boasts four Italian chefs and, whilst the menu is rather 'Italian by numbers', the food is excellent. Pizzas are wood fired in plain sight, the antipasti buffet is varied and tasty, and the pastas are just right. GS

Food ●●●●○ Serv ●●●◐○ Venue ●●●◐○ Value ●●●●○

Andiamo!

Bacchus

Location → Fairmont Hotel · Trade Centre 1&2 | 311 8000
Hours → 11:00 - 03:30 07:00 - 23:00
Web/email → www.fairmont.com Map Ref → 9-E1

250

Bacchus goes out of its way to bring a little piece of Italy to Dubai. Using the finest ingredients and an al forno oven, an array of creative pizzas (named after Bacchus' Roman circle of 'friends') are served. Try to not watch the calories and just dive into the dessert. The service is attentive and friendly without being intrusive, while candlelight, marble tables, Sheikh Zayed on one end and the pool on the other set the mood for a lovely evening out. AD

Food ●●●●○ Serv ●●●●○ Venue ●●●●◐ Value ●●●●◐

BiCE

Location → Hilton Jumeirah · Marsa Dubai | 399 1111
Hours → 12:00 - 15:00 19:00 - 24:00
Web/email → www.hilton.com Map Ref → 2-D2

200

Stylish and relaxing with exemplary staff and sensational food, BiCE continues to be a popular choice for lovers of premier, if pricier, Italian cuisine. A broad range of culinary delights include fresh, perfectly cooked pasta, luscious pizza and delicious specials; the oven baked sea bream is exceptional. Attractive wooden furnishings, pristine linen napery, an entertaining and talented pianist, and brilliant service turn any meal into a special occasion. A stiff contender on the list of Dubai's fabulous places. PL

Food ●●●●◐ Serv ●●●●● Venue ●●●●● Value ●●●●○

BiCE

Carnevale

Location → Jumeirah Beach Htl · Umm Suqeim | 406 8181
Hours → 12:30 - 15:00 19:00 - 23:00
Web/email → www.jumeirahinternational.com Map Ref → 4-B2

150

Carnevale offers a personalised, intimate and homey Italian ambience rare to Dubai. A rich and impressive à la carte menu comprises a range of pasta, poultry and red meat (pizzas are not included), but fish dishes seem to be the focus. The wine selection has some Italian gems that are rarely seen in this part of the world. Sit on the balcony if the climate permits, and let the eloquent and attentive staff guide you through a pleasurable authentic Italian experience. JT

Food ●●●◐○ Serv ●●●◐○ Venue ●●●●○ Value ●●●◐○

Casa Mia

Location → Le Meridien Dubai · Al Garhoud | 702 2506
Hours → 12:30 - 14:45 20:00 - 23:30
Web/email → casamia@le-meridien-dubai.com Map Ref → 14-E3

This atmospheric Italian eatery is particularly popular with residents and business clientele. The

a la carte menu offers traditional fare (such as pasta and stone baked pizza) along with the more intricate dishes (pork fillet or fish). The wine menu is extensive, the portions are generous and the staff is of a silver service standard. Greatly appreciated is the option of small or large servings. Set in the quaint Le Meridien Village, Casa Mia is a cut above when it comes to an Italian experience in Dubai. EAT

Food ●●●●◐ Serv ●●●●◐ Venue ●●●●◐ Value ●●●●●

Come Prima

Location → Al Bustan Hotel · Al Garhoud | 282 0000
Hours → 12:00 - 15:00 19:00 - 23:00
Web/email → www.rotana.com | Map Ref → 14-E3

Come Prima is notable for outstanding food, service to match, and an excellent value for money Dhs.95 all-you-can-eat and drink antipasti night. The décor is upmarket 'Manhattan', with understated, elegant and trendy, but not at all stuffy surroundings. The menu's attention to detail and creativity are subtle, and can be superb. There are monthly special menus and lunch specials offer an opportunity to try a variety of dishes. Reservations are advisable, especially on Wednesdays. S

Food ●●●●◐ Serv ●●●◐○ Venue ●●●●○ Value ●●●●○

Cucina

Cubo

Location → Ibis World Trade Centre · Shk Zayed Rd | 318 7139
Hours → 12:00 - 15:00 19:00 - 24:00 none
Web/email → novotel.ibis@accorwtc.ae | Map Ref → 9-E3

Fill a cube with goodness and feel the spirit of Cubo, the chic Italian restaurant in the Ibis Hotel at the World Trade Centre. Cubo generously fills its patrons with superb tastes. Carlo, the genial genius of the Cubo kitchen, leads with his pastas, especially the comforting gnocchi with creamy four cheese sauce. Its gentle touch of sage prefigures the creativity of main course offerings. Glorious desserts like mascarpone mousse with fresh diced fruit and apricot coulis intensify Cubo's satisfying dimensions. AP

Food ●●●●◐ Serv ●●●●○ Venue ●●●●○ Value ●●●●○

Cucina

Location → JW Marriott Hotel · Deira | 607 7977
Hours → 12:30 - 15:00 19:30 - 23:30
Web/email → www.marriott.com | Map Ref → 12-A3

The light scent of a wood fire sets the tone and welcomes you to Cucina. Delicious fresh bread whets your appetite as you catch a verse or two from the singing staff. Their occasional outbursts shouldn't distract you from the extensive menu – you'll find a great selection for all tastes and prices. The variety, the generous portions, the wonderfully unpretentious feel of the place, and (most important) the flavours, keep Cucina lively. Make a reservation and save room for dessert. CG

Food ●●●●○ Serv ●●●●○ Venue ●●●●○ Value ●●●●○

Da Vinci's

Location → Millennium Airport Hotel · Al Garhoud | 703 9123
Hours → 12:00 - 24:00 Thu 12:00 - 01:00
Web/email → apothotl@emirates.net.ae | Map Ref → 14-D3

Da Vinci's is a deservedly popular midrange Italian restaurant. Spacious, yet still managing an intimate feel in the manner of an Italian country house, it appeals to both larger and smaller groups. Da Vinci's rolls out a selection – solid rather than outstanding – of the usual suspects in substantial portions, and at reasonable prices. There is an affordable wine list too. Couple this with spot on service, and you have a reliable restaurant that delivers good value for money. SE

Food ●●●◐○ Serv ●●●●○ Venue ●●●◐○ Value ●●●◐○

About time your favourite waiter got a pat on the posterior for good service? Prompt a pay raise or promotion by shouting 'good service' from the rooftops! Eat Out Speak Out is the perfect way to get your 'pat' across. Not only will we publish your 'pat' online, we'll also make sure that it is transported straight from your hands to the 'back' of the establishment.

Don Corleone

Location → Metropolitan · Jct 2, Shk Zayed Rd | 343 0000
Hours → 12:30 - 14:30 19:00 - 23:00
Web/email → www.methotels.com | Map Ref → 5-C4

White plaster walls, gingham tablecloths and the voice of Dean Martin greet you as you enter this cosy restaurant. Whether inside or on the terrace, pleasant and efficient staff receive you with a warm welcome. Although not extensive, the menu does offer interesting salads and a selection of pasta and sauces for mixing and matching. The food itself is flavoursome, and represents value for money for a restaurant of this standard. However, expect to pay over the odds for alcohol. AB

Food Serv Venue Value

Gardenia

Location → Towers Rotana · Trade Centre 1&2 | 312 2210
Hours → 06:00 - 23:00
Web/email → www.rotana.com | Map Ref → 9-B2

The Pirates of Penzance have set up shop at the Towers Rotana, where guys in feathered hats and plastic swords serve up a mean roast beef. Fish and chips, meat pies, and 'all you can drink' wine and beer are offered on British theme night. The real sinker is the dessert bar; home to what may be the world's best chocolate mousse and toffee torte. For the early birds, the breakfast buffet and a Friday brunch are good options in this buffet restaurant. LA

Food Serv Venue Value

Il Rustico

Location → Rydges Plaza Hotel · Al Satwa | 398 2222
Hours → 12:00 - 15:00 18:00 - 24:00
Web/email → rhrdxb@emirates.net.ae | Map Ref → 7-A4

For rustic charm and good value Italian fare, this restaurant is hard to beat. The friendly staff and congenial clientele provide an instant welcome. Bare wooden floorboards, beamed ceilings and intimate candlelit tables combine to provide a warmth and cosiness in which to enjoy the selection of pasta, wood fired pizzas and more. Indulge your palate with the temptations on offer and don't worry if you can't make it to dessert. This little gem has become very popular; booking is essential. LS

Food Serv Venue Value

Italian Connection

Location → Nr Lamcy Plaza · Oud Metha | 335 3001
Hours → 12:00 - 15:30 19:00 - 23:30
Web/email → n/a | Map Ref → 10-D4

Italian Connection is a quality neighbourhood restaurant. Its bright, modern décor and busy tables give it more atmosphere than many hotel outlets. The food is good and plentiful; the menu offers a lot of choice, including a wide range of interesting salads and a huge selection of tasty and authentic pizzas. Italian Connection doubles as a café outside restaurant hours, and if you work or live in the Lamcy Plaza area, it could easily become a second home. SB

Food Serv Venue Value

Johnny Carinos

Location → Beh Rihab Rotana Suites · Deira | 295 7080
Hours → 11:00 - 02:00
Web/email → na | Map Ref → 14-D1

Sinatra and Dino croon out hits, and checked tablecloths and cosy alcoves create the ambience of a traditional Italian trattoria rather than an American franchised theme in the heart of Deira. Your best bet would be to try out any of JC's signature dishes – the twelve layer lasagne, five cheese pizza or the very rich tiramisu. Be warned though, the servings can feed an average man for a week! For a night out with the family, JC's will be a hit and worth the drive across the Creek. KM

Food Serv Venue Value

La Moda

Location → Hotel InterContinental · Deira | 205 7333
Hours → 13:00 - 15:00 20:00 - 02:30
Web/email → intercon_bc@itcdubai.co.ae | Map Ref → 8-C4

La Moda is a place to be seen. On most evenings, it is packed with beautiful people enjoying average Italian cuisine in a lively and relaxed environment. The menu is varied, and generally reasonably priced, although the meat and fish dishes seem expensive for what you get. The huge pizzas and ample pasta dishes represent better value. Despite the crowds, service is good and contributes to an enjoyable evening in a venue where the atmosphere, perhaps more than the food, is the attraction. VB

Food Serv Venue Value

La Veranda

Location → Mövenpick Hotel Bur Dubai · Oud Metha | 336 6000
Hours → 12:00 - 15:00 19:00 - 24:00
Web/email → hiburdxb@emirates.net.ae Map Ref → 10-D4

In Florentine style, La Veranda has an easygoing pleasant ambience, with a concise menu and efficient, friendly staff. The food is light and fresh (though at times inconsistent) without an over reliance on complicated heavy sauces. Save room for later; if the Italian desserts don't tempt, the famous Movenpick ice-creams will nudge you to loosen the belt buckle and indulge. The overall experience is more Leonardo da Vinci, prescriptive and controlled than the hedonistic passion of Boticelli; while perfectly fine, it lacks Italian passion. LG

Food ●●○○○ Serv ●●●●○ Venue ●●○○○ Value ●●◐○○

La Vigna

Location → Century Village · Al Garhoud | 282 0030
Hours → 11:30 - 01:00
Web/email → dagama@emirates.net.ae Map Ref → 14-C3

100

La Vigna shares one of the most attractive alfresco settings of central Dubai – Century Village. Sit outside and enjoy the surroundings: trees lit with fairy lights, water fountains and a buzzing courtyard atmosphere. The food is generally agreeable (try the excellent grilled vegetable antipasti), and the service slick. There is certainly classier Italian food in Dubai, but La Vigna is distinctive in offering an affordable meal in great surroundings. SB

Food ●●●◐○ Serv ●●●●○ Venue ●●●●◐ Value ●●●●○

Luciano's

Location → Metropolitan Resort · Marsa Dubai | 399 5000
Hours → 12:30 - 14:30 19:00 - 23:30 Fri 12.30 - 16.00
Web/email → www.methotels.com Map Ref → 2-E2

If you're a hotel guest or in the neighbourhood, Luciano's offers a pleasant enough, midrange, unhurried Italian experience. The menu contains an ample selection of antipasti, soups, pizzas, pastas, seafood and meat dishes – which are generous in size but not consistent in quality. Service is knowledgeable and efficient within the rustic style surroundings. Desserts are inedible and must be missed. This eatery seems to be little more than a 'tourist restaurant', catering largely for hotel patrons. NQ

Food ●●◐○○ Serv ●●●◐○ Venue ●◐○○○ Value ●●○○○

Mosaico

Location → Emirates Towers · Shk Zayed Rd | 319 8754
Hours → 24 hrs
Web/email → www.jumeirahinternational.com Map Ref → 9-C2

In the Emirates Towers hotel is Mosaico; a stylish and relaxed Italian eatery containing the largest mosaic in the Middle East. At times, the unruffled laissez-faire ambience can stretch to include the service, and the upmarket Italian menu can be inconsistent. Some menu items are fantastic (the aubergine rigatoni is a tasty sun dried surprise), but others, like the calamari and broccoli salad are less exciting. A well selected wine list offers great choice. Open 24 hours, Mosaicio is perfect for a late night dinner al fresco amongst fairy lit trees. JAW

Food ●●◐○○ Serv ●●◐○○ Venue ●●●●○ Value ●●●◐○

Mosaico

Ossigeno

Location → Le Royal Meridien · Marsa Dubai | 399 5555
Hours → 19:00 - 24:00
Web/email → www.leroyalmeridien-dubai.com Map Ref → 2-E2

Ossigeno is more than a cut above your average Italian restaurant. From its modern décor to its imaginatively conceived dishes, this is a classy act. The quality is evident in the ingredients (superb mozzarella, for example), and the wide selection of

inventive combinations, all pleasingly presented. The superior nature of this modern establishment is somewhat reflected in the prices, but these should not deter you from making the journey: Ossigeno is an excellent restaurant. SB

Food ●●●●◐ Serv ●●●●◐ Venue ●●●●○ Value ●●●●◐

Pax Romana

Location → Dusit Dubai · Trade Centre 1&2 | 343 3333
Hours → 19:30 - 01:00
Web/email → foodbev@dusitdubai.com | Map Ref → 9-A2

For Italian food that is delicious and beautifully presented, Pax Romana demands a visit. The interior is bright and spacious, decorated in classic Italian style. Window seats allow diners to take advantage of the views towards the coastline. Diners have the option of a reasonably priced four course set menu (Dhs.125), or an inviting a la carte menu with the standard array of pizzas, pastas, soups, antipasti and mains... and a definite leaning towards seafood. Make sure you leave room for the delightful dolci. NQ

Food ●●●●○ Serv ●●●●○ Venue ●●●●○ Value ●●●●○

San Lorenzo

Location → Metropolitan Palace · Deira | 227 0000
Hours → 12:30 - 15:30 19:30 - 23:30
Web/email → www.methotels.com | Map Ref → 11-D2

Pleasant, if somewhat tired, surroundings, subdued lighting and a menu full of promising Italian standards greet you on arrival. Food comes in generous portions, but is lacking in quality, presentation and taste, especially for the price. Antipasti can be an excessive mountain of samples, while the pasta and risotto are tasty enough but unmemorable. Music from the adjacent bar can dominate a romantic meal. Service could be more attentive and generally more professional. This is a restaurant past its prime in more ways than one. CH

Food ●●○○○ Serv ●○○○○ Venue ●◐○○○ Value ●●○○○

Splendido Grill

Location → Ritz-Carlton · Marsa Dubai | 399 4000
Hours → 12:30 - 16:30 19:0 - 24:00
Web/email → emanuele.raffuzzi@ritzcarlton.com | Map Ref → 2-E2

Weather permitting, dine alfresco in the patio with picturesque views of the Arabian Sea to compliment the candlelit surroundings and live band. Pastas, risottos and salads prep your appetite before heading on to main course options, such as paellas, pizzas, seafood and grilled meats. Uninitiated diners to the cuisine need only look puzzled before knowledgeable waiters offer insight on dishes, down to preparation and history! Accentuated by the 'Ritz experience', Splendido offers authentic Italian cuisine at a premium. OF

Food ●●●●○ Serv ●●●●● Venue ●●●●○ Value ●●●◐○

Venezia

Location → Metropolitan · Jct 2, Shk Zayed Rd | 343 0000
Hours → 24:00 - 24:00 19:00 - 24:00
Web/email → www.methotels.com | Map Ref → 5-C4

While the ambitious décor of Venezia attempts to evoke Italian dreams, the reality falls a little flat. Despite the faux canals and gondolas, the mediocre food and cavernous dining room are more likely to stir up memories of a catering hall than Venice. The menu features standard, but uninspired, pasta, pizza, meat and seafood dishes, with many of the more popular choices available in family sized portions. The high point is definitely the wine cellar, where you can choose your own bottle. ABH

Food ●●◐○○ Serv ●●●◐○ Venue ●●○○○ Value ●●◐○○

Verdi

Location → Taj Palace Hotel · Deira | 223 2222
Hours → 12:00 - 15:00 19:00 - 23:30 Fri 12:00- 23.30
Web/email → tajdubai@emirates.net.ae | Map Ref → 11-D2

Bright and impersonal, Verdi offers the usual Italian fare, in a pseudo Romanesque setting. Wednesday and Friday are buffet nights; you might want to give these nights a miss and go any other day of the week, when you can choose from a selection of fresh a la carte dishes. The extensive array of soft beverages more than makes up for the lack of alcohol. For Dhs.100, a family of four can enjoy the Friday brunch, an international buffet compiled from all of the hotel's restaurants. Otherwise, the takeaway pizzas are recommended. LS

Food ●●◐○○ Serv ●●○○○ Venue ●●◐○○ Value ●●●○○

Hidden Charges

When the bill arrive, subtly check out th dreaded small print (sly lurking at the bottom the bill) that sa 'INCLUSIVE +15% +5% Be careful what you touch as you may find that eve the most innocent e contact with a nut bowl c result in surplus charges

Vivaldi

Location → Sheraton Hotel & Towers · Deira | 207 1717
Hours → 12:00 - 15:00 15:00 - 01:30 06:30 - 12:00
Web/email → www.starwood.com | Map Ref → 11-C1

Lovers of Italian cuisine with a flavour of sophistication will find Vivaldi hard to beat. After a pre-dinner drink in the lounge complete with pianist, take a table with views of the Creek or the activity of the open kitchen around which the restaurant is structured. Authentically prepared and beautifully presented food is complimented by professional, friendly service. The selection of delicious antipasti, soups, fresh pasta, seafood, meat dishes and pizza, together with your favourite Italian dessert, make for a truly tantalising dining experience. Reservations essential.

Food Serv Venue Value

Japanese

Other options → **Karaoke Bars [p.452]**

Benihana

Location → Al Bustan Hotel · Al Garhoud | 282 0000
Hours → 12:00 - 14:45 19:00 - 23:30
Web/email → www.rotana.com | Map Ref → 14-E3

Saturday and Tuesday sushi nights at Benihana are well established on the list of great, affordable buffets in Dubai. The sushi may not be of spectacular range or quality, but throw in some sashimi, tempura, soup, fine appetisers and house drinks, all for Dhs. 95, and you have yourself a winner. Also popular is teppanyaki night on Sunday. Ordering a la carte can be a much pricier proposition. Benihana may not be the most authentic, but is surely one of the more popular Japanese restaurants in town.

Food Serv Venue Value

Creekside

Location → Sheraton Hotel & Towers · Deira | 207 1750
Hours → 12:30 - 15:00 18:30 - 24:00
Web/email → www.starwood.com | Map Ref → 11-C1

For good Japanese food without the frills of super upscale dining, Creekside fits the bill. This practical, no nonsense restaurant serves excellent authentic Japanese cuisine in abundant quantities and affordable prices. Theme nights (Dhs.80++ for teppanyaki and Dhs.70++ for sushi) are quite the crowd puller with natives making up a sizeable chunk of the crowd (a confirmation of 'genuine' fare). Although hard back straight chairs drop the physical comfort a notch, the friendly wait staff more than make up for a casual and filling evening.

Food Serv Venue Value

ET Sushi

Location → Emirates Towers · Shk Zayed Rd | 319 8790
Hours → 12:30 - 15:00 19:30 - 00:00
Web/email → www.jumeirahinternational.com | Map Ref → 9-C2

In the five minutes and 12 seconds it takes the conveyor to do one full circuit of ET Sushi, the now 'favourites' in raw fish cuisine are presented before you. While the classics are the mainstay, the skilled chefs can prepare something from the a la carte menu for the more adventurous eel eaters. An almost clinical cleanliness and DIY service make this place less conducive to lingering but perfect for a pit stop before sampling the other attractions of Emirates Towers.

Food Serv Venue Value

Hana

Location → Riviera Hotel · Deira | 222 2131
Hours → 12:00 - 15:00 19:00 - 23:00
Web/email → riviera@emirates.net.ae | Map Ref → 8-C3

Hana is a real culinary tour of Asia. Situated in one of Dubai's oldest hotels, this multi cuisine locale overlooks the Creek and is charming and elegant, offering an incredibly extensive Asian menu. You can opt for an intimate dinner in the tatami room or have fun with friends at the teppanyaki tables. The menu tends to overwhelm a bit in size, losing some attention to quality with the more obscure dishes. For a sure bet, try the sushi and sashimi, and don't miss the Chinese vegetables.

Food Serv Venue Value

Kiku

Location → Le Meridien Dubai · Al Garhoud | 282 4040
Hours → 12:30 - 15:00 19:00 - 23:30
Web/email → kiku@le-meridien-dubai.com | Map Ref → 14-E3

A taste of Tokyo without the travel, Kiku is about as authentic as it gets; the staff, many of the

Seafood
by the Creek

clientele, menu, music and décor are genuine Japan. Seating options include the teppanyaki bar, sushi counter, booths and private tatami rooms, but wherever you sit, you're guaranteed an excellent experience. Seafood is particularly good, as traditional dishes have been adapted to the local catch of the day. If you're ready to kick the tried and tested sushi joints and go up a notch, Kiku is your venue of choice. LG

Food Serv Venue Value

Minato

Location → Hotel InterContinental · Deira | 222 7171
Hours → 13:00 - 15:00 15:00 - 23:30
Web/email → n/a | Map Ref → 8-C4

Minato offers an authentic Japanese dining experience in traditional surroundings that will add flavour to any occasion. Both expert and novice Japanese cuisine diners are in good hands with the friendly staff. While the extensive menu offers all the Japanese standards, the fresh sushi and sashimi come with the highest recommendation. Try the ice-cream for something different if you've still got space. For the more price conscious, Monday's sushi and Thursday's teppanyaki buffets are a good option at Dhs.125 net. FA

Food Serv Venue Value

Miwako Japanese Lounge

Location → Metropolitan · Jct 2, Shk Zayed Rd | 407 6928
Hours → 19:00 - 24:00
Web/email → www.methotels.com | Map Ref → 5-C4

Tucked away in a corner of the Metropolitan, Miwako is a pleasant surprise and quite a find for

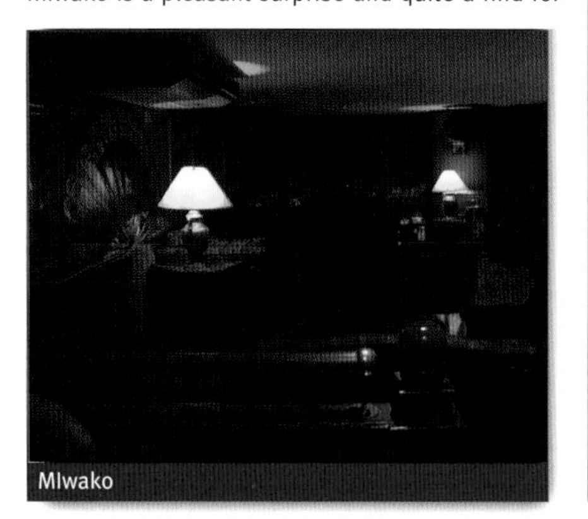

MIwako

lovers of lounge. Within a dim lit cave like space, the décor is an exciting mish mash of battered wood, exotic candelabras and chintzy sofas. Choose your spot, be it at the flashy bar or the cosy corner table, and order away from a modest menu. Stick with the sushi and sashimi choices; other dishes are a hit and miss, but for such amazingly low prices, some errors can be easily overlooked. LM

Food Serv Venue Value

Miyako

Location → Hyatt Regency · Deira | 209 1222
Hours → 12:30 - 15:00 19:00 - 23:00
Web/email → www.dubai.hyatt.com | Map Ref → 8-D2

Like a gleaming pearl inside an oyster, Miyako impresses highly. A mind boggling array of dishes features everything you could possibly wish for in a Japanese restaurant, and the food is astoundingly good. Master chefs prepare perfect sushi, exquisite tempura prawns and superb yakitori, and the Shabu Shabu is a table cooked treat without equal. Exquisite Geisha style service and an authentic, serene environment work their magic in easing the price conscious mind. JK

Food Serv Venue Value

Noodle Sushi

Location → Above Safestway · Trade Centre 1&2 | 321 1500
Hours → 12:00 - 16:00 19:00 - 24:00
Web/email → seawfood@emirates.net.ae | Map Ref → 5-D3

V 100

Joining in the festivities of converting the Safestway supermarket roof into several culinary delights, Noodle Sushi is also set to open its doors in mid December. Dim lighting and authentic decor enhance the intimate surroundings. Although no menu has at present been released, the ornamental attention to detail suggests that we're in for a real treat. And with Sea World next door, there will be no shortage of sushi.

www.EAT OUT SPEAK OUT.com

Did we pan your favourite pasta? Or celebrate a soggy pudding? If you think our food critic needs to be strung up on the nearest specials board, then log on to Eat Out Speak Out. Add your comments to our restaurant reviews, and we'll not only publish them online but will also send them to the restaurants themselves.

See also: *Ayotaya Restaurant, R.G.L.A. and Sea World, all located in the same venue.*

Food n/a Serv n/a Venue n/a Value n/a

Sakura

Location → Crowne Plaza · Trade Centre 1&2 | 331 1111
Hours → 19:00 - 23:00
Web/email → www.dubaicrowneplaza.com Map Ref → 9-D2

This venue is worth a visit for the tasty and entertainingly prepared teppanyaki. Don't bother with the mediocre starters or sushi – just skip ahead to the main event: melt-in-the-mouth beef, chicken and seafood accompanied with fresh vegetables and either steamed or fried rice, all cooked before your eyes by a charismatic chef. The Japanese style décor, polite staff in kimonos and a porcelain complexioned woman tinkling out background music on the koto, add to the overall Sakura experience. JJR

Food Serv Venue Value

Sakura

Location → Taj Palace Hotel · Deira | 223 2222
Hours → 12:00 - 15:00 19:00 - 23:30
Web/email → tajdubai@emirates.net.ae Map Ref → 11-D2

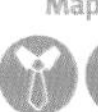

If it is a serene Asian setting of delicate Japanese elegance with quality food you are looking for, then Sakura is the place. It's hard to beat for a satisfying all round dining experience. Teppanyaki aficionados will have several set dinners to choose from, and then be able to watch it cooked up right before you. The selection of melt in your mouth sushi and sashimi is even wider, and includes both imported and local catch presented in classical aesthetically appealing style. For fine Japanese dining, Sakura is it. DM

Food Serv Venue Value

Sho Cho

Location → Dubai Marine Beach · Jumeira | 346 1111
Hours → 19:30 - 02:00
Web/email → www.dxbmarine.com Map Ref → 6-D2

Slick, chic and fantastic, Sho Cho's delights with its unique aquatic location and Japanese food. Book a table on the outdoor terrace overlooking gently lapping waves and feast on delectable fresh traditional and quasi Japanese delicacies. Local seafood is widely used and expertly prepared: dishes such as Hammour Yaki with green chilli mayonnaise and prawn spring rolls with mint and wasabi pepper cream are not to be missed. Reasonable bar prices make this place good for a special night out. JK

Food Serv Venue Value

Sumo

Location → Pink Bld · Trade Centre 1&2 | 343 5566
Hours → 11:00 - 23:00
Web/email → www.sumosushi.com Map Ref → 9-A2

Sumo is a healthy fast food lover's best option for good quality, fresh, fast, and inexpensive Japanese cuisine. The restaurant specialises in bento boxes, but the menu does have a selection of sushi (try the Banzai roll) and sashimi as well. The staff are always welcoming, though most people tend to takeaway from this sparsely decorated venue. You won't find an extensive menu or many traditional Japanese dishes, but you will find good value, quality food, and a quick fix for simple sushi cravings. HP

Food Serv Venue Value

Sushi Bar

Location → Grand Hyatt Dubai · Umm Hurair (2) | 317 2222
Hours → 12:30 - 15:00 19:00 - 23:30
Web/email → www.dubai.grand.hyatt.com Map Ref → 13-E3

V 300

With sushi bars running amok in Dubai, the Grand Hyatt introduces its own novel venue, Sushi, which is well prepared to take on its fellow

Sushi Platter

comrades. Sit and watch the sushi master whip up a feast, or if in the 'seen it all before' phase, there are several side tables ideal for a quick business lunch. Although prices are a little steep and it may seem difficult to zone out from the daily hubbub of the busy hotel, the relaxing Zen water feature and melt in your mouth sushi will have you mesmerised.

Food ●●●●● Serv ●●●●○ Venue ●●●●○ Value ●●●◐○

Sushi Sushi

Location → Century Village · Al Garhoud | 282 9908
Hours → 12:30 - 24:00
Web/email → n/a | Map Ref → 14-C3

Valet it

Still single because you're always late for your date? In Dubai, finding a parking space is a time wasting exercise. If you're dining at a restaurant in a hotel, don't stress for a spot. Boldly drive your beaten up bandwagon to the main entrance, and hand over your keys to a valet. Just make sure he does work for the hotel... or you'll be walking home.

Fresh, funky décor and the best alfresco option of all the Japanese restaurants in Dubai ensure this place remains popular. Diehard Japanese aficionados may frown at the food; this is a social venue to see and be seen rather than a temple of Japanese cuisine. Grilled and non traditional dishes are recommended. The 'all you can eat' Dhs.89 dinner (Tuesdays) continually draws hip crowds. A pleasant, Japanese inspired venue.

Food ●●●◐○ Serv ●●●●○ Venue ●●●●◐ Value ●●●◐○

Sushi Times

Location → Dubai Media City · Al Sufouh | 391 0199
Hours → 13:00 - 24:00
Web/email → n/a | Map Ref → 3-A2

Experience great Japanese food this side of Japan. An a la carte menu, daily set menus and lunchbox specials come in generous helpings. The menu has a decent range of raw and cooked items, including tempura, teriyaki, sashimi, sushi and some variations on the salad theme. Veggies should try the vegetarian teriyaki. The décor is pleasing, the food delicious and its presentation stunning with great attention to detail. Call to find out more on the various daily promotions.

Food ●●●◐○ Serv ●●●●○ Venue ●●●◐○ Value ●●●◐○

tokyo@the towers

Location → Emirates Towers · Shk Zayed Rd | 319 8793
Hours → 12:30 - 15:00 19:30 - 24:00
Web/email → www.jumeirahinternational.com | Map Ref → 9-C2

Roll yourself into a California roll or some ebi maki tempura with a touch of style. The settings are deceptively simple in contrast to the excellent, melt in your mouth food served from an extensive (but pricey) menu. The seasonal specials offer even more variety; make a prior reservation for a teppanyaki table and watch the sumo inspired chefs slice and dice the food before your eyes. Later, cap the night with your favourite tune at the karaoke bar next door.

Food ●●●●○ Serv ●●●◐○ Venue ●●●●○ Value ●●●◐○

Yakitori

Location → Ascot Hotel · Bur Dubai | 352 0900
Hours → 12:30 - 15:00 18:30 - 23:30
Web/email → www.ascothoteldubai.com | Map Ref → 7-E3

For advocates of real Japanese food, this is a hidden treasure trove. An extensive menu offers an unrivalled choice of delicious fresh food prepared by a Japanese chef whose standards clearly delight a regular Japanese clientele. The staff is helpful and informative, but this restaurant will most likely not be best enjoyed by the novice. The décor, in red and black, is evocative and stylish. One may find venues with more subtle ambience but rarely better food. Once visited, Yakitori will become a regular haunt.

Food ●●●●◐ Serv ●●●●○ Venue ●●●●○ Value ●●●●◐

YO! Sushi

Location → BurJuman Centre · Bur Dubai | 336 0505
Hours → 11:00 - 23:00
Web/email → yo_sushi@emirates.net.ae | Map Ref → 11-A1

London based chain Yo!Sushi has hit the Dubai streets, and what better place to set its anchor – none other than the groovy BurJuman Centre. The pace is fast but the quality of the food unblemished, and as fresh fish arrives daily, dishes are expertly prepared, colour/price coded and set spinning on the conveyor belt. A trendy setting, top quality sushi fit for a whale and reasonable prices all reflect in YO!Sushi's international success.

Food ●●●●○ Serv ●●●◐○ Venue ●●●◐○ Value ●●●◐○

Korean

Seoul Garden Restaurant

Location → Zomorodah · Al Karama | 337 7876
Hours → 12:00 - 15:30 18:00 - 23:30 Fri 18:00-23:30
Web/email → n/a | Map Ref → 10-E3

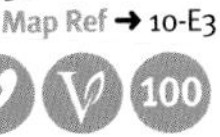

In true Korean style, this simply decorated restaurant features tables with a built in barbecue. If you're not familiar with this dining style, the helpful staff will advise on everything, from what to select to how to cook and even how to eat! Korean specialities include pan fried seasoned beef or chicken, and grilled beef rib served with kimchi, a hot, spicy, cabbage – not for the faint hearted, but must be tried once. Recommended is the wok casserole – it's brought to your table bubbling and is a feast for two. CH

Food ●●●◐○ Serv ●●●●○ Venue ●●●○○ Value ●●●◐○

Silla

Location → Ramada Continental · Hor Al Anz | 266 2666
Hours → 11:00 - 15:00 18:00 - 23:00
Web/email → ramadadb@emirates.net.ae | Map Ref → 12-B4

Silla is one of Dubai's few Korean restaurants, providing good value in authentic (though dated) East Asian surroundings. The menu offers a plentiful range of predominantly meat dishes to explore and entice; vegetarians are not well catered for with this type of cuisine. The flavours are strong and distinctive – it's not for everyone; the restaurant is mostly patronised by Koreans. The service is courteous, though at times hindered by language barriers; look for the friendly manager to help out if need be. DIP

Food ●●◐○○ Serv ●●●◐○ Venue ●◐○○○ Value ●●●◐○

Latin American

Pachanga

Location → Hilton Jumeirah · Marsa Dubai | 399 1111
Hours → 18:30 - 24:00
Web/email → www.hiltondubai.com | Map Ref → 2-D2

Pachanga weaves threads of Argentinean, Brazilian, Mexican and Cuban cultures into a stunning tapestry. The decadent Cuban lounge opens out onto a rustic 'courtyard' replete with Corinthian columns and a trio of sizzling South American musicians. Traditional dishes are imaginatively transformed into things of wonder and are presented with flair and style. The overall effect is akin to being entertained in a royal hacienda. You'll pay for the Pachanga experience, but like all great works of art, price is somewhat irrelevant here. Go! JK

Food ●●●●◐ Serv ●●●●◐ Venue ●●●●● Value ●●●●○

Malaysian

Other options → **Chinese [p.363]**

Fusion

Location → Le Royal Meridien · Marsa Dubai | 399 5555
Hours → 19:00 - 24:00
Web/email → www.leroyalmeridien-dubai.com | Map Ref → 2-E2

An elegant combination of service, fresh ingredients, artistic presentation and tranquil surroundings, this Malaysian/Indonesian restaurant rates highly. The tasty and creative selection of seafood dishes is offered with the option of spicy or mild, plus there is a wide choice of vegetarian and meat dishes. The ultra chic décor, with the choice of bar, terrace or indoor dining affords plenty of options. The staff are discreet and unassuming, mirroring the minimalist nature of the surroundings. A fab introduction to the region's cuisine. DK

Food ●●●●○ Serv ●●●○○ Venue ●●●●◐ Value ●●●○○

Mediterranean

Other options → **Italian [p.392]**

Focaccia

Location → Hyatt Regency · Deira | 209 1600
Hours → 12:30 - 15:00 19:30 - 23:30
Web/email → hyattbus@emirates.net.ae | Map Ref → 8-D2

Saunter into this Mediterranean villa, nicely hidden away with great hospitality and fresh foods. Sink into warm focaccia bread with an accomplice of freshly roasted garlic cloves that you can slather on (if your dinner company is fine with it!). Then, curl into deep conversation as you wait for your plate of perfectly cooked pasta, seafood or paella. The cosy setting offers a different theme in every room (the wine cellar is particularly hypnotising), and rooms can be booked for private parties.

Food ●●●●◐ Serv ●●●●○ Venue ●●●●○ Value ●●●◐○

Focaccia

Gozo Garden

Location → Millennium Airport Hotel · Al Garhoud | 282 3464
Hours → 06:00 - 24:00
Web/email → apothotl@emirates.net.ae | Map Ref → 14-D3

Gozo Garden is a large terrace type restaurant set off the main lobby of the hotel. It features different food themes every night, (except Saturday) where, for a set price, you can eat and drink to your stomach and liver's content. Sample British, Chinese, Indian, or Hawaiian offerings, though there can be a great similarity in taste between certain dishes and quality can be somewhat low overall. There is a loud resident band playing throughout the evening, and the ambience is convivial.

Food ●●●○○ Serv ●●●○○ Venue ●●◐○○ Value ●●●○○

La Villa

Location → Sofitel City Centre · Al Garhoud | 603 8300
Hours → 12:30 - 15:30 19:00 - 23:30
Web/email → cityhotl@emirates.net.ae | Map Ref → 14-D1

La Villa views its Mediterranean motif across a French stove. Smart young women serve stylishly presented cuisine in a dining room of uplifting yellows and golds, conveying an unmistakable Gallic accent. Although fish dominate the main courses, one might still begin with medallions of lobster paired with mango, or follow that with splendidly sauced slices of duck breast aside warmed figs. Among several irresistible desserts, the simple apple tart emphasises the skill of La Villa's admirable kitchen.

Food ●●●●◐ Serv ●●●●◐ Venue ●●●○○ Value ●●●●○

Majlis Al Bahar

Location → Burj Al Arab · Umm Suqeim | 301 7600
Hours → 12:00 - 15:00 19:30 - 00:00
Web/email → www.jumeirahinternational.com | Map Ref → 4-A1

Dinner at the understated Majlis Al Bahar may well be the best way to visit the Burj. A fantastic view of the hotel complements the delicious food, with a small but well planned Mediterranean menu offering a wide range (pizzas and pastas to sea food, chicken, lamb veal and more). A trio of excellent roaming musicians entertains diners with an eclectic mix of songs. Relaxing and comfortable, with pleasant, informed waiters, this venue delivers luxury without the usual snobbery: overall an outstanding dining experience. The restaurant is only accessible to non Burj al Arab guests for dinner.

Food ●●●●○ Serv ●●●●○ Venue ●●●●◐ Value ●●◐○○

Medzo

Location → Pyramids · Umm Hurair (2) | 324 4100
Hours → 12:30 - 15:00 19:30 - 23:30
Web/email → www.pyramidsdubai.com | Map Ref → 13-D2

Medzo is simple yet chic. In a relaxed setting, enjoy a combination of fine Italian foods with a cheeky twist of the Mediterranean. Sample the imaginative menu, which bravely plays with variety: the tomato sorbet is worth trying for curiosity alone and the stone baked pizza comes with a la carte style toppings (not for the simple 'pizzaholic'). This intimate dining experience requires you to leave the kids at home, don your glad rags and head for their spacious terrace, which is perfect during the cooler evenings.

Food ●●●●○ Serv ●●●●○ Venue ●●●●○ Value ●●●●○

Olive House

Location → Nr One Tower · Trade Centre 1&2 | 343 3110
Hours → 12:00 - 13:30
Web/email → na | Map Ref → 9-A2

A hit with local business bods, Olive House is also a welcome retreat for passers by, there to take in

the architectural splendour of the area. There are tables outside, but the traffic noise may prove a little overpowering. A quaint interior with a trendy décor of cream walls and dark wooden furniture plays host to a variety of Mediterranean dishes, salads, fish and Arabic meze, and true to it name, different flavoured olive oils are for sale. HP

Food ●●●◐○ Serv ●●●◐○ Venue ●●●◐○ Value ●●●◐○

Oregano

Location → Oasis Beach Hotel · Marsa Dubai | 399 4444
Hours → 18:30 - 24:00
Web/email → n/a | Map Ref → 2-D2

Treat the one you love to an evening of enchantment at this warm and welcoming venue, which offers notable Mediterranean cuisine and impressive service. Choose wisely from the menu, as certain dishes are rich, and portions generous. Desserts are made for sharing! Throw in the great Polish accordion player, squeezing out both jovial and melancholic tunes while you gaze at your partner through the candlelight, and you'll agree that this must be one of the most romantic settings in Dubai. JJR

Food ●●●◐○ Serv ●●●●○ Venue ●●●●◐ Value ●●●◐○

Prasino's

Location → Jumeirah Beach Club · Jumeira | 344 5333
Hours → 12:30 - 15:00 19:30 - 23:00
Web/email → www.jumeirahinternational.com | Map Ref → 5-D1

Even on a dark evening, Prasinos manages to convey a light Mediterranean feel. In the cooler months, the terrace is a pleasant place to be. Refreshingly different Chilean musicians blend the guitar and the flute with entrancing Latin vocals. The food has a definite seafood bias with some interesting meat dishes to add variety, but vegetarians may find their options limited – the menu sounds great on the page and doesn't disappoint on the plate. Although pricey, Prasinos combines style with substance. GS

Food ●●●●◐ Serv ●●●●○ Venue ●●●●◐ Value ●●●◐○

Maria Bonita

Vu's

Location → Emirates Towers · Shk Zayed Rd | 319 8771
Hours → 12:30 - 15:00 19:30 - 24:00
Web/email → www.jumeirahinternational.com | Map Ref → 9-C2

Located 50 floors up, and offering fabulous views of the city, it's no surprise that you need to book early for the best tables (next to the panoramic floor to ceiling glass). A Mediterranean menu comprises the regulars plus all the meats (fish steak, lamb, chicken and more); the Steak Rossini (in a bed of spinach sprinkled with mushrooms) is delectable. Staff is friendly, unobtrusive and ultra efficient. Chic, modern and delicious, with a view to melt the coldest of hearts, this restaurant aces across the board. CH

Food ●●●●◐ Serv ●●●●● Venue ●●●●● Value ●●●●◐

Mexican

Maria Bonita

Location → Nr Spinneys Cen. · Umm Suqeim | 395 5576
Hours → 12:30 - 23:30
Web/email → n/a | Map Ref → 5-A2

The ONLY authentic Mexican restaurant in Dubai, this taco shop and grill offers both carnivores and veggies delicious dishes based on traditional recipes – and none of its Tex Mex (thankfully!). The 'Guacamole on the Spot' is made at your table, and is definitely the best you'll find outside of Mexico. All ingredients are shipped in from Mexico, and tortillas are made in-house. There's no Corona or tequila here, but on the flip side, you're not going to pay hotel prices for your excellent experience. PG

Food ●●●●◐ Serv ●●●◐○ Venue ●●●●◐ Value ●●●●◐

Middle Eastern

There is no one distinct Middle Eastern or Arabic cuisine, but it is instead a blend of many styles of cooking from the region. Thus, an Arabic meal will usually include a mix of dishes from countries as far afield as Morocco or Egypt to Lebanon and Iran. However, in Dubai, modern Arabic cuisine almost invariably means Lebanese food. Typical ingredients include beef, lamb, chicken, rice, nuts (mainly pistachios), dates, yoghurt and a range of seafood and spices. The cuisine is excellent for meat eaters and vegetarians alike.

A popular starter is a selection of dishes known as 'mezze' (meze or mezzeh), which is often a meal in its own right. It is a variety of appetisers served with flat bread, a green salad and 'radioactive' pickles. Dishes can include 'humous' (ground chickpeas, oil and garlic), 'tabouleh' (parsley and cracked wheat salad, with tomato), 'fatoush' (lettuce, tomatoes and grilled Arabic bread) and 'fattayer' (small, usually hot, pastries filled with spinach or cottage cheese).

Charcoal grilling is a popular cooking method, and traditionally dishes are cooked with many spices including ginger, nutmeg and cinnamon. An authentic local dish is 'khouzi' (whole lamb, wrapped in banana leaves, buried in the sand and roasted, then served on a bed of rice mixed with nuts), which is most often available at Ramadan for the evening meal at the end of the day's fast ('Iftar'). It would also have been served at the 'mansaf'; the traditional, formal Bedouin dinner, where various dishes were placed on the floor in the centre of a ring of seated guests.

Other typical dishes include 'kibbeh' (deep-fried balls of mince, pine nuts and bulgar (cracked wheat), and a variety of kebabs. Seafood is widely available, and local varieties of fish include hammour (a type of grouper), chanad (mackerel), beyah (mullet) and wahar, which are often grilled over hot coals or baked in an oven.

Meals end with Lebanese sweets, which are delicious, but very sweet. The most widely known is 'baklava' (filo pastry layered with honey and nuts) and 'umm Ali' (mother of Ali in English), which is a rich, creamy dessert with layers of milk, bread, raisins and nuts - an exotic bread and butter pudding.

Moroccan

Other options → **Arabic/Lebanese [p.356]**

Al Khaima

Location → Le Royal Meridien · Marsa Dubai | 399 5555
Hours → 10:00 - 18:00 20:00 - 01:00
Web/email → www.leroyalmeridien-dubai.com Map Ref → 2-E2

Shisha by the sea sets the Al Khaima theme. Operating under theatrical tents on mild evenings, the restaurant offers a slender menu of Arabic specialities featuring mixed grill but not mixed meze, fruit juices but no vegetables. The food in no way undercuts shisha satisfaction or the two pleasing musicians who appear after 21:00. While the service is outstanding, and the prices reasonable, the romantic beach setting with plentiful shisha options is the main draw here. AP

Food Serv Venue Value

Marrakech

Location → Shangri-La Hotel · Trade Centre 1&2 | 343 8888
Hours → 13:00 - 15:00 20:00 - 24:00
Web/email → www.shangri-la.com Map Ref → 9-A2

A Moroccan chef and a culinary team combined with an authentic décor make Marrakech a total Moroccan experience. A canopied marble archway, semi private alcoves, 'mashrabbiyeh' screens, rustic lanterns and candelabras whisk the diners back in time, creating a charming authentic acquaintance. Couscous dishes and tajine specialties are baked and served in traditional ceramics, and refreshing mint tea poured from elegant silver pots cap off a perfect evening. Dining here is a highly delightful (though pricey) culinary experience. DIP

Food Serv Venue Value

Tagine

Location → One&Only Palace · Al Sufouh | 399 9999
Hours → 19:00 - 23:00
Web/email → www.oneandonlyresort.com Map Ref → 3-A2

The dimly lit classically Moroccan interior transports diners well away from the hustle and bustle of everyday Dubai. An expansive menu offers delicious starters – the 'pastilla bil hamam' (pigeon

One&Only
Royal Mirage
Dubai
Welcome to the Magic of Arabia

pie topped with cinnamon and icing sugar) is superb. For mains, try the tagine (stew) or couscous (semolina). A limited dessert menu offers an excellent 'kenaffa' and the reasonably extensive wine list is definitely not cheap. Staff donning traditional garb double as live entertainers. Authentic Moroccan cuisine, gorgeous décor and quality service make this a star venue in town. NQ

Food ●●●●◐ Serv ●●●◐○ Venue ●●●●◐ Value ●●●●○

Tagine

Pakistani

Other options → Indian [p.376]

Karachi Darbar

Location → · Various locations | 334 7272
Hours → 04:00 - 02:00
Web/email → n/a | Map Ref → n/a

A top option for tasty, friendly, and cheap Indo-Pakistani fare, this restaurant chain is a perennial favourite in Dubai. The simple décor, plain menus, and utilitarian settings may not pull visitors off the street: this is a shame. The no-nonsense but very welcoming service, the range of high-quality food, and the generous portions make these restaurants exceptional. Amazingly, service and food are consistently good across the various branches, which further confirms that this is one local eatery that is worth seeking out. CC

***See also:** Karama Shopping Centre, near the large car park (334 7434); Bur Dubai, near HSBC (353 7080); Qusais Road (261 2526); Naif Road, near Hyatt Regency Hotel (272 3755); Al Satwa (349 0202); Hor Al Anz, behind Dubai Cinema (262 5251); Al Qusais, Sheikh Colony (263 2266); Rashidiya (285 9464).*

Food ●●●●○ Serv ●●●◐○ Venue ●●◐○○ Value ●●●●●

Ravi's

Location → Nr Satwa R/A · Al Satwa | 331 5353
Hours → 24 hours
Web/email → n/a | Map Ref → 6-E4

Satwa's legendary Ravi's is probably the cheapest eatery in the book. This 24 hour Pakistani diner offers a delicious and not too spicy range of curried favourites, such as biryani, alongside more quirky dishes like fried brains. The venue is basic and parties including women should head for the more welcoming 'family' section. The clientele is mainly Pakistani bachelors and clued in Westerners collecting takeouts. Portions are shareable. Ravi's is perfect for generous curry in a hurry on a budget. JAW

Food ●●●●◐ Serv ●●●●○ Venue ●●◐○○ Value ●●●●●

Persian

Other options → Arabic/Lebanese [p.356]

Al Borz

Location → Al Durrah Tower · Trade Centre 1&2 | 331 8777
Hours → 11:00 - 24:00
Web/email → n/a | Map Ref → 9-D2

One of Tehran's best kebab houses has finally crossed the Gulf and set up shop on Sheikh Zayed Road, providing Dubai-ites the chance to sample their famous kebabs and rich rice specialities. The lunch buffet is an ideal introduction to Iranian cuisine, including soups and desserts, and is very moderately priced. A family setting and large portions make Al Borz especially popular among natives familiar with Persian fare. If lazy, opt for takeout – the delivery service is timely. LA

Food ●●●◐○ Serv ●●●○○ Venue ●●●○○ Value ●●●◐○

Pars Iranian Kitchen

Location → Al Diyafah Street · Al Satwa | 398 4000
Hours → 10:00 - 01:00 18:00 - 01:00
Web/email → pars@emirates.net.ae | Map Ref → 7-A3

Pars Iranian Kitchen offers a casual Arabic atmosphere. Relax on the various outdoor

majlises, listen to Arabic music and enjoy a shisha while the wait staff brings you a host of appetisers and freshly baked bread. Start with the classics, such as humous, moutabel, tabouleh and soups. Tasty kebabs and grills accompanied with rice or chips make up the limited main courses. The restaurant has two branches but alfresco dining is available only at the Al Diyafah Street branch. VML

Food ●●●◐○ Serv ●●●○○ Venue ●●●◐○ Value ●●●◐○

Shabestan

Location → Hotel Inter-Continental · Deira | 205 7333
Hours → 13:00 - 15:00 20:00 - 23:00
Web/email → n/a Map Ref → 8-C4

For a taste of exotic Persian hospitality, Shabestan is sure to please the most discerning of diners. Candlelit with a Persian band, choose from a view overlooking the Creek or private dining alcoves for groups. The menu abounds with delights from the region: a fine selection of starters, soups, salads and generous mains. A variety of sumptuously laden platters of lamb, seafood and chicken can feed three to four. Don't miss the fresh Persian bread – straight out of the clay oven and into your basket! AK

Food ●●●●○ Serv ●●●●● Venue ●●●◐○ Value ●●●◐○

Shahrzad

Shahrzad

Location → Hyatt Regency · Deira | 209 1200
Hours → 12:30 - 15:30 19:30 - 23:00
Web/email → hyattbus@emirates.net.ae Map Ref → 8-D2

Shahrzad serves delicious, plentiful Persian fare in a beautiful, stirring setting. Arrive after 20:30, and you'll notice the band, which fills the lobby with vociferous delirium; reserve a table on the balcony if you prefer quiet conversation. The freshly baked bread and hot starters are delectable, and the otherworldly blend of aubergine, egg, ginger, and tomatoes is a must try. The mutton and seafood rice dishes are also outstanding; tender, wholesome flakes of lamb drop from the bone, sumptuous fresh shrimps overflow the plate. Undoubtedly peerless Persian cuisine. JAW

Food ●●●●● Serv ●●●○○ Venue ●●●◐○ Value ●●●●○

Pizzerias

Other options → **Italian [p.392]**

Biella Caffé Pizzeria Ristorante

Location → Wafi Mall · Umm Hurair (2) | 324 4666
Hours → 12:00 - 23:30
Web/email → www.pyramidsdubai.com Map Ref → 13-D2

Biella features an attractive dimly lit terrace and a pleasant, bright non smoking interior in the mall. The service here is outstanding and the generous food portions are exquisitely presented: the minestrone casareccio is a rustic delight, the calamari fritti tender but rather oily, the rugby ball sized calzone farcito stuffed with tasty morsels and the linguini al cartoccio trimly wrapped in delicious pizza crust. By 20:00, Biella is packed, mostly with locals enjoying great value and wholesome Italian fare. JAW

Food ●●●●○ Serv ●●●●● Venue ●●●◐○ Value ●●●●◐

Ciro's Pomodoro

Location → Le Meridien Mina · Al Sufouh | 399 3333
Hours → 12:00 - 16:00 19:00 - 03:00
Web/email → www.lemeridien-minaseyahi.com Map Ref → 3-A2

Pizzeria meets nightclub is the flavour of Ciro's Pomodoro. This late night venue with live music and a small dance floor offers a wide range of Italian favourites, including pizza and excellently cooked pasta. The carpaccio of tuna and seafood salad starters are delicious and generous enough to share. A selection of grills and salads offers some menu diversity. The desserts are somewhat disappointing, as is a rather hefty bill, but it still does not deter friends from meeting up in this lively spot. PL

Food ●●●●○ Serv ●●●○○ Venue ●●●○○ Value ●●○○○

La Fornace

Location → Le Royal Meridien · Marsa Dubai | 399 5555
Hours → 18:00 - 24:00
Web/email → www.leroyalmeridien-dubai.com Map Ref → 2-E2

La Fornace seems to be based on an authentic Italian farmhouse – the interior, however, is nothing short of tacky and fake. Food is a little more appealing with pizzas naturally dominating the menu. Other meat and fish dishes, pastas and salads are available. While the quality is reasonable, this is still, standard Italian fare that is lacking in imagination. A lack of more organic produce could have given the concept more authenticity. Service is good to average, but overall, the experience is not worth the trip. SC

Food ●●◐○○ Serv ●●◐○○ Venue ●○○○○ Value ●●◐○○

Pizza Corner

Location → Nr Riviera Htl, Baniyas St · Deira | 228 4330
Hours → 11:00 - 01:00
Web/email → n/a Map Ref → 8-C3

Dubai's 'original' pizza restaurant was established in 1973, and it's certainly showing its age. Back in the dark ages when fresh food was hard to come by, it might have been okay to use tinned mushrooms and vegetables, but not today. Pizzas are crisp and tasty but not astounding, and other meals are also fairly ordinary. The service is friendly and helpful, but the tired looking venue and cafeteria quality food combine to make this an unattractive option. Observation and conclusion: 'Original' is not always best. JK

Food ●◐○○○ Serv ●●●○○ Venue ●○○○○ Value ●●◐○○

Pizza Express

Location → Bin Sougat Centre · Rashidiya | 285 2393
Hours → 11:30 - 24:00 Fri 11:30 - 01:00
Web/email → n/a Map Ref → n/a

The glistening new branch of Pizza Express at Bin Sougat Centre will tempt delivery recipients to visit, and takeout customers to linger. Bright colours, abstract paintings and perky service distinguish the small dining area. Notable soups, abundant salads, good looking pastas and, of course, pizzas freshly topped in 21 creatively different ways, satisfy hunger most pleasantly. Add delicious fresh juice and some tasty, albeit conventional, desserts, and you have nourishment that somehow makes you feel healthy for having taken it. AP

Other locations: *Atrium Centre, Bank Street (355 2424); next to Park'nShop, Jumeira (359 2463)*

Food ●●●○○ Serv ●●●●◐ Venue ●●●●○ Value ●●●●○

Pizzeria Uno Chicago Grill

Location → City Centre · Deira | 294 8799
Hours → 08:00 - 24:00
Web/email → www.pizzeriauno.com Map Ref → 14-D1

This famous chain was established in Chicago in 1943, and their Deira City Centre version, with its Chicago 'steakhouse' décor, is almost true to the original. The menu is authentically American, with portions large enough to choke a buffalo, some of the most decadent desserts in town, and free soft drink and coffee refills. They claim to have invented the deep dish pizza, and it's delicious. Also on offer is an extensive range of appetisers, burgers, pasta and sandwiches, though enormous portions don't make up for blandness; you may prefer to stick to their signature pizzas. CC

Food ●●●●○ Serv ●●●◐○ Venue ●●●○○ Value ●●●◐○

Round Table Pizza

Location → Al Diyafah Street · Al Satwa | 398 6684
Hours → 11:00 - 04:00 Thu & Fri 11:00 - 01:00
Web/email → n/a Map Ref → 7-A3

Primarily known for its excellent takeaway and home delivery pizzas, Round Table Pizza also has two restaurants; on Al Diyafah Street in Satwa, and in Al Garhoud. The outlets have bright, clean dining areas and a large selection of pizzas, most with wacky names – the 'King Arthur's supreme' or 'zesty Santa Fe chicken and shrimp pesto' are firm favourites. Recommended are the 'garlic parmesan twists' and the thin pan 'gourmet veggie' pizza, which is excellent! The list of possible additional toppings is 34 items long, so you can create the wildest combinations possible.

Other locations: Near Dubai Tennis Stadium, Al Garhoud (282 0666); Karama (396 6999). HP

Food ●●●●○ Serv ●●◐○○ Venue ●●○○○ Value ●●●◐○

Polynesian

Other options → **Chinese [p.363]**

Bamboo Lagoon

Location → JW Marriott Hotel · Deira | 262 4444
Hours → 19:30 - 24:30
Web/email → www.marriott.com | Map Ref → 12-A3

Original and enticing dishes in this large sculpted tropical garden present comprehensive Polynesian and Far Eastern dining within a five star restaurant budget. Trot along little paths and round ponds to seek out your favourite sushi, teppanyaki and fresh fish from the market, delivered to your nook with a flourish. Or experiment a la carte for some novel delicacies, ably advised by the obliging waiters. The all inclusive food and beverage options are also well worth trying for a group. DM

Food ●●●●◐ Serv ●●●●○ Venue ●●●●● Value ●●●●○

Beachcombers

Location → Jumeirah Beach Htl · Umm Suqeim | 406 8181
Hours → 12:00 - 16:30 19:00 - 24:00
Web/email → www.jumeirahinternational.com | Map Ref → 4-B2

Lovers of romantic settings should not miss Beachcombers. With a breathtaking view of the beach and the Burj Al Arab, diners relax in faux rustic Polynesian surroundings and sample quality international cuisine. By day, the menu is a la carte; by night, it's buffet. Theme nights with live entertainment take place regularly, dramatically changing the atmosphere of the restaurant and providing fun for everyone. The wait staff are attentive and the food is good, but it is the venue that pulls the crowds. JM

Food ●●●●○ Serv ●●●●◐ Venue ●●●●◐ Value ●●●○○

Tahiti

Location → Metropolitan Palace · Deira | 205 1731
Hours → 19:30 - 24:00
Web/email → www.methotels.com | Map Ref → 11-D2

Tahiti, as the name implies, sets the theme. A bridge at the entrance leads you into a very decorated restaurant with bamboo furniture, a water feature and lots of grassy things hanging about. A live cooking station takes up the centre. The buffet menu changes nightly from seafood to steaks, but does not offer great variety. However, the food is fresh and the price (at Dhs.140 with unlimited beverages) is worth it. Friendly service, a 'flame-buoyant' chef, and a live band make for an entertaining evening. DL

Food ●●●◐○ Serv ●●●●○ Venue ●●●◐○ Value ●●●●○

Trader Vic`s

Location → Crowne Plaza · Trade Centre 1&2 | 331 1111
Hours → 12:30 - 15:00 19:30 - 23:30
Web/email → cpdxb@cpdxb.co.ae | Map Ref → 9-D2

Please see review under Cocktail Lounges - On the Town [p.447]. HP

Food ●●●●◐ Serv ●●●●● Venue ●●●●◐ Value ●●●●○

Portuguese

Other options → **Spanish [p.419]**

Da Gama

Location → Century Village · Al Garhoud | 282 3636
Hours → 12:30 - 01:00
Web/email → dagama@emirates.net.ae | Map Ref → 14-C3

Its location in the Century Village is perhaps Da Gama's finest feature. This pleasant and refreshingly quiet outdoor eating area is lined with a variety of restaurants, and crammed with plants and trees. Da Gama's welcoming and efficient staff is another appealing feature. The menu, with an emphasis on seafood, offers a mix of authentically salty Portuguese specialities, such as pork in red wine sauce, and Mexican classics. Although the food is a tad pricey and somewhat disappointing, the restaurant's location probably makes up for this. AB

Note: *At 22:00 this venue turns into a loud Arabic style nightclub.*

Food ●●●○○ Serv ●●●●○ Venue ●●●●◐ Value ●●●◐○

Places for Pork

Remember that you are in a Moslem country. Nevertheless, all you pork freaks out there curbing your fetish, know that, although rare, you can still find pork on the menu. Understandably, the local, independent outlets are unlikely to serve any, but hotel restaurants are more accommodating to the cause. The bacon butty lives on.

Russian

Troyka

Location → Ascot Hotel · Bur Dubai | 359 5908
Hours → 12:00 - 15:00 19:00 - 03:00
Web/email → www.ascothoteldubai.com
Map Ref → 7-E3

Dining at Troyka is a mini holiday. Traditionally dressed staff serve hearty Russian favourites in a large dining room decorated with snowy murals, while Russian musicians and dancers perform. The flavourful borscht, beef stroganoff, savoury pies and potato dishes are sure hits from the extensive menu. If you fancy something more delicate, sample some of the famed caviar. Very popular with Russian expats, Troyka is at its best after 22:00, when reservations are essential. ABH

Food ●●●●○ Serv ●●●●○ Venue ●●●◐○ Value ●●●●○

Seafood

Other options → **Dinner Cruises [p.426]**

Al Bandar

Location → Heritage & Diving Village · Al Shindagha | 393 9003
Hours → 19:00 - 01:00
Web/email → n/a
Map Ref → 8-B1

Nestled on the edge of the Creek, good international seafood and an idyllic setting make Al Bandar a choice venue for the more dress down crowd. This is an ideal place to introduce visitors to a more Arabesque experience, and a welcome break from the many plush restaurants in five star hotels. The seafood choice is abundant in variety and the prices are cheap. Tradition is the theme with the added photographic thrill of the resident camels nearby. CC

Food ●●●◐○ Serv ●●●○○ Venue ●●●●○ Value ●●●◐○

Al Mahara

Location → Burj Al Arab · Umm Suqeim | 301 7600
Hours → 12:30 - 15:00 19:00 - 24:00
Web/email → www.jumeirahinternational.com
Map Ref → 4-A1

Plutocrats, Mafiosi and 'entrepreneurs' will feel right at home at this Burj extravaganza. Calculated to impress with excess, the restaurant curls around an enormous aquarium. As expected, the mostly seafood menu is meticulously interesting – every dish seems to have truffles, caviar, champagne and lobster worked into it somehow. Such palatable pleasure could become addictive, but the prices keep frequent trips in check. Truly well executed food distracts from the mesmerising aquarium and formal service makes the evening elegant. CC

Food ●●●●◐ Serv ●●●●○ Venue ●●●●● Value ●●●◐○

Al Mahara

Aquarium

Location → Creek Golf Club · Al Garhoud | 295 6000
Hours → 12:00 - 15:00 19:30 - 23:00
Web/email → creekfnb@dubaigolf.com
Map Ref → 14-C2

The central attraction here, as the name suggests, is a giant ceiling to floor circular aquarium. Luckily for Nemo, these fish do not go on the grill, but provide graceful entertainment. Look the other way and there's a beautiful view of the Creek. The décor is modern, but slightly lacking in atmosphere and the menu has a strong emphasis on seafood which is expertly prepared, presented and served at reasonable prices. HP

Food ●●●●◐ Serv ●●●●○ Venue ●●●●○ Value ●●●●○

Beach Bar & Grill, The

Location → One&Only Palace · Al Sufouh | 399 9999
Hours → 19:00 - 23:00
Web/email → www.oneandonlyresorts.com
Map Ref → 3-A2

On the menu, starters include a tranquil walk through the gardens to reach your destination, the main course is the tasteful Moroccan décor, unpretentious seating and thoughtful finishing touches, and for dessert the stunning view of the Arabian Gulf lapping almost at your feet. This is

one chic lunch venue with an imaginative selection of seafood, prepared and presented with the same quality and care devoted to the surroundings. LG

Food ●●●●○ Serv ●●●●◐ Venue ●●●●◐ Value ●●●●○

Fish Bazaar

Location → Metropolitan · Jct 2, Shk Zayed Rd | 407 6867
Hours → 12:30 - 15:00 19:00 - 24:00
Web/email → www.methotels.com Map Ref → 5-C4

150

The Fish Bazaar offers fresh seafood with a South East Asian slant. One of Dubai's older restaurants, its tasty food is more of a draw than the somewhat tired décor and pricey drinks. The staff are knowledgeable and helpful, giving advice on ingredient selection, preparation and accompaniments – sauces, vegetables etc. There are livelier and more stylish restaurants in Dubai, but the Fish Bazaar is convenient for seafood aficionados on the Jumeira side of town. SB

Food ●●●●○ Serv ●●●●◐ Venue ●●◐○○ Value ●●●◐○

Fish Market, The

Location → Hotel InterContinental · Deira | 205 7333
Hours → 13:00 - 15:00 20:00 - 23:30
Web/email → intercon_bc@itcdubai.co.ae Map Ref → 8-C4

As much an experience as a meal. Donning an apron after being seated, you are invited to partake of pre-dinner French fries, and in the absence of a menu, admire the view of the Creek. Before long your server approaches with a large basket and accompanies you round the impressive selection of the day's catch stacked on ice. Serving suggestions and accompaniments entice you to order enough for an army. With chefs waiting in the wings, it just doesn't get fresher or tastier than this. Great for a special occasion. LG

Food ●●●●◐ Serv ●●●●○ Venue ●●●◐○ Value ●●●◐○

Golden Fork

Location → Various locations · Dubai | 228 2662
Hours → 12:00 - 03:00
Web/email → n/a Map Ref → n/a

If you're craving a healthy, but fast and cheap Asian meal, you've found your match. The seafood is fresh and the noodles are delicious. The curries are full of masala and the portions generously family style. The chain has many locations; some have an in-house bakery. For dining in, try the Diyafah Street location, where you can watch the world cruise by. Otherwise, go for a takeout and enjoy your meal in front of the TV. LA

Locations: Nasr Square (221 1895); near Astoria Hotel (393 3081); Al Riqqa Street (222 9802); Satwa (345 9846)

Food ●●◐○○ Serv ●●◐○○ Venue ●●◐○○ Value ●●●◐○

Marina Seafood Market

Location → Jumeirah Beach Htl · Umm Suqeim | 406 8181
Hours → 12:30 - 15:00 19:00 - 01:00 Thu & Fri 12:30 - 16:00
Web/email → www.jumeirahinternational.com Map Ref → 4-B2

Look outside for views of the Burj Al Arab and the marina, or focus inside for an interesting underwater world. Fish, oysters and giant shrimps are displayed on ice as well as in tanks, which are home to lobsters, other edible crustaceans and smaller marine life. The menu ranges from fish, scallops, crabs, prawns, chicken, steak, duck and quail to even some veggie options. Be daring and try the fish market; select your choice and then advise on the style of cooking. CH

Food ●●●○○ Serv ●●●●◐ Venue ●●●●○ Value ●●●◐○

Mi Vida

Location → Le Royal Meridien · Marsa Dubai | 399 5555
Hours → 19:00 - 24:00
Web/email → www.leroyalmeridien-dubai.com Map Ref → 2-E2

'Of claws your welcome!' Promising an ocean of fresh seafood, they keep to their word here. Delicious soups, stuffed olives and fresh bread are a prelude to your selected crustaceans or fish, prepared to perfection according to your cooking preference, along with your selection of sauces. An extensive wine list adds an elegant touch. Service is attentive, alert and helpful. If weather permits, dine on the relaxing terrace. This is a true haven for seafood lovers. AD

Food ●●●●◐ Serv ●●●●◐ Venue ●●●◐○ Value ●●●●○

Sammach Restaurant

Location → Beach Centre, The · Jumeira | 349 4140
Hours → 11:30 - 23:30
Web/email → www.binhendi.com Map Ref → 6-B2

Sammach means fisherman in Arabic, and this will become very obvious once you enter into Mr Fadi's

piscine realm. Choose from the range of local seafood on display and pay by weight, or select from the Lebanese influenced a la carte menu. Either way, you can be assured that your meal was swimming just a few hours back. Fresh fish, friendly staff and the obvious dedication of the owner to his craft make this a good option for late night shoppers. JK

Food ●●●●○ Serv ●●●◐○ Venue ●●●◐○ Value ●●●◐○

Sea World

Location → Above Safestway · Al Wasl | 321 1500
Hours → 12:00 - 16:00 19:00 - 24:00
Web/email → www.seaworld-dubai.com | Map Ref → 5-D3

100

This venue brings the novelty of a seafood market to a mass audience. The large tank in the centre of the restaurant is home to a selection of live seafood. The dining area is comfortable, with an impressive 500 seating capacity. Alternatively, there are private cabins for larger or private parties. Place selections in your trolley, add vegetables, and select your preferred cooking method. With fairly reasonable prices, this is a good place for the biggest party to chomp crustaceans in this vast, family friendly restaurant. HP

> **www.EAT OUT SPEAK OUT.com**
>
> *Did we pan your favourite pasta? Or celebrate a soggy pudding? If you think our food critic needs to be strung up on the nearest specials board, then log on to Eat Out Speak Out. Add your comments to our restaurant reviews, and we'll not only publish them online but will also send them to the restaurants themselves.*

See also: *Ayotaya Restaurant, Noodle Sushi, and R.G.L.A, all located in the same venue.*

Food ●●●○○ Serv ●●●●○ Venue ●●●◐○ Value ●●●○○

Seafood Market

Location → Le Meridien Dubai · Al Garhoud | 282 4040
Hours → 12:30 - 15:00 19:30 - 23:30
Web/email → seafoodmkt@le-meridien.dubai.com | Map Ref → 14-E3

250

The menu here is of little importance; it provides more of an idea of the myriad of different ways your fish selection can be prepared. Complimentary starters begin your experience, then move on to the 'market style' counter of seafood and vegetables, select your ingredients, decide how you'd like it all cooked (sautéed, steamed, grilled, fried etc), then sit back and wait for your meal to arrive (all cooked to perfection). Help is at hand to lead you through the difficult decision making process. HP

Food ●●●●○ Serv ●●●◐○ Venue ●●●●○ Value ●●●◐○

Wharf, The

Location → Mina A'Salam · Umm Suqeim | 366 8888
Hours → 12:00 - 03:00 19:00 - 23:30
Web/email → www.jumeirahinternational.com | Map Ref → 4-A2

150

The twinkling lights of illuminated palm trees reflected in still dark waters, Arabian wind towers, abras gliding by and the distant sound of waves breaking on a sandy beach – this is the backdrop to The Wharf. A predominantly seafood restaurant, The Wharf offers innovative cuisine that is both superbly cooked and beautifully presented. Whilst there is a good selection of vintage wines for the adults, the separate children's menu ensures its popularity with families, and the busy staff aim to please. LS

Food ●●●●● Serv ●●●○○ Venue ●●●●◐ Value ●●●●○

Wharf, The

Singaporean

Other options → Chinese [p.363]

Peppercrab

Location → Grand Hyatt Dubai · Umm Hurair (2) | 317 2222
Hours → 19:00 - 24:00
Web/email → www.dubai.grand.hyatt.com | Map Ref → 13-E3

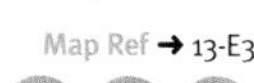

250

Looking for a taste to complement the opulence of the Grand Hyatt? Peppercrab's live grilled rock lobster is well worth the splurge – rich but delicate, char grilled to perfection and served with three sweet and spicy sauces. The Singaporean menu features mud crab, frog's legs, squid and sushi. Peppercrab's interior is tastefully grand but minimal and the kitchen is in an aquarium!

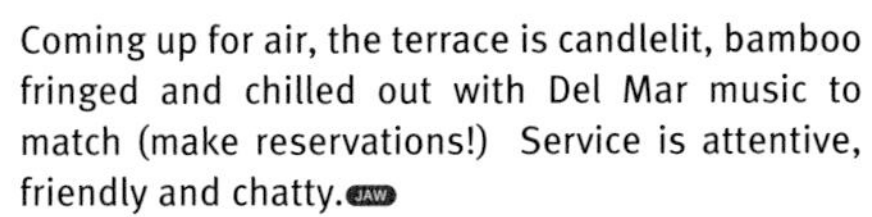

Coming up for air, the terrace is candlelit, bamboo fringed and chilled out with Del Mar music to match (make reservations!) Service is attentive, friendly and chatty. JAW

Food Serv Venue Value

Peppercrab

Singapore Deli Café

Location → Nr. Bur Juman Centre · Bur Dubai | 396 6885
Hours → 09:00 - 15:00 19:00 - 23:30
Web/email → delimd@hotmail.com Map Ref → 11-A1

   100

When it comes to noodles, Singapore Deli is as authentic as it gets. This small restaurant may look like a deli with pink walls and flower prints, but it serves up crispy deep fried wontons and spring rolls, and generous portions of steaming noodles. For noodle fans, the 'Hawker noodles' are not to be missed. The menu includes brunch items, such as muffins, waffles, sandwiches, cookies and speciality coffees as well. Those who discover Singapore Deli are likely to return for a regular (and reasonable) fix. CG

Food Serv Venue Value

Singapura

Location → Oasis Beach Hotel · Marsa Dubai | 399 4444
Hours → 18:00 - 24:00
Web/email → obh@jaihotels.com Map Ref → 2-D2

 150

Friendly and casual, Singapura caters to the package holiday crowd. The menu offers a good chance to try a variety of Asian food without getting too far from the familiar tastes of a European diet. The friendly staff are the highlight of the restaurant and will help you select from the menu, the daily specials, or the fresh fish market on display. They'll even provide both children and adults with traditional Singaporean games. Balcony seating during the cooler months offers an ocean and pool view. CG

Food Serv Venue Value

Spanish

Other options → **Tapas Bars [p.454]**

Bodega

Location → Le Meridien Dubai · Al Garhoud | 282 4040
Hours → 12:30 - 14:45 19:00 - 11:45
Web/email → f&bsec@le-meridien-dubai.com Map Ref → 14-E3

 100

To experience authentic Spanish cuisine without breaking the bank, go to Bodega. This restaurant is a culinary treat with food that is both authentic and well presented. A wide selection of dishes caters to all tastes. The tapas menu, in particular, gives the opportunity to try either small or medium sized dishes before you hit the main courses (or not, as the case may be). Service is efficient and pleasant, and the ambience, especially in the outdoor courtyard, is very relaxing. Bodega suits both the intimate evening diners as well as the flock out to enjoy a bite. BD

Food Serv Venue Value

Bodega

Seville's

Location ➔ Wafi City · Umm Hurair (2) | 324 7300
Hours ➔ 12:00 - 02:00 Thu & Fri 12:00 - 03:00
Web/email ➔ phsales@emirates.net.ae | Map Ref ➔ 13-D2

Please see review under Tapas Bars - Going Out [p.454].

Food ●●●◐○ Serv ●●●●○ Venue ●●●●◐ Value ●●●◐○

Steakhouses

Other options ➔ American [p.347]

49'ers

Location ➔ Sea Shell Inn · Bur Dubai | 393 4477
Hours ➔ 19:00 - 24:00
Web/email ➔ seashellinnhotel@yahoo.com | Map Ref ➔ 7-E2

Casual American style eating and drinking, with a DJ or live band playing most nights of the week, is 49ers' appeal. Tuesdays and Sundays offer two free drinks for the ladies. Cowboy and cowgirl waiters are efficient though not personable. The open kitchen displays a selection of steaks, fish, chicken, prawns and even a veggie burger option, barbecued to your choice of temperature. A simple concept, but pleasant for a casual dinner or drinks (followed by dancing).

Food ●●●○○ Serv ●●◐○○ Venue ●◐○○○ Value ●●●◐○

Dress Up

Dubai seems to have an unspoken (smart) dress code on the social scene. You could, perhaps, get away with shorts in some of the pubs and hotels. However, it is recommended that you check out the dress code beforehand (particularly for nightclubs) in order to avoid the embarrassment of being refused entry and your pals aren't. (Also a good test of friendship!)

Beach Comber Bar & Carvery Grill

Location ➔ Metropolitan Resort · Marsa Dubai | 399 5000
Hours ➔ 16:30 - 24:00
Web/email ➔ www.methotels.com | Map Ref ➔ 2-E2

With dimly lit secluded tables outside and very few Dubai residents present, this is not a bad place for a clandestine meeting! Good barbecued meats are on offer here; just remember to self serve the first course. The clientele are mainly hotel guests and prices are reasonably good value, especially for the fixed menu.

Food ●●●◐○ Serv ●●◐○○ Venue ●●●◐○ Value ●●●○○

Grill Room, The

Location ➔ Sheraton Jumeirah Beach · Marsa Dubai | 399 5533
Hours ➔ 19:00 - 24:00
Web/email ➔ www.starwood.com | Map Ref ➔ 2-D2

This small, understated venue is big on surprises. Between courses, the enthusiastic wait staff brings forth various complimentary nibbles, from Parma ham to crudités. The menu focuses on quality cuts of US and Australian beef, but also includes many seafood selections. Can't decide? Opt for the surf and turf – a tender beef fillet and succulent Omani lobster, grilled to perfection. The Grill Room is a worthy contender in the competition for carnivorous diners.

Food ●●●●◐ Serv ●●●●◐ Venue ●●●◐○ Value ●●●●◐

JW's Steakhouse

Location ➔ JW Marriott Hotel · Deira | 262 4444
Hours ➔ 12:30 - 15:00 19:30 - 23:30
Web/email ➔ www.marriott.com | Map Ref ➔ 12-A3

The JW's Steakhouse has gathered a justifiably sound reputation amongst Dubai's carnivore set over the last eight years. Within the cosy and luxurious setting of the restaurant, service is superbly warm, knowledgeable and efficient. In addition to a lavish selection of imported Black Angus US beef, a range of equally good seafood, poultry and vegetarian offerings are also available. Desserts include the popular crème brulee and their speciality, bourbon bread & butter pudding . While food and service are excellent, this all comes at a steep price – caveat emptor.

Food ●●●●◐ Serv ●●●●○ Venue ●●●●○ Value ●●●◐○

Legends

Location ➔ Creek Golf Club · Al Garhoud | 295 6000
Hours ➔ 19:00 - 23:00
Web/email ➔ creekfnb@dubaigolf.com | Map Ref ➔ 14-C2

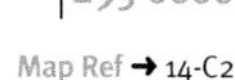   

Set under the main 'sail' of the Dubai Creek Golf & Yacht Club, this impressive restaurant is one of the best fine dining experiences in Dubai. The main dining room has the chic style of any of London's Michelin starred restaurants. The food is of very good quality, and the presentation excellent, however, the menu favours carnivores with its divine steaks. Service is attentive and staff are knowledgeable and friendly. An impressive wine list and a live pianist only add to the overall quality of this establishment.

Note: Legends will be closed from January to September, while the club undergoes renovations.

Food Serv Venue Value

Links Terrace

Location → Nad Al Sheba Club · Nad Al Sheba | 336 3666
Hours → 12:30 - 15:30 19:30 - 23:30
Web/email → www.nadalshebaclub.com Map Ref → 17-A3

With a serene, sophisticated outdoor terrace, Links Terrace commands magnificent views of the Nad Al Sheba track, enclosures and stands. Simple, self serve salads are fresh and crunchy, butterfly cut steaks are delicious (if a little thin) and the dessert selection is extraordinary – the sizzling fruit 'Toban Yaki' should not be missed. The service, although friendly, is disjointed. Like a newborn baby, Links Terrace has yet to develop a unique personality of its own. Will it become a creative genius or...???

Food Serv Venue Value

M's Beef Bistro

Location → Le Meridien Dubai · Al Garhoud | 282 4040
Hours → 12:30 - 14:45 19:30 - 23:45
Web/email → beefbistro@lemeridien-dubai.com Map Ref → 14-E3

Ravenous carnivores take note – you need to come here for one of the finest steaks in town. Tucked away in a quiet corner of the Le Meridien, the Beef Bistro exists for only one purpose: eating meat. Carpaccio, tartar, fondue and succulent steaks are the prime attractions, and you would be hard pressed to find better tenderloin elsewhere. This casual, low key eatery features both US and New Zealand cuts with the Americans winning on superior tenderness. You'll pay for the privilege, but satisfaction is guaranteed.

Food Serv Venue Value

Manhattan Grill

Location → Grand Hyatt Dubai · Umm Hurair (2) | 317 2222
Hours → 19:30 - 23:30
Web/email → www.dubai.grand.hyatt.com Map Ref → 13-E3

This bright, gleaming and sophisticated corner of the Grand Hyatt is definitely for steak lovers. Large 'bone-in' rib eye, tenderloin and New York strip cuts are the stars of the show. The supporting cast (sauces, salads and vegetables) can be less successful and let down what otherwise would be a grand production. The service though, is impeccable. You will need an all star cast budget to dine here.

Food Serv Venue Value

Prime Rib

Location → Le Royal Meridien · Marsa Dubai | 399 5555
Hours → 19:00 - 24:00
Web/email → www.leroyalmeridien-dubai.com Map Ref → 2-E2

An elegant place to dine with the added attraction of the kitchen being an energetic centrepiece for diners to watch the chefs at work. The restaurant

JW's Steakhouse

exudes style and the staff complements the ambience delivering very efficient service. The menu is uncomplicated and revolves around US Angus beef, although there is something for everyone. The deserts, in particular, are impressive in taste and presentation. The wine list is excellent and will cater for expensive tastes as well as regular chug-ers. In all, a very pleasant place to dine. AR

Food ●●●●◐ Serv ●●●●○ Venue ●●●●◐ Value ●●●◐○

Rib Room, The

Location → Emirates Towers · Shk Zayed Rd | 319 8741
Hours → 12:30 - 15:00 19:30 - 24:00
Web/email → www.jumeirahinternational.com Map Ref → 9-C2

200

If budget is not an issue, and first rate grilled American beef is the order of the day, then The Ribroom is worth a visit. This stylish venue does not compromise on presentation or quality. Steaks, obviously, feature high on the menu, although the fish options, and some imaginative vegetarian choices, cannot be overlooked; the wine cellar stocks up an educated selection that complements the menu. A good pick for those 'impress the client' evenings. JT

Food ●●●●○ Serv ●●●●○ Venue ●●●●○ Value ●●●◐○

Rodeo Grill

Location → Al Bustan Hotel · Al Garhoud | 705 4620
Hours → 12:00 - 15:00 19:00 - 24:00
Web/email → www.rotana.com Map Ref → 14-E3

200

Want an uptown, classy restaurant with a twist? This is the place especially for meat lovers. With all the trappings you'd expect of a five star deluxe romantic restaurant – great starters (especially the foie gras), tasty mains, delectable desserts, intimacy, outstanding service – the Rodeo Grill goes further. Guess the weight of your selected US or Australian prime beef within six grams – and it's free! Not as easy as it sounds, but loads of fun. KR

Food ●●●●◐ Serv ●●●●◐ Venue ●●●●○ Value ●●●●○

Western Steak House

Location → Crowne Plaza · Trade Centre 1&2 | 331 1111
Hours → 12:00 - 15:00 19:00 - 23:30
Web/email → www.dubaicrowneplaza.com Map Ref → 9-D2

Regular patrons probably hope that nothing ever changes at Western Steak House, corralled sedately at the western end of the Crowne Plaza lobby. If it looks like a smart Omaha favourite, let it be, for the beef always meets its sky high standard. Filet, tournedos, rib-eye – every flawlessly cooked piece of aged prime beef testifies to tender care and reliability. Nothing, not even a seductive Stilton mousse, can or should divert attention from the beef. Just let it be, night after night. AP

Food ●●●●◐ Serv ●●●●◐ Venue ●●●○○ Value ●●●●○

Tex Mex

Alamo, The

Location → Dubai Marine Beach · Jumeira | 349 3455
Hours → 12:00 - 15:00 19:00 - 23:30
Web/email → www.dxbmarine.com Map Ref → 6-D2

The Alamo presents a good selection of Tex Mex food in a lively atmosphere. The extensive menu ensures that vegetarians get a good selection and also provides quite a few non Tex Mex dishes. Prices are moderate, flavours are great and portions are more than generous – sharing is always an option. Sports events, a live band most nights and drink specials midweek draw a crowd

More

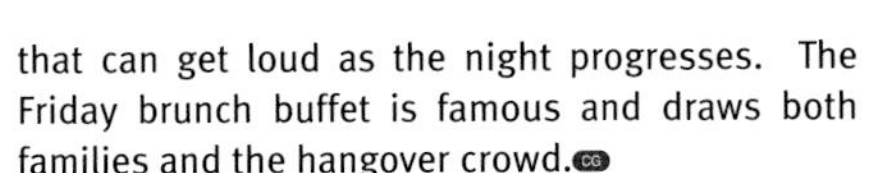

that can get loud as the night progresses. The Friday brunch buffet is famous and draws both families and the hangover crowd.

Food ●●●◐○ Serv ●●●○○ Venue ●●●○○ Value ●●●◐○

Cactus Cantina

Location → Rydges Plaza Hotel · Al Satwa | 398 2274
Hours → 12:00 - 23:15
Web/email → www.cactuscantinadubai.com | Map Ref → 7-A4

It may not be sophisticated, but this well known Tex Mex venue has lots to offer if you're in the mood for a fiesta. Expect crowds on Thursdays with free margaritas for ladies. On other days, the drinks are cheap with plenty of 'two-for-one' food specials. The food is tasty but typically American style Mexican (refried beans and melted cheese with everything), and portions are muy grandes. You can, however, work it off (if so inclined) with in-house salsa classes on Saturday and Sunday nights.

Food ●●●◐○ Serv ●●●◐○ Venue ●●●○○ Value ●●●●○

Cactus Jacks

Location → Millennium Airport Hotel · Al Garhoud | 703 9167
Hours → 12:00 - 15:00 19:00 - 24:00
Web/email → apothotl@emirates.net.ae | Map Ref → 14-D3

Cactus Jack may exhibit a minor acquaintance with the idea of a Mexican restaurant. Famished families welcome huge portions; fajita fans puzzle at nothing but its architectural mysteries; beverage boosters celebrate their wisdom in reordering and skipping dessert; guacamole guardians bring hot sauce. Depressed diners drag themselves in and smile at the way a 30% discount drives Cactus Jack toward a measure of some authenticity ie, real Mexican restaurant prices.

Food ●●○○○ Serv ●●◐○○ Venue ●◐○○○ Value ●●○○○

El Rancho

Location → Marco Polo Hotel · Hor Al Anz | 272 0000
Hours → 19:00 - 03:00
Web/email → marcohot@emirates.net.ae | Map Ref → 8-E4

The upbeat band & DJ running this passable Tex Mex toon town means a late night for cowboys and many Indians. Under a very dark 'night sky' and UV lighting, it becomes more disco than barn dance once the burritos are cleared away. The menu is wide ranging, even if undistinguished in novelty and quality (with apparently no need for desserts). Look out for when an Indian DJ rides into town for a night of dance music at this pinewood pueblo.

Food ●●○○○ Serv ●●○○○ Venue ●●●○○ Value ●●○○○

Pancho Villa's

Location → Astoria Hotel · Bur Dubai | 353 2146
Hours → 12:00 - 15:00 19:00 - 02:00
Web/email → www.astamb.com | Map Ref → 8-A2

Once the reigning king of Dubai nightlife, this venue seems in something of a slump. The Mexican food has always been acceptable, but the room is large enough that dinner in a sparsely populated hall feels desperately sombre. As the evening wears on, people do come in, and it does eventually get going, though with a quirky mix of guests looking for a wide range of, ahem, evening's activities. Good for groups and for a look if in the mood for something less pretentious.

www.EAT OUT SPEAK OUT.com

Just had a disastrous dining experience at a top nosh spot? Was your knickerbocker glory less than glorious, or your pizza a bit pathetic? Don't bottle it all up. Explode online with Eat Out Speak Out; we'll publish your pain, advertise your agony and forward your constructive criticism to the restaurant itself.

Food ●●●○○ Serv ●●●●○ Venue ●●◐○○ Value ●●●◐○

Thai

Other options → **Chinese [p.363]**

Ayotaya

Location → Above Safestway · Al Wasl | 321 1500
Hours → 12:00 - 16:00 19:00 - 24:00 Fri 12:00 - 24:00
Web/email → seawfood@emirates.net.ae | Map Ref → 5-D3

If you are a Thai cuisine fanatic, here's a new place to add to your list of 'To Do's'. Set to open in mid December, Ayotaya is one of several new restaurants to appear above Safestway on Sheikh Zayed Road. The location may seem odd, but the traditional Thai wooden décor immediately creates a chic and authentic mood. Once opened, a special business lunch will be on offer for Dhs. 25. Watch this space or the *Weekly Explorer* for more...

Food n/a Serv n/a Venue n/a Value n/a

Bangkok Thai Cellar, The

Location → Highland Lodge, The · Al Karama | 337 9470
Hours → 19:00 - 01:00
Web/email → thelodge@emirates.net.ae | Map Ref → 10-E4

Recently opened...

Food n/a Serv n/a Venue n/a Value n/a

Benjarong

Location → Dusit Dubai · Trade Centre 1&2 | 343 3333
Hours → 19:30 - 23:30
Web/email → foodbev@dusitdubai.com | Map Ref → 9-A2

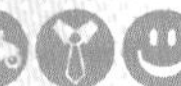

On the 24th floor of the Dusit, Benjarong blends sleek Dubai and elegant Thai brilliantly. The décor is refined, presentation excellent, and the prices are surprisingly affordable, with beer and a wide selection of wines available. Traditional Thai favourites are the base of the extensive menu and knowledgeable staff offer advice when needed. Special promotions are offered each month. Whether you are looking for a romantic night out, a sophisticated business dinner or an outing with friends, Benjarong fits all.

Food Serv Venue Value

Plate smashing is a form of expression, culturally acceptable only in Greek restaurants. You can now get your point across for all other eateries and still avoid costly lawsuits. Just log on to Eat Out Speak Out, UAE's first online restaurant review forum and freely spill all thoughts about the dining experience.

Blue Elephant

Location → Al Bustan Hotel · Al Garhoud | 705 4660
Hours → 12:00 - 15:00 19:00 - 23:30
Web/email → www.rotana.com | Map Ref → 14-E3

This restaurant boasts the best far eastern experience in town, and it's not difficult to see why. A magical ambience, tables overlooking the fish filled lagoon, and even just the *sawadee* (welcome in Thai) from the staff immediately transport you to an authentic oriental world. The food is of excellent quality; for a Thai culinary taster, try the Bangkok Symphony or the Royal Thai Banquet. You can be as daring (or not) as you like when selecting the spice level. Be sure to make reservations, as this place is a local favourite.

Food Serv Venue Value

Lemongrass

Location → Nr Lamcy Plaza · Oud Metha | 334 2325
Hours → 12:00 - 24:00
Web/email → n/a | Map Ref → 10-D4

Named after the reed like herb growing in pots at the door, Lemongrass is a beautiful, bright, contemporary Thai restaurant with attitude. The warm interior is extremely welcoming and the exquisite cuisine aptly celebrates its being with a refreshing lemongrass juice – a great collaborator to a mouth watering appetiser of chicken satay and a mound of prawn crackers with dip. The all Thai staff is attentive and, being open from noon to midnight, means that any Thai food cravings mid afternoon will be catered for.

Food Serv Venue Value

Sukhothai

Location → Le Meridien Dubai · Al Garhoud | 282 4040
Hours → 12:30 - 15:00 19:30 - 23:45
Web/email → sukhothai@lemeridien-dubai.com | Map Ref → 14-E3

Sukothai exudes eastern promise with its warm wooded interior and fragrant smells of traditional Thai cooking. The menu is well balanced, offering an array of curries, seafood and vegetarian dishes. The staff is very accommodating, adding to the atmosphere in their traditional Thai dress. The restaurant's terrace option allows you to people watch at the surrounding restaurants in the

Sukhothai

Going Out
Thai

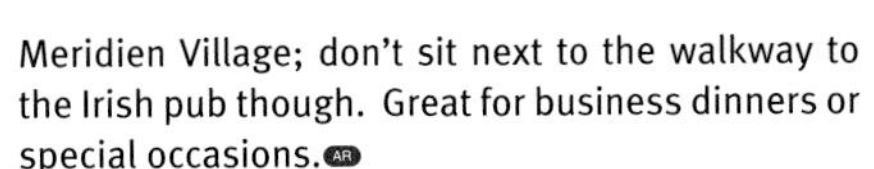

Meridien Village; don't sit next to the walkway to the Irish pub though. Great for business dinners or special occasions. AR

Food ●●●●○ Serv ●●●●○ Venue ●●●●◐ Value ●●●●○

Thai Bistro

Location → Dubai Marine Beach · Jumeira | 346 1111
Hours → 19:00 - 23:30
Web/email → www.dxbmarine.com | Map Ref → 6-D2

150

This popular Thai restaurant rates highly for its wonderful setting: alfreco seating overlooking the pool/cove. Unfortunately, the service, while friendly and knowledgeable, tends to be quite slow. The food is pleasing enough, featuring a diverse selection of seafood items, but does not rival the best of the increasingly competitive Thai restaurants. That said, few diners seem to leave hungry or unhappy, so when seeking ambience and a generally elegant evening, Thai Bistro is a decent choice. CC

Food ●●●●○ Serv ●●●◐○ Venue ●●●●◐ Value ●●●○○

Thai Chi

Location → Pyramids · Umm Hurair (2) | 324 4100
Hours → 12:00 - 15:00 19:30 - 24:00
Web/email → www.pyramidsdubai.com | Map Ref → 13-D2

Duality masquerades in the form of Thai Chi, bringing two popular Far Eastern cuisines under one roof. While mood and ambience are determined by your choice of setting – formal fare, intimate Thai, or casual laid back Chinese – your choice of cuisine is interchangeable. No nonsense, time conscious diners may prefer the set menus bundling appetisers, main courses and dessert options, or if you're feeling a bit adventurous, try combining the Thai Chi Talay Pao with some crispy fried Peking duck – exotica guaranteed! DP

Food ●●●●○ Serv ●●●○○ Venue ●●●◐○ Value ●●●●◐○

Thai Paradise

Location → Al Ain Centre · Bur Dubai | 351 8808
Hours → 12:00 - 23:30
Web/email → n/a | Map Ref → 8-A4

Nestled in Al Ain Centre's Computer Plaza is Thai Paradise. Don't be put off by the décor; here you'll discover some of Dubai's finest Thai cuisine – and for less than the price of a posh pizza! Soups are flavourful and loaded with exotic ingredients. The pad Thai is scrumptious, and the prawn red curry is a 'more-ish' marvel; a perfect blend of zest, spice and seafood. Whether new to Thai or an old hand, you can't go wrong with the extensive menu offerings here. JAW

Food ●●●●◐ Serv ●●●●◐ Venue ●●●○○ Value ●●●●◐

Thai Terrace

Location → Trade Centre Rd · Al Karama | 396 9356
Hours → 12:00 - 14:00 19:00 - 23:30
Web/email → suwabhan@emirates.net.ae | Map Ref → 10-E1

Thai Terrace was the first Thai restaurant to open in the UAE and, although the menu is packed with traditional Thai offerings, it is not a greatly talked about venue. The staff is extremely genial and the gentle atmosphere makes up for the slightly complacent quality, prices and portions of their dishes. 'Tom Kha Kai' and the red curry are particular favourites, and take away seems to be the more preferred option. CC

Food ●●●○○ Serv ●●●●○ Venue ●●●◐○ Value ●●●○○

Turkish

Other options → **Arabic/Lebanese [p.356]**

Topkapi

Location → Taj Palace Hotel · Deira | 223 2222
Hours → 12:00 - 15:00 19:00 - 23:30
Web/email → tajdubai@emirates.net.ae | Map Ref → 11-D2

A relatively undiscovered gem, Topkapi offers great Turkish food at very decent prices. Reserve one of the tables against the wall and take advantage of the comfortable couch seating complete with cushions, while enjoying the sounds of the oud player. The Arabic influence across the menu is unmistakable; the food is of first rate quality. The menu includes an extensive array of authentic starters, salads, grills, stews and pide (Turkish pizza). For dessert, ask for the sampler menu. NQ

Food ●●●●○ Serv ●●●◐○ Venue ●●●◐○ Value ●●●●○

Vegetarian

Vegetarians may be pleasantly surprised by the range and variety of veggie cuisine that can be found in restaurants in Dubai. Although the main

course of Arabic food is dominated by meat, the staggering range of meze, often vegetarian, and the general affection for fresh vegetables should offer enough variety to fill even the most ravenous herbivore!

Nowadays, most outlets offer at least one or two veggie dishes. However, if you want a little more variety, choices include the numerous Indian restaurants, which cater for the large number of Indians who are vegetarian by religion. These offer so many styles of cooking and such a range of tasty dishes, that Indian cuisine is hard to beat for vegetarians. Check out the Indian section of Eating Out for dedicated meat free outlets. Other highlights include loads of excellent Italian, Far Eastern and international restaurants all over the city offering something for every type of veggie.

Vietnamese

Other options → **Chinese [p.363]**

Hoi An

Location → Shangri-La Hotel · Trade Centre 1&2 | 343 8888
Hours → 19:30 - 01:00
Web/email → www.shangri-la.com | Map Ref → 9-A2

Hoi An is fine Asian dining with a difference, serving authentic Vietnamese cuisine in a traditional setting. The interior does its namesake (the ancient city of Hoi An) justice, with fine woodwork, turquoise shutters and pale tangerine walls. Crispy crab rolls, shitake mushrooms and the famous Vietnamese soup, Pho Ga, are just a few of the mouthwatering temptations, and a relaxing bar at the front caters to wine connoisseurs. A healthy selection of uniquely blended teas are a wonderful end to the Hoi An experience. VML

Food●●●●◐ Serv●●●●○ Venue●●●●◐ Value●●●●○

Indochine

Location → Grand Hyatt Dubai · Umm Hurair (2) | 317 2222
Hours → 19:00 - 23:30
Web/email → www.dubai.grand.hyatt.com | Map Ref → 13-E3

Indochine, one of Dubai's most handsome and rewarding restaurants, limits itself to dinner, but its quality knows no limit. The graceful staff primarily delivers Vietnamese dishes: chicken with banana flowers and dried beef with papaya as a prelude to veal with lemon grass, spicy soft shell crabs and morning glories gloriously prepared. These creations, along with other starters and main courses, fresh fruit and exquisite tea constitute Dhs.120 value that diners in love with beauty, will soon seek again. AP

Food●●●●◐ Serv●●●●● Venue●●●●● Value●●●●◐

Dinner Cruises

Other options → **Belly dancing [p.321]**

Al Boom Tourist Village

Location → Nr Al Garhoud Bridge · Umm Hurair (2) | 324 3000
Hours → 20:00 - 22:30
Web/email → www.alboom.co.ae | Map Ref → 14-A3

Al Boom Tourist Village, next to Garhoud bridge, is the surprising base for this relaxing dinner and

Al Boom Tourist Village

tour of the city. Their two hour cruise leaves at 20:30, gently guiding you past many sites and giving a fascinatingly different perspective of Dubai. The food is standard – an assortment of tasty Lebanese appetisers and a meat and seafood barbecue, followed by Arabic sweets. Regardless of whether you're a resident or an out of towner, your stay in Dubai is not complete without the dinner cruise experience. CG

Food Serv Venue Value

Al Mansour

Location → Hotel InterContinental · Deira | 205 7333
Hours → 13:00 - 15:00 20:30 - 23:00
Web/email → n/a
Map Ref → 8-C4

    150

Indulge in a nicely prepared Arabic buffet while cruising along the Creek. Diners board the well maintained, traditional wooden dhow at set sailing times in the afternoon and evening, and relax upstairs on the open air deck or down below in the windowed buffet area. The views are spectacular, the food adequate. Friendly, almost eager staff caters to all whims and live Arabic music, a majlis and shisha complete the experience. This is a fantastic option for neophytes or guests from out-of-town. CG

Food Serv Venue Value

Bateaux Dubai

Location → Nr British Embassy · Bur Dubai | 337 1919
Hours → 12:30 - 15:00 20:30 - 23:00
Web/email → www.bateauxdubai.com
Map Ref → 8-C4

   200

Al Minsaf is the new state of the art boat on the block. Catering for up to 350 people, this mostly glass venue offers spectacular lunch, dinner, sunset and private cruises. A delicious menu of Eastern and Western dishes prepared by the chef on board takes cruising with a 360 degree panoramic view of the Creek to new heights. Carefully designed to cater for all, kids too are very welcome, and you have the option of booking the boat for a party – with live music, fireworks and laser shows, it will be quite a memorable experience! Lunch or dinner cruises range from Dhs.130-290 per adult. Call for specific timings and costs. PR

Food Serv Venue Value

Creek Cruises

Location → Nr DCCI · Deira | 393 9860
Hours → 20:30 - 22:30
Web/email → www.creekcruises.com
Map Ref → 11-C2

  150

Surf the Dubai waters as you delve into an authentic buffet meal catered by a four star hotel, and enjoy the swaying rhythms of live musicians and a talented bellydancer. Then relax and take in the sights along the Creek. The cost of one such evening is Dhs.150 per person. The cruise starts at 20:30 and lasts for about two hours. Here's an idea – cater a private party (from 20 – 200 persons) and design your own genuinely remarkable dinner experience. AR

Food Serv Venue Value

Creekside Leisure

Location → Opp Dubai Municipality HQ · Deira | 336 8406
Hours → Timings on request
Web/email → www.tour-dubai.com
Map Ref → 11-C1

100

For a unique view of Dubai, try a floating majlis dinner cruise by Creekside Leisure. As the dhow floats past both shores of the Creek, you can dine from the limited but hearty international buffet. Efficient service brings your drink order promptly. The reasonable price includes hotel pickup as well as an after dinner bellydancing show. You also have the option of special bookings for groups that might want something more than the standard buffet or usual entertainment. RC

Food Serv Venue Value

Dhow Cruises

Danat Dubai Cruises

Location ➔ Nr British Embassy · Bur Dubai | 351 1117
Hours ➔ 08:00 - 18:30
Web/email ➔ www.danatdubaicruises.com | Map Ref ➔ 8-C4

Enjoy a sumptuous five star international buffet dinner under the stars and take in the sparkling lights of Dubai as you sail through the Creek. Evening cruises feature a range of dishes with a live cooking station and entertainment, including music and a dance floor. If you're looking for a non traditional Arabian dhow cruise experience, this is the one to choose.

Costs: *Adults – Dhs.195; children Dhs.120.*

Timings: *Departs at 20:30; returns at 23:00*

Food ●●●○○ Serv ●●●●○ Venue ●●●◐○ Value ●●◐○○

Cafés & Coffee Shops

Dubai is a wonderful city for those who love café culture – take a break from work or shopping, relax with the newspapers, a cup of tea and a cake, or simply enjoy the chance to catch up on gossip with friends. The numerous cafés around the city vary from outlets that border on being a restaurant and serve an excellent variety of cuisine, from cake to a full blown three course meal, to those that have more of a cake and coffee with a few sandwiches approach. Because of the limitations on opening a restaurant serving alcohol outside of a hotel or certain clubs, plus a high number of people who do not drink alcohol, cafés enjoy a popularity here that they do not perhaps have in other parts of the world. The following section encompasses cafés, coffee shops, ice-cream parlours, Internet and shisha cafés.

Basta Art Café

Location ➔ Bur Dubai · Bastakiya, Bur Dubai | 353 5071
Hours ➔ 10:00 - 20:00
Web/email ➔ bastaartcafe@yahoo.com | Map Ref ➔ 8-B3

The quiet courtyard of Basta Art Café seems a world away from frenetic, modern Dubai. Set within a traditional building in historic Bastakiya, the café provides a refreshing array of juices, salads, pita wraps and jacket potatoes. The salads are big and fresh, and the salmon avocado wrap is a good bet for a light meal. Get a seat in the corner majlis (if you're lucky enough) and do browse the small gallery filled with local handicrafts before stepping back into the world outside.

Food ●●●◐○ Serv ●●●◐○ Venue ●●●●◐ Value ●●●●○

Basta Art Café

Bella Donna

Location ➔ Mercato · Jumeira | 344 7701
Hours ➔ 11:00 - 23:00
Web/email ➔ n/a | Map Ref ➔ 5-E1

If you want a great bowl of pasta before a stroll around the shops, or a pizza after your movie, this place is a good option. Tucked away in the upstairs corner of Mercato Shopping Mall, the open kitchen and classy monochrome decor make this a very stylish eatery. The menu is simple Italian fare, but the choice is delicious and healthy. Try the salmon and cream cheese pizza, served cold, and sit outside on the terrace watching the best of Jumeira going about their business.

Food ●●●○○ Serv ●●●◐○ Venue ●●●●○ Value ●●●●○

Bella Donna

Bocadillo Café

Location → Khalid Al Attaar Tower · Trade Centre 1&2 | 331 3133
Hours → 10:00 - 02:00 Fri 12:00 - 02:00
Web/email → n/a Map Ref → 9-C2

If you are a crêpe fan, this is the place for you. Small, cosy and with a tavern like feel, the main seating area is upstairs beyond the open plan kitchen, where you'll find tables and some relaxing sofas. The menu is Mediterranean in style, but favours a good selection of savoury and sweet crêpes. Generous portions may have you needing a siesta before returning to work. Popular with the younger office set and busy at lunch, arrive early, or enjoy a take away. DM

Food Serv Venue Value

Café Ceramique

Location → Town Centre · Jumeira | 344 7331
Hours → 08:00 - 24:00
Web/email → www.cafeceramique.com Map Ref → 5-E1

Unleash the artist in you. Paint pots over coffee, a bagel and lovely sea vistas. This relaxed and cheery café lets you decorate your choice of available crockery with paints, brushes, and a bit of professional guidance. Your creations are glazed in-house and can be collected later. The staff is helpful, especially with children. The draw here is certainly the novelty and activity rather the food. A fun place for hobby enthusiasts. LG

Food Serv Venue Value

Café Havana

Location → City Centre · Deira | 295 5238
Hours → 08:30 - 24:00
Web/email → www.binhendi.com Map Ref → 14-D1

Cafe Havana is the perfect pit stop for an energy boost and some people watching. Coffee and chocolate cake provides a welcome break for shopping stragglers. Sandwiches, pasta and pizza are also on the menu, and the open air mall location sets the tone for a lunchtime venue. Wicker chairs and plants relax the mood; the service is at breakneck speed, but there's no pressure on you if you wish to linger and get a second wind for the next round of shopping. SB

Other Locations: *Spinneys Umm Suqeim (394 1727)*

Food Serv Venue Value

Café Mozart

Location → Nr Carlton Tower Htl · Deira | 221 6565
Hours → 08:00 - 23:00
Web/email → n/a Map Ref → 8-C4

Relaxed and calm, Cafe Mozart is a handy retreat from the busy streets of Deira. Set up by Austrian born Suzan nine years ago, this café is quaint and welcoming, if a little kitsch, with Mozart-o-rama adorning the walls. Curiously, it also serves Thai food from a comprehensive menu, somewhat skewing the Vienna theme. Otherwise, there's a typical cafe range of sandwiches, salads, some main courses and cakes etc, the latter being most tempting. The café also undertakes private parties and outside catering. CC

Food Serv Venue Value

Coffee Bean & Tea Leaf

Location → Bank Street · Bur Dubai | 352 2225
Hours → 07:30 - 00:30
Web/email → www.coffeebean.com Map Ref → 8-A4

A great place to settle down with the morning paper and catch up with the news. Indulge in a spot of breakfast (or not); hard coffee drinkers can make use of the pink card system. Nine... yes... nine cups of coffee win you a free cup (and a sleepless night!). If in a hurry, grab a quick lunch – the Chinese chicken and the Mediterranean salad are great, and with many hungry office goers in the vicinity, delivery (over Dhs.20) is extremely popular. LG

Other locations: *La Plage, Jumeira (342 9992); World Trade Centre, Shk Zayed Road (332 6655); new outlet opening soon in Jumeirah Plaza*

Food Serv Venue Value

Costa

Location → Mercato · Jumeira | 344 5705
Hours → 08:00 - 22:00
Web/email → n/a Map Ref → 5-E1

There are now nine branches of this popular chain in town. Comfy seating, low coffee tables, outdoor terraces (venue dependant) with basic tables and chairs serve as the core formula for this popular coffee chain. The menu offers traditional coffee shop treats and sandwiches, while hungry patrons can opt for a more filling lunch buffet. For a bit of zing in your coffee, note that the Century Village outlet is licensed, to cure whatever ails you.

Other locations: *City Tower II, Shk Zayed Rd (331 2499); Deira City Centre (294 0833); DNATA Airline Centre, Shk Zayed Rd (321 0978); Mercato Mall (344 5705); Dubai International Airport (Departure Lounge – 220 0179) ; Dubai International Airport (Concourse I & II – 220 0225); Dubai Internet City (391 8896); Century Village (286 9216)*

Food ●●●◐○ Serv ●●●●○ Venue ●●●◐○ Value ●●●◐○

Dome Café

Location → BurJuman Centre · Bur Dubai | 355 6004
Hours → 07:30 - 23:30
Web/email → n/a | Map Ref → 11-A1

This Australian franchise has a lively atmosphere with business meetings on one table and gossip on the next. A diverse menu ranges from Far Eastern specials to pizzas, pies, gourmet sandwiches on various fresh breads, and a good salad bar. Excellent home baked cakes, ice creams and pastries satisfy a sweet tooth. Open early until late, this café works for both, a quick coffee or a leisurely light meal.

Other Locations: *BurJuman (355 6004), Jumeirah Plaza (349 0383) & Bin Sougat Centre (284 4413).*

Food ●●●●○ Serv ●●●○○ Venue ●●●●○ Value ●●●●◐

Elements

Location → Wafi City · Umm Hurair (2) | 324 4252
Hours → 10:00 - 01:00 Some Fridays 12:00 onwards
Web/email → www.elements-cafe.com | Map Ref → 13-D2

Elements offers a relaxed meal, a shisha or a cup of tea within upmarket, minimalist surroundings. Overseen by the charismatic manager (Olivier), attentive, friendly staff assists with food selection. You could also 'be your own chef'; pick your choice of fish, meat or pasta, select a cooking style as well as additional ingredients to round the meal. Recommended are the 'Signature Elements' with mocktails and chocolate fondant. The cuisine is fusion, the portions generous, packed with flavour, and definitely focused on retaining the purity of fresh ingredients.

Food ●●●●◐ Serv ●●●●○ Venue ●●●●◐ Value ●●●●○

Elements

French Connection

Location → Wafa Tower · Trade Centre 1&2 | 343 8311
Hours → 07:00 - 24:00
Web/email → n/a | Map Ref → 9-A2

This 'hot spot' for Internet connectivity is ideal for grabbing a quick salad or sandwich. The cheerful yet calm environment is attractively decorated allowing for a pleasant cup of coffee while browsing or chatting with a friend. A nice selection of breads (baked fresh twice daily) and desserts are always tempting. Specials of the day, including salads, soups and sandwiches, are tasty and filling, though a bit pricey. There are two more branches in the Golden Sands area (359 4545) and Al Qouz (339 4141).

Food ●●●◐○ Serv ●●●●○ Venue ●●●◐○ Value ●●●●○

Gerard

Location → Magrudy Shopping Mall · Jumeira | 344 3327
Hours → 07:30 - 23:00 Fri 07:30 - 22:30
Web/email → gerard07@emirates.net.ae | Map Ref → 6-C2

Gerard's is one of the oldest European style cafés in town, and attracts a loyal clientele of both expats and locals. Stop in at the counter to peruse the pastry and croissant selection before finding a seat underneath the cool canopy of bougainvillaea outside. While the cappuccinos are of a modest size, the delicious and affordable desserts more than make up for this. Sandwiches, salads and freshly made crepes are on offer as well. Gerard's displays a personal touch that is missing from many of the chain cafés around town.

Other Locations: *Al Ghurair City*

Food ●●●◐○ Serv ●●●◐○ Venue ●●●●○ Value ●●●●○

IKEA

Location → City Centre · Deira | 295 0434
Hours → 10:00 - 22:00 14:00 - 22:00
Web/email → www.ikeadubai.com
Map Ref → 14-D1

In the middle of epic IKEA excursions, don't forget the calm cafe nestled inside the IKEA universe. Reasonable, tasty and most of all, relatively quiet, this self service food bar offers dozens of food options, including a daily vegetarian special. Fresh 'Swedish' food is the theme: try the prawn mayonnaise open sandwich or the heartier Swedish meatballs. The cappuccino and hot chocolate is surprisingly good, but in this climate, why bother? A clearly superior option to the chaos of the food court. HP

Food Serv Venue Value

La Brioche

Location → Jumeirah Centre · Jumeira | 349 0588
Hours → 10:00 - 22:00
Web/email → www.binhendi.com
Map Ref → 6-C2

A favourite with Jumeira shoppers, La Brioche offers a superb café style dining experience, as perfect for an evening bite as for a lunchtime snack. Located in the mall lobby, it has the feel of a conservatory with its wicker furniture and airy ambience. Food ranges from delicious pastries to a good selection of international favourites . The French onion soup will make you swoon, the fruit juices are a must, and the generous portions won't leave you desiring anything else. AH

Food Serv Venue Value

La Marquise

Location → Palm Strip · Jumeira | 345 8433
Hours → 08:00 - 01:30
Web/email → frbakery@emirates.net.ae
Map Ref → 6-D2

Shisha is the main attraction of this Palm Strip café. Tucked away on the first floor, it lacks the location benefits of those downstairs with the outdoor terrace opening onto the street. The menu is rather confusing, seemingly having several add-ons to give wider appeal. Staff, while friendly, regularly perform disappearing acts; make sure you order everything you want when they do appear. The food is uninspiring in selection and bland in presentation. The fruit cocktails are a chink of light in an otherwise forgettable experience. LG

Other Locations: Next to BP off Defence R/A (343 3320).

Food Serv Venue Value

Lime Tree

Location → Nr Jumeira Mosque · Jumeira | 349 8498
Hours → 07:30 - 20:00
Web/email → limetree@emirates.net.ae
Map Ref → 6-D2

The funky little Lime Tree Café, popular with the Jumeira Jane set, is an oasis of green, both inside and out. Choose your meal from a daily changing variety of fritatas, quiches, sandwiches, salads and other delectables from the deli counter. Try to leave room for the tasty treats (particularly their delicious cakes and cookies). Weather permitting, relax outside in the garden. Service is efficient and portions are presented with no frills, straight from the display. Veggies be warned: ask for a full ingredient list before selecting! CH

Food Serv Venue Value

Lobby Lounge, The

Location → Ritz-Carlton Dubai · Marsa Dubai | 399 4000
Hours → 10:00 - 24:30 Thu 10:00-01:30
Web/email → rcdubai@emirates.net.ae
Map Ref → 2-E2

This is probably as good as gets in Dubai without having to be a multimillionaire. This exquisitely appointed colonial style locale overlooking the beach offers a range of afternoon teas, but don't miss the Royal Tea, which includes champagne, finger sandwiches, freshly baked scones with clotted cream and homemade jams, and pastries. There is also a dazzling selection of twenty different gourmet teas to choose from. For truly special occasions or just to relax in style, the Lobby Lounge offers guaranteed satisfaction at a very reasonable price. DM

Food Serv Venue Value

More

Location → Nr Welcare Hospital, · Al Garhoud | 283 0224
Hours → 08:00 - 22:00
Web/email → n/a
Map Ref → 14-D4

Once seekers of More's great bread discover that 'next to Welcare' means hidden behind the

supermarket, no obstacle remains to further satisfaction. So called starters – gallons of glorious soup or bushels of basil dressed spinach almost concealed by roasted pumpkin and pine nuts – should be enough to convince anyone not captured by the More mantra. Sturdy paella and other enticing fish or meat dishes, accompanied by juice make More as good as it gets. The desserts don't fall short either. AP

Food Serv Venue Value

Lobby Lounge, The

Paul

Location → Mercato · Jumeira | 344 3505
Hours → 12:00 - 15:00 19:00 - 24:00
Web/email → n/a | Map Ref → 5-E1

100

Often mistaken for a hair salon (a whimsical choice of name), Paul offers a scenic setting (if you like people watching) and a great place to safely leave shopping stragglers without too much protest. Paul has a French bistro theme and rustic wooden decor, plus an affordable menu with an exciting choice, but hit and miss service. Most tantalising is the French deli takeout section. Guaranteed to tempt even the most 'laden down with bags' shoppers and add to their growing collection of purchases. PR

Food Serv Venue Value

R.G.L.A.

Location → Above Safestway · Al Wasl | 321 1500
Hours → 19:00 - 24:00
Web/email → seawfood@emirates.net.ae | Map Ref → 5-D3

 50

Resembling a small fort with two large cannons on either side of the large wooden entrance door, this newly opened shisha café is a favourite spot for the largely Arabic clientele. Private cabins are available to enjoy the wide selection of juices, beverages and Arabic snacks. A perfect venue to relax and puff away to your heart's content on some hubbly bubbly.

Food n/a Serv n/a Venue n/a Value n/a

Sahn Eddar

Location → Burj Al Arab · Umm Suqeim | 301 7600
Hours → 07:00 - 02:00
Web/email → www.jumeirahinternational.com | Map Ref → 4-A1

      150

Tea for two and two for tea in this decadent setting from where the luxurious carpets and gold trimmings of the Burj plus the ocean can be viewed. Order a la carte or partake in the long and languid, traditionally English, afternoon tea. Sit back and let the staff pamper you with four courses of sweets, sandwiches, scones, chocolates and a pot of fragrant tea or coffee of your choice. It's a bargain compared to the unforgettable impression you'll make on your mom – who, by the way, would love you forever for this! LA

Food Serv Venue Value

Second Cup

Location → Oasis Tower · Trade Centre 1&2 | 343 5314
Hours → 07:30 - 24:00
Web/email → www.binhendi.com | Map Ref → 9-B2

 50

If caffeine is your weakness, do yourself a favour and give Second Cup a second glance. Delicious brews served in oversized cups come hot and foamy to your table, transporting you to Seattle or New York. But when the coffee runs out, it's time to move on. With an delicious looking but ultimately disappointing selection of cakes, there is nothing else on offer to tempt you to linger for lunch. Best bet; eat at Japengo next door, then retire to Second Cup and let the dust settle. LG

Food Serv Venue Value

Shakespeare & Co.

Location → Kendah House · Trade Centre 1&2 | 331 1757
Hours → 07:00 - 01:30
Web/email → shakesco@emirates.net.ae | Map Ref → 9-B2

The only thing that this venue shares with its namesake in Paris is a truly eclectic concept. Something of an insider haunt, the food is good and the ambience relaxing. Choosing between the charmingly rustic interior and the terrace is the first challenge; choosing a meal from the diverse, creative menu is another. Arabic, Moroccan, and some continental dishes appear (sometimes slowly) out of the smallish kitchen, destined to delight. LG

Other locations: *Gulf Towers (335 3335).*

Food ●●●◐○ Serv ●●●◐○ Venue ●●●●○ Value ●●●●○

Spot Café

Location → Nr Four Points Sheraton · Bur Dubai | 352 1215
Hours → 08:00 - 24:00 Fri 10:00 - 24:00
Web/email → n/a | Map Ref → 8-A4

This bright café is especially popular with the bankers on that street during lunchtimes. Hip and healthy French and Italian food is served all through breakfast, lunch and dinner, and a decent brunch of Mediterranean and continental cuisine is a Friday regular. Although service can be spotty, this is a good choice for a quick snack or a light meal. Perhaps not the best choice for a quiet cup of coffee and a book though. LG

Food ●●●◐○ Serv ●●●○○ Venue ●●●○○ Value ●●●○○

THE One

Location → Nr Jumeirah Mosque · Jumeira | 342 2499
Hours → 09:00 - 22:00 Fri 14:00 - 22:00
Web/email → purchase@theoneme.com | Map Ref → 6-D2

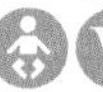

This is popular spot (especially with the Jumeira Jane crowd and local ladies) for a quick coffee or a bite to eat if you're in the area or shopping at THE One. The dining area is separated from the main shop by curtains. Offerings from the clearly imaginative chef include tasty sandwiches, pastries and a wide range of shakes and juices. A different homemade soup is available each day. The cakes (carrot, walnut, chocolate) are superb, but order straight away – they disappear quickly. LG

Food ●●●●○ Serv ●●●○○ Venue ●●●◐○ Value ●●●◐○

Vienna Cafe

Location → JW Marriott Hotel · Deira | 262 4444
Hours → 24 hours
Web/email → www.marriott.com | Map Ref → 12-A3

Catering for the sophisticated executive and the young at heart, this comfortable coffee stop offers intimate booths and an array of Viennese delicacies ranging from the smoked salmon breakfast to schnitzels and strudels. You could just plop there with an alcoholic milkshake and a jar of jelly bears! An hour's Internet use, including tea or coffee, is Dhs.38, and with unlimited refills, it doesn't matter how small the cups are. Popular with businessmen and, well... just a little different. LS

Food ●●●○○ Serv ●●◐○○ Venue ●●●○○ Value ●●○○○

Vivel

Location → · Beach Rd, Jumeira | 344 3232
Hours → 07:30 - 23:30
Web/email → na | Map Ref → 5-C2

A quaint little coffee shop for the privacy seeking non Starbucks crowd. Hidden behind the more 'glamorous' Coffee Bean & Tea Leaf, this little venue is often overlooked. A French-ish décor spreads through to a tiny terrace, ideal for a romantic sojourn on cooler evenings. The cuisines lean towards Iranian, Arabic and European, with a selection of pastries, chocolates, confectionaries and cakes. The menu also includes sandwiches and salads. For a crisp start of the day, opt for the daily breakfast between 07:30 - 11:00.

Other Locations: *Al Rigga St (285 7005)*

Food ●●●○○ Serv ●●●◐○ Venue ●●●◐○ Value ●●●○○

West One

Location → Jumeirah Centre · Jumeira | 398 7177
Hours → 07:30 - 23:00
Web/email → www.dubaishoppingmalls.com | Map Ref → 6-C2

This refreshingly casual, café style eatery is a great place for a light meal or a quick sandwich on the run. The food is tasty and fresh, the service fast and friendly, and with a set lunch starting from Dhs.25, it's also good value. Now at a new location, the menu too has undergone a makeover, with kids' meals, a Friday brunch and 24 hour delivery. However, their speciality is outside catering – from

corporate functions to private cocktail parties, they'll tailor make menus to suit any occasion. HK

Food ●●●●○ Serv ●●●●○ Venue ●●●○○ Value ●●●●○

Zyara Café

Location → Nr Al Salam Tower · Trade Centre 1&2 | 343 5454
Hours → 08:00 - 24:00
Web/email → zyara@emirates.net.ae | Map Ref → 9-B2

V 50

The relaxed atmosphere, eclectic décor and laissez-faire service are all conducive to taking your time over a coffee or a light meal. Zyara is Arabic for visit, and a wide variety of magazines, books and games help you pass the time while you wait for your order. The mainly Arabic buffet attracts a largely Lebanese clientele and a predominantly sandwich and salad menu is popular with the business lunchers. Another branch of Zyara Café is located at Dubai Media City (391 8031). CC

Food ●●●○○ Serv ●●●○○ Venue ●●●○○ Value ●●●○○

Internet Cafés

If you want to surf the Web, visit a chat room, email friends or play the latest game, but want to be a little bit sociable about it, or perhaps do not have your own facilities for being online, Internet cafés are perfect to visit. Over the last few years, this type of café has become a common feature throughout Dubai. The mix of coffee, cake and technology has proved an irresistible draw, and this particular niche of café will doubtless continue to expand. As always, facilities, ambience, prices and clientele vary considerably, so poke your head in the door and then make your decision. Prices are typically Dhs.5 - 15 per hour. Happy surfing!

Just had a disastrous dining experience at a top nosh spot? Was your knickerbocker glory less than glorious, or your pizza a bit pathetic? Don't bottle it all up. Explode online with Eat Out Speak Out; we'll publish your pain, advertise your agony and forward your constructive criticism to the restaurant itself.

Current hotspot locations include: French Connection, Sheikh Zayed Road, Spot Cafe, Bank Street, Bur Dubai (Dhs.7/hour) and Al Jalssa Internet C@fe, Al Ain Centre (Computer Plaza) (Dhs.10/hour), but great cafés are springing up all the time, so check out what suits you.

Shisha Cafés

Shisha cafés are common throughout the Middle East, offering relaxing surroundings and the chance to smoke a shisha pipe (aka 'hubble bubble' or 'narghile') with a variety of aromatic flavours. They are traditionally the preserve of local men who meet to play backgammon and gossip with friends. However, the cafés are popular with locals and visitors alike, especially in the cooler winter evenings.

Most outlets offer a basic menu; generally Arabic cuisine and a few international options, plus coffees, teas and fruit juices. So, choose your flavour of shisha and sit back – this is what life is all about! Prices are typically around Dhs.15 - 25, and loads of cafés continue to spring up around town. Many literally offer door to car door service, so you can roll up, wind down your window or smoke on the pavement next to your car – especially good if you want to impress that date on the back seat! Oud Metha's got some great (conveniently dark) areas for car shisha...

If you get 'hooked' (pun intended), and wish to have your own, Carrefour and Al Karama market (see [p.168]), among many trinket shops all over the city, are particularly good places to get started, offering a variety of pipes and some of the basic tobacco flavours. It can be a very satisfying experience, puffing on a pipe around a campfire in the desert, watching the stars...

Shisha	
Al Hadiqua	Sheraton Jumeirah Beach
Al Hakawati	Sheikh Zayed Rd
Al Khayma	Dubai Marine
Al Koufa	Nr American Hospital
Aroma Garden	Nr Maktoum Bridge
Awafi	JW Marriott
Cosmo Café	Sheikh Zayed Rd
Courtyard	Royal Mirage Hotel
Fakhreldine	Holiday Inn Bur Dubai
Fatafeet	Next to Dubai Creek
QD's	Dubai Creek Golf & Yatch Club
Mazaj	Century Village
Shakespeare & Co	Sheikh Zayed Rd
Elements	Wafi City

Food on the Go

Bakeries

In addition to bread, bakeries offer a wonderful range of pastries, biscuits and Lebanese sweets. Arabic foods include 'borek' (flat pastries, baked or fried with spinach or cheese) and 'manoushi' (hot bread, doubled over and served plain or filled with meat, cheese or 'zatar' (thyme seeds)). Biscuits are often filled with ground dates. All are delicious, and must be tried, at least once.

Panini

Location → Grand Hyatt Dubai · Umm Hurair (2) | 317 2222
Hours → 08:00 - 01:00
Web/email → www.dubai.grand.hyatt.com | Map Ref → 13-E3

50

Nestled in the Grand Hyatt, next to Andiamo!, this Italian bakery specialises in oven fresh crusty breads, homemade cakes, pastries, the finest praline chocolates, freshly baked biscotti and quality Italian ice-cream. Their significant highlight is their takeaway business, but whether munching there or picking up an order to go, the entry of a better bakery in town is always a good thing. BD

Fruit Juices Etc.

Fresh juices are widely available, either from shawarma stands or juice shops. They are delicious, healthy and cheap, and made on the spot from fresh fruits such as mango, banana, kiwi, strawberry and pineapple (have the mixed fruit cocktail if you can't decide).

Yoghurt is also a popular drink, often served with nuts, and the local milk is called 'laban' (a heavy, salty buttermilk that doesn't go well in tea or coffee). Arabic mint tea is available, but probably not drunk as widely as in other parts of the Arab world; however, Arabic coffee (thick, silty and strong) is extremely popular and will have you buzzing on a caffeine high for days!

Shawarma

Throughout the city, sidewalk stands sell 'shawarma', which are rolled pita bread filled with lamb or chicken carved from a rotating spit, and salad. Costing about Dhs.3 each, these are inexpensive, well worth trying, and are an excellent alternative fast food to the usual hamburger. The stands usually sell other dishes, such as 'foul' (a paste made from fava beans) and 'falafel' (or ta'amiya), which are small savoury balls of deep fried beans. You can also buy a whole grilled chicken, salad and humous for about Dhs.11.

While most shawarma stands offer virtually the same thing, slight differences make some stand out from the rest. People are often adamant that their particular favourite serves, for example, the best falafel in town. These can often be the first place you eat when you come to the UAE, however, look around – every restaurant has its own way of doing things and you might find that the best is, surprisingly, the smallest, most low-key restaurant you happen on by chance.

Panini

Al Mallah

Location → Al Diyafah St · Al Satwa | 398 4723
Hours → 06:30 - 03:30
Web/email → n/a | Map Ref → 6-E3

Among the throngs of small Arabic joints, this one stands out. Situated on one of the busiest streets, it mainly offers pavement seating with a few tables and chairs inside. The shawarmas and fruit juices are excellent here, the cheese and zatar manoushi good and they have, possibly, the biggest and best falafel in Dubai! Grab an evening snack and watch the world drive by, or stay and order a bigger meal. Another branch of Al Mallah is located on Al Mateena Road, Deira (272 3431).

Food●●●○○ Serv●●●○○ Venue●●◐○○ Value●●●◐○

Al Shera'a Fisheries Centre

Location → Nr. Marks & Spencers · Deira | 227 1803
Hours → 10:00 - 01:00
Web/email → n/a | Map Ref → 11-E1

We all know the lovely but ubiquitous shawarma that spins on spits everywhere in town. If you think you've tried them all, think again! This venue takes a winning concept and, well, let's say, adapts it. This is the only joint in town that serves fish shawarma, which is actually quite tasty and a pleasant change. This very casual shop is worth a visit, if only for the novelty. What's next, date hummous?

Food●●●●○ Serv●●●◐○ Venue●●◐○○ Value●●●◐○

Friday Brunch

An integral part of life in Dubai, Friday brunch is a perfect event for a lazy start or end to the weekend, especially once the really hot weather arrives. Popular with all sections of the community, it provides Thursday night's revellers with a gentle awakening, and often much needed nourishment. For families, brunch is a very pleasant way to spend the day, especially since many venues organise a variety of fun activities for kids, allowing parents to fill themselves with fine food and drinks, and to simply relax. Different brunches appeal to different crowds; some have fantastic buffets, others are in spectacular surroundings, while some offer amazing prices for all you can eat.

Parties at Home

Caterers

A popular and easy way to have a party, special occasion or business lunch, in-house catering allows you to relax and enjoy yourself, or to concentrate on... anything but the cooking! Numerous outlets offer this service, so decide on the type of food you want – Indian, Chinese, Italian, Lebanese, finger food, etc, and ask at your favourite or local restaurant or café to see if they do outside catering. Alternatively, most of the larger hotels have an outside catering department, usually capable of extravagant five star functions.

There are also specialist companies who provide a variety of services at very reasonable prices. You don't even have to stay at home to get in-house catering – how about arranging a party in the desert with catering? Depending on what you require, caterers can provide just the food or everything from food, crockery, napkins, tables, chairs and even waiters, doormen and a clearing up service afterwards. Costs vary according to the number of people, dishes and level of service, etc, required.

For a list of hotel numbers, check out the hotel table in General Information. For restaurant and cafés, browse the Going Out section of the book. You can also refer to the catering section in the telephone books, especially the Hawk A - Z business pages.

Room Service Deliveries

Location → Nr. Capitol Htl · Satwa | 345 5444
Hours → 24 hrs
Web/email → www.roomservice-uae.com | Map Ref → 7-A2

The concept, successful in most international cities, is to deliver food from your favourite restaurant. Peruse the directory of participating restaurants, make a selection from the menu, and call it in: food should be on its way in an hour. Minimum orders are Dhs.40 for lunch and Dhs.60 for dinner with a Dhs.10 - 20 delivery charge. Deliveries can be made anywhere in central Dubai and Jebel Ali anytime between 11:00 - 23:00, with deliveries to Sharjah and 'Greater Dubai' outside rush hour times.

Friday Brunch

Restaurant	Location	Phone	Buffet	A La Carte	Breakfast	Lunch	Kid Friendly	Alcohol	Outside Terrace	Cost		Timings
										Adult	Child	
Al Muntaha	Burj Al Arab	301 7777	y	n	n	y	n	y	n	240	120	11:00 - 15:30
Al Shindagha	Metropolitan Palace hotel	227 0000	y	n	y	y	n	y	n	89	u	11:00 - 15:00
Alamo	Dubai Marine	346 1111	y	n	y	y	n	y	n	60	30	11:00 - 15:00
Antigo	Le Meridien Dubai	282 4040	y	n	y	y	y	y	y	98	50	12:30 -15:30
Aquarium	Creek Golf & Yacht Club	295 6000	y	n	y	y	y	n	n	75	35	11:30 - 15:00
Bazaar, The	Oasis Beach Hotel	399 4444	y	n	y	y	y	n	y	70	35	12:30 - 15:30
Bella Vista	Jumeirah Rotana Hotel	345 5888	y	n	y	y	y	y	n	75	37	11:30 - 15:30
Benjarong	Dusit Dubai	343 3333	y	n	y	y	y	y	n	95	u	12:30 - 15:00
Biggles	Millenium Airport Hotel	282 3464	y	n	y	y	n	n	y	38	19	11:00 - 15:30
Boston Bar, The	Jumeirah Rotana Hotel	345 5888	y	n	n	y	n	y	n	40	20	12:00 - 16:00
Brasserie	Le Royal Meridien	399 5555	y	y	y	y	y	n	y	120	60	12:30 - 16:00
Cactus Jacks	Millenium Airport Hotel	282 3464	y	y	y	y	n	n	y	28	15	12:00 - 16:00
Café Boulvar	Hotel Inter-Continental	222 7171	y	n	y	y	n	n	n	99	57	12:00 - 16:00
Cafe Insignia	Ramada Hotel	351 9999	y	n	y	y	y	y	n	110	38	12:00 -15:00
Carter's	Pyramids	324 0000	y	n	y	y	y	n	y	65	30	11:30 - 15:00
Cascades	Fairmont Hotel	332 5555	y	n	y	y	n	n	n	95	45	09:00 - 15:15
Cellar, The	Aviation Club, The	282 4122	n	y	y	y	n	y	y	60	u	11:30 - 16:30
Cheers	Lodge, The	337 9470	y	n	n	n	y	n	n	40	20	11:30 - 15:30
Coconut Grove	Rydges Plaza Hotel	398 2222	y	n	y	y	n	n	n	30	15	12:30 - 15:00
Colonnade, The	Jumeirah Beach Hotel, The	348 0000	y	y	y	y	n	y	y	130	65	12:00 - 15:30
Dubai Restaurant	Nad Al Sheba Racecourse	336 3666	y	n	n	y	y	n	y	70	25	12:00 - 16:30
Dubliner's	Le Meridien Dubai	282 4040	n	y	y	n	n	y	n	40	40	11:00 - 23:45
Finnegans	Palm Hotel Dubai, The	399 2222	y	n	y	y	y	y	y	59	30	12:00 - 15:00
Fontana	Al Bustan Rotana Hotel	282 0000	y	n	y	n	y	n	n	99	50	12:00 - 15:00
Gozo Garden	Millenium Airport Hotel	282 3464	y	y	y	y	y	n	y	38	19	12:00 - 15:30
Handi	Taj Palace Hotel	223 2222	y	n	n	y	y	n	n	88	44	12:00 - 16:00
Long's Bar	Towers Rotana Hotel	343 8000	y	n	y	y	n	y	n	49	25	12:00 - 16:00
Market Place	JW Marriott Hotel	262 4444	y	n	y	y	y	n	y	99	m	12:30 - 16:00
More	Al Garhoud	283 0224	y	y	y	y	n	n	y	65	35	11:00 - 16:00
New York Deli	Regal Plaza Hotel	355 6633	y	n	y	y	n	n	n	50	25	12:00 - 17:30
Oceana	Hilton Dubai Jumeirah	399 1111	y	y	y	n	y	y	n	95	u	12:30 - 15:30
Olives	One&Only Royal Mirage, The	399 9999	y	n	n	y	n	n	y	115	25	12:30 - 15:30
Pax Romana	Dusit Dubai	343 3333	y	n	y	y	n	y	n	95	u	12:00 - 15:00
Planet Hollywood	Wafi City	324 4777	y	y	y	y	y	n	n	65	35	11:30 - 15:00
Prasino's	Jumeirah Beach Club	344 5333	y	n	n	y	n	n	y	130	65	12:30 - 15:00
Rainbow Room	Aviation Club, The	282 4122	y	n	n	y	n	n	n	30	15	12:00 - 16:00
Rock Bottom Café	Regent Palace Hotel	396 3888	y	n	y	y	y	y	n	49	u	12:00 - 15:30
Sakura	Taj Palace Hotel	223 2222	y	n	y	y	y	n	n	88	44	12:30 - 16:00
Scarlett's	Emirates Towers Hotel	319 8768	y	n	y	y	y	n	y	70	u	11:30 - 16:00
Spice Island	Renaissance Hotel	262 5555	y	n	y	n	y	y	n	91	71	12:00 - 14:30
Splendido	Ritz-Carlton	399 4000	y	n	y	n	y	n	y	140	70	12:30 - 15:30
Taverna	Dubai Marine Beach Resort & Spa	346 1111	y	n	y	y	y	n	y	125	70	12:30 - 15:30
Topkapi	Taj Palace Hotel	223 2222	y	n	n	y	y	n	n	88	44	12:00 - 16:00
Verdi	Taj Palace Hotel	223 2222	y	n	y	y	y	n	n	88	44	12:00 - 16:00
Vivaldi	Sheraton Dubai Creek Hotel	207 1717	y	n	y	y	n	n	y	70	35	12:30 - 15:30
Waxy O'Conner's	Ascot Hotel	352 0900	y	n	y	y	n	y	n	50	15	12:00 - 18:00
Windtower	Dubai Country Club	333 1155	y	n	y	y	y	n	y	49	20	12:00 - 16:00
Zyara Cafe	Sheikh Zayed Road	343 5454	y	n	y	y	n	n	y	50	25	11:00 - 15:00

m-metre (charged by height) ~5% off u-under 12 is free ^1st child is free

In-house Catering

In-house Catering	
Dubai World Trade Centre	308 6944
Emirates Abela	282 3171
Happy Home	396 7644
Intercat	334 5212
Master Chef	282 9100
Metropolitan Catering Services	881 7100
Sandwich Express	343 5212
Something Different	267 1639
West One	349 4500

Kids' Video Services

Shooting Stars

Location → Jumeira Rd · Jumeira | 344 7407
Hours → Timings on request
Web/email → n/a | Map Ref → 6-A2

Shooting Stars is an adventure video production company that produces keepsake videos of children in imaginative situations. Using the latest digital technology, they can turn children into the stars of their own video adventure: a popular choice is 'My Arabian Adventure' (the background tape is filmed in the dunes at Hatta). It's a unique and unusual gift to send back to the grandparents! For more information contact the above number or (050 798 8209).

Party Organisers

Flying Elephant

Location → Warehouse · Jct 3, Shk Zayed Rd | 347 9170
Hours → Timings on request
Web/email → www.flyingelephantuae.com | Map Ref → 4-D4

Flying Elephant offers everything you would expect from a party planning company: from adding special effects for a product launch or providing a turnkey service for annual family days to entertainment on your little one's first birthday party in your back garden. The company can bring a wide range of products to the occasion, such as balloons and decorations, or the Gulf's largest outdoor confetti blaster. Flying Elephant also offers theme decoration, theme parties, balloon printing and balloon decoration/sculpting.

On the Town

If you're out on the town in Dubai, you'll soon find that there are a good many places to go and things to do. It may not be quite the buzzing city found in other parts of the world, but Dubai is without doubt the 'Party Capital of the Gulf', with enough choice to keep even the most ardent socialite happy. The following section covers the 'cultural' entertainment such as theatre and comedy clubs, as well as cafés, bars, pubs and nightclubs.

In Dubai people tend to go out late, usually not before about 21:00. Even on weeknights, kick off is surprisingly late and people seem to forget, after about the tenth drink, that they really ought to be at work the next day. If you're venturing out to Arabic nightclubs or restaurants, you're likely to find them almost deserted before about 23:00.

Wednesday and Thursday, being the start of most peoples' weekend, are obviously busy, but you will also find that during the week many bars and restaurants offer promotions and special nights to attract customers and to create a lively atmosphere. Particularly popular is Ladies Night, which is traditionally on a Tuesday (and the busiest night of the week for some places). Women are given tokens on the door offering them free drinks – the number varies from one to an endless supply, and it may be limited to certain types of drink. This ploy certainly seems to attract male customers too! With men outnumbering women in Dubai (by two to one), it's an unbalanced world where women, for once, can take full advantage. The following are the main places that have a Ladies Night/s at some point during the week:

Bar hopping in Dubai

Cafés and restaurants generally close between 23:00 and 01:00, with most bars and nightclubs split between those who close 'early' at 01:00 and those who stay open 'late' until 02:00 or 03:00. Little is open all night. To complement the bars and nightclubs, refer also to the information on Eating Out. Many restaurants have a very good bar and some also have a dance floor which kicks in towards midnight. However, they are usually reviewed only once – as a restaurant. In this section, you will also find further information on, for instance, Dubai's alcohol laws.

Bars

Dubai has an excellent number of bars with a good variety of different styles. Most are located in hotels, and while many bars come and go, the more popular ones are always busy. In addition to the bars reviewed here, there are plenty of others (usually in the smaller hotels), which do not attract the regular crowds of the more popular venues. If you're looking for somewhere different... get out there and explore! The city's more upmarket locations range from terminally hip cocktail lounges to decadent wine bars, from jazz bars to cigar bars – all providing salubrious surroundings for those opulent and self indulgent moments. For more details on where and when people in Dubai go to drink, refer to the start of the On the Town section. For information on the individual bars read on...

Door Policy

Even with the mix of nationalities that makes up the cultural melting pot of Dubai, there are certain bars and nightclubs that have a selective entry 'policy'. Sometimes the 'Members Only' sign on the entrance needs a bit of explaining. Membership is usually introduced to control the clientele frequenting the establishment, but is often only enforced during busy periods. At quieter times, non members may have no problem getting in, even if unaccompanied by a member. Basically, the management uses the rule to disallow entry if they don't like the look of you or your group, and they will point to their sign and say 'Sorry'. Large groups (especially all males), single men and certain nationalities are normally the target. You can avoid the inconvenience, and the embarrassment, by breaking the group up or by going in a mixed gender group.

If you find yourself being discriminated against, don't get mad – get even! In most cases it's not worth trying to discuss this rationally with the doorman – it won't work. Most companies hate bad publicity – try taking the issue up with some of the local media. Other possible solutions include taking out membership for that particular club, shamelessly trying to bribe the doorman, getting there early (around 19:00), going with Kylie Minogue, or staying at home.

Dress Code

Most bars have a reasonably relaxed attitude to their customers' dress sense. Some places, however, will insist on no shorts, jeans or sandals, while others require at least a shirt with a collar. Nightclubs generally have a dressier approach, so dress to impress. As Dubai is well on its way to becoming *the* trendy tourist destination, the dress code will continue to lean towards the latter extreme.

Specials

Many places hold occasional promotions with different themes and offers. These run alongside special nights, such as Ladies Night, which are usually held weekly. For the promotions, you can find out what's coming up in the weekly and monthly entertainment publications and from the venues concerned. Special nights such as the popular quiz nights, are mainly promoted in the bar or pub, and many attract quite a following. As a bonus, the prizes are often quite good.

Balcony Bar

Location → Shangri-La Hotel · Trade Centre 1&2 | 343 8888
Hours → 12:00 - 02:00
Web/email → www.shangri-la.com | Map Ref → 9-A2

All your needs will be attended to at the Shangri-La, where service reigns. The Balcony Bar is no exception. Stunning décor and good music are the Asian fusion backdrop to a cosy bar overlooking the lower lobby. The bar is home to a large selection of wine, and a small but adequate collection of cigars. Full bar staff mixes up your late night ambrosia with a touch of elegance, as you curl up in a corner with your tangy cigar and relaxed company. LA

Food ●●●○○ Serv ●●●●○ Venue ●●●◐○ Value ●●●◐○

Bhari Bar

Location → Mina A'Salam · Umm Suqeim | 366 8888
Hours → 12:00 - 02:00
Web/email → www.jumeirahinternational.com Map Ref → 4-A2

This is a cocktail bar with something special. The view from the popular terrace takes in the Venetian waterway, the lapping sea and the towering neighbour, Burj Al Arab. This venue can easily be added to Dubai's list of fabulous places to spend quality time with good company. A menu of wines, spirits and cocktails entices all tastes and pockets, and the beverages are palatably superior and good value for money. Attentive service ensures that glasses are full at all times and the tasty nibbles never run out. DIP

Food ●●●●◐ Serv ●●●●◐ Venue ●●●●◐ Value ●●●●◐

Marina Roof Deck

Location → Jumeirah Beach Htl · Umm Suqeim | 348 0000
Hours → Oct to May 12:00 - 24:00
Web/email → www.jumeirahinternational.com Map Ref → 4-B2

At the end of the jetty and up a flight of stairs (reminiscent of a cruise ship), you'll find a pleasant place to drink and pass time. The scenery and the company you keep are what sustain you, for the cocktails are not too well concocted, nor delivered in a timely manner. The drinks menu is extensive, but try and sample ones that don't need mixing. Stunning night views of Jumeira Beach and the Burj Al Arab make up for the drinks and make the overall experience a good one. KR

Food ●●◐○○ Serv ●●◐○○ Venue ●●●◐○ Value ●●◐○○

Nakhuda Bar

Location → Mina A'Salam · Umm Suqeim | 366 8888
Hours → 12:00 - 15:00 19:00 - 02:00
Web/email → www.jumeirahinternational.com Map Ref → 4-A2

The description says, 'a rustic, harbour side retreat'. And Nakhuda is indeed that and more. A very extensive drinks list, comfortable seating (inside or out) and a menu that doubles as a storybook, all add up to an enjoyable place for before or after dinner drinks and light snacks. With over forty wines available, and no house wine offered, making a decision becomes a little tough. Seek help from the manager if you must, or just be adventurous. KR

Food ●●●●◐ Serv ●●●○○ Venue ●●●●● Value ●●●●◐

Bahri Bar

P.m. Bar

Location → Ibis World Trade Centre · Shk Zayed Rd | 332 4444
Hours → 12:00 - 01:00
Web/email → www.accorhotels.com Map Ref → 9-E3

This is a handy retreat when a major exhibition or conference is in town. Tucked away on the ground floor of the Ibis Hotel, this brightly lit bar is comfortable but not intimate. A central TV dominates, and is popular with those preferring a bar stool. A drinks menu includes teas, coffees and softies, which can also be served in an adjoining lounge. Some very strong beers and breezers, and only house wines are on offer. Overall, a place worth knowing about. CH

Food ●●●○○ Serv ●●●◐○ Venue ●●●◐○ Value ●●●●○

American Bars

Billy Blues

Location → Rydges Plaza Hotel · Al Satwa | 398 2272
Hours → 18:00 - 02:00
Web/email → cactus1@emirates.net.ae Map Ref → 7-A4

Please see review under American – Going Out.

Food ●●●○○ Serv ●●●◐○ Venue ●●●●○ Value ●●●●○

Blues & Cues

Location → Ramada Continental · Hor Al Anz | 266 2666
Hours → 16:00 - 03:00
Web/email → ramadadb@emirates.net.ae | Map Ref → 12-B4

As the name suggests, this gently lit bar on the first floor of the Ramada Continental in Deira is a nice place to shoot pool. While the Colombian band isn't exactly 'Blues', it's still good live music. The food is mostly bar snacks; there are a few beers on tap but more in bottles. The place has a nice vibe, but can get pretty crowded, so it's a good idea to reserve a pool table. Darts are also available if the pool tables are full. CC

Food ●●○○○ Serv ●●●◐○ Venue ●●◐○○ Value ●●◐○○

Boston Bar, The

Location → Jumeira Rotana · Al Satwa | 345 5888
Hours → 12:00 - 03:00
Web/email → www.rotana.com | Map Ref → 6-E3

Its intimate atmosphere and open setting make the Boston Bar very popular as a friendly tavern, sports bar and eatery. Starting with English breakfast at noon, the bar serves daily specials with afternoon discounts that include Dubai's longest happy hour (between 12:00 and 20:00!). However, the place really takes off at night, especially on the two ladies' nights (Tuesdays and Thursdays). Appetisers, salads, soups, pasta, fish, grilled meat and sandwiches are all offered on a hearty menu that favours English cuisine. RC

Food ●●●◐○ Serv ●●●●◐ Venue ●●●●◐ Value ●●●●○

> ***Ramadan Timings***
>
> *During Ramadan, opening and closing times of restaurants change considerably. Be sure to call and check before landing somewhere, only to find all the lights off and nobody home. Many nightclubs remain open, but the dance floor is closed off... so you'll just have to save those jiggy jiggy moves for a later date!*

Harry's Place

Location → Renaissance Hotel · Hor Al Anz | 262 5555
Hours → 12:00 - 16:00 18:00 - 24:30
Web/email → rendubai@emirates.net.ae | Map Ref → 12-A3

Please see review under American – Going Out Section.

Food ●●●◐○ Serv ●●●○○ Venue ●◐○○○ Value ●●◐○○

Rock Bottom Café

Location → Regent Palace Hotel · Bur Dubai | 396 3888
Hours → 12:00 - 03:00
Web/email → www.ramee-group.com | Map Ref → 11-A1

The rough and ready ending to any big night out, this joint rocks at full volume. The resident bands tend to be among the town's finest, belting out cover songs until the DJ takes over. Quieter early on, steak and burgers hog the all American menu. The smoky pool tables and Harley Davidson Motorcycles parked outside kick start the rock'n'roll atmosphere, and the 'too late in the evening to care' revellers do the rest. Over 21's only and ID may be required. The door 'policy' is very strict (i.e. favours Westerners). CC

Food ●●◐○○ Serv ●●◐○○ Venue ●●●●○ Value ●●●◐○

Scarlett's

Location → Emirates Towers · Shk Zayed Rd | 319 8768
Hours → 12:00 - 03:00
Web/email → www.jumeirahinternational.com | Map Ref → 9-C2

Contemporary music, tans and browns, screens for sports, faux Dixie decorations, gallons of refreshing liquids, inattentive service, expensive but edible food, patrons in dishabille, delicious apple and berry crumble, a surfeit of decibels – can anyone imagine spotting a reincarnated Margaret Mitchell among Scarlett's expats? Only her parting words would verify the vision: 'As God is my witness, I'll never be that hungry again.' This is not Tara; this is the more familiar gentility of our age. Welcome home to Scarlett's. AP

Food ●●●○○ Serv ●●○○○ Venue ●●●○○ Value ●●●○○

Ladies Nights

Boston Bar	21:30 - 02:30	Tue
Boudoir	22:30 - 03:00	Tue
Carters	22:00 - 24:00	Sun & Tues
Jimmy Dix	22:00 - 01:00	Sun & Tues
Lodge, The	20:00 - 01:00	Wed & Sun
Long's Bar	22:00 - 01:00	Tue & Wed
Oxygen	21:00 - 03:00	Mon & Wed
Planetarium	23:00 - 03:00	Tues & Wed
Rockbottom	20:00 - 02:00	Everyday - not Fri, Wed
Scarlett's	21:00 - 23:00	Tue
Seville's	23:00 - 24:00	Tue & Fri
Waxy O'Connors	20:30 - 01:30	Thu
Zinc	19:00 - 23:00	Tue

Beach/Waterfront Bars

Barasti Bar

Location → Le Meridien Mina · Al Sufouh | 399 3333
Hours → 08:30 - 02:00 18:00 - 23:00
Web/email → f&b@lemeridien-minaseyahi.com Map Ref → 3-A2

Location, location, location! Whether for a relaxing sundowner or a romantic meal, this beachside terrace and bar is truly a delightful spot. However, this is let down slightly by poorly trained staff, a limited wine list and hit and miss cuisine. The seafood platter though, is a hit, comprising a huge selection of local produce, (lobster, shrimps, clams, mussels and oysters and more). The atmosphere is especially lively on Friday evenings when those in the know gather to hear the resident 'Scratch Band'. SC

Food ●●●◐○ Serv ●●●○○ Venue ●●●●◐ Value ●●●○○

Beach Bar, Al Hadiqa Tent, The

Location → Sheraton Jumeirah Beach · Marsa Dubai | 399 5533
Hours → 12:00 - 01:30
Web/email → www.starwood.com Map Ref → 2-D2

You can choose between the 'tent' (with glass sides, a canvas roof and plenty of a/c units to keep it nice and chilled) or alfresco dining on the outside patio. Enjoy typical Arabic dishes, such as meze, falafel, shawarma, shish taouk, kebabs and kofta. Portions are large, very tasty and cooked to perfection. End your meal with an aromatic shisha; choose from a number of fruity or cappuccino flavours. Barring the lack of efficient service, this a true Arabian experience. CH

Food ●●●○○ Serv ●◐○○○ Venue ●●●○○ Value ●●●◐○

QD's

Location → Creek Golf Club · Al Garhoud | 295 6000
Hours → 18:00 - 02:00 18:00 - 02:00
Web/email → creekfnb@dubaigolf.com Map Ref → 14-C2

Situated next to the gently lapping waters of the Creek, QD's lets you relax with drinks before or after a meal. Shisha and bar snacks are available, and a recently installed pizza oven will further expand the menu. The wine selection is pretty good, but cocktails and beer are the order of the day. Speakers placed around the edges allow for good sound balance – you can hear the music (or DJ) everywhere. This trendy outdoor bar is a great place to party through the cooler winter evenings. CG

Food ●●◐○○ Serv ●●●◐○ Venue ●●●●○ Value ●●◐○○

Sunset Bar

Location → Jumeirah Beach Club · Jumeira | 344 5333
Hours → 17:00 - 22:00
Web/email → www.jumeirahinternational.com Map Ref → 5-D1

A sundowner experience requires the right blend of sandy beaches, uninterrupted views of the horizon, happy hours, shisha, music and utter relaxation. The Sunset Bar offers all that and, situated on one of Dubai's finest private beaches, is possibly the best local example of such. Clearly, Friday is the

Sunset Bar

day to be seen there, but make sure you arrive well before sunset, as seating goes fast. Just grab a beach carpet, plonk down on a giant cushion and shisha the evening away.

Food●●●○○Serv●●●○○Venue●●●●○Value●●●●○

Cigar Bars

Cigar Bar

Location ➜ Fairmont Hotel · Trade Centre 1&2 | 332 5555
Hours ➜ 19:00 - 02:00
Web/email ➜ www.fairmont.com
Map Ref ➜ 9-E1

This luxurious hideaway lets you slip comfortably into Cuba without raising eyebrows at the CIA. The staff can find treats for both experts and rookies from a huge selection, and the ventilation system keeps the place fresh (for the non smokers). Port, wine and a full bar round things out, with drinks made with Brazilian alcohol to add that special taste. You don't have to be an aficionado to enjoy the Cigar Bar – an introduction into the world of Cubans makes this a perfect starting point for novices.

Too much pepper in your prawn balls... and the muscle bound chef looks like he wouldn't take criticism lightly? Smile politely, go home, and log on to Eat Out Speak Out. Rant and rave to your hearts content! We'll not only publish your comments, we will also pass them on to the chef - anonymously of course...

Food●●◐○○Serv●●●●○Venue●●●●○Value●●◐○○

Library & Cigar Bar, The

Location ➜ Ritz-Carlton Dubai · Marsa Dubai | 399 4000
Hours ➜ 17:00 - 24:30
Web/email ➜ rcdubai@emirates.net.ae
Map Ref ➜ 2-E2

Dark wood, Chesterfields, soft yellow lighting and moody 20's style jazz make this the perfect place for the idle smoker with too much time and money on their hands. The room is dark and luxurious, and offers aficionados a huge array of classic stogies. The drinks list caters primarily to the scotch, single malt and cognac crowd, although good cocktails are available along with a range of wines by the glass. Kick back, relax, and let your worries drift away.

Food●●●◐○Serv●●●○○Venue●●●●●Value●●◐○○

Cocktail Lounges

Al Samar Lounge

Location ➜ Mina A'Salam · Umm Suqeim | 366 8888
Hours ➜ 08:30 - 01:00
Web/email ➜ www.jumeirahinternational.com
Map Ref ➜ 4-A2

Located in the lobby, the Al Samar Lounge is the meeting place of Mina A' Salam. Watch in comfort amidst the bustle of this animated area, as the world and its people go by. The lounge features an extensive selection of non alcoholic and alcoholic cocktails, traditional high teas in the afternoon, and live entertainment in the evening. Adjacent is an outdoor shisha terrace overlooking the lagoon and beyond. Service is extra friendly and helpful. A visit here is recommended for its lively atmosphere.

Food●●●●○Serv●●●●●Venue●●●●◐Value●●●●○

Boudoir

Location ➜ Dubai Marine Beach · Jumeira | 345 5995
Hours ➜ 19:30 - 03:00
Web/email ➜ www.myboudoir.com
Map Ref ➜ 6-D2

French Renaissance makes a revival at Boudoir, blending opulence and sophistication with slicker, 21st century crowds. Deep reds, oud scents and soft lighting set the mood for your dining or chill out experience. Savour French cuisine at its finest with traditional dishes – tartar of salmon with crème fraîche or a cassolette of lobster thermidor are divine. After hours, Boudoir transforms into the ultimate lounge, with the help of DJ Igor and the various drink deals (free for the fairer sex... tough luck guys!)

Food●●●◐○Serv●●●◐○Venue●●●●○Value●●●◐○

Ginseng

Location ➜ Wafi City · Umm Hurair (2) | 324 8200
Hours ➜ 19:00 - 02:00 19:00 - 03:00 Thu
Web/email ➜ www.ginsengdubai.com
Map Ref ➜ 13-D2

This upmarket restaurant/cocktail lounge, which looks like a set from 'Miss Saigon', provides the perfect opportunity to taste the culinary delights of the Far East without hurting your wallet. The bar keeps the mood focused on the fantastic cocktails and creates a trendy but relaxed meeting place for

a night out. The tapas sized portions allow for the option to select a variety of dishes from soup through to tempura and share with friends. Offering a selection of meats, fish, seafood and vegetarian dishes that represent the very best of Asian cuisine, one can't fail to be impressed. EAT

Food Serv Venue Value

La Moda

Location → Hotel InterContinental · Deira | 205 7333
Hours → 13:00 - 15:00 19:00 - 03:00
Web/email → intercon_bc@itcdubai.co.ae | Map Ref → 8-C4

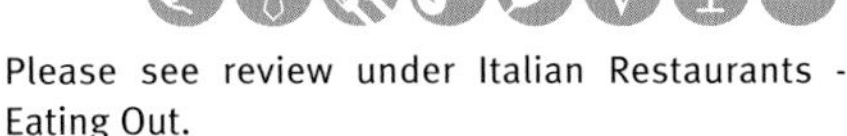

Please see review under Italian Restaurants - Eating Out.

Food Serv Venue Value

Martini Lounge

Location → Sofitel City Centre · Al Garhoud | 603 8500
Hours → 12:00 - 00:30
Web/email → www.deiracitycentre.com | Map Ref → 14-D1

The Martini Lounge is City Centre's cheesy chill out room. If you need an escape from the City Centre crowds, and fancy something stronger than a coffee, head here. This dimly lit bar is only two minutes from the bustling mall, and offers an endless list of martini combinations, inexpensive cocktails, mocktails, shorts and every kind of beer. Also present is a dinner menu and an occasional live pianist. If the place is too smoky, try the outside terrace. JAW

Food Serv Venue Value

Piano Bar, The

Location → Crowne Plaza · Trade Centre 1&2 | 331 1111
Hours → 00:00 - 00:30 18:00 - 01:30
Web/email → www.crowneplaza.com | Map Ref → 9-D2

Dark, discreet, and discerning, the Piano Bar caters to the late night business crowd. Middle age wheeler dealers come here for the fine selection of whiskies, old world wines and cigars, and regulars keep their expensive private bottles in locked signature cabinets. Happy hour features two for one bottles of scotch with complimentary hot meze, but curiously, there are few takers. Latecomers are rewarded with songs sung blue, sleek service and sumptuous snacks. This is an elegant bar that takes its traditions seriously. JK

Food Serv Venue Value

Rooftop Lounge & Terrace

Location → One&Only Arabian Court · Al Sufouh | 399 9999
Hours → 19:00 - 01:00
Web/email → www.oneandonlyresort.com | Map Ref → 3-A2

This bar takes lounging and relaxation to new heights. Slouch on the circular couch surrounding a large spherical half moon, and rest your legs on the supplied puffies. Sip one of their many exotic cocktails while taking in the ocean vistas beyond. If required, choose a more formal seating option at one of the tables. A wide selection of drinks includes non alcoholic beverages too, but it is their Arabian Comfort (a mint mixture) and Desert Dunes that heighten the already romantic setting under the stars. AR

Food Serv Venue Value

La Moda

Trader Vic`s

Location → Crowne Plaza · Trade Centre 1&2 | 331 1111
Hours → 18:30 - 02:00
Web/email → cpdxb@cpdxb.co.ae | Map Ref → 9-D2

Trader Vic's exalts the theme of south pacific paradise with high quality food, drinks, singers and service. The bar serves exotic cocktails

perfected over 60 years (many in their own signature goblets) and island titbits of tasty snacks play finger food to the cocktails or act as appetisers to the entrees. A mouth watering menu includes tasty wok meals and specialties from the large Chinese wood fire oven. Flambé dishes cooked at your table further the exotic theme. Not cheap, but worth it for the more special occasions.

Food Serv Venue Value

General Bars

Alamo, The

Location → Dubai Marine Beach · Jumeira | 349 3455
Hours → 12:00 - 15:30 19:00 - 00:45
Web/email → www.dxbmarine.com | Map Ref → 6-D2

Please see The Alamo review under Tex Mex.

Food Serv Venue Value

Blue Bar

Location → Novotel Wrld Trade Centre · Shk Zayed Rd | 332 0000
Hours → 12:00 - 01:00
Web/email → www.novotel.com | Map Ref → 9-E3

Not so blue! The Blue Bar's dark wood and caramel hues exude class and sophistication, setting the tone for a business lunch or a relaxing drink after the close of a corporate deal. Thankfully, the ambience is lightened with plasma screens on either side of the room showcasing the latest international sporting event. Being the first bar in Dubai to specialise in Belgian beers, one must disregard the conventional bottled beers and venture into the draft section. The Blue Bar's extensive drinks menu does not disappoint.

Food Serv Venue Value

Bridges

Location → Fairmont Hotel · Trade Centre 1&2 | 332 5555
Hours → 09:00 - 01:45
Web/email → www.fairmont.com | Map Ref → 9-E1

For personal comfort, ambience and choice of beverages, Bridges located on the ground floor of The Fairmont Hotel is a good meeting place. Just settle into one of the 'chat show style' swivel chairs, high chairs at the bar, or lounges, and choose from a tremendous array of cocktails (many with historical explanations in the menu). Reasonably priced beers, wines by the glass, fresh juices or hot drinks are available with bar snacks and the complimentary nuts/crisps. Well worth a visit.

Food Serv Venue Value

Carter's

Location → Pyramids · Umm Hurair (2) | 324 4100
Hours → 12:00 - 01:00 12:00 - 02:00
Web/email → www.pyramidsdubai.com | Map Ref → 13-D2

Themed to colonial Egypt, wicker chairs and ceiling fans adorn three dining areas – two indoor and one alfresco, better suited for casual get togethers rather than intimate encounters. Stroking midnight, Carter's comes alive as strobe lights pulse hypnotically to DJ Matt's house beats. Grab those drinks early though, with the various drinks deals on hand, the bar area can get crowded sooner than you think. Carter's is a well balanced formula that works on all level – Tutan Khamen would have been proud.

Food Serv Venue Value

Gulf Pavilion, The

Location → Ritz-Carlton Dubai · Marsa Dubai | 399 4000
Hours → 11:30 - 18:00
Web/email → rcdubai@emirates.net.ae | Map Ref → 2-E2

Walking into The Ritz-Carlton, you are engulfed by a superior and 'upper' sensation. This stylishly elegant hotel sweeps you down a palatial staircase to The Gulf Pavilion, situated between two pools and surrounded by palm trees and gardens. Ideal for an informal lunch or a casual dinner, the ambience is relaxed, the food excellent and the service second to none. A kids' menu is offered in an environment that is perfect to feed them in and watch them play. Dining here is not cheap, but not expensive either, considering the entire package.

Food Serv Venue Value

Jules Bar

Location → Le Meridien Dubai · Al Garhoud | 282 4040
Hours → 11:00 - 03:00
Web/email → julesbar@le-meridien-dubai.com | Map Ref → 14-E3

Not exactly one of the jewels in the Le Meridien's culinary crown, Jules Bar nonetheless, offers tolerable

options for beverage obsessed stomachs. Enchiladas, fajitas, burritos and chimichangas dominate the menu and this may come as a surprise, but the thirty or so dishes have travelled far enough from their origins to be non threatening. In daylight, scars on interior surfaces framed by rival TV sets bespeak rollicking good times, with bands and beverages at night (when, despite its food, Jules Bar shines). BD

Food ●●◐○○ Serv ●●◐○○ Venue ●●●◐○ Value ●●◐○○

ku-bu

Location → Hotel InterContinental · Deira | 205 7773
Hours → 19:00 - 03:00
Web/email → infocentre@ihcdubai.co.ae | Map Ref → 8-C4

Shadowed in a corner of the InterContinental Dubai is the tattoo themed bar, Ku-Bu. Japanese influences apparent, you'd be forgiven for landing the occasional karate chop in the dojo-esque surroundings. Space is restricted so it's wise to arrive early or make reservations beforehand. With a theme night everyday of the week, you're bound to get the best drink deals around town. The perfect venue for a pre-party buzz. DP

Food ●●●◐○ Serv ●●●◐○ Venue ●●●◐○ Value ●●●◐○

Long's Bar

Location → Towers Rotana · Trade Centre 1&2 | 343 8000
Hours → 12:00 - 03:00
Web/email → www.rotana.com | Map Ref → 9-B2

Very popular with Dubai residents both on weekends and ladies nights, Long's has the longest bar in the Middle East. Quiet and desolate early on, the venue starts hopping as the crowds descend on the bar. The dedicated dining area is a haven when things get noisy in the bar, offering a good selection (except vegetarian) of tasty dishes in all categories, particularly European. Catch up with friends, the prowl crowd circling the bar, or settle in the restaurant for a more intimate stay. BD

Food ●●●◐○ Serv ●●●◐○ Venue ●●●○○ Value ●●●◐○

Piano Bar, The

Location → Le Royal Meridien · Marsa Dubai | 399 5555
Hours → 17:00 - 01:00
Web/email → www.leroyalmeridien-dubai.com | Map Ref → 2-E2

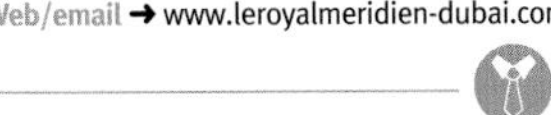  

This bar exudes a certain style but is, nevertheless, uncomplicated in approach and appearance. The atmosphere relaxes, and then energises you as you sip one of their many cocktails. The drinks list is extensive and boasts every drink imaginable, and if you decide to satisfy your hunger pangs, a snacks menu is also available. Friendly staff is eager and helpful. The selection of cigars is limiting, however, more than adequate for the layman smoker. AR

Food ●●●●○ Serv ●●●○○ Venue ●●●●○ Value ●●●◐○

Rainbow Room

Location → Aviation Club, The · Al Garhoud | 282 4122
Hours → 19:00 - 02:00
Web/email → www.aviationclubonline.com | Map Ref → 14-C3

  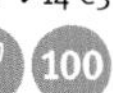

This quiet pub condones a one on one evening; sit and chat, and maybe play some cards or watch TV. Although sectioned off with an Internet café, the area is nice and the pub food, decent enough, with a late night kitchen and a full bar with cocktails to boot. Pour your heart out to a friend over a pina colada, snacks and some poker – for you get the feeling that here, everyone's doing just that. LA

Food ●●●○○ Serv ●●◐○○ Venue ●●●○○ Value ●●◐○○

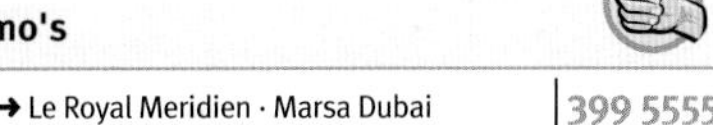

Satchmo's

Location → Le Royal Meridien · Marsa Dubai | 399 5555
Hours → 17:30 - 02:30 17:30 - 02:30
Web/email → www.leroyalmeridien-dubai.com | Map Ref → 2-E2

 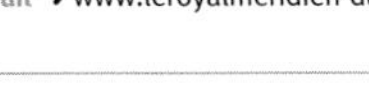 

This place is hip without the pressure of the club scene. Late night entertaining comes with all the gloss and service of a five star hotel venue, plus live jazz six nights a week. An intriguing cocktail menu even extends to fun, low calorie choices. Their signature blends show off the talents of the bar staff, who will be delighted to stir up something unique for you. Ideal for celebrating a special anniversary or event. KM

Food ●●●◐○ Serv ●●●●○ Venue ●●●●◐ Value ●●●●○

Siam

Location → Dusit Dubai · Trade Centre 1&2 | 343 3333
Hours → 17:00 - 03:00
Web/email → foodbev@dusitdubai.com | Map Ref → 9-A2

Dark wood and an intriguing Thai ambience makes Siam the perfect spot to unwind after a difficult day under florescent lighting. Stick to international cocktails and drinks served off their really long bar.

Snacks cover Thai, Indian and Arab specials, and delightfully appeal to a myriad of palates. Choose to watch the world go by on Sheikh Zayed below, or keep up with the scores on the large screen TV. Also a welcome setting for the working bachelor after a long hard day! AD

Food●●●○○Serv●●◐○○Venue●●●◐○Value●●●○○

Spectrum On One

Location ➜ Fairmont Hotel · Trade Centre 1&2 | 311 8101
Hours ➜ 17:30 - 19:00
Web/email ➜ www.fairmont.com | Map Ref ➜ 9-E1

This modern and trendy bar on the first floor of the dazzling Fairmont hotel ranks highly as a plush and pleasant venue. The glass fronted cellar tempts wine aficionados with the goodies on offer, while the staff's efficiency, courtesy and genuine enthusiasm when advising about cocktails, is matchless. Perhaps this is the perfect mellow place for a drink before your meal, as it's located between all the other hotel restaurants. Go easy on the cocktails though, or order a taxi in advance. LM

Food●●●◐○Serv●●●●●Venue●●●●○Value●●●◐○

Spectrum On One

Spikes Bar

Location ➜ Nad Al Sheba Club · Nad Al Sheba | 336 3666
Hours ➜ 07:00 - 01:00
Web/email ➜ www.nadalsheba.com | Map Ref ➜ 17-A3

Looking for a good meal and interested in sport? This golf bar could be a great choice. A varied a la carte menu, catering to all appetites and ages, is available throughout the day. Items range from sandwiches, salads and burgers to more substantial entrees; the prawn curry and lamb fillet being delicious examples. TVs dotted around, offer the chance to relax and unwind in front of your favourite sport, and attentive service creates a pleasant environment. RL

Food●●●◐○Serv●●●◐○Venue●●●○○Value●●●◐○

Studio One

Location ➜ Hilton Jumeirah · Marsa Dubai | 399 1111
Hours ➜ 16:00 - 03:00
Web/email ➜ www.hilton.com | Map Ref ➜ 2-D2

The latest revamped locale of Hilton's food and beverage outlets, Studio One is a small but hip sports bar with a difference. Complete with a dartboard, foosball and pool table, this place is perfect for the big game, or for a drink or two after a night out. The normal fare of snacks and finger food is available: fish and chips, club sandwiches, chicken nuggets and more. The happy hour, though, is the real enticement, with 50% off drinks from 20:00 – 22:00 everyday! HK

Food●●●●○Serv●●●●○Venue●●●◐○Value●●●◐○

Uptown

Location ➜ Jumeirah Beach Htl · Umm Suqeim | 406 8181
Hours ➜ 18:00 - 02:00
Web/email ➜ www.jumeirahinternational.com | Map Ref ➜ 4-B2

Glide up to the 24th floor and presented with an amazing sundowner view. This is certainly the place to be if you want to relax on the terrace, or chill out to soft tunes woven by the 'requests welcomed' pianist. Serving a mixture of fine cocktails, wines, beers and speciality coffees, all natures and appetites are pretty well covered. Do observe the uniqueness of the slanting glasses, which are all pre-chilled to make your drink that much more special. If you're feeling a little peckish, try the tasty 'lite bites'. EAT

Food●●●●◐Serv●●●●◐Venue●●●●●Value●●●◐○

Vu's

Location ➜ Emirates Towers · Shk Zayed Rd | 319 8783
Hours ➜ 12:30 - 15:00 19:30 - 24:00
Web/email ➜ www.jumeirahinternational.com | Map Ref ➜ 9-C2

You haven't seen the city until you've caught the view from the 51st floor of Emirates Towers. Vu's

tucks you into a corner under a starry Dubai night where you can sip what is arguably the world's best cocktail. Do try the Level 51 – an ambrosia like drink and quite the mood setter. The ambience and sheer novelty of Vu's is not to be missed, especially if you're looking for a place that instantly propels you into a world of quiet class. LA

Food Serv Venue Value

Karaoke Bars

Other options → **Filipino [p.370]**

Harry Ghatto's

Location → Emirates Towers · Shk Zayed Rd | 319 8796
Hours → 19:30 - 03:00
Web/email → www.jumeirahinternational.com | Map Ref → 9-C2

This upscale sing-along bar is small and very noisy, but then again, that's exactly how it should be. Ever popular with a very mixed crowd, it is cosy and modern with a full bar and (mediocre) food. The staff energetically keep things rolling. Although the song selection is not the widest, they'll sing with you if you need support. Self conscious karaoke neophytes may appreciate the private room that can be reserved. Go for a laugh and a change of pace, and have dinner beforehand. PL

Food Serv Venue Value

Hibiki Karaoke Lounge

Location → Hyatt Regency · Deira | 209 1444
Hours → 19:30 - 03:00
Web/email → hyattbus@emirates.net.ae | Map Ref → 8-D2

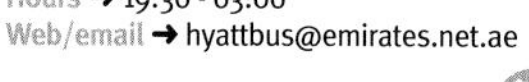

This Japanese karaoke bar invites all prima donnas to take the stage. More reserved crooners may prefer to hire a private room with a group of friends. The service is exceptional, and a vast range of expensive cocktails brings an elegant executive feel to a fun evening's entertainment. Happy hour increases the good value experience. The cosy atmosphere attracts more singles, but if it's a fine Cuban you prefer, have a look at the cigar menu. DP

Food Serv Venue Value

Sports Bars

Other options → **Activities [p.257]**

Aussie Legends

Location → Rydges Plaza Hotel · Al Satwa | 398 2222
Hours → 15:00 - 03:00 Thu 12:00 - 03:00
Web/email → rhrdxb@emirates.net.ae | Map Ref → 7-A4

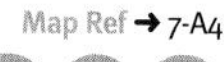

This convivial and fun Aussie sports bar is a favourite of local expats and has a wide variety of drinks, food, and a pool table. The atmosphere and service are friendly and relaxed, and the menu is varied, but this is not the place to come for a light meal as most items on the menu are continent sized and calorie laden. Aussie Legends also shows numerous sporting events on their big screen TV's. DM

Food Serv Venue Value

Champions

Location → JW Marriott Hotel · Deira | 262 4444
Hours → 12:00 - 01:00 Fri 18:00 - 02:00
Web/email → www.marriott.com | Map Ref → 12-A3

One of Dubai's better sports bars, Champions offers large portions of fresh, tasty American cuisine at great value prices. From bar snacks to steaks with all the trimmings, diverse tastes are catered for on the surprisingly comprehensive menu. Lunchtime specials are the biggest bargain at Dhs.25 for a choice from six main courses with a drink. The atmosphere can be quiet and relaxed (ideal for a nice game of pool) or rowdy, depending on which game is on the screens around the bar. SC

Food Serv Venue Value

Cricketers Sports Bar

Location → Ramada Continental · Hor Al Anz | 266 2666
Hours → 12:00 - 15:30 18:30 - 03:00
Web/email → ramadadb@emirates.net.ae | Map Ref → 12-B4

Pop into the Cricketer for a quick drink on the way home from work. This casual bar is served by welcoming staff and decorated with assorted cricket paraphernalia: photos, bats, shirts and shields. The menu is varied, with BBQ and fried options dominating, a limited veggie selection,

and a chicken curry with rice or naan that's just right (spicy and filling). Unwind and listen to the (loud) band with a free pint accompanying the BBQ meal. CC

Food ●●●○○ Serv ●●●○○ Venue ●●●○○ Value ●●●◐○

Tapas Bars

Other options → **Cuban [p.367]**

Pachanga Terrace

Location → Hilton Jumeirah · Marsa Dubai | 399 1111
Hours → 18:30 - 24:00
Web/email → www.hilton.com | Map Ref → 2-D2

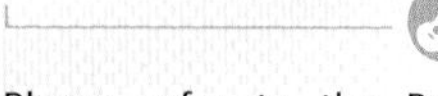

Please refer to the Pachanga review under Argentinian restaurants.

Food ●●●●◐ Serv ●●●●◐ Venue ●●●●● Value ●●●●○

Seville's

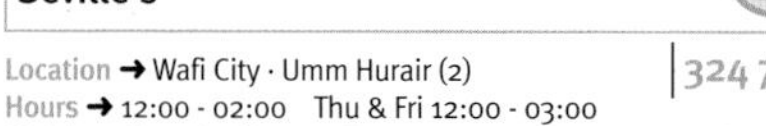

Location → Wafi City · Umm Hurair (2) | 324 7300
Hours → 12:00 - 02:00 Thu & Fri 12:00 - 03:00
Web/email → phsales@emirates.net.ae | Map Ref → 13-D2

The original tapas bar in Dubai, Seville's is a fine place to meet friends, sip sangria and explore the diverse tastes on offer. A beautifully designed outdoor terrace is pleasant and very popular on the weekends, while live Spanish music enhances the cosier ambience inside. Adequate portion sizes allow you to sample a range of Spanish cuisine, and the menu offers enough variety to please any palate. A good choice to kick off a night on the town. DK

Food ●●●◐○ Serv ●●●●○ Venue ●●●●◐ Value ●●●◐○

Wine Bars

Agency, The

Location → Emirates Towers · Shk Zayed Rd | 319 8785
Hours → 12:30 - 01:00 Fri 15:00 - 01:00
Web/email → www.jumeirahinternational.com | Map Ref → 9-C2

If you need to unwind at the end of a particularly taxing day's work, the Agency may be just what you need. The setting is tranquil and suitably relaxed (assuming you get a seat inside the bar), albeit on the smarter side of casual. Budgets for wines start at around Dhs.100 for a bottle or Dhs.25 per glass. A limited food menu offers Mediterranean tapas style snacks. This is definitely an early evening venue at which to be seen. JT

Food ●●●●○ Serv ●●●◐○ Venue ●●●●○ Value ●●●●○

Chianti's

Location → Ibis World Trade Centre · Shk Zayed Rd | 319 7151
Hours → 12:00 - 01:00
Web/email → www.ibishotel.com | Map Ref → 9-E3

A new wine bar is always welcome in a city that has a greater interest in beer. Chianti's is a blend of glass, mirrors and dark wood, with an open layout giving it the feel of a stylish lobby bar. The wine list is adequate without being huge, and a small selection of bar snack-ish antipasti and spuntini (such as open tomato and mozzarella sandwiches, or grilled prawns) is on offer. Although this may not be a typical self contained wine bar, Chianti's is a nicer alternative to the many pubs that proliferate in this city. SB

Food ●●●○○ Serv ●●●◐○ Venue ●●●●○ Value ●●●◐○

Vintage

Location → Pyramids · Umm Hurair (2) | 324 0000
Hours → 19:00 - 02:00
Web/email → www.pyramidsdubai.com | Map Ref → 13-D2

Nicely balanced between classy and casual, Vintage maintains a tranquil and mellow mood. Polite and knowledgeable staff indulge the palate with a seriously impressive selection of wines and cheeses (if the names appear Greek to you, request shavings and go by the taste buds). Wine prices range from extremely reasonable to the king's drink. If out for a quiet nip n sip, avoid the popular Fondue Nights (Mondays & Fridays), when fabulous deals transform this quiet haven into the pre and post dinner nibbler's hotspot. LM

Food ●●●◐○ Serv ●●●●○ Venue ●●●◐○ Value ●●●●○

Pubs

Pubs in Dubai generally look close enough to the real thing to transport you from the brown desert to the green, green grass of home – not most people's vision of the Middle East! Some of these pubs (the English ones especially) are very well established and were among the first modern places for

socialising in Dubai. The Irish pubs are some of the favourite and best drinking venues around town. Popular with all nationalities, a good number of pubs manage very successfully to recreate the warm, friendly atmosphere of a typical hostelry. Thousands of miles from their proper location, these places have become genuine locals for many people, offering just what they've always done – good beer, tasty food and great crack.

Biggles

Location → Millennium Airport Hotel · Al Garhoud | 282 3464
Hours → 12:00 - 01:30
Web/email → apothotl@emirates.net.ae | Map Ref → 14-D3

  100

Biggles is a quirky British pub with grub, a band, a brunch, quizzes, a carvery and a big screen for sports fans. Archaic aviation paraphernalia adorns the walls and a propeller sweeps the ceiling. The menu features staple couplets: steak n' kidney pie, bangers n' mash, bread n' butter pudding and fish n' chips (the fish is authentic but unspectacular and the fries are Mcfries). The service and atmosphere are great – an ideal setting for the homesick northern European or the unsubscribed footie fan. JAW

Food ●●●○○ Serv ●●●●● Venue ●●●●◐ Value ●●●◐○

Carpenter's Bar

Location → Hyatt Regency · Deira | 209 1400
Hours → 12:00 - 15:00 18:00 - 02:00
Web/email → hyattbus@emirates.net.ae | Map Ref → 8-D2

   50

Carpenter's Bar is small and friendly with a feel good atmosphere and a happy hour and a half. Despite its location in the lobby, it maintains considerable character, looking (and smelling) like a proper British pub with dark wood, mirrors, stools at the bar, a stand up section and a small TV in the corner for the footy. There's also a raucous Filipino band every night from 21:00 onwards, so get there early if you're looking to just booze and banter. JAW

Food ◐○○○○ Serv ●●●●◐ Venue ●●●●○ Value ●●●●○

Chelsea Arms, The

Location → Sheraton Hotel & Towers · Deira | 207 1721
Hours → 12:00 - 16:00 18:00 - 02:00
Web/email → www.starwood.com | Map Ref → 11-C1

  100

In keeping with the name, this British style pub has plenty of wood panelling and a menu which is reminiscent of 'back home'. The variety of food is extensive, the service prompt and friendly, and the ambience more laid back rather than noisy and busy. A dartboard indulges those seeking some right hand practice. Overall, The Chelsea Arms sits at the smarter end of the generic pub experience, and for this reason, the atmosphere is perhaps closer to that of a hotel lounge. BD

Food ●●●○○ Serv ●●●○○ Venue ●●●○○ Value ●●●○○

Churchill's

Location → Sofitel City Centre · Al Garhoud | 603 8400
Hours → 12:00 - 02:00 12:00 - 11:00
Web/email → cityhotl@emirates.net.ae | Map Ref → 14-D1

   50

A large, bright and comfortable pub, Churchill's offers drinkers and diners respite from the hustle and bustle of the City Centre. Featuring live English Premiership matches on large TV screens, a separate pool table area and a quiet leather clad lounge, Churchill's has something for everyone. A pub menu lists lively versions of classic favourites and there are many quiet nooks to enjoy a sly glass or two. Clean and cheerful, Churchill's is both welcoming and refreshing. JK

Food ●●●○○ Serv ●●●○○ Venue ●●●◐○ Value ●●●◐○

Dhow & Anchor

Location → Jumeirah Beach Htl · Umm Suqeim | 406 8181
Hours → 12:00 - 00:30
Web/email → www.jumeirahinternational.com | Map Ref → 4-B2

   100

The view over the beach ranks the Dhow & Anchor amongst Dubai's best located pubs. While there's substantial outside seating during the cooler

Dhow & Anchor

Going Out · Pubs

months, the interior is tight but cosy. An extensive range of typical pub grub is on offer, including salads, curries, seafood, meat, sandwiches and simple well executed desserts. The wine list too, does not fall short of your expectations, quite unlike the service, which can be inconsistent. For those not in a hurry, this is a good choice for a nice, simple and reasonably priced meal. NO

Food ●●●●○ Serv ●●◐○○ Venue ●●●●○ Value ●●●◐○

Dubliner's

Location → Le Meridien Dubai · Al Garhoud | 282 4040
Hours → 11:00 - 15:00 15:00 - 01:00
Web/email → dubliners@le-meridien-dubai.com Map Ref → 14-E3

Serving what is arguably the best kept pint of Guinness in Dubai, Dubliners is a great example of the global phenomenon of the Irish Bar. Although not as big as the Irish Village or as trendy as Waxy O'Connors, it has great beer, great food and great prices, which all add up to a genuine pub atmosphere. The food is well prepared; the fish & chips and all day breakfast are extremely popular, especially with black pudding fans. After a few visits, Dubliners could easily become your regular. LG

Food ●●●●○ Serv ●●●◐○ Venue ●●●○○ Value ●●●●●

George & Dragon

Location → Ambassador Hotel · Bur Dubai | 393 9444
Hours → 11:00 - 16:00 18:00 - 00:30 Fri 18:00 - 01:00
Web/email → ambhotel@astamb.com Map Ref → 8-A2

Situated just off the busy, bustling streets of Bur Dubai, the George & Dragon welcomes the weary traveller with friendly service and a tasty meal. If craving authentic pub grub, you've come to the right place. The music is unobtrusive, the portions generous, and if the dartboard or sports channels don't strike your fancy, why not shoot some pool while unwinding over a cool beer. GS

Food ●●●●○ Serv ●●●○○ Venue ●●●○○ Value ●●●●○

Harvester's Pub

Location → Crowne Plaza · Trade Centre 1&2 | 331 1111
Hours → 12:00 - 01:00 19:00 - 01:00
Web/email → www.dubaicrowneplaza.com Map Ref → 9-D2

If you fancy a pub night with great food, beer and quizzes or a glimpse of the latest match, then this is the place to go. With its very English 'local' feel, the bar offers something for everyone. There are ladies nights on Sundays and Tuesdays, quiz nights on Mondays, and happy hours that lasts from 12.00 - 20.00! The service is pleasant and prompt, the portions are large, a decent menu ranges from sandwiches to 12 oz steaks, and the prices are just not five star hotel level! EAT

Food ●●●●◐ Serv ●●●●○ Venue ●●●●○ Value ●●●●○

Humphrey's

Location → Trade Centre Hotel · Trade Centre 1&2 | 331 4000
Hours → 12:00 - 02:00
Web/email → www.jumeirahinternational.com Map Ref → 10-A2

 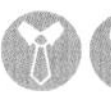 

Humphrey's is one of Dubai's remaining venues offering a straightforward, value for money pub meal in a 'local' pub atmosphere. The lunch specials, at Dhs.20, are the equivalent of a shopping festival bargain and vary from day to day – paying a visit on the 'beef roast and Yorkshire pudding' day would be a shrewd move. Various pies and a pint are offered at an economical Dhs.38 – great value for money (unless you order a bottle of water!). JT

Food ●●●○○ Serv ●●◐○○ Venue ●●◐○○ Value ●●●◐○

Irish Village

Location → Aviation Club, The · Al Garhoud | 282 4750
Hours → 11:00 - 01:30 Wed & Thu 11:00 - 02:30
Web/email → www.aviationclubonline.com Map Ref → 14-C3

The Irish Village has to be one of Dubai's favourite eating and watering holes amongst expats. The

Irish Village

Pubs

Going Out

Crystal Clear...

Isn't it annoying when you ask for a bottle of mineral water and are cleverly served the most expensive one on the menu?! Be aware, the imported brands may be much dearer but the Emirati water is just as good. So don't be shy – specify! Or pay the price

pub offers hearty traditional food, an excellent selection of beers, and (mostly) friendly service. An indoor section is decorated in the classic Irish pub theme, and a spacious (and more popular) outdoors serves as an occasional music venue for rock bands, keeping the place humming with activity. Nothing spells relief after a hard day's work than retiring to the Irish Village for a pint. VML

Food ●●●●○ Serv ●●◐○○ Venue ●●●●◐ Value ●●●●◐

Old Vic

Location → Ramada Hotel · Bur Dubai | 351 9999
Hours → 12:00 - 01:00
Web/email → www.ramadadubai.com/theoldvic.htm Map Ref → 7-E3

A place where regulars all seem to have their own barstools, this local watering hole has the feel of a well worn small town English pub, complete with television sets, sports channels, a pool table, dartboard and karaoke. Patrons can enjoy their pints and listen to live music in the bar area, or fill up on traditional English fare on the other side in the dining area – but stick to the menu specials. Old Vic's is unique in that it's lively but relaxed at the same time. VML

Food ●●○○○ Serv ●●◐○○ Venue ●●●◐○ Value ●●●○○

Red Lion

Location → Metropolitan · Jct 2, Shk Zayed Rd | 343 0000
Hours → 12:00 - 01:00
Web/email → www.methotels.com Map Ref → 5-C4

Lapsing two decades, the Red Lion pub remains amongst the few old school joints fuelled by devoted patrons and hotel guests. A traditional sports bar at heart, the walls are adorned with various sports memorabilia, while pool tables, dartboards and baby foot tables make for friendly challenges with your mates. Ample TV screens hover over the dining area, offering unrestricted football viewing while attentive waitresses make sure your pints are regularly topped and your plates constantly filled with English grub. DP

Food ●●●○○ Serv ●●●◐○ Venue ●●◐○○ Value ●●●●○

Somerset's

Location → Mövenpick Hotel Bur Dubai · Oud Metha | 336 6000
Hours → 12:00 - 15:00 18:00 - 02:00
Web/email → hiburdxb@emirates.net.ae Map Ref → 10-D4

In the heart of Bur Dubai, this authentic English pub, complete with wood and leather, serves up hearty fare such as Irish stew with sourdough and pepper steak pie. A couple of discreet TVs offer a sneak peek at the sports, but it is the dartboard that attracts the regulars. While there's no live music, the background is easy rock and allows the focus to remain on conversation rather than entertainment. Brimming with lively banter, this is the perfect meeting place for a wind down after a long workweek. KM

Food ●●●○○ Serv ●●●●○ Venue ●●●●○ Value ●●●●○

Thatcher's Lounge

Location → Ascot Hotel · Bur Dubai | 352 0900
Hours → 12:00 - 02:00
Web/email → www.ascothoteldubai.com Map Ref → 7-E3

Hidden away on the first floor of the hotel, Thatcher's Lounge offers a quiet, TV free retreat for cosy drinks in a convivial atmosphere. Unobtrusive, live music does not hinder conversation; service is efficient and friendly with a good rapport between staff and regulars. A limited menu covers some pub grub favourites, including fish and chips and club sandwich; the seafood platter, fresh and excellently cooked, is worth a try. This intimate venue is an old fashioned, traditional style bar that caters to a more mature clientele, PL

Food ●●●○○ Serv ●●●◐○ Venue ●●●○○ Value ●●●●○

Viceroy, The

Location → Four Points Sheraton · Bur Dubai | 397 7444
Hours → 12:00 - 03:00
Web/email → www.starwood.com Map Ref → 8-A4

The Viceroy combines all the nuances of an Olde English Tavern with the big screen entertainment of a sports bar. The smoky air, friendly service and bustling tables exude an atmosphere of contentment. Cheap, palatable pub grub is the order of the day, with a few Indian specialities thrown in for good measure.

However, don't save any room for puddings. Daily promotions of beer and spirits, and theme nights make this a popular venue with the local business community.

Food ●●◐○○ Serv ●●◐○○ Venue ●●●○○ Value ●●●◐○

Waxy O'Conner's

Location → Ascot Hotel · Bur Dubai | 352 0900
Hours → 12:00 - 03:00
Web/email → www.ascothoteldubai.com | Map Ref → 7-E3

If tourists rarely visit Ireland for the food, one should not expect the cuisine to concern the joyous crowd at Waxy O'Conner's. It is, after all, an Irish pub, and a brilliant one at that! A burger, any number of pies, puddings and stews, or simply the wonderful Dublin fries, will satisfy any hunger. It will also not distract the faithful from the beverages, the startlingly clear views of arsenals , and the lavish distribution of free beverage benefits for the lads and lassies. AP

Food ●●◐○○ Serv ●●◐○○ Venue ●●●●◐ Value ●●●◐○

Nightclubs

Packed with all nationalities, Dubai's nightclubs are very popular from about 23:00 until well into the small hours. Even on weeknights, there's a good scene, and at the weekend, many places are full to overflowing. There's a reasonable number of dedicated nightclubs, as well as numerous other venues with schizophrenic personalities that are bars or restaurants earlier in the evening, then later turn into the perfect place to cut loose and shake your thang. For authentic club nights, look out for the increasingly common visits by international DJs and the special nights held all over Dubai by various event organisers (these are mostly held in winter).

Additionally, since you're in the Middle East, don't forget the option of Arabic nightclubs. Here you can sample a variety of Arabic food and enjoy a night of traditional Arabic entertainment, usually with a bellydancer, a live band and singer. These venues only start getting busy very late in the evening, and can still be empty when most other nightspots are packed, reflecting the Arabic way of starting late and finishing, well... later. For information on door policy and dress code, refer to the introduction to Bars.

Amnesia

Location → Dubai Park · Al Sufouh | 399 2222
Hours → 19:00 - 03:00
Web/email → dxbprkht@emirates.net.ae | Map Ref → 3-A3

Previously called Atlantis, this nightclub still retains its aquatic theme. Reasonably priced drinks and a limited Arabic menu, but young Arabs people are here more to dance, chill out and meet other singles. The door policy is very strict, though more so for men than women, and they charge a Dhs.100 cover. A singer accompanied by a keyboard player, and DJ later on, entertain with popular Arabic songs, attracting people onto the small central dance floor. The gallery area at bar level is good for people watching and there's a private VIP lounge now. CC

Venue ●●●○○ Value ●●◐○○

Cyclone

Location → Nr American Hospital · Oud Metha | 336 9991
Hours → 21:00 - 03:00
Web/email → cyclone@emirates.net.ae | Map Ref → 10-D4

Cyclone has remained the 'infamous' late night spot due to a mostly male clientele out to meet the many 'international' girls who 'hang' there. Once past the strict doormen (who may relieve you of Dhs.50), the large oval bar anchors the action, although a good sized dance floor does exist. Cyclone is an interesting venue for an adult night out in varied company, and you may find yourself waking up not quite in the circumstances you're accustomed to. DP

Venue ●●○○○ Value ●●○○○

Jimmy Dix

Location → Mövenpick Hotel Bur Dubai · Oud Metha | 336 8800
Hours → 12:00 - 16:00 18:00 - 03:00
Web/email → jimmydixdxb@hotmail.com | Map Ref → 10-D4

This popular restaurant/bar/night club is based on the concept of a 1920's American speakeasy complete with a richly coloured interior, dark wood panelling, deep red velvet curtains and intimate lighting. The live band, The Usual Suspects, which has excellent stage presence, and DJ Pete Martin, guarantee great music and draw the crowds, especially on theme nights and their 'Thursday

Thump' weekend party. Flavourful Tex Mex is also served, making this a good one stop eating/drinking/partying venue.

Venue ●●●●◐ Value ●●●●○

Kasbar

Location → One&Only Palace · Al Sufouh | 399 9999
Hours → 21:00 - 03:00
Web/email → www.oneandonlyresort.com Map Ref → 3-A2

With an expansive cocktail menu and wine list, three levels of entertainment, and an almost romantic ambience, Kasbar redefines nightclubs, as we know them. Featuring an Arabian theme, candles make up the majority of the venue's lighting, giving it a warm appeal. Catering to all moods, the main level consists of a dance floor and tables; a spiral staircase takes you up to a mezzanine overlooking the dance floor, and down to an Arabian lounge style area. A well balanced theme and ambience make this a venue that should not be missed.

Venue ●●●●◐ Value ●●●○○

Kasbar

Lodge, The

Location → Al Nasr Leisureland · Oud Metha | 337 9470
Hours → 11:00 - 03:00
Web/email → www.alnasrleisureland.ae Map Ref → 10-E4

The Lodge is unique for its substantial open air dance floor. Around the edge, you can mingle without the usual smoke or crushed bodies. Split into several bars, restaurants and a nightclub, such as Rockefellas and Tahiti Garden, this is a refreshingly unpretentious late night venue. Getting in (and getting served!) may be tough at times – especially if your face doesn't fit – but the prospect of unbridled revelry under the stars means The Lodge will always attract a boisterous crowd.

Venue ●●●●○ Value ●●◐○○

MIX

Location → Grand Hyatt Dubai · Umm Hurair (2) | 317 2570
Hours → 18:00 - 03:00
Web/email → www.dubai.grand.hyatt.com Map Ref → 13-E3

Set apart as the only 'superclub' in town, this three tiered newcomer boasts an island bar, sprawling dance floor, seating/lounge area, two VIP rooms, a cigar bar and a sound proofed live music room... not to mention the kitchen sink! Bartenders flair their magic, while you flip through the almost endless cocktail and wine list. Wide open spaces, a luxury amongst the competition, ensures even the most hardened claustrophobic doesn't break into a sweat. Already peaking its 800 capacity venue, MIX is a welcome addition to Dubai's booming nightlife scene.

Venue ●●●●◐ Value ●●●●○

Mix

Planetarium

Location → Wafi City · Umm Hurair (2) | 324 0072
Hours → 23:00 - 03:00
Web/email → www.planetariumdubai.com | Map Ref → 13-D2

Planetarium still remains the number one venue for international DJs to showcase their talents. Settle down to resident DJ Charlie C's house and R'nB tunes, while the ambient lighting compliments your experience of this better seasoned club. With theme nights five days a week and no less than four major events every month, you're guaranteed to get some mileage out of your dancing shoes. Strict entrance policies apply so dress to impress! DP

Venue Value

Premiere, The

Location → Hyatt Regency · Deira | 209 1333
Hours → 22:00 - 03:00
Web/email → hyattbus@emirates.net.ae | Map Ref → 8-D2

Stuck with a tired 80's feel and a severe decor that has scarcely altered in 15 years, this bar/club may have seen better days. Still, it's extremely popular with the late night singles crowd who, at nearly 01:00, are clearly more interested in 'people watching' than in dancing. The well situated, central dance floor sees little use until very late. Patrons prefer to gather around the edges of the room chatting and drinking. Couples and groups are discouraged, as seating is limited, and the ambience... slightly hungry. DP

Venue Value

Tangerine

Location → Fairmont Hotel · Trade Centre 1&2 | 332 5555
Hours → 20:00 - 03:00
Web/email → www.starwood.com | Map Ref → 9-E1

This rich red underworld maintains exclusivity with strict bouncers and stiffer prices. Torch glow lit, the heavy set Arabic décor and cushion clad lounge sofas behind curtained alcoves invoke cavernous comfort. The bar staff proffer superior beverages and can tailor rich cocktails to individual tastes. Very slick, very Buddha Bar-esque and very 'upmarket' cool! One of the must dos in the bar hopping tour list. DM

Venue Value

Tangerine

Zinc

Location → Crowne Plaza · Trade Centre 1&2 | 331 1111
Hours → 19:00 - 03:00
Web/email → sean@crowneplaza.co.ae | Map Ref → 9-D2

No more platters of fried scampi elegantly washed down at the side of the dance floor. The latest trend hitting nightspots is a more avant garde menu, which, although unappealing to young clubbers, is a more refined way for the older contingent to sneak through. The overcomplicated bar system often delays swift service and the prices are customary hotel, but with live 70's music, disco and R&B, this spacious metallic interior is a hot and happening local haunt. SC

Venue Value

Entertainment

Cinemas

A trip to the cinema is one of the most popular forms of entertainment in the Emirates, and movie lovers here are reasonably well catered for, although showings are generally limited to the latest Arabic, Bollywood or Hollywood releases. At

present there are five cinemas in Dubai and three in Sharjah showing English language films, with another few showing Indian and Arabic films, including the unique Rex Drive-In cinema at the Mirdif Interchange, Airport Road.

The newer cinemas are generally multi-screen sites, while the older cinemas tend to be larger, with fewer screens and a traditional, crowded cinema atmosphere. Dubai has seen an explosion in the number of screens available over the past couple of years, with the opening of an eleven screen complex near Wafi City and another eleven screen outlet as part of Deira City Centre Mall. These two sites alone have a capacity of 6,000 seats. These will be added to with multi screen cinemas as part of the expansion of both Al Ghurair City and BurJuman Centre.

Cinema timings can be found in the *Weekly Explorer* – contact Explorer Publishing if you would like to register as a free subscriber. Alternatively, timings are in the daily newspapers, as well as in an entertainment special in the *Gulf News* every Wednesday.

Release dates vary considerably, with new Western films reaching the UAE anywhere from four weeks to a year after release in the USA. New movies are released every Wednesday. Films often don't hang around for too long, so if there's something you really want to see, don't delay too much or it will be gone! The cinemas tend to be cold, so make sure you take a sweater. During the weekends, there are extra shows at midnight or 01:00 – check the press for details. Tickets can be reserved, but usually have to be collected an hour before the show. With so many screens around now, you will often find cinemas half empty, except for the first couple of days after the release of an eagerly awaited blockbuster.

Comedy

The regular comedy scene in Dubai is unfortunately limited, however, there are regular visits from the occasional comical theatre production or one off event. Comedy shows tend to be aimed at British expats, and other nationalities may not find the sense of humour as funny as the Brits in the audience do. Events are often promoted only a short time before they actually take place, so keep your ears to the ground, or your eyes on your *Weekly Explorer* for what's coming up.

Concerts

Throughout the year, Dubai hosts a variety of concerts and festivals, with visits from international artists, bands and musicians. Most events are held in the winter, as well as during the Dubai Shopping Festival and international sporting events. Ticket prices are around the same, or a bit higher, than you would expect to pay elsewhere. There's no regular calendar of events for music lovers, so for details of what's going on, check out the *Weekly Explorer* – contact Explorer Publishing if you would like to register as a free subscriber. You can also check the daily press, magazines, and listen out for announcements and adverts on the radio. Promoters may be able to supply information on events, but usually no long term programmes exist, and details are only available about a month in advance. Tickets go on sale at the

Cinemas

Name	Tel No.	Map	Location	Languages	No. of Screens	Prices Normal	Prices Special
Al Nasr	337 4353	10-E3	Oud Mehta	M, T	1	15.00	20.00
Century Cinemas	349 9773	5-E1	Mercato Mall	A, E, H	7	30.00	–
CineStar	294 9000	14-D1	Deira City Centre	A, E, H	11	30.00	40.00
Deira Cinema	222 3551	11-D1	Deira	M, T	1	15.00	20.00
Dubai Cinema	266 0632	12-A3	Deira	H	1	15.00	20.00
Galleria	209 6469 / 70	8-D2	Hyatt Regency	H, M, T	2	20.00	–
Grand Cinecity	228 98 98	11-D1	Al Ghurair City	E, A, H	8	25.00	30.00
Grand Cineplex	324 2000	13-D3	Umm Hurair 2	A, E	12	25.00	30.00
Lamcy	336 8808	10-D4	Lamcy Plaza	H	2	20.00	–
Metroplex	343 8383	5-C4	Sheikh Zayed Rd	A, E	8	30.00	55.00
Plaza	393 9966	8-A2	Bur Dubai	H, M	1	15.00	20.00
Rex Drive-In	288 6447	Overview	Madinat Badr	H	1	15.00	–
Strand	396 1644	11-A2	Al Karama	H	1	15.00	20.00

Key: A = Arabic; E = English; H = Hindi; M = Malayalam; T= Tamil

venues and through other outlets, such as Virgin Megastore. Tickets for some concerts can also be purchased online at www.ibuytickets.com or www.itptickets.com.

Classical Concerts

There is only a small number of classical music events held each year in the city. Most notably, the Crowne Plaza Hotel hosts visiting orchestras, musicians and singers from all over the world. Other venues have performances by musical groups or artistes, mainly during special events such as the gala dinners of large trade exhibitions.

Dance Events

Dubai is building itself a surprisingly good club scene, offering some great nights on a fairly regular basis. Different themed nights are organised by international promoters at various clubs around the city, as well as special events like the 'In The Mix' and Ministry of Sound events, which bring in international DJs for epic line ups and non stop action. Previous names include Ravin, Sasha, Grooverider, Ian Van Dhal, Judge Jules, Claude Challe and Roger Sanchez. Like many events in Dubai, dance events are often announced at very short notice, and while the main action is widely publicised, other events can sometimes be promoted in a more underground sort of way.

Pop Concerts

Cynics could say that Dubai, and the Gulf in general, are only honoured by visits from Western bands that are 'on their way down'. However, over the last few years there have been improvements in the standard of performer, and 'big' names have included Elton John, Jamiroquai, Deep Purple, Roger Waters, UB40, Bryan Adams, Rod Stewart, Tom Jones, Sting, Maxi Priest and James Brown. Concerts are usually held at venues such as the Dubai Tennis Stadium, Irish Village, Dubai Creek Golf & Yacht Club and the Dubai International Marine Club (DIMC). Smaller venues, notably the Cyclone and Premiere nightclubs, and Rock Bottom Café, have hosted the likes of Bad Manners or Leo Sayer, as well as Abba or Madness tribute bands. Good fun, if not exactly cutting edge stuff. For Asian and Arabic music lovers, there is a range of concerts and musical programmes held in venues like Al Nasr Leisureland and DIMC. These feature some of the biggest names from the Middle East, India, Pakistan and Sri Lanka.

See also: *Nightclubs [p.458].*

Fashion Shows

Complementing Dubai's reputation as one of the best places to shop for clothes in the Middle East, there are regular fashion shows held in the city. However, very little is arranged on a long term basis. Check out the *Weekly Explorer* from Explorer Publishing or keep an eye out in hotels, local newspapers, etc, for what's happening in the month to come. During Dubai Shopping Festival, there are up to 30 fashion shows organised over the month. These are mainly held in hotels and shopping malls; the press during the Festival usually carries information on dates and times.

Concert / Dance Event Venues	
Al Nasr Leisureland	337 1234
Aviation Club	282 4122
Creekside Park	336 7633
Crowne Plaza	331 1111
Dubai Creek Golf and Yacht Club	295 6000
Dubai International Marine Club	399 3333
Irish Village	282 4750
Jimmy Dix	336 6000
Media City	343 1110
Mix, The	317 1234
M-Level	227 1111
Oxygen	282 0000
Planetarium	324 0072
Regent Palace Hotel	396 3888
Rooftop Gardens	324 4426
Tangerine	332 5555
Virgin megastore	295 8955

Theatre

The theatre scene in Dubai is rather limited, with fans relying chiefly on touring companies and the occasional amateur dramatics performance. The amateur theatre scene always welcomes new members, either on stage or behind the scenes. There are also the occasional murder mystery dinners where you're encouraged to display your thespian skills by being part of the performance.

One restriction on regular theatre performances is that every time a local or international group performs, a stage has to be created from scratch. To remedy this, there were plans in 2003 to build Dubai's first community theatre for amateur and professionals groups. However, this has been put on hold since its location cannot be agreed upon.

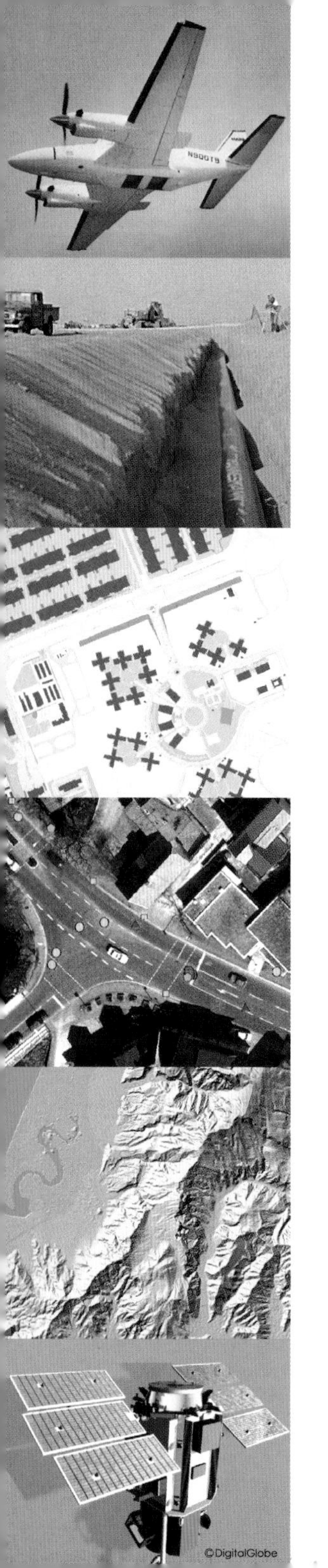
©DigitalGlobe

Maps

EXPLORER

Maps

User's Guide

To further assist you in locating your destination, we have superimposed additional information, such as main roads, roundabouts and landmarks on the maps. Many places listed throughout the guidebook also have a map reference alongside, so you know precisely where you need to go (or what you need to tell the taxi driver).

To make it easier to find places, and give better visualisation, the maps have all been orientated parallel to Dubai's coastline rather than the customary north orientation. While the overview map on this page is at a scale of approximately 1:180,000 (1 cm = 1.8 km), all other maps range from 1:12,000 (1 cm = 120 m) to 1:48,000 (1cm = 480 m).

Technical Info – Satellite Images

The maps in this section are based on rectified QuickBird satellite imagery taken in 2003.

The QuickBird satellite was launched in October 2001 and is operated by DigitalGlobe™, a private company based in Colorado (USA). Today, DigitalGlobe's QuickBird satellite provides the highest resolution (61 cm), largest swath width and largest onboard storage of any currently available or planned commercial satellite.

MAPS geosystems are the Digital Globe master resellers for the Middle East, West, Central and East Africa. They also provide a wide range of mapping services and systems. For more information, visit www.digitalglobe.com (QuickBird) and www.maps-geosystems.com (mapping services) or contact MAPS geosystems on 06 572 5411.

What's new?

Street Map Explorer

At last! The most accurate and up to date map of Dubai has arrived. The Street Map Explorer (Dubai) provides a concise, comprehensive and cross referenced compendium of street names, with a full A to Z index of businesses and tourist attractions. This handy book will soon become your favourite travel mate and a standard tool for navigating the streets of Dubai.

Map Legend

Activity	*Café/Cinema*	*Shopping/Souk*
Area/Roundabout	*Embassy/Hospital*	*Important Landmark*
Business	*Hotel*	*Exploring*

Online Maps

If you want to surf for maps online, Dubai Municipality's www.exploredubai.ae is an excellent Website for navigating through maps and routes. On www.dubailocator.com, you can actually pin point your location and will be a supplied with a Web address for your personal map. Just give out this URL for your next party! For those owning property, the Land Department's Website, www.dubailand.gov.ae is worth a bookmark.

Dubai Overview Map (Map Sheet Index)

Community & Street Index

The following is a list of the main streets in Dubai, which are referenced on the map pages. Many roads are longer than one grid reference, in which case the main grid reference has been given.

Community	Map Ref	Community	Map Ref
Al Barsha	3-D4	Emirates Hill 1	2-E4
Al Garhoud	14-D4	Emirates Hill 2	3-A3
Al Hamriya	12-C3	Hor Al Anz	12-B3
Al Jafilia	7-B4	Jaddaf	13-E4
Al Karama	10-D2	Jebel Ali FZ	1-B2
Al Mamzar	12-E2	Jumeira	6-B3
Al Mankhool	7-C4	Jumeira 2	5-E2
Al Quoz	5-B4	Jumeira 3	5-B2
Al Quoz Ind. 1	4-E4	Marsa Dubai	2-D2
Al Quoz Ind. 3	4-B4	Mirdif	16-B4
Al Qusais	15-D2	Muhaisnah	16-D3
Al Qusais Ind.	15-E3	Oud Mehta	10-D4
Al Safa 1	5-B3	Port Rashid	7-C2
Al Safa 2	4-E3	Port Saeed	11-C2
Al Satwa	6-C4	Rashidiya	16-A2
Al Satwa East	10-B1	Shindagha	8-B1
Al Sufouh	3-E3	Trade Centre 1	9-B1
Al Tawar	15-C2	Trade Centre 2	9-C2
Al Wasl	5-D3	Umm Hurair 2	13-E1
Bastakiya	8-B3	Umm Suqeim 1	4-E2
Bur Dubai	8-A3	Umm Suqeim 2	4-C2
Deira	8-C3	Umm Suqeim 3	4-B2
Dubai Int. Airport	15-A2	Za'abeel	10-B3

Street	Map Ref	Street	Map Ref
2nd Za'abeel Rd	17-C1	Al Wasl Rd	4-B3
Abu Hail Rd	12-B4	Algiers Rd	16-D3
Airport Rd	14-E2	Baghdad Rd	15-D3
Al Adhid Rd	7-C4	Beirut Rd	15-B4
Al Diyafah	7-A3	Beniyas Rd	8-B3
Al Garhoud Rd	14-C2	Casablanca Rd	14-D3
Al Ittihad Rd	12-A4	Damascus Rd	15-E2
Al Jumeira Rd	4-B2	Doha Rd	17-A1
Al Khaleej Rd	8-A1	Dubai - Al Ain Rd	17-A4
Al Khawaneej Rd	15-A4	Dubai - Sharjah Highway	12-D4
Al Maktoum Rd	11-D2	Khalid Bin AlWaleed Rd	7-E2
Al Manara Rd	4-D2	Muscat Rd	5-C4
Al Mankhool Rd	7-B3	Oud Mehta Rd	13-B2
Al Mina Rd	7-B2	Rabat Rd	16-A4
Al Muraqqabat Rd	11-E2	Riyadh Rd	13-E3
Al Musallah Rd	8-A3	Salah Al Din Rd	12-A4
Al Naif Rd	8-D3	Sheikh Zayed Rd	2-B3
Al Quds Rd	15-B2	Trade Centre Rd	10-B1
Al Quta'eyat Rd	13-D3	Tunis Rd	16-D2
Al Rasheed Rd	12-B3	Umm Hureir Rd	10-E3
Al Rigga Rd	11-D2	Za'abeel Rd	10-D3
Al Satwa Rd	6-C4		
Al Sufouh Rd	3-B2		

Dubai Address System

Dubai is in the process of completing a Comprehensive Addressing System that consists of two complementary number systems – the Route Numbering System and the Community, Street & Building Numbering System. The former helps an individual to develop and follow a simple series of directions for travelling from one area to another in Dubai; the latter helps a visitor to locate a particular building or house in the city.

Routes Numbering System

Various routes connecting Dubai to other emirates of the UAE, or to main cities within an emirate, are classified as 'Emirate-Routes' or 'E-Routes'. They comprise of two digit numbers on a falcon emblem as shown on the UAE Map. Routes connecting main communities within Dubai are designated as 'Dubai-Routes' or 'D-Routes'. They comprise of two digit numbers on a fort emblem. D-Routes parallel to the coast are even numbered, starting from D94 and decreasing as you move away from the coast. D-Routes perpendicular to the coast are odd numbered, starting from D53 and decreasing as you move away from the Abu Dhabi border.

Community, Street Numbering System

This system helps an individual to locate a particular building or house in Dubai. The emirate is divided into nine sectors.

Sectors 1, 2, 3, 4 and 6 represent urban areas.
Sector 5 represents Jebel Ali.
Sectors 7, 8 and 9 represent rural areas
Sectors are sub-divided into communities, which are bound by main roads. A three digit number identifies each community. The first is the number of the sector, while the following two digits denote the location of the community in relation to neighbouring communities in sequential order.

Buildings on the left hand side of the street have odd numbers, while those on the right hand side take even numbers. Again, building numbers increase as you move away from the city centre. The complete address of a building in Dubai is given as Community Number, Street Number and Building Number.

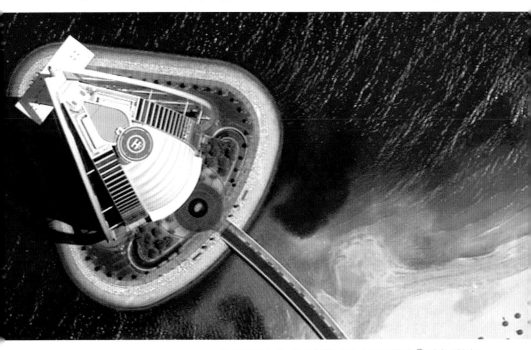

A
B
C
MAPSgeosystems
1
2
3
4
Palm, Jebel Ali (u/c)
Jebel Ali Beach
Jebel Ali Hotel
& Golf Resort
Emirates
Kart Club
Jebel Ali
Shooting Club
Jebel Ali Free Zone
Interchange
No-9
Interchange
No-8
E 11

DIGITALGLOBE
Arabian Gulf
DUBAL
Interchange
No - 6
Interchange
No - 7
Jebel Ali Village
Maps

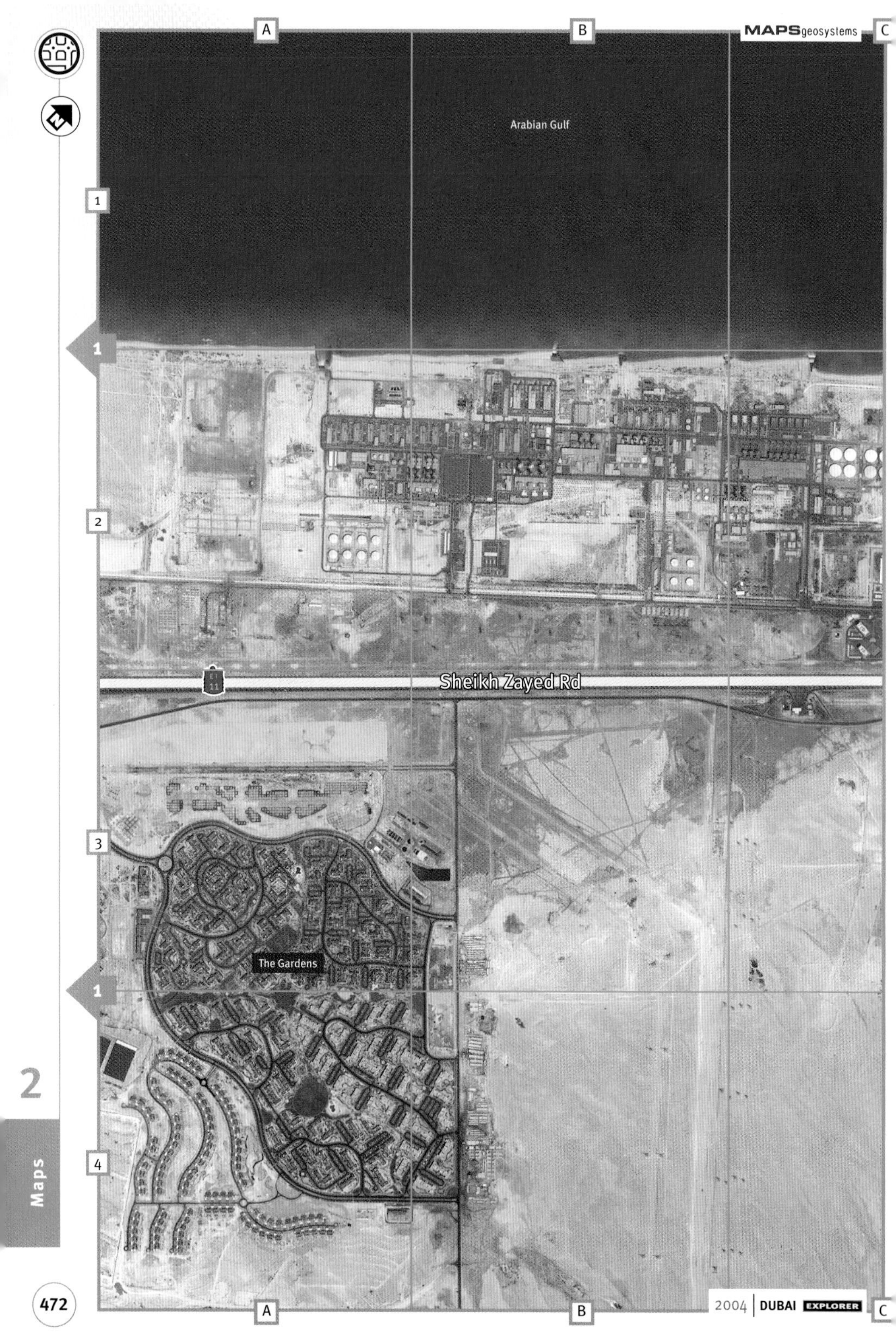

MAPSgeosystems
Arabian Gulf
Sheikh Zayed Rd
E 11
The Gardens
A
B
C
1
2
3
4

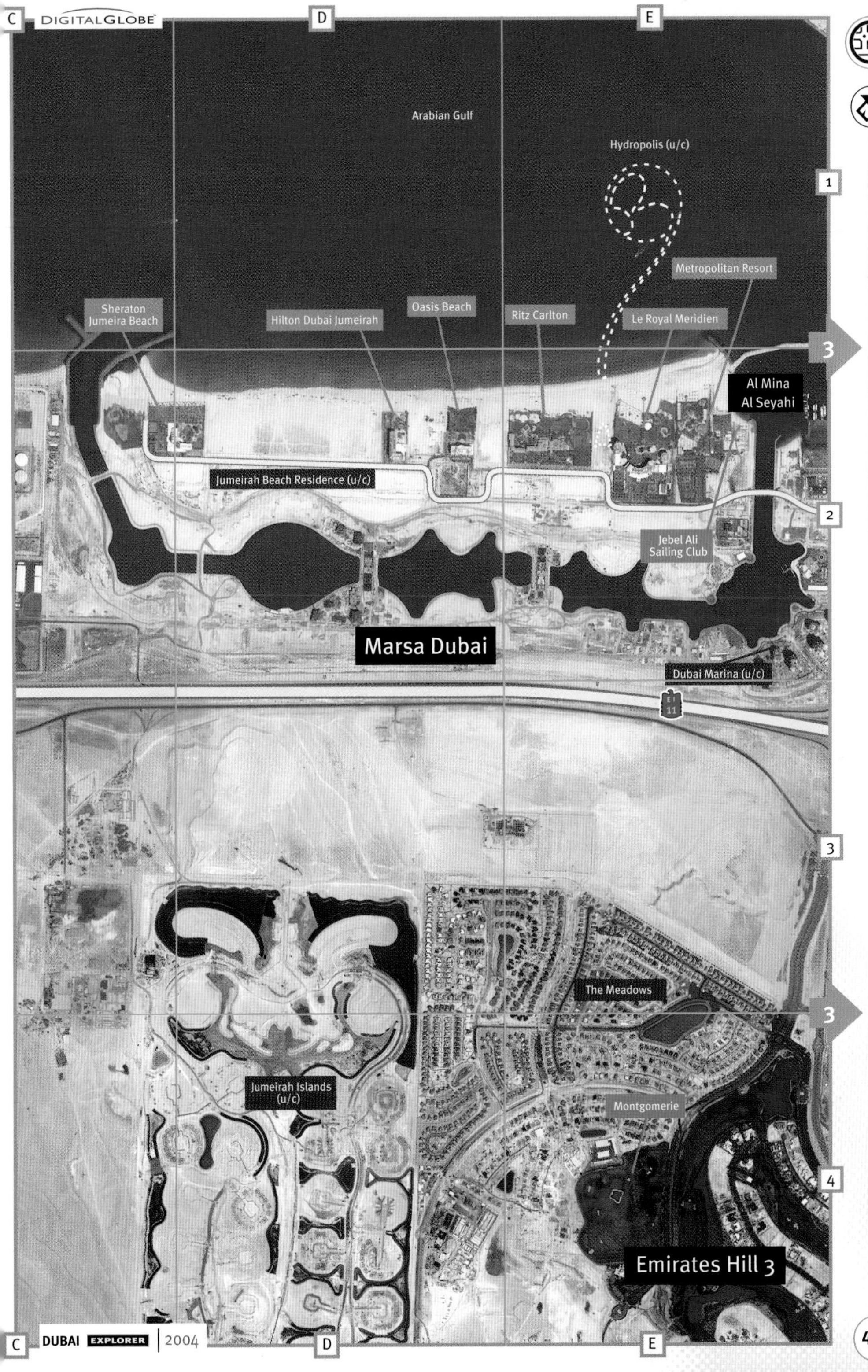

DIGITALGLOBE
Arabian Gulf
Hydropolis (u/c)
Metropolitan Resort
Sheraton Jumeira Beach
Hilton Dubai Jumeirah
Oasis Beach
Ritz Carlton
Le Royal Meridien
Al Mina Al Seyahi
Jumeirah Beach Residence (u/c)
Jebel Ali Sailing Club
Marsa Dubai
Dubai Marina (u/c)
The Meadows
Jumeirah Islands (u/c)
Montgomerie
Emirates Hill 3
Maps

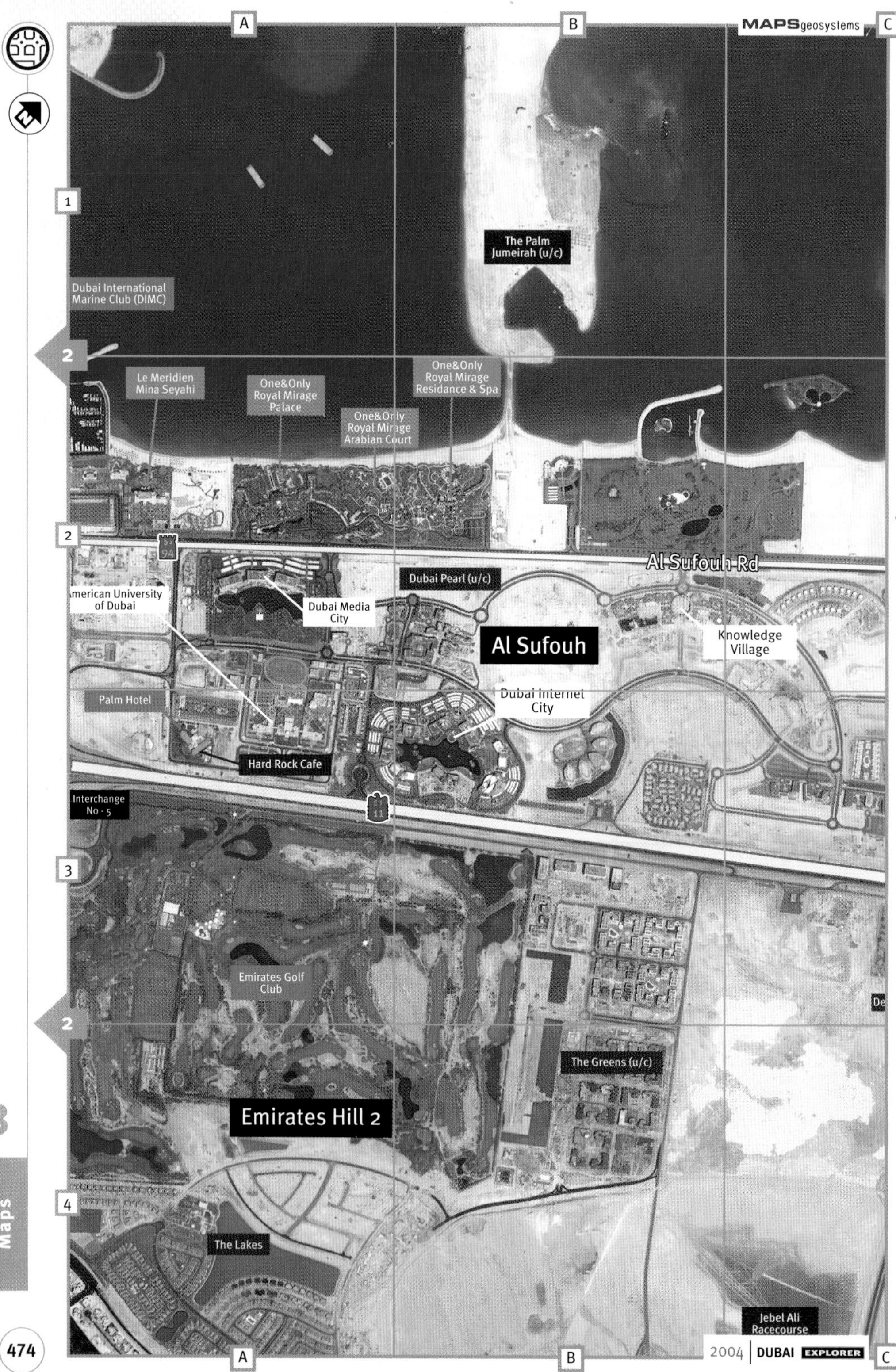

MAPSgeosystems
A
B
C
1
2
3
4
The Palm Jumeirah (u/c)
Dubai International Marine Club (DIMC)
Le Meridien Mina Seyahi
One&Only Royal Mirage Palace
One&Only Royal Mirage Arabian Court
One&Only Royal Mirage Residance & Spa
Al Sufouh Rd
Dubai Pearl (u/c)
American University of Dubai
Dubai Media City
Al Sufouh
Knowledge Village
Palm Hotel
Dubai Internet City
Hard Rock Cafe
Interchange No - 5
Emirates Golf Club
The Greens (u/c)
Emirates Hill 2
The Lakes
Jebel Ali Racecourse
Maps

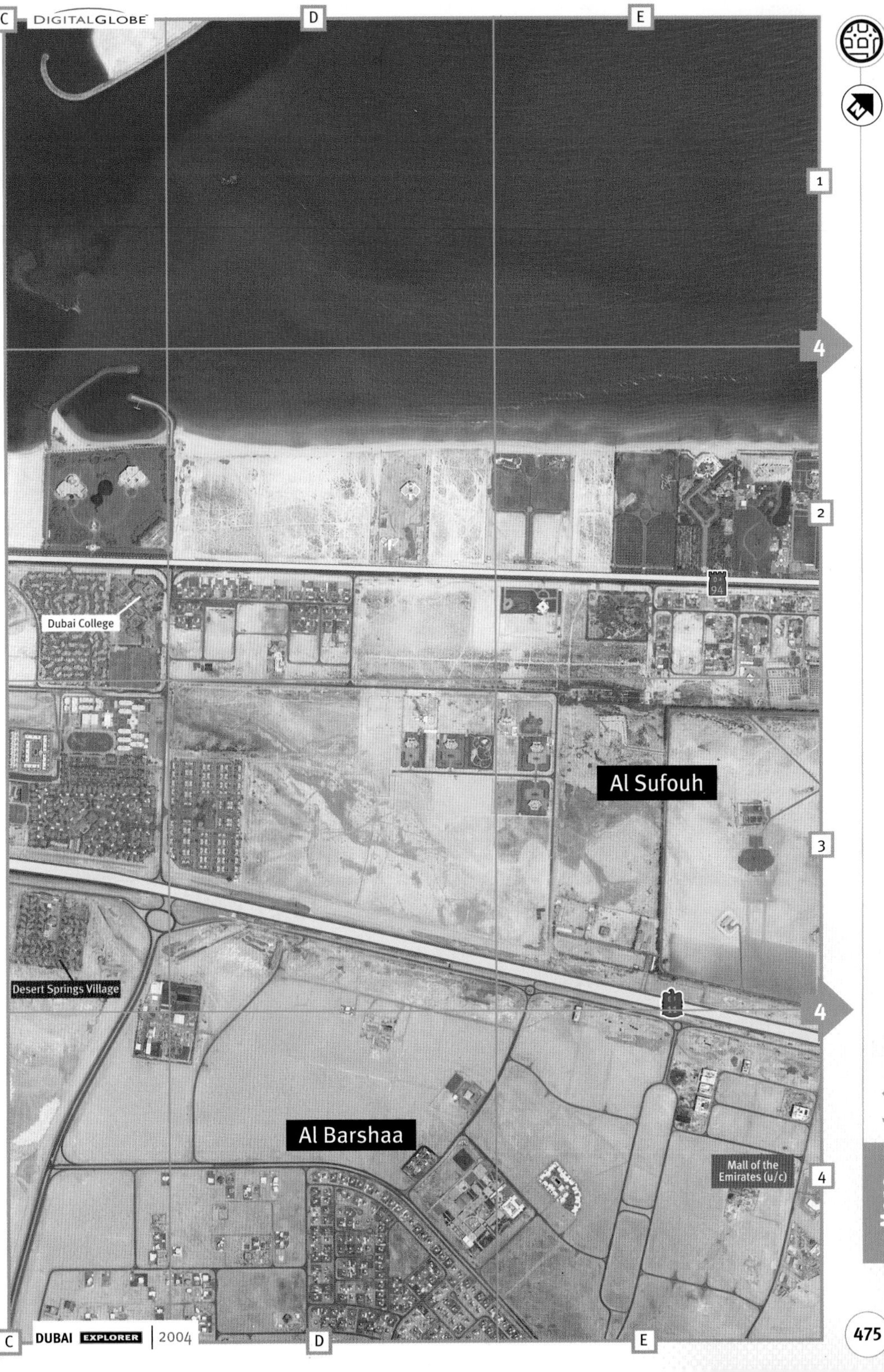
DIGITALGLOBE
C
D
E
1
2
3
4
Dubai College
Al Sufouh
Desert Springs Village
Al Barshaa
Mall of the Emirates (u/c)
3
Maps

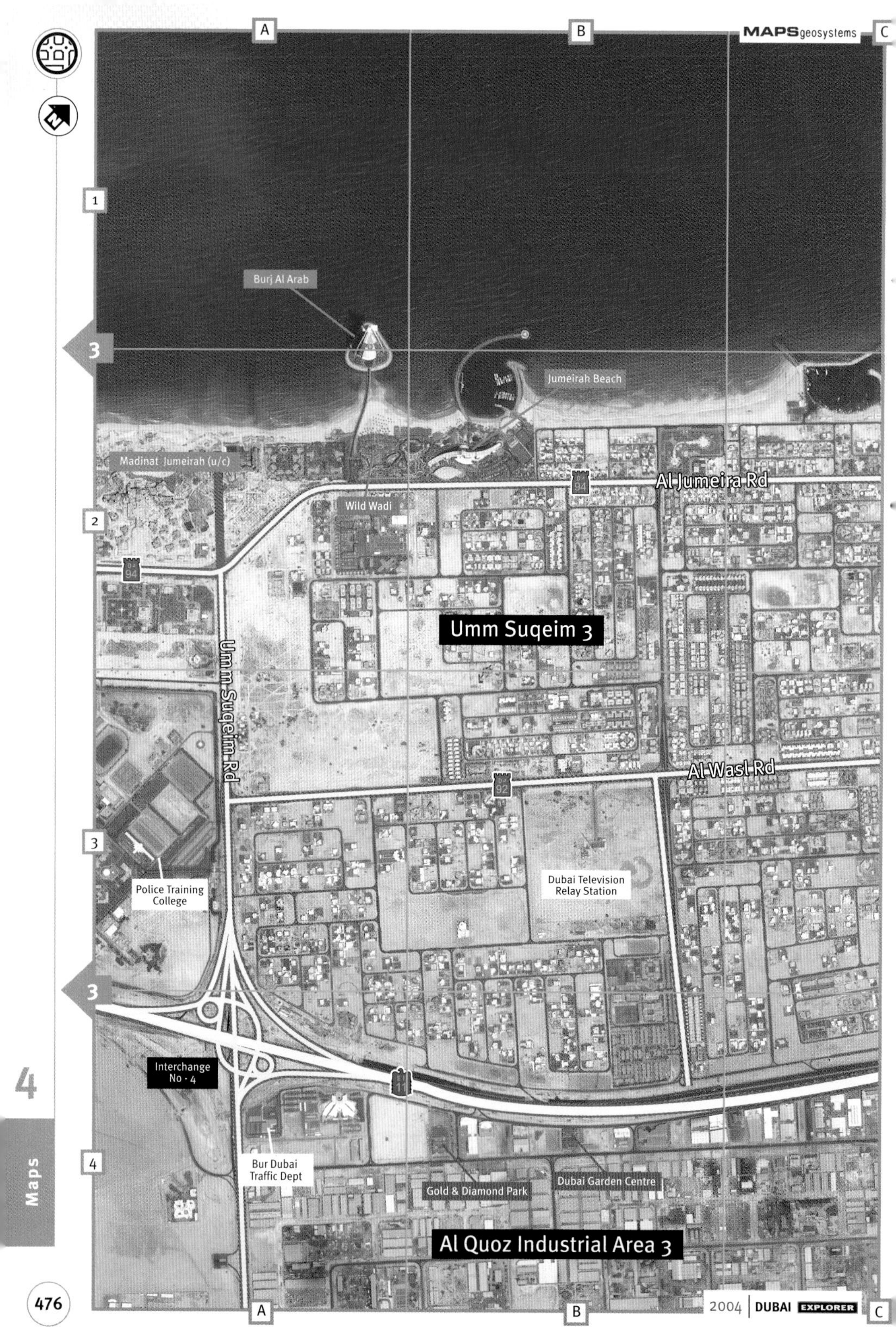
MAPSgeosystems
A
B
C
1
2
3
4
Burj Al Arab
Jumeirah Beach
Madinat Jumeirah (u/c)
Wild Wadi
Al Jumeira Rd
94
Umm Suqeim 3
Umm Suqeim Rd
Al Wasl Rd
92
Police Training College
Dubai Television Relay Station
Interchange No - 4
Bur Dubai Traffic Dept
Gold & Diamond Park
Dubai Garden Centre
Al Quoz Industrial Area 3

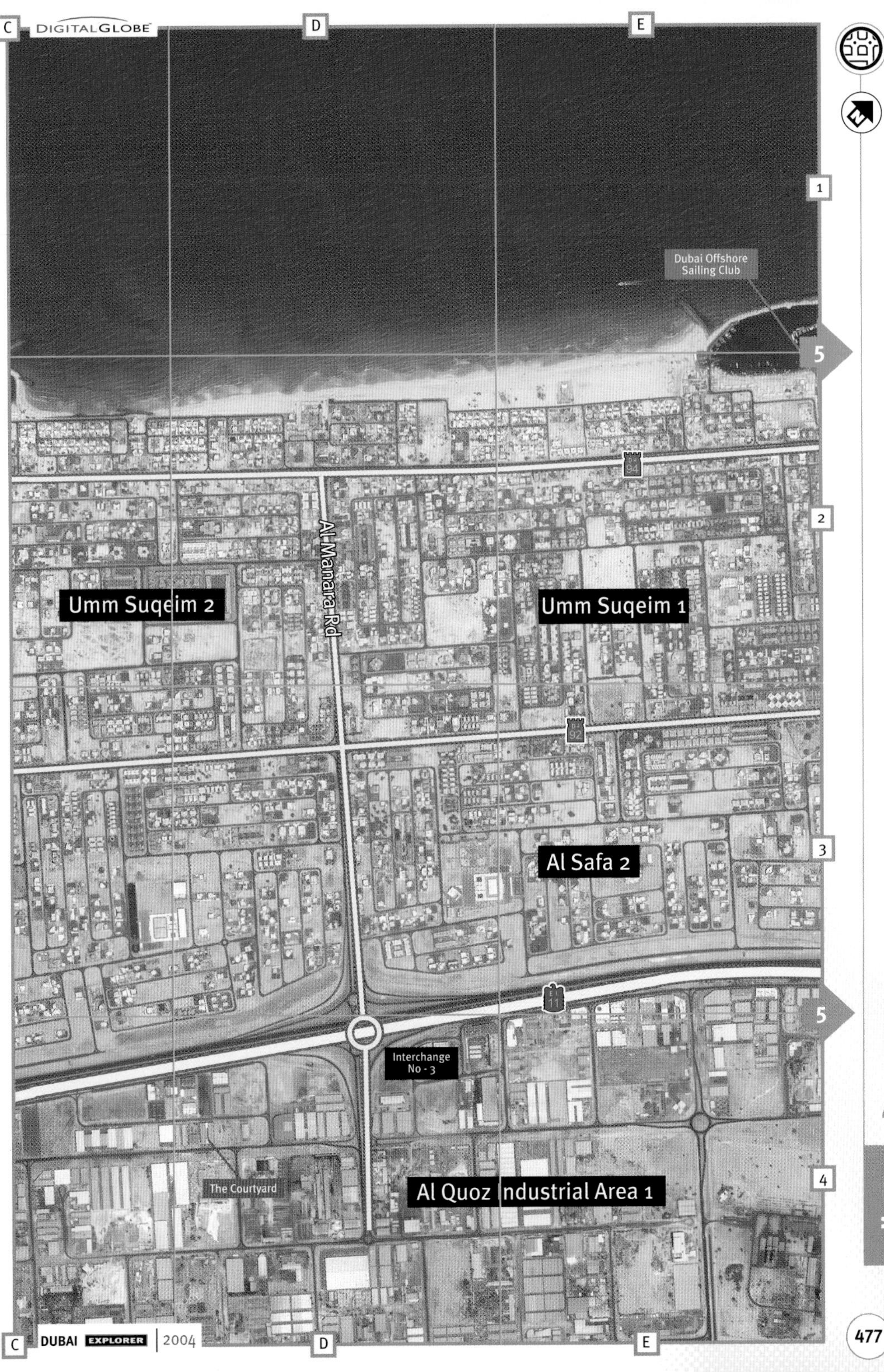
DIGITALGLOBE
C
D
E
1
2
3
4
5
5
Dubai Offshore Sailing Club
Umm Suqeim 2
Umm Suqeim 1
Al Manara Rd
Al Safa 2
Interchange No - 3
The Courtyard
Al Quoz Industrial Area 1
94
92
11

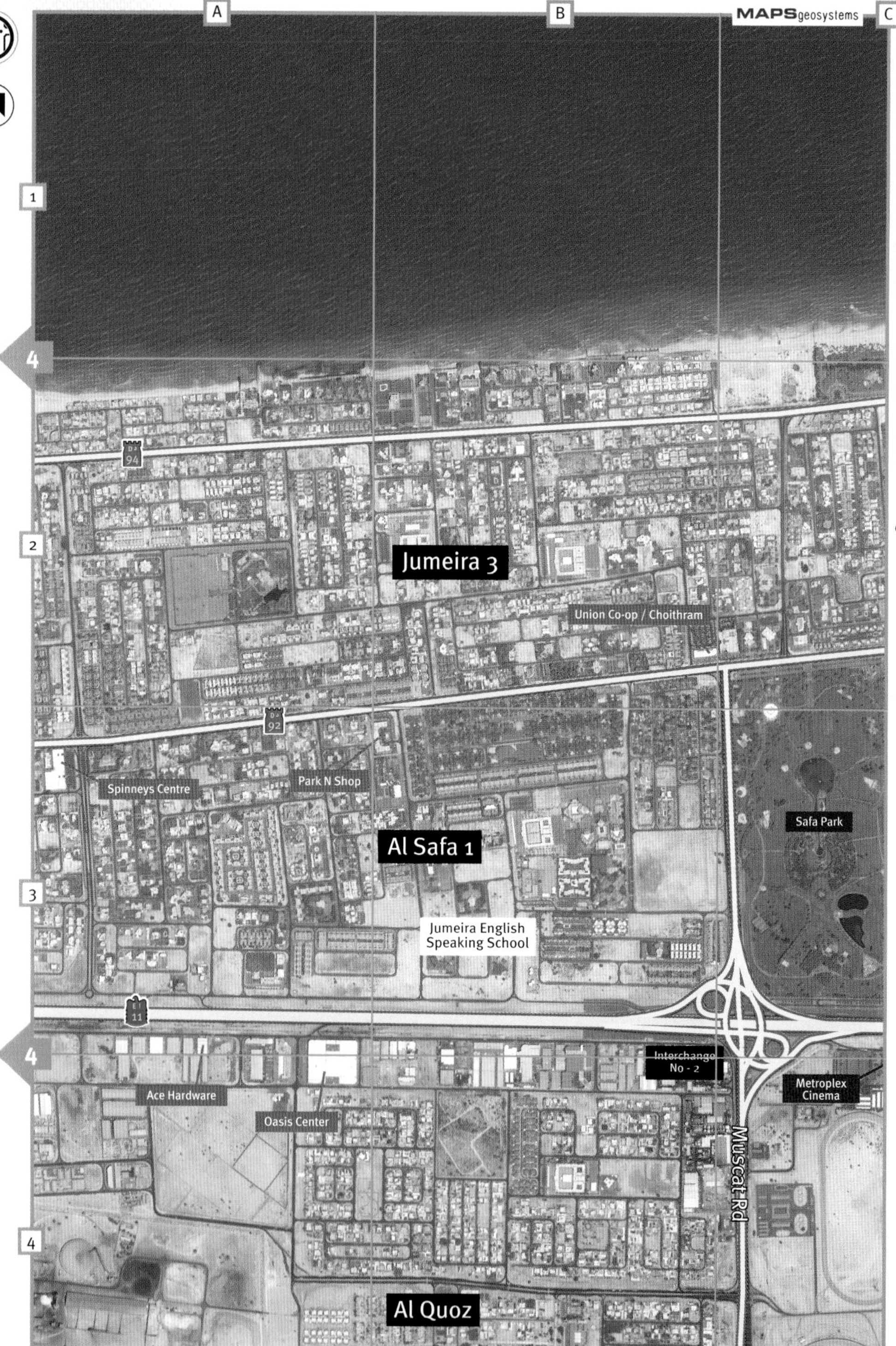
MAPSgeosystems
A
B
C
1
2
3
4
4
4
94
92
11
Jumeira 3
Union Co-op / Choithram
Spinneys Centre
Park N Shop
Al Safa 1
Safa Park
Jumeira English
Speaking School
Interchange
No - 2
Metroplex
Cinema
Ace Hardware
Oasis Center
Muscat Rd
Al Quoz

5
Maps

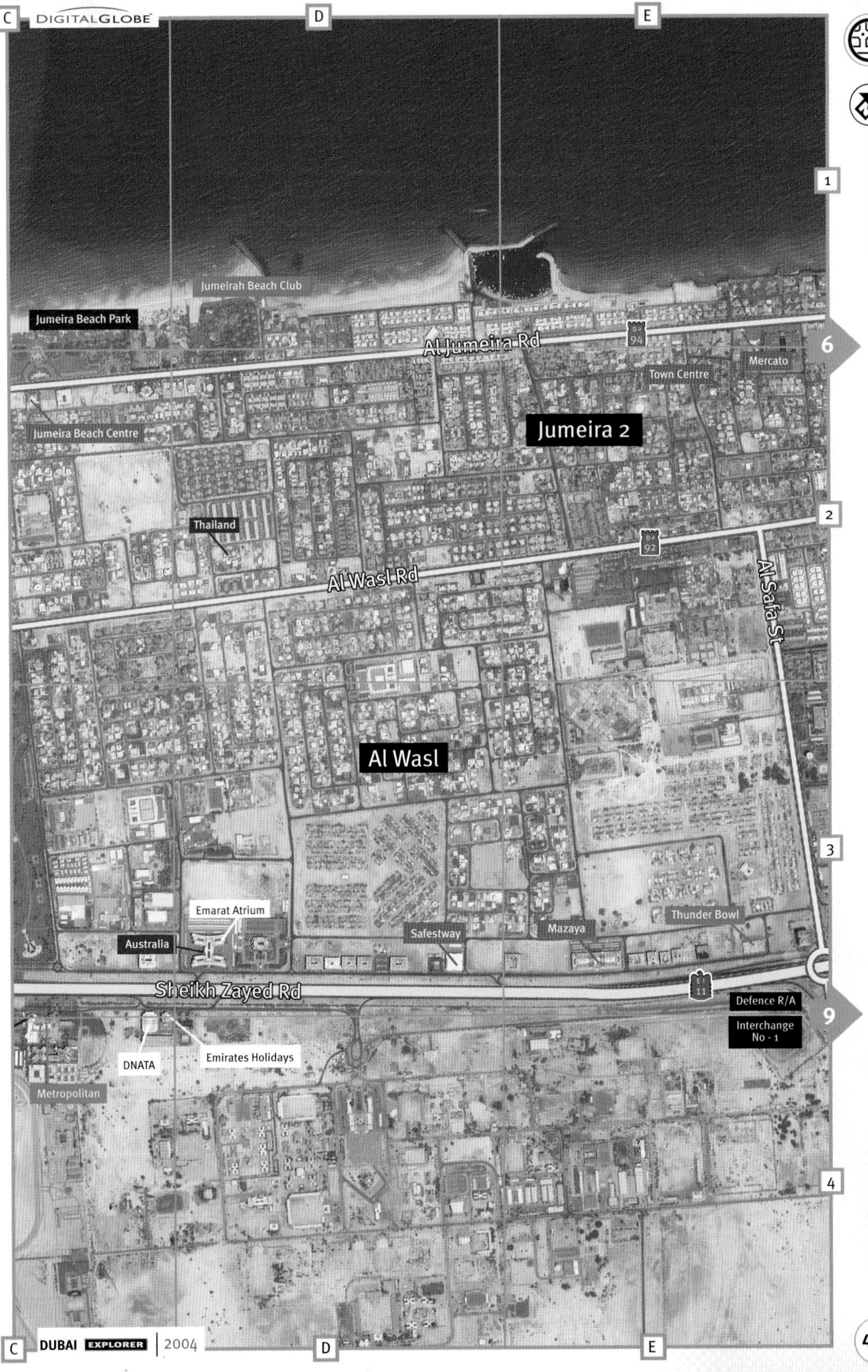

DIGITALGLOBE
C
D
E
1
2
3
4
6
9
Jumeirah Beach Club
Jumeira Beach Park
Al Jumeira Rd
94
Mercato
Town Centre
Jumeira Beach Centre
Jumeira 2
Thailand
92
Al Wasl Rd
Al Safa St
Al Wasl
Emarat Atrium
Australia
Safestway
Mazaya
Thunder Bowl
Sheikh Zayed Rd
11
Defence R/A
Interchange No - 1
DNATA
Emirates Holidays
Metropolitan

Maps

A
B
C
MAPSgeosystems
1
2
3
4
5
5
9
Dubai International Art Centre
Al Jumeira Rd
Beach Centre
Century Plaza
Jumeirah Plaza
Dubai Zoo
Jumeira
American School
Al Wasl Rd
Al Satwa
Al Satwa Rd
94
92
90

6

Maps

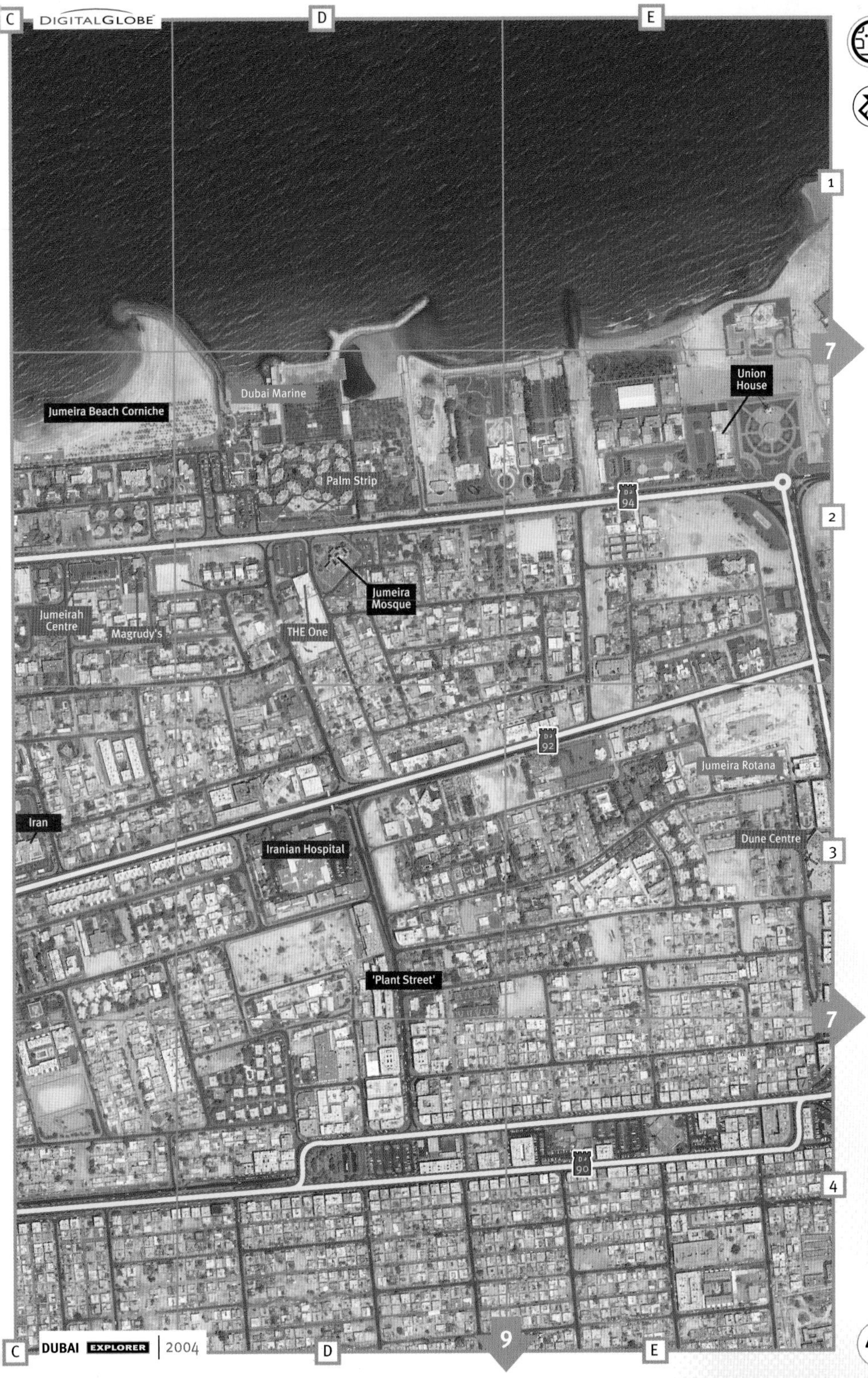
DIGITALGLOBE
Jumeira Beach Corniche
Dubai Marine
Palm Strip
Union House
94
Jumeira Mosque
Jumeirah Centre
Magrudy's
THE One
92
Jumeira Rotana
Iran
Iranian Hospital
Dune Centre
'Plant Street'
90
7
7
9
C
D
E
1
2
3
4

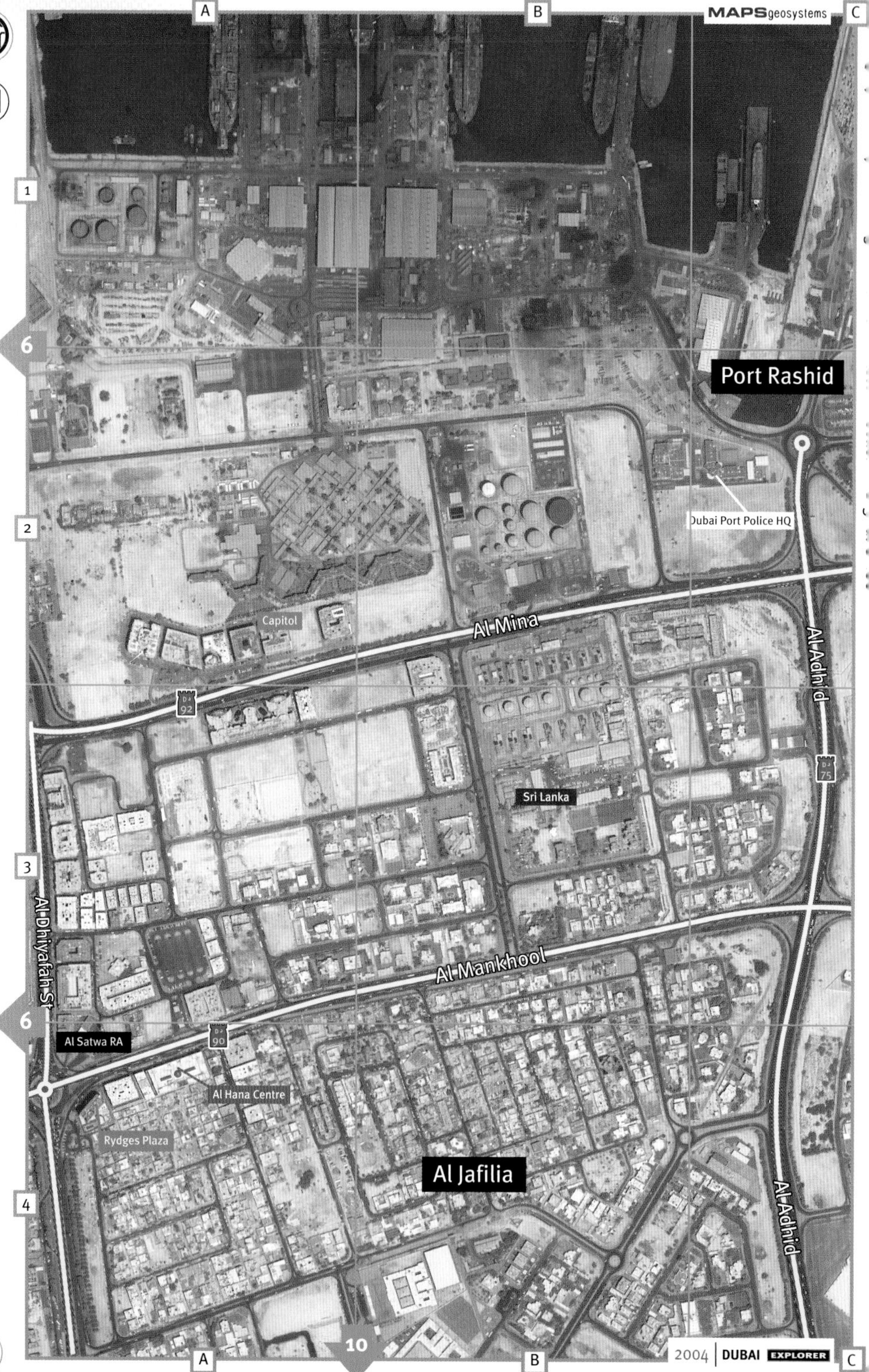

A
B
C
MAPSgeosystems
1
2
3
4
6
Port Rashid
Dubai Port Police HQ
Capitol
Al Mina
92
Al Adhid
75
Sri Lanka
Al Dhiyafah St
Al Mankhool
Al Satwa RA
90
Al Hana Centre
Rydges Plaza
Al Jafilia
Al Adhid
10

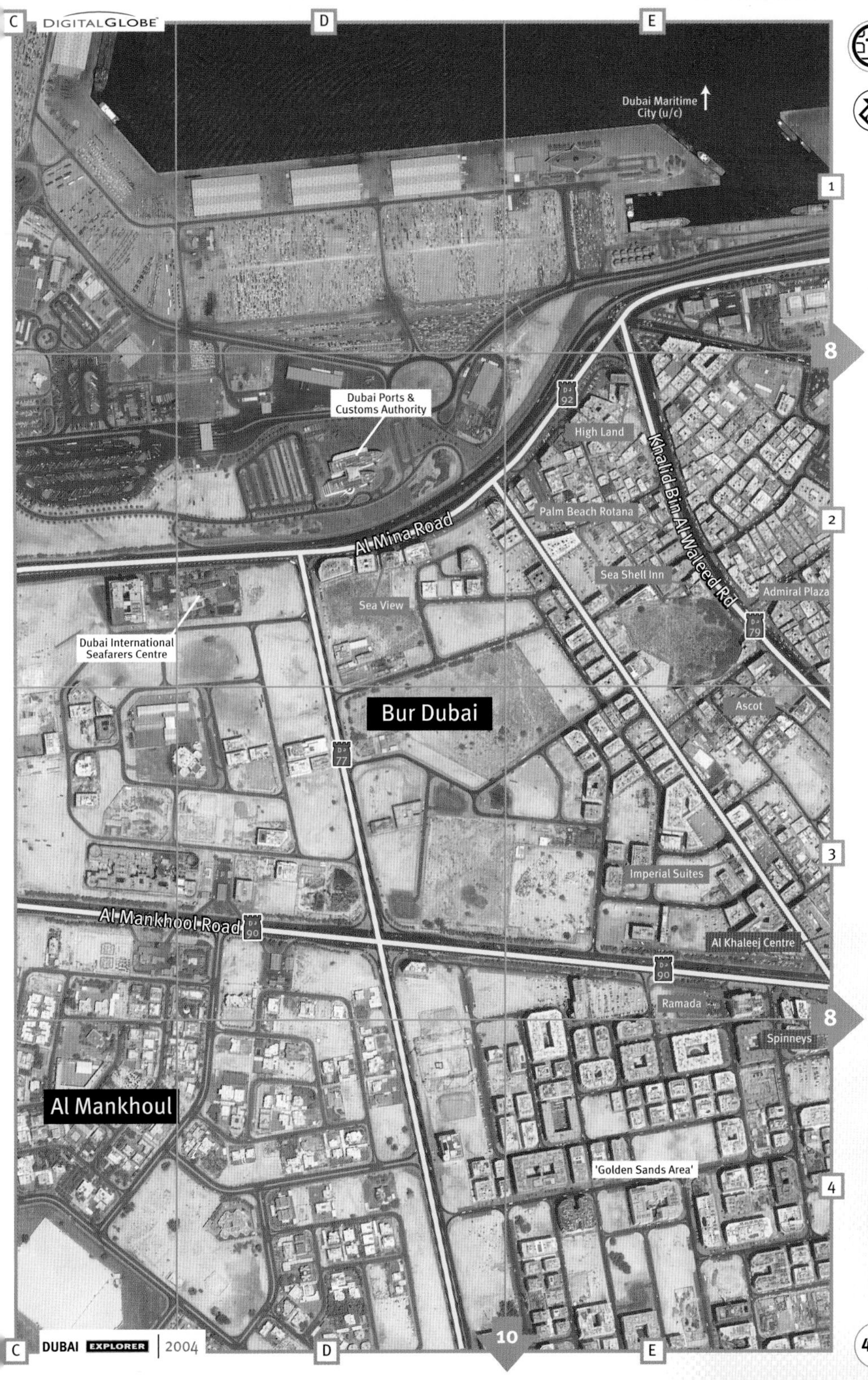
DIGITALGLOBE
C
D
E
Dubai Maritime City (u/c)
1
8
Dubai Ports & Customs Authority
92
High Land
Khalid Bin Al Waleed Rd
Palm Beach Rotana
2
Al Mina Road
Sea Shell Inn
Admiral Plaza
Sea View
79
Dubai International Seafarers Centre
Ascot
Bur Dubai
77
3
Imperial Suites
Al Mankhool Road
90
Al Khaleej Centre
90
Ramada
8
Spinneys
Al Mankhool
'Golden Sands Area'
4
10

7

Maps

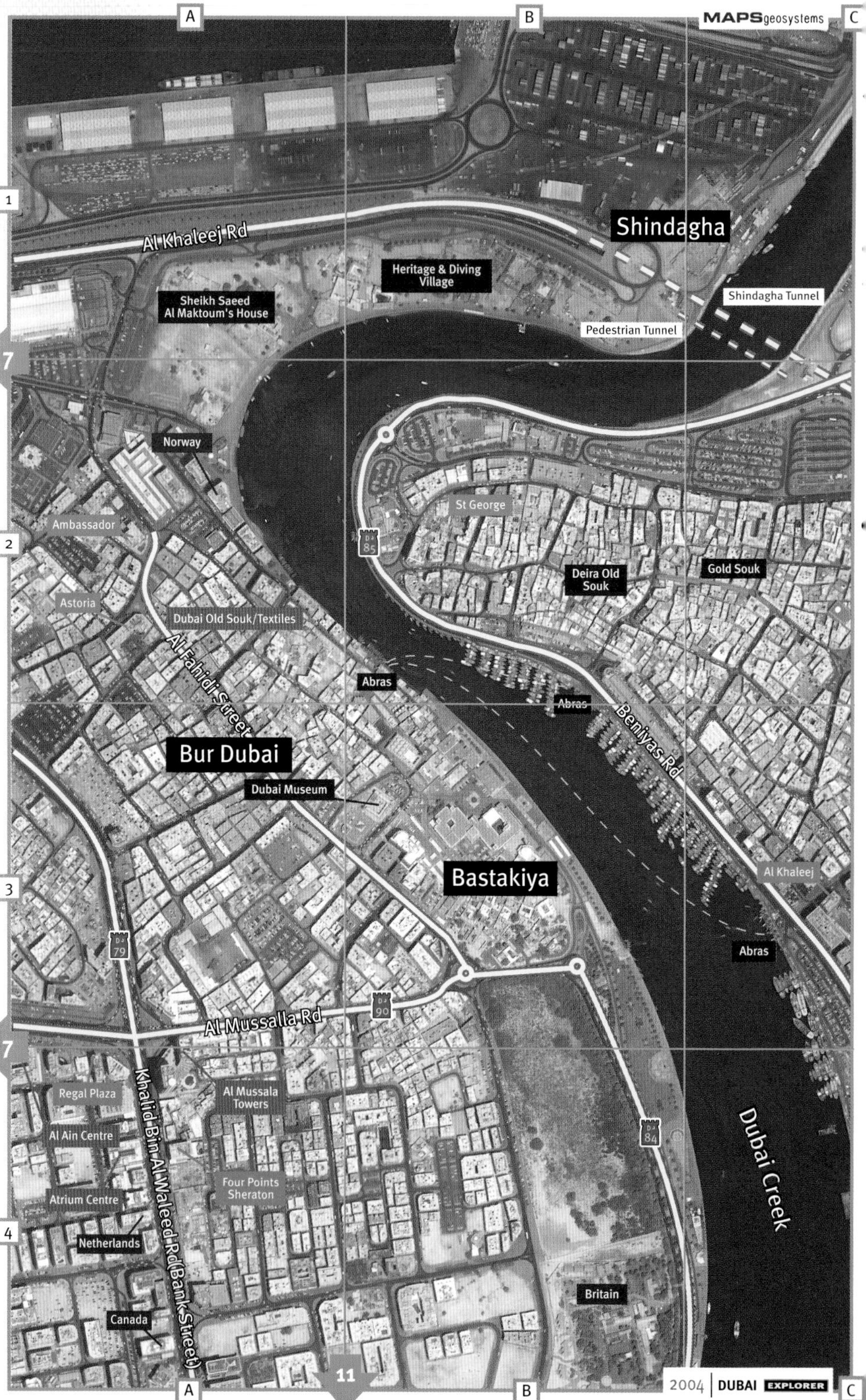

A
B
C
MAPSgeosystems
1
2
3
4
7
7
11
Al Khaleej Rd
Shindagha
Heritage & Diving Village
Sheikh Saeed Al Maktoum's House
Shindagha Tunnel
Pedestrian Tunnel
Norway
St George
Ambassador
Astoria
Dubai Old Souk/Textiles
Deira Old Souk
Gold Souk
Al Fahidi Street
Abras
Abras
Beniyas Rd
Bur Dubai
Dubai Museum
Bastakiya
Al Khaleej
Abras
Al Mussalla Rd
Regal Plaza
Al Mussala Towers
Al Ain Centre
Khalid Bin Al Waleed Rd(Bank Street)
Four Points Sheraton
Atrium Centre
Netherlands
Canada
Britain
Dubai Creek

DIGITALGLOBE
Deira Fish, Meat & Vegetable Market
Hyatt Regency
Hyatt Golf Park
Al Khaleej Rd
Deira
Deira Covered Souk
Naif RA
Naif Park
Al Naif Rd
Carlton Tower
Riviera
Twin Towers
Al Maktoum Hospital
Inter Continental
Fish RA
Marco Polo
85
92
88
82
80
89
12
11
C
D
E
1
2
3
4

MAPSgeosystems
A
B
C
6
1
2
3
4
5
5
17
Al Safa
Al Moosa 2
Zabeel
Al Rostamani
Al Salam
Al Moosa
Trade Centre 1
Kalantar
Doha
Sahara
Wafa
Towers Rotana
Number One
Shk Ahmed
Oasis
Shangri-La
Sheikh Zayed Rd
E 11
21st Century Tower
Oasis
Al Attar
Sky
Al Ghadier
Capricorn
Al Kawakeb
Ghaya Residence
Interchange No 1
Jumeira
Kendah House
Dusit
Dubai International Financial Centre (u/c)
The Gate (u/c)
Etisalat
Al Murooj Complex (u/c)

DIGITALGLOBE
C
D
E
6
Al Satwa
1
Khalid Al Attaar
Al Wasl
City
City 2
Al Durrah
Saeed
White Swan
White Crowne
API World Tower
France
Fairmont
Crowne Plaza
10
11
Sheikh Zayed Road
Trade Centre 2
Trade Centre Apartments
Ibis
2
The Tower
Emirates Towers
Emirates Towers Office
Dubai International Conference Centre
Dubai International Exhibition Centre
Novotel
3
10
4
17

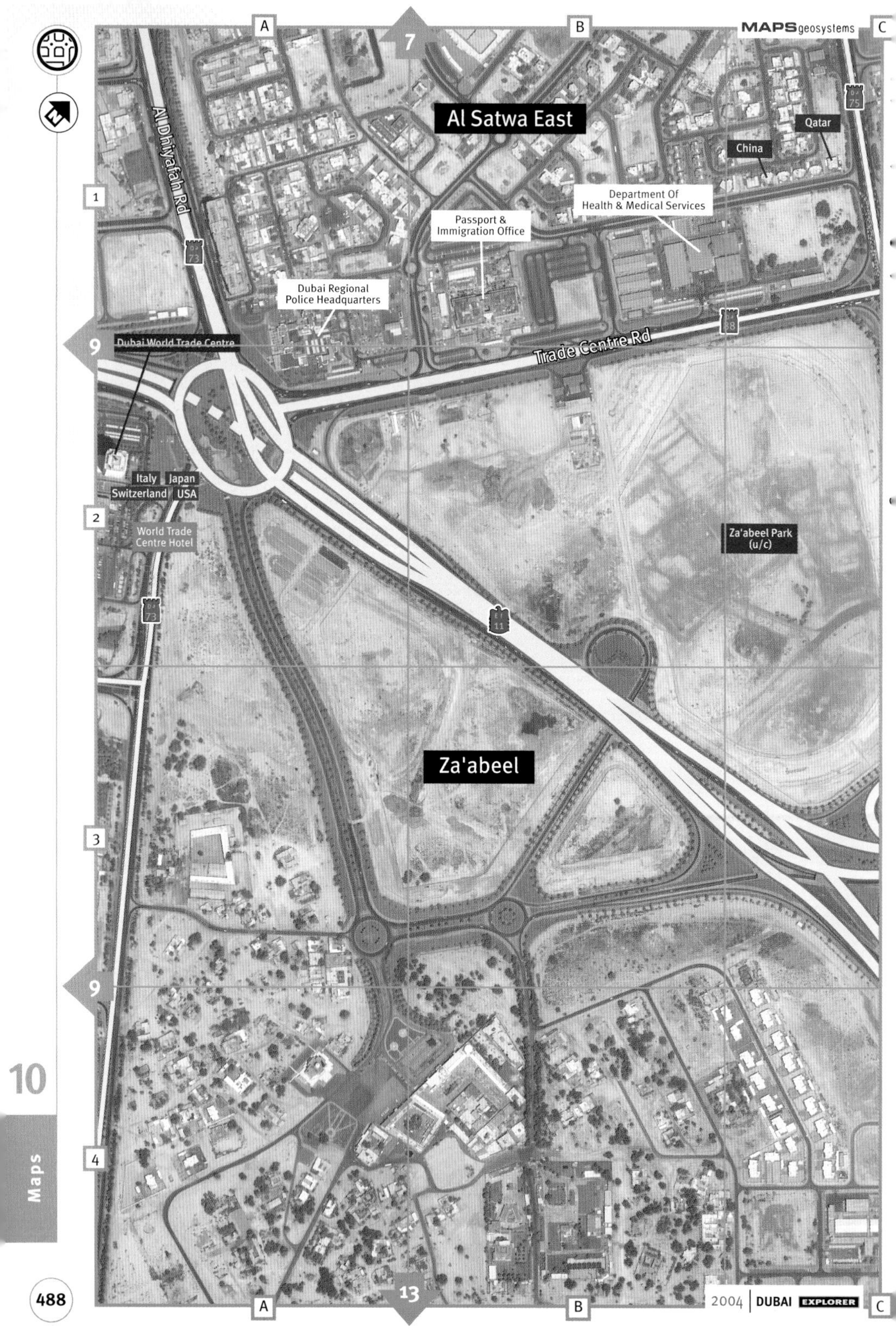

MAPSgeosystems
Al Satwa East
Al Dhiyafah Rd
Qatar
China
Department Of
Health & Medical Services
Passport &
Immigration Office
Dubai Regional
Police Headquarters
Dubai World Trade Centre
Trade Centre Rd
Italy
Japan
Switzerland
USA
World Trade
Centre Hotel
Za'abeel Park
(u/c)
Za'abeel
A
B
C
1
2
3
4
7
9
13
10
Maps

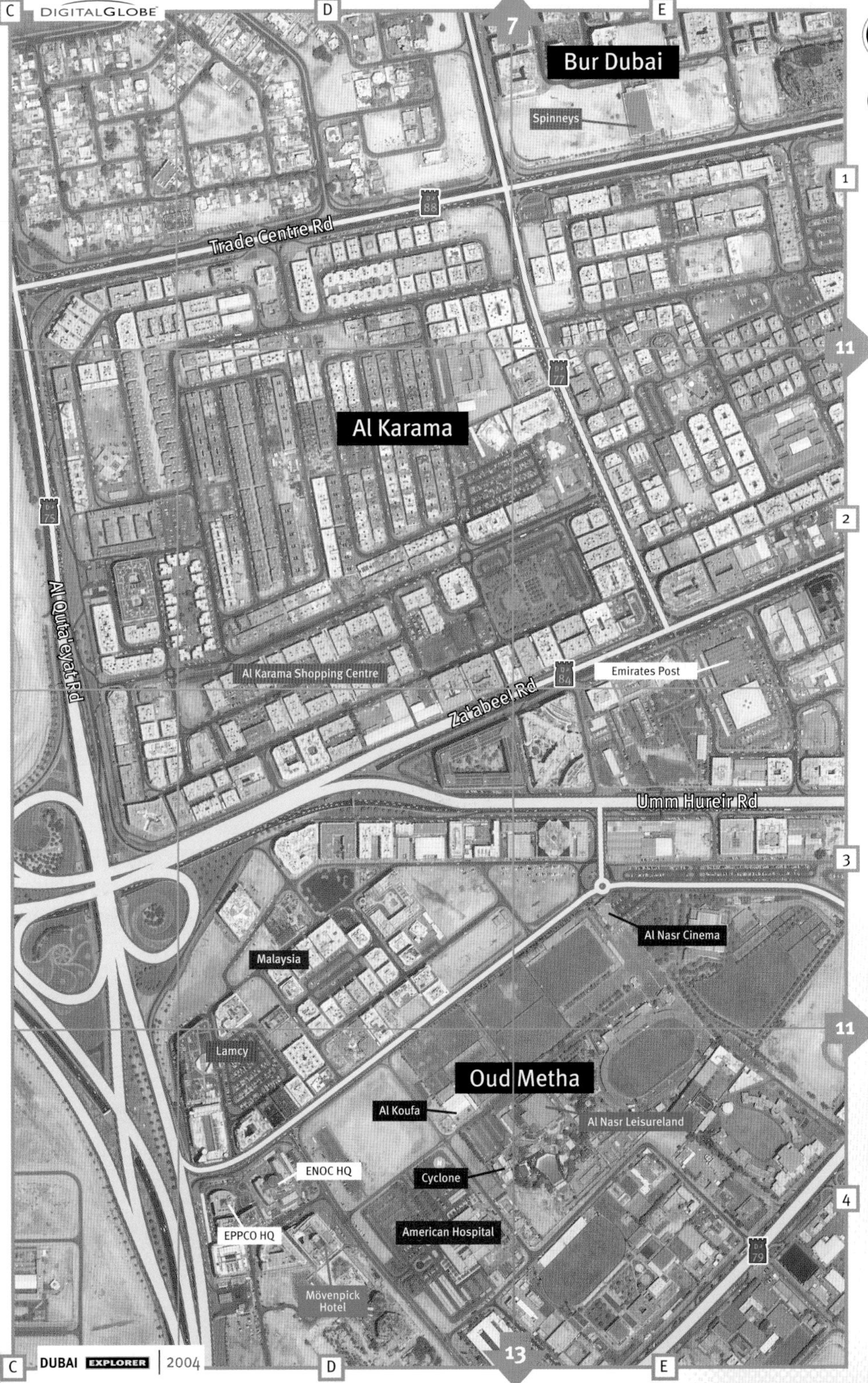

DIGITALGLOBE
C
D
E
7
Bur Dubai
Spinneys
1
88
Trade Centre Rd
11
77
Al Karama
75
2
Al Quta'eyat Rd
Al Karama Shopping Centre
84
Emirates Post
Za'abeel Rd
Umm Hureir Rd
3
Al Nasr Cinema
Malaysia
11
Lamcy
Oud Metha
Al Koufa
Al Nasr Leisureland
ENOC HQ
Cyclone
4
EPPCO HQ
American Hospital
79
Mövenpick Hotel
13
C
D
E

10

Maps

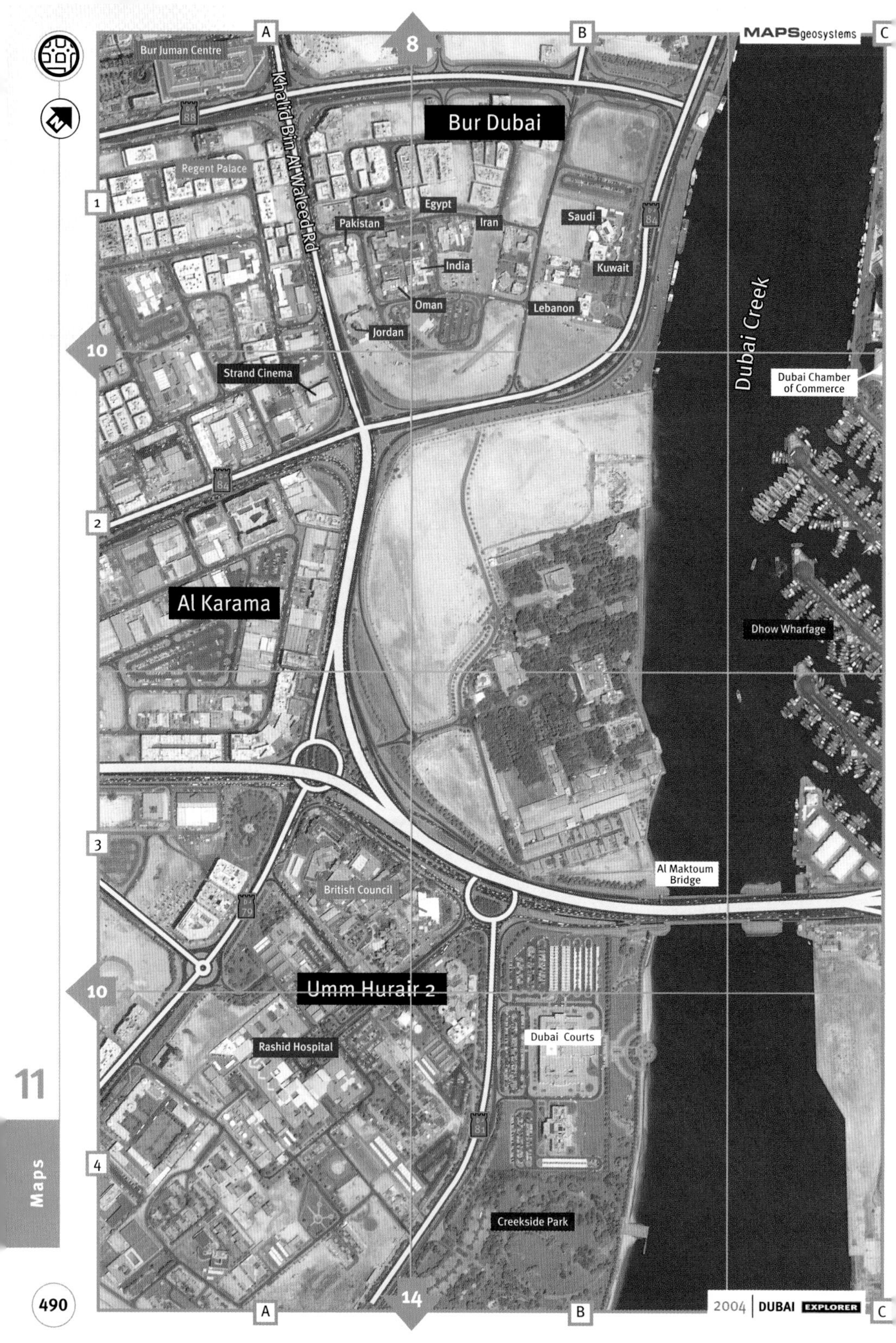
MAPSgeosystems
Bur Juman Centre
Khalid Bin Al Waleed Rd
Bur Dubai
Regent Palace
Egypt
Pakistan
Iran
Saudi
India
Kuwait
Oman
Lebanon
Jordan
Strand Cinema
Dubai Creek
Dubai Chamber of Commerce
Al Karama
Dhow Wharfage
Al Maktoum Bridge
British Council
Umm Hurair 2
Dubai Courts
Rashid Hospital
Creekside Park
A
B
C
1
2
3
4
8
10
10
14

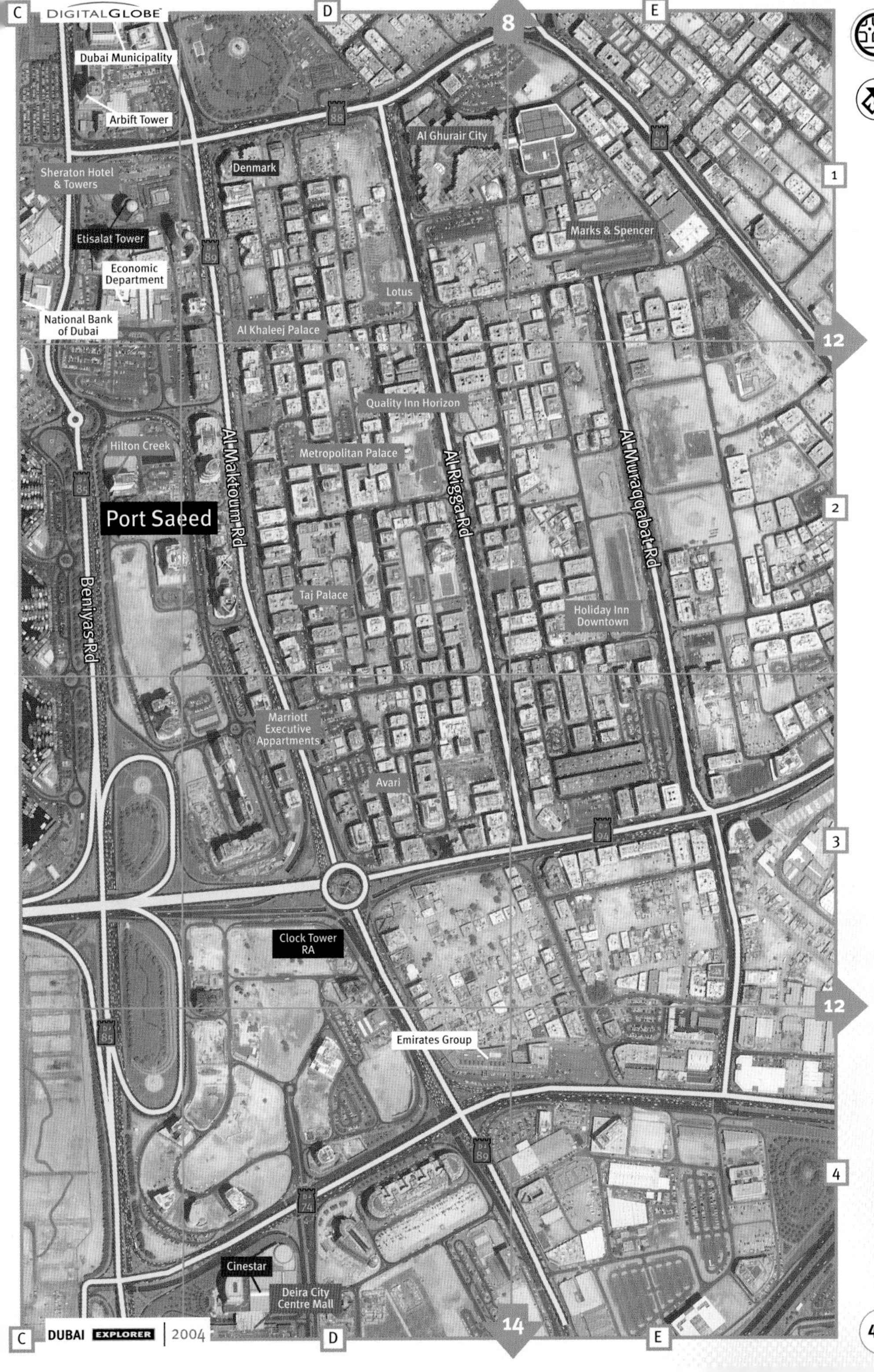
DIGITALGLOBE
Dubai Municipality
Arbift Tower
Sheraton Hotel & Towers
Etisalat Tower
Economic Department
National Bank of Dubai
Hilton Creek
Port Saeed
Beniyas Rd
Denmark
Al Khaleej Palace
Al Maktoum Rd
Lotus
Quality Inn Horizon
Metropolitan Palace
Taj Palace
Marriott Executive Appartments
Avari
Clock Tower RA
Emirates Group
Cinestar
Deira City Centre Mall
Al Ghurair City
Marks & Spencer
Al Rigga Rd
Al Muraqqabat Rd
Holiday Inn Downtown
8
12
12
14
C
D
E
1
2
3
4

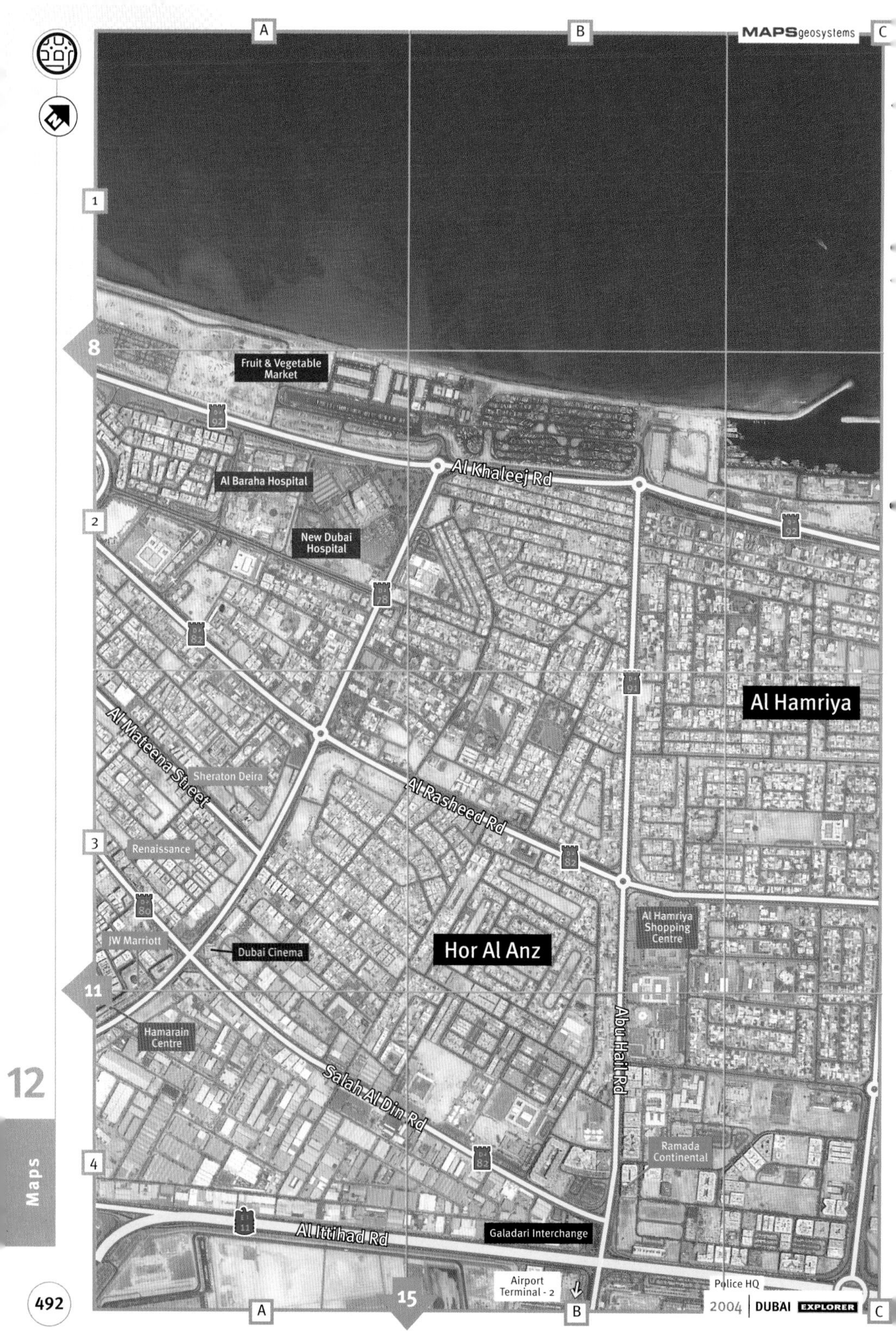
MAPSgeosystems
A
B
C
1
2
3
4
8
11
15
Fruit & Vegetable Market
Al Baraha Hospital
New Dubai Hospital
Al Khaleej Rd
Al Hamriya
Al Mateena Street
Sheraton Deira
Renaissance
Al Rasheed Rd
JW Marriott
Dubai Cinema
Hor Al Anz
Al Hamriya Shopping Centre
Hamarain Centre
Abu Hail Rd
Salah Al Din Rd
Ramada Continental
Al Ittihad Rd
Galadari Interchange
Airport Terminal - 2
Police HQ

DIGITALGLOBE
C
D
E
1
2
3
4
Al Mamzar Beach Park
Al Mamzar
Al Hamriya Port
Khor Al Mamzar
Dubai - Sharjah Highway
Sharjah
Al Mulla Plaza
15

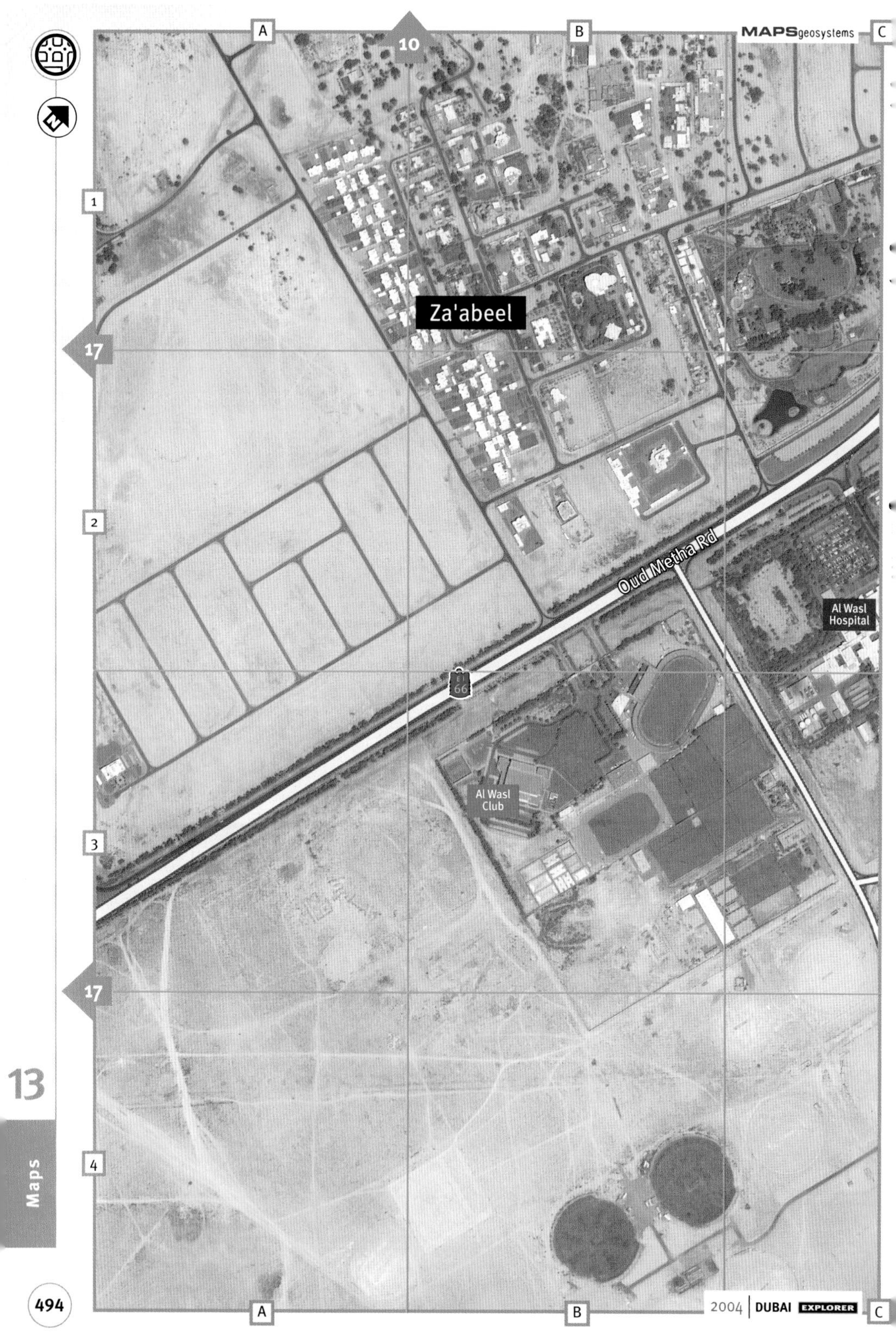

A
B
C
10
MAPSgeosystems
1
2
3
4
17
17
Za'abeel
Oud Metha Rd
Al Wasl Hospital
Al Wasl Club
E 66
13
Maps

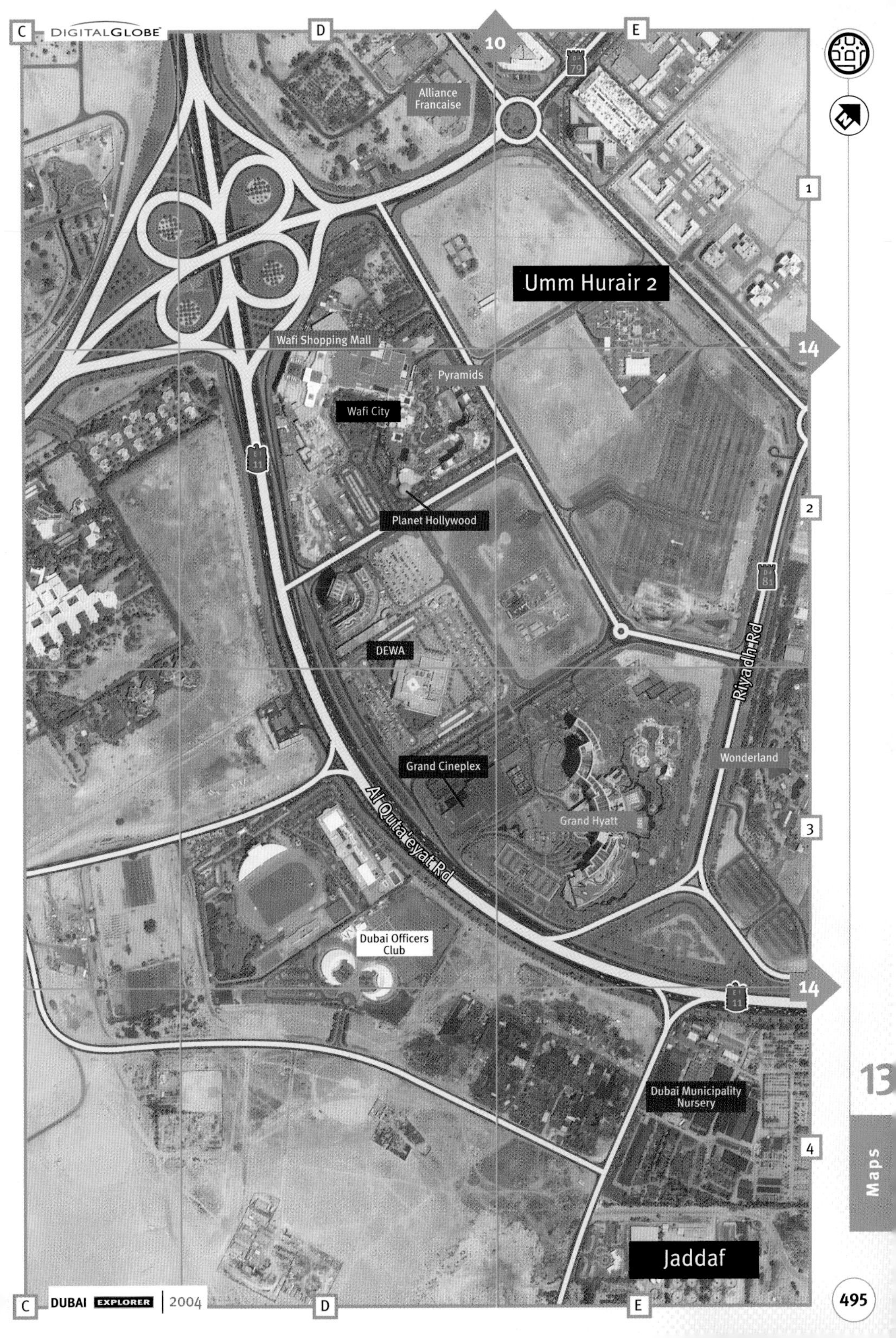
C
D
10
E
Alliance Francaise
1
Umm Hurair 2
14
Wafi Shopping Mall
Pyramids
Wafi City
11
Planet Hollywood
2
81
Riyadh Rd
DEWA
Wonderland
Grand Cineplex
Al Quta'eyat Rd
Grand Hyatt
3
Dubai Officers Club
14
11
Dubai Municipality Nursery
4
Jaddaf
79

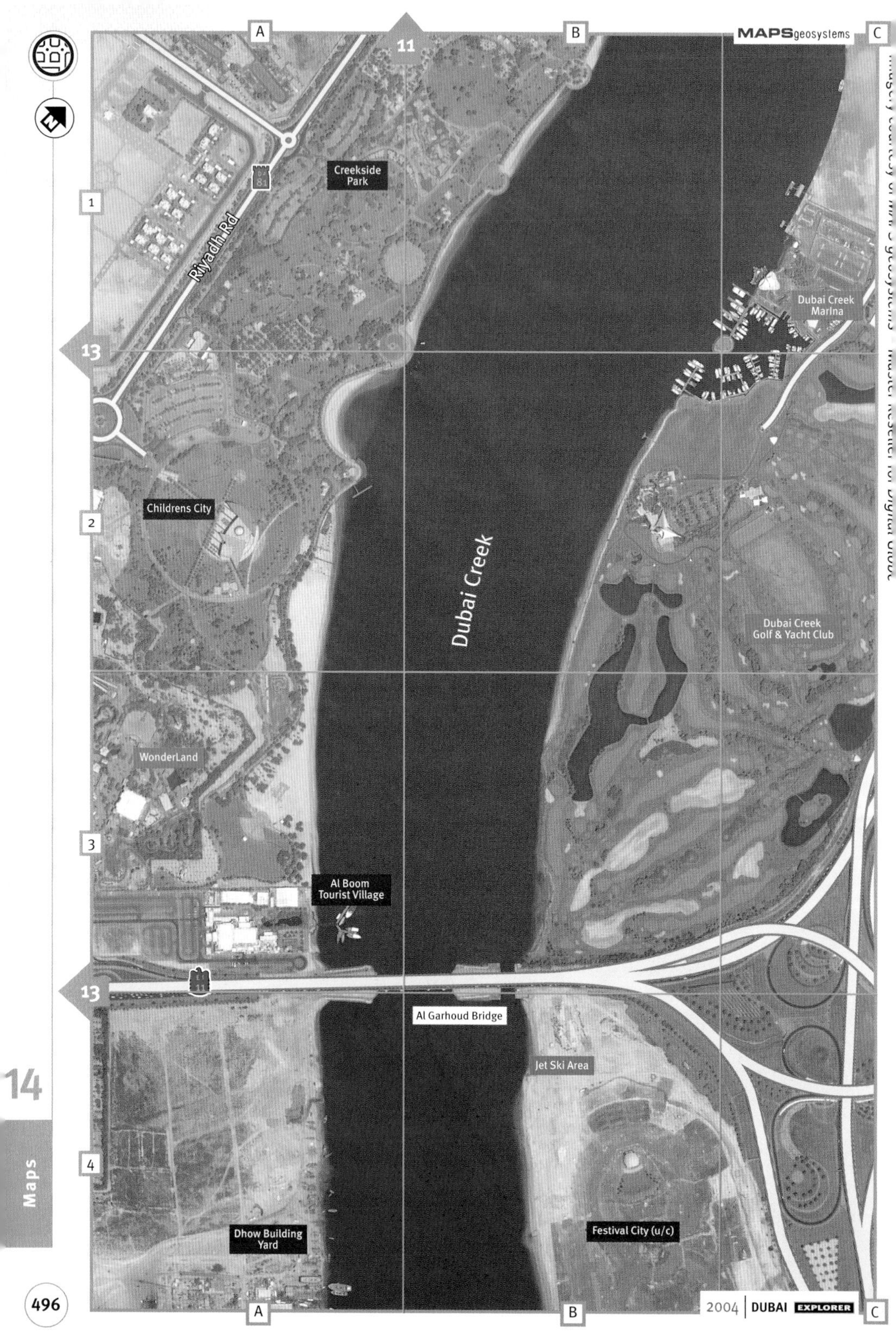
MAPSgeosystems
A
B
C
1
2
3
4
11
13
Creekside Park
Riyadh Rd
Childrens City
Dubai Creek
Dubai Creek Marina
Dubai Creek Golf & Yacht Club
WonderLand
Al Boom Tourist Village
Al Garhoud Bridge
Jet Ski Area
Dhow Building Yard
Festival City (u/c)

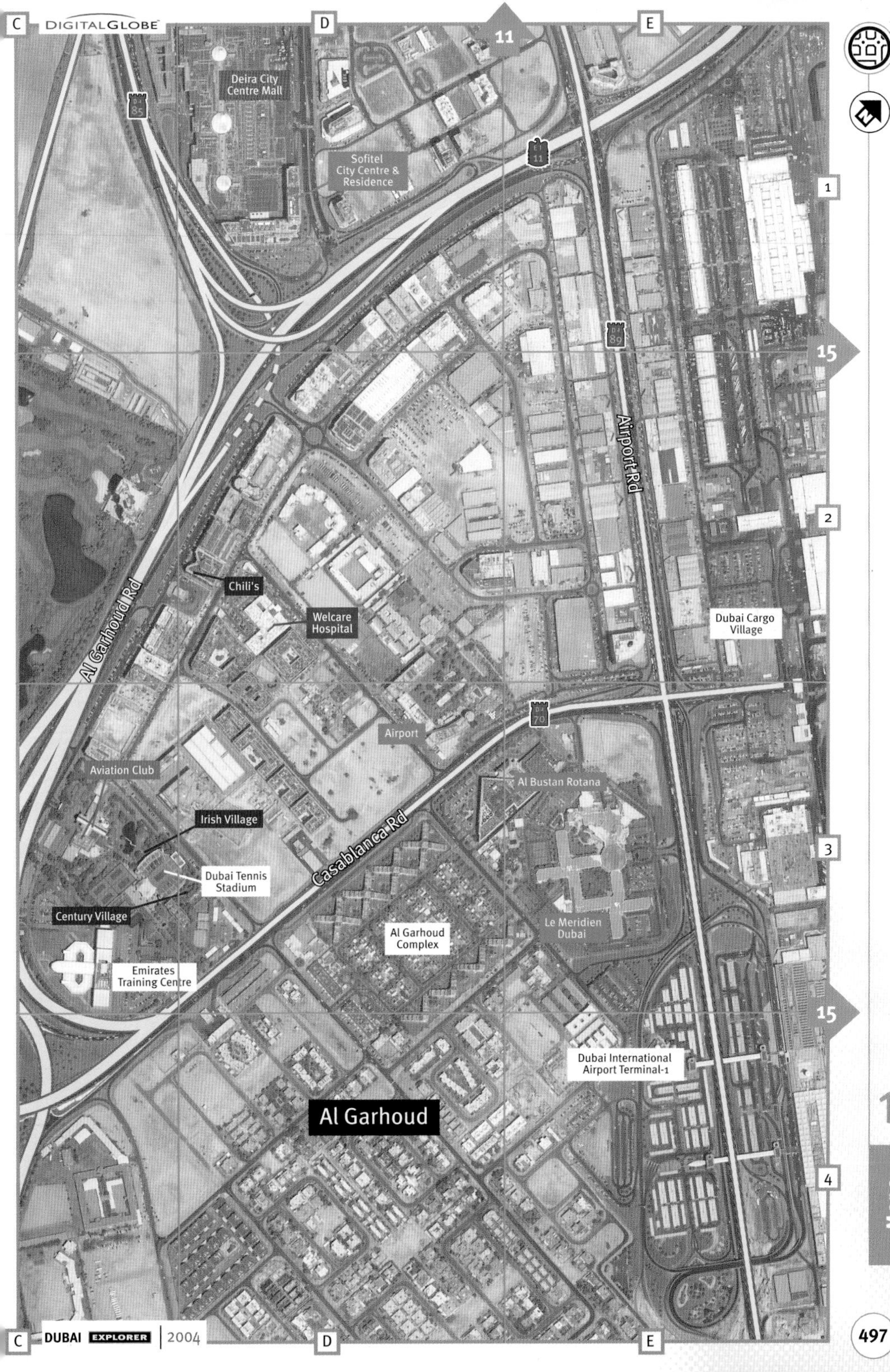
DIGITALGLOBE
C
D
E
11
15
1
2
3
4
Deira City Centre Mall
Sofitel City Centre & Residence
Airport Rd
Al Garhoud Rd
Chili's
Welcare Hospital
Dubai Cargo Village
Airport
Aviation Club
Al Bustan Rotana
Irish Village
Casablanca Rd
Dubai Tennis Stadium
Century Village
Al Garhoud Complex
Le Meridien Dubai
Emirates Training Centre
Dubai International Airport Terminal-1
Al Garhoud

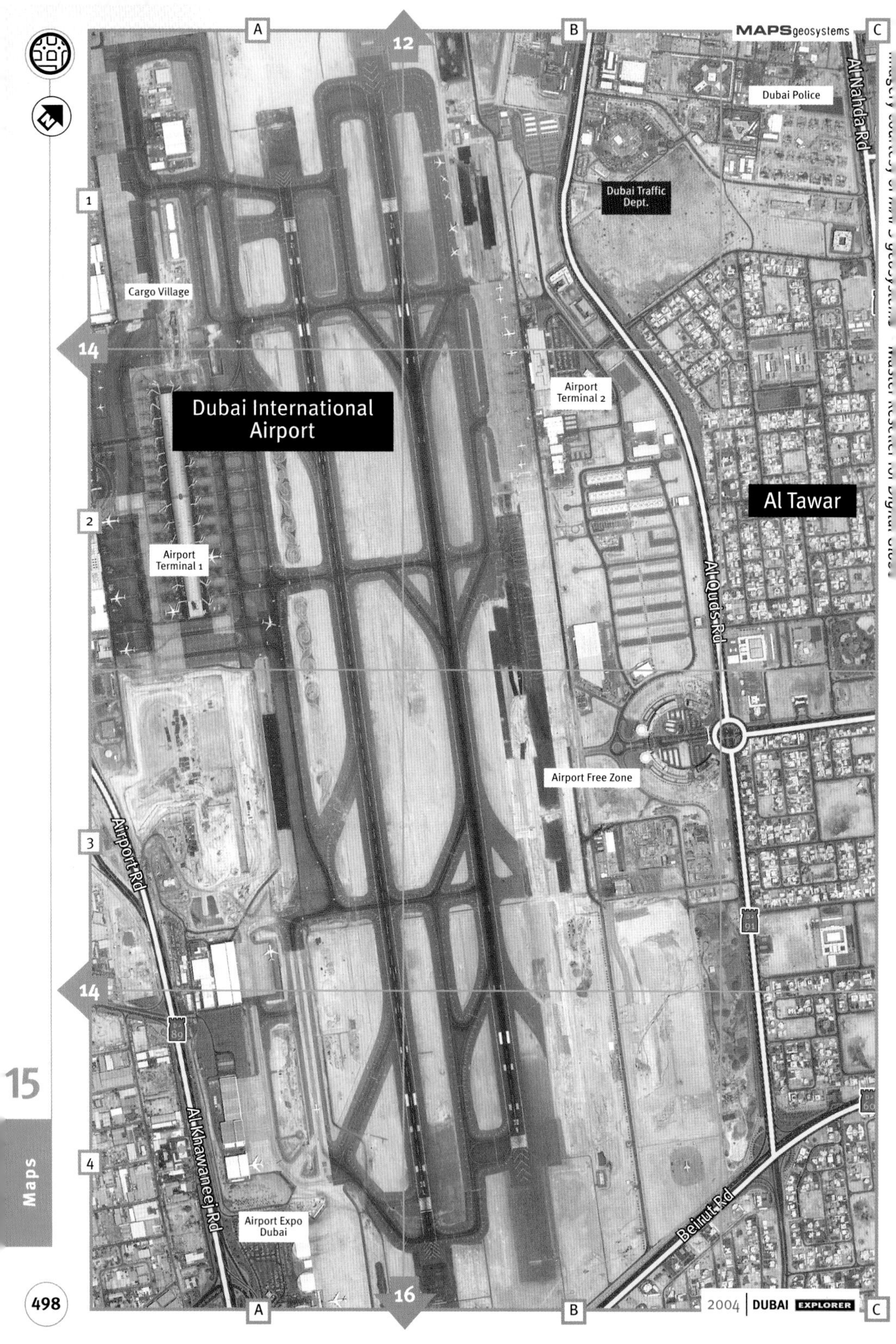
MAPSgeosystems
A
B
C
12
14
14
16
1
2
3
4
Dubai Police
Al Nahda Rd
Dubai Traffic Dept.
Cargo Village
Dubai International Airport
Airport Terminal 2
Al Tawar
Airport Terminal 1
Al Quds Rd
Airport Free Zone
Airport Rd
Al Khawaneej Rd
Beirut Rd
Airport Expo Dubai
2004 DUBAI EXPLORER
15
Maps

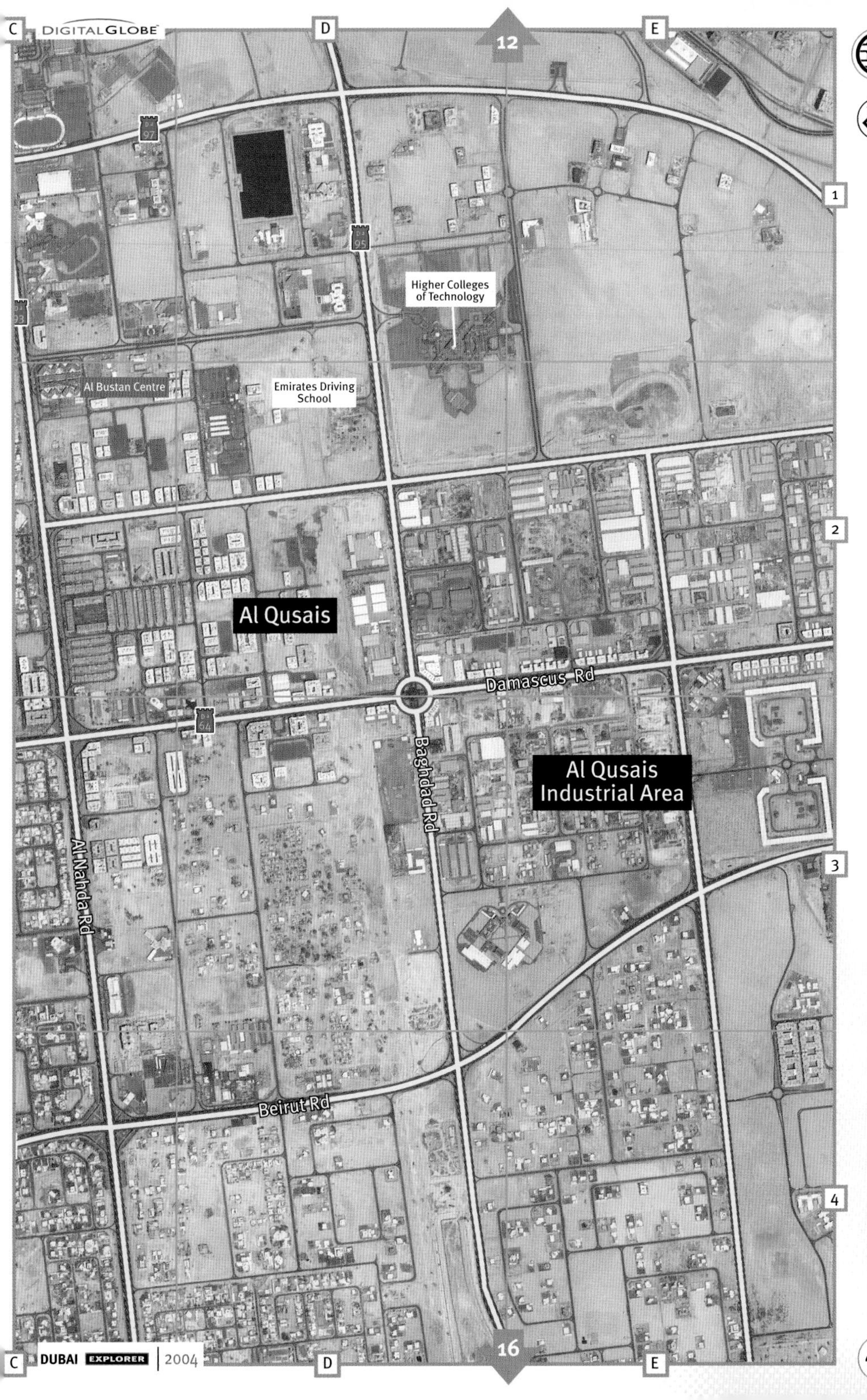
DIGITALGLOBE
C
D
E
12
1
2
3
4
16
97
95
93
64
Higher Colleges of Technology
Al Bustan Centre
Emirates Driving School
Al Qusais
Damascus Rd
Baghdad Rd
Al Qusais Industrial Area
Al Nahda Rd
Beirut Rd

15
Maps

MAPSgeosystems
15
A
B
C
1
2
3
4
Airport Expo Dubai
Bin Saugat Centre
Al Tawar
Rashidiya
Mirdif
Rabat Rd
60
89
311
83
56
2004 DUBAI EXPLORER
16
Maps

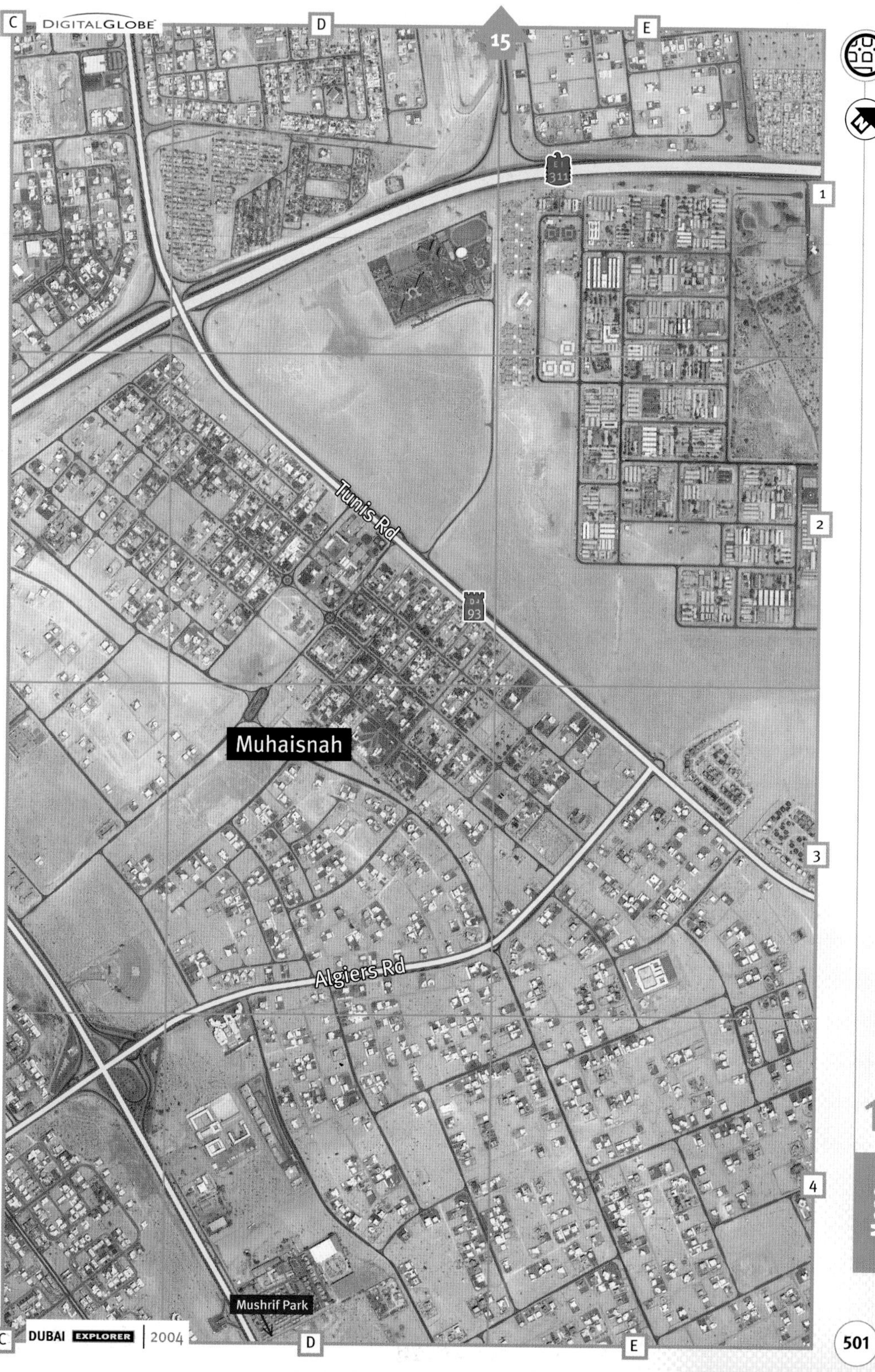

DIGITALGLOBE
C
D
E
15
1
2
3
4
Tunis Rd
Muhaisnah
Algiers Rd
Mushrif Park
311
93
16
Maps

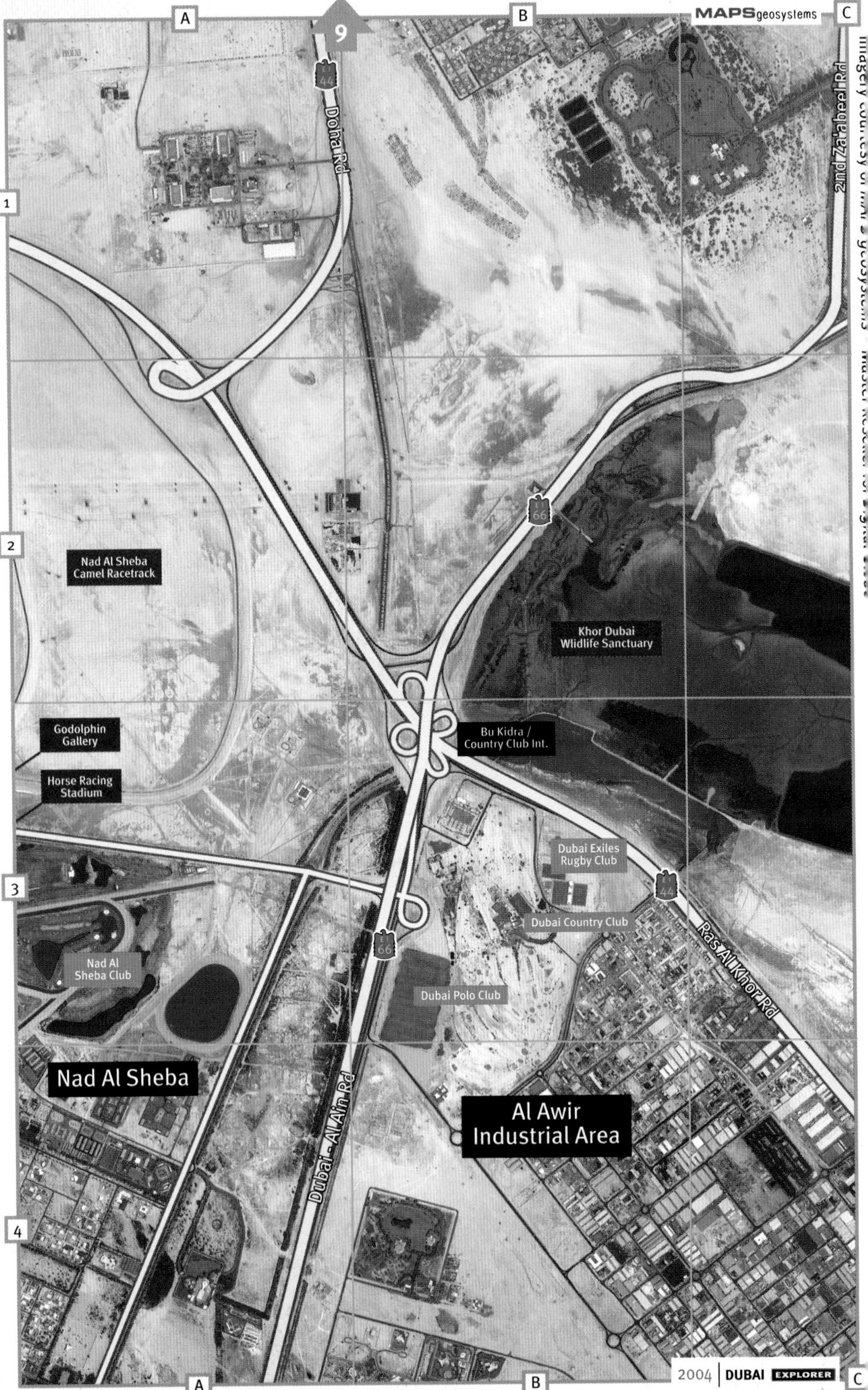
MAPSgeosystems
A
B
C
9
1
2
3
4
E 44
Doha Rd
2nd Za'abeel Rd
E 66
Nad Al Sheba
Camel Racetrack
Khor Dubai
Wildlife Sanctuary
Godolphin
Gallery
Bu Kidra /
Country Club Int.
Horse Racing
Stadium
Dubai Exiles
Rugby Club
E 44
Dubai Country Club
Ras Al Khor Rd
E 66
Nad Al
Sheba Club
Dubai Polo Club
Nad Al Sheba
Dubai - Al Ain Rd
Al Awir
Industrial Area

Index

EXPLORER

# #

A

B

Index

C

D

E

F

G

H

I

J

K

L

P

Q

R

S

T

U

V

W

Y

Z

Quick Reference

Emergencies

General

Police	999
Ambulance	998 / 999
Fire	997
DEWA	991
Dubai Police HQ	229 2222
Municipality 24 Hour Hotline	223 2323
Operator	181

Pharmacies/Chemists – 24 hours

Each emirate has at least one pharmacy open 24 hours. The location and telephone numbers are in the daily newspapers. The Municipality has an emergency number (223 2323) which gives the name and location of open chemists.

Cinemas

Al Nasr	337 4353
Metroplex	343 8383
Century Cinemas	349 9773
Cinestar	294 9000
Deira Cinema	222 3551
Dubai Cinema	266 0632
Galleria	209 6469 / 70
Grand Cinecity	228 98 98
Grand Cineplex	324 2000
Lamcy	336 8808
Plaza	393 9966
Rex Drive-In	288 6447
Strand	396 1644

Hospitals

Al Amal Hospital	344 4010
Al Baraha Hospital	271 0000
Al Maktoum Hospital	222 1211
Al Wasl Hospital	324 1111
American Hospital	336 7777
Belhoul European Hospital	345 4000
Dubai Hospital	271 4444
International Private Hospital	221 2484
Iranian Hospital	344 0250
Rashid Hospital	337 4000
Welcare Hospital	282 7788

Telephone Codes

Directory Enquiries	181	Etisalat Information	144
Operator	100	Fault Reports	171
Etisalat	633 3111	Billing Info	140

Airlines

Air Arabia	06 508 8888
Air France	294 5899
Air India	227 6787
Alitalia	224 2256
Austrian Airlines	294 5675
British Airways	307 5777
Cathay Pacific Airways	295 0400
CSA Czech Airlines	295 9502
Cyprus Airways	221 5325
Emirates	214 4444
Etihad	02 505 8000
Gulf Air	271 3111
KLM Royal Dutch Airlines	335 5777
Kuwait Airways	228 1106
Lufthansa	343 2121
Malaysia Airlines	397 0250
Olympic Airways	221 4761
Oman Air	351 8080
PIA	222 2154
Qatar Airways	229 2229
Royal Brunei Airlines	351 4111
Royal Jet	02 575 7000
Royal Jordanian	266 8667
Royal Nepal Airlines	295 5444
Saudi Arabian Airlines	295 7747
Singapore Airlines	223 2300
South African Airways	397 0766
SriLankan Airlines	294 9119
Swiss	294 5051
United Airlines	316 6942

Private Centres/Clinics

Al Borj Medical Centre	321 2220
Al Zahra Private Medical Centre	331 5000
Allied Diagnostic Centre	332 8111
Belhoul European Hospital	297 6203
Dr Akel's General Medical Clinic	344 2773
Dubai London Clinic	344 6663
Dubai Physiotherapy Clinic	349 6333
General Medical Centre	349 5959
Health Care Medical Center	344 5550
Jebel Ali Medical Centre	881 4000
Manchester Clinic	344 0300
New Medical Centre	268 3131

Dubai Airport

DNATA	295 1111
Dubai Airport	224 5555
Flight Enquiry	216 6666

Hotels

Five-Star	Phone
Al Bustan Rotana Hotel	282 0000
Al Maha Resort	832 9900
Burj Al Arab	301 7777
Crowne Plaza	331 1111
Dubai Marine Beach Resort & Spa	346 1111
Dusit Dubai	343 3333
Emirates Towers Hotel	330 0000
Fairmont Hotel	332 5555
Grand Hyatt Dubai	317 1234
Hilton Dubai Creek	227 1111
Hilton Dubai Jumeirah	399 1111
Hotel Inter-Continental Dubai	222 7171
Hyatt Regency Hotel	209 1234
Jebel Ali Golf Resort & Spa	883 6000
Jumeirah Beach Club, The	344 5333
Jumeirah Beach Hotel, The	348 0000
JW Marriott Hotel	262 4444
Le Meridien Dubai	282 4040
Le Meridien Mina Seyahi	399 3333
Le Royal Meridien Beach Resort & Spa	399 5555
Metropolitan Palace Hotel	227 0000
Mina A'Salam	366 8888
Mövenpick Hotel Bur Dubai	336 6000
Palace at One&Only Royal Mirage, The	399 9999
Renaissance Hotel	262 5555
Ritz-Carlton Dubai	399 4000
Safir Deira Hotel	224 8587
Shangri-La Hotel	343 8888
Sheraton Deira	268 8888
Sheraton Dubai Creek Hotel & Towers	228 1111
Sheraton Jumeirah Beach Resort	399 5533
Sofitel City Centre Hotel	295 5522
Taj Palace Hotel	223 2222
World Trade Centre Hotel, The	331 4000

Four-Star	
Al Khaleej Palace Hotel	223 1000
Ascot Hotel	352 0900
Avari Dubai International	295 6666
Best Western Dubai Grand	263 2555
Capitol Hotel	346 0111
Carlton Tower, The	222 7111
Four Points Sheraton	397 7444
Golden Tulip Aeroplane Hotel	272 2999
Holiday Inn Downtown	228 8889
Ibis World Trade Centre	332 4444
Jumeira Rotana Hotel	345 5888
Marco Polo Hotel	272 0000
Metropolitan Deira	295 9171
Metropolitan Hotel	343 0000
Metropolitan Resort & Beach Club Hotel	399 5000
Millennium Airport Hotel	282 3464
Novotel World Trade Centre	332 0000
Oasis Beach Hotel	399 4444

Hotels

Four Star	Phone
Ramada Continental Hotel	266 2666
Ramada Hotel	351 9999
Regent Palace Hotel	396 3888
Riviera Hotel	222 2131
Rydges Plaza Hotel	398 2222
Sea View Hotel	355 8080
Towers Rotana Hotel	343 8000

Three Star	
Admiral Plaza, The	393 5333
Al Khaleej Holiday Hotel	227 6565
Ambassador Hotel	393 9444
Astoria Hotel	353 4300
Claridge Hotel	271 6666
Comfort Inn	222 7393
Dubai Palm Hotel	271 0021
Gulf Inn Hotel	224 3433
Imperial Suites Hotel	351 5100
Kings Park Hotel	228 9999
Lords Hotel	228 9977
Lotus Hotel	227 8888
Nihal Hotel	295 7666
Palm Beach Rotana Inn	393 1999
Palm Hotel Dubai, The	399 2222
Princess Hotel	263 5500
Quality Inn Horizon	227 1919
Sea Shell Inn	393 4777
Vendome Plaza Hotel	222 2333

Two Star	
Deira Park Hotel	223 9922
New Peninsula Hotel	393 9111
Phoenicia Hotel	222 7191
President Hotel	334 6565
Ramee International Hotel	224 0222
San Marco	272 2333

One Star	
Dallas Hotel	351 1223
Middle East Hotel	222 6688
Vasantam Hotel	393 8006
West Hotel	271 7001

Taxi Companies

Cars Taxis	269 3344
Dubai Transport Company	208 0808
Gulf Radio Taxi	223 6666
Metro Taxis	267 3222
National Taxis	336 6611
Sharjah: Delta Taxis	06 559 8598